CEQA Deskbook

Third Edition

CEQA Deskbook

Third Edition

Ronald E. Bass
Kenneth M. Bogdan
Antero A. Rivasplata

Solano Press Books
Point Arena, California

CEQA Deskbook
Third Edition

Printed in the United States of America.

Third Edition: 2012
Second Printing: 2014

Solano Press Books
Post Office Box 773
Point Arena, California 95468
telephone: (800) 931-9373
facsimile: (707) 884-4109
email: spbooks@solano.com
Internet: www.solano.com

Photos by Chris Austria and Antero A. Rivasplata, ICF International
Book design by Solano Press Books
Index by Lee Humphrey
Printed by Sentinel Printing, St. Cloud, Minnesota

ISBN 978-0-923956-48-6

IMPORTANT NOTICE
Before you rely on the information in this book, please be sure you have the latest edition and are aware that some changes in statutes, guidelines, or case law may have gone into effect since the date of publication. The book, moreover, provides general information about the law. Readers should consult their own attorneys before relying on the representations found herein.

The authors wish to dedicate this book to Robert Jones (1917–1994) who was instrumental in the early development of the California Environmental Quality Act. In 1970 he served as the lead consultant to the State Assembly Select Committee on Environmental Quality. The committee's report, known as the Environmental Bill of Rights, contained the recommendation to enact CEQA. A year later the Legislature followed Bob's advice, and California became the first state to have an environmental impact assessment law. His leadership in guiding CEQA through the Legislature and his subsequent founding of one of the state's first environmental consulting firms were truly pioneering efforts in the field of environmental management in California.

Preface

The California Environmental Quality Act (CEQA) is California's preeminent environmental law. It requires state, local, and other California public agencies to evaluate and disclose to the public and other agencies the potential environmental implications of their proposed actions before committing to them. Furthermore, it requires agencies to avoid or reduce, when feasible, the significant environmental impacts of their actions.

CEQA establishes substantive procedures to ensure that agencies accomplish the purposes of the law. The California Natural Resources Agency has adopted regulations, known as the State CEQA Guidelines, which provide detailed procedures that agencies must follow to implement the law. The key to compliance with CEQA is understanding the procedural steps and key decision points involved in the environmental review process established by the statute (Public Resources Code 21000 et seq.), the Guidelines (14 Cal. Code Reg. 15000 et seq.), agency CEQA procedures, if applicable, and relevant court decisions.

In the four decades since its enactment, CEQA has been praised by many as giving the public the ability to influence public agencies and the information to improve environmentally damaging projects, and criticized by others as a major impediment to California's economic progress and development. It has become a familiar topic whenever discussions about environmental protection, land use planning or economic development arise. Despite the divergent viewpoints on its relative benefits, CEQA is inextricably woven into the fabric of California governance, decision-making, and politics.

The authors of this deskbook have devoted their careers to achieving excellence in CEQA compliance. They have participated in many of the CEQA improvement efforts over the years and deeply believe that a solid knowledge of CEQA's policies, procedures and practices leads to successful implementation of the law. *CEQA Deskbook: A Step-by-Step Guide on How to Comply with the California Environmental Quality Act* presents the user with a handy, easy-to-understand approach to CEQA. This 2012 edition contains new and improved materials designed to help public agency staff, consultants, attorneys, developers, and interested citizens understand the environmental review process, and identifies, in a simplified fashion, most of the key steps, requirements, and decision points necessary to comply with the law. This edition reflects the most recent changes to CEQA (as of June 2012), including all legislative and regulatory changes adopted through 2011, as well as the most important principles established by recent court decisions. Additionally, it includes the author's practical advice to help CEQA practitioners through the process of environmental review.

With this book users will be better able to:

- Determine whether CEQA applies to proposed projects and when exemptions are applicable
- Learn when a Negative Declaration is appropriate or whether an Environmental Impact Report (EIR) must be prepared
- Prepare a legally defensible Negative Declaration, Mitigated Negative Declaration, or EIR
- Prepare a "program level" EIR and understand how to streamline CEQA by "tiering" later analyses from that EIR
- Write feasible, enforceable, and effective mitigation measures
- Meaningfully review, evaluate, and comment on CEQA documents prepared by other public agencies
- Prepare joint CEQA/NEPA documents to satisfy both CEQA and the federal National Environmental Policy Act (NEPA)
- Understand the environmental review process and determine the roles and responsibilities of state and local agencies
- Make better decisions that take into account environmental factors

The book is intended to be used as a general guide to implementing the provisions of CEQA, for more detailed interpretations users should consult the CEQA statute, the State CEQA Guidelines, and relevant case law.

The legal citations in the book are not exhaustive. The handbook selectively cites CEQA (Pub. Res. Code Secs. 21000–21177), the State CEQA Guidelines (14 Cal. Code Reg. 15000-15387) other relevant statutes, case law, and other references when doing so clarifies the underlying legal authority for a particular requirement. The CEQA Statues and the Guidelines are included as appendices. For detailed legal citations, users should refer to the applicable CEQA publications listed in the suggested reading section after the appendices.

For up-to-date information about changes in CEQA, the CEQA Guidelines, and CEQA case law, see the ICF website: website at: www.icfi.com

Acknowledgments

The author's want to acknowledge and thank Albert Herson for his work as author on previous editions of the book. The authors wish to thank the following staff members at ICF International for their assistance in producing this book:

- Pauline Cueva – coordination
- Susan Jansen – editing
- Susy DellVeneri - graphic designer

Special thanks goes to Chris Austria who contributed his beautiful photography. Sadly, Chris passed away before the book was published. His creative abilities and congenial personality will be missed by all who worked with him.

Finally, the authors also wish to acknowledge the valuable input from colleagues at ICF International and many environmental professionals who have worked with the authors and attended CEQA training workshops over the years and shared their ideas for improving the book.

About the Authors

Ronald E. Bass, J.D., AICP is a Senior Consultant with ICF International (formerly Jones & Stokes Associates). Mr. Bass has a professional and academic background in environmental law and planning. He has participated in a broad variety of planning and environmental studies under the California Environmental Quality Act (CEQA), the National Environmental Policy Act (NEPA), and other state and federal environmental laws. He provides strategic advice, peer review and issue resolution related to the implementation of CEQA and NEPA. Mr. Bass is a frequent speaker at professional workshops on environmental impact assessment. Mr. Bass received a J.D. from the Washington College of Law at American University, Washington, D.C.; an M.A. in environmental planning from California State University, Sacramento; and a B.A. in Anthropology from Ohio State University, Columbus, Ohio.

Mr. Bass is co-author, with Mr. Bogdan, of *THE NEPA BOOK: A Step-By-Step Guide on How to Comply with the National Environmental Policy Act.* He is also a co-author of the CEQA chapters of California Environmental Law and Land Use Practice and a member of the on the editorial board of the *California Environmental Law Reporter*, published by LexisNexis/Mathew Bender.

Kenneth M. Bogdan, Esq., was environmental counsel and environmental education team leader and project director at ICF International for twenty-three years and is now with the California State Water Resources Control Board's Office of General Counsel. Ken's expertise is in analyzing issues regarding compliance with the California Environmental Quality Act, the National Environmental Policy Act, and other federal and state environmental laws and regulations and assisting practitioners with understanding the complexities of environmental permitting requirements and developing strategies for compliance. Ken has conducted scores of CEQA and other environmental law training courses during the past decade, including tailored land use planning and CEQA courses. Ken graduated with a Bachelor of Sciences in Environmental Management from Rutgers University and a Juris Doctorate from the University of California, Davis, King Hall School of Law.

Mr. Bogdan, as well as being co-author of The NEPA Book: A Step-By-Step Guide on How to Comply with the National Environmental Policy Act, is an author of "Wetlands, Streams and Other Waters"; and the League of Cities: Guide to Conservation Planning in California. He has authored numerous CEQA and other environmental law case reviews for the *California Environmental Law Reporter*, published by LexisNexis/Mathew Bender.

Antero A. Rivasplata, AICP, is a technical director at ICF International, specializing in CEQA, land use planning, and environmental education. He manages the preparation of EIRs, Negative Declarations, and NEPA documents. In addition, he works with California planning law, Williamson Act, and zoning issues. In addition to being an instructor in CEQA and NEPA through the UC Extension, he is the editor of the Association of Environmental Professionals' "Environmental Assessor" quarterly. He is a past director of the State Clearinghouse in the Governor's Office of Planning and Research (OPR) and, in addition to participating in the CEQA Guidelines amendments of the 1990s, was a co-author of several editions of the General Plan Guidelines while working there. Prior to OPR, Mr. Rivasplata worked as a county planner. Mr. Rivasplata received a B.S. from the University of California, Davis.

Chapters at a Glance

Contents

Contents

Contents

Contents

Contents

Contents

Short Articles

Figures

Tables

Appendices

Chapter 1

Background and Implementation of CEQA

Overview

Introduction

Since 1970, the California Environmental Quality Act (CEQA) has been regarded as the foundation of environmental law and policy in California. CEQA requires California public agencies to participate in an environmental review process to identify significant environmental impacts and adopt feasible mitigation prior to making a final decision on a proposed project. As described by CEQA, this environmental review is generally a three-phase process (CEQA Guidelines § 15002(k), *see* Figure 1-1, page 2):

- **Phase 1.** The public agency determines if the proposed action is considered a "project" and if it fits under an exemption where no detailed environmental analysis is required.
- **Phase 2.** If no exemption applies, the public agency determines whether it should be the lead agency for the detailed document preparation, and if so, it conducts an initial study (IS) to determine if the proposed project has the potential to cause significant environmental impacts.
- **Phase 3.** If the lead agency determines that the proposed project does not have the potential to cause significant impacts, it prepares either a negative declaration (ND) or mitigated negative declaration (MND). If there is the potential to cause significant impacts, and mitigation will not fully address the standard for an MND, it prepares an environmental impact report (EIR).

This book addresses each phase and detailed steps within the CEQA process and presents a detailed discussion of the practical implications of CEQA compliance. These three phases will be discussed in Chapters 2, 3, and 4. For an activity that is not a "project" as defined under CEQA, or that is exempt from CEQA (exemptions are discussed in Chapter 2), the

Introductory CEQA Glossary

- **Project:** a discretionary action with potential physical effects on the environment
- **Statutory Exemption:** legislative exclusion from preparation of CEQA documents
- **Categorical Exemption:** regulatory exclusion from preparation of CEQA documents, limited to when there is no possible significant impact
- **Lead Agency:** agency with primary responsibility for CEQA compliance when preparing an initial study, negative declaration, mitigated negative declaration, or EIR
- **Responsible Agency:** California agenc(ies) other than the lead agency with discretionary authority over the project
- **Initial Study (IS):** document prepared to study project for potential significant effects
- **Negative Declaration (ND):** document prepared when there are no potential significant impacts
- **Mitigated Negative Declaration (MND):** document prepared when there are no potential significant impacts after application of mitigation
- **Environmental Impact Report (EIR):** document prepared when there are potential significant impacts

Figure 1-1 Overview of the CEQA Process

Phase 1 — Preliminary Review

- ◆ Pre-application consultation
- ◆ Application submitted to Lead Agency
- ○ Application determined to be complete (30 days from submittal; start of EIR/Negative Declaration time limits)
- ◆ Determination that project is subject to CEQA
- ◆ Review for exemptions

Phase 2 — Initial Study

- ◆ Checklist completed
- ◆ Consultation with responsible and trustee agencies
- ○ Decision to prepare EIR or Negative Declaration (30 days from acceptance of complete application)

Phase 3

Environmental Impact Report

- ◆ Notice of Preparation sent to responsible and trustee agencies
- ○ Responses to Notice of Preparation sent to Lead Agency (30 days from acceptance)
- ○ Contract for EIR preparation executed (45 days from decision to prepare EIR)
- ◆ Preliminary Draft EIR prepared
- ◆ Independent review by Lead Agency
- ◆ Draft EIR completed and submitted for review
- ◆ Notice of completion filed
- ◆ Public notice and review of Draft EIR
- ○ Public hearing on Draft EIR (optional) (30–45 days)
- ◆ Written comments received
- ◆ Responses to comments prepared
- ○ Responses sent to commenting agencies (10 days before decision)
- ○ Final EIR certified by Lead Agency (1 year from acceptance)
- ○ Lead Agency makes decision on project (6 months from final EIR certification)
- ◆ Findings written and adopted
- ◆ Mitigation reporting and monitoring program adopted
- ○ Notice of Determination filed (5 days from approval)
- ○ Notice of Determination posted (24 hours from filing)
- ○ Responsible agency makes decision on project (180 days from Lead Agency decision)

or

Negative Declaration

- ○ Contract for Negative Declaration preparation executed (45 days from decision to prepare Negative Declaration)
- ◆ Mitigation measures identified and agreed to by project proponent
- ◆ Draft Negative Declaration prepared
- ○ Public notice and review (20–30 days)
- ◆ Responses to Negative Declaration received
- ◆ Comments considered
- ○ Negative Declaration completed (180 days from acceptance)
- ◆ Commenting agencies notified of date of hearing on project
- ◆ Negative Declaration adopted
- ○ Mitigation reporting and monitoring program adopted
- ○ Lead Agency makes determination on project (2 months from Negative Declaration adoption)
- ○ Notice of Determination filed (5 days from project approval)
- ○ Notice of Determination posted (24 hours from filing)
- ○ Responsible agency makes decision on project (180 days from Lead Agency decision)

CEQA Process Complete

Legend

- ◆ CEQA process actions
- ○ CEQA process actions with time constraints

CEQA process ends after Phase 1. Projects requiring a negative declaration or mitigated negative declaration will be subject to all three phases of review, as discussed in Chapter 3 and 4. Most projects requiring an EIR will also go through all three phases, as discussed in Chapter 5. However, if an agency decides to prepare an EIR from the start, it is not required to prepare an initial study and may skip Phase 2.

Figure 1-1 presents an outline of the three phases of CEQA, incorporating the steps of CEQA's environmental review requirements.

> **Phases in the Environmental Review Process under CEQA**
>
> - **Phase 1:** preliminary review of an agency action to determine whether the action is subject to CEQA or the underlying project is exempt from CEQA
> - **Phase 2:** preparation of an initial study to determine whether the project may have a significant environmental effect
> - **Phase 3:** preparation of an EIR if the project may have a significant environmental effect or of a negative declaration or mitigated negative declaration if no significant effects will occur

Objectives

When CEQA was enacted, in the early 1970s, many of the most important environmental laws and their implementing regulations were enacted at the federal level. These include the National Environmental Policy Act (NEPA), as well as the Clean Water, Clean Air, and Endangered Species Acts. CEQA, which was modeled after NEPA, encourages the protection of all aspects of the environment by requiring California state and local agencies to prepare multidisciplinary environmental impact analyses and to make decisions on projects based on those studies. Since its enactment, CEQA has been praised, criticized, and amended often, and has been subject to considerable litigation. In spite of this, it has maintained its position as the backbone of California's environmental program. The full text of CEQA, codified in the California Public Resources Code, is found in Appendix 1. The full text of the regulations to implement CEQA, referred to as the State CEQA Guidelines (Guidelines), codified in Title 14 of the California Code of Regulations, is found in Appendix 2.

> **CEQA Objectives**
>
> - Disclose to decisionmakers and the public the significant environmental effects of proposed activities
> - Identify ways to avoid or reduce environmental damage
> - Prevent environmental damage by requiring implementation of feasible alternatives or mitigation measures
> - Disclose to the public reasons for agency approval of projects with significant environmental effects
> - Foster interagency coordination in the review of projects
> - Enhance public participation in the planning process

Through its comprehensive policies and rigorous procedural requirements, CEQA has made an indelible mark on both government and private decisionmaking in California. CEQA's main objectives are to disclose to decisionmakers and the public the significant environmental effects of proposed activities, and to require agencies to avoid or reduce those environmental effects by implementing feasible alternatives or mitigation measures (consistent with the constitutional requirements summarized in the State CEQA Guidelines § 15002(a)). Other objectives of CEQA focus on public disclosure of the reasons for agency approval of projects with significant environmental effects, interagency coordination in the review of projects, and enhancement of public and other state and local agencies' participation in the planning process (Pub. Res. Code §§ 21000–21004; Guidelines §§ 15002, 15044, 15072, 15073, 15086, 15087, and 15200–15209).

Application to Government Activities in California

CEQA applies to all discretionary activities considered "projects" (*see* Chapter 2 for a detailed discussion of what is a project under CEQA) proposed to be carried-out or approved by California public agencies—including state, regional, county, and local agencies—unless an exemption applies (*see* Chapter 2 for a detailed discussion of statutory and categorical exemptions under CEQA). This includes projects proposed and implemented by

California public agencies, as well as the issuance of a permit or land use entitlement from a California public agency for private development, subject to certain exemptions discussed below (Pub. Res. Code §§ 21001.1, 21002, 21080; Guidelines § 15002(c)).

CEQA requires analysis of potential impacts on the physical environment, including agricultural resources.

Policies Encouraging Protection of the Environment

CEQA sets forth a series of sweeping policy statements encouraging environmental protection (Pub. Res. Code §§ 21000–21004; Guidelines §§ 15002, 15003). These policy statements in CEQA provide that:

- Maintenance of a quality environment is of statewide concern.
- There is a need to maintain ecological systems and the general welfare of the people.
- Government agencies should identify critical thresholds for health and safety and prevent conditions from reaching those thresholds.
- Every citizen has the responsibility to preserve and enhance the environment.
- Public and private interests must make systematic and concerted efforts to enhance environmental quality and control pollution.
- Government agencies must give major consideration to preventing environmental damage.
- All actions necessary to protect, rehabilitate, and enhance the environmental quality of the state should be taken.
- All actions necessary to provide the people with clean air and water and the enjoyment of aesthetic, natural, scenic, and historic qualities should be taken.
- The elimination of fish and wildlife species should be prevented by ensuring that their populations do not drop below self-perpetuating levels.

These broad, environmentally-oriented policies have led the courts to interpret CEQA "so as to afford the fullest protection of the environment within the reasonable scope of the statutory language (*Friends of Mammoth v. Board of Supervisors* (1972) 8 Cal. 3d 247)."

Policies Encouraging Efficient and Streamlined Implementation

In addition to encouraging the protection of the environment, CEQA also encourages agencies to implement the Act in an efficient and streamlined manner through policies that require them to:

- Integrate CEQA with other planning and environmental laws to encourage concurrent review and processing.
- Organize and write environmental documents to make them useful to decisionmakers and the public.
- Omit unnecessary project descriptions and emphasize feasible alternatives and mitigation measures.

Figure 1-2
Objectives and Procedures

CEQA Objectives	CEQA Procedural Requirements to Meet Objectives
Disclose environmental impacts	• Initial studies • Negative declarations • Environmental impact reports
Identify and prevent environmental damage	• Mitigation measures • Alternatives • Mitigation monitoring
Disclose agency decision making	• Findings • Statements of overriding consideration
Enhance public participation	• Scoping • Public notice requirement • Response to comments • Legal enforcement procedures • Citizen access to the courts
Foster intergovernmental coordination	• Early consultation • Scoping meetings • Notices of preparation • State Clearinghouse review

- Incorporate information from environmental impact reports into a database that can be used to reduce delays and duplication in preparing subsequent documents.
- Carry out CEQA efficiently and expeditiously to conserve financial, governmental, physical, and social resources so that those resources may be applied toward mitigation of environmental impacts.
- Make decisions with environmental consequences in mind.
- Consider the whole of an action, not simply its constituent parts, when determining whether it will have a significant environmental effect.
- Prepare sufficient but not necessarily technically perfect informational documents that are complete and contain a good-faith effort at full disclosure.
- Make decisions that are informed and balanced, and not use CEQA as an instrument for the oppression and delay of social, economic, or recreational development or advancement.

Source: Pub. Res. Code § 21003; Guidelines §§ 15003, 15006

Procedural and Substantive Requirements

CEQA requires all California public agencies to comply with both procedural and substantive requirements (Pub. Res. Code § 21080; Guidelines § 15002). Failure to follow either set of requirements may be considered a violation of CEQA, and an agency's decision may be set aside by a court (Pub. Res. Code §§ 21005, 21168, 21168.5). It should be noted that if CEQA procedural requirements are not met, a court may invalidate the public agency's decision, without consideration of the substantive merits of the agency's CEQA decision.

Procedural Requirements. CEQA sets forth a series of detailed procedural requirements to ensure that each of the law's objectives are accomplished (*see* Figure 1-3, page 8). The fundamental premise on which the Act is based is that environmental protection can be achieved through compliance with these rigorous, action-forcing procedures. Also, CEQA's procedural requirements involving notice and opportunity for comment, are directly related to its main objective of disclosure. Figure 1-2 outlines some of the procedural requirements designed to accomplish each objective. They are linked with specific timing requirements that must be met in order for an agency to have complied with CEQA. Detailed procedural requirements within each phase of CEQA are discussed throughout this book.

Substantive Requirements. CEQA also contains substantive provisions requiring agencies to mitigate environmental impacts, whenever feasible (*City of Marina et al, v. Board of Trustees of the California State University* (2006) 39 Cal. 4th 341). Therefore, to comply with CEQA, it is not enough for agencies to prepare a report that merely meets the procedural requirements. Rather, agencies must actually avoid or minimize environmental damage unless doing so is not feasible (Pub. Res. Code § 21002; Guidelines §§ 15002, 15021). If avoiding or minimizing environmental damage is not feasible, CEQA requires agencies either to disapprove the project or to prepare a written statement of overriding considerations that explains why they approved a project that will cause significant effects on the environment (Pub. Res. Code § 21002; Guidelines §§ 15021, 15040–15043). The statement of overriding considerations must be supported by substantial evidence in the record (Pub. Res. Code § 21081; Guideline § 15091).

Authorities Granted to Public Agencies

No New Powers. CEQA should be used in conjunction with a public agency's existing discretionary powers granted by other laws (Guidelines § 15040). Although it requires agencies to mitigate or avoid significant impacts when feasible, CEQA does not grant an agency new, independent powers to impose or carry out mitigation measures. Rather, an agency must rely on its existing discretionary powers granted by other laws to mitigate or avoid significant environmental effects. Thus, a state agency might have the authority to require mitigation in its enabling statute, or a local government may rely on its police power or specific authority in a local ordinance (Pub. Res. Code § 21004; Guidelines § 15040). Although the public agency might not have the authority to require mitigation under its jurisdiction, CEQA still requires that all mitigation be disclosed. As part of this disclosure, the lead agency must discuss the other agencies that would have the power to implement the mitigation.

> **CEQA Authorizes Agencies to:**
>
> - Require changes in a project to lessen or avoid significant effects, when feasible. Guidelines § 15041(a)
> - Disapprove a project to avoid significant effects. Guidelines § 15042
> - Approve a project with significant effects if there is no feasible way to lessen or avoid the significant effects and the project's benefits outweigh these effects. Guidelines § 15043
> - Impose fees on project applicants for CEQA implementation. Guidelines § 15045(a)

Agency Authorities Granted by CEQA. CEQA does grant public agencies several basic types of authorities to enable them to carry out the objectives of the Act. As discussed later in this chapter, the Act anticipates that there may be several agencies that will be required to comply with CEQA for a particular project. The agency with the most authority over the action will be the agency that takes the lead—referred to as the "lead agency"—in preparing the CEQA document (initial study, negative declaration, mitigated negative declaration, or environmental impact report). All other California public agencies required to use the document for compliance will be considered "responsible agencies" and assist the lead agency in preparation of the document.

- **Authority to Comment.** CEQA authorizes all persons or entities, including public agencies other than responsible agencies, to comment on other agencies' environmental documents (Pub. Res. Code § 21104; Guidelines § 15044). A responsible agency must limit its comments to those project activities that are within its areas of expertise or regulatory authority (Guidelines § 15096(d)).
- **Authority to Mitigate or Disapprove.** CEQA authorizes lead and responsible agencies to require feasible changes in a project to substantially lessen or avoid significant effects, or to disapprove a project to avoid significant effects (Pub. Res. Code § 21002.1; Guidelines §§ 15041, 15042). Since each agency's underlying law determines its authority, the ability to mitigate impacts differs from agency to agency. Thus, a general purpose agency, such as a city or county, would typically have greater authority to require mitigation that would a single-purpose agency, such as an air or water quality agency.
- **Authority to Approve Projects Despite Impacts.** CEQA authorizes lead agencies to approve a project with significant effects if there is no feasible way to lessen or avoid them, and the project's benefits outweigh these effects (Pub. Res. Code § 21002.1; Guidelines § 15043).
- **Authority to Impose Fees.** CEQA allows lead agencies to impose fees on project applicants for CEQA implementation, including preparing environmental documents, and for procedures necessary for compliance for an applicant's project. Litigation expenses are not recoverable under this authorization, but may be under other laws or arrangements (Pub. Res. Code § 21089; Guidelines § 15045(a)). The concept of lead, responsible, and trustee agencies is discussed later in this chapter under Key Participants in the CEQA Process.

For CEQA analysis, the environment includes both natural and man-made conditions.

Legislative and Judicial History

Enactment and Early Enforcement

Enacted in 1970, CEQA was modeled after the National Environmental Policy Act (NEPA, 42 U.S.C. 4321–4327). NEPA was enacted by Congress in 1969 and signed into law by President Nixon on January 1, 1970. California was the first state to enact an environmental impact assessment law modeled after NEPA, sometimes referred to as the "mini-NEPA process." See Figure 1-4 for a map of why states have similar law. Like NEPA, CEQA requires agencies to prepare environmental impact assessments of proposed projects and to circulate these documents to other agencies and the public for comment before making decisions on the proposed action (*see* Chapter 9). However, CEQA is considered to be more substantive than NEPA because it not only requires agencies to disclose environmental impacts, but also to avoid or mitigate impacts when feasible to do so. NEPA, on the other hand, only requires impacts to be disclosed through an environmental analysis, and does not necessarily require

Figure 1-3. CEQA Process Flow Chart

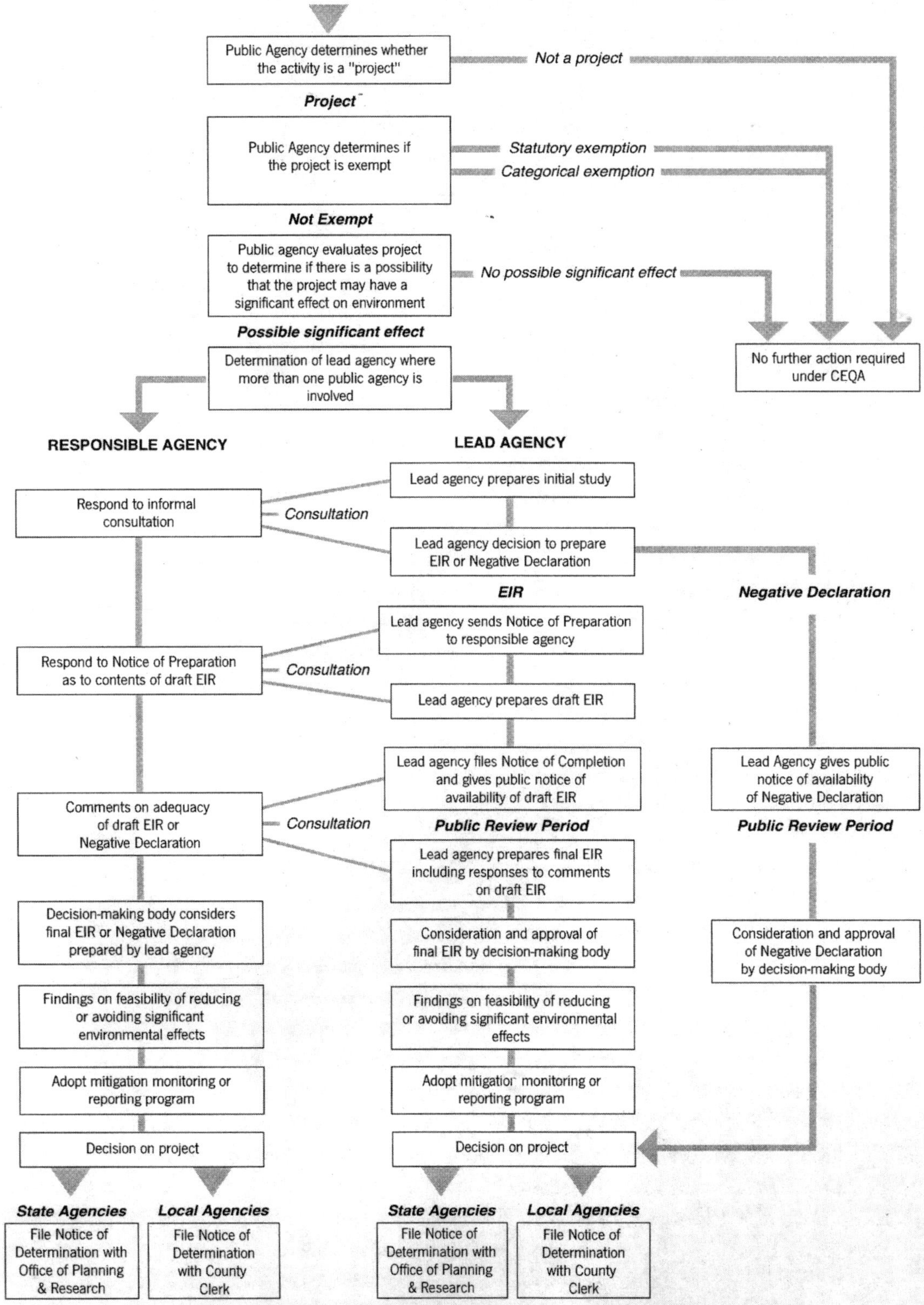

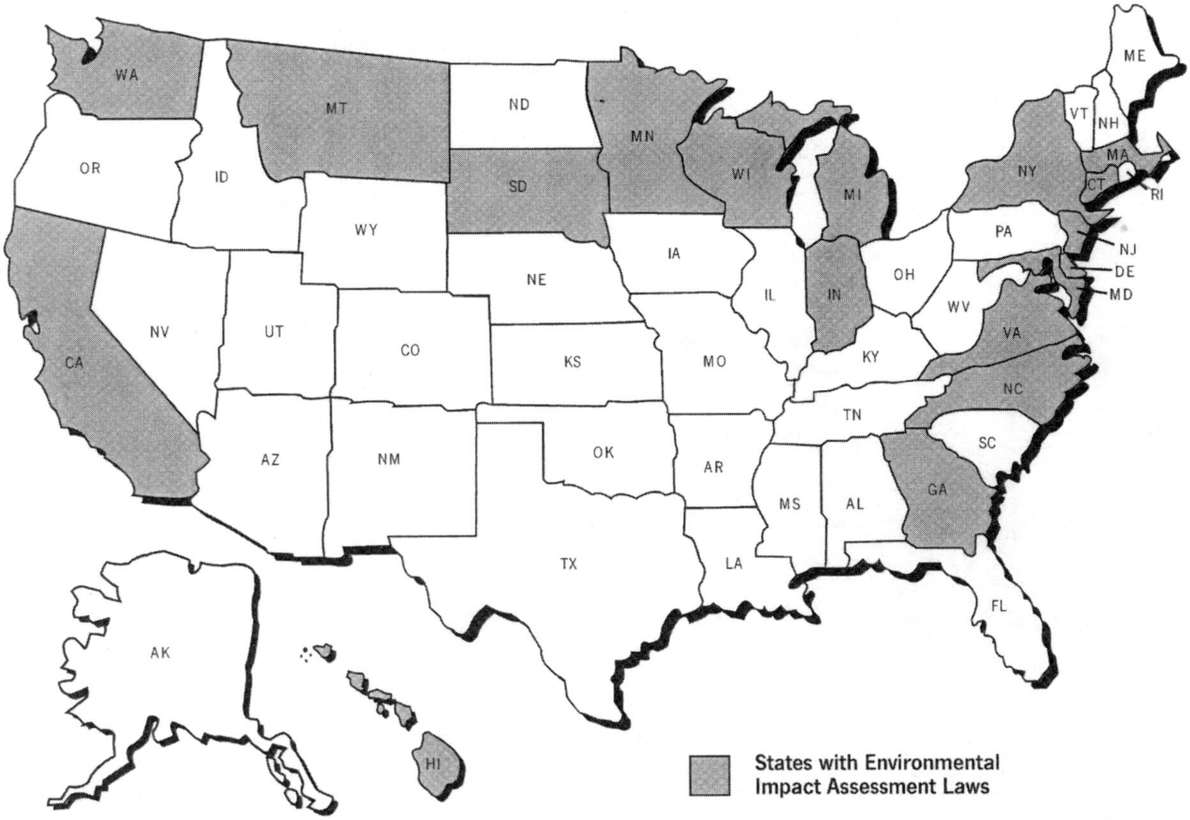

Figure 1-4. States with Environmental Impact Assessment Laws

federal agencies to adopt mitigation measures, regardless of their feasibility (*see* chapter 6 for a detailed comparison of CEQA and NEPA).

CEQA was drafted in response to *The Environmental Bill of Rights*, a report issued by the California Assembly Select Committee on Environmental Quality in 1970. This report called for adoption of an environmental quality act modeled after NEPA. The *Bill* included a proposal to make CEQA a constitutional amendment, but the Legislature instead chose to enact it as a statute. Following the recommendation of the Assembly Select Committee on Environmental Quality, Assemblyman John T. Knox introduced Assembly Bill 2045. CEQA was eventually passed by the Legislature on August 21, 1970, and was signed by Governor Reagan on September 18, 1970.

Court Decisions and Subsequent Amendments

The CEQA that exists today is not the same CEQA that was signed into law by Governor Reagan. What may have been interpreted at the time as a law requiring environmental review of only projects proposed to be built by public agencies, CEQA has evolved into an expansive requirement for environmental review of practically all discretionary actions by public agencies, including approval of most private projects needing California agency approval. Since its enactment, CEQA has been amended almost every year. Also, the State CEQA

The Court's Role in Developing CEQA Policy

The courts have played a key role in the evolution of CEQA, particularly in its enforcement. As discussed in Chapter 8, there is no separate agency explicitly authorized to enforce CEQA. Therefore, CEQA enforcement has been accomplished primarily through the courts. As such, important CEQA court decisions throughout the years have shaped CEQA practice. Intertwined in many of the sections of the CEQA Guidelines, important policy statements are presented as derived from CEQA court decisions. These concepts will be described in more detailed in the proceeding chapters. Starting with State CEQA Guideline § 15003, the Guidelines acknowledge that "in addition to the policies declared by legislature... the courts of this state have declared the following policies to be implicit in CEQA:"

- CEQA was intended to be interpreted in such manner as to afford the fullest possible protection to the environment within the reasonable scope of the statutory language. *Friends of Mammoth v. Board of Supervisors of Mono County,* [1972] 8 Cal. 3d 247
- The environmental impact report requirement is the heart of CEQA. *County of Inyo v. Yorty,* [1973] 32 Cal. App. 3d 795
- The EIR serves not only to protect the environment, but also to demonstrate to the public that it is being protected. *County of Inyo v. Yorty,* [1973] 32 Cal. App. 3d 795
- The EIR serves to inform other governmental agencies and the public generally of the environmental impact of a proposed project. *No Oil, Inc. v. City of Los Angeles,* [1974] 13 Cal. 3d 68
- The EIR serves to demonstrate to an apprehensive citizenry that the agency has, in fact, analyzed and considered the ecological implications of its action. *People ex rel. Department of Public Works v. Bosio,* [1975] 47 Cal. App. 3d 495
- The EIR process enables the public to determine the environmental and economic values of their elected and appointed officials, thus allowing for appropriate action come election day should a majority of the voters disagree. *People v. County of Kern,* [1976] 39 Cal. App. 3d 830
- The purpose of CEQA is not to generate paper, but to compel government at all levels to make decisions with environmental consequences in mind. *Bozung v. LAFCO,* (1975) 13 Cal. 3d 263
- The lead agency must consider an action in its entirety, not simply its constituent parts, when determining whether it will have a significant environmental effect. *Citizens Assoc. For Sensible Development of Bishop Area v. County of Inyo,* (1985) 172 Cal. App. 3d 151
- CEQA does not require technical perfection in an EIR, but rather adequacy, completeness, and a good-faith effort at full disclosure. A court does not pass upon the correctness of an EIR's environmental conclusions, but only determines if the EIR is sufficient as an informational document. *Kings County Farm Bureau v. City of Hanford,* (1990) 221 Cal. App. 3d 692
- CEQA requires that decisions be informed and balanced. It must not be subverted into an instrument for the oppression and delay of social, economic, or recreational development or advancement. *Laurel Heights Improvement Assoc. of San Francisco v. Regents of U.C.*, (1993) 6 Cal. 4th 1112; *Citizens of Goleta Valley v. Board of Supervisors,* (1990) 52 Cal. 3d 553

Friends of Mammoth v. Board of Supervisors: Court Establishes that CEQA Applies to Government Approval of Private Projects

CEQA was not taken seriously by many public agencies during the first year following its enactment, and the law was not originally applied to private development projects requiring government permits or approvals. Early EIRs looked more like the initial studies and negative declarations prepared by today's standards.

The application of CEQA greatly expanded with the California Supreme Court's decision in *Friends of Mammoth v. Board of Supervisors* (1972) 8 Cal. 3d 247, which specifically addressed whether CEQA applied to government approval of private projects. In that case, Mono County, assuming that its action was not subject to the newly enacted law, approved a conditional use permit for a complex of 184 condominium units, a restaurant, and specialty shops without any environmental study. Friends of Mammoth, an unincorporated association, was formed by a group of Mono county citizens for the purpose of challenging the approval of the project. Specifically, the organization filed suit against the county seeking a writ of mandate to set aside the county's approval, pending compliance with CEQA.

Although the Court of Appeal held for the county, the State Supreme Court reversed the lower court's decision, holding that the county's grant of a conditional use permit was a "project" as defined under CEQA. The court stated that the State Legislature enacted CEQA to require an agency, in its regulatory capacity, to analyze the significant environmental effects of its actions, including privately-initiated projects for which government approvals are needed. Therefore, the term "project" includes not only agency actions that directly involve physical impacts on the environment, but also activities such as approving permits, which have indirect environmental effects. In addition to holding that CEQA applied to issuance of permits for private projects, the court announced that all aspects of CEQA should be interpreted expansively "so as to afford the fullest protection of the environment within the reasonable scope of the statutory language." In 1972, the Legislature amended the law to indicate that CEQA clearly applied to government approval of private projects as well as to direct government activities.

The California Supreme Court's decision in *Friends of Mammoth* was a landmark decision in the history of environmental protection in California. It established the courts as the ultimate enforcers of CEQA and provided a clear message that agency noncompliance would not be tolerated.

HISTORICAL NOTE: *The formation of Friends of Mammoth was led by former Olympic Gold Medal skier Andrea Mead Lawrence. Her ongoing efforts to protect the environment in Mono County have earned her a place as one of California's true environmental pioneers and she went on to serve sixteen years as supervisor. In 2000, the California Chapter of the American Planning Association recognized Ms. Lawrence with a Distinguished Leadership Award for her lifelong contributions to planning in California. She passed away in 2009.*

Justice Mosk was the author of the majority opinion in the *Friends of Mommoth* case.

Guidelines have been revised according to legislative amendments as well as in reaction to court decisions interpreting CEQA. Most of the legislative amendments have been minor—however, fundamental changes have been made every few years. For example, in 1972, CEQA was amended to codify the key holding of *Friends of Mammoth v. Board of Supervisors of Mono County* (1972) 8 Cal. 3d 247, 104 Cal. Rptr. 76 (that CEQA applies not only to public projects but also to private activities requiring discretionary governmental approval; *see* previous section). Other important amendments, generally intended to streamline CEQA, were enacted in 1976, 1978, 1984, 1989, and 1993.

The CEQA Revision Acts of 1993 resulted in numerous technical revisions intended to streamline the CEQA process. These revisions included such measures requiring an update of the Guidelines every two years, expediting the responsible agency permit process, streamlining the process of granting CEQA compliance for environmentally mandated projects, limiting judicial remedies, and new procedures for preparing master and focused EIRs. The 1993 legislation also encouraged the use of mitigated negative declarations and added a definition of "substantial evidence." Since then, the Legislature has adopted revisions to CEQA but has not altered its fundamental structure. The primary changes for CEQA practitioners have come from changes to the State CEQA Guidelines, California Supreme Court decisions, and published appellate court decisions.

The Politics of CEQA Compliance

Discretion and Risk. CEQA is a flexible law that gives state and local agencies a broad array of choices regarding implementation. An agency has the discretion in determining whether CEQA is triggered and the method of compliance. The lead agency also has the responsibility to weigh the evidence before it and determine whether a "fair argument" exists for preparation of an EIR. In addition, the lead agency has discretion related to the scope and content of the document being prepared. With such broad discretion comes considerable responsibility, risk, and challenges from conflicting interests. Throughout the environmental review process, public agencies must make a series of important decisions, any one of which may be challenged by project opponents. Lead agencies and their staffs must continually balance the time, effort, and expense of proper compliance against the risks of making unpopular decisions and the potential for legal challenge. To a great extent, the success of CEQA depends on the way in which agencies manage this risk.

In practice, the lead agency is often subject to political and economic influences to shorten the process and lessen the document preparation by either allowing the project to proceed under an exemption when a negative declaration may be more appropriate (*see* Chapter 2), or preparing a negative declaration when an EIR may be more appropriate (*see* Chapter 3). When deciding which type of document to prepare, the agency should be mindful of the legal and political risks inherent in taking shortcuts. Generally, the risk of being successfully challenged in court increases as less time and effort is devoted to preparing the CEQA document and the administrative record on which the agency has based its decision (*see* Figure 1-3, page 8). Covered in

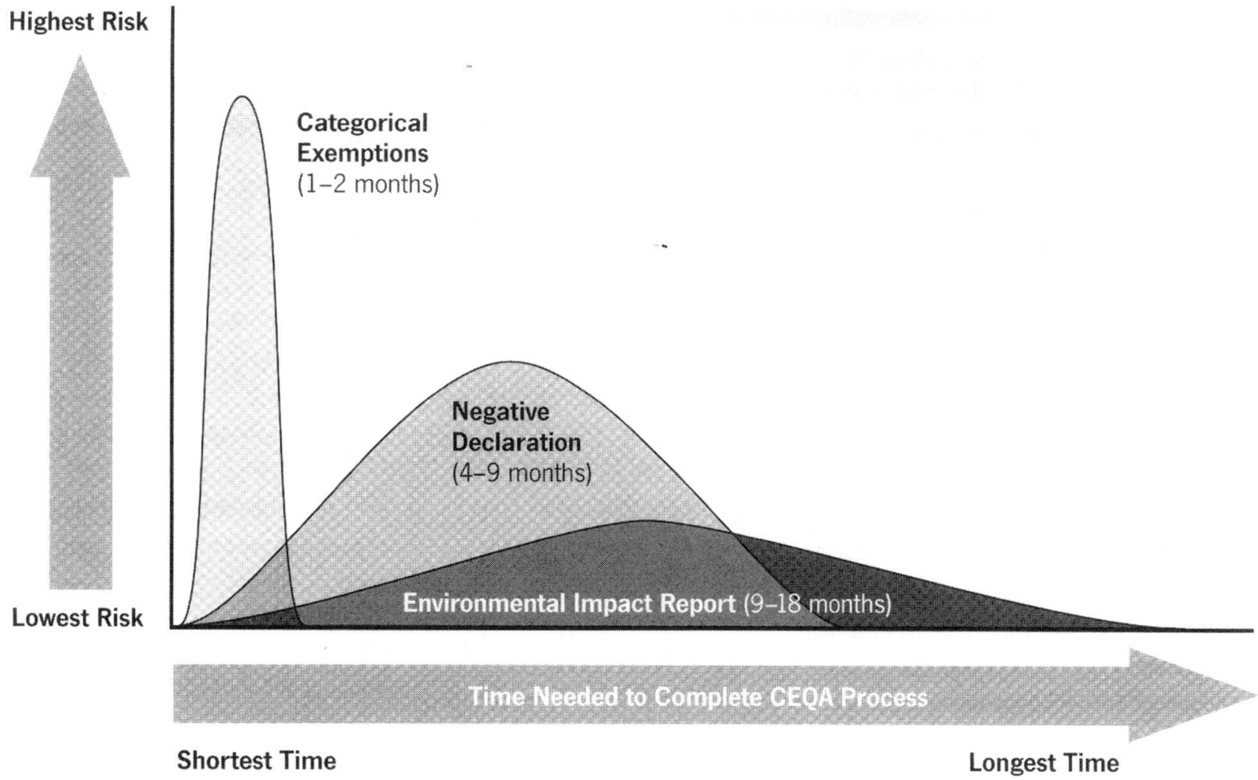

Figure 1-5
Risk Versus Approximate Time in CEQA Compliance

more detail in Chapter 8, the adequacy of the administrative record is directly related to the judicial review of the agency's CEQA compliance.

Variations in CEQA Compliance among Projects and Agencies. An additional challenge for public agencies is that the degree of public scrutiny of their actions or community concern regarding a type of project or sensitive resource, is generally a factor in determining the level of CEQA compliance. Consequently, the standard for determining adequate compliance often differs among project, communities, and agencies. For example, a project that requires an EIR in one jurisdiction may require only a negative declaration in another because of differing environmental thresholds of the public agency, or because of the amount of information on adverse environmental impacts generated by differing levels of public scrutiny or community concerns.

One way to think of these levels of CEQA compliance is: "bare legal minimum," "good practice," and "highly conservative approach." Examples of these levels can vary between different California jurisdictions, and within the same jurisdiction depending on a number of factors including the risk of legal challenges. In instances where the project effects and controversy surrounding the project's adverse effects are minimal, it may be appropriate to achieve CEQA compliance through the "bare legal minimum," where minimal environmental review and notice is prepared. However, where project effects are numerous and complicated, and where there is controversy (and threat of legal challenge), it may be in the agency's (and project proponent's) best interest to achieve compliance though a highly conservative approach to document preparation that goes over and above the more routine CEQA document.

CEQA as a Bridge between Science and Politics. The intent of CEQA is to use an interdisciplinary approach in agency decision making to ensure integration of the natural and social sciences and the consideration of the qualitative as well as quantitative factors (Guidelines § 15142). In addition to being highly discretionary and subject to local variations, CEQA compliance is also a challenge sometimes because of the interdisciplinary nature of many environmental impacts. As described in Chapter 3, CEQA requires an agency to review the effects of its actions on numerous environmental resources, including air, water, fish, and wildlife. Proper implementation may require extensive coordination between a variety of professional disciplines. The goal of CEQA's interdisciplinary focus is to ensure that government agencies consider a broad range of environmental factors, and that trade-offs between various resources are publicly considered.

Prior to the passage of CEQA, government decision making was often two-dimensional, focusing only on economic and technical factors. Environmental issues rarely entered into the political debate. Generally, the negative aspects of a project—often environmental in nature—were not even presented to the public.

By requiring multi-disciplinary scientific inquiry, CEQA has clearly filled a void. The EIR, in particular, has proved to be a valuable tool for bridging the gap between science and politics, fostering informed public debate over a broad range of environmental impacts.

State Administration and Oversight

Two state agencies, the Governor's Office of Planning and Research (OPR) and the California Natural Resources Agency, are responsible for CEQA's basic administration and oversight. Their responsibilities center on administering some of CEQA's procedural requirements and issuing the State CEQA Guidelines. Additionally the State Attorney General's Office may review and comment on CEQA documents and, if appropriate, may initiate or intervene in litigation to enforce CEQA compliance.

OPR Responsibilities

OPR is responsible for the following CEQA-related activities:

- Reviewing and recommending changes to the State CEQA Guidelines
- Recommending categorical exemptions to be included in the State CEQA Guidelines
- Resolving lead agency disputes upon request
- Assisting in identifying responsible agencies upon request
- Ensuring that responsible agencies respond to notices of preparation (NOPs)

- Operating the State Clearinghouse (SCH) to set the review period for state review of environmental documents and to coordinate that review
- Posting notices of completion, exemption, and determination submitted to the SCH
- Providing environmental documents received in electronic form to the state library for filing and posting on the internet
- Publishing the SCH newsletter
- Collecting California Department of Fish and Game review fees for projects triggering the requirement to send documents to the SCH
- Maintaining a database to assist agencies in CEQA implementation and making that database available on the Internet

Sources: Pub Res. Code §§ 21080.4, 21083, 21159.9; Guidelines §§ 15023, 15053

Natural Resources Agency Responsibilities

The California Natural Resources Agency is responsible for the following CEQA-related activities:

- Formal rulemaking and adoption of the Guidelines, including the establishment of classes of a categorical exemption
- Certifying state agency regulatory programs as being the "functional equivalent" of CEQA's environmental review process
- Receiving notices of determination filed for certified regulatory programs
- Maintenance of Internet information about CEQA

Sources: Pub. Res. Code § 21083(c); Guidelines §§ 15024, 15252

CEQA and the State CEQA Guidelines. CEQA, codified in the California Public Resources Code at § 21000 *et. seq.*, is the collection of CEQA legislation passed by the Senate and Assembly and signed by the Governor (*see* Appendix 1). CEQA specifically directs the Resources Agency, with advice from OPR, to adopt regulations to implement the general directives contained in the Act (Pub Res Code 21083). The State CEQA Guidelines (*see* Figure 1-6, page 16) are the official administrative interpretation of CEQA for agency implementation (*see* Appendix 2).

Legal Effect of the State CEQA Guidelines. Although the Guidelines are formally adopted with public notice and comment, and are contained in Title 14 of the California Code of Regulations, there is some legal question as to whether the Guidelines are regulatory mandates for all agencies to follow or merely discretionary aids to interpreting CEQA. Although the courts have been reticent to make a dispositive conclusion to this issue, they generally defer to the Guidelines and refer to them in much the same way they would other regulations, unless there is a direct conflict with the legislation. The California Supreme Court has noted that at a minimum "courts should afford great weight to the Guidelines except where a provision is clearly unauthorized or erroneous under CEQA."

Figure 1-6. CEQA Guidelines Contents

Article 1	General Provisions
Article 2	General Responsibilities
Article 3	Authorities Granted to Public Agencies by CEQA
Article 4	Lead Agency
Article 5	Preliminary Review of Project and Conduct of Initial Study
Article 6	Negative Declaration Process
Article 7	EIR Process
Article 8	Time Limits
Article 9	Contents of EIR
Article 10	Considerations in Preparing EIRs
Article 11	Types of EIRs
Article 12	Special Situations
Article 13	Review and Evaluations of EIRs and Negative Declarations
Article 14	Projects Also Subject to NEPA
Article 15	Litigation
Article 16	EIR Monitor
Article 17	Exemptions for Certified State Regulatory Programs
Article 18	Statutory Exemptions
Article 19	Categorical Exemptions
Article 20	Definitions
	Appendices

(*Laurel Heights Improvement Assoc. of San Francisco v. Regents of University of California* (1988) 47 Cal. 3d 376) (Guidelines § 15005).

Revision and Update of CEQA Guidelines. OPR is directed to review the Guidelines at least once every two years and recommend amendments to the Natural Resources Agency (Pub. Res. Code 21083). The process for adoption of Guidelines starts with recommendations from OPR or through a request from a public agency. The Natural Resources Agency sometimes convenes a task force or working group, representing diverse interests, to recommend Guidelines revisions. After proposing a draft that goes through public notice and comment pursuant to the Administrative Procedures Act, the Natural Resources Agency certifies and adopts the Guidelines. The Natural Resources Agency is directed to certify and adapt Guideline amendments at least once every two years (Pub. Res. Code 21083). After adoption but prior to the Guidelines becoming effective, the California Office of Administrative Law reviews the adopted Guidelines to ensure compliance with state requirements for promulgating regulations (*See* Government Code 11346.4, 11346.5, 11346.8). Compliance with amendments to the Guidelines becomes mandatory 120 days after the amendments have become "effective," although a public agency may choose to implement the amendment beginning on the Guideline amendment's effective date (Guidelines § 15007). This process may have a much shorter administrative review period when the CEQA Guidelines amendments are considered minor, non-substantive non-regulatory rulemaking.

The complete text of the CEQA Guidelines can be found in Appendix 2, or is available online at the State Office of Administrative Law (http://ccr.oal.ca.gov/ccrmain.htm under Title 14 Natural Resources, Division 6 Resources Agency, Chapter 3).

Since the Guidelines are not always current with legislative changes and published court opinions, practitioners are advised to keep abreast of new laws adopted by the State Legislature and to review the latest judicial opinions for the most recent interpretations of CEQA. CEQA cases are also reported on the CERES website.

Other Responsibilities of OPR

Beginning in March 1994, OPR has been required to implement a public assistance and information program to help agencies implement CEQA. As part of this program, OPR started a CEQA technical advice series to explain complex issues that frequently arise in CEQA practice. It has issued the very useful advice memoranda including (available at http://www:opr.ca.gov):

- Tracking Mitigation Measures under AB 3180 (March 1996)
- Focusing on Master EIRs (November 1997)
- Mitigated Negative Declarations (December 1997)
- CEQA, NEPA, and Base Closure: Recipes for Streamlining Environmental Review (March 1996)

- Thresholds of Significance: Criteria for Defining Environmental Significance (September 1994)
- Circulation and Notice Under the California Environmental Quality Act (July 2001)
- CEQA and Climate Change: Addressing Climate Change through CEQA Review (June 2008)
- CEQA and Low-Impact Development Stormwater Design: Preserving Stormwater Quality and Stream Integrity through CEQA (August 2009)
- Cities and Counties Addressing Climate Change (November 2010)

OPR's technical advice series booklets on CEQA and archaeological and historical resources have been superseded by the advice of the California Office of Historic Preservation. The publication, "Technical Advice Series #1: California Environmental Quality Act (CEQA) and Historical Resources," is available online from the Office of Historic Preservation at http://ohp.parks.ca.gov.

Additionally, OPR is required to maintain an information database to help agencies prepare environmental documents (Pub. Res. Code § 21159.9). The database is available online, as discussed below. A listing of recent environmental documents submitted to the SCH is available through the CERES website (discussed below).

State Clearinghouse

In 1973, the State Clearinghouse was established within OPR as the single point of contact in state government to receive and distribute environmental documents prepared pursuant to NEPA, and to coordinate the environmental review process under CEQA when state agencies are involved. The categories of documents required to be sent to the SCH are described in Chapter 3. The SCH does not actually review CEQA documents, but instead circulates them for review to those state agencies likely to be interested in the projects, and receives and transmits comments from those state agencies to the agencies responsible for preparing the CEQA documents.

The review period for environmental documents submitted to the SCH is set by CEQA Guidelines § 515105. Under specific criteria, a shortened SCH review may be granted (Guidelines Appendix K). The SCH may refuse to circulate documents that are incomplete or lack an accompanying notice of completion form. Pursuant to state law, the SCH has up to three working days to distribute an environmental document to state agencies once SCH is satisfied that the filing is complete (Pub. Res. Code § 21091; Guidelines § 15105).

The SCH maintains a computerized database of all environmental documents it receives for state review. Although the SCH does not receive all EIRs, its database is the only source of information regarding the number of EIRs prepared in California. This database is now available online at the OPR website: http//www.ceqanet.ca.gov. The database will become increasingly interactive and will someday allow for the filing of notices with the SCH electronically.

California Resources Agency—California Environmental Resource Evaluation System

CERES is a web-based information system developed by the State of California to facilitate access to a variety of electronic data describing California's environment. The goal of CERES is to improve environmental analysis and planning by integrating natural and cultural resource information from multiple contributors and making it available and useful to a wide variety of users.

The CERES website contains CEQA Web that contains the web links to text of CEQA, the regulations, including proposed amendments, and a growing collection of online environmental documents. CERES may be found online at http://ceres.ca.gov. Information available online includes:

- The CEQA Statute
- The CEQA Guidelines, including proposed amendments
- Most CEQA court decisions
- Recent Statutory Changes/Amendments to CEQA
- Other information related to CEQA

One component of CERES, under supplemental materials, is an interactive CEQA process flow chart, an innovative legal research tool to help CEQA practitioners. Using the interactive version of the familiar CEQA flow chart, a person may select any aspect of the environmental review process and the following information will immediately appear:

- A narrative summary of that component of the process
- The relevant Public Resources Code sections
- The CEQA Guideline references related to that topic
- A list of the most significant cases dealing with that topic

The flow chart helps bring the details of CEQA's legal framework to anyone who uses it. Additionally, it helps bridge the gap between the visually oriented world of planners and the written world of attorneys.

Also located within CERES, the Land Use Planning Information Network (LUPIN) contains numerous data sources on land use planning in California.

Attorney General Responsibilities

The Attorney General is a statewide, elected official who serves the chief law officer of California. It is the duty of the Attorney General to see that the laws of the state are uniformly and adequately enforced (California Constitution, Article V, Section 13). The Attorney General carries out responsibilities of the office through the California Department of Justice.

To alert the Attorney General of pending CEQA lawsuits, any party initiating CEQA litigation must notify the Attorney General (Pub. Res. Code 21167.7). This enables the Attorney General to participate in the litigation on behalf of the people of California (*See* Chapter 10 for a discussion of CEQA litigation).

As the state's chief law enforcement agency, the Attorney General has taken on an oversight responsibility for ensuring the proper implementation of

CEQA by state and local agencies. In this capacity, the Attorney General's office occasionally comments on EIRs and Negative Declarations, particularly when impacts of regional and statewide importance are involved, or where the underlying project also involves potential violations of other state laws (e.g. water quality laws, air quality laws, housing laws, etc.).

The Attorney General's role has been especially influential in how lead agencies currently evaluate greenhouse gas emissions and climate change impacts. In addition to commenting on the climate change components of CEQA documents, several lawsuits in 2007 and 2008 involving the Attorney General have resulted in important settlement agreements, which have had precedent-setting effects on how these issues are evaluated by other agencies.

Copies of the Attorney General's comments on CEQA documents, settlement agreements, and other CEQA-related documents can be found on the agency's website: http://ag.ca.gov/globalwarming/ceqa.php.

CEQA Implementation by Public Agencies

CEQA applies to all government agencies subject to the jurisdiction of California law at all levels, including state agencies, state boards, state commissions, cities, counties, regional agencies, and special districts (Pub. Res. Code §§ 21000, 21001; Guidelines §§ 15002, 15368, 15379, 15383). However, CEQA does not apply to the legislature, the governor, or the judiciary. Additionally, CEQA does not apply to non-state entities such as federal agencies, tribal governments, and the bi-state Tahoe Regional Planning Agency (although actions by these agencies may require a state or local zoning approval, thereby triggering CEQA).

While many types of actions are subject to CEQA, both the Legislature and the Resources Agency have established exemptions for certain types of activities (*see* Chapter 2 for a detailed discussion of the definition of a "project," and statutory and categorical exemptions).

Agency Requirement to Adopt CEQA Procedures

Each state and local agency must adopt CEQA implementation procedures that are consistent with CEQA and the State CEQA Guidelines. A public agency's implementing procedures should contain the provisions for:

- Identifying activities that are exempt from CEQA
- Conducting initial studies
- Preparing negative declarations
- Consulting with other agencies
- Ensuring adequate opportunities for public review and comment
- Evaluating and responding to comments
- Assigning responsibility for determining the adequacy of environmental documents
- Reviewing and considering environmental documents by decision makers
- Filing environmental documents

- Submitting comments to other agencies
- Assigning CEQA functions to agency staff
- Providing time periods for performing CEQA functions

Source: Pub. Res. Code § 21082; Guidelines § 15022

A public agency may adopt the State CEQA Guidelines by reference, but the agency's procedures must still include specific provisions to tailor the general provisions to its specific operations (Guidelines § 15022).

Because public participation is an essential part of the CEQA process, each public agency should include provisions in its CEQA procedures to encourage both formal and informal public involvement. Such procedures should be designed to receive and evaluate public comments on environmental issues related to agency activities. Additionally, an agency's CEQA procedures should include, whenever possible, making environmental information available in electronic format on a website maintained or utilized by the public agency (Guidelines § 15201).

In practice, most state and local agency CEQA procedures have not been updated and tend to mainly incorporate the Guidelines by reference. Practitioners will rarely need to check with a particular agency's CEQA procedures, as they do not vary from the State CEQA Guidelines. However, agencies should consider updating their CEQA procedures to maximize CEQA's usefulness within their jurisdiction.

Key Participants in the CEQA Process

For any given project, many agencies and groups may be involved in the CEQA process (*see* Figure 1-5, page 13). The potential roles of the various agencies involved in CEQA are described below. An agency may serve in different roles for different projects.

Lead Agency. A lead agency is the California government agency that has the principal responsibility for carrying out or approving a project, and therefore has the principal responsibility for preparing the CEQA document. A lead agency is responsible for deciding whether a negative declaration or an EIR will be required, and for determining the scope and content of that document. Additionally, the lead agency is responsible for the preparation and adequacy of the document, and has the ultimate discretion for significance conclusions and appropriateness of mitigation within the mitigated negative declaration or EIR. The lead agency is required to make changes in a project to lessen or avoid significant effects, when feasible, or to disapprove a project to avoid significant effects unless the project's benefits outweigh these effects (Pub. Res. Code § 21067; Guidelines §§ 15367, 15050) (*see* chapter 2). A lead agency has a duty to produce a comprehensive environmental document that, in most instances, must be used by all responsible agencies in making their decisions. As discussed below, in certain limited instances, a responsible agency may take over the lead agency role in the CEQA process.

Determining the Lead Agency. Identification of the lead agency is an important initial step in the CEQA process. This agency will be the focal point for all the procedural and substantive decisions for CEQA compliance. In general, the lead agency is the agency with the greatest responsibility for approving or carrying out the project. The following are the criteria outlined in the State CEQA Guidelines for determining the lead agency:

- For public projects subject to CEQA, a public agency is the lead agency for its own projects, even if the project will be located within the jurisdiction of another agency.
- For private projects requiring government approval, an agency with general governmental powers (*e.g.*, city or county) prevails as the lead agency over an agency with a single or limited purpose.
- For rezoning, the city approving the rezoning will be the lead agency.
- When criteria are equal, the agency that acts first typically becomes the lead agency. However, in this instance, agencies may designate a lead agency by mutual agreement.

Source: Guidelines § 15051

The designation by mutual agreement only applies when agencies have equal claim to lead agency status. Agencies must use that authority carefully because the designation of the wrong lead agency can lead to CEQA compliance being set aside by a court. For example, in *Planning and Conservation League v. Department of Water Resources* (2000) 83 Cal. App. 4th 892, the Court of Appeal found that the Department of Water Resources, not an individual participating water agency, should have been the lead agency for a multi-agency water supply agreement affecting DWR's operation of the State Water Project. In that case, the parties decided that one of the individual water districts, not DWR, should serve as the lead agency. The court affirmed the Guidelines provision that the lead agency must be the agency with the principal responsibility for carrying out or approving the project. In arriving at its decision, the court noted that DWR had a statewide perspective and expertise in water issues that the water district lacked.

Lead Agency Disputes. Lead agency disputes may be submitted to OPR for resolution (Pub. Res. Code § 21165; Guidelines §§ 15023, 15053). OPR issued lead agency dispute regulations setting forth procedures agencies must follow to formally resolve disputes (*see* Title 14, Cal. Code Regs. §§ 16012 *et seq.* and OPR's Regulations for Designation of Lead Agency, Appendix 3). State law limits those who may petition OPR for a determination of lead agency status to the disputing agencies and the project applicant (in cases where there is an applicant) (Pub. Res. Code § 21165). OPR does not have the authority to designate a lead agency absent a request.

Although OPR has informally mediated numerous lead agency disputes, there have been only a handful of occasions where the OPR director has had to formally designate a lead agency.

Multiple Lead Agencies. Although CEQA does not expressly prohibit having more than one lead agency for preparation of a CEQA document, the concept of lead agency is typically considered a single entity that is the final decision maker related to CEQA compliance. Both the Act and the State

Figure 1-7
Key Participants in the CEQA Process

Trustee Agencies

California Department of Fish and Game (fish and wildlife of the state)

State Lands Commission (state-owned sovereign lands)

Department of Parks and Recreation (units of the state park system)

University of California (natural land and water reserves system)

CEQA Guidelines always refer to this entity as "*the* lead agency," in the singular (Pub. Res. Code 21067; Guidelines § 15367).

In most cases, it is not recommended to have two agencies serve as CEQA co-lead agencies. Many difficult decisions related to CEQA compliance need to be made, and having two agencies share the decision making powers does not lend itself to an efficient process. Thus, if two or more agencies decide to serve as co-leads, it is recommended that the agencies sign an agreement at the start of the CEQA process to delineate how decisions will be made and how disputes will be resolved. Where two (or more) agencies have equivalent authority over an action and none wish to give up the decisionmaking authorities associated with the lead agency, the agencies may opt to form a "joint powers authority" (JPA), where two or more agencies form a separate single public agency for the purposes of preparing the CEQA document. The JPA operating instrument would address how decisions were made in the CEQA process.

A joint powers authority (JPA) is formed when two or more agencies enter into an agreement to share specified powers for some particular purpose. The agreement will describe those powers that the agencies will share. A JPA does not require the agencies to share all of their powers. A common example is a Council of Government, where several cities and one or more counties consider planning issues of common interest, but which have none of the land use regulatory power that the cities and county wield.

A more common form of "co-lead agencies" is when there is one CEQA lead agency and a separate lead agency for compliance with NEPA is discussed in Chapter 9.

Responsible Agency. A responsible agency is an agency other than the lead agency that also has a legal responsibility for carrying out or approving a project. A responsible agency must actively participate in the lead agency's CEQA process, review the lead agency's CEQA document, and use that document when making a decision on the project (Pub. Res. Code § 21069; Guidelines §§ 15050, 15052, 15096, 15381). A responsible agency is required to rely on the lead agency's environmental document in acting on whatever aspect of the project requires its approval, but must prepare and issue its own findings regarding the project (Guidelines § 15096). The responsible agency must require changes to the project under its jurisdiction that would avoid or substantially reduce all significant impacts. A responsible agency generally must consider the lead agency's CEQA document legally adequate, subject to narrow exceptions (Pub. Res. Code § 21167.3; Guidelines §§ 15052, 15096) (*see* Chapter 4). In certain cases, a responsible agency may take over a lead agency's role (Guidelines § 15052).

Switch in Lead Agency Status. Where a responsible agency is called on to grant an approval for a project subject to CEQA for which another public agency was the appropriate lead agency, the responsible agency must use the lead agency's document. A responsible agency may only step into the lead agency role and prepare a separate CEQA document when:

- It successfully challenges the lead agency document in court.
- A subsequent EIR, supplement to the EIR, or subsequent negative declaration is required pursuant to Sections 15162 or 15163 and
  - The lead agency no longer has discretionary authority over the project, and
  - The statute of limitations for challenging the lead agency's action under CEQA has expired.
- The lead agency prepared inadequate environmental documents without consulting with the responsible agency as required by Sections 15072 or 15082, and the statute of limitations has expired for a challenge to the action of the appropriate lead agency.

(Guidelines §§ 15052. 15096(e)).

If the lead agency determines that the appropriate CEQA compliance is through a statutory or categorical exemption (*see* Chapter 2), the "responsible agency" is not bound to follow the lead agency's determination and may step into the lead agency role if it determines an initial study leading to a negative declaration, mitigated negative declaration, or an EIR is required.

Trustee Agencies. Trustee agencies, as defined in CEQA, have jurisdiction over certain resources held in trust for the people of California but do not have a legal authority over approving or carrying out the project (Guidelines § 15386). These trustee agencies may also have separate discretionary authority based on other statutory mandates and may, depending on their particular role in a given project, serve as the lead or responsible agency, as well as a trustee agency for a particular project. Only four agencies are specifically identified by the State CEQA Guidelines as trustee agencies:

- The California Department of Fish and Game, with regard to fish and wildlife of the state, native plants designated as rare or endangered, game refuges, and ecological reserves

Determining the Lead Agency

Public projects

- A public agency is the lead agency for its own projects, even if the project will be located within the jurisdiction of another agency

Private projects requiring government approval

- An agency with general governmental powers (*e.g.*, city or county) prevails over an agency with a single or limited purpose
- The city prezoning an area prior to annexation will be the lead agency rather than the Local Agency Formation Commission (LAFCO)
- When criteria are equal, the agency that acts first becomes the lead agency
- Agencies may designate a lead agency by mutual agreement

- The State Lands Commission, with regard to state-owned "sovereign" lands, such as the beds of navigable waters and state school lands
- The California Department of Parks and Recreation, with regard to units of the state park system
- The University of California, with regard to sites within the Natural Land and Water Reserves System

(Guidelines § 15386).

Although other agencies have jurisdiction by law over certain resources (*see* below), they are not necessarily considered trustee agencies for purposes of CEQA compliance. Trustee agencies are generally required to be notified of CEQA documents relevant to their jurisdiction, whether or not these agencies have actual permitting authority or approval power over aspects of the underlying project (Guidelines § 15086). Involvement of a trustee agency mandates that the negative declaration or EIR be submitted to the SCH for review.

Agencies with Jurisdiction by Law. In addition to contacting all responsible and trustee agencies, the lead agency, when preparing an EIR, must consult with and seek comments from every public agency that has *jurisdiction by law* with respect to the project. Agencies with jurisdiction by law include each city or county that borders on a city or county within which the project is located; and state, federal, and local agencies that exercise authority over resources that may be affected by the project (*e.g.*, U.S. Fish and Wildlife Service for species listed under the Federal Endangered Species Act) (Pub. Res. Code §§ 21104, 21153; Guidelines § 15086) (*see* also State CEQA Guidelines Appendix B for statutory authority of state departments).

Authority and Obligations of Agencies. Lead and responsible agencies have the authority to require changes in the project to lessen or avoid, or to refuse to approve the project to avoid significant impacts and to deny project approval where there are significant impacts that cannot be mitigated. CEQA does not give an agency any authority beyond what it already wields under its statutory and regulatory powers (Pub. Res. Code §§ 21104(c), 21153(c); Guidelines §§ 15041(b), 15042).

Public Participation

Importance of Public Involvement

Public involvement is an essential feature of CEQA (Guidelines § 15201). The environmental review process introduced by CEQA has greatly expanded the opportunities for interested citizens and interest groups to participate in project planning and government decisionmaking. The EIR and the negative declaration have become well-established tools by which the public can gain access to information and influence the outcome of a broad variety of projects. In fact, the California Supreme Court has stated that members of the public hold a "privileged position" in the CEQA process (*Concerned Citizens of Costa Mesa v. 32nd District Agricultural Association* (1986) 42 Cal. 3d 929).

The environmental review process established by CEQA provides ample opportunities for the public to participate through scoping (Guidelines § 15083), public notice and public review of CEQA documents (Guidelines §§ 15072, 15087), and public hearings, and by requiring agencies to respond to public comments in Final EIRs (Guidelines § 15088).

Also, the public plays a major role in the judicial enforcement of CEQA. The vigilance of private citizens has been instrumental in ensuring that agencies comply with the law. Without the active involvement of citizen "watchdogs," many instances of noncompliance would have gone unchallenged. Many Californians have come to expect full compliance with CEQA and are ready and, willing to challenge agencies that do not take CEQA seriously, especially in view of the possibility to recover attorney's fees and other litigation costs.

Lead Agency Responsibility for Public Involvement

The success of CEQA as an environmental disclosure and problem-solving law is based on transparent decisionmaking. Therefore, state and local agencies must make diligent efforts to involve the public in implementing CEQA throughout the environmental review process. Each public agency must include provisions in its CEQA procedures for wide public involvement, both formal and informal, to encourage the public to react to environmental issues related to the agency's proposed projects (Guidelines § 15201). The objectives of public review of agency proposals include sharing expertise, disclosing agency analysis, checking for accuracy, detecting omissions, discovering public concerns, and soliciting counter proposals (Guidelines § 15200). The specific public noticing requirements for EIRs and negative declarations are discussed in Chapters 4 and 5.

E-Mail Notice and Comments

If a public agency offers to provide notice of a proposed negative declaration, notice of preparation, or draft EIR by e-mail, a person may request that the notice be provided to them by e-mail (Pub. Res. Code § 21092.2). Whether or not it has provided notice by e-mail, an agency must accept comments by e-mail and treat e-mail comments as the equivalent to written comments (Pub. Res. Code § 21091(d)).

How to Effectively Participate in the CEQA Process

CEQA provides ample opportunities for members of the public to participate in the environmental review process. Citizens and interest groups should learn the organizational structure, the decision making lines of authority, and the administrative appeal process for the agencies of concern and identify the key individuals who may be responsible for CEQA implementation within the agency. It is important for citizens to write to those individuals and request to be put on the list of persons to be notified of CEQA actions. Joining forces with established associations, environmental groups, and other organizations will assist citizens to address similar environmental issues and pool financial resources. It is also helpful for concerned citizens to regularly monitor local newspapers or agency websites for any formal announcements or articles about agency activities in their community. Some agencies maintain e-mail lists to notifying concerned citizens.

When concerned about a particular agency action, citizens should submit comments at each opportunity afforded by the agency. The comments should be substantive, well written and presented, and supported by the weight of evidence. Conjecture, speculation, and argumentative posturing, without the support of factual information, may be counterproductive to participation in the CEQA process. Citizens must be willing to meet with agency staff to discuss views about the proposed actions. If all other efforts to influence agency decisionmaking are unsuccessful, a person or organization may challenge the agency's decision through litigation.

A vigilant, informed, and well-prepared citizenry is the key to CEQA enforcement and better environmental decisionmaking by state and local officials.

Time for Preparation of CEQA Documents

CEQA provides that a negative declaration for a private project is to be adopted within six months of the application being accepted as complete. An EIR for a private project is to be certified within one year from acceptance. of a complete application. There are no time requirements for preparation of CEQA documents for public projects. In practice, the time limits for private projects are not strictly adhered to by lead agencies (see Chapter 2 for additional discussion of CEQA and the Permit Streamlining Act). The time extended for environmental analysis preparation depends on the complexities of the environmental resources and project effects. In general, Phase 1 documentation to support a CEQA exemption should take one to three months; Phase 2 preparation of an initial study to support a negative declaration or mitigated negative declaration should take four to nine months; Phase 3 development of an environmental impact report should take ten to eighteen months.

The length of time needed for CEQA compliance also depends on CEQA's required public review periods, number and level of detail of comments, and the public agency's own particular approval process.

Integration with Existing Planning Procedures

The environmental review process established by CEQA is not a stand-alone process, but rather, it must be integrated into project planning and decisionmaking. To the maximum extent feasible, these procedures should run concurrently, not consecutively (Guidelines § 15004(c)) (*see* Figure 1-6, page 16). As described in detail in Chapter 3, CEQA should be coordinated with the project planning process, when CEQA requirements are directly linked to the phases of the agency's planning process.

Integration with Related Environmental Review Requirements

To the fullest extent possible, the lead agency should integrate CEQA with other state and federal environmental review and consultation requirements (Guidelines § 15124). CEQA document preparers need to proactively determine all applicable environmental review requirements applicable to a proposed project and develop a comprehensive environmental review strategy. See Chapter 9 for a discussion of coordinating CEQA, NEPA, and various environmental review requirements.

Tips for Successful Compliance

This chapter covered the historical background, legal framework, the roles agencies play, and overview of CEQA's environmental review process. As the chapter reveals, CEQA is fundamental part of California's system of environmental management. However, its implementation can be complex and sometimes controversial. The following are some tips for successful CEQA compliance:

- **Remember CEQA's objectives**—As you implement the law, keep in mind that CEQA's polices and legislative purpose are still relevant after forty years and routinely guide the courts in litigation.
- **Learn the process**—CEQA document preparation and review can be complex; you should take the time to learn the process in a step-by-step fashion.

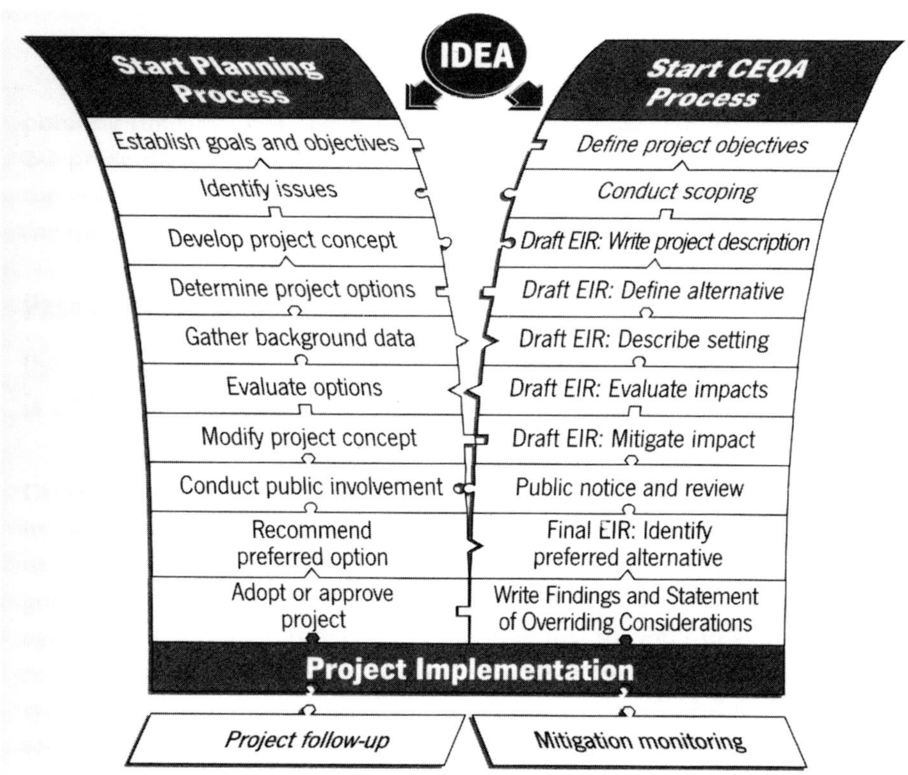

Figure 1-8 Integrating CEQA with Planning

- **Read the CEQA Guidelines**—The CEQA Guidelines form the basis of the environmental review process and knowing them inside and out is essential to successful CEQA implementation.
- **Keep abreast of court decisions**—Although CEQA Guidelines provide the fundamentals, understanding how the courts have interpreted CEQA is also necessary.
- **Determine the appropriate roles of agencies**—Since agencies may assume different roles on different projects, it is essential to understand those roles and each agency's respective responsibilities before starting the CEQA process.
- **Involve the public**—CEQA is a public-oriented law and the environmental review process should be as interactive as possible.

Chapter 2

Preliminary Review and Exemptions

Phases in the Environmental Review Process

Chapter 1 presents an overview of the three phases of CEQA, incorporating the steps of CEQA's environmental review requirements. Figure 2-1 presents the questions raised during the three phases of CEQA and the resulting documents that are prepared depending on the answers to the questions.

CEQA is triggered by a "project," including discretionary decisions related to existing facilities.

Initial Trigger to Comply with CEQA

Lead agencies should prepare CEQA documents during the agency planning process, and must complete and certify those documents before project "approval," which is the decision committing an agency to a definite course of action on the project (Guidelines § 15352(a)). CEQA documents should be prepared early enough in the planning process to enable environmental factors to influence project design, but late enough so that useful information is available for environmental assessment (Guidelines § 15004(b)).

With public projects, the project sponsors must incorporate environmental considerations into project conceptualization, design, and planning. With private projects, the lead agency must encourage the project proponent to incorporate environmental considerations in their project conceptualization, design, and planning at the earliest feasible time. In either case, public agencies must not undertake any action concerning a proposed project that would have a significant adverse effect or limit the choice of alternatives or mitigation measures before completion of CEQA compliance. As seen in the *Save Tara v. City of West Hollywood* ((2008) 45 Cal. 4th 116) decision, how strongly a lead agency commits to a proposed project may determine how early in the process CEQA compliance should occur.

Additionally, an agency may not formally make a decision to proceed with the use of a site until after CEQA compliance. However, an agency may

Figure 2-1
Screening Projects for CEQA Applicability

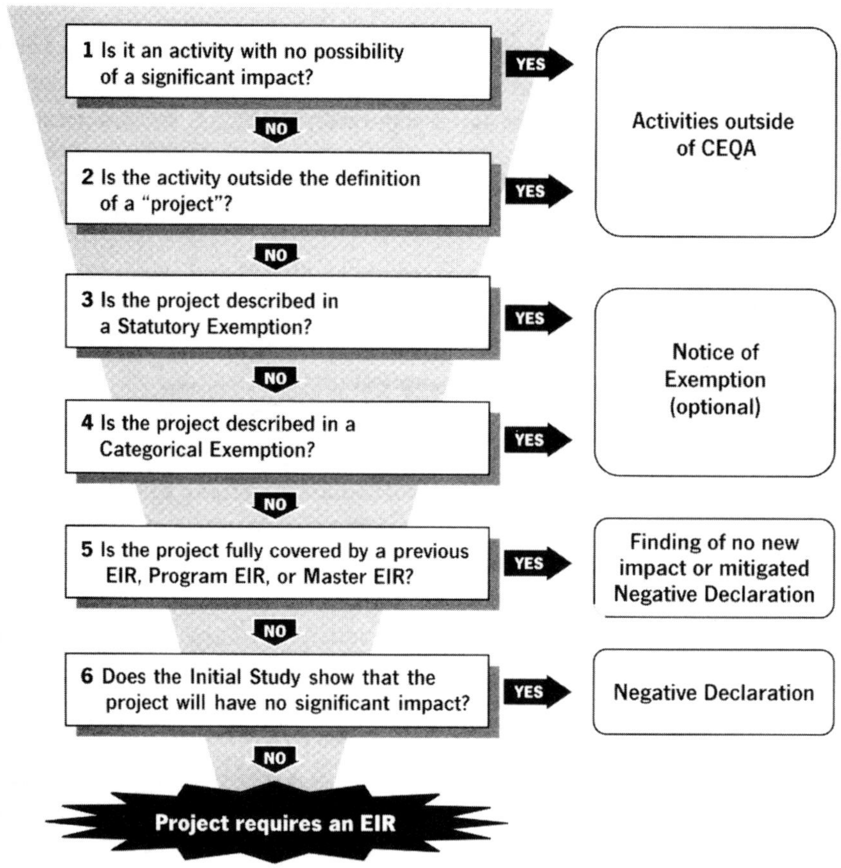

designate a preferred site for CEQA review and may enter into a land acquisition agreement, so long as the agreement is conditioned on any future use of the site being subject to CEQA compliance (Guideline § 15004(b)(2)(A)). This subsection of the State CEQA Guidelines is somewhat confusing and has been interpreted differently by different public agencies. Some public agencies read this provision to allow the final purchase of property as long as the agency has not designated it for a particular use (which would require CEQA compliance). Other more conservative interpretations read this as merely allowing an agency to proceed with the initial purchase process and possibly buying a "right to purchase;" however, the final purchase of the property is contingent on and prior to completing CEQA. This seems the more reasonable approach, as many agencies have specific authorities to purchase property for specific uses (e.g., transportation agencies purchasing land for transportation related uses). Allowing agencies to proceed to final purchase without CEQA completion or compliance would possibly taint the future CEQA analysis once the use was designated—the already owned site could preclude the feasibility of other alternative sites.

Further, an agency may not commit or solicit funding for a project or otherwise take any action that gives impetus to a planned-for foreseeable project in a manner that forecloses alternatives or mitigation measures that would ordinarily be part of CEQA compliance (Guidelines § 15004).

CA Supreme Court Reviews Definition of "Project" and Trigger For CEQA Compliance: *Save Tara v. City of West Hollywood* (2008) 45 Cal. 4th 116.

In May of 2004, the City of West Hollywood approved an agreement with a developer for the reuse and redevelopment of a large historic home (nicknamed "Tara" after the home in *Gone with the Wind*) that had been willed to the City by a wealthy widow. The agreement would convey the property to the developer, provide the developer a substantial loan, and allow the construction of thirty-five units of housing on the site. While the agreement provided that all CEQA requirements be satisfied at some future time, it also gave the City Manager authority to waive those requirements. The historic home would be retained as part of the project, but would have been altered by the development. The agreement would allow the developer to receive final approval of a grant from the federal Housing and Urban Development Department (HUD) that would provide funding for the project. A "Scope of Development" discussion attached to the draft agreement described the construction related to the project in some detail. At the time of the approval, the City's housing manager assured the Council that the project would be subject to further planning approvals and these were "not a rubber stamp" for the project.

Save Tara sued the City in July 2004 alleging that the City had violated CEQA by failing to prepare and consider a CEQA document prior to approving the agreement. In August, the City and the developer executed a revised agreement that specified that CEQA requirements would apply and could not be waived by the City Manager. The trial court held for the City, finding that the provision for future CEQA compliance was satisfactory.

The Court of Appeal reversed, opining that conditioning a development agreement on future CEQA compliance is insufficient because CEQA "is intended to be part of the decision-making process itself, not an examination, *after the decision has been made*, of the possible environmental consequences of the decision." The Court of Appeal was satisfied that prior to the May approval the City knew enough about the project to prepare a CEQA analysis. Meanwhile, between the time of the trial court decision and consideration by the Court of Appeal, the City had prepared and certified a Final EIR for the project. The Court of Appeal, by a 2 to 1 vote, ordered the City to prepare a new EIR. The dissenting justice argued that the case was moot in light of the certified EIR.

The Supreme Court upheld the decision of the Court of Appeal in most regards. The City asserted that certification of the Final EIR rendered the case moot. The Supreme Court disagreed. "No irreversible physical or legal change has occurred during pendency of the action, and Save Tara can still be awarded the relief it seeks, an order that City set aside its approvals."

The Court set out two considerations important to the timing of EIR preparation: "(1) that CEQA not be interpreted to require an EIR before the project is well enough defined to allow for meaningful environmental evaluation; and (2) that CEQA not be interpreted as allowing an EIR to be delayed beyond the time when it can, as a practical matter, serve its intended function of informing and guiding decision makers." The Court held that the decision over when a project is sufficiently defined to allow CEQA analysis is a legal question (which allows independent judicial review). Citing its 2007 *Muzzy Ranch* decision, the Court noted that it had already found the question of whether an action is in fact a project is one of law. The Court opined that:

> *To accord overly deferential review of agencies' timing decisions could allow agencies to evade CEQA's central commands. While an agency may certainly adjust its rules so as to set "[t]he exact date of approval" (Cal. Code Regs., tit. 14, §15352, subd. (a)), an agency has no discretion to define approval so as to make its commitment to a project precede the required preparation of an EIR.*

The City argued that the August 2004 agreement committed the City to future CEQA compliance, thereby eliminating the need to prepare a CEQA document before entering into the agreement. Save Tara countered that allowing deferral of CEQA analysis rendered the EIR requirement a "dead letter." The Court adopted what it called "an intermediate position:"

> A CEQA compliance condition can be a legitimate ingredient in a preliminary public-private agreement for exploration of a proposed project, but if the agreement, viewed in light of all the surrounding circumstances, commits the public agency as a practical matter to the project, the simple insertion of a CEQA compliance condition will not save the agreement from being considered an approval requiring prior environmental review.

The Court distinguished the Court of Appeal decisions in *Stand Tall on Principles v. Shasta Union High Sch. Dist.* (1991) 235 Cal. App. 3d 772 and *Concerned McCloud Citizens v. McCloud Community Services Dist.* (2007) 147 Cal. App. 4th 181 from the present case. Neither case convinced the Court that a "broad rule exists permitting EIR preparation to be postponed in all circumstances by use of a CEQA compliance condition." Section 15004(b)(2)(A) provides an exception for land purchases, but that should not be interpreted as allowing the deferral in situations other than that described in the section. The City argued to limit the need for a CEQA analysis to "unconditional agreements irrevocably vesting development rights." The Court disagreed:

> Such a rule would be inconsistent with the CEQA Guidelines' definition of approval as the agency's "earliest commitment" to the project. (Cal. Code Regs., tit. 14, §15352, subd. (b), italics added.) Just as CEQA itself requires environmental review before a project's approval, not necessarily its final approval (Pub. Resources Code, §§21100, 21151), so the guideline defines "approval" as occurring when the agency first exercises its discretion to execute a contract or grant financial assistance, not when the last such discretionary decision is made.

The Court rejected the notion that CEQA can be "postponed until the last governmental step is taken." Here, the City had expressed its favor for the project, defended it publicly, devoted substantial public resources to it, and announced a detailed agreement to go forward with the project, all without CEQA review. Under those circumstances, it is not practical to assume that a later CEQA review would be more than a post hoc rationalization of the project's approval.

In keeping with its theme of taking an intermediate road, the Court refused to find that "any agreement, conditional or unconditional, would be an 'approval' requiring prior preparation of CEQA documentation if at the time it was made the project was sufficiently well defined to provide 'meaningful information for environmental assessment.'" Approval is not the same as an agency's mere interest in, or inclination to support a project, no matter how well-defined the project may be. In the Court's words: "we look both to the agreement itself and to the surrounding circumstances, as shown in the record of the decision, to determine whether an agency's authorization or execution of an agreement for development constitutes a 'decision . . . which commits the agency to a definite course of action in regard to a project.' (Cal. Code Regs., tit. 14, §15352.)"

Here, the City had committed to the project by advising HUD the City had approved the sale of property and had committed up to $1 million in financial aid; announcing that the HUD grant would be used to redevelop Tara; advising residents who opposed the project that while variations in the project might be considered, the City must fulfill its obligation to redevelop the property; and ruling out other public uses of the property such as a library, park, or cultural center. Furthermore, the City was proceeding with relocating the existing tenants of the property.

The Supreme Court disagreed with the Court of Appeal only on the issue of whether to require the City to prepare a new EIR. Save Tara did not challenge the adequacy of the Final EIR certified by the City in 2006. As a result, that EIR "is conclusively presumed to comply with CEQA's standards unless a subsequent or supplemental environmental EIR is needed for any of the reasons set out in [Public Resources Code] section 21166." Since the 2006 EIR was based on the City's invalidated approvals, it may need revision. Whether that is so can be decided by the City, subject to review of the superior court under the substantial evidence standard.

Preapplication Consultation

A potential project applicant may request a meeting with the lead agency to consider:

- Range of actions
- Potential alternatives
- Mitigation measures, particularly those relating to the mandatory findings of significance.
- Potential significant effects on the environment

The lead agency may involve:

- Responsible agencies
- Trustee agencies
- Other interested agencies

Phase One: Preliminary Review—Determining Whether an Action Is a "Project" as Defined by CEQA and Reviews for Exemptions

Review for Application of CEQA. During the preliminary review phase of CEQA, the lead agency must determine whether CEQA applies to the activity being evaluated. The CEQA Guidelines (§ 15060(c) outline three preliminary questions:

1. Does the action involve exercising discretionary powers by a public agency (discussed below, under Statutory Exemption for Ministerial Projects)?
2. Will the action result in a direct or reasonably foreseeable indirect physical change in the environment (discussed below, under General Exemption)?
3. Is the action considered a "project" (as defined in CEQA Guidelines § 15378)

The agency must conduct a preliminary screening to determine whether the activity is a "project," as defined by CEQA, or whether it is exempt. A government activity is only subject to CEQA if it involves the exercise of an agency's discretionary powers, has the potential to result in a direct or reasonably foreseeable indirect physical change in the environment, and falls within the definition of a "project" as defined by the Guidelines (Guidelines § 15060). All of these concepts are discussed further below.

Definition of a Project. CEQA applies only to discretionary government activities that are defined as "projects." A project is defined as "the whole of an action which has the potential for resulting in either a direct physical change in the environment or a reasonably foreseeable indirect physical change in the environment" (Pub. Res. Code § 21065; Guidelines § 15378(a)). Projects can include activities that have no direct effect on the environment, but that will open the way for indirect effects. For example, a general plan adoption or amendment, enactment or amendment of a zoning ordinance, and city annexation for purposes of future development are all projects under CEQA.

Project Segmenting Not Permitted. In determining when a proposed activity is indeed a project, a lead agency must first determine the extent of the activity being evaluated. An agency is generally not permitted to "segment" or "piecemeal" a project into small parts if the effect is to avoid full disclosure of environmental impacts. CEQA defines a project to include the "whole of the action (Guidelines § 15378(a))." This phrase has been interpreted by the California Supreme Court to mean that it is generally inappropriate to chop a project into small segments to avoid preparing an EIR. In an early but frequently cited decision, the California Supreme Court affirmed this principle when it held that an annexation was a "project" even though it was only the first step in the eventually development of the land being annexed (*Bozung v. Local Agency Formation Commission* (1975) 13 Cal. 3d 263). Therefore, an agency may not treat each separate permit or approval as a separate project for purposes of evaluating environmental impacts. Rather, "project" refers to the underlying activities being approved by an agency, not just the government permits necessary to develop such an undertaking (Guidelines § 15378(c)) (*see* Chapter 7 for more detail on requirements of the project description in an EIR).

The rule against segmenting does not mean that every activity related to a proposed project must be included in the project description of the CEQA document. The California Supreme Court held that related actions only had to be included in a CEQA document when they were reasonably foreseeable, but not when they were remote and speculative (*Laurel Heights Improvement Association of San Francisco v. Regents of the University of California* (1988) 47 Cal. 3d 376). The *Laurel Heights* case also noted that the decision whether related actions must be evaluated in a single CEQA document is determined by the facts and circumstances of each case. Even if these actions are not considered as part of the proposed project, the action's effects may be required for inclusion in the CEQA document either because of the indirect impacts as a reasonably foreseeable consequence of the proposed project or in the cumulative impacts discussion (*see* Chapter 7).

Definition of a Project

- An activity directly undertaken by a public agency, including:
  - Public works construction activities
  - Clearing or grading of land
  - Improvements to existing public structures
  - Enactment and amendment of zoning ordinances
  - Adoption and amendment of local general plans
- An activity that is supported, in whole or in part, through public agency contracts, grants, subsidies, loans, or other assistance from a public agency
- An activity involving the public agency issuance of a lease, permit, license, certificate, or other entitlement for use by a public agency

"Projects" under CEQA

- an activity directly undertaken by a public agency;
- an activity that is supported, in whole or in part, through public agency contracts, grants, subsidies, loans, or other assistance from a public agency; and
- an activity involving the public agency issuance of a lease, permit, license, certificate, or other entitlement for use by a public agency. As used in CEQA, the term "project" is very broad. In considering whether an activity is a "project" an agency must look at all of the parts, components, and phases of the activity.

Figure 2-2. Evaluation of Related Activities in a CEQA Document Illustrative Case Examples

When must related activities be evaluated in the same CEQA document?

When "Action B" is a reasonably foreseeable consequence of "Action A"

Bozung v. Local Agency Formation Commission (1975) 13 Cal. 3d 263 (successive government approvals for the same underlying project must be considered together); *Laurel Heights Improvement Association v. Regents of the University of California* (1988) 47 Cal.3d 376 (future phases of a single building must be evaluated in the EIR on the first phase because they are foreseeable)

When "Action B" is a future expansion of "Action A" and will be significant because it will likely change the scope, nature, and impacts of "Action A"

Laurel Heights Improvement Association v. Regents of the University of California (1988) 47 Cal.3d 376 (future phases of a single building must be evaluated in the EIR on the first phase because they will contribute to the project's impacts)

When "Action A" cannot proceed without essential public services that would be provided by "Action B"

Santiago County Water District v. County of Orange (1981) 118 Cal. App. 3d 818 (EIR on a mining project must include impacts of water delivery system to serve the project); *San Joaquin Raptor/Wildlife Rescue Center v. County of Stanislaus* (1995) 27 Cal. App. 4th 713 (EIR on a housing project must include impacts of additional sewer capacity to serve the project)

When "Action A" and "Action B" are integral parts of the same project

No Oil, Inc. v. City of Los Angeles (1987) 196 Cal. App. 3d 223 (Pipelines to deliver oil must be evaluated in an EIR for an oil drilling project)

When may related activities be deferred to a future CEQA document? *

When "Action A" is being evaluated at a time when meaningful information about "Action B" is not capable of being obtained (e.g., is " remote and speculative")

No Oil, Inc. v. City of Los Angeles (1987) 196 Cal. App. 3d 223 (information about pipeline locations was not yet available and did not have to be evaluated in an EIR on an oil drilling project)

When information about "Action B" is not necessary to make an intelligent decision whether to proceed with "Action A"

No Oil, Inc. v. City of Los Angeles (1987) 196 Cal. App. 3d 223 (detailed information about pipelines to deliver oil was not necessary for a decision to be made whether to approve an oil drilling project)

When "Action A" is being evaluated in a first-tier EIR and "Action B" will be evaluated in a second-tier EIR.

Rio Vista Farm Bureau Center v. County of Solano (1992) 5 Cal. App. 4th 351 (program EIR on hazardous waste management plan need not evaluate project-specific impacts of activities that will be subject to future, second-tier EIRs)

When "Action A" merely establishes criteria for "Action B" but does not commit to its implementation

Rio Vista Farm Bureau Center v. County of Solano (1992) 5 Cal. App. 4th 351 (EIR on hazardous waste management plan need not evaluate future facilities that might be developed under the plan)

When "Action B" is independent of, and not a contemplated future part of, "Action A"

Christward Ministry v. County of San Diego (1993) 13 Cal. App. 4th 31 (EIR for a proposed landfill expansion need not evaluate impacts of other solid waste projects in the county)

When "Action A" is part of a large highway project with logical termination points and independent utility and does not foreclose consideration of alternatives

Del Mar Terrace Conservancy, Inc. v. City Council of the City of San Diego (10 Cal. App 4th. 712) (EIR on 1.8 mile highway project was appropriate because it had independent use for local and state service even if no other phases were constructed)

* **When a Lead Agency elects to exclude or limit the evaluation of related activities, it should include the following in the CEQA document:**

1) A description of the potential future activities and how they relate to the proposed project
2) A brief explanation of the types of impacts that those related actions might produce
3) A discussion of why it is not necessary or possible to evaluate the related actions at the current time
4) An explanation of when, and in what type of CEQA document, the related actions will be evaluated (e.g., second-tier EIR)

A variety of other exceptions to the "segmenting" rule have also been recognized over the years. Figure 2-2 summarizes the current state of the law regarding when related activities must be considered in a single environmental document and when they may be segmented into separate environmental documents or deferred to future documents. In the table, "Action A" refers to the proposed project under current evaluation, and "Action B" refers to the related activity in question (often a future activity).

The related components of the action, depending on the relation to the underlying agency approval may be characterized several different ways. The components may be characterized as parts of the project within the project description, where the impacts are addressed as part of the "direct environmental effects" of the action. The related components of the action may be characterized a part of the "indirect effects analysis"—where it is technically not part of the project but is a reasonably foreseeable consequence of the action. The related components of the action may most appropriately be characterized as foreseeable consequences, not as an indirect effect, of the proposed action and analyzed in the "growth inducement section"—where the project either removes an obstacle to or otherwise enhances the possibility for related development to occur. Lastly, the related components of the action characterized within the "cumulative effects analysis" as reasonably foreseeable probable future projects—where the proposed project's effects are discussed in combination with the contributions of the effects of these and other probable future projects.

Nonprojects. The Legislature has the authority to establish whether activities are or are not subject to CEQA. Thus, some government activities are not subject to CEQA because they have been excluded, by statute, from the term "project," as defined by the law. Although they are listed separately in CEQA, for practical purposes "nonprojects" are treated the same as statutory exemptions (Guidelines § 15378). Under the definition of project, CEQA specifically lists the following actions to be outside the definition of a project:

- Proposals for legislation to be enacted by the State Legislature
- Certain continuing administrative or maintenance activities
- Submissions of proposals to a statewide vote by citizens petitions
- School closing and student transfer when the only physical changes involved are categorically exempt
- A city council action placing a voter initiative on the ballot. This applies only to initiatives that are qualified for the ballot by voter petition—it does not include an initiative that the city council itself places on the ballot. In *Friends of Sierra Madre v. City of Sierra Madre,* (2001) 25 Cal. 4th 165, the state Supreme Court held that a city council-sponsored initiative placed on the ballot by that city council was subject to CEQA
- Creation of government funding mechanisms or other government fiscal activities that do not involve any commitment to any specific project that may result in physical environmental impacts
- Organizational or administrative activities of governments that will not result in direct or indirect physical changes in the environment

Documentation of Nonproject. Although CEQA does not require any specific documentation of an agency's interpretation that an action does not fit into the definition of a "project," it is recommended that the agency create some record of its decision citing the public resource code or CEQA Guideline section and the rationale why the action does not trigger specific CEQA compliance. An agency may choose to file the optional notice of exemption (NOE) (*see* below) to further document its determination and to take advantage of the shortened statute of limitations that corresponds with the filing of the NOE.

Exemptions from CEQA

Review for Exemptions. Once a lead agency has determined that an activity is a "project" subject to CEQA, it should determine whether an exemption applies. Generally, exemptions fall into two broad categories: "statutory exemptions," and "categorical exemptions." Other activities, while not falling specifically under either a statutory or categorical exemption, may nevertheless be exempt under the "general rule" or "common sense" exemption (Guidelines § 15061(b)).

Although an exemption allows the agency to approve the action without specific CEQA documentation, a notice of exemption, as discussed below, may be filed. Also, due to the possibility of litigation, it is recommended that the agency create some kind of record of its decision that the action is exempt from CEQA. This "record" does not necessarily need to be circulated to the public, but should provide the background and rationale for why the particular exemption applies, and may be supported by some environmental analysis, where appropriate.

Agencies are not required to solicit input regarding the use of a particular exemption or the need to proceed with more detailed environmental review of a proposed action. However, it may be in the agency's best interest to obtain an opinion regarding the use of the exemption from all other agencies that may be required to approve the same action. Because there is no "lead agency determination" with the use of CEQA's exemptions (although Guidelines § 15061 refers to the "lead agency"), the other agencies who must also comply with CEQA for approval of the same action are not required to follow the first agency's use of the exemption and may, in fact, determine that the exemption used by the previous agency should not apply. This can cause a certain amount of vulnerability in the first agency's use of the exemption and may have the effect of an agency with less authority over the action actually stepping into the lead agency role, even if it is a project proposed by another public agency (where that agency has used an exemption for CEQA compliance).

General Exemption. The CEQA Guidelines provide that "where it can be seen with certainty that there is *no possibility* that the activity in question may have a significant effect on the environment" (emphasis added), the activity is not subject to CEQA (Guidelines § 15061(b)). This rule, known as the "general rule" or "common sense" exemption, relates directly to the concept that CEQA covers actions with the potential to cause direct or indirect physical effects on the environment consistent with CEQA's definition of "project." If it is certain that no environmental effects will occur, there is no need to comply with CEQA. In practice, this may be somewhat hard to prove, as most activities can have some foreseeable consequence on the physical environment. However, as will be discussed in Chapter 3 with regard to baseline, the approval or re-license of certain existing facilities, where there are no proposed changes in operation, may fit into this general rule exemption. The California Supreme Court found that approval of an airport land use plan that simply incorporated existing county general plan and zoning provisions that were already in place, qualified under the common sense exemption (*Muzzy Ranch Co. v. Solano County Land Use Commission* (2007) 41 Cal. 4th 372).

Statutory Exemptions. Because CEQA is legislative in origin, the Legislature has the authority to exempt activities from its jurisdiction. A project that falls within a statutory exemption is not subject to CEQA's disclosure and mitization requirements even if it has the potential to significantly affect the environment (unless the statutory exemption explicitly conditions the exemption on particular environmental provisions, see for example the exemption for "qualified housing projects" (Public Resources Codes § 21159.21). The Legislature has established a variety of statutory exemptions from CEQA *see* Figure 2-3, pages 42-43). A project that is statutorily exempt is entitled to a blanket exemption from all of CEQA's procedures and policies, as delineated by the statutory language. Although there are dozens of statutory exemptions from CEQA, most apply to very specific types of projects, or in some cases even individually-named projects. However, there are several categories that are of general application and more commonly used. Some of the more commonly used statutory exemptions are discussed below.

Not all statutory exemptions are found within the CEQA statute. For reasons of its own, the Legislature has also placed some CEQA exemptions in other California Codes. Article 18 of the CEQA Guidelines has attempted to compile a comprehensive list of the statutory exemptions, with cross-references to the particular California Code section where the exemption is specifically located. §15260 *et. seq.*

Ministerial Projects. The exemption from CEQA review for ministerial projects is the most widely used statutory exemption. "Ministerial" describes a decision applying fixed, objective standards with little or no judgment required as to the wisdom or manner of carrying out the project (Pub. Res. Code § 21080(b)(1); Guidelines §§ 15268, 15369). Basically, an action is considered ministerial where an agency must issue the authorization if the proponent has met all the specified conditions of the action, regardless of environmental considerations.

A "discretionary project," on the other hand, requires the exercise of judgment or deliberation when a project decision is made (Guidelines § 15357). If a project contains both ministerial and discretionary elements, it is not exempt (Guidelines § 15268(d)). Examples of ministerial projects include final subdivision map approvals and most building permits.

The determination of whether an agency action is "ministerial" or "discretionary" requires a careful analysis of the language of the statute or ordinance by which the action was authorized. For example, a building permit is considered ministerial if the ordinance requiring the permit limits the public official to determining whether the zoning allows the structure to be built in the requested location, the structure will meet the requirements of the Uniform Building Code, and the applicant has paid the required fee.

Building, grading, and demolition permits, although often ministerial, may be considered discretionary if the particular permit ordinance allows the exercise of at least some discretion that can be used to reduce environmental impacts. This exercise of discretion varies from jurisdiction to jurisdiction. Generally, courts have interpreted the scope of the ministerial project exemption narrowly, and it should therefore be applied with caution. For example, in *Friends of Westwood v. City of Los Angeles* (1987) 191 Cal. App. 3d 259, the City's issuance of a building permit authorizing high rise buildings was considered discretionally prohibiting the use of the ministerial project statutory exemption.

Emergency Projects. Most emergency projects are exempt from CEQA review (Pub. Res. Code §§ 21080(b)(2), (3), (4); Guidelines § 15269). A situation is considered an "emergency" if it is a sudden, unexpected occurrence involving a clear and imminent danger that demands immediate action to prevent or mitigate loss of or damage to life, health, property, or essential public services. Emergencies include such occurrences as fires, floods, earthquakes, or other soil or geologic movements, as well as riots, accidents, or sabotage (Pub. Res. Code § 21060.3; Guidelines § 15359). The Legislature recognizes that the CEQA process should not stand in the way of an agency's response to emergencies and their aftermath, nor should the agency be limited by the time necessary to comply with CEQA where there are imminent threats.

The types of emergency actions covered by this exemption are:

- Projects to maintain, repair, restore, demolish, or replace property or facilities damaged or destroyed as a result of a disaster in a disaster-stricken area in which a state of emergency has been proclaimed by the governor. This includes projects that would adversely affect historical resources when that resource represents an imminent threat to bodily harm or damage to adjacent properties.
- Emergency repairs to publicly or privately owned service facilities necessary to maintain service essential to the public health, safety, or welfare.
- Specific actions necessary to prevent or mitigate an emergency, but not including long-term projects undertaken to fix short-term problems. For example, in *Calbeach Advocates v. City of Solana Beach*, (2002) 103 Cal. App. 4th 529, the city's use of an emergency exemption to allow construction of a seawall to shore up a crumbling cliff was upheld where there was substantial evidence, in the form of an engineer's report, that the cliff was in imminent danger of collapse.
- Projects carried out or approved by a public agency to maintain, repair, or restore an existing highway damaged by a natural disaster, excluding official state scenic highways and excluding projects to expand or widen highways initiated within one year of the occurrence of damage.

An action to drive away the giant blue bear that is pushing on a downtown office building could be the subject of an emergency exemption. (Photo courtesy of Antero Rivasplata)

A CEQA exemption may apply where there are minor modifications to existing facilities.

- Certain seismic retrofit work on highways and bridges.

(Pub. Res. Code §§ 21080(b)(2), (3), (4); Guidelines § 15269)

Rejected or Disapproved Projects. Projects that are rejected or disapproved by the agency's decision-making body are exempt from CEQA. The policy underlying this exemption is that that agencies should be allowed to screen projects on their merits, and disapprove or deny them prior to initiation or completion of the sometimes costly and time-consuming CEQA process, when the agency can clearly determine that the project cannot or should not be approved (*see Sunset Skyranch Pilots Assoc. v. County of Sacramento* (2009) 47 Cal. 4th 902). This situation might arise, for example if a project is inconsistent with a local general plan. This exemption does not relieve an applicant from paying the costs associated with preparing an environmental document for a project prior to the agency's disapproval but after normal evaluation and processing (Pub. Res. Code § 21080(b)(5); Guidelines § 15270).

Setting of Certain Rates, Tolls, Fares, or Charges. The setting, modification, structuring, or restructuring of certain rates, tolls, fares, or charges other than rate increases to fund system expansions are exempt from CEQA review. These fees must be for the purpose of meeting operating expenses, including employee wage rates and fringe benefits; purchasing or leasing supplies, equipment, or materials; meeting financial reserve needs and requirements; or obtaining funds for capital projects necessary for maintenance of services within an existing service area or as authorized by city charter. Rate increases to fund capital projects for the expansion of a system are not part of this exemption and are subject to CEQA (Pub. Res. Code § 21080(b)(8); Guidelines § 15273).

Feasibility or Planning Studies for Possible Future Actions. Exempt from CEQA review are feasibility or planning studies carried out, funded, or otherwise approved by a public agency when the agency has not approved, adopted, or funded the underlying future project. This provision does not apply to adoption of any plan that would have a legally binding effect on later activities (e.g., a city or county general plan) (Pub. Res. Code §§ 21102, 21150; Guidelines § 15262). Although this statutory exemption specifically mandates "consideration of environmental factors," even though it is "exempted from the preparation of an environmental impact report," most agencies do not prepare a separate environmental analysis to support use of this exemption.

Specified Residential Projects for Agricultural Employees and Urban Infill Projects. As discussed in Chapter 5, where a community-level environmental review has been certified, three classes of qualified CEQA exemptions may apply for specified residential projects for agricultural employees and for urban infill residential projects of up to 100 units for moderate-, low- and very low-income residents (Pub. Res. Code §§ 21159.22, 21159.23, and 21159.24; Guidelines §§ 15193, 15194, and 15195.

Transit Priority Projects. As discussed in Chapter 5, where a transit priority project complies with certain environmental and land use criteria and is

CA Supreme Court Rules on Use of General Exemption: *Muzzy Ranch Co. v. Solano County Airport Land Use Commission* (2007) 41 Cal. 4th 372.

Muzzy Ranch sued the County Airport Land Use Commission (ALUC) over its adoption of the Travis Air Force Base airport land use compatibility plan (TALUP) without preparation of a CEQA document. The TALUP establishes land use compatibility policies for future development in the area surrounding Travis AFB. Compatibility Zone C of the TALUP encompasses hundreds of thousands of acres that are subject to noise levels exceeding 60 dB CNEL and low altitude overflights. The TALUP policies freeze development within Zone C at currently allowed levels (no new general plan amendments or zone changes would be approved). The ALUC concluded that the TALUP is not a "project" for CEQA purposes and was exempt from CEQA's requirements under CEQA Guidelines Section 15061(b)(3), the general rule or "common sense" exemption.

The Court of Appeal held in favor of Muzzy Ranch finding that the TALUP is subject to CEQA. The Court opined that because development pressures are high in Solano County, there is a reasonable argument that adoption of the TALUP will push into surrounding areas future development that might have occurred within Zone C, even though the existing general plans would not allow such development. The court found that "it is reasonable to assume that general plans will be amended to accommodate some of that development pressure, absent an obstacle to amendment such as the TALUP."

The Supreme Court unanimously reversed the decision. CEQA is a three-tiered review process. The first tier involves determining whether an action is a "project"; the second, whether the project may result in a significant impact; and the third, the type of CEQA document prepared in review of the project's impacts. This case involved the first two tiers.

The ALUC argued that the TALUP was not a project. They claimed that potential housing displacement was too speculative to address, particularly the level of housing expansion that might have occurred in Zone C as a result of future general plan amendments, absent the TALUP. The Court disagreed. "[N]othing inherent in the notion of displaced development places such development, when it can be reasonably anticipated, categorically outside the concern of CEQA." Additionally, the TALUP "can operate like a multi-jurisdictional general plan," so, like a general plan, it would be subject to CEQA. Therefore, the ALUC erred in concluding that adopting the TALUP is not a project.

Discussing the second-tier issues, the Court looked at the ALUC's filing of the Notice of Exemption (NOE). Case law provides that the agency is obligated to produce substantial evidence supporting its exemption decision. The ALUC didn't do this when filing its NOE. "An agency obviously cannot declare 'with certainty that there is not possibility that the activity in question may have a significant effect on the environment' (citation) if it has not considered the facts of the matter." The ALUC "is mistaken in its suggestion that agencies have no obligation to consider geographically distant environmental impacts of their activities."

However, notwithstanding the ALUC's error, the Court found that the administrative record as a whole demonstrated that Commission had reached the correct result. The record reflects that the TALUP's restriction on land use simply incorporates the County's existing general plan and zoning restrictions. Further, the County's existing plan calls for nearly all the land in this area to remain in agricultural or open space uses. Therefore, "any potential displacement the TALUP might otherwise have effected *already* has been caused by the existing land use policies and zoning regulations to which the TALUP is keyed" (emphasis added). There is no reason to assume that local agencies will change their policies in the future to permit increased development within Compatibility Zone C.

considered to be a sustainable community's project pursuant to a Sustainable Communities Stategy, it is otherwise exempt from further CEQA review.

Categorical Exemptions. CEQA acknowledges that there may be categories of activities that have minimal adverse environmental effects and, therefore, specifically directs the Resources Agency to designate categories of projects that should be exempt from CEQA review (Pub. Res. Code §§ 21080(b)(9), 21084). As discussed in detail below, unlike statutory exemptions, categorical exemptions are *subject to certain exceptions*, related to potential environmental effects (Guidelines § 15300.2).

Figure 2-3. Statutory Exemptions

The Legislature has enacted a variety of statutory exemptions from CEQA. This table summarizes the exemptions and provides citations to the appropriate code sections. Please refer to the statutory provision for the complete statutory language. The table does not include certain project-specific exemptions for certain facilities already approved or constructed.

Type of Action	Exempt Activities	Statutory Provision
Agency Actions	• Ministerial projects (e.g., issuance of building permits or business licenses)	Pub. Res. Code 21080(b)(1)
	• Projects that a public agency rejects or disapproves	Pub. Res. Code 21080(b)(5)
	• Local actions implementing a state rule or regulation pursuant to a state-certified regulatory program, except certain site-specific activities	Pub. Res. Code 21080(b)(15)
	• Feasibility or planning studies for possible future actions that the agency has not approved, adopted, or funded	Pub. Res. Code 21102, 21150
Emergency Actions	• Emergency repairs to public service facilities necessary to maintain service	Pub. Res. Code 21080(b)(2)
	• Projects to maintain, repair, restore, demolish, or replace property or facilities damaged or destroyed in an area proclaimed as an emergency by the Governor	Pub. Res. Code 21080(b)(3)
	• Actions necessary to prevent or mitigate an emergency (not including long-term projects with low probability of short-term occurrence)	Pub. Res. Code 21080(b)(4)
	• Projects to maintain, repair, or restore an existing highway	Pub. Res. Code 21080.33
Energy Projects	• Actions relating to thermal power plants	Pub. Res. Code 21080(b)(6)
	• Solar energy systems on roofs and parking lots	Pub. Res. Code 21080.35
	• Local ordinances regarding solar shade control requirements	Pub. Res. Code 25985
Transportation-Related Projects	• Actions to establish, modify, or restructure rates, tolls, fares, or other charges for certain designated public purposes	Pub. Res. Code 21080(b)(8)
	• Projects instituting or increasing passenger or commuter service on existing rail or highway rights-of-way	Pub. Res. Code 21080(b)(10)
	• Projects instituting or increasing passenger or commuter service on existing high-occupancy vehicle lanes	Pub. Res. Code 21080(b)(11)
	• Mass transit extensions of less than 4 miles for the transfer of passengers	Pub. Res. Code 21080(b)(12)
	• Regional or state transportation improvement programs	Pub. Res. Code 21080(b)(13)
	• Congestion Management Program by a county agency	Pub. Res. Code 21080(b)(13)
	• Railroad grade separation projects	Pub. Res. Code 21080.12
	• Restriping of streets or highways to reduce traffic congestion	Pub. Res. Code 21080.19
	• Transportation rights-of-way in designated transportation corridors for which an EIR was certified	Pub. Res. Code 33911
Categorically Exempt Projects	• All classes of projects designated pursuant to Pub. Res. Code 21084 (i.e., categorical exemptions)	Pub. Res. Code 21080(b)(9)
Out-of-State/ NEPA Projects	• Projects or portions of projects located in another state that will be subject to NEPA or state environmental review consistent with NEPA	Pub. Res. Code 21080(b)(14)
Housing-Related Projects	• Housing or neighborhood commercial facilities in urbanized areas that are consistent with a comprehensive regulatory document and meet certain criteria	Pub. Res. Code 21080.7
	• Conversion of existing rental mobile home parks to condominium ownership	Pub. Res. Code 21080.8
	• Adoption of ordinances related to certain senior citizen units or second units	Pub. Res. Code 21080.17
	• Approval of day-care homes providing family daycare for up to 12 children	Health and Safety Code 1597.46
	• Actions related to the construction, conversion, or use of low-income agricultural employee housing	Pub. Res. Code 21801.01
	• Sustainable communites project	Pub. Res. Code 21155.1
	• Agricultural employee housing	Pub. Res. Code 21159.21/21159.22
(continued next page)	• Low-income housing	Pub. Res. Code 21159.21/21159.23

Figure 2-3. Statutory Exemptions (continued)

Type of Action	Exempt Activities	Statutory Provision
Housing-Related Projects (continued)	• Infill housing and limited mixed use	Pub. Res. Code 21159.21/ 21159.24
	• Actions related to the construction, conversion, or use of lower-income housing projects of 100 units or less in urban areas	Pub. Res. Code 21080.14
	• Regional housing needs determinations made by the Department of Housing and Community Development, a council of governments, or a city or county	Gov. Code 65584
Local Coastal Programs	• Activities and approvals by local governments or state colleges and universities related to local coastal programs	Pub. Res. Code 21080.9
School Projects	• Closing of any K-12 public school or the transfer of students from such a school, if the associated physical changes are categorically exempt	Pub. Res. Code 21080.18
Timberland Preserve Projects	• Local adoption of timberland preserve zones	Gov. Code 51119
Water-Related Projects	• Temporary water transfers of up to 1 year in duration	Water Code 1729
	• Repiping, redesign, or use of reclaimed water for certain irrigation, cooling, or air conditioning purposes	Water Code 13552.4(c)(1), 13552.8(c)(1)
	• Minor alterations to utilities to comply with public water system fluoridation requirements	Pub. Res. Code 21080.26
	• Preparation and adoption of Urban Water Management Plans	Water Code 10652
Waste Disposal Projects	• Non-disposal facilities of local solid waste management plans	Pub. Res. Code 41375
	• Certain pipelines for the transport of certain hazardous or volatile wastes	Pub. Res. Code 21080.23
	• Cooperative agreements for the development of solid waste management facilities on Indian lands	Pub. Res. Code 44203(g)
Specific Agency Actions	• General plan time extensions granted by the Office of Planning and Research	Pub. Res. Code 21080.10a
	• General plan actions required to comply with a court order	Gov. Code 65759
	• Funding of low- or moderate-income housing projects by the California Department of Housing and Community Development or Housing Finance Agency	Pub. Res. Code 21080.10(b)
	• Settlements of title and boundary problems and related exchanges and leases by the State Lands Commission	Pub. Res. Code 21080.11
	• Adoption of waste discharge requirements under the federal Clean Water Act, except for certain new sources, by the State Water Resources Control Board and Regional Water Quality Control Boards	Water Code 13372, 13389
	• Issuance of bonds by the California Pollution Control Financing Authority	Health and Safety Code 44561
	• Local general plan amendments required by the Delta Protection Commission	Pub. Res. Code 21080.22
	• Issuance, modification, or renewal of "Title V" permits under the Clean Air Act that do not involve physical or operational changes by an Air Quality Management District	Pub. Res. Code 21080.24
	• Issuance of permits relating to automotive painting by an Air Quality Management District	Chapter 1131 Statutes of 1993, Section 1
	• Bidding, hosting, or staging of and funding and carrying out of the Olympic Games	Pub. Res. Code 21080(b)(7)
	• Notification of discovery of Native American burial sites	Pub. Res. Code 5097.98(c)
	• Specified prison facilities	Pub. Res. Code 21080.01, 21080.03, 21080.07
	• Purchase of rail right-of-way for the San Francisco Peninsula commute service	Pub. Res. Code 21080.05
	• Project funding by the Rural Economic Development Infrastructure Panel	Pub. Res. Code 21080.08
	• Installation of new or repair or removal of an existing pipeline under 1 mile	Pub. Res. Code 21080.21
	• Actions by the Industrial Development Authority	Gov. Code 91543

The Resources Agency has from time to time proposed additions and editorial changes to the categorical exemptions, as part of its requirement to revise the CEQA Guidelines every two years. The process requires the Resources Agency to provide appropriate public notice and opportunity for comment and separate review through the Office of Administrative Law. Currently, there are thirty-three classes of categorical exemptions (*see* Fig. 2-4, pg. 48. Guidelines §§ 15301–15333). Each public agency must establish its own list of specific activities falling within each class (Guidelines § 15300). However, the majority of agencies have simply relied on the list of categorical exemptions found in the State CEQA Guidelines.

As with statutory exemptions, some categorical exemptions are more commonly used than others. The following are generalized summaries of the more frequently used categorical exemptions. Agencies interested in relying on a particular exemption should refer to the specific language contained in the Guidelines to make sure the proposed activity falls within the exemption.

Class 1: Existing Facilities. This categorical exemption applies to the operation, repair, maintenance, permitting, leasing, licensing, or minor alteration of existing public or private structures, facilities, mechanical equipment, or topographical features involving "negligible or no expansion of use" beyond that existing at the time of the agency's determination. The exemption includes interior and exterior alterations (Guidelines § 15301). For example, in *Santa Monica Chamber of Commerce v. City of Santa Monica* (2002) 101 Cal. App. 4th 786, the court upheld the use of a Class 1 exemption for adoption of regulations giving residents priority in the issuance of on-street parking permits. The program involved no change in streets or parking patterns and the city had prepared a parking study that indicated there would be no impacts resulting from the ordinance.

Class 2: Replacement or Reconstruction. This categorical exemption applies to the replacement or reconstruction of existing structures and facilities where the new structure will be located on the same site as the original one and will have substantially the same purpose and capacity as the original. However, according to this exemption, replacement or reconstruction of existing schools or hospitals for earthquake retrofit may actually expand capacity up to fifty percent. The exemption specifically states that replacement or reconstruction of existing utility facilities must involve "negligible or no expansion of capacity (Guidelines § 15302)."

Class 3: New Construction or Conversion of Small Facilities. This categorical exemption applies to the construction and location of limited numbers of new small facilities or structures; the installation of small new equipment and facilities in small structures; and the conversion of existing small structures from one use to another when only minor modifications are made to the exterior of the structure. The exemption includes a list of structures with maximum allowable sizes. For example, it applies to the construction of three or fewer single-family homes in urbanized areas (Guidelines § 15303). In *Fairbank v. City of Mill Valley* (1999) 75 Cal. App. 4th 1243, the court found that a retail/office building project qualified for a Class 3 exemption because it fell within the description established by the 1998 Guidelines revision.

Class 4: Minor Alterations to Land. This categorical exemption applies to minor public or private alterations in the condition of land, water, or vegetation that do not involve removal of healthy, mature, scenic trees except for forestry and agricultural purposes. The exemption includes grading on land with a slope of less than ten percent or new gardening or landscaping (Guidelines § 15304).

Class 5: Minor Alterations in Land Use Limitations. This categorical exemption applies to minor alterations in land use limitations in areas with an average slope of less than twenty percent when they do not result in any changes in land use or density. The exemption includes lot line adjustments and variances that do not create new parcels (Guidelines § 15305).

Class 6: Information Collection. This categorical exemption applies to basic data collection, research, experimental management, and resource evaluation activities that do not result in a serious or major disturbance to an environmental resource. These activities may involve information gathering only or be part of a study that leads to an action not yet approved, adopted, or funded by the public agency (Guidelines § 15306).

Classes 7 and 8: Actions by Regulatory Agencies for Protection of Natural Resources or the Environment. These two closely related categories consist of actions taken by regulatory agencies, as authorized by state law or local ordinance, to ensure the maintenance, restoration, or enhancement of natural resources or the environment when regulatory processes involve procedures for environmental protection. This exemption does not apply to any construction activities or relaxation of standards allowing environmental degradation (Guidelines §§ 15307, 15308).

Class 9: Inspections. This categorical exemption applies to activities limited entirely to inspections to check for performance of an operation or for the quality, health, or safety of a project, including related activities such as inspection for possible mislabeling, misrepresentation, or adulteration of products (Guidelines § 15309).

Class 11: Accessory Structures. This categorical exemption applies to construction, or replacement, of "minor structures accessory to (appurtenant to) existing commercial, industrial, or institutional facilities." This exemption includes the construction of on-premise signs, small parking lots, and temporary or seasonal items (Guidelines § 15311).

Class 14: Minor Additions to Schools. This categorical exemption applies to "minor additions to existing schools within existing school grounds." The addition cannot increase the "original student capacity by more than twenty-five percent or ten classrooms, whichever is less." The addition of portable classrooms is included in this exemption (Guidelines § 15314).

Class 21: Enforcement Actions by Regulatory Agencies. This categorical exemption applies to actions taken by "regulatory agencies" to enforce or revoke a lease, permit, license, certificate, or other entitlement. This exemption

Supreme Court Argues Denial Is Not a Project:

***Sunset Skyranch Pilots Assoc. v. County of Sacramento* (Dec. 28, 2009) 47 Cal. 4th 902**

The County of Sacramento denied the conditional use permit that would have allowed Sunset Skyranch, a small private airport, to remain in operation. Notwithstanding the possibility of indirect physical effects on the environment, the county cited Public Resources Code § 21080(b)(5), the statutory exemption which allows denial of a project without preparing a CEQA analysis, in determining that no CEQA analysis would be prepared. The Court of Appeals found that the statutory exemption embodied in Section 21080(b)(5) did not apply in a situation like this one where denial would reasonably lead to the possibility of significant impacts related to the airport closure and transferral of pilots and operations to other airports.

The Supreme Court overturned the Court of Appeals. While the Court has traditionally construed CEQA broadly "to afford the fullest protection to the environment within the reasonable scope of statutory language," it does not balance the policies served by statutory exemptions against the goal of environmental protection. The Supreme Court held that:

"The Court of Appeal erred by deeming the consequences of a project denial to be part of the project itself. Its reasoning would effectively abrogate the statutory exemption for projects disapproved by a public agency. (citation) In many cases, disapproval of a proposed project could have possible environmental impacts associated with alternative courses of action. 'Yet the Legislature has determined for reasons of policy to exempt project disapprovals from environmental review under CEQA. Our state legislators evidently concluded that public agencies should not be forced to commit their resources to the costly and time-consuming environmental review process for proposed private development projects slated for rejection, whatever the reason for agency disapproval. This court does not sit in judgment of the Legislature's wisdom in balancing such competing public policies. (*Napa Valley Wine Train, Inc. v. Public Utilities Com.* [*supra*,] 50 Cal. 3d 370, 376.)' (*Main San Gabriel Basin Watermaster v. State Water Resources Control Bd., supra*, 12 Cal. App. 4th at pp. 1383-1384.) As we noted in *Napa Valley Wine Train*, the very purpose of the statutory CEQA exemptions is to avoid the burden of the environmental review process for an entire class of projects, even if there might be significant environmental effects. (*Napa Valley Wine Train, supra*, 50 Cal. 3d at p. 381.)"

also applies to "law enforcement activities by peace officers acting under any law that provides criminal sanctions." This exemption specifically does not include "construction activities undertaken by the public agency taking the enforcement or revocation action (Guidelines § 15321)."

Class 31: Historical Resource Restoration/Rehabilitation. This exemption applies to projects limited to maintenance, repair, stabilization, rehabilitation, restoration, preservation, conservation, or reconstruction of historical resources consistent with the Secretary of Interior's "Standards for the Treatment of Historic Properties with Guidelines for Preserving, Rehabilitating, Restoring, and Reconstructing Historic Buildings" (published 1995) (Guidelines § 15331).

Class 32: In-fill Development Projects. This categorical exemption applies to projects "characterized as in-fill development" that are consistent with the applicable general plan and zoning designations, are "within city limits," are on a project site of "no more than 5 acres substantially surrounded by urban uses," are on a site with no value as habitat for endangered, rare, or threatened species, are on a site that can be adequately served by all required utilities and public services, and whose approval would not result in any significant effects relating to traffic, noise, air quality, and water quality (Guidelines § 15332). Because this exemption does not specify what type of "project" is authorized, many agencies use this exemption for any and all types of construction activities that fits within the general conditions, including housing, commercial, industrial, and public infrastructure.

To use the Class 32 exemption, the agency must specifically determine that a project would not result in significant traffic, noise, air quality, and water quality impacts (beyond the general requirement under § 15300.2); this may require technical studies of some or all of those topics. Such studies would provide substantial evidence supporting the conclusion that no significant impacts exist. If the study indicates that there is a possibility of a significant impact, then the exemption cannot be invoked. For example, in *Banker's Hill, Hillcrest, Park West Community Preservation Group v. City of San Diego* (2006) 139 Cal. App. 4th 249, the Court upheld the use of the Class 32 Categorical exemption, where the City had prepared a traffic study and, along with other evidence, concluded there was no possibility of significant impacts.

Class 33: Small Habitat Restoration Projects. This exemption applies to restoration projects on sites of five acres or less that have no potential for significant effects and where there is no hazardous or toxic waste on the site. Examples cited in the Guidelines include: revegetation with native plants; wetland restoration to improve waterfowl conditions; stream or bank restoration to benefit native fish or amphibian habitat; habitat restoration or enhancement projects being undertaken with hand, rather than mechanized, labor; stream or bank stabilization with native vegetation for the purpose of eliminating erosion and sedimentation; and culvert replacement conducted in accordance with DFG or NOAA Fisheries guidelines for the purpose of improving habitat and reducing sedimentation.

Cal/EPA Toxic Site Database

The Department of Toxic Substances Control administers the Enviro-star database of hazardous waste sites. http://www.envirostor.dtsc.ca.gov/public/

Exceptions to Categorical Exemptions. Categorical exemptions represent activities that generally do not result in significant environmental impacts. Thus, unlike most statutory exemptions, categorical exemptions are not absolute, but rather are subject to six exceptions (Pub. Res. Code §§ 21084(b), (c), (e); Guidelines § 15300.2).

A categorical exemption does not apply if "unusual circumstances" create a reasonable possibility that the activity may have a significant environmental impact. The Court in *Fairbank v. City of Mill Valley* (1999) 75 Cal. App. 4th 1243, clarified that "unusual circumstances" refers to the existence of one or more of the exceptions described in Guidelines § 15300.2(c). Another court defined unusual circumstances of a particular project as those that "differ from the general circumstances of the projects covered by a particular categorical exemption, and create an environmental risk that does not exist for the general class of exempt projects (*See Citizens for a Better Environment*, *citing Azusa Land Reclamation Co. v. Main San Gabriel Basin Watermaster* (1997) 52 Cal. App. 4th 1165)." In addition, a categorical exemption does not apply where the action would cause a considerable contribution to a significant cumulative impact (Guidelines § 15300.2(b)).

A Categorical Exemption Does Not Apply If:

- A reasonable possibility exists that the activity may have a significant environmental impact because of unusual circumstances.
- Project cumulative impacts would be considerable and therefore significant.
- A project within certain categories of exemption occurs in certain specified sensitive environments.
- A project affects scenic resources within official state scenic highways.
- A project is located on a toxic site listed by the California Environmental Protection Agency.
- A project causes substantial adverse changes in significant historic resources.

Additionally, a categorical exemption does not apply if the project occurs in certain specified sensitive environments (for classes 3, 4, 5, 6, and 11 (Guidelines § 15300.2(a)), affects scenic resources within official state scenic highways (Guidelines § 15300.2(d)), or is located on listed hazardous waste sites in the database maintained by the California Environmental Protection Agency (Guidelines § 15300.2(e)). Also, a categorical exemption does not apply if the project causes substantial adverse changes in the significance of a historical resource (Guidelines § 15300.2(f)).

A categorical exemption cannot be used if mitigation measures must be applied to the project (or added to the project description) in order for the project to offset the impacts of "unusual circumstances." The need for mitigation triggers the need to prepare an initial study leading to either a mitigated negative declaration or an EIR. See, for example, *Salmon Protection and Watershed*

Figure 2-4. Categorical Exemptions

The Secretary for Resources has adopted a variety of categorical exemptions from CEQA. This table summarizes the exemptions (referred to as "classes") and provides citations to the appropriate Guidelines sections. Many of the categories include special limitations and examples of exempt projects. Please refer to the Guidelines section for complete Guidelines language. Also, unlike statutory exemptions, categorical exemptions are subject to certain exceptions found in Guidelines Section 15300.2.

Class	Exempt Activity	Guidelines Section
Class 1	Operation, repair, maintenance, or minor alteration of existing structures or facilities not expanding existing uses	15301
Class 2	Replacement or reconstruction of existing structures or facilities on the same site having substantially the same purpose and capacity	15302
Class 3	New construction of limited small new facilities; installation of small, new equipment and facilities in small structures; and conversion of the use of small existing structures (e.g., construction of three or fewer single-family homes in urban areas)	15303
Class 4	Minor alterations in the condition of the land, such as grading, gardening, and landscaping, that do not affect sensitive resources	15304
Class 5	Minor alterations to land use limitations, such as lot line adjustments, variances, and encroachment permits on land with a slope of less than 20%, that do not result in changes in land use or density	15305
Class 6	Basic data collection, research, experimental management, and resource evaluation activities that do not result in major disturbances to an environmental resource	15306
Class 7	Certain actions by regulatory agencies to maintain, restore, or enhance natural resources, other than construction activities, where the regulatory process includes procedures to protect the environment	15307
Class 8	Certain actions by regulatory agencies to maintain, restore, or enhance the environment, other than construction activities, where the regulatory process includes procedures to protect the environment	15308
Class 9	Inspections to check for the performance of an operation, or for quality, health, or safety of a project	15309
Class 10	Certain Department of Veterans Affairs loans and mortgages for purchases of certain existing structures	15310
Class 11	Construction or placement of minor structures accessory to existing facilities (e.g., signs, small parking lots, portable structures)	15311
Class 12	Sales of surplus government property, except in environmentally sensitive areas	15312
Class 13	Acquisition of land for fish and wildlife habitat conservation purposes	15313
Class 14	Minor additions to existing schools that do not increase capacity by more than 25%	15314
Class 15	Subdivision of certain properties in urban areas into four or fewer parcels	15315
Class 16	Certain acquisitions or sales of land in natural condition or containing cultural resource sites to establish a park	15316
Class 17	Establishment of agricultural preserves, making and renewal of Williamson Act contracts, and acceptance of open space property	15317
Class 18	Designation of wilderness areas under the California Wilderness System	15318
Class 19	Annexations of certain areas containing existing structures and certain small parcels	15319
Class 20	Local government reorganizations requiring no changes in the areas where previous powers were exercised, such as the establishment of subsidiary districts, consolidations, and mergers	15320
Class 21	Actions by regulatory agencies to enforce a lease, permit license, or other entitlement; actions by law enforcement officials	15321
Class 22	Actions related to educational or training programs involving no exterior physical changes	15322
Class 23	Normal operations of existing facilities for public gatherings for which the facilities were designed	15323
Class 24	Actions taken by regulatory agencies related to wages, hours, and working conditions	15324
Class 25	Transfers of interest in land to preserve open space	15325
Class 26	Actions needed to implement a housing assistance plan by acquiring an interest in housing units	15326
Class 27	Leasing of new or unoccupied private facilities in a building exempt from CEQA	15327
Class 28	Installations of certain hydroelectric facilities of less than 5 megawatts capacity at existing facilities	15328
Class 29	Installation of certain cogeneration equipment of less than 50 megawatts capacity at existing facilities	15329
Class 30	Minor actions to prevent, minimize, stabilize, mitigate, or eliminate the release or threat of release of hazardous waste or substances	15330
Class 31	Historical resource restoration or rehabilitation consistent with Secretary of Interior guidelines	15331
Class 32	Certain in-fill development projects in urban areas	15332
Class 33	Small habitat restoration projects	15333

Network v. County of Marin (2005) 125 Cal. App. 4th 1098, where the court struck down the use of a Class 3 categorical exemption for a discretionary permit for residence in a sensitive stream corridor because the County applied mitigation as a condition of approval. The court stated that there is no such thing as a "mitigated categorical exemption under CEQA."

Although an agency cannot add mitigation measures in order for a project to qualify for a categorical exemption, a project can include features within the project description that would avoid potential impacts. The project features would have to be part of the project design (*see Wollmer v. City of Berkeley* (2011) 193 Cal. App. 4th 1329).

The lead agency is not required by CEQA to write findings support the use of a categorical exemption or to explain why the exceptions to the exemption do not apply. It is recommended, however, that the lead agency prepare enough information within the administrative record to support the use of a categorical exemption and explain why exceptions to the exemption arise in this particular instance. Many agencies prepare a "mini-initial study" to support the use of a categorical exemption and explain the reasons why none of the exceptions to the exemptions under section 15300.2 apply. Most courts use the standard of review similar to Negative Declarations requiring a person challenging the use of a categorical exemption to produce substantial evidence creating the fair argument that the project has the potential for significant environmental impacts in order to show that an exception applies.

A CEQA exemption may apply for information collection.

Notice of Exemption. In most cases, a public agency has the option to file a notice of exemption when it decides that a project is exempt from CEQA and approves or determines to carry out the project (an NOE is mandatory when using certain statutory exemptions for housing, see below). If an NOE is filed at all, it should include a brief description of the project, a finding that the project is exempt, citations to the applicable exemption in the law or Guidelines, and a brief statement of reasons supporting the finding of exemption (Guidelines § 15062), and it should be filed with the county clerk or OPR, depending on the public agency filing notice, after approval of the project. NOEs must be posted and made available for public inspection on a weekly basis. In addition to posting NOEs in the customary manner, agencies are encouraged to make postings of the notices available in electronic format on the Internet. Appendix E of the CEQA Guidelines (*see* Appendix 2 of this book) is a recommended notice of exemption form.

When a public agency has utilized one of the qualified statutory exceptions for agricultural employee housing or affordable infill housing under Public Resources Code §§ 21159.22–21159.24, the NOE is mandatory, and the agency or the project applicant is required to file a notice with the State Clearinghouse (Guidelines § 15062(e)). The Clearinghouse will post the notice for at least thirty days (Pub. Res. Code § 21152.1).

In practice, agencies are strongly advised to file the optional notice of exemption. If the notice of exemption is filed and posted, a thirty-five-day statute of limitations will commence from the date of project approval; if the notice is not filed, a 180-day statute of limitations will apply (Guidelines § 15062(d)) (*see* the discussion of CEQA litigation in Chapter 10). Thus, agencies are encouraged to file NOEs to limit their exposure to legal challenge.

State Certified Regulatory Programs

CEQA provides the Secretary of Resources with the authority to *certify* certain state agency regulatory programs as the "functional equivalent" of CEQA, thereby allowing project approvals under a "partial exemption" from CEQA where these state agency processes do not follow some of CEQA's normal procedures. Under a certified regulatory program, the lead agency is exempt from the requirements to prepare separate EIRs, initial studies, and negative declarations (Pub. Res. Code § 21080.5; Guidelines §§ 15250–15253). A certified program, and the substitute document prepared thereunder, however, remains subject to all substantive provisions of CEQA, such as the requirement to evaluate and avoid significant adverse effects on the environment.

In programs where the state regulatory agency prepares a "substitute document," sometimes referred to as a "functional equivalent document" or "substitute environmental document," that contains the environmental evaluation, involves the public, and responds to comments, and the agency prepares written findings, the Secretary of Resources may find it meets the requirements of CEQA and deem that separate CEQA compliance is not required. The concept of a certified regulatory program is modeled after the NEPA concept of "functional equivalence," and is based on the theory that for an agency whose regulatory program includes all necessary components of CEQA process and analysis, it would be redundant to require a separate CEQA process and analysis to repeat the same information (Guidelines § 15252). The following programs have been certified by the Secretary of Resources:

- Regulation of timber harvesting operations by the California Department of Forestry and Fire Protection and the State Board of Forestry
- The regulatory program of the Fish and Game Commission
- The regulatory program of the California Air Resources Board involving protection and enhancement of ambient air quality
- The regulatory program of the State Board of Forestry under the Forest Practices Act
- California Coastal Commission preparation, approval, and certification of local coastal programs
- The Water Quality Control and Section 208 planning programs of the State Water Resources Control Board and the Regional Water Quality Control Board
- The Pesticide Regulatory Program administered by the Department of Pesticide Regulation of the California Environmental Protection Agency and the county agricultural commissioners
- California Department of Water Resources regulation of water resources management projects
- The Power Plant Site Certification Program of the Energy Resources Conservation and Development Commission
- The regulatory program of the State Water Resources Control Board to establish in-stream beneficial use protection programs

Notice of Exemption

- A brief description of the project
- A finding that the project is exempt
- Citations to the applicable exemption in the law or Guidelines
- A brief statement of reasons supporting the finding of exemption

Notice of Exemption Filing and Posting Time Periods

- File with county clerk
- County clerk posts notice within 24 hours
- Posting lasts 30 days
- Notice retained by Lead Agency for 9 months

Partial Exemption for State-Certified Regulatory Programs

Not Required
- Notices of Preparation
- Draft EIRs
- Final EIRs

Required Content in Program
- Project description
- Alternatives
- Environmental impacts
- Cumulative impacts
- Mitigation measures

Required within Agency's Process
- Consultation with other agencies
- Public notice and review requirements
- Response to comments
- Findings
- Mitigation monitoring
- Notice of decision (filed with Resource Agency)

- The planning program of the Sacramento–San Joaquin Delta Protection Commission
- Portions of the regulatory program of the South Coast Air Quality Management District
- The incidental take of Endangered and Threatened Species Permit Program of the Department of Fish and Game under Fish and Game Code § 2081
- The regulatory program of the Department of Fish and Game for review and approval of voluntary local programs for routine and ongoing agricultural activities under the California Endangered Species Act, pursuant to Fish and Game Code § 2086

(Guidelines § 15251).

While certified regulatory programs have some common elements, the specifics of each program contains unique procedural and evaluation requirements that are integrally related to the agency's mission. Thus, persons interested in a particular regulatory program must review the respective regulations of that agency.

Duties of Lead Agencies with Certified Programs. A certified regulatory program is only a partial exemption from some of CEQA's procedural requirements. Agencies responsible for implementing a certified program must continue to comply with CEQA's goals and policies, provide public review of the substitute document, respond to comments, and adopt CEQA findings. Also, an agency must consider the cumulative effects of its actions. In the substitute document, the agency must evaluate impacts and identify alternatives and mitigation measures. The document must include a description of the project activity, along with either alternatives to the activity and mitigation measures to avoid or reduce the significant environmental effects or a statement, and supporting checklist or other documentation, that there would be no significant environmental effects and therefore no alternatives or mitigation measures proposed. When approving a project on the basis of a certified regulatory program, the agency must file a notice of determination with the Resources Agency (Guidelines § 15252).

Duties of Responsible Agencies where Lead Agency Has Certified Program. Responsible Agencies are required to use the substitute documents of a lead agency's certified regulatory program for CEQA compliance if certain conditions are met (Guidelines § 15253). The certified state regulatory agency must be the first agency to grant discretionary approval for the project and must consult with the responsible agencies (although a written exchange of notices is not required), including the opportunity to review the project site. In addition, as well as meeting all of CEQA's substantive requirements, the certified regulatory program's substitute document must identify the significant environmental effects within the responsible agencies' jurisdiction.

Duties of the California Natural Resources Agency Relative to Certified Programs. The Natural Resources Agency is responsible for determining whether an agency's regulatory program meets the requirements for certification. Upon determining that the requirements are met (although CEQA currently contains no specific criteria), the Secretary of the Agency must undertake an administrative rulemaking to certify the program. The Secretary may also withdraw certification in the same manner if they determine that the regulatory program has been altered as such that it no longer meets certification requirements. The Secretary has developed a protocol for reviewing prospective applications for certification, and has the authority to revoke previous certifications when found to be out of compliance. However, as of this writing, no certification has ever been revoked (Pub. Res. Code § 21080.5).

In 2001, Public Resources Code § 21080.5 was amended to require the secretary to develop specific protocols for reviewing and approving whether a state regulatory agency's program was actually consistent with the requirements of CEQA. In addition, the legislation required the Secretary to report to the Legislature about the need to obtain additional authority to review existing certified regulatory programs (Pub. Res. Code § 21080.5). This report was presented in 2002, but the Legislature has not taken action to amend the certified regulatory process. Currently, there is no specific review process, and commenters have noted that many of the regulatory programs that were certified many years ago no longer meet the current requirements of CEQA.

Relying on Prior CEQA Documents

CEQA provides a variety of methods by which an agency may rely on previously prepared documents in lieu of preparing a new EIR or Negative Declaration. While these are not exemptions from CEQA, they can result in substantially reduced analyses requirements thereby leading to savings in cost and time. As discussed in Chapter 5, each of these approaches contain very different and specific requirements to which agencies must carefully adhere:

- Prior CEQA Coverage (Program or Project).
- "Within the Scope" of a Prior CEQA Document.
- Tiering.
- Projects Consistent with a Community Plan or Zoning.

Project Has Prior NEPA Document.

CEQA Guidelines § 15221 provides that when a project will require compliance with both CEQA and NEPA, the lead agency can use a previously prepared environmental impact statement (EIS) or finding of no significant impact (FONSI) when the following two conditions occur:

- The EIS or FONSI is prepared before the EIR or negative declaration; and
- The EIS or FONSI otherwise complies with the CEQA Guidelines.

When NEPA has been complied with in such a way that it also meets the requirements of CEQA, the lead agency can rely on that NEPA analysis and no additional CEQA analysis is necessary. This does not apply where the project is exempt under a federally adopted categorical exclusion (NEPA's equivalent to CEQA's categorical exemption).

Before taking this approach, the lead agency should first assure itself that the NEPA document and its review process met the requirements that would otherwise apply to an EIR or negative declaration under the CEQA Guidelines. Because NEPA and CEQA have different requirements, a document written to meet NEPA requirements should not automatically be assumed to meet CEQA requirements. Typical things to look out for include:

- **Baseline**—be sure that the NEPA document used a baseline equivalent to existing conditions for analyzing impacts of the project.
- **Determination of significance**—be sure that the NEPA document (particularly a FONSI) took into account the "fair argument" for preparation of an EIR. *See* Chapter 3 (The Initial Study) for more about the fair argument standard.
- **Thresholds of significance**—be sure that the EIS identifies the level of significance of each project impact.
- **Mitigation measures**—be sure that there is a mitigation measure for each significant impact, and that the mitigation measures are feasible and "fully enforceable" as required under CEQA.
- **Alternatives**—be sure that the EIS includes a reasonable range of feasible alternatives that avoid one or more of the project's significant effects while meeting most of its objectives.
- **State Clearinghouse involvement**—be sure that the NEPA document was sent to the State Clearinghouse for review, when applicable.

Where the lead agency is using the NEPA document for CEQA compliance, the lead agency will still need to make the applicable findings for an EIR or negative declaration and adopt a mitigation monitoring or reporting program.

Review of Entitlement Applications under the Permit Streamlining Act

Purpose of the Permit Streamlining Act. For project proposals from nonpublic entities (also referred to as "private projects"), the lead agency must determine whether the project being evaluated is subject to the Permit Streamlining Act (PSA). The PSA requires government agencies complying with CEQA for certain types of private "development projects" to process those projects within state-mandated time limits (*see* Figure 2-5). It was enacted to ensure that government agencies process certain private development projects expeditiously.

The PSA applies only to "development projects," as defined by the act. This definition includes "quasi-judicial" (e.g., administrative) decisions, and not "legislative" actions. Thus, for example, at the local level, projects that are subject to the PSA include conditional use permits, design reviews, and tentative tract maps. On the other hand, general plan amendments and rezonings are not subject to PSA because they are "legislative." At the state level, most agency permits would be generally be subject to the PSA (Gov. Code §§ 65920–65960).

Preapplication Consultation. A lead agency must, upon request by a non public agency project applicant, provide for consultation concerning CEQA compliance prior to the filing of a permit application. The purpose of this

A state agency regulatory program may be certified as being the "functional equivalent" to CEQA.

preapplication consultation is for the lead agency to discuss with the applicant the scope and content of the CEQA requirements for the project. The objective of a preapplication meeting is to identify as many issues as possible early in the permit process to encourage efficient and expeditious CEQA compliance. Among the topics that should be discussed at the preapplication meeting are:

- The range of actions the project would include
- The potential alternatives to be evaluated in the environmental document
- The likely significant environmental impacts of the project
- Mitigation measures for any significant impacts

(Pub. Res. Code § 21080.1(b); Guidelines § 15060.5).

Review for Completeness of Application. The lead agency or responsible agency, during "preliminary review," is allowed thirty days to review a permit application for completeness. The lead agency must inform the applicant in writing if the applicantion is complete or specify what information would make the application complete.

The application will be deemed complete if the agency does not make a determination as to whether an application is complete within thirty days of receipt (Gov. Code § 65943(a); Guidelines § 15101). If the application is returned as incomplete, the applicant may complete and resubmit the application, and the agency again has 30 days to determine the completeness of the resubmitted application (Gov. Code § 64943(b); Guidelines § 15060).

Each agency must publish and make available to the project applicant the information required for submitting entitlement applications. An agency may require enough information to determine whether an EIR must be prepared, but may not require the informational equivalent of an EIR as a condition of accepting an application as complete (Gov. Code § 65941). The purpose of this prohibition is to encourage simultaneous CEQA and permit processing. However, accepting an application as complete does not limit the authority of the lead agency to require the applicant to submit additional information needed for environmental evaluation of the project. Requiring such additional information after the application is complete does not change the status of the application (Guidelines § 15060).

PSA and CEQA Time Limits Initiated by Completion of the Application. CEQA, in coordination with the PSA, contains strict time limits that a lead agency is required to, but does not always follow. Once an application is deemed complete, a lead agency must determine if the activity is subject to CEQA before conducting an initial study (Guidelines § 15060) (*see* Chapter 3 for discussion of Initial Studies). The lead agency must decide whether to prepare an EIR or a negative declaration within thirty days, complete a negative declaration within 180 days, and complete an EIR within one year (Guidelines §§ 15102, 15107, 15108). An applicant's unreasonable delay in providing information will, however, suspend these time limits (Guidelines § 15109) (*see* Figure 2-5, page 56).

CA Supreme Court Reviews Timber Harvest Plan Certified Regulatory Program: in *Ebbetts Pass Forest Watch, et.al. v. California Department of Forestry and Fire Protection* (2008) 43 Cal. 4th 936.

Forest Watch sued CDF over the Department's approval of three Timber Harvest Plans (THPs) in Tuolumne County. The THP process is a certified regulatory program under CEQA. The CDF has adopted voluminous regulations for the preparation of a THP for and assessment of the potential environmental impacts of timber cutting operations.

The Supreme Court reversed the decision. The Court held that a functional equivalent program such as a THP is subject to the CEQA standard of review. Under that standard, the courts' inquiry extends only to determine whether there was a prejudicial abuse of discretion. A prejudicial abuse exists when either the agency has not proceeded in a manner required by law or its determination or decision is not supported by substantial evidence.

CDF's rules for the preparation of THPs require a single, watershed-based study area for all the affected species rather than individually pertinent areas, by species (Forest Practices Rules Technical Rule Addendum No.2). In some instances, that approach would not be sufficient to analyze cumulative impacts on a species. However, when the Court examined the actual analyses and responses to comments contained in the THP at issue, it found that the analyses and responses properly considered the effects of the THPs on the Pacific fisher and spotted owl along the Sierra Nevada range, including National Forest lands. The studies provided to CDF as part of the THP application and separate federal studies addressing conditions throughout the Sierra showed that the analysis actually considered the broader view beyond the watershed.

The Court concluded, with regard to whether a THP comply with the letter of Technical Rule Addendum No. 2's methodology for analysis, that "the technical addendum is properly read to direct that a timber harvest plan's cumulative-impacts assessment be reasonably tailored, in geographic scope as in other respects, to the species under discussion, but not to require rigid adherence to a particular analytical process." Because this argument was over the procedure being followed, the Court held that it could reach its conclusion without examining whether CDF had substantial evidence to support its impact conclusions.

With regard to herbicide use, the THPs asserted that the precise application of herbicides to any given site was not reasonably foreseeable and that, assuming the herbicides were applied as intended, their impact would be less than significant. The Court concluded that the THP incorrectly stated that analysis of herbicide use was not reasonably foreseeable. But that did not mean the general, non-site-specific analysis included in the THPs was inadequate. "Applying the substantial evidence standard to this predominantly factual question, we conclude CDF did not abuse its discretion by accepting the plans' finding that the precise parameters of future herbicide use could not be predicted, and hence failing to demand a more detailed, site-specific analysis of impacts and mitigation measures."

Moving to the question of the THPs' reliance on DPR registration to avoid examining the effects of specific herbicides, the Court stated that "we agree with plaintiffs that the fact a sister agency had assessed the environmental effects of various herbicides in general and registered them for use did not excuse CDF from assessing those herbicides' use as part of a particular timber harvest plan. (original emphasis)" DPR does not certify that herbicides will not cause a significant environmental effect. The Court found that:

> "CDF therefore had no grounds to state in its response to public comments that because of the Department of Pesticide Regulation's registration program "we do not have the authority to approve or disapprove any project regarding the use of chemicals." To the contrary, as the lead agency evaluating timber harvests, CDF has not only the authority but also the duty to approve, disapprove, and impose mitigation measures on timber harvest plans, including measures to address the foreseeable use of herbicides in planned silvicultural operations."

However, as earlier, when examining the content of CDF's responses to comments on the THP, the Court found that the responses provided "an extensive discussion of potential impacts, mitigation measures, and alternatives to herbicide use. CDF thus did not erroneously rely on the DPR's regulatory program and fail to conduct its own environmental impacts assessment."

Project Approval by the Lead Agency. The PSA requires the lead agency to approve or disapprove the project within sixty days from the date of adoption of a negative declaration or the determination that a project is exempt. For projects involving an EIR, the lead agency must approve or disapprove the project within 180 days from the date of certification of the EIR (Gov. Code § 65950). If a combined EIR and environmental impact statement is prepared in compliance with CEQA and NEPA, the lead agency must approve or disapprove the project within ninety days after the document was completed and adopted (Gov. Code § 65951).

An agency may not, however, disapprove an application for a development project merely for the purpose of satisfying the time limits in the PSA. Rather, any disapproval of an application must specify the reasons for disapproval, other than failure to meet the specified time limits (Gov. Code § 65959).

Project Approval by the Responsible Agency. A responsible agency, at the request of a project applicant, must begin processing a permit application for a development project prior to final lead agency action on the project, to the extent that needed information is available (Gov. Code § 65941(c)).

A responsible agency must act within 180 days either of accepting the application as complete or of the lead agency's action, whichever is later (Gov. Code § 65952).

Execution of Consultant Contracts. Although not specifically a PSA requirement, CEQA adds the time constraint that if an EIR or negative declaration is to be prepared by a private consultant under contract with the lead agency, the contract must be executed within forty-five days from the lead agency's determination that either a negative declaration or an EIR is required. The lead agency may take longer to execute the contract if compelling circumstances exist and the project applicant consents. This requirement, however, may result in practical timing difficulties, especially if consultant contracts must be placed on an agenda and formally approved by lead agency decision-making bodies (Pub. Res. Code § 21151.5(b)).

Extensions. The PSA allows for a one-time, limited extension for most of the time limits with mutual consent of the project applicant and lead agency. The PSA specifically disallows any other extensions or waivers of the time limits (Gov. Code § 65957).

Enforcement. The project may be "deemed approved" if an agency fails to act within the time limits for project approval, provided public notice

Figure 2-5
Permit Streamlining Act Time Limits

Environmental Document Time Limits Lead Agency	• 30 days from applicant's acceptance as complete: Lead Agency must decide to prepare Negative Declaration or EIR
	• 45 days from decision to prepare Negative Declaration or EIR: Lead Agency must execute consultant contract • 180 days from application's acceptance as complete: Lead Agency must complete Negative Declaration • 1 year from application's acceptance as complete: Lead Agency must certify EIR
Project Approval Time Limits	• 2 months from exemption decision or adoption of Negative Declaration • 6 months from date of EIR certification
Responsible Agency Project Approval Time Limits	• 180 days after responsible agency accepts application as complete or after Lead Agency action, whichever is later

requirements have been met (Gov. Code § 65956(b)). However, it should be noted that the PSA is a confusing law subject to conflicting judicial interpretations. For example, the court in *Schellinger Brothers v. City of Sebastopol* (2009) 179 Cal. App. 4th 1245, held that CEQA's inclusion of the PSA one-year period for the lead agency to complete an EIR was not fixed "in cement." For projects subject to the law, public agencies must carefully document the dates on which permit applications are submitted and determined to be complete. Although in practice few projects are "deemed approved" by a lapsed time limit, decision-making agencies should avoid such inadvertent lapses because the courts have occasionally deemed projects approved under such circumstances and allowed project implementation without CEQA review and requirement of appropriate mitigation.

CEQA compliance for private projects may trigger the need for compliance with the Permit Streamlining Act.

Tips for Successful Compliance

This chapter covered preliminary review of projects to determine if CEQA applies, when statutory and categorical exemptions apply, as well as certified regulatory programs. The following are some tips for successful implementation of these aspects of CEQA:

- **Consider the "whole of the action"**—CEQA prohibits the "segmenting" of projects into small parts to avoid or minimize the type of environmental document that must be prepared.
- **Learn the list of exemptions**—You should study the list of statutory and categorical exemptions and determine which ones are most likely to apply to your projects.
- **Understand the difference between Statutory and Categorical Exemptions**—A statutory exemption means CEQA does not apply to a qualifying project, regardless of whether environmental impacts might result. A Categorical Exemption, on the other hand, has exceptions, which may mean that a Negative Declaration or EIR must still be necessary.
- **Document the use of exemptions**—Beyond just filing a Notice of Exemption, a lead agency should provide some documentation for why an exemption applies and, in the case of a Categorical Exemption, why no exceptions apply.
- **Determine if a project is a "development project" subject to the Permit Streamlining Act**—If a project is subject to the Permit Streamlining Act then additional deadlines and legal requirements apply.
- **Remember that Certified Regulatory Programs are not truly exemptions**—While certified regulatory programs typically eliminate the need for an EIR or Negative Declaration, many of CEQA's other rules and requirements still apply.

State legislation is statutorily exempt from CEQA.

Chapter 3

The Initial Study

Once it determines that an activity is subject to CEQA and no statutory or categorical exemptions apply, a lead agency needs to determine if an EIR is necessary or if it is appropriate to prepare a Negative Declaration or Mitigated Negative Declaration. The initial study is used to make this determination, unless the lead agency determines at the outset that an EIR is warranted.

Phase Two of CEQA: Preparation of an Initial Study

Purposes of an Initial Study

An initial study is a preliminary analysis prepared by a lead agency, in consultation with other relevant agencies, to determine whether an EIR or a negative declaration is needed. If the initial study concludes that the project, without mitigation, may have a significant effect on the environment, an EIR must be prepared; otherwise, the lead agency may prepare a negative declaration or mitigated negative declaration (Guidelines § 15063). The significant effects to be considered in the initial study include the direct, reasonably foreseeable indirect, cumulative, and growth-inducing impacts of the project. A project with both positive and adverse effects (as opposed to only adverse effects) is not absolved from the responsibility of preparing an initial study. For example, in *County Sanitation District No. 2 of Los Angeles County v. County of Kern* (2005) 127 Cal. App. 4th 1544, the courts held that a project with both positive and potentially significant adverse effects still requires an EIR.

Tools for Determining Whether Environmental Effects Are Significant

- Model Initial Study Checklist (Appendix G of the Guidelines)
- CEQA's mandatory findings of significance
- Agency adopted regulatory standards
- Consultation with other agencies
- Agency thresholds of significance

Where the lead agency has decided to prepare an EIR, the initial study can still be used to focus the EIR on the potential significant effects and allows the lead agency to avoid unnecessary analysis on those effects that are not potentially significant. If a negative declaration is to be prepared, the initial study is used to support the finding that a project will not have a significant unmitigated environmental impact (Guidelines § 15063(c)). The initial study

> **Thresholds May Be Based on a Variety of Factors, Including:**
>
> - Established health standards, such as air pollution emission standards, water pollution discharge standards, or noise levels
> - Public service capacity standards, such as traffic level of service (LOS) or water supply capacity
> - Ecological tolerance standards, such as the physical carrying capacity of a particular ecosystem, measurable sensitive species habitat needs, or farmland conversion acreage limits
> - Guidelines established by agencies or professional associations, such as local registers, including the National and State Registers of Historic Places or the California Native Plant Society's Inventory of Rare and Endangered Plants of California
> - Other standards relating to environmental quality, such as those listed in the model initial study checklist

can be used to assist a lead agency in avoiding preparation of an unnecessary EIR when, prior to public review of the proposed negative declaration, appropriate measures can be incorporated into the project description to mitigate the potential significant impacts identified and, therefore, allow for preparation of a mitigated negative declaration. See Chapter 7 for a discussion of mitigation measures.

After preparing and issuing the initial study and negative declaration or mitigated negative declaration for public review, the lead agency has several options when it determines that there is substantial evidence that any aspect of the project, either individually or cumulatively, may cause a significant effect on the environment, regardless of whether the overall effect of the project is adverse or beneficial. The lead agency must either prepare an EIR, use a previously prepared EIR that adequately analyzes the project at hand, or use one of CEQA's allowable tiering methods to determine which of the project's effects have already been adequately examined in an earlier EIR or negative declaration (Guidelines § 15063(b)(1)).

If the lead agency determines that there is no substantial evidence that the project may cause a significant effect on the environment, it may either prepare a negative declaration or mitigated negative declaration (Guidelines § 15063(b)(2)). This determination is based on the "fair argument standard" described below.

Process for Preparation of the Initial Study

CEQA does not specify a particular process for preparing initial studies. The lead agency may prepare the initial study based on many sources, including information submitted by the applicant. When the initial study is prepared by anyone other than the agency, the lead agency must independently review the information and appropriately incorporate it into the administrative record.

There is no requirement in CEQA to circulate the initial study for public or agency review independently of the negative declaration or mitigated negative declaration. However, the lead agency may choose to informally circulate the "draft" initial study, either only to other agencies or also to the public, in order to get early input regarding potential impact issues. This may further assist in the development of mitigation measures to support a mitigated negative declaration and avoid preparation of unnecessary environmental impact reports. The initial study, where it serves to support a negative declaration or integrated negative declaration, will be part of the review process for the ND or MND. Where the EIR is being prepared, the lead agency may circulate the initial study as an attachment to the notice of preparation.

Contents of the Initial Study

CEQA requires initial studies to include a description of the project, environmental setting, potential environmental impacts, and mitigation measures for any significant effects. In describing the project, the initial study must look at all phases including project planning, implementation, and operation. The initial study must address consistency of the proposed project with existing plans and policies. Names of preparers of the document are also required for inclusion in the initial study (Guidelines § 15063(d)).

When describing potential environmental effects in an initial study, the lead agency may use a checklist, matrix, or other form so long as the entries are briefly explained to indicate that substantial evidence exists to support the entries. The brief explanation may be provided through either a narrative or a reference to another information source such as attached maps, photographs, or earlier EIRs or negative declarations. A reference to another document should include, where appropriate, a citation to the page or pages where the information is found (Guidelines § 15063(d)(3)).

In preparing an initial study, the lead agency may rely upon expert opinion supported by facts, technical studies, or other substantial evidence to document its conclusions. An initial study is neither intended nor required to include the level of detail that is typically found in an EIR (Guidelines § 15063(a)(3)). However, many provisions of the CEQA Guidelines dealing with EIR preparation may be helpful in preparing an initial study. Additionally, in preparing an initial study, the lead agency may use an environmental assessment or environmental impact statement prepared by a federal agency pursuant to NEPA, if one has been prepared (Guidelines § 15063(a)(2)). If necessary, pertinent technical reports (e.g., traffic study, air quality analysis, biological survey, archaeological survey) must be attached to the initial study to document its findings.

Format of Initial Study

The initial study may use a checklist format but must present the factual data or evidence used to reach conclusions regarding impact significance. An initial study without appropriate explanations is sometimes referred to as a "naked checklist" and should be avoided. The lead agency must undertake a reasonable investigation of potential impacts when it prepares an initial study. Thus, fact-based explanations must be used to support the checklist.

Most public agencies rely on initial studies composed of checklists similar to the model checklist found in Appendix G of the Guidelines. The checklist contains a comprehensive listing of potential environmental impacts, many tied to other environmental laws and regulations. Although the items presented in the checklist should not necessarily be thresholds of significance, as the language added to Appendix G with the 2010 CEQA Guidelines Amendments specifically states, a lead agency may use them when determining whether the proposed project effects are significant.

Practitioners should note that Appendix G is a *model* checklist and may or may not address all of the issues that are pertinent to a particular jurisdiction and a particular project. Appendix G specifically states that it is a "sample form and may be tailored to satisfy individual agencies' needs and project circumstances." An environmental issue not on the model checklist does may nevertheless be pertinent to the project, as Appendix G states, "substantial evidence of potential impacts that are not listed on this form must also be

Required Contents of an Initial Study

- Project description
- Environmental setting
- Potential environmental impacts
- Mitigation measures for any significant effect
- Consistency with plans and policies
- Names of preparers

Lead Agency Choices When Initial Study Concludes Project May Significantly Affect the Environment

- Develop mitigation for the significant impact in order to prepare a mitigated negative declaration
- Prepare an EIR
- Use a previously prepared EIR that adequately analyzes the project at hand
- Use one of CEQA's allowable tiering methods to determine which of the project's effects have already been adequately examined in an earlier EIR or negative declaration

considered." For example, in one case, the impacts on nearby streams of eliminating the canal leakage that had fed those streams during the summer was found to be pertinent even though that issue is not explicitly described in Appendix G (*Protect the Historic Amador Waterways v. Amador Water Agency* (2004) 117 Cal. App. 4th 590). Therefore, even with the revised more comprehensive model checklist, a lead agency may want to develop its own comprehensive checklist, adding issues that are unique to its jurisdiction, including more detail on potential resources affected and cumulative impacts. Of particular note, the model checklist does not necessarily integrate the mandatory findings of significance (Guidelines § 15065) and merely lists them at the very end of the checklist.

The model checklist includes four possible levels of environmental effects: "potentially significant impact," "less than significant with mitigation incorporation," "less than significant impact," and "no impact." These possible checklist responses correspond directly to the legal standards for preparing EIRs, mitigated negative declarations, and negative declarations, respectively (Guidelines § 15063(f) and Appendix G of the Guidelines). If there are any checks in the "potentially significant impact" column, this is tells the reader that an EIR must be prepared.

Conclusions of an Initial Study: The Fair Argument Standard

When Must an EIR Be Prepared? The "Fair Argument" Standard. In addition to the mandatory EIRs described at the end of this chapter (CEQA Guidelines § 15981.5), a lead agency must prepare an EIR when the lead agency determines that:

It can be fairly argued, based on substantial evidence, in light of the whole record before the agency, that a project may have a significant effect on the environment (Pub. Res. Code secs. 21080(d), 21082.2(d)).

Thus, if such substantial evidence of significant impacts is developed by or presented to the lead agency, it must prepare an EIR, even though it may be presented with other evidence that the project would *not* have significant impacts (Guidelines § 15064). Known as the "fair argument" test, this standard for preparation of an EIR turns on whether the administrative record contains expert, factual, analytical, or other substantial evidence from which a fair argument can be made that significant effect may result from the proposed project.

The "Fair Argument" standard is the linchpin of CEQA's approach to determining when an EIR is necessary. It purposely sets a low threshold for preparation of an EIR in order that where there is a question of the presence of a significant effect, these potential environmental impacts are disclosed to the public and decisionmakers, and means of avoiding or reducing those impacts identified and implemented in the larger, more detailed CEQA document, the environmental impact report. It also makes information (i.e., substantial evidence) that may be received from other agencies and the public as important as the information provided by the lead agency. The "whole record" consists of the administrative record before the lead agency from the time the project begins the process of consideration (when an application is deemed complete for processing, for example) until a final decision is rendered. The whole record includes evidence that is received after the end of the negative declaration's review period, but before final action is taken on the project.

Under the "fair argument" test, an EIR is required even if the lead agency considers the net, overall impact of the project to be beneficial. "For projects that may cause both beneficial and adverse significant impacts on the environment, preparation of an EIR is required because the consideration of feasible alternatives and mitigation measures might result in changes to the project that decrease its adverse effects on California's environment (*County Sanitation District No. 2 of Los Angeles County v. County of Kern* 127 Cal. App. 4th 1544)."

The "fair argument standard" is unique to CEQA, and is arguably one of the most controversial aspects of the law. It differs from the traditional substantial evidence standard in that it favors evidence submitted by project opponents, rather than deferring to an agency's expertise on a particular topic. Under the "fair argument standard," if project opponents present substantial evidence that a project may result in significant effects, the agency must either mitigate the impact to a less than significant level (and prepare a mitigated negative declaration) or prepare an EIR, even if its own substantial evidence supports a contrary conclusion. In addition, the fair argument standard can be used to discredit the mitigation proposed to reduce the impact to a less-than-significant level in a mitigated negative declaration (*see* below).

The "fair argument standard" means that a lead agency must seriously consider any comments it receives calling for the preparation of an EIR. If such comments are supported by substantial evidence and create a fair argument as to the significance of an impact, then the agency is required to prepare an EIR. In practice, however, the lead agency may want to discuss the comments with the organization or person submitting them to find out if there are ways to mitigate or avoid such impacts. If the lead agency can reach an agreement with the commenter that mitigation can reduce the potentially significant impacts, and commits to such mitigation, an EIR may be avoided, and a mitigated negative declaration prepared instead.

Definition of Substantial Evidence. "Substantial evidence" includes facts, fact-related reasonable assumptions, and expert opinions based on facts. According to CEQA, substantial evidence does not include arguments, speculation, unsubstantiated opinion or narrative, clearly inaccurate or erroneous evidence, or socioeconomic impacts not related to the physical environment (Pub. Res. Code secs. 21080(e), 21082.2(c); Guidelines § 15384). Substantial evidence on the record may come from any source–agencies, project applicants, neighbors, project opponents, project supporters–and is not limited to "expert opinion" where the resource impacts are based merely on fact or are non-technical and subjective, such as aesthetics.

Substantial Evidence

Substantial evidence for an initial study means enough relevant information and reasonable inferences from that information to make a fair argument, and consists of:

- Facts
- Reasonable assumptions predicated on facts
- Expert opinion supported by facts

Substantial evidence does not include:

- Argument
- Speculation
- Unsubstantiated opinion or narrative
- Evidence that is clearly erroneous or inaccurate
- Evidence of social or economic impacts that do not contribute to or are not caused by physical impacts on the environment

What Effects Trigger which Document under CEQA?

EFFECTS	ACTION
Potentially Significant	Prepare EIR
Less Than Significant with Mitigation	Prepare MND
Less-Than Significant	Prepare ND
No Impact	Prepare ND

For example, in *Ocean View Estates Homeowners Assoc., Inc. v. Montecito Water District* (2004) 116 Cal. App. 4th 396, the Court overturned a mitigated negative declaration based on the presence of substantial evidence of a potentially significant impact in the form of a memo from the district's own consultant warning about residual water quality impacts and statements by non-expert residences that there would be an aesthetic impact. Regarding the aesthetic impact, the court noted that, because of the subjective nature of aesthetic effects, "[p]ersonal observations on these nontechnical issues can constitute substantial evidence." See also, *The Pocket Protectors v City of Sacramento* (2004) 124 Cal. App. 4th 903, where a mitigated Negative Declaration was overturned. The Court specifically held that the testimony by "neighbors familiar with the site and the planned unit development (PUD)" who "offered detailed factual observations on these points, not mere general opinions" counted as substantial evidence that there was a fair argument related to aesthetic impacts and consistency with the PUD.

When May a Negative Declaration Be Prepared? A negative declaration may only be prepared when no substantial evidence exists, in light of the whole record, that the project may have a significant environmental effect (Pub. Res. Code § 21080(c); Guidelines § 15070). Conversely, if the administrative record contains any substantial evidence of a potentially significant effect (and the requirements of a mitigated negative declaration cannot be met), the lead agency must prepare an EIR (Guidelines § 15064). Similarly, if there is a disagreement among experts and both are supported by substantial evidence, the lead agency must prepare an EIR.

When May a Mitigated Negative Declaration Be Prepared? A mitigated negative declaration may be prepared if the initial study identifies a potentially significant effect for which the project's proponent, before public release of a proposed negative declaration, has made or agrees to make project revisions that clearly mitigate the effects. A mitigated negative declaration may not be used, however, if any substantial evidence indicates that the revised project with mitigation may still have a significant environmental effect (Pub. Res. Code § 21064.5; Guidelines § 15070). For such a mitigated negative declaration, specific mitigation measures must be developed and agreed to before the notice of intent to adopt the MND has been published. No format for the mitigation agreement is specified in CEQA–the project proponent's agreement regarding mitigation commitments may take the form of either a letter or a revised project application. For additional information about mitigated negative declarations, *see* "Mitigated Negative Declarations," a CEQA advice memorandum published by OPR (December 1997) (Appendix 8). Chapter 7 contains a detailed discussion of what constitutes mitigation under CEQA.

Evolution of the "Fair Argument" Standard

Despite its fundamental importance to the CEQA process, the fair argument standard does not appear in the statute. Rather, it was a creation of the courts very early in the development of CEQA. In 1974, the California Supreme Court, in *No Oil, Inc. v. City of Los Angeles* 13 Cal. 3d 68 (1974). enunciated an early version of the "fair argument" standard when it held that "an agency should prepare an EIR whenever it perceives some substantial evidence that the project may have a significant effect environmentally (13 Cal 3d 68 (1974))." That court, citing a NEPA decision, noted that "an environmental impact report should be prepared whenever the action arguably will have an adverse environmental impact." From this combination of language, the "fair argument" standard emerged.

After the *No Oil* decision, the fair argument standard was added to the CEQA Guidelines (§ 15064). In 1980, an appellate court strongly affirmed the fair argument standard in *Friends of B Street v. City of Hayward,* (1980) 106 Cal. 3d 988. Since those early decisions, the fair argument standard has been raised in dozens of CEQA decisions, but it has withstood the test of time. Today, it is one of the cornerstones of CEQA practice.

Determining Whether Effects Are Potentially Significant

Determining whether a project may have a significant effect on the environment calls for careful judgment on the part of the lead agency. To the extent feasible, the decision should be based on scientific and factual data. An ironclad definition of "significant effect" is not possible because the significance of an activity may vary with the setting. For example, an activity that may not be significant in an urban area may be significant in a rural one (Guidelines § 15064(b)). The Guidelines' recommended tools for determining the potential for significant environmental effects include the model initial study checklist (Appendix G of the Guidelines), CEQA's mandatory findings of significance (Guidelines § 15065), consultation with other agencies, and particular agency thresholds of significance.

Fair Argument Standard
- It can be fairly argued
- Based on substantial evidence
- In light of the whole record before the agency
- That the project may have a significant effect on the environment.

A significant effect on the environment is generally defined as a substantial or potentially substantial adverse change in the physical environment (Guidelines § 15358). "Environment" as used in this definition means the physical conditions that exist within the area affected by a proposed project, including, but not limited to, land, air, water, minerals, flora, fauna, ambient noise, and objects of historical or aesthetic significance. The "environment" includes both natural and man-made conditions. "The area that will be affected" means the area in which significant effects would occur either directly or indirectly as a result of the project (Guidelines § 15360). Such areas of potential impact will typically differ from impact to impact. For example, the area affected by a noise source will likely be more localized than the area affected by air pollution; even though both are emitting from the same source.

CEQA's Mandatory Findings of Significance

CEQA sets forth certain mandatory findings of significance. The presence of these impacts will cause the preparation of an EIR unless mitigation can be incorporated to offset the effect (Pub. Res. Code § 21083; Guidelines § 15065). According to the CEQA Guidelines, a project would have a significant effect on the environment if the project would:

- Substantially degrade the quality of the environment
- Substantially reduce fish or wildlife habitat
- Cause a fish or wildlife habitat to drop below self-sustaining levels
- Threaten to eliminate a plant or animal community
- Substantially reduce the numbers or range of a rare, threatened, or endangered species
- Eliminate important examples of the major periods of California history or prehistory; or
- Achieve short-term goals to the disadvantage of long-term goals
- The project's possible environmental effects are individually limited but cumulatively considerable, when viewed in connection with past, current, and reasonably anticipated future projects, the project would be deemed to have a significant effect
- The project would have environmental effects that will directly or indirectly cause substantial adverse effects on human beings

(Guidelines § 15065).

In addition, the Guidelines specify that a project with an effect that may cause a substantial adverse change in the significance of an historical resource will have a significant effect on the environment (Guidelines § 15064.5).

CA Supreme Court Rules Holds Evidence Not Sufficient to Trigger EIR:

In the case *Save the Plastic Bag Coalition v. City of Manhattan Beach* (2011) 52 Cal. 4th 155, the Court upheld a Negative Declaration for the City of Manhattan Beach ordinance banning plastic bags at the point of sale within the City.

Although opponents to the ordinance had submitted studies finding that the increase in paper bag use is "generally associated with a variety of negative environmental impacts," the Court stated that "no evidence [submitted on the record] suggests that paper bag use by Manhattan Beach consumers in the wake of a plastic bag ban would continue to those impacts in any significant way." The Court stated that "common sense" is an important consideration "in all levels of CEQA review." Applying common sense to these types of "generic studies of live cycle impacts," the Court concluded that the "environmental impacts discernible from the lifecycle of plastic bags are not significantly implicated " by a plastic bag ordinance for a small city like Manhattan Beach.

Mandatory Findings of Significance

A project will have a significant effect if it will:

- Substantially degrade environmental quality
- Substantially reduce fish or wildlife habitat
- Cause a fish or wildlife habitat to drop below self-sustaining levels
- Threaten to eliminate a plant or animal community
- Substantially reduce the numbers or range of a rare, threatened, or endangered species
- Eliminate important examples of the major periods of California history or prehistory
- Achieve short-term goals to the disadvantage of long-term goals
- Have possible environmental effects that are individually limited but cumulatively considerable when viewed in connection with past, current, and reasonably anticipated future projects
- Have environmental effects that will directly or indirectly cause substantial adverse effects on human beings

Effective mitigation agreed to before environmental documentation begins can allow the lead agency to avoid a mandatory finding of significance.

Because several of these "mandatory" findings are written with vague modifiers, such as "substantially," they are somewhat open to lead agency interpretation as to when a project meets the trigger for significance (e.g., defining when a project feature would substantially reduce the range of an endangered species). A lead agency should not modify these mandatory findings in a way that could be construed as more lenient than section 15065. *Endangered Habitats League v. County of Orange* (2005) 131 Cal. App. 4th 777 struck down an EIR that had modified the language of the mandatory finding to limit significance to situations where a plant or animal community drops below self-perpetuating levels on a "statewide or regional basis." As stated by the court in *Defend the Bay v. City of Irvine* (2004) 119 Cal. App. 4th 1261, "any project that reduces the habitat of a wildlife species, or reduces the number or range of an endangered, rare or threatened species is deemed to have a significant impact on the environment as a matter of law."

For example, in *San Bernardino Audubon Society v. Metropolitan Water District* (2001) 89 Cal. App. 4th 1097, the court held that a mitigated negative declaration could not be adopted where there was a fair argument that the project would reduce the numbers or range of rare, threatened, or endangered species, and that the proposed mitigation measures were inadequate to avoid that outcome. Although specific mitigation was included to avoid this impact, the presence of substantial evidence to support a fair argument turned the case against the District.

Agencies May Mitigate Where Mandatory Findings Are Triggered. Amendments to section 15065 adopted in 2004 clarified that a project may avoid a mandatory finding of significance if:

> Prior to commencement of preliminary review of an environmental document, a project proponent agrees to mitigation measures or project modifications that would avoid any significant effect specified by [section 15065] or would mitigate the significant effect to a point where clearly no significant effect on the environment would occur.

(Guidelines § 15065(b)).

In addition, section 15065 provides that where a project would have the potential to substantially

Sundstrom v. County of Mendocino: Court Establishes Rules for Mitigation Detail in Initial Studies and Negative Declarations

In *Sundstrom v. County of Mendocino* (1988) 202 Cal. App. 3d 296, court interpretation of negative declarations came to a head. An individual citizen challenged the Mendocino County Board of Supervisors' decision to approve construction of a sewage treatment plant to serve an existing development consisting of a small motel, restaurant, and filling station, to which a larger motel, a restaurant, and apartments would be added.

The county had prepared an Initial Study supporting a negative declaration for the proposed project. The Initial Study/negative declaration conditioned certain mitigation measures to be developed and implemented at a later date. One of the reasons the Initial Study/ negative declaration concluded there would be no potential for significant effects was because it required the applicant to prepare a future hydrologic study to evaluate the project's potential environmental effects on soil stability, erosion, sediment transport, and flooding of downslope properties. This future study was required to recommend appropriate mitigation measures for the significant impacts reported.

The Court of Appeal held that the Initial Study/negative declaration violated CEQA. The court stated that, before approving the project, the county must first resolve the uncertainties regarding the project's potential significant environmental effects. The court concluded that the success of the mitigation determined by a later study was uncertain; therefore, the county could not have reasonably concluded that the project would not have the potential to have significant environmental effects. Also, the court found that the county's deferral of the analysis of significant effects to a study the applicant was preparing in the future was an inappropriate delegation of its CEQA duties. Although the county had included a permit condition requiring subsequent county approval of a sludge disposal plan, the court found it inadequate because there was evidence that an environmentally sound disposal plan might not be achievable. The court also noted that both the county public works department and the Coastal Commission had recommended project denial until the potential problems could be solved.

The court held that the Initial Study/negative declaration was ultimately invalid because of a lack of substantial evidence supporting the county's finding of no potential for significant impact. The court stated that the county had "evaded its responsibility to engage in comprehensive environmental review." This fact pattern and associated court ruling have been used as a reference guide for assessing the adequacy of mitigation included in Initial Study/negative declarations. An Initial Study/negative declaration that relies on a future study to determine if there are potentially significant effects is considered "classic Sundstrom mitigation" and does not comply with CEQA.

Since 1988, there have been many court decisions that have reached similar conclusions, but the *Sundstrom* case still stands as the landmark decision relating to whether analysis and mitigation can be deferred to a timeframe after the initial study was prepared and MND adopted.

reduce the number or restrict the range of an endangered, rare, or threatened species, no EIR needs to be prepared if all of the following conditions are met:

- The project proponent is required to implement mitigation requirements relating to such species and habitat pursuant to an approved Habitat Conservation Plan (HCP) or Natural Community Conservation Plan (NCCP).

- The HCP or NCCP was approved by a federal or state agency on the basis of an environmental impact statement or EIR.
- The requirements of the HCP or NCCP avoid any net loss of habitat and net reduction in number of affected species or the requirements preserve, restore, or enhance sufficient habitat to mitigate the reduction in habitat and number of the affected species to below a level of significance.

Consultation with Other Agencies

In determining whether to prepare an EIR, a lead agency must consult with responsible and trustee agencies through the CEQA process. Additionally, a lead agency is authorized to consult informally with these agencies as well as any other agency with jurisdiction over resources affected by the proposed project (Pub. Res. Code § 21080.3). The purpose of interagency consultation is to ensure that all affected agencies have a voice in the threshold decision.

If an agency with jurisdiction over an affected environmental resource recommends that an EIR be prepared and presents substantial evidence to support that recommendation, the lead agency should either prepare an EIR or develop mitigation measures that satisfy the requirements of the other agency for inclusion in a mitigated negative declaration.

Lead agencies must take comments from responsible or trustee agencies or federal regulatory agencies particularly seriously. Such agencies, by definition, have expertise over the resources under their jurisdiction, and their comment letters are usually based on scientific data developed by their staff. Thus, if a responsible or trustee agency submits comments to the lead agency requesting than an EIR be prepared, and if such request is based on substantial evidence the lead agency should follow that advice.

Where a project could impact fish or wildlife resources, the lead agency may be required to consult with DFG as a Trustee or Responsible Agency.

Not every comment letter submitted by a responsible or trustee agency automatically triggers an EIR. Rather, the lead agency should discuss the comments with the agency submitting comments to determine the factual basis for their opinion that an EIR is necessary. Additionally, the two agencies should discuss whether it is possible to mitigate any potential impacts, thereby enabling the lead agency to prepare a mitigated negative declaration rather than an EIR.

For example, if the Department of Fish and Game indicates that the potential impacts from a project would significantly affect the habitat of a particular species and that an EIR should, therefore, be prepared, rather than merely accepting or rejecting that request, the lead agency should contact the DFG and find out what data they have to support their request for an EIR. They should also find out if DFG has suggestions for mitigating the potential impacts. Although the lead agency has the discretion to make significance conclusions for biological resources, and has the ultimate authority to make the decision to prepare an EIR or negative declaration, the information provided by DFG will inform which document should be prepared. If DFG's recommendation to prepare an EIR is, indeed, based on substantial evidence, and the lead agency refuses to follow DFG's mitigation advice, then proceeding with a negative declaration would be very risky.

Thresholds of Significance

Each public agency is encouraged to develop and publish thresholds of significance to aid that agency in determining the significance of environmental effects. A threshold of significance is an identifiable quantitative, qualitative, or performance level of a particular environmental effect. Noncompliance with this performance level would normally be determined to be significant by the agency, and compliance would normally be determined to be considered less than significant (Guidelines § 15064.7). In practice, those agencies that have developed thresholds of significance treat exceedences as a rebuttable presumption of significance and non-exceedances as presumptions of nonsignificance.

Thresholds of significance to be adopted for general use must be developed though a public review process with advance public notice. If thresholds are formally adopted, they must be adopted by ordinance, resolution, rule, or regulation. Some agencies, however, have developed advisory thresholds to be used by their staffs, but have stopped short of having their decisionmakers formally adopt them. Thresholds must be supported by substantial evidence (Guidelines § 15064.7).

However, the thresholds developed for a particular project are not required to be adopted by ordinance or other formal means (*see* for example, *Oakland Heritage Alliance v. City of Oakland* (2011) 195 Cal. App. 4th 884).

Relationship to Adopted Regulatory Standards

Regulatory standards adopted by agencies with jurisdiction over particular resources based on other laws or regulations (e.g., Regional Water Quality Control Board Basin Plan standards) may be used as one basis for determining the significance of a project impact to the extent they reduce the project's impact. The same is true for compliance with development standards such as the California Building Code (*Oakland Heritage Alliance v. City of Oakland* (2011) 195 Cal. App. 4th 884). However, if there is a fair argument that the project's compliance with the standard would still not reduce its impacts to a less-than-significant level, then an EIR is required. The Court in *Communities for a Better Environment v. California Resources Agency* (2002) 103 Cal. App. 4th 98 made this issue clear in overturning an amendment to the State CEQA Guidelines. The Resources Agency had adopted a language in Section 15064(h) of the State CEQA Guidelines to state that a "change in the environment is not significant if the change complies with a standard (defined as a regulatory standard adopted by a public agency to protect the environment)." The court overturned this language as being contrary to the fair argument standard. The court stated that, in effect, the Guideline language would have a lead agency ignore substantial evidence that shows there is still the potential for a significant impact, notwithstanding the projects compliance with a "regulatory standard."

The sample environmental checklist in Appendix G of the CEQA Guidelines contains several regulatory standards within particular resource areas. However, it is not intended to identify all regulatory standards that may apply to a project, nor is it intended to be used, by itself, as a threshold of significance where more practical, measurable thresholds exist. The essential purposes of the checklist are to assist in the examination of potential project impacts and to direct the agency to explain its rationale for its impact determinations. The examination must also be informed by other sources, depending on the resources potentially effected by the proposed project.

Environmental Effects to Be Considered in Conducting an Initial Study

Direct and Indirect Effects. In evaluating the potential significance of an impact, the lead agency must consider both the direct and reasonably foreseeable indirect impacts of the project (Guidelines § 15064(c)). A more detailed discussion of direct and indirect impacts can be found in Chapter 7. Although CEQA does not specify the level of analysis necessary to analyze direct and indirect effects in an initial study, in practice the initial study typically contains less information than an EIR because if there is a potential for a significant impact, the lead agency should be proceeding with the preparation of an EIR. However, many lead agencies prepare detailed initial studies supporting a negative declaration or mitigated negative declaration to create a larger administrative record to support the conclusion that the fair argument has not been raised.

Socioeconomic Effects. An economic or social change alone is not considered a physical effect on the environment (*see* CEQA Guidelines §§ 15064, 15382) and, therefore, is not part of the significance determinations in an initial study. An economic or social change that is causally related to a physical change may be taken into consideration when determining the significance of the physical change (Guidelines §§ 15064(e), 15064(f), 15382). For example, where a project would result in urban decay (i.e., long-term vacancies, deteriorating structures, etc., leading to aesthetic impacts on the physical environment) as a result of its economic impacts on existing development, the economic impact must be disclosed and analyzed in relation to the indirect significance of the physical effect (related to aesthetics) on the environment in the initial study (*see* for example, *Bakersfield Citizens for Local Control v. City of Bakersfield* (2004) 129 Cal. App. 4th 1184).

Cumulative Effects. In assessing whether a cumulative effect requires an EIR, the lead agency must consider whether the cumulative impact is significant, and whether the project's contribution is "cumulatively considerable." An EIR must be prepared if the project's incremental contribution, though it may be individually limited, is "cumulatively considerable to a significant cumulative impact." Cumulatively considerable means that the incremental effects of an individual project are considerable when viewed in connection with the effects of past, current, and probable future projects (Guidelines §§ 15064(i)(1), 15130).

In conducting an initial study, a lead agency may determine that a project's contribution to a significant cumulative impact is not cumulatively considerable and thus is not a potentially significant impact related to the proposed project. When a project might contribute to a significant cumula-

Making the Threshold Decision: Are Effects Potentially Significant?

Factors to consider that must be based on substantial evidence in the record:

- Direct effects
- Reasonably foreseeable indirect effects
- Expert disagreement
- Public controversy (no EIR required unless based on substantial evidence that a significant effect may occur)
- "Considerable" contribution to cumulative effects
- Special thresholds for historical and archaeological resources

Factors not relevant:

- Speculative indirect physical changes to the environment
- Economic and social effects

Keep in mind that the baseline for analysis is the existing environmental setting. It is not the projected buildout of the site under an adopted general plan, nor, in most cases, is it the future no-project scenario.

tive impact, but would be rendered less than cumulatively considerable through mitigation, the initial study must briefly indicate and explain how the contribution has been mitigated (Guidelines § 15064(h)(2)).

A lead agency may also determine that a project's contribution to a cumulative impact is not "cumulatively considerable" if the project will comply with the requirements in a previously approved plan or mitigation program that provides specific requirements that will avoid or substantially lessen the cumulative problem within the geographic area in which the project is located. Such plans or programs must be specified in law or adopted by the public agency with jurisdiction over the affected resources through a public review process. Examples of this concept include project-specific compliance with mitigation measures in a water quality control plan, air quality plan, or integrated waste management plan. However, if there is substantial evidence that the effects of the project are still cumulatively considerable, despite compliance with a plan or mitigation program, then an EIR must be prepared (Guidelines § 15064(h)(3)).

An increase in traffic is a common concern for neighbors. (Photo courtesty of Antero Rivasplata)

The court in *Communities for a Better Environment* invalidated a 1998 Guidelines provision that a lead agency may determine that the incremental impacts of a project are not "cumulatively considerable" when they are so small that they make a *de minimis* contribution to a significant cumulative impact caused by other projects that would exist in the absence of the project (the decision voided previous Guidelines §§ 15064(i)(4), 15130(a)(4), and 15152(f)(2)). The court noted that where cumulative impacts are particularly acute, even a very small individual contribution may be important. The *de minimis* approach would therefore have resulted in a failure to identify such impacts. The court also held that using a ratio approach to determine whether a project's cumulative contribution is considerable was improper because the ratio approach masks the importance of individual contributions when the cumulative impact is acute.

Public Opinion and Controversy. A lead agency must consider public opinion when determining the magnitude and significance of an impact (Pub. Res. Code §§ 21080(c)(2), 21082.2(b); Guidelines § 15064(c)). The existence of public controversy alone, however, does not trigger an EIR if the public controversy has not raised substantial evidence in light of the whole record shows that the project may have a significant environmental effect. Nevertheless, in marginal cases in which it is unclear whether substantial evidence of a potential significant effect exists, the presence of public controversy may indicate that an EIR is necessary if the controversy is related to the project's potential significant environmental effects (Guidelines § 15064(h)).

Expert Disagreement. As with public controversy, expert disagreement alone does not trigger an EIR unless the experts disagree about the significance of an effect and their opinions are based on substantial evidence (Guidelines § 15064(h)). Thus, when experts disagree, based on substantial evidence, a mitigated negative declaration is not the appropriate CEQA document.

For example, in *City of Carmel-by-the-Sea v. Board of Supervisors* (1986) 183 Cal. App. 3d 229, the existence of disagreement among experts was a factor in the court overturning the negative declaration adopted by the city. Plaintiffs supplied expert opinion that differed from the lead agency's experts on the definition of "wetlands" and, therefore, the extent of wetlands affected by the proposed development project that would be made possible by the city's rezone. The court noted that the EIR was a "necessity" to add a "degree of factual certainty for tentative opinion."

A lead agency is entitled to discount expert testimony that lacks credibility. For example, in *Bowman v. City of Berkeley* (2004) 122 Cal. App. 4th 572, the court upheld the city's negative declaration for a senior housing project where the suppositions by plaintiff's "expert" on toxic plumes within the groundwater was found by the city to not be expert testimony because the person had no special training, knowledge, or experience. In this case, the court stated that "a complex scientific issue such as migration of chemicals through land calls for expert evaluation."

Lay Person Testimony as Substantial Evidence. Included in the definition of "substantial evidence" is both facts and "reasonable assumption predicated on fact (Pub Res Code Section 21080(e)(1))." Therefore, in certain instances, testimony by a lay person (i.e., not considered an expert) may qualify as substantial evidence and possible triggering the "fair argument" standard for preparing an EIR. Where input from non-experts is credible and does not purport to embody analysis that would require specialized training, it can be considered substantial evidence. For example, in the Bowman case cited above, the court held that "statements of area residents who are not environmental experts may qualify as substantial evidence if they are based on relevant personal observations or involve non technical issues." In *Ocean View Estates Homeowners Assn v. Montecito Water District* (2004) 116 Cal.App.4th 396, the court overturned the lead agency water district's negative declaration on a proposal to construct an aluminum covering over a reservoir, based in part on opinions by residents living uphill from the reservoir regarding the potential aesthetic impact of the project (where the lead agency had concluded there would be no impact). Regarding the subjective concerns of aesthetic impacts, the court stated that this "is not the special purview of experts. Personal observations on these nontechnical issues can constitute substantial evidence."

Baseline for Analysis. To determine whether a potential impact is significant or not, the lead agency must compare that impact to a baseline condition. CEQA Guidelines § 15125 specifies that a project's environmental setting normally is the "baseline" for environmental analysis. The CEQA Guidelines defines the "environmental setting" as being the physical conditions in the vicinity of a project as they exist at the time the notice of preparation (NOP) is published (for preparation of an EIR) or, in the absence of an NOP (as would be the case in preparation of an initial study), at the time environmental analysis is commenced (Guidelines § 15125). Although environmental setting is described under a Guidelines section discussing the elements of an EIR, the concept of the environmental setting as baseline is equally applicable to an initial study.

Future impacts resulting from the proposed project (both directly and indirectly) are compared to the "baseline," and their "significance" is measured as a function of the difference between the baseline environmental setting and the future condition when the project is implemented. One of the fundamental principles of CEQA is that an adequate baseline discussion is necessary to have an adequate impact evaluation.

Despite the Guideline's attempt to define the "baseline" for determining impacts, the question of determining the proper baseline still perplexes many professionals. This is so because the concept of a "baseline" is multi-dimensional. It involves both a temporal dimension (e.g. when existing conditions are defined); a spatial dimension (e.g. what the geographic area is to be described); and a functional dimension (e.g. what description of existing activities and uses must be described). While no single rule captures all of these aspects of baseline, a lead agency should describe its baseline carefully and should explain, in the CEQA document, why a particular baseline or baselines (they may differ for different resources) were used. Additionally there must be substantial evidence on the reload to support the choice of a baseline. In most cases, the baseline is not the same as the "no-project" alternative (Guidelines § 15126.6).

Table 3-1 Selected Historic Resources Court Decisions Lead Agency's Action Set Aside

League for Protection of Oakland's Architectural and Historical Resources v. City of Oakland (1997) 52 Cal. App.4th 60	Montgomery Ward building proposed for demolition was listed on City plan of historic resources. Mitigated negative declaration inadequate to avoid substantial adverse effect to the resource.
Architectural Heritage Assoc. v. County of Monterey (2004) 122 Cal. App. 4th 1095	Old county jail proposed for demolition was eligible for California Register. Mitigated negative declaration inadequate to avoid substantial effect.
Valley Advocates v. City of Fresno (2008) 160 Cal. App.4th 1039	Categorical exemption for proposed demolition of old apartment building invalidated. Despite finding that the building was not on the State, Federal or local registers and was not eligible for listing, the City failed to make finding under CEQA Guidelines § 15164.5 that the building was not historically significant.
Committee to Save the Hollywoodland Specific Plan and Hollywood Heritage v. City of Los Angeles (2008) 161 Cal. App. 4th 1168	Categorical exemption for fence to be built on top of a listed, historic rock wall invalidated. City failed to analyze potential adverse effect of the fence on the wall's historic significance. CEQA Guidelines § 15300.2 *prohibits use of a categorical exemption where potential for adverse effect on historic resource.*

Recent court decisions provide additional guidance and examples that may help agencies define proper baseline. As some of the cases in Table 3-2 illustrate, baseline issues are particular problematic when existing on-going activities are involved, and the current document is being prepared on a continuation of those activities in the future (e.g. a permit renewal).

The California Supreme Court has clarified the use of baseline related to existing facilities. In *Communities for a Better Environment v. South Coast Air Quality Management District* (2010) 48 Cal 4th 310, the court overturned a Negative Declaration adopted by the Air District for an existing facility that was proposing modifications to refine a different type of diesel fuel. The Air District used the previously permitted emissions as the baseline for the impact analysis, although the existing air emission operations were not nearly as high as the permitted level. Therefore, although the change in refinery operations from existing conditions would exceed the Air District's published significance thresholds, the Negative Declaration concluded that there was no impact because the proposed operations would still be under the baseline (permitted level of emissions allowed under prior operating permits). The Court noted that CEQAs "general rule" related to baseline is that it "must be the existing physical conditions in the affected area, [reflecting] the real conditions on the ground, rather than the level of development or activity that could or should have been present according to a plan or regulation." Therefore, the Court rejected the District's baseline stating that "by comparing the proposed project to what could happen rather than to what was actually happening, the District set the baseline not according to established levels of a particular use but by merely hypothetical conditions allowable under the permits. An approach using hypothetical allowable conditions as the baseline results in illusory comparisons that can only mislead the public as to the reality of the impacts and subvert full consideration of the actual environmental impacts, a result at direct odds with CEQA's intent."

A particularly contentious issue is whether an agency can use a future baseline instead of existing conditions. The use of a future baseline is often the preferred approach among those evaluating traffic impacts as well as air quality and noise impacts, which are based on traffic impacts. The appellate courts have issued divergent opinions regarding whether a future baseline is acceptable and the California Supreme Court has yet to resolve the issue.

For updated material on this topic, please see the 2013 Addendum at www.solano.com

In *Sunnyvale West Neighborhood Assoc. v. City of Sunnyvale City Council* (2010) 190 Cal. App. 4th 1351, and EIR for a road extension was invalidated because it used 2020 conditions without the project (2020 conditions) as its baseline for traffic analysis (this baseline was also reflected in the air quality and noise analyses). The Court of Appeal could find no statute or case law that allowed the use of a future condition as the baseline for analysis and cited the *Communities for a Better Environment* decision for the proposition that the baseline cannot be a hypothetical future condition. At most, in the opinion of this court, the baseline might be the time at which the project is approved. Accordingly, the court held that the 2020 baseline precluded an adequate analysis of the project's incremental traffic impacts and obscured the severity of the project's impacts. The air quality and noise analyses based on the baseline for traffic analysis were similarly inadequate.

In *Pfeiffer v. City of Sunnyvale* (2011) 200 Cal. App. 4th 1552, the same appellate court softened its position on the use of a future baseline. In that case, the lead agency used several different baselines, including: existing conditions, future "background" conditions, project conditions, and cumulative conditions. Background conditions included future planned and funded road improvements, as well as future traffic that would be generated by approved but as yet unbuilt projects expected to be in place at the time of the project's opening. Unlike the situation in the *Sunnyvale West* case, this EIR used existing conditions as one of its baselines and made a significance determination on that basis. The court upheld the EIR's inclusion of a future baseline.

In *Neighbors for Smart Rail v Exposition Metro Line Construction Authority* (2012), a different appellate court addressed the issue of whether the future baseline used for evaluating traffic and air quality impacts, including greenhouse gas impacts, was proper. The EIR for the project was commenced in 2009 and certified in 2010. However, the Authority did not use existing conditions as the baseline for determining the significance traffic and air quality impacts because "the population and traffic level that were current in 2009 did not provide a reasonable baseline for determining the traffic and air quality impacts of the project are significant." Instead, the Authority used a future baseline–the year 2030. The future baseline was developed from the 2008 Southern California Association of Governments (SCAG) regional transportation model and included "improvements explicitly committed to be constructed by the year 2030." The impacts were then determined by comparing "future with project" to "future without project." Curiously, the year 2030 was selected as the baseline even though the project was expected to be constructed and operational by 2015. The Appellate Court held that the use of the 2030 baseline was appropriate because it was based on reliable projections (e.g. SCAG transportation models) and because of the inevitability of traffic increases in the future. In reaching its decision, the court specifically rejected the reasoning applied by the *Sunnyvale West* court.

Selecting the correct baseline for analysis is critical to accurate impact assessment under CEQA.

At this writing, this case has been granted review by the California Supreme Court and is, therefore, no longer available for citation. The Supreme Court is expected to reconcile this split between the appellate courts.

As these decisions illustrate, the question of whether a future baseline is appropriate is unresolved. Unfortunately, the California's Supreme Court's refusal to accept any of these decisions for review leaves the issue very uncertain. Even though some courts have allowed the use of a future baseline, an agency must remember that existing conditions is normally supposed to be the baseline and that a hypothetical future baseline cannot be used. Therefore, the use of existing conditions as the baseline is always a safe bet. If, however an agency chooses to rely on a future baseline, the CEQA document must contain a thorough explanation of why that baseline is reasonable and must support that explanation with substantial evidence on the record. Even with a great explanation and supporting evidence, the uncertainty in case law means that no non-normal baseline is foolproof.

A lead agency assessing whether an EIR is required for a general plan amendment, rezoning, or other land use change must compare the proposed uses

Table 3-2 Selected Environmental Setting (e.g., "Baseline") Court Decisions	
Lead Agency's Choice of Baseline Upheld	
Benton v. Board of Supervisors (1991) 226 Cal. App. 3d 1467	Negative declaration for the expansion of a winery was adequate where the baseline for impact analysis was the previously approved smaller winery for which the applicant already had approved permit and had begun construction. (e.g., building with vested rights was correct baseline)
Temecula Band of Luiseño Mission Indians v. Rancho California Water District (1996) 43 Cal. App. 4th 425	Supplemental EIR to measure incremental effects of a pipeline realignment project was upheld where realignment was considered a modification of the previously approved pipeline project, which was included as part of the baseline conditions.
Fairview Neighbors v. County of Ventura (1999) 70 Cal. App. 4th 238	EIR for permit renewal of operating sand and gravel mine properly used activity levels allowed under existing permit as baseline for impact evaluation of proposed expansion as opposed to using actual activity levels (e.g., vested right levels of operation was correct baseline).
Riverwatch v. County of San Diego (1999) 76 Cal. App. 4th 1428	EIR for permit renewal of operating sand and gravel mine properly used existing conditions as the baseline for impact analysis even though those conditions were caused by applicant's prior illegal activities (e.g., illegal operations were part of baseline).
Kenneth F. Fat v. County of Sacramento (2002) 97 Cal. App. 4th 1270	Negative declaration upheld where conditions existing at the time environmental analysis was commenced as the baseline for evaluating the impacts of a permit to allow continued operation of an airport that never had proper permits (e.g., illegal operations were part of baseline)
Wal-Mart Stores inc. v. City of Turlock (206) 138 Cal. App. 4th 273	Decision that no additional CEQA necessary upheld where baseline considered existing general plan and comparisons of impacts of a proposed Wal-Mart Super Store to those of hypothetical, smaller shopping centers were inappropriate
In re Bay-Delta Programmatic EIR Co- ordinated Proceedings (2008) 43 Ca. 4th1143	Proofs in EIRs baseline for purposes of selecting alternatives upheld using existing conditions of the Bay-Delta, not future conditions with the project.
Cherry Valley Pass Acres and Neighbors v. City of Beaumont (2010) 190 Cal. App. 4th 316.	EIR for specific plan approval upheld where baseline for water use included existing entitlements within an adjudicated water basin that went beyond current use.
Pfeiffer v. City of Sunnyvale (2011) 200 Cal. App. 4th 1552	EIR for medical office expansion was adequate where it used several baselines, including future conditions and existing conditions, and the significance determination was made based on comparison to existing conditions.
Neighbors for Smart Rail v Exposition Metro line Construction Authority (2012) 205 Cal. App. 4th 552	EIR for passenger rail line extension was adequate even though it used future conditions as the baseline, because those conditions were based on reliable agency projections.

with existing environmental conditions rather than with existing land use designations. Mere conformity of a project with a general plan does not independently justify a finding of no significant effect.

A more detailed discussion of setting the baseline or "environmental setting" for significance determinations can be found in Chapter 5.

Special Rules for Determining the Significance (and Mitigation) of Certain Impacts

Historical and Archaeological Resources. CEQA provides special rules for determining whether impacts on historical and archaeological resources are potentially significant. The Guidelines specify that a substantial adverse change in the significance of an historical resource is a significant effect requiring preparation of an EIR. The demolition, destruction, relocation, or alteration of a significant historical resource would be considered a substantial adverse change, and therefore, a significant effect (Guidelines § 15064.5). Thus, there is a dual meaning of the term "significant" when addressing historic resource impacts. First, the lead agency is required to determine whether the historic resource is considered signifi-

Table 3-3 Selected Environmental Setting (e.g., "Baseline") Court Decisions

Lead Agency's Choice of Baseline Set Aside	
Environmental Planning and Information Council v. County of El Dorado (1982) 131 Cal. App. 3d 350	EIR prepared for new county general plan was inadequate where it relied on the future environmental conditions under the existing general plan, as opposed to existing environmental conditions, as the baseline for assessing the impacts of the new plan.
City of Carmel-by-the Sea v. Board of Supervisors(1986) 183 Cal. App. 3d 229	Negative declaration prepared for the rezoning of site to allow a resort hotel was inadequate where it relied on the future environmental conditions under existing zoning, as opposed to existing environmental conditions, as the baseline for assessing the impacts of the new zoning designation.
Chirstward Ministry v. Superior Court (1985) 184 Cal. App. 3d 180.	EIR overturned where impact of general plan amendment to redesignate existing landfill site examined impact on what might occur in the future undersite's land use designation.
San Joaquin Raptor/Wildlife Center v. County of Stanislaus (1994) 27 Cal App. 4th 713	EIR for residential development was inadequate where it failed to identify and describe the existing wetlands on and adjacent to the project site.
Cadiz Land Company v. County of San Bernadino (2000) 83 Cal.App.4th 74	EIR for a proposed landfill in the desert was inadequate where it failed to discuss the volume and size of an existing groundwater aquifer underlying the proposed project (e.g., impacts were evaluated without first describing existing groundwater conditions).
Save Our Peninsula Committee v. Monterey County Board of Supervisors (2001) 87 Cal. App. 4th 99	EIR for a proposed residential project was inadequate because county used erroneous and constantly changing numbers for the level of existing water usage as the environmental baseline for evaluation of water supply impacts (e.g., actual pre-project water usage was misleadingly distorted as baseline).
County of Amador v. El Dorado County Water Agency(2002) 76 Cal. App. 4th 931	EIR for proposed water storage project was inadequate because the "environmental setting" failed to account for the location, extent, and nature of actual historic water releases as the baseline for impact evaluation. (e.g., baseline description was too general).
Woodward Park Homeowners Assn, Inc. v. City of Fresno (2007) 150 Cal. App. 4th 683	EIR for commercial development was inadequate because it used prospective land use under existing zoning rather than existing use as the baseline.
Communities for a Better Environment v. South Coast Air Quality Management District (2010) 48 Cal. App. 4th 310	Negative Declaration for modification of existing refinery overturned where baseline used previously permitted allowable air emissions rather than existing emissions level.
Sunnyvale West Neighborhood Assoc. v. City of Sunnywale (2010) 190 Cal. App. 4th 1351	EIR for major highway improvements was inadequate because it used future no-project conditions (general plan build-out) as baseline for traffic and traffic-related impact analysis.

cant, based on eligibility criteria. Second, the lead agency is required to determine if the proposed project's effect on the significant historic resource is considered significant, based on the adverse change to the resource's defining elements (warranting its label as a significant historic resource in the first instance).These rules are described in greater detail in Chapter 7 under the Contents of an EIR.

Water Supply. CEQA requires that a city or county consult with the affected public water supplier or, where there is no supplier, to prepare a long-term water supply assessment for certain large projects (PRC § 21151.9; Water Code § 10910, *et seq.*; Guidelines § 15155). The purpose of the assessment is to disclose the availability of groundwater and surface water supplies to serve the proposed project in the context of demand and supply over the next twenty years. This requirement, generally called an "SB 610 water supply assessment" (added to the Water Code § 10910 by SB 610 in 2003), highlights the need for environmental analyses to consider the actual availability of water to serve projects into the future. See DWR's handbook http://www.water.ca.gov/pubs/use /5b_610_5b_221_guidebook/guidebook.pdf.

While the SB 610 assessment applies only to certain "large" projects, there is an expanding line of case law that emphasizes the need to consider water availability even when smaller projects are being analyzed. See Chapter 7 for a detailed discussion of this requirement.

An analysis of available water supply should focus on supplies that can actually be delivered to the project in light of future demand. Agencies must avoid basing water supply analyses on "paper water"—that is, water that is available to community merely on contractual rights, but for which there are insufficient water supplies or no existing or planned delivery system.

In preparing an initial study for a proposed project that does not have adequate water supplies available, the lead agency should attempt to estimate the additional sources necessary to support the project. Depending on these sources and indirect environmental impacts associated with delivering the water to the project, the lead agency may be required to conclude that the project has a potentially significant impact and prepare an EIR.

Advantages of a Lead Agency Adopting Thresholds of Significance Include Providing:

- Consistency in significance determinations for different projects and as applied by different staff within the lead agency's jurisdiction
- Efficiency within the agency regarding staff time and effort
- Greater certainty for project applicants regarding mitigation requirements and whether preparation of an EIR will be necessary
- Encouragement to project applicants to incorporate mitigation into projects to bring their projects below the significance thresholds
- Greater assurance to courts that an agency is acting reasonably in its CEQA determinations

County Projects Affecting Oak Woodlands. If the lead agency is a county, it must determine whether the project may result in a significant effect on oak woodlands. If a project may have a significant effect on oak woodlands, CEQA mandates the use of specific mitigation measures. Pub. Res. Code § 21083.4. The specific mitigation measures include:

- Conservation of oaks through conservation easements
- Replacement through planting program
- Contribution to Oak Woodlands Conservation Fund

However, CEQA specifically provides that other measures, as appropriate, may be developed by the county.

Situations Where an Initial Study Is Not Required

An initial study is not mandatory, and the lead agency may encounter a situation where it is appropriate to proceed straight to preparation of an EIR. Although an initial study is not required when the lead agency has already concluded that an EIR will be prepared, it may nonetheless be worthwhile to prepare an initial study because an initial study serves to focus the EIR on only the potentially significant effects.

The situations where the lead agency is not required to prepare an initial study and may proceed directly to prepare an EIR are:

- The lead agency may determine during phase 1 that the proposed activity *does* have the potential to significantly affect the environment and that preparation of an EIR will be required, and, therefore, bypasses preparation of the initial study (Guidelines § 15063).
- The lead agency is involved in a project approval for which the State Legislature has decided that preparation of an EIR is always required:
  - Construction of new facilities involving the burning of municipal wastes, hazardous wastes, or refuse-derived fuel, including tires (Pub. Res. Code § 21151.1(a)).
  - Expansion of an existing facility that burns hazardous waste increasing capacity by more than ten percent (Pub. Res. Code § 21151.1(a)).
  - Issuance of a hazardous waste facilities permit to a land disposal facility or large treatment facility. Pub. Res. Code § 21151.1(a).

- Location of a campus or development of a long-range development plan for all public community colleges, the California State University, and the University of California. Pub. Res. Code § 21080.09(b).
- Open pit mining operations subject to the Surface Mining and Reclamation Act (Pub. Res. Code § 2710 *et seq.*) that utilize a cyanide heap-leaching process for producing gold or other precious metals.

(Guidelines § 15081.5).

Tips for Successful Compliance

This chapter covered the preparation of Initial Studies and the determination of whether an EIR is necessary. The following are some tips for successful implementation of this part of CEQA:

- **Beware of the "Naked Checklist"**—Initial Studies typically take the form of environmental checklists, based on Appendix G of the CEQA Guidelines. However such checklists must be well-documented to justify the conclusions found in them. Often, this means that technical studies (i.e., biological survey, traffic impact analysis, air quality impact analysis, etc.) are necessary to support the conclusions on whether there is no impact, a less than significant impact, or a less than significant impact only after mitigation is required.
- **Don't get tripped up by the "Fair Argument" standard**—CEQA's "fair argument" standard establishes a very low bar for triggering an EIR; if any substantial evidence points to the potential for significant effects to occur that cannot be mitigated, then an EIR must be prepared. This "argument" is not necessarily made by project opponents, but is "in light of the whole record" and can be based on information prepared by the lead agency's own staff.
- **Consider direct, indirect and cumulative impacts**—When preparing an Initial Study a lead agency must consider direct, indirect and cumulative impacts. There is no exemption from analyzing these impacts because the lead agency is merely preparing an initial study.
- **Use the correct baseline**—The normal baseline for determining the proposed project impacts and whether the fair argument is triggered is "existing conditions"; use of another baseline must be carefully explained. The lead agency should take care that the analyses in the initial study that rely on the same data (traffic, noise, and air quality, for example) use the same baseline.
- **Explain criteria used to evaluate "significance"**—In determining if impacts are significant, lead agencies should explain the thresholds or other criteria they are using to make such determinations. This information must be supported by substantial evidence.
- **Solicit and consider the views of other agencies and the public**—Initial Studies should not be prepared in a vacuum, but rather should

be based on consultation with other agencies and the public. Although formal scoping and circulation of a draft initial study is not required prior to issuance of the notice of intent to adopt the negative declaration, the lead agency should request input from the agencies with expertise regarding a particular resource and interested public before finalizing the initial study.

Keep in mind that CEQA's mission is to protect the environment.

Chapter 4

Preparation of Negative Declarations, Including Mitigated Negative Declarations

This chapter addresses situations in which the lead agency determines, based on the initial study, that no fair argument has been raised regarding the proposed project's potential to cause significant impacts. The lead agency, therefore, determines that preparation of an EIR is not necessary and that a negative declaration or mitigated negative declaration may be prepared. As explained in greater detail in Chapter 3, during the preparation of the initial study, the lead agency must determine whether it can be fairly argued based on substantial evidence in light of the whole record that a project may have a significant effect on the environment. If the lead agency concludes that there is no fair argument, a negative declaration or mitigated negative declaration should be prepared (Guidelines § 15063). Unless otherwise noted, all discussions regarding negative declarations in this chapter also apply to mitigated negative declarations (*see also* OPR's CEQA advice memoranda, "Mitigated Negative Declarations").

The preparation of a negative declaration or a mitigated negative declaration represents one option for Phase 3 of the CEQA process. Chapters 5, 6, and 7 include discussions of the third phase of CEQA as it pertains to preparation of an EIR if the project may have a significant environmental effect.

Contents of a Negative Declaration

A negative declaration is a written statement that briefly explains why a proposed project will not have a significant environmental effect. It must include a brief description of the project and location, identification of the project proponent, and a proposed finding of no significant effect. The negative declaration is also required to include a copy of the initial study justifying the conclusion that no significant impacts would occur. For mitigated negative declarations, the negative declaration must describe the mitigation measures included in the project description that will avoid potentially significant environmental effects (Guidelines § 15371; Pub. Res. Code § 21092.6(a)).

Required Contents of a Negative Declaration

- Project description
- Project location
- Identification of project proponent
- Proposed finding of no significant effect
- Attached copy of the initial study justifying the finding
- For mitigated negative declarations, mitigation measures included in the project description to avoid significant effects

Although the CEQA Guidelines requirements for preparing a negative declaration are not extensive, in practice, a lead agency should consider adopting many of the rules governing the preparation and content of EIRs. For example, while a negative declaration does not have to include formal responses to comments received in response to the notice of intent to adopt the negative declaration, the lead agency should consider preparing a "responses to comments document" as part of the final version of the negative declaration in order to create a clear record on why none of the comments change the conclusions in the negative declaration or why none of the changes warrant recirculation of the notice or the preparation of an EIR.Therefore, persons preparing negative declarations should familiarize themselves with the required procedural requirements (*see* Chapter 6) and contents of EIRs (*see* Chapter 7) and include relevant information in a negative declaration when necessary to improve the planning and decision-making process.

If a negative declaration for non-public projects is to be prepared by a consultant under contract to the lead agency, then the contract must be executed within forty-five days from the lead agency's determination that a negative declaration is required. The lead agency may take longer to execute the contract if compelling circumstances exist and the project applicant consents. According to the Permit Streamlining Act, the negative declaration for non-public projects must be completed and approved within 180 days from determination that the application was complete (Pub. Res. Code § 21151.5(c); Guidelines § 15107).

Mitigated Negative Declaration

Mitigated negative declarations have been used by numerous agencies for many years. However, it was not until the Legislature approved the 1993 CEQA amendments that specific legislation authorized their use (Pub. Res. Code § 21064.5; Guidelines § 15074).

A mitigated negative declaration is typically used when a lead agency prepares an initial study and determines that a project's impacts may be potentially significant, but the agency can apply mitigation measure to avoid or reduce those impacts to a less-than-significant level. A mitigated negative declaration can only be used when the mitigation measures are agreed to by the project proponent prior to public review of the MND and initial study (Pub. Res. Code § 15070(b)(1)). Although there is no specified format for this agreement, many lead agencies require a written commitment by the proponent at a minimum. Thus, in practice, this relatively straightforward concept sometimes leads to extended negotiations between the lead agency, the project proponent, other concerned agencies, and even concerned individuals or organizations. Such negotiations are often informal and, with the concurrence of a project applicant, may prolong the formal negative declaration review process for months. However, the goal of CEQA to apply all feasible mitigation for potentially significant impacts is often better achieved through such negotiations, making the extra time worthwhile, especially in light of the time and effort necessary to complete the EIR process.

Although the previsions in the Guidelines related to MND are written from the perspective of a lead agency reacting to a non-public entity proponent's proposed project (*see* for example Guidelines § 15070(b)(1)–"revisions in the project plans or proposals made by or agreed to by the *applicant*"), in practice the MND also applies to public agency projects where the lead agency is also the project proponent. Most public agency projects that incorporate mitigation to reduce impacts to a less-than-significant level do so through an MND even though there is no "applicant" and no separate acceptance of the mitigation. The MND in these instances makes clear that a good faith effort at full disclosure was made to address potential significant impacts. It also adds a firm commitment to implement the mitigation and monitor it through the MMRP that must be adopted for all mitigation measures made a condition of approval.

The flexibility permitted by the MND has been praised by its supporters and criticized by its detractors. People favoring its use cite as the main advantage the virtual certainty that impacts will be mitigated to below the level of significance. Unlike the use of an EIR, which allows unavoidable significant impacts to ultimately be overridden by decisionmakers, the use of an MND is only permissible if all potentially significant impacts will definitely be mitigated. When there is a fair argument that the measures would not reduce the potential impact below the level of significance, a MND would not be appropriate and an EIR must be prepared. Therefore, many people feel that the MND is a far more effective tool than an EIR to ensure environmental protection.

Public Review

Every negative declaration is subject to the requirement of public review and comment, as well as interagency review. After a lead agency has prepared an initial study, and prepared a proposed negative declaration, including the development of any necessary mitigation measures, it must notify the public of the availability of the document and the opportunity to comment prior to adopting the negative declaration as final. The Notice of Intent to Adopt a Negative Declaration must specify the review period, identify any public meetings or hearings on the project, briefly describe the project, and state where the proposed negative declaration and all reference documents are available for review (Pub. Res. Code § 21092(b)(1)). A copy of the notice of intent and the proposed negative declaration must be mailed to responsible and trustee agencies and agencies with jurisdiction by law and to all parties previously requesting notice (Guidelines §§ 15073, 15072). The notice of intent must be posted in the county clerk's office for a minimum of twenty days (Pub. Res. Code § 21092.3). The clerk must post the notice within twenty-four hours of receipt (Pub. Res. Code § 21092.3). In addition, where a state agency is the lead agency, a state agency is a responsible agency, where a trustee agency's involvement is required, or where the project is of statewide, regional, or areawide importance, sufficient copies (currently fifteen are required by the SCH) of the proposed negative declaration and initial study are required to be sent to the SCH for transmittal to other agencies (Pub. Res. Code § 21091,

Required Contents of a Notice of Intent to Adopt a Negative Declaration or Mitigated Negative Declaration

- Brief description of project and location
- Starting and ending dates for public review
- Date, time, and place of any scheduled public meetings or hearings
- Address where copies of the negative declaration or mitigated negative declaration are available for review
- Whether listed toxic sites are present
- Other information required by statute or regulation for a particular type of project

Guidelines § 15205). The copies submitted to the SCH must be accompanied by a notice of completion form (Guidelines § 15205, Guidelines Appendix C).

The minimum public review period for a proposed negative declaration or MND is twenty days. When the document is sent to the State Clearinghouse for review, the public review period is thirty days, unless a shorter period (not less than twenty days) is approved by the SCH (*see* Chapter 4 for a discussion of when SCH distribution procedures apply) (Pub. Res. Code § 21091(b)). The public review period must be at least as long as the period established by the SCH. The SCH review period begins on the day the SCH distributes its copies (Guidelines § 15105(c)).

Special Consultation Requirements

Water Agency Consultation. Certain large projects must also be referred to the applicable water provider(s) for preparation of a water supply assessment. The assessment, which is required to describe available supplies into the future, would be included in the negative declaration or mitigated negative declaration. See Chapters 3 and 6 for a detailed discussion of this requirement. (Water Code § 10910, *et seq.*, Guidelines § 15155.).

Military Consultation. A proposed negative declaration or mitigated negative declaration is also required to be sent to the United States Department of Defense or a military branch when either has notified the lead agency and provided it with the specific boundaries of a low-level flight path, military impact zone, or special use airspace, and the project meets any of the following criteria:

- It includes a general plan amendment.
- It is of statewide, regional, or areawide significance.
- It is required to be referred to the airport land use commission.

CEQA provides that while a project's effect on military activities may cause, or be associated with, adverse environmental effects, the project's effect or potential effect does not itself constitute an adverse effect (Pub. Res. Code § 21098, Guidelines § 15072(f)).

Recirculation of a Negative Declaration

If a negative declaration (and supporting initial study) must be substantially revised after public review and before adoption, the lead agency is required to recirculate the proposed negative declaration for an additional public review period. A negative declaration is considered to be "substantially revised" if:

- A new, avoidable significant effect is identified and mitigation measures or project revisions must be added to reduce the effect to a less than significant level.
- The lead agency determines that the proposed mitigation measures or project revisions will not reduce potential significant effects and new measures or revisions must be required.

Recirculation is not required under the following circumstances:

- Mitigation measures are replaced with equal or more effective measures (*see* below).
- New project revisions are added in response to comments on the project's effects identified in the proposed negative declaration that are not new avoidable significant effects.
- Measures or conditions of project approval are added after circulation of the proposed negative declaration that are not required by CEQA, that do not create new significant environmental effects, and are not necessary to mitigate an avoidable significant effect.
- New information is added to the negative declaration that merely clarifies, amplifies, or makes insignificant modifications to the negative declaration .

(Guidelines §§ 15073.5(a), (b), (c)).

Switching from a Negative Declaration to an EIR

If during the negative declaration process substantial evidence is developed by or presented to the lead agency that the project may have a significant effect on the environment that cannot be mitigated or avoided, raising the "fair argument," the lead agency must cease preparation of the ND or MND and instead must proceed with the EIR process prior to project approval. When it circulates the EIR for consultation and public review, the lead agency must advise reviewers in writing that a proposed negative declaration had previously been circulated for the project (Guidelines § 15073.5(d)).

Consideration of Comments on the Proposed Negative Declaration and Consideration of Adoption of the Negative Declaration

The lead agency must consider the proposed negative declaration and supporting initial study, together with any comments received and changes to the proposed negative declaration and initial study (if applicable), before approving the project (Pub. Res. Code § 21091(f); Guidelines § 15074). The lead agency must accept and *consider* comments from all sources and by all methods, including those submitted via e-mail, and must treat e-mail comments as the equivalent of written comments (Pub. Res. Code § 21091(d)). Unlike in the case of an EIR, the lead agency is not required to prepare formal written responses to comments on the proposed negative declaration, but it may be good practice to do so. In any case, the lead agency must have adequate information on the record explaining why the comment does not affect the conclusion that there are no potential significant environmental effects. The lead agency is required to notify in writing any commenting agencies of the date of the public hearing on the project for which a negative declaration is prepared (Pub. Res. Code § 21092.5(b); Guidelines § 15073).

Substitution of Mitigation Measures

Before approving the project for which a mitigated negative declaration was prepared, the lead agency is permitted to substitute equivalent mitigation measures without having to recirculate the mitigated negative declaration. The lead agency

Substitution of Mitigation Measures in a Mitigated Negative Declaration

A lead agency may substitute one mitigation measure for another if:

- The new measure is equivalent or more effective.
- The agency considers the matter at a public meeting.
- The agency adopts a written finding that:
  - The new measure is equivalent or more effective.
  - The new measure will not cause a significant effect.

must, however, hold a public hearing (that may overlap with the hearing on project approval) on the matter and find that the new mitigation measures are at least as effective as the original ones in mitigating significant environmental impacts and do not themselves cause any potentially significant effects. A lead agency may also use this process, and avoid new environmental review, if a court or administrative body sets aside a condition of project approval (Pub. Res. Code secs. 21080(f), (g); Guidelines § 15074.1).

The ability to substitute one mitigation measure for another provides agencies with considerable flexibility in the project approval process. However, this provision is also subject to potential abuse if an agency substitutes questionable or untested measures that have not been reviewed by the public. Therefore, to ensure that substitution of mitigation is legally adequate and justified, the lead agency must not only hold the required hearing but also carefully explain, on the record, why the original mitigation measure is not feasible and why the newly proposed mitigation is "equivalent." This explanation must be supported by substantial evidence.

Mitigation Monitoring and Reporting

When approving a mitigated negative declaration, the lead agency must also adopt a monitoring or reporting program for those mitigation measures made a condition of project approval to mitigate or avoid significant environmental effects (Pub. Res. Code § 21081.6; Guidelines § 15074(d)). See Chapter 8 for a full discussion of mitigation monitoring and reporting.

Notice of Determination

A Notice of Determination (NOD) for approval of a project based on a negative declaration or mitigated negative declaration must be filed within five working days after approval of a project for which a negative declaration has been prepared as follows:

- State agency acts as lead agency—NOD is filed with OPR's SCH
- Local agency acts as lead agency—NOD is filed with county clerk(s) of the county or counties in which the project will be located; if a state agency will be a responsible agency, the local lead agency must also file the NOD with OPR's SCH

The Department of Fish and Game filing fee must accompany the NOD. The NOD must be posted by the county clerk within twenty-four hours of receipt (Pub. Res. Code § 21092.3; Guidelines § 15075). The NOD for a negative declaration must identify and describe the project, indicate the date of project approval, and state that the project will have no significant environmental effect and that a negative declaration has been prepared. In addition to the customary noticing and posting requirements, agencies are encouraged to make copies of all NODs available online (Guidelines § 15075(f)).

The NOD must be posted for at least thirty full calendar days. The first day of posting does not count toward the thirty. The NOD must remain posted during regular business hours. (*Latinos Unidos de Napa v. City of Napa* (2011) 196

Required Contents of an NOD on a Project for Which a Negative Declaration or Mitigated Negative Declaration Has Been Approved

- Project name
- Project description
- Project location
- Date of project approval
- Determination that the project will not have any significant effects on the environment
- Statement that a negative declaration or mitigated negative declaration has been prepared
- Address where the document may be reviewed

Payment of Environmental Review Fees to California Department of Fish and Game

The California Fish and Game Code was amended in the late 1980s to require payment of environmental review fees to the California Department of Fish and Game for all negative declarations and EIRs prepared pursuant to CEQA. In an interesting case of "single agency focus" (no other trustee or responsible agency has a similar provision), the Legislature agreed that project proponents should help offset the costs DFG incurs by participating in the CEQA projects as a trustee agency or responsible agency on so many projects that go through CEQA review as NDs, MNDs, or EIRs. As of January 1, 2007, DFG is authorized to increase the fee when necessary. CEQA practitioners should check with DFG or the Governor's Office of Planning and Research for the current amount. The fee is paid to the to the county clerk (or to the Governor's Office of Planning and Research in the case of a state lead agency) at the time the notice of determination is filed.

This fee is transmitted to DFG to fund its environmental review staff. A project approval is not considered final until the fee was paid or a "no effect" determination form is submitted and has been approved by DFG. California Fish and Game Code § 711.4.

From the outset, the requirement for these review fees was controversial. Payment of this fee is not contingent on the amount of actual DFG review time, if any, or on the underlying project's potential environmental effects on fish and wildlife resources. Private applicants dislike the requirement because of both the added costs to prepare a negative declaration or EIR, and being required to pay a "tax" without a definable relationship to actual DFG review. Public agencies other than DFG may dislike the requirement because of their added administrative burden to collect and distribute the fees (although legislation authorizes them to collect a $50 administrative fee) and because many other agencies' review time was not covered by similar fees.

The DFG environmental review fee issue has been resolved through the courts in favor of the Department. In 2000, the California Court of Appeal found that DFG's fee is a "regulatory fee" related to the overall cost of reviewing CEQA documents and is not an unconstitutional tax. *California Association of Professional Scientists et al. v. Department of Fish and Game* 79 Cal. App. 4th 935. As a regulatory fee, its amount is not required to be directly related to the actual cost of reviewing any given CEQA document. This decision ended the debate over the validity of DFG's environmental review fees. For any project subject to the fees, approval is not considered final until the fees are paid. Many County Clerks will not accept the NOD without the DFG review fee. The fee, however, must only be paid once notwithstanding the fact that several responsible agencies may also be filing NODs for the same project.

The courts will not consider a project approval final without payment of the DFG review fee.

Cal.App.4th 1154). At the end of that time, the county clerk is to notify the lead agency and the lead agency is to keep a copy of the NOD on file for at least twelve months. OPR is also required to keep a copy of any NOD filed with it for at least twelve months after the end of the posting date (Pub. Res. Code Secs 21108, 21152).

The filing of the NOD starts the thirty-day statute of limitations to challenge the lead agency's project approval for failure to comply with CEQA (*see* Chapter 10 for more information on CEQA litigation).

A Subsequent Negative Declaration Is Required When:

- Substantial changes are proposed for the project that will involve new, significant environmental effects or substantially increase the severity of previously identified effects
- Substantial changes occur with respect to the circumstances under which the project is undertaken that involve new significant environmental effects or substantially increase the severity of previously identified ones
- New information of substantial importance shows:
  - The project will have one or more significant effects not discussed in the previous negative declaration
  - Significant effects previously examined will be substantially more severe than shown in the previous negative declaration
  - Mitigation measures or alternatives previously found not to be feasible would in fact be feasible and would substantially reduce one or more significant effects of the project, but the project proponents decline to adopt them
  - Mitigation measure or alternatives that are considerably different from those analyzed in the previous document would substantially reduce one or more significant effects, but the project proponents decline to adopt them
- There is no substantial evidence in light of the whole record that a project, or a project with mitigation agreed to by the project proponent, may have a significant effect on the environment

Process for Responsible Agency

Under the provisions of CEQA, each project shall have one document prepared for it and, after the lead agency has made a decision on the project, based on the negative declaration prepared, the responsible agency is expected to take its action to approve. A responsible agency complies with CEQA by considering the negative declaration or mitigation negative declaration prepared by the lead agency and reaching its own conclusions on whether and how to approve the proposed project. When considering mitigation measures in the MND, a responsible agency has responsibility for mitigating only the environmental effects of those parts of the project which it decides to carry out or approve or deny the project. The responsible agency should file a notice of determination in the same manner as the lead agency under CEQA Guidelines § 15075 except that the responsible agency need not state that the negative declaration complies with CEQA. The responsible agency should state, however, that it considered the negative declaration as prepared by the lead agency prior to making the project approval (CEQA Guidelines § 15096).

If the responsible agency believes the negative declaration prepared by the lead agency is not adequate, the responsible agency must take the issue to court within thirty days after the lead agency has filed the notice of determination. Otherwise, the responsible agency is deemed to have waived any objection to the adequacy of the negative declaration or mitigated negative declaration. If warranted, the responsible agency can step into the lead agency's position to prepare a subsequent negative declaration if there are new significant impacts or EIR or substantially more severe impacts due to new information or changes in the project or circumstances (per CEQA Guidelines § 15162). Even where a lead agency has prepared a CEQA, an agency can assume lead agency role where the former lead agency did prepare an inadequate document as determined by the courts or no notice or consultation was provided to the responsible agency (CEQA Guidelines § 15052) (CEQA Guidelines § 15096(e)).

Subsequent Negative Declarations

Generally, only one negative declaration is adopted for a project. Once a project has been approved, the lead agency's role in it is completed unless further discretionary approval on that project is required. Information appearing after an approval usually does not require reopening that approval. However, if the lead agency does have to exercise further discretionary approvals, or a responsible agency has yet to act on the project, and if new information arises, then further environmental review may be necessary.

An agency must prepare a subsequent negative declaration or mitigated negative declaration for a project if it determines, on the basis of substantial evidence in light of the whole record, that one or more of the following has occurred, *and* there is no substantial evidence in light of the whole record that the project may have a significant effect on the environment:

- Substantial changes are proposed for the project that will require major revision of a previous negative declaration due to the involvement of new, significant environmental effects or a substantial increase in the severity of previously identified effects.

- Substantial changes occur with respect to the circumstances under which the project is undertaken, requiring major revision to a previous negative declaration due to the involvement of new significant environmental effects or a substantial increase in the severity of previously identified ones.
- New information of substantial importance that was not known or could not have been known without the exercise of reasonable diligence at the time the previous negative declaration was adopted shows any of the following:
  - The project will have one or more potentially significant effects (prior to mitigation) not discussed in the previous negative declaration.
  - Significant effects (that can be mitigated) previously examined will be substantially more severe than shown in the previous negative declaration.
  - Mitigation measures previously found not to be feasible would in fact be feasible and would substantially reduce one or more significant effects of the project, but the project proponents decline to adopt them.
  - Mitigation measure that are considerably different from those analyzed in the previous document would substantially reduce one or more significant effects, but the project proponents decline to adopt them.

(Guidelines § 15162(a)).

If the project was approved by the lead agency prior to the occurrence of conditions that trigger preparation of a subsequent negative declaration, the subsequent document must be prepared by the public agency, i.e., responsible agency, that grants the next discretionary approval for the project (Guidelines § 16162(c)). If no further discretionary authorities are necessary for the project to move forward, no supplemental document is required.

A subsequent negative declaration is subject to the same notice and public review requirements as the original document and must state whether the previous document is available for review (Guidelines § 15162(d)).

Addendum to a Negative Declaration

An agency may prepare an addendum to an adopted negative declaration if only minor technical changes or additions are necessary or if none of the conditions triggering a subsequent negative declaration are present. An addendum need not be circulated for public review but can be included in or attached to the adopted negative declaration. The decision-making body shall consider the addendum with the adopted negative declaration before making a decision on the project. A brief explanation supported by substantial evidence justifying the decision not to prepare a subsequent negative declaration or EIR should be included in the addendum or elsewhere in the record (Guidelines § 15164).

MNDs must have a commitment to implement all mitigation to reduce impacts to less than significant levels.

Judicial Review of Negative Declarations

As previously stated, an EIR, rather than a negative declaration, must be prepared if it can be "fairly argued on the basis of substantial evidence in light of the whole record" that the project may have a significant environmental effect, even though the agency has other substantial evidence that the project will not have a significant effect (Pub. Res. Code §§ 21080(d), 21082.2(d); Guidelines § 15064(g)(1)).

Thus, in reviewing an agency decision to rely on a negative declaration, the court will review the entire record to determine whether any substantial evidence was presented to the lead agency that a significant impact could occur. Substantial evidence must include facts, fact-based reasonable assumptions, or expert opinion based on fact. It does not include speculation or clearly inaccurate evidence (Pub. Res. Code secs. 21080(e), 21082.2(e) (*see* Chapter 10 "CEQA Litigation").

Tips for Successful Compliance

This chapter covered the preparation and review of Negative Declarations and mitigated negative declarations. The following are some tips for the successful use of these documents:

- **Consider the EIR requirements when preparing NDs and MNDs**—Although NDs and MNDs are typically more abbreviated than EIRs, the requirements and approaches for preparing EIRs are also useful in preparing these documents
- **Obtain proponent commitments when using MNDs**—When an MND is prepared, the lead agency must obtain the proponents commitment to the mitigation identified in the initial study before the mitigated negative declaration can be released for public review
- **Commit to mitigation.** An MND's mitigation measures should be anticipated by project proponents and committed to as early in the process as possible.

Chapter 5

Environmental Impact Reports—Making the Right Choice for Your Project

Definition and Purpose of an EIR

The preparation of an EIR is part of the third phase of CEQA's environmental review process. After the lead agency decides that an activity is a project, is not exempt from CEQA, and may result in significant effects on the environment that could not be addressed by a mitigated negative declaration, an EIR must be prepared (Pub. Res. Code §§ 21080(d), 21082.2(d); Guidelines § 15064). This chapter reviews the types of EIRs provided for by CEQA and when the use of each is appropriate. Chapters 6 and 7 discuss the preparation and contents of EIRs.

An EIR is a detailed informational document prepared by a lead agency that analyzes a project's potential significant effects and identifies mitigation measures and reasonable alternatives to avoid or reduce those significant effects (Guidelines §§ 15121(a), 15362). The primary purposes of an EIR are to inform decisionmakers and the public about a project's significant environmental effects and ways to reduce them, to demonstrate to the public that the environment is being protected, and to ensure political accountability by disclosing to citizens the environmental values held by their elected and appointed officials (Guidelines §§ 15003, 15121(a)). CEQA does not require technical perfection in an EIR, but rather adequacy, completeness, and a good faith effort at full disclosure (Guidelines § 15003(i)). See Chapter 7 for more information on the substantive requirements for writing an EIR.

Purposes of an EIR

- Inform decisionmakers and the public about a project's significant environmental effects and ways to reduce them
- Demonstrate to the public that the environment is being protected
- Ensure political accountability by disclosing to citizens the environmental values held by their elected and appointed officials

Matching the EIR to the Decisionmaking Process

CEQA provides for a variety of different types of EIRs. A lead agency should select the appropriate type of EIR based on the particular decisionmaking process and project being evaluated. Although CEQA requirements for EIR procedures and content are generally applicable to all types of EIRs, certain ones may assist the lead and responsible agencies in streamlining and focusing the environmental review of the proposed action. Figure 5-2 lists various kinds of projects that may require an EIR and the correlated type of EIR that may be prepared to most appropriately review the potential effects of the proposed project. Appendix J of the CEQA Guidelines compares and contrasts the different types of EIRs.

CEQA practitioners should keep in mind that, in general, the content of the EIR is more important than the title given to the EIR. A good faith effort at full disclosure should always be the practitioner's guiding objective for an EIR, whether it is a "project EIR," a "program EIR," or some other type of EIR.

Tiering

Tiering refers to the preparation of environmental documents using a multilevel approach where the first tier includes analysis of general matters contained in a broader EIR (analyzing the impacts of an entire plan, program, or policy) and subsequent tiers include analysis of narrower projects with later EIRs and negative declarations (incorporating by reference the general discussions from the broader EIR and focusing only on the impacts of individual projects that implement the plan, program, or policy) (Guidelines § 15152; Figure 5-1).

CEQA provides several methods of tiering, as described below and illustrated in Figure 5-2. Each has its own specific procedural requirements, and some methods are limited to particular circumstances. Review the applicable statutory and CEQA Guidelines requirements when using a particular method.

First tier documents are usually program EIRs, master EIRs, general plan EIRs, redevelopment plan EIRs, or similar EIRs that evaluate the broad-scale impacts of an entire plan, program, or policy. Second-tier (or later) documents are typically project EIRs, focused EIRs, or mitigated negative declarations that evaluate the impacts of a single activity undertaken to implement the plan, program, or policy.

Tiering is a method to streamline EIR preparation by allowing a lead agency to focus on the issues that are ripe for decision and exclude from consideration issues already decided or not yet ready for decision, or which have already been evaluated in an earlier document (Guidelines §§ 15152; 15385).

Agencies are encouraged to tier the environmental analyses whenever possible when they prepare CEQA analyses for separate but related projects including general plans, zoning changes, and developments projects. This approach can eliminate repetitive discussions of the same issues and focus the later EIR or negative declaration on the actual issues ripe for decision at each level of environmental review. Tiering is appropriate when the sequence of analysis is from an EIR prepared for a general plan, policy, or program to an EIR or negative declaration for another plan, policy, or program of lesser scope, or to a site-specific EIR or negative declaration. Tiering does not excuse the lead agency from adequately analyzing reasonably foreseeable significant environmental effects of the project currently being considered and does not justify deferring such analysis to a later tier EIR or negative declaration. However, the level of detail contained in a first-tier EIR need not be greater than that of the program, plan, policy, or ordinance being analyzed according to the specificity of the project description (Guidelines § 15152(b)).

Various Types of EIRs That May Be Used in a Tiering Situation

- General plan EIR
- Staged EIR
- Program EIR
- Master EIR
- Multiple-family residential development/residential and commercial or retail mixed-use development
- Redevelopment project
- Projects consistent with community plan, general plan, or zoning

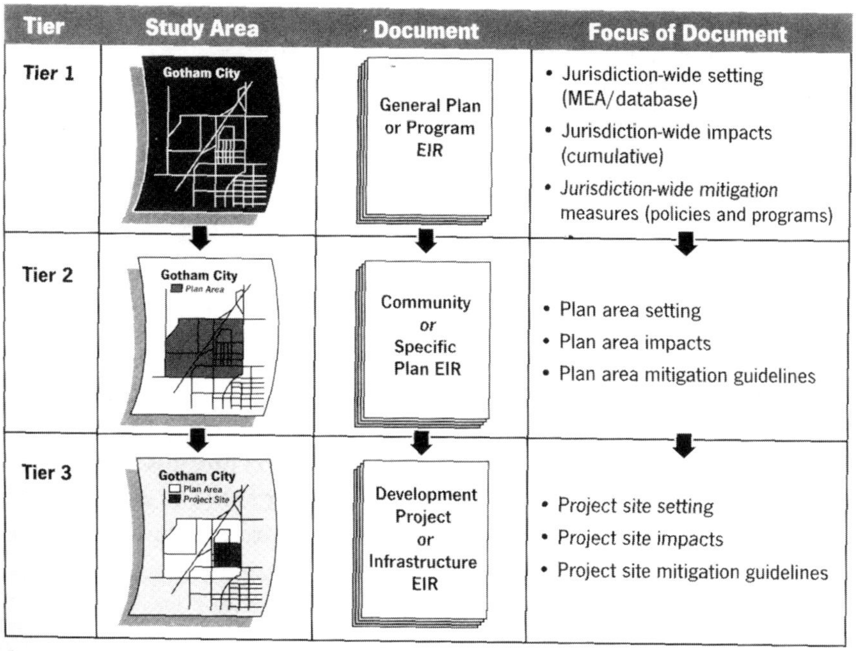

Figure 5-1
Tiering under CEQA

Where a lead agency is using the tiering process in connection with an EIR for a large-scale planning approval, such as a general plan or component thereof (an area plan or community plan), the development of detailed, site-specific information may not be feasible but can be deferred, in many instances, until such time as the lead agency prepares a future environmental document in connection with a project of a more limited geographical scale, as long as deferral does not prevent adequate identification of significant effects of the planning approval at hand (Guidelines § 15152(c)).

Additionally, a first-tier EIR may contain generalized mitigation criteria and policy-level alternatives. The subsequent tiered CEQA documents contain the focused analysis for site-specific mitigation requirements and a specific set of alternatives. For example, tiered CEQA documents for development projects that are consistent with a general plan or community plan may be limited to those site-specific issues or worsened significant effects not disclosed in the first-tier EIR (Pub. Res. Code § 21083.3; Guidelines § 15183).

Where an EIR has been prepared and certified for a program, plan, policy, or ordinance consistent with CEQA's tiering requirements, any lead agency for a later project pursuant to or consistent with the program, plan, policy, or ordinance should limit the EIR or negative declaration on the later project to effects that were not examined as significant effects on the environment in the prior EIR or are susceptible to substantial reduction or avoidance by the choice of specific revisions in the project, by the imposition of conditions, or other means. Tiering under this section shall be limited to situations where the project is consistent with the general plan and zoning of the city or county in which the project is located, except that a project requiring a rezone to achieve or maintain conformity with a general plan may be subject to tiering (Guidelines §§ 15152(d), (e)).

Practice Tip: Simultaneous tiering and project level compliance

Sometimes, an agency will be considering a program level decision at the same time that it is considering a project-level decision within that program. For example, a city or county may be preparing a community plan while it is simultaneously processing an individual project within the community plan area. In those situations, the agency may want to prepare a first-tier document on the plan and a second-tier document on the project at the same time, and possibly in the same EIR.

There is nothing in either CEQA to prohibit such "simultaneous tiering." However, the lead agency must assure that the appropriate level of specificity is presented for each tier and must carefully explain the relationship between the two. If a single document is prepared, it must exhibit the requisite level of detail so that both the general and specific actions are adequately analyzed.

Required Contents of an EIR

- Table of contents or index
- Summary
- Project description
- Environmental setting
- Significant environmental impacts
  - Direct
  - Indirect
  - Short-term
  - Long-term
  - Cumulative
  - Unavoidable
- Areas of known controversy
- Alternatives
  - No Project alternative
  - Environmentally superior alternative
- Mitigation measures
- Growth-inducing impacts
- Significant irreversible changes (required only in EIRs on plans, policies, ordinances, LAFCO actions, and joint NEPA documents)

Tiering does, however, have some limitations. Any agency may only rely on tiering when the first tier CEQA document has been certified and has not been declared inadequate by a court. There have been several examples of situations where a second tier EIR was declared inadequate because the earlier tier document had been found to be inadequate. *Friends of the Santa Clara River v. Castaic Lake Water Agency* (2002) 95 Cal. App. 4th 1373 and *California Oak Foundation, et al. v. City of Santa Clarita* (2005) 133 Cal. App. 4th 1219.

Additionally, when relying on tiering, the lead agency must be certain that the information in the first-tier document is still up-to-date and relevant to the project being evaluated.

When using a tiered analysis, a lead agency should prepare an initial study to decide whether and to what extent the first-tier document is still adequate. A later EIR is required when the initial study or other analysis finds that the later project may cause significant effects on the environment that were not adequately addressed in the prior EIR (the fair argument test). Otherwise, a negative declaration is required.

Cumulative effects have been a difficult issue to address for later-tiered CEQA documents. CEQA clarifies that where a lead agency determines that a cumulative effect has been adequately addressed in the prior EIR (and found to be mitigated to a less significant level), that effect is not treated as significant for purposes of the later EIR or negative declaration, and need not be discussed in detail. When assessing whether there is a new significant cumulative effect, the lead agency must consider whether the incremental effects of the project would be considerable when viewed in the context of past, present, and probable future projects. At this point, the question is not whether there is a significant cumulative impact, but whether the project' contribution are cumulatively considerable (Guidelines §§ 15064(i), 15152(f)).

For purposes of tiering, significant environmental effects have been "adequately addressed" in the first-tier document if the lead agency determines that the significant environmental effects:

- Have been mitigated or avoided as a result of the prior EIR and findings adopted in connection with that prior EIR
- Have been examined at a sufficient level of detail in the prior EIR to enable those effects to be mitigated or avoided by site-specific revisions, the imposition of conditions, or by other means in connection with the approval of the later project, or
- Cannot be mitigated to avoid or substantially lessen the significant impacts despite the project proponent's willingness to accept all feasible mitigation measures, and the only purpose of including analysis of such effects in another EIR would be to put the agency in a position to adopt a statement of overriding considerations with respect to the effects.

When a lead agency decides to prepare a second-tier CEQA document, the document must include a statement that it is a "tiered" EIR or negative declaration, make reference to the first-tier CEQA document, and

Figure 5-2. Types of EIRs or Other Documents for Which Tiering May Be Appropriate

EIR Type (Authority)	Applicable Programs or Projects
Program EIR (14 CCR 15168)	Programs composed of a series of actions that are: • related geographically • logical parts in a chain of contemplated actions • connected as part of a continuing program • carried out under same authorizing statute or regulatory authority and have similar environmental impacts that can be mitigated in similar ways
Master EIR (Pub. Res. Code sec. 21156–21158.5)	Programs for approval of: • general plan (including individual elements and amendments) • specific plan • project consisting of smaller, phased projects • regulation to be implemented by subsequent projects • project pursuant to or furthering a redevelopment plan • state highway or transit project subject to multiple reviews or approvals • Department of Fish and Game hunting and fishing regulations
Staged EIR (14 CCR 15167)	Programs or projects that are larger in nature and will: • involve many years of planning • require numerous discretionary approvals from several government agencies, some of which would be required before detailed project plans would be formulated • require several approvals, one of which is scheduled to occur more than 2 years before construction will begin
Community Plan EIR/ Zoning Ordinance EIR	• A project with proposed land uses that are consistent with zoning/community plan designations that were evaluated in a previous community plan EIR (Pub. Res. Code sec. 21083.3) • A multifamily residential development of not more than 100 units or residential and commercial or retail mixed-use development of not more than 100,000 square feet that is consistent with a community plan or zoning ordinance for which an EIR was prepared within the preceding 5 years if the project site: – is surrounded by immediately contiguous urban development – was previously developed with urban uses – is within 0.5 mile of an existing rail transit station (Pub. Res. Code sec. 21158.5)
General Plan/Specific Plan/ Coastal Program EIR	• A housing or neighborhood commercial facilities development project in an urbanized setting that is consistent with a specific plan or coastal program adopted within the preceding 5 years (Pub. Res. Code sec. 21080.7) • A residential development project consistent with a specific plan for which an EIR was certified after January 1, 1980 (Govt. Code sec. 65457) • A multifamily residential development of not more than 100 units or residential and commercial or retail mixed-use development of not more than 100,000 square feet that is consistent with a community plan or zoning ordinance for which an EIR was prepared within the preceding 5 years if the project site: – is surrounded by immediately contiguous urban development – was previously developed with urban uses – is within 0.5 mile of an existing rail transit station (Pub. Res. Code sec. 21158.5)
Redevelopment Plan EIR	• A project that is consistent with a redevelopment plan (Pub. Res. Code sec. 21090)
Environmentally Mandated Projects	• A project undertaken to comply with a performance standard or treatment requirement of the Air Resources Board or an air quality management or control district, the State Water Resources Control Board, a regional water quality control board, the Department of Toxic Substances Control, or the Integrated Waste Management Board (Pub. Res. Code sec. 21159.2)
Installation of Pollution Control Equipment	• Installation of pollution control equipment required by a rule or regulation of the Air Resources Board or an air quality management or control district, the State Water Resources Control Board, a regional water quality control board, the Department of Toxic Substances Control, or the Integrated Waste Management Board (Pub. Res. Code sec. 21159.1)
Environmental Analysis of Rivers and Wetlands	• Adoption of rules and regulations by the Air Resources Board, Department of Toxic Substances Control, Integrated Waste Management Board, State Water Resources Control Board or Regional Water Quality Control Boards, and Air Pollution Control Districts

indicate where the first-tier document is available for review (Guidelines § 15152).

Tiering can be used in a variety of situations under CEQA. These options and the projects to which they apply are summarized in Figure 5-2. Appendix J of the CEQA Guidelines (*see* Appendix 2 of this book) further explains the concept of tiering with examples of tiered situations.

Project EIRs analyze the impacts of a specific project.

Specific Types of EIRs

Project EIR

The most common type of EIR, the "project EIR" analyzes the impacts of an individual activity or specific project. The project EIR, like all EIRs, must include the contents required by CEQA and the Guidelines and must examine all phases of the project, including planning, construction, operation, and reasonably foreseeable future phases (Guidelines § 15161). Examples of project EIRS are those prepared for:

- Residential, commercial, and mixed use projects
- Industrial and energy facilities
- Public works projects such as roads, sewers, and water storage

Program EIR

When Applicable. The program EIR, a type of first-tier document (*see* Tiering, page 88), is prepared for an agency program or series of related actions that can be characterized as one large project. Typically, a large project involves actions that are closely related either geographically or temporally, such as a multiphased development project. Program EIRs are also prepared for agency plans, policies, or regulatory programs. Program EIRs generally analyze broad environmental effects of the program with the acknowledgment that site-specific environmental review may be required for particular aspects of portions of the program when those aspects are proposed for implementation (Guidelines § 15168).

A lead agency should prepare a program EIR, rather than a project EIR, when the agency is considering a program or series of related actions that are linked geographically, are logical parts of a chain of contemplated events, rules, regulations, or plans that govern the conduct of a continuing program, or are individual activities carried out under the same authorizing statutory or regulatory authority and having generally similar environmental effects that can be mitigated in similar ways (Guidelines § 15168(a)).

Environmental Review of Subsequent Activities. Once a program EIR has been prepared, subsequent activities within the program will be evaluated to determine whether an additional CEQA document needs to be prepared. However, the lead agency may not need to prepare a new CEQA document in all situations. Section 15162 of the CEQA Guidelines, regarding the triggers for a subsequent or supplemental EIR, applies to this analysis and acts to limit the need prepare a new EIR unless there have been substantial changes in the project or its circumstances or substantial new information that indicates the project would now have a new or more severe impact not analyzed in the original program EIR (*Citizens for Responsible Equitable Environmental Development v. City of San Diego Redevelopment Agency, et al.* (2005) 134 Cal. App. 4th 598). When the subsequent activities involve site-specific operations, the lead agency should use a written checklist (an initial study checklist) to document its determination that the environmental effects of the operation were already covered in the program EIR. This determination is not subject to the fair argument test. If the program EIR addresses the program's effects as specifically and comprehensively as possible, many subsequent activities could be found to be within the program EIR scope, and additional environmental documents would not be required (Guidelines § 15168(c)).

Types of Actions For Which a Program EIR May Be Appropriate

- Activities that are linked geographically
- Activities that are logical parts of a chain of contemplated events
- Rules, regulations, or plans that govern the conduct of a continuing program
- Individual activities carried out under the same authorizing statutory or regulatory authority and having generally similar environmental effects that can be mitigated in similar ways

There is no expiration date, or "freshness date," on a program EIR under CEQA. The program EIR is appropriate for use as long as the information remains relevant to the agency's decision making process and the underlying environmental analysis. Further, the analysis of the later activity may be limited to the criteria in CEQA Guidelines Section 15162 to whether substantial changes in the project or its circumstances or substantial new information that indicates the project would now have a new or more severe impact. The analysis for the underlying project approval need not re-examine the original program EIR (*Citizens for Responsible Equitable Environmental Development v. City of San Diego Redevelopment Agency, et al.* (2005) 134 Cal. App. 4th 598 *See* Chapter 8 for a discussion of Guidelines Section 15162).

If a subsequent activity would have effects that are not within the scope of the program EIR, the lead agency must prepare a new initial study leading to either a negative declaration, mitigated negative declaration, or an EIR. This initial study is subject to the "fair argument test." In this case, the program EIR still serves a valuable purpose as the first-tier environmental analysis. The program EIR can be incorporated by reference into the subsequently prepared document to address program wide issues such as cumulative impacts and policy alternatives, allowing the subsequent environmental document to focus on new or site-specific impacts (Guidelines §§ 15168(d), 15152. Chapter 7 includes a more detailed discussion of cumulative impact analysis).

When a program EIR is relied on during implementation of subsequent activities, the lead agency must incorporate the feasible mitigation measures and alternatives developed in the program EIR into the subsequent activities (Guidelines § 15168(c)(3)). If a public notice is required for the subsequent activities, the lead agency must state in that notice that the proposed activity is *within the scope of* the program EIR (Guidelines § 15168(e)).

Practical Implications of Program EIRs and Tiering for Subsequent Activities. Although the legally required contents of a program EIR are the same as those of a project EIR, in practice there are considerable differences in level of detail. Because of the general nature of the programs being evaluated, program EIRs are typically more conceptual and abstract. Courts have indicated that a program EIR may contain a more general discussion of impacts, alternatives, and mitigation measures (see for example, *Sierra Club v. City of Orange* (2008) 163 Cal. App. 4th 523).

The level of detail in the program EIR must match the level of detail known about the project. When all or a portion of the program is known in detail, then the program EIR must include detailed analyses of the related issues. For example, if a program EIR is being prepared for a phased development project, the analysis of the first phase will be more detailed than the analyses of later phases about which less is currently known. Put another way, a program EIR can include project-level detail as well as broader program-level analyses, depending upon the project being analyzed.

In developing a program EIR for a regulatory program (as opposed to a large land use project), the lead agency should try to anticipate likely future scenarios that could ultimately develop under the program. Uncertainty over future scenarios often leads agencies to prepare program EIRs as alternative-based documents, evaluating more than one possible set of future outcomes in equal levels of detail. In a program EIR, once a reasonable range of assumptions about the future is developed, the agency will generally evaluate the impacts using quantitative and qualitative methods similar to those used for project-specific EIRs.

Lack of adequate funding is sometimes a deterrent to the preparation of program EIRs for public projects, because CEQA does not readily provide a system for recouping the cost of the program EIR from future projects that develop under the program.

Despite these shortcomings, the program EIR, used by a variety of agencies, is considered a useful tool for evaluating community-wide and regional impacts and for saving agencies time and money as they comply with CEQA on subsequent projects.

Advantages of Program EIRs

The Guidelines encourage the use of program EIRs, citing five advantages:

- Provision for a more exhaustive consideration of impacts and alternatives than would be practical in an individual EIR
- Focus on cumulative impacts that might be slighted in a case-by-case analysis
- Avoidance of continual reconsideration of recurring policy issues
- Consideration of broad policy alternatives and programmatic mitigation measures at an early stage when the agency has greater flexibility to deal with them
- Reduction of paperwork by encouraging the reuse of data (through tiering)

(Guidelines § 15168(b))

Master EIR

General. Master EIRs are a type of first-tier document that are similar to program EIRs and staged EIRs. According to CEQA, master EIRs may be prepared for general plans (including elements and amendments), specific plans, projects consisting of smaller individual projects to be implemented in phases, regulations to be implemented by subsequent projects, state highway or transit projects subject to multiple reviews or approvals, regional transportation plans, congestion management plans, California Department of Fish and Game regulations for hunting and fishing, and federal military base reuse plans (Pub. Res. Code §§ 21157(a), (c)).

Background. The Legislature intended in its 1993 amendments to CEQA to include the provision for master EIRs to streamline the CEQA process by allowing that a Master EIR evaluate cumulative, growth-inducing, and irreversible significant environmental effects of subsequent projects to the greatest extent feasible. The Legislature further intended that environmental review of subsequent projects be substantially reduced to the extent that the Master EIR reviews project impacts and sets forth mitigation measures (Pub. Res. Code §§ 21156–21159).

Specific Requirements. A Master EIR must describe and present sufficient information about anticipated subsequent projects within its scope. Information required about subsequent projects includes size, location, intensity, and scheduling. The Master EIR must also preliminarily describe potential impacts of anticipated subsequent projects for which insufficient information is available to support a full impact assessment. A lead agency may impose a fee program to pay for a Master EIR (Pub. Res. Code §§ 21157(a), (c)).

Limited Environmental Review for Subsequent Projects. The lead agency and responsible agencies identified in the master EIR may use the master EIR to limit review of subsequent projects. There are several alternative ways that a lead agency may limit the scope of a subsequent document. Whenever it is evaluating a subsequent project, the first step is for the lead agency to prepare an initial study to determine whether the subsequent project and its alternatives, impacts, and mitigation measures were already addressed in the Master EIR.

If the lead agency determines that the subsequent project is "within the scope" of the Master EIR and therefore will have no additional significant environmental effect, and that no new mitigation measures or alternatives may be required, it may prepare a written finding to that effect without preparing a new environmental document or findings. The lead agency must provide public notice of its intent to approve or carry out the project and incorporate all feasible applicable mitigation measures or alternatives (Guidelines § 15177). This notice of conformance with the master EIR scope must be provided "within a reasonable time" prior to action on the project, but does not trigger a comment period (Pub. Res. Code § 21092(a)).

Projects "Identified in" the Master EIR. If the subsequent project is not within the scope of the Master EIR, but has been "identified in" the master EIR and the lead agency cannot make the above findings, it may prepare either a mitigated negative declaration or a focused EIR for the subsequent project (Guidelines § 15178).

Small Residential and Mixed-Use Project Not Identified in the Master EIR. Even if the subsequent project was not identified in the Master EIR, it may nevertheless be the subject of a Focused EIR if it is a multiple-family residential projects of 100 units or less or residential and commercial or retail mixed use projects of not more than 100,000 square feet and meets certain specific criteria (Guidelines § 15179.5).

Restrictions on Use and Practical Implications of Master EIRs. The Master EIR cannot be used to limit subsequent project reviews if it was certified more than five years before the application for a subsequent project was filed, or if subsequent approval of a project that was not described in the Master EIR may affect the adequacy of the environmental review in the Master EIR. In these cases, the lead agency must find that no substantial changes or no new information related to the Master EIR exists, or certify a subsequent or supplemental EIR or mitigated negative declaration that makes appropriate modifications to the Master EIR. (Pub. Res. Code § 21157.6, Guidelines § 15179).

If a subsequently approved project that is not within the scope of the Master EIR makes substantial changes or provides new, relevant information to the Master EIR, the lead agency for the Master EIR must take one of three steps:

Master EIRs May Be Prepared for:

- General plans (including elements and amendments)
- Specific plans
- Projects consisting of smaller individual projects to be implemented in phases
- Regulations to be implemented by subsequent projects
- Projects pursuant to or furthering a redevelopment plan
- State highway or transit projects subject to multiple reviews or approvals
- Regional transportation plans
- Congestion management plans
- Federal military base reuse plans
- California Department of Fish and Game for hunting and fishing regulations

Special Master EIR Content Requirements

- Anticipated future projects
  - Type
  - Location
  - Intensity
- Scheduling of capital improvements
- Location of alternative sites
- Preliminary evaluation of anticipated future project-specific impacts and mitigation measures
- Cumulative impacts
- Growth-inducing impacts
- Significant irreversible environmental changes

Figure 5-3
Relationship between Master EIR and Subsequent Documents

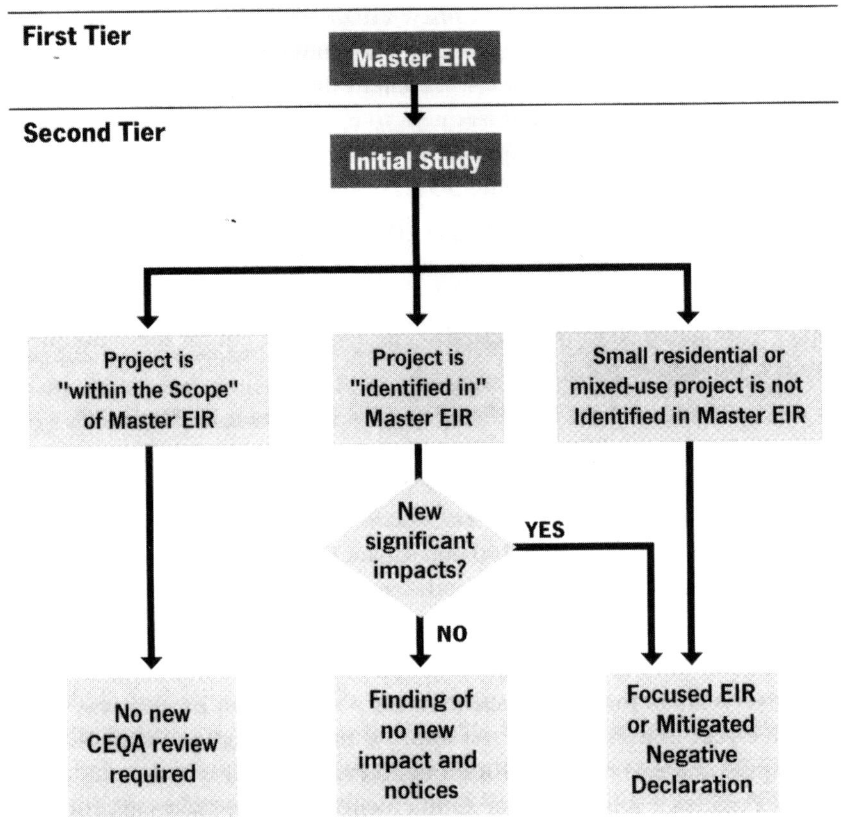

- Prepare a subsequent or supplemental Master EIR to include additional subsequent projects
- Prepare a mitigated negative declaration for a subsequent project within the scope of the Master EIR
- Prepare a focused EIR for all subsequent projects within the scope of the Master EIR

The Master EIR (and Focused EIR) (*see below*) provisions added to CEQA establish for the first time a detailed statutory process for tiering CEQA documents. Agencies using processes will have greater certainty about their ability to withstand legal challenges to tiered documents.

The provisions for master EIRs (and Focused EIRs), however, are considered by some practitioners to have shortcomings. The procedures for use of the Master EIR for subsequent project review are detailed and highly complex, and the Master EIR may be difficult to use for this purpose more than five years after preparation. Although, a subsequent project can be found to be within the scope of a Master EIR through an initial study and administrative finding, CEQA does not specify the procedures for filing the notice of this finding and the standards of review for judicial challenges to such an administrative finding.

Limited Environmental Review Process for Projects within the Scope of a Master EIR

No new EIR or findings are required if the lead agency:

- Incorporates in the project all feasible mitigation measures or alternatives as set forth in the Master EIR
- Prepares initial study that concludes:
  - The proposed project was described in Master EIR
  - No additional significant impacts would result
- Prepares findings that:
  - Project is within scope of Master EIR
  - No additional significant impacts would result
  - No new additional mitigation or alternatives would be required
- Prepares public notice pursuant to Guidelines § 15075

Focused EIR

General. A Focused EIR, also provided for by the legislation creating master EIRs, is an EIR for a subsequent project identified in a Master EIR. It may be used only if the lead agency finds that the Master EIR analyses of cumulative, growth-inducing, and irreversible significant environmental effects are adequate for the subsequent project (Pub. Res. Code § 21158(a). Focused EIRs may be prepared for future projects that were identified in the Master EIR, small multifamily and mixed-use projects not identified in a Master EIR (subject to certain conditions), and installation of pollution control equipment required by specific agency regulation (subject to certain conditions).

The Focused EIR must analyze additional project-specific significant environmental effects not addressed in the Master EIR and any new mitigation measures or alternatives not included in the Master EIR. It must also examine significant effects discussed in the Master EIR for which substantial new information exists showing that those effects may be more significant than described in the Master EIR. The Focused EIR must also examine those mitigation measures found to be infeasible in the Master EIR for which substantial new information exists that shows those measures may now be feasible (Guidelines §§ 15178, 15179.5).

Transit priority projects may be exempt from CEQA.

Focused EIRs for Small Multifamily and Mixed-Use Projects (Not Analyzed in Master EIR). A Focused EIR may be prepared for a multifamily residential project not exceeding 100 units or a mixed-use residential project not exceeding 100,000 square feet, even though the project was not identified in a Master EIR, if the following conditions are met:

- The project is consistent with a general plan, specific plan, or zoning ordinance for which an EIR was prepared within five years of the Focused EIR's certification
- The project does not require preparation of a subsequent or supplemental EIR
- The parcel is bordered by urban development, was previously developed by urban uses, or is within one-half mile of a rail transit station

A Focused EIR for these projects should be limited to analyzing site-specific significant effects and significant effects that substantial new information shows will be more significant than described in the Master EIR (Guidelines § 15178).

Focused EIRs for Installation of Pollution Control Equipment. If certain conditions are met, a Focused EIR may be prepared for a project consisting solely of the installation of pollution control equipment required by a regulation of the Air Resources Board, local air pollution control districts, the State Water Resources Control Board, the Regional Water Quality Control Boards, the Department of Toxic Substances Control, and the Integrated Waste Management Board. The agency must have certified an EIR on the regulation or reviewed it pursuant to a certified regulatory program within five years of certification of the Focused EIR. The scope of the Focused EIR must be limited to project-specific, potentially significant effects not discussed in the prior environmental analysis and to alternative means of compliance with the regulation (Pub. Res. Code § 21159.1; Guidelines § 15188). These provisions overlap considerably with those for preparation of EIRs for environmentally mandated projects (Pub. Res. Code §§ 21159–21159.4; Guidelines § 15187).

General Plan and Other Plan-Level EIRs

Scope and Content. A general plan EIR is one prepared for a city or county general plan, and is often prepared as a program EIR. The plan itself may serve as the EIR if all required topics in CEQA are covered and identified (Guidelines § 15166). Preparation of the EIR parallels the development of the general plan so that evaluation of the effects of land uses on the environment may dictate where land uses are located. Preparing a general plan EIR allows an economizing of time and money and results in a more comprehensive document, although in some cases combining the two documents may not be practical. For further information and advice about preparing general plan EIRs, see the *General Plan Guidelines* issued by OPR. That document encourages the integration the EIR process with the planning process and the merger of the EIR into the plan.

The environmental review process for a general plan EIR should be initiated at the outset of general plan preparation. The lead agency would prepare a general plan EIR on the proposed general plan's overall land use designations, policies, and implementation measures. When combined with an EIR, the general plan must address all the topics required for an EIR by CEQA and the Guidelines, and must contain a special section or cover sheet identifying where the general plan document addresses each of the points required in an EIR. The development and evaluation of alternatives for the general plan can be the basis for the alternatives analysis of the general plan EIR. Special studies prepared for the general plan may provide useful information for the analysis of the environmental effects in the general plan EIR (e.g., a study developed to analyze traffic at various land use intensities can be used to evaluate traffic impacts).

All CEQA reviews on subsequent actions as authorized by the general plan should be based on the general plan EIR using CEQAs tiering provision. A well-prepared general plan EIR can increase the possibility that negative declarations can be issued at a later time for specific project proposals within the planning area.

Projects Consistent with a General Plan, a Community Plan, or Zoning. A project that is consistent with the development density established by the existing general plan, community plan, or zoning policies for which an EIR was certified does not require additional environmental review, except where there are project-specific significant impacts that are "peculiar to the project or the site." When relying on this form of tiering, the lead agency must limit its examination of environmental effects to those that the agency determines in an initial study or other analysis to be impacts peculiar to the project or project site that were not evaluated in the first-tier EIR. It must also determine if there are any potentially significant off-site impacts or cumulative impacts that were not discussed in the prior EIR. Further, it must determine if any impacts identified in the prior EIR are more severe than previously determined, due to substantial new information.

An effect of a project on the environment cannot be considered "peculiar to the project or the site" for the purposes of this tiering provision if uniformly applied development policies or standards have been previously adopted by the city or county with a finding that the development policies or standards will substantially mitigate that environmental effect when applied to future projects, unless substantial new information shows that the policies or standards

Focused EIRs May Be Prepared for:

- Future projects that were identified in the Master EIR
- Small multifamily and mixed-use projects not identified in a Master EIR
- Installation of pollution control equipment required by specific agency regulation

Practice Tip: "Focused EIR" versus "focused EIR"

There is considerable confusion regarding the terms "Focused EIR" versus "focused EIR." The formal designation of "Focused EIR" (with a capital "F") is a defined type of EIR that is only prepared after a lead agency prepares a Master EIR. It includes very specific content requirements relating to the Master EIR and has a special relationship with the Master EIR. On the other hand the phrase "focused EIR" (with a small "f") refers to the concept of *focusing* an EIR on the significant environmental effects. In practice, all EIRs should be focused (as opposed to unfocused).

will not substantially mitigate the environmental effect. The finding must be based on substantial evidence, which need not include an EIR.

Such development policies or standards need not apply throughout the entire city or county, but can apply only within the zoning district in which the project is located, or within the area subject to the community plan on which the lead agency is relying. Moreover, such policies or standards need not be part of the general plan or any community plan, but can be found within another pertinent planning document such as a zoning ordinance. Where a city or county, in previously adopting uniformly applied development policies or standards, fails to make a finding as to whether such policies or standards would substantially mitigate the effects of future projects, the decision-making body of the city or county, prior to approving such a future project pursuant to this section, may hold a public hearing for the purpose of considering whether the standards or policies would substantially mitigate the effects of the project. Such a public hearing need only be held if the city or county decides to apply the standards or policies as permitted in this section (Pub. Res. Code § 21083.3).

This provision is discussed in detail in *Wal-Mart Stores, Inc. v. City of Turlock* (2006) 138 Cal. App. 4th 273, which upheld the city's use of Pub. Res. Code § 21083.3 to support a change to its zoning ordinance restricting certain types of big box stores where the change was consistent with the general plan. Turlock successfully relied on its general plan EIR to address the impacts of the ordinance and was not required to prepare an individual EIR for the adoption of the ordinance.

Focused EIR

Contents must:

- Focus on project-specific impacts and mitigation measures
- Evaluate any new significant effects not in Master EIR
- Include no new evaluation of:
  - Cumulative impacts
  - Growth-inducing impacts
  - Significant irreversible environmental changes

Redevelopment Projects. When preparing an EIR prepared for a redevelopment plan the lead agency has the option of specifying whether it is a master EIR, program EIR, or project EIR. When the EIR is a project EIR, all public and private activities or undertakings pursuant to or in furtherance of a redevelopment plan are considered a single project, and are deemed approved at the time of adoption of the redevelopment plan by the legislative body. Therefore, once a project EIR is prepared for a redevelopment plan, no subsequent EIR need be prepared for activities undertaken under the plan, unless the rules governing subsequent or supplemental EIRs (i.e., Guidelines §§ 15162 and 15163) trigger the need for further CEQA compliance (Pub. Res. Code § 21090). However, if the lead agency elects to prepare a project EIR, then all aspects of the redevelopment plans must be evaluated in site specific detail to the extent such impacts are foreseeable. When the EIR is a Master EIR or program EIR, later activities under the redevelopment plan will be considered pursuant to the master EIR and program EIR provisions of CEQA and the CEQA Guidelines (Guidelines § 15180). With the dissolution of California's redevelopment agencies in 2011, these provisions are obsolete.

For updated material on this topic, please see the 2013 Addendum at www.solano.com

Project for Which a Community-Level Environmental Review Has Been Certified. In 2002, CEQA's provisions for the review of agricultural employee, affordable, and urban infill housing projects were consolidated (Pub. Res. Code § 21159.20 *et seq.*; Guidelines § 15191 *et seq*). This statute establishes three classes of qualified statutory exemptions for specified residential projects for agricultural employees and for urban infill residential projects of up to 100 units for moderate-, low-, and very low-income residents (Pub. Res. Code §§ 21159.22, 21159.23, and 21159.24; Guidelines §§ 15193, 15194, and 15195). Whenever a lead agency utilizes one of these exemptions, it must file a notice of exemption with the State Clearinghouse in the Office of Planning and Research, where it will be posted for a period of at least thirty days (Pub. Res. Code § 21152.1, Guidelines § 15062(e)).

This statute is extremely detailed. Refer to Guidelines § 15191-15196 for more information.

In order to qualify for one of the three exemptions, a project must first meet all of the following criteria:

- The proposal is consistent with the applicable general plan, specific plan, and local coastal program and with any applicable zoning.
- A community-level environmental review has been adopted or certified. A "community-level environmental review" is either an EIR certified for a general plan, general plan land use and circulation element update, applicable community plan, applicable specific plan, general plan housing element, or a subsequent negative declaration based on an EIR for a general plan, community plan, or specific plan.
- The project and prior projects can be adequately served by existing utilities and all applicable in-lieu or impact fees will be paid.
- The project site doesn't contain wetlands or have value as wildlife habitat, the project does not harm any special-status species, and the project would not destroy or affect any species protected by local ordinance.
- The project site is not included on the "Cortese List" of toxic or hazardous sites (*see* Gov. Code § 65962.5).
- The project site has had a preliminary endangerment assessment prepared by a Registered Environmental Assessor and remediation completed, if necessary.
- The project does not have a significant effect on historical resources.
- The project site is not subject to wildland fire hazard, an unusually high risk of fire or explosion from materials used or stored nearby, risk of public health exposure exceeding state or federal standards, location within an earthquake fault or seismic safety zone as delineated, location in a landslide hazard or flood hazard zone, location on developed public open space, or location within the boundaries of a state conservancy.

(Pub. Res. Code § 21159.21, Guidelines § 15192).

Agricultural Employee Housing. The statute exempts the construction, conversion, or use of agricultural employee housing that is either:

- Affordable to lower income households, as defined; lacks public financial assistance; and the developer provides legal commitments to ensure availability to lower income households for at least fifteen years; or
- Affordable to very low-, low-, or moderate-income households; has public financial assistance; and the developer provides legal commit-

ments to ensure availability to low- and moderate-income households for at least fifteen years.

(Pub. Res. Code § 21159.22(a), Guidelines § 15193).

Wildlife protection is an important facet of CEQA.

This exemption can be applied to a project in either a city, certain unincorporated urbanized areas, or a site zoned for general agricultural use. If this housing is located in either a city or a "census defined place" (*see* Pub. Res. Code § 21159.20(a) for the definition), it is limited to not more than forty-five individual units or housing for not more than forty-five agricultural employees in group housing. If the project is located in a general agricultural area, it is limited to not more than twenty individual units or twenty agricultural employees in group housing. There is a limit on the maximum area for such projects of either two or five acres, depending upon the population density of the area (Pub. Res. Code § 21159.22(b) and (c); Guidelines § 15193(c)).

There is an exception to this exemption when a project is proposed in either a city or census-defined place of at least 1,000 persons per square mile, but less than 5,000 persons per square mile. In such locations, the exemption does not apply if there is "a reasonable possibility" that the completed project would have a significant effect on the environment due to unusual circumstances or cumulative impacts. The language used in describing this exception is similar to that used in Guidelines § 15300.2 (Pub. Res. Code § 21159.22(d); Guidelines § 15193(c)(1)(A)).

Affordable Housing. CEQA creates a qualified exemption for the construction, conversion, or use of up to 100 units of housing on up to five acres of land where the developer has provided legal commitments to ensure the continued use of the units by lower income households (as defined in Health and Safety Code § 50079.5) for at least thirty years. The project site must either have been previously developed for "qualified urban uses" (defined by Pub. Res. Code § 21072 as residential, commercial, public institutional, transit or transportation passenger facility, retail use, or any combination of these), or at least seventy-five percent of the site must adjoin qualified urban uses and the remaining twenty-five percent adjoin parcels previously developed with qualified urban uses and the site not subdivided or developed for urban uses within ten years of the proposal. Pub. Res. Code § 21159.3 (a) and (b), Guidelines § 15194.

The project must be located in one of the following areas:

- An urbanized area or a census-defined place with a population density of at least 5,000 persons per square mile
- If the project has fifty or fewer units, a city with a population density of at least 2,500 persons per square mile and a total population of at least 25,000 people
- A city or a census-defined place with a population density of at least 1,000 persons per square mile

(Pub. Res. Code § 21159.3 (a) and (b); Guidelines § 15194(c)).

There is an exception to this exemption when a project is proposed in a city or census-defined place with a population of at least 1,000 persons per square mile. In such locations, the exemption does not apply if there is "a reasonable possibility" that the completed project would have a significant effect on the environment due to unusual circumstances or cumulative impacts. The language used in describing this exception is similar to that used in CEQA Guidelines §. Pub. Res. Code § 21159.3 (c); Guidelines § 15194(c)(1)(C) (dealing with exceptions to categorical exemptions).

Residential Infill. CEQA creates a qualified exemption for infill projects within urbanized areas where the project is limited to 100 or fewer residential units, the site is not more than four acres in area, the project is within a specific distance of a major transit stop, the project doesn't contain any single-level building exceeding 100,000 square feet in area, and the project promotes "higher density infill housing" (as described in the statute). In order to apply this exemption, the community-level environmental review must have been certified not more than five years before the project application was deemed complete (Pub. Res. Code § 21159.24(a); Guidelines § 15195).

The infill exemption is limited to particular circmstances. (Courtesy of Antero Rivasplata)

This exemption is limited to affordable housing projects. In order to qualify, a project must include at least ten percent moderate-income housing units for sale, or at least ten percent low-income housing for rent, or at least five percent very low-income housing for rent. The developer must provide legal commitments to ensure the availability and use of these affordable units. Alternatively, the developer may pay fees pursuant to a local ordinance in an amount sufficient to develop an equivalent number of units, if allowed by the lead agency. Pub. Res. Code § 21159.24(a)(7); Guidelines § 15195(a)(5).

This exemption does not apply when either there's a reasonable probability that the project will have a project-specific, significant effect due to unusual circumstances; there are substantial changes with respect to the circumstances under which the project is being undertaken that are related to the project that have occurred since the community-level environmental review was certified or adopted; or new information becomes available regarding the circumstances under which the project is being undertaken and that is related to the project that was not known and could not have been known at the time that community-level environmental review was certified or adopted. These exceptions are unlike those found elsewhere in CEQA. To an extent, they blend the provisions of Guidelines § 15300.2 and Public Resources Code § 21166. Unlike § 21166, for example, the change in circumstances or new information is not required to be substantial enough to require major changes in the EIR. This is a lower threshold than section 21166 would provide. When a project is prohibited from using this exemption due to any of these three circumstances, later analyses shall be limited to an analysis of the project-specific effects, changed circumstances, or new information (Pub. Res. Code § 21159.24(b) and (c); Guidelines § 15195(b)).

Military Base Reuse Projects. An EIR for a military base reuse project is subject to special rules and procedures. Among these procedures are the authority to use the federal EIS as the EIR, the establishment of a specific baseline for impact analysis, and the requirement to conduct a special public hearing on the project (Pub. Res. Code §§ 21083.8, 21083.81).

Sustainable Communities Strategy or Alternative Planning Strategy Projects

Under legislation adopted in 2009 (commonly referred to as "SB 375"), provisions were made for streamlining project approvals for certain types of projects that have been planned to minimize vehicle miles traveled and therefore minimize greenhouse gas (GHG) emissions. Certain projects which are consistent with a regional Metropolitan Planning Organization's (MPOs) Sustainable Communities Strategy (adopted as part of the Regional Transportation Plan) or Alternative Planning Strategy, that has been reviewed and approved by the California Air Resources Board (ARB), may be eligible for CEQA streamlining. The streamlining provisions apply to qualifying "transit priority projects" (Pub. Res. Code § 21155, *et seq.*) and certain residential/mixed use projects (Pub. Res. Code § 21159.28). CEQA was amended to provide for a qualified exemption for these projects, and creating a shortened "environmental assessment" process for transit priority projects that do not otherwise qualify for the exemption. SB 375 is unclear as to what constitutes "the prior environmental impact reports." This may be intended to mean the EIR prepared and adopted for the sustainable communities strategy. If that's the case, then an Alternative Planning Strategy adopted without an EIR could not be the basis for this streamlining provision.

Transit Priority Projects

A transit priority project is consistent with the general use designation, density, building intensity, and applicable policies in either a Sustainable Communities Strategy or Alternative Planning Strategy in which ARB has concurred that the plan would meet the established GHG reduction targets; contains at least fifty percent residential use; has a Floor-Area Ratio (FAR) of 0.75 or more if the project has between twenty-six and fifty percent nonresidential uses; has a minimum net density of at least twenty dwelling units per acre; and is within 0.5 mile of a major transit stop or high quality transit corridor included in a Regional Transportation Plan.

Qualified Exemption

A transit priority project that complies with certain enumerated environmental and land use criteria (see below) and one of the three other criteria is determined to be a "sustainable community's project" is exempt from further CEQA review. This determination is to be made by the lead agency (typically a city, county, or redevelopment agency) after a public hearing. The qualifying criteria are as follows:

Environmental criteria (project must meet all):

- The project is adequately served by existing utilities and the project applicant has paid or committed to pay all applicable in-lieu or development fees.
- The project:
    - * Does not contain wetlands or riparian areas.

Practice Tip
Transit Priority Projects

The transit priority project exemption is available only in those regions where an Air Resources Board-approved Sustainable Communities Strategy or Alternative Planning Strategy has been adopted. The decision whether to apply the exemption rests with the city or county considering the proposed project. All city or county plan and ordinance requirements continue to apply.

  * Does not have significant value as a wildlife habitat.
  * Does not harm any species protected by the federal Endangered Species Act, the California Endangered Species Act, or the Native Plan Protection Act.
  * Does not cause the destruction or removal of any species protected by local ordinance.
- The project site is not included on any list of facilities and sites compiled pursuant to section 65962.5 of the Government Code (Cortese list of hazardous waste sites).
- The project site has been the subject of a preliminary endangerment assessment to determine the existence of any release of a hazardous substance and the potential for exposure of future occupants to significant health hazards from any nearby property or activity. If release of a hazardous substances or exposure to hazards from surrounding areas is found, then the release shall be removed, the hazard abated or otherwise mitigated to a less than significant level in compliance with state and federal requirements.
- The project would not have a significant effect on historic resources.
- The project site would not be subject to any of the following:
  * Wildland fire hazard (unless local requirements contain provision to mitigate the risk)
  * Unusually high risk of fire or explosion from materials stored or used on nearby properties
  * Risk of a public health exposure exceeding state of federal standards
  * Seismic risk due to being within a delineated earthquake fault zone or seismic hard zone unless the applicable local regulations contain provisions to mitigate associated risks
  * Landslide hazard, floodplain, floodway, or restriction zone unless applicable local regulation contain provisions to mitigate the risk of a landside or flows
- The project cannot be located on "developed open space."
- The project buildings must be fifteen percent more energy efficient than what is required in Title 24 regulations.
- The buildings and landscaping must use twenty-five percent less water than average household use in the region.

Land use criteria (project must meet all):

- The project site is not more than eight acres in area.
- The project does not contain more than 200 residential units.
- The project does not result in a net loss in the number of affordable housing units in the project area.

- The project does not include any single level building greater than 75,000 square feet.
- Mitigation measures/performance measures from the prior applicable adopted EIRs will be incorporated.
- The project site does not conflict with nearby operating industrial uses.
- The project site is located within 0.5 mile of a rail transit station or a ferry terminal included in a Regional Transportation Plan or within 0.25 mile of a high-quality transit corridor included in a Regional Transportation Plan.

Other criteria (the project must meet at least one):

- The transit priority project will provide twenty percent moderate income housing, ten percent low income housing, or five percent very low income housing and the transit priority project developer provides assurances for the period required by the applicable financing. Rental units shall be affordable for at least fifty-five years. Ownership units shall be subject to resale restrictions or equity sharing requirements for at least thirty years.
- The transit priority project developer has paid or will pay in-lieu fee sufficient to result in the development of an equivalent number of units that would otherwise be required pursuant to the above paragraph.
- The transit priority project provides public open space equal to or greater than five acres per 1,000 residents of the project.

Sustainable Communities Environmental Assessment and EIR

A transit priority project that does not qualify as a sustainable community project because it fails to meet the requisite environmental, land use, or other criteria (described above) can be processed under CEQA through one of two ways, depending upon its impact:

Sustainable Communities Environmental Assessment: This is a new type of CEQA document, similar to a traditional initial study supporting a mitigated negative declaration. Although an initial study must be prepared under the sustainable communities' environmental assessment, the scope of the initial study may be limited to project-specific impacts. The IS supporting the sustainable communities environmental assessment is not required to address growth inducing impacts, nor any project-specific or cumulative impacts from cars and light-duty truck trips generated by the project on global warming or the regional transportation network. The IS must, however, identify any cumulative effects that have been adequately addressed and mitigated pursuant to CEQA in prior applicable certified EIRs. Where the lead agency determines that a cumulative effect has been adequately addressed and mitigated, that cumulative effect shall not be treated as cumulatively considerable for CEQA purposes. A sustainable community's environmental assessment must include measures to avoid or mitigate all impacts to a less than significant level (other than the precluded impact subjects). Unlike a standard initial study supporting a mitigated negative declaration, a sustainable communities environmental assessment is subject to the substantial evidence, not the "fair argument," standard.

The public review and approval process for a sustainable community's environmental assessment is as follows:

- The draft of the sustainable communities' environmental assessment must be circulated for public comment for a period of not less than thirty days. Notice shall be provided in the same manner as required for an EIR.
- Prior to acting on the sustainable communities' environmental assessment, the lead agency must consider all comments received. Like a Negative Declaration, no written responses are required.
- Prior to approving a sustainable communities environmental assessment, the lead agency must conduct a public hearing, review the comments received, and find the following:
    - * All potentially significant or significant effects required to be identified in the initial study have been identified and analyzed.
    - * With respect to each significant effect on the environment required to be identified in the initial study, either of the following apply:
        - o Changes or alterations have been required in or incorporated into the project that avoid or mitigate the significant effects to a level of insignificance.
        - o Those changes or alterations are within the responsibility and jurisdiction of another public agency and have been, or can and should be, adopted by that other agency.
- If local ordinances allow a direct appeal of approval of a sustainable community's environmental assessment, legislative body of the lead agency shall conduct the public hearing.

If litigated, the lead agency's decision to review and approve a transit priority project with a sustainable community's environmental assessment will be reviewed under the substantial evidence standard.

Sustainable Communities EIR: Where the transit priority project does not meet the conditions of the exemption and the limited scope initial study shows there is a potential for a significant impact to occur, the lead agency is required to prepare an EIR. The EIR however need only address the significant or potentially significant impacts identified in the Initial Study, and no analysis of off-site alternatives is required. Presumably, the EIR may be limited in scope related to growth-inducing impacts and cumulative impacts from cars and light-duty truck trips generated by the project on global warming or the regional transportation network.

Residential/Mixed-Use Projects

If a residential or mixed-use residential project is consistent with the use designation, density, building intensity, and applicable policies specified for the project area in either a Sustainable Communities Strategy or Alternative Planning Strategy, for which the Air Resources Board has concurred meets the regional greenhouse gas reduction targets, and if the project incorporates the mitigation measures required by an applicable prior environmental document, then the CEQA documentation need not discuss either growth-inducing impacts or any project specific or cumulative impacts from cars and light-duty truck trips generated by the project on global warming or the regional transportation network. Any EIR prepared for such a project shall not be required to reference, describe, or discuss a reduced residential density alternative to address the effects of car and light-duty truck trips generated by the project. (Pub. Res. Code § 21159.28)

The statute specifies that a project can still be subject to conditions, exactions or fees for mitigation of project impacts on the structure, safety, or operations of the regional transportation network or local streets and roads. Presumably this means that transit priority projects are still subject to traffic impact fees, even though the impacts on the regional transportation network are exempt from CEQA analysis. Analysis of impacts on local streets and roads is still required.

Senate Bill 226

CEQA provides (Pub. Res. Code Sec. 21094.5) an alternative streamlining method for infill projects, pursuant to SB 226 (Chapter 469, Statutes of 2011). An infill project is defined as a project located in an urban area on a previously developed site or a vacant site where at least seventy-five percent of the perimeter adjoins or is across a public road from developed urban parcels that any one or more of the following uses: residential; retail or commercial where not more than half the site is used for parking; a transit station; a school; or a public office building. "Urban area" includes urbanized, unincorporated areas as well as cities.

For updated material on this topic, please see the 2013 Addendum at www.solano.com

Where an EIR was certified for a planning level decision of a city or county, CEQA review shall be limited to the effects on the environment that are specific to the later project or its site and were not addressed as significant effects in the prior EIR, or substantial new information shows the effects will be more significant than described in the prior EIR. An environmental effect of a project would not be considered project-specific or a significant effect that was not considered significant in a prior EIR, or an effect that is more significant than was described in the prior EIR if uniformly applicable development policies or standards adopted by the city, county, or the lead agency, would apply to the project and the lead agency makes a finding, based upon substantial evidence, that the development policies or standards would substantially mitigate that effect.

Residential or Mixed-Use Resident Projects

A residential or mixed-use residential project is defined as a project where at least seventy-five percent of the total building square footage of the project consists of residential use, or a project that is a transit priority project.

If an infill project would result in project-specific significant effects, or if the significant effects of the infill project were not addressed in or are more significant than the effects addressed in the prior EIR, and if a mitigated negative declaration or a sustainable communities environmental assessment could not be otherwise adopted, then the EIR prepared for the infill project to analyze those impacts need not consider alternative locations, densities, and building intensities, nor growth-inducing impacts.

The infill project would be required to satisfy both of the following:

- Any of these three conditions:
  - ◇ Is consistent with the general use designation, density, building intensity, and applicable policies specified for the project area in either an approved sustainable communities strategy or alternative planning strategy.
  - ◇ Consists of a small walkable community project located in an area designated by a city for that purpose.
  - ◇ Is located within the boundaries of a metropolitan planning organization that has not yet adopted a sustainable communities strategy or alternative planning strategy, and the project has a residential density of at least twenty units per acre or a floor area ratio of at least 0.75.
- All applicable statewide performance standards contained in the guidelines adopted pursuant to Section 21094.5.5.

At this writing in 2012, the Natural Resources Agency is amending the CEQA Guidelines to establish the statewide standards for projects on infill sites. The rule-making process is expected to be completed in 2013. The provisions of SB 226 cannot be applied to a project until the statewide standards are adopted as part of the CEQA Guidelines.

Staged EIRs may be prepared for large-scale, capital-intensive projects, such as telecommunication projects.

Staged EIR

A "staged EIR," similar to a program EIR, may be prepared for large-scale, capital-intensive projects that are planned and developed over a long period of time, or similar actions. The first stage of a staged EIR must include a general discussion of the entire project, including cumulative impacts; however, unlike a program EIR, the first stage EIR contemplates that there will be future environmental documentation, including project EIRs, prepared. The second-stage EIR supplements the first, focusing on more detailed impact analysis related to second-stage approval (Guidelines § 15167).

Reuse of Certified EIRs for Different Actions

A lead agency may reuse an EIR, previously prepared and certified for one project, for a later project if an initial study shows that the previous EIR adequately describes the later project's setting, impacts, alternatives, and mitigation measures. Prior to the reuse of a previous EIR, the lead agency must: (1) provide public notice that the previous EIR will be used as a draft EIR; (2) respond to public comments received in response to the notice; and (3) complete the remaining steps in the CEQA process. Guidelines § 15153.

Master Environmental Assessment

The master environmental assessment (MEA) is not the same thing as a master EIR, but rather an inventory of resources within a jurisdiction (Guidelines § 15169). It is recommended as a tool to identify environmental characteristics and constraints of an area during the first phase of comprehensive planning. Preparation of an MEA does not replace the need to prepare an EIR; however, an MEA may be incorporated by reference into an EIR for addressing the environmental characteristics of the proposed project site. In practice, MEAs are rarely prepared as stand-alone documents. Rather, the "environmental setting" section of a program EIR or a Master EIR, or a general plan is sometimes referred to as an MEA.

Environmental Impact Report/Environmental Impact Statement

An environmental impact statement is the NEPA equivalent of an EIR. An EIR/EIS is a document prepared jointly by a lead agency subject to CEQA and a federal lead agency subject to NEPA to satisfy the requirements of both CEQA and NEPA (Guidelines § 15170). CEQA provides that a scoping meeting held for purposes of an EIS may also serve the same purpose for a related EIR when notice has been given pursuant to CEQA (Pub. Res. Code § 21083.9(d); Guidelines § 15082(c)). See Chapter 9 for a complete discussion of EIR/EISs and other joint CEQA/NEPA documents.

Substitute Document for Certified Regulatory Programs

As described in Chapter 2, an agency's actions when involving the implementation of certain state regulatory programs (required to be certified by the Secretary of Resources) are exempt from the CEQA requirement to prepare an EIR (or negative declaration). For an action to qualify for this partial exemption, the regulatory program requires preparation of a "substitute document" that must include several specific environmental protection requirements. The substitute document prepared for the agency action within the certified regulatory program must comply with many of the substantive CEQA requirements for preparation of an EIR, including the requirement to avoid significant adverse effects on the environment where feasible. Each state agency with a certified regulatory program has particular requirements specific to the regulatory program that must be followed notwithstanding the CEQA procedural requirements (*see* Partial Exemptions for Certified Regulatory Programs in Chapter 2).

Environmental Analysis for Adoption of New Regulations for Environmentally Mandated Projects

CEQA provides special rules for environmental analyses of regulations adopted by the Air Resources Board, local air pollution control districts, the State Water Resources Control Board, the Regional Water Quality Control Boards, the Department of Toxic Substances Control, and the Integrated Waste Management Board. These agencies, when adopting a regulation, must conduct an environmental review of reasonably foreseeable methods of compliance (e.g., installation of pollution control equipment). The regulatory review must include reasonably foreseeable impacts of methods of compliance, mitigation measures, and alternative means of compliance. This requirement will be satisfied by an EIR prepared when a regulation is adopted (Pub. Res. Code § 21159; Guidelines § 15187).

If a subsequent project consists solely of compliance with a performance standard or treatment requirement imposed by the above-listed regulatory agencies, the lead agency must use the previously prepared regulatory review to the greatest extent feasible. Any EIR required for the compliance project must be limited in scope to project-specific issues not discussed in sufficient detail in the regulation's environmental review, mitigation measures for significant environmental effects only, and alternative means for compliance with the regulation (Pub. Res. Code §§ 21159.2, 21159.3). These procedures overlap considerably with those for preparation of Focused EIRs for installation of pollution control equipment.

Subsequent EIR, Supplemental EIR, and Addendum

Subsequent EIRs, supplemental EIRs, and addenda to an EIR are required when there is a change in the conditions analyzed in an EIR, after the EIR has been certified but before all lead or responsible agency discretionary authorities have been granted for the project. These documents are discussed in chapter 8 under Subsequent EIR, Supplemental EIR, and Addendum to an EIR.

Tips for Successful Compliance

This chapter explained the different types of EIRs and the many different approaches to using them, including tiering. The following are some tips for successfully making the correct choice of CEQA document for your project.

- **Match the EIR to the decision at hand**—With so many different types of EIRs and approaches to tiering, lead agencies should make sure to select the one that best fits the project and circumstances.
- **Be careful of what you tier from**—although tiering can be a valuable tool to saving time and effort on CEQA compliance, agencies should make sure that the document to which they are tiering is adequate and up-to-date, and is not the subject of ongoing litigation over its adequacy
- **Do not use tiering as an excuse to defer impact analysis**—In preparing first-tier document, agencies must evaluate impacts that are reasonably foreseeable at the time, and not defer their analysis to future tiers.
- **Remember, content is more important than title**—Although there are many different types of EIRs and approaches to tiering, regardless of which one is selected, the content of the document is of primary importance.

Chapter 6

Environmental Impact Reports: Preparation, Review, and Certification

EIR Preparation Process

After the lead agency decides—either through preparation of an initial study or at the outset of project planning—that substantial evidence exists that the proposed project may have a significant effect on the environment, it must prepare an EIR. This multiple-step process is designed to provide opportunities to integrate environmental factors into project planning and decisionmaking. (Guidelines § 15080. *See* Figure 6-1, page 116). The primary steps for the lead agency in the EIR and project approval process include issuance of Notice of Preparation (NOP) and determination of scope, content, and focus of EIR; preparation of a draft EIR/analysis of significant environmental impacts and alternatives; notice and circulation of the draft EIR for agency and public comment; preparation of a final EIR/response to substantive issues raised during comments; certification of EIR and decision on the project; adoption of findings regarding significant impacts and appropriate mitigation and alternatives; and possible adoption of a statement of overriding considerations for significant and unavoidable impacts.

This chapter explains the EIR process from the notice of preparation to the final EIR. Chapter 7 discusses required EIR substantive contents. EIR certification, decisionmaking, and follow-up are discussed in Chapter 8.

Key Steps for in EIR Preparation and Project Approval

- Issuance of NOP
- Determination of scope, content, and focus
- Issuance of a draft EIR/analysis of significant environmental impacts
- Notice and circulation of the draft EIR for agency and public comment
- Preparation of a final EIR/response to substantive issues raised during comments
- Certification of EIR and decision on the project
- Adoption of findings regarding significant impacts and appropriate mitigation
- Adoption of statement of overriding considerations for significant and unavoidable impacts
- Adoption of a mitigation monitoring or reporting program
- File notice of determination

Time of Preparation of the EIR

The incorporation of environmental factors into all levels of government planning and project implementation is one of the fundamental objectives of CEQA. To accomplish this goal, EIR preparation should begin as early as possible in the planning process—to allow environmental considerations to influence project design—but late enough to provide meaningful information for environmental assessment (Guidelines § 15004(b)). *See* Initial Trigger to Comply with CEQA, page 29. Too often, project design is finalized before beginning the

Figure 6-1
EIR Process

Start

- ◆ **Notice of Preparation sent to Responsible and Trustee Agencies**
- ○ **Responses to Notice of Preparation sent to Lead Agency** (30 days from acceptance)
- ○ **Contract for EIR preparation executed** (45 days from decision to prepare EIR)
- ◆ **Preliminary Draft EIR prepared**
- ◆ **Independent review by Lead Agency**
- ◆ **Draft EIR completed and submitted for review**
- ◆ **Notice of completion filed**
- ◆ **Public notice and review of Draft EIR** (30–45 days)
- ○ **Public hearing on Draft EIR (optional)**
- ◆ **Written comments received**
- ◆ **Responses to comments prepared**
- ○ **Responses sent to commenting agencies** (10 days before decision)
- ○ **Final EIR certified by Lead Agency** (1 year from acceptance)
- ○ **Lead Agency makes decision on project** (6 months from final EIR certification)
- ◆ **Findings written and adopted**
- ◆ **Mitigation reporting and monitoring program adopted**
- ○ **Notice of Determination filed** (5 days from approval)
- ○ **Notice of Determination posted** (24 hours from filing)
- ○ **Responsible Agency makes decision on project** (180 days from Lead Agency decision)

Finish

Legend
◆ CEQA process actions
○ CEQA process actions with time constraints

CEQA process. This often leads to costly design changes and a project proponent's resistance to analyzing alternatives and including mitigation measures.

For private development projects, EIR preparation is to be completed within one year from the time an application is accepted as complete by the lead agency. Figure 2-5, page 56 and 6-1, above.

Determining the Scope, Focus, and Content of the EIR

Purpose of Scoping

The process of determining the scope, focus, and content of an EIR is known as "scoping." Scoping helps to identify the range of actions, alternatives, environmental effects, methods of assessment, and mitigation measures to be analyzed in depth and eliminates from detailed study those issues that are not important to the decision-making. Scoping is also an effective way to bring together and resolve the concerns of interested federal, state, and local agencies; the proponent of the action; and other interested persons, including opponents of the project (Guidelines § 15083). As a result of scoping, including preparation of an initial study, the lead agency may limit EIR discussion of nonsignificant environmental effects to a brief explanation of why those effects are not considered potentially significant (Pub. Res. Code § 21002.1; Guidelines § 15143).

Tools used to determine the scope of an EIR include the initial study, early public and interagency consultation, the NOP, and scoping meetings with agencies and the public.

Early Public and Agency Consultation

Prior to or during preparation of an EIR, the lead agency may, consult with any person, organization, or government agency it believes will be concerned with the environmental effects of the project (Guidelines § 15083). Many lead agencies have found that early consultation solves potential problems that would arise in more serious forms later in the review process.

Notice of Preparation

A notice of preparation informs agencies and the public that an EIR will be prepared. Its purpose is to solicit input on the scope and content of the EIR, including information needs, project effects, and possible alternatives and mitigation measures. CEQA requires an NOP to include a brief description of the proposed project and project location (including a map); probable environmental effects of the project; date, time, and place of the scoping meeting (if required); the address where documents or files relating to the proposed project are available for review and where written comments on the scope of the EIR may be sent; and the deadline for submitting comments (Guidelines § 15082). To be effective, an NOP must contain sufficient detail to allow recipients to prepare a meaningful response.

A sample NOP form can be found in Appendix I of the CEQA Guidelines (Appendix 2 of this book). The NOP must be posted in the county clerk's office for thirty days (Pub. Res. Code § 21092.3). The county clerk must post the notice within twenty-four hours of receipt (Pub. Res. Code § 21092.3).

Methods for Notices of Preparation. Immediately after deciding that an EIR is required, the lead agency must send an NOP to responsible and trustee agencies and involved federal agencies; to the State Clearinghouse (SCH) within OPR; and to parties previously requesting notice in writing (Guidelines § 15082(a)). The CEQA Guidelines state that the NOP "shall use either certified mail or any other method of transmittal that provides it with a record that the notice was received" (Guidelines § 15082(a)(3)). Because this can sometimes be costly, lead agencies minimize the use of certified mail and rely on other methods of publication, including regular mail and publishing in newspapers and on websites.

The NOP must always be sent to the SCH, even where a state responsible or trustee agency is not involved in the project. The SCH will assign a Clearinghouse number and may comment on the NOP; however, in practice, comments from OPR are rare. Sending copies of the NOP to the SCH does not necessarily fulfill the requirement to send an NOP directly to any state responsible or trustee agencies.

An NOP is also required to be sent to the U.S. Department of Defense or a military branch when either has notified the lead agency and provided it with

Required Contents of a Notice of Preparation

- Brief description of the proposed project
- Description of the proposed project's location
- Date, time, and place of the public hearing (if the lead agency decides to hold one)
- Address where documents or files relating to the proposed project are available for review
- Address where written comments on the scope of the EIR may be sent
- Deadline for submitting comments

the specific boundaries of a low-level flight path, military impact zone, or special use airspace, and the project meets any of the following criteria:

- The project includes a general plan amendment.
- The project has of statewide, regional, or areawide significance.
- The project must required to be referred to the airport land use commission.

CEQA provides that while a project's effect on military activities may cause—or be associated with—adverse environmental effects, the project's effect or potential effect does not itself constitute an adverse effect (Public Resources Code § 21098; Guidelines § 15082).

Although not required, the lead agency should also consider sending the NOP to all parties that may be interested in the project, including neighboring landowners, adjacent communities, special districts, and federal agencies (Pub. Res. Code § 21092.2; Guidelines § 15082).

Responses to a Notice of Preparation. Responsible and trustee agencies that receive the NOP must submit comments to the lead agency within the thirty-day review period. Each response must provide specific details about the scope and content of the environmental information related to the responsible agency's jurisdiction to be included in the EIR. If no response is issued within thirty days (and there is no well-justified request for additional time), the lead agency may presume the responsible agency has no comment. The lead agency must include in the EIR any appropriate information requested in response to the NOP (Guidelines § 15082). The lead agency must accept comments via e-mail and treat them as the equivalent of written comments on the NOP (Pub. Res. Code § 21091(d)).

Scoping Meetings

Scoping is one of the methods lead agencies use to identifying the key issues to be examined in the EIR. Formal scoping meetings are required by CEQA when a lead agency has decided to prepare an EIR in the following situations:

- Caltrans has requested a scoping meeting in which the project may affect highways or other facilities of the department.
- The project is of "statewide, regional, or areawide significance" (as defined in Guidelines § 15206).

(Public Resources Code § 21083.9).

The CEQA Guidelines also provide that the lead agency, a responsible or trustee agency, or a project applicant may request a meeting between involved agencies to help the lead agency determine the scope and content of environmental information that the responsible or trustee agencies may require (Guidelines § 15082(c)).

At the lead agency's discretion, however, scoping meetings with responsible and trustee agencies—and other interested agencies or the public—may be held in other situations as well. Scoping meetings offer a useful opportunity for obtaining information about the scope and content of an EIR. When a project scoping meeting has been held pursuant to NEPA, and notice has also been provided pursuant to CEQA, the meeting is deemed to have met CEQA requirements (Public Resources Code § 21083.9(d); Guidelines § 15082(c)).

Notice for Scoping Meeting. When a scoping meeting is held for a project that has statewide, regional, or areawide significance, the lead agency must provide notice of that meeting to any responsible agency, any agency with jurisdiction by law, any individual or organization that has filed a written request for notice, and any county or city that borders the county or city in which the project is located (Guidelines § 15082(c)). The notice of a scoping meeting can be included in a general public meeting notice. Although the notice for the scoping meeting may be combined with the NOP, the notice requirements for the scoping meeting go beyond the requirements of the NOP, and the lead agency should provide this combined notice to the more expansive mailing list.

Limitations on the Scope of Certain State-Mandated Local Projects

An EIR prepared for a local project mandated by a state agency order must be limited to factors and alternatives consistent with the order (Guidelines § 15184). If a local agency undertakes a project to implement a rule or regulation imposed by a certified state regulatory program listed in the Guidelines (§15251), the scope of the local agency's CEQA compliance is limited to site-specific effects of the project that were not analyzed by the certified state agency as a significant effect on the environment. The local agency is not required to reexamine the general environmental effects of the state rule or regulation.

Preparation of a Draft EIR

The lead agency must allow at least thirty days from the issuance of the NOP to solicit comments regarding the scope of the EIR. However, the lead agency may start collecting preliminary information and preparing the impact analysis for the EIR directly after deciding to prepare an EIR (and not necessarily waiting for the NOP comment period to end). The lead agency cannot, however, circulate a draft EIR for public review before the thirty-day time period for responses to the NOP has expired (Guidelines § 15082(a)(4)).

Contents of a Draft EIR

The scoping process assists the lead agency in determining the basic substantive content of the EIR and the methodologies by which impacts will be evaluated. Through scoping–both internally with the agency staff and externally with agency and public input–the lead agency identifies the range of actions, alternatives, environmental effects, and mitigation measures to be analyzed in detail in the draft EIR. The EIR's discussion of nonsignificant environmental effects may be limited to a brief explanation of why those effects are not considered potentially significant (Pub. Res. Code § 21002.1; Guidelines § 15143).

CEQA and the Guidelines outline the specific content requirements for a draft EIR:

- Table of contents or index
- Summary of discussion contained in the draft EIR

Practice Tips: Scoping Meeting

- While the lead agency has some discretion in determining whether if a project has statewide, regional, or areawide significance, it is recommended to hold the scoping meeting to achieve a somewhat simple procedural requirement and to meet the important objective of public outreach.
- Although not required, some agencies hold two scoping meetings on the same date in order to accommodate the different needs of public agencies and the public. The agency scoping meeting is typically held during business hours. The scoping meeting for the public is held after business hours so that members of the working public can attend without taking time off from work.
- A scoping meeting offers the lead agency a good opportunity to identify those issues that may require particular attention in the EIR. These might include areas of confusion about the project, environmental issues or resources of local interest, and site-specific information about the environment.
- While there is no formal requirement to summarize the results of scoping, some agencies prepare "scoping reports" that explain how they conducted scoping and summarizing the information obtained during scoping. Other agencies include a summary of their scoping efforts in the introductory section of the EIR.

- Project description
- Environmental setting
- Significant environmental effects of the project (including direct, indirect, short-term, long-term, cumulative, and unavoidable impacts)
- Areas of known controversy
- Alternatives to the proposed project, including the no-project alternative, and identification of the environmentally superior alternative
- Mitigation measures for significant environmental effects
- Growth-inducing impacts
- Significant irreversible changes due to the proposed project (required only for EIRs on plans, policies, ordinances, local agency formation commission actions, and EIR/EISs)

See Chapter 7 for more detail on the contents of an EIR.

Who May Prepare a Draft EIR

The EIR may be prepared either by the lead agency's own staff or by another public or private entity, project applicant or project applicant's consultant, or a combination of these parties. The lead agency may also rely on another lead agency's EIR and use the previously prepared EIR as its own (Guidelines § 15084(d)). However, regardless of who proposes the project or prepares the EIR, the lead agency is ultimately responsible for the adequacy of the draft (and final) EIR under CEQA, including the scope, content, and impact conclusions of the draft EIR and final EIR. At the end of the CEQA process, the lead agency must make findings that the EIR reflects its independent judgment.

A Draft EIR May Be Prepared by...

- Lead agency staff
- Another public or private entity
- Project applicant or project applicant's consultant
- Three-part contract involving the lead agency, project applicant, and consultant

The preparation of an environmental impact report is a difficult and challenging task that is sometimes beyond the expertise or time constraints of an agency's own staff. Consequently, many lead agencies rely on private consultants to prepare all or parts of EIRs.

When the lead agency is considering a private applicant's proposal, there is a wide variety of preferences for approaches to the preparation of an EIR. Even when they use consultants, lead agencies must maintain a firm control on the scope, content, and adequacy of the EIR. Agencies typically send requests for proposals to private consultants and directly retain the consultants under a two-party contract. In these situations, the private applicants are given only minimal, if any, involvement in the process, even though they typically pay the cost of EIR preparation under a separate fee arrangement with the lead agency (Guidelines § 15045).

Other lead agencies utilize a three-party contract under which the agency, consultant, and applicant participate in EIR preparation. In these situations, applicants are often given a limited degree of review of the EIR (typically regarding project description issues) while it is prepared. Still other agencies allow project applicants to have the primary role in consultant selection and contracting. Because of the appearance of inappropriateness for an applicant-funded consultant to prepare an EIR, every lead agency should review its consultant selection procedures and its standard consultant contract to ensure that they support the concept that the lead agency should control all aspects of the CEQA process. Any agency that gives too much control to project applicants may jeopardize its legal counsel's ability to successfully defend the EIR if it is ever challenged. As discussed below, the lead agency must subject the draft EIR to its own independent review and analysis (Guidelines § 15084(e)).

Lead Agency Responsibilities. No matter who prepares the initial version of an EIR, CEQA requires that the EIR must be subject to the lead agency's own review and analysis and reflect the lead agency's independent judgment with regard to scope, content, and adequacy. The lead agency is responsible for the objectivity of the draft EIR. When a draft EIR is prepared by another party, such as the applicant or a consultant, the lead agency should require the submittal of administrative drafts of the EIR to enable the lead agency staff to review the document and exercise its independent judgment concerning the EIR's scope, content, and general CEQA adequacy. At the time of certifying the EIR (Chapter 8), the lead agency must make a written finding that the EIR does in fact reflects its own independent judgment (Pub. Res. Code § 21082.1(c); Guidelines § 15084(e)).

Time Limits for Consultant Contracting. If a draft EIR is to be prepared under contract with a consultant, the contract must be executed within 45 days of the decision of the lead agency to prepare the draft EIR (Pub. Res. Code § 21151.5(c)). To assist in meeting this time constraint, some lead agencies maintain a list of qualified consultants from which to choose for preparing the EIR.

Practice Tip: "Administrative" or "Screen Check" Draft EIRs

When a lead agency relies on consultants to prepare an EIR, the common practice is for the consultants to submit an "administrative draft" EIR to the lead agency for internal review by agency staff. Some jurisdictions refer to this as a "screen check" draft EIR. While not specifically mentioned in the CEQA Guidelines, this is a very important step in EIR preparation because the draft EIR that is released for public review must reflect the independent judgment of the lead agency. Without an opportunity for independent review by the lead agency, the document would merely represent the consultant's and possibly the project proponent's judgment, not that of the agency. In practice, several rounds of review and change are sometimes necessary before the lead agency is satisfied that the document reflects its views. The administrative record should reflect the changes the lead agency makes to the administrative or screen check EIR.

Public Notice and Review of a Draft EIR

Once a draft EIR is prepared, the lead agency must issue notices of availability and completion (below) and distribute the document for review and comment and consultation with other agencies. The lead agency must ensure that other agencies and the public have been adequately notified of the availability of the draft EIR. *See* OPR's CEQA Technical Advice Series report, "Circulation and Notice under CEQA," found in Appendix 11.

Consultation with Other Agencies Concerning a Draft EIR

A lead agency must consult with and request comments on a draft EIR from the following agencies:

- Responsible agencies
- Trustee agencies
- Any other state, local, or federal agencies that have jurisdiction by law with respect to the project
- Any city or county that borders on the city or county where the project is located
- For a project of statewide, regional, or areawide significance, the transportation planning agency and other agencies that have major transportation facilities within their jurisdiction

Contents of a Public Notice of Draft EIR

- Brief description of the proposed project and location
- Dates of review period
- List of anticipated significant environmental effects
- Location for public review of documents
- Presence of any hazardous waste sites

A Notice of Draft EIR Availability Must Contain...

- Project description, including the project name
- Project location
- Identification of significant environmental impacts
- Specification of the review period
- Identification of the public hearing date, time, and place (if applicable)
- Address where the draft EIR is available for review
- Identification of the location of documents referenced in the draft EIR
- Statement of whether the project site is a listed toxic site

- For development projects meeting the requirements of Guidelines § 15083.5, water agencies affected by the project
- For a state lead agency when the EIR is prepared for a highway or freeway project, the State Air Resources Board
- For a subdivision project located within one mile of the State Water Project, the California Department of Water Resources
- For certain projects within specific boundaries of a low-level flight path, military impact zone, or special use airspace, the Department of Defense or military branch that has notified the lead agency of those boundaries

In addition to these required consultations, a lead agency may consult with any person or agency who is interested in or has expertise with regard to the project (Guidelines § 15086). The EIR must contain a list of all the entities or persons consulted (Guidelines § 15129).

Public Notice of Draft EIR Availability

In General. As discussed in Chapter 1, public involvement is one of the fundamental objectives of CEQA. Thus, adequate notification to the public of the availability of a draft EIR is important to achieving this objective. CEQA requires state and local agencies to make diligent efforts to involve the public throughout the environmental review process. Each lead agency must include provisions in its CEQA procedures for wide public involvement, both formal and informal, to encourage the public to react to environmental issues related to the agency's proposed projects. In addition to the notice requirements discussed below, an agency should, whenever possible, make environmental information available in electronic format on the Internet or on a website maintained or utilized by the public agency (Guidelines § 15201).

Objectives of Public Review of Agency Proposals

- Sharing expertise
- Disclosing agency analysis
- Checking for accuracy
- Detecting omissions
- Discovering public concerns
- Soliciting counterproposal

Notice of Availability. The notice that the draft EIR is available for public review must contain a description of the project and location; identification of significant environmental impacts; specification of the review period; identification of the public hearing date, time, and place (if applicable); address where the draft EIR and documents referenced in the draft EIR are available for review; and a statement of whether the project site is a listed toxic site (Pub. Res. Code §§ 21092(b), 21092.6; Guidelines §§ 15087, 15105). Although the lead agency is not required to provide a copy of the draft EIR with the notice, it must make it available for copying and can charge a reasonable fee for copying costs.

Methods of Notice of Availability. CEQA requires that the public notice announcing that the draft EIR is available for review be issued to the county clerk, all responsible and trustee agencies (below), and any person or organization requesting, or who previously requested, a copy of the notice. The public notice must either be published in a general circulation newspaper, posted on and off the project site, or directly mailed to owners and occupants of contiguous property. If the lead agency uses a newspaper notice, and if more than one area will be affected, the notice must be published in the largest circulation newspaper in the affected areas (Pub. Res. Code §§ 21092(b), 21092.3; Guidelines

§ 15087(a)). The agency may also send additional notice by e-mail. If it does so, then it must send e-mail notice to any member of the public who may have asked for such notice (Pub. Res. Code § 21092.2).

The notice must be posted in the county clerk's office for thirty days, and the clerk must post the notice within twenty-four hours (Pub. Res. Code § 21092.3).

Notice of Completion

At the same time the lead agency provides public notice of the availability of a draft EIR, the lead agency must file a notice of completion with the State Clearinghouse. The notice must include a brief project description and information on the project location, the address where the draft EIR is available, and the public review period (Guidelines § 15085). A model notice of completion form is in Appendix L of the State CEQA Guidelines. The notice of completion may be filed as a printed hard copy or electronically via a diskette or e-mail (Guidelines § 15085).

Posting on Agency Website

While not required, an excellent way to enhance public participation objectives of CEQA is for the lead agency to establish a link on its website for posting CEQA documents. Some agencies not only post documents for review, but also offer commenters the opportunity to submit e-mail comments directly to the agency. When posting documents, file size and accessibility are two important considerations. The agency should be sensitive to the fact that many potential viewers do not have high-speed Internet access. Large documents should be split into pieces (chapters, for example) so that individual files are not too large to download in a reasonable amount of time. Also, the agency should consider the program in which the document is presented. Graphics or engineering program files are generally not accessible to the average internet user. Many agencies avoid this problem by posting their documents as PDF files, using this easily obtained and commonly accepted format.

Online documents are not a substitute for print copies. The lead agency must continue to make print copies available to the public and agencies, as provided in CEQA. They should also place copies in public areas such as the agency office or public library where they are available for review.

State Review Process Administered by the State Clearinghouse

The SCH was established to coordinate the systematic review of environmental documents by state agencies. The SCH must be used to distribute draft EIRs (and negative declarations) to state agencies whenever the project meets any of the criteria shown in the sidebar on page 114 (Guidelines §§ 15205, 15206).

The lead agency is required to identify to the SCH those state agencies that are likely to be interested in the project. The lead agency must send at least fifteen copies of the draft EIR to the SCH and a copy of the notice of completion (Appendix C of the CEQA Guidelines is a sample SCH notice).

A Lead Agency Assures Public Participation by Providing for ...

- Issuance of the Notice of Preparation
- Scoping meetings
- Public notice and public review of the draft EIR
- Public hearings on the draft EIR
- Response to public comments in the final EIR
- Public hearing on the project decision

Public Notice of a Draft EIR Must Be Sent to...

- County clerk
- All responsible and trustee agencies
- Any person or organization requesting, or who previously requested, a copy
- A water supply agency, under certain circumstances
- The Department of Defense or military branch, under certain circumstances

Public Notice of a Draft EIR Must Be Issued in at Least Any One of the Following Ways ...

- Publication in a newspaper of general circulation
- Posting on and off the project site
- Direct mailing to owners and occupants of contiguous property

When Is State Clearinghouse Review Required?

- State agency is a lead agency, responsible agency, trustee agency, or agency with jurisdiction by law
- The project is of "statewide, regional, or areawide significance," defined as follows:
  - General plan, element, or amendment for which an EIR was prepared
  - Project with extraterritorial impacts
  - Residential project (more than 500 units)
  - Commercial projects (more than 1,000 occupants or greater than 500,000 square feet)
  - Office buildings (more than 1,000 occupants or greater than 250,000 square feet)
  - Hotels or motels (more than 500 rooms)
  - Industrial projects (more than 1,000 occupants or greater than 650,000 square feet) (Guidelines § 15206)
- The project is for cancellation of a Williamson Act contract covering more than 100 acres
- The project is in one of the following Environmentally Sensitive Areas:
  - Lake Tahoe Basin
  - Sacramento-San Joaquin River Delta
  - Suisun Marsh
  - Coastal Zone, as defined by the California Coastal Act (including San Francisco Bay Conservation and Development Commission jurisdiction)
  - An area within one-quarter mile of a river designated as wild and scenic
- The project affects sensitive wildlife habitats or the habitats of any rare, threatened, or endangered species
- The project interferes with water quality standards
- The project is within 10 miles of a nuclear power plant

The SCH transmits the draft EIR to those agencies identified for review and receives comments on the draft EIR from reviewing agencies for transmittal to the lead agency. In addition to submitting printed copies of environmental documents to the State Clearinghouse, the lead agency must include a copy of the document in electronic format, on a diskette or by e-mail, if available (Guidelines § 15205; *see* Figure 6-2).

As of this writing, an EIR cannot be submitted to the SCH solely in electronic form. However, the SCH will accept EIRs on CD-ROM instead of print copies. The lead agency must submit 15 copies of the CD-ROM with the EIR file in either PDF or Microsoft Word format. These must be accompanied by 15 print copies of the EIR's executive summary and a notice of completion. For large projects, the SCH reserves the right to request print copies in addition to those submitted on CD-ROM.

Public Comments

As explained in Chapter 1, public participation is an essential part of CEQA (Guidelines § 15201). Although a member of the public is free to comment on any aspect of a proposed project, when reviewing draft EIRs, people should focus on the sufficiency of the document regarding the identification of environmental impacts and methods to avoid or mitigate those impacts (Guidelines § 15204). The lead agency is required, when responding to comments on the draft EIR, to respond to the significant environmental issues raised (Guidelines § 15088).

Persons who submit comments or otherwise participate in the public review process provided by CEQA are afforded protection from legal retaliation by project proponents or others who may disagree with their comments. Such lawsuits, known as "strategic lawsuits against public participation" (SLAPP), have been frowned on by the courts in California, and the Legislature has enacted an anti-SLAPP law to deter this type of offensive litigation (*Dixon v. Superior Court* (1994) 30 Cal. App. 4th 733; Code Civ. Proc. § 425.16).

Agency Comments

A public agency is limited to submitting comments on only those aspects of a project within its area of expertise or required to be carried out or approved by the agency. Agency comments must be supported by substantial evidence (Guidelines §§ 15204(f), 15209).

If, in commenting on a draft EIR, a responsible or trustee agency identifies any significant environmental effects, it should submit mitigation measures to address those effects and must notify the lead agency of detailed performance objectives for mitigating those impacts or refer the lead agency to readily available guidelines or reference documents concerning mitigation measures. If the responsible or trustee agency is not aware of any appropriate mitigation measures, it must state that to the lead agency (Guidelines §§ 15204(f), 15086).

Figure 6-2: State Clearinghouse Operation

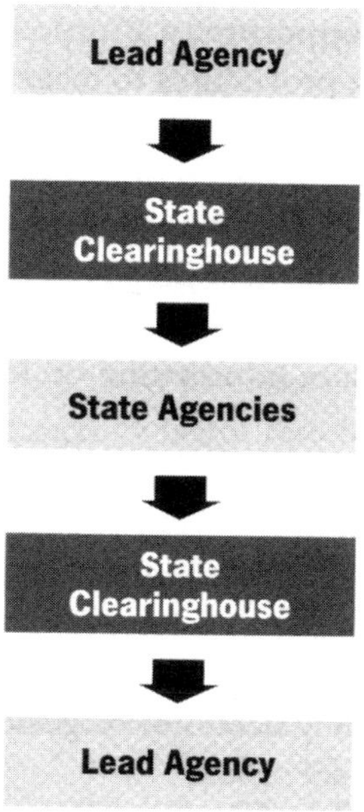

Submits Draft EIRs and Negative Declarations to State Clearinghouse

Distributes Draft EIRs and Negative Declarations to State Agencies

Submit comments to State Clearinghouse

Sends comments to Lead Agencies

Receives comments from State Clearinghouse

Agencies frequently involved in reviewing CEQA documents:

- Air Resources Board
- Bay Conservation and Development Commission
- California Coastal Commission
- California Environmental Protection Agency
- Department of Conservation
- Department of Fish and Game
- Department of Forestry and Fire Protection
- Department of Parks and Recreation
- Department of Transportation
- Department of Water Resources
- Integrated Waste Management Board
- State Lands Commission
- State Water Resources Control Board

Methods of Public Comment

Comments on a draft EIR may take the form of both oral and written comments. The lead agency must accept comments from agencies or the public via e-mail and treat e-mail comments as the equivalent of written comments on the draft EIR (Pub. Res. Code § 21091(d)). If the agency holds a public hearing on the draft EIR, it should have some means of collecting comments. Some agencies have a "court reporter" to transcribe the oral comments while other agencies use comment cards or record the hearing to capture oral comments.

Public Hearings

CEQA does not require a public hearing on draft EIRs (Guidelines § 15087(I)), although in practice many agencies conduct some type of public meeting that affords concerned citizens and agencies the opportunity to voice their opinions. This type of "hearing" is typically held for the lead agency to receive comments on the draft EIR and is not a formal evidentiary hearing. Participants have no right to cross-examine the preparers of the draft EIR, and the lead agency is not required to respond to questions or comments raised at the hearing. If the lead agency conducts a hearing on the merits of the project during the draft EIR phase of CEQA compliance, the agency should include draft EIR review as part of that larger hearing. To the extent that an agency maintains or utilizes a website, notice of all public hearings should be made available in electronic format on that site (Guidelines § 15202).

How to Comment Effectively

To effectively participate in the CEQA review process, members of the public as well as interested organizations and agencies must be diligent and focused in their comments. In reviewing EIRs, people should address the sufficiency of the document in identifying and analyzing possible significant environmental impacts and how they may be avoided or mitigated. Comments are most helpful when they disclose additional impacts, alternatives, or mitigation measures, or when they address the methods of analysis used by the lead agency to evaluate these issues. Commenters should explain the basis for their comments and should support them by substantial evidence such as data, references, expert opinion, or other facts. Mere opinions about the document or the underlying project, while permissible, are not helpful to the agency in developing an adequate EIR. At the same time, commenters should be aware that the adequacy of an EIR is determined in terms of what is reasonable. CEQA does not require a lead agency to conduct every test or perform all research, study, and experimentation recommended or demanded by commenters. Perfection is not required for an EIR to be adequate (Guidelines §§ 15151, 15204).

All commenters should include the name of a contact person who would be available for later consultation if necessary (Guidelines § 15204(d)).

Exhausting Administrative Remedies. Under the legal doctrine known as "exhaustion of administrative remedies," a court generally will not allow a person or organization to bring a legal challenge on an agency's decision unless that person or organization has participated during the agency's administrative review process (Pub. Res. Code. § 21177). To most effectively participate in the environmental review process, and to preserve the right to later bring a legal action regarding particular CEQA issues, a person should take advantage of every opportunity afforded by CEQA, the Guidelines, and the lead agency's own procedures to make his or her views known.

Exhaustion of administrative remedies requires that a person preparing written or oral comments on an environmental document must allege specific violations of CEQA procedures or substantive findings. Mere objections to the project, as opposed to the procedures or environmental information, are not sufficient to alert an agency to an objection based on CEQA. For more information on legal remedies, see Chapter 10, CEQA Litigation.

Failure to Comment or Late Comment

When a person or organization who has been consulted about a draft EIR (or negative declaration) fails to comment within the lead agency time limits provided, the lead agency may assume that the person or agency has no comment (Guidelines § 15207). This does not mean that the lead agency may ignore late comments; rather it must handle late comments carefully. While the Guidelines and judicial precedent indicate that a lead agency need not respond to a late comment in writing, the agency should exercise discretion because all comments—including

Practice Tips for Effective Participation

- Learn the organizational structure, the decision-making lines of authority, and the administrative appeal process for the agencies of concern.
- Identify key individuals who may be responsible for CEQA implementation within the agency.
- Write to key individuals and request to be put on the list of persons to be notified of CEQA actions.
- Join forces with established associations, environmental groups, and other organizations to address similar environmental issues.
- Regularly monitor local newspapers and agency sites for any formal announcements of or articles about agency activities in your community.
- Submit comments at every possible opportunity afforded by the agency.
- Make sure your comments are substantive, well written or presented, and supported by the weight of evidence.
- Be willing to meet with agency staff to discuss your views about their proposed actions.
- If all other efforts to influence agency decisionmaking are unsuccessful, a person or organization may challenge the agency's decision through litigation.

Practice Tip: Disclosure of personal information

Individuals submitting comments must realize that the full text of their comments, including the letterhead and signature, will typically be included in the final EIR. Thus, if they do not want personal information—such as addresses and phone numbers—to be made public, they should not put it on their comments. However, the commenter's name must be indicated. Agencies are advised to inform would-be commenters about this, in their notices of availability or in the EIR's Introduction.

late ones—become part of the project's administrative record (*Galante Vineyards v. Monterey Peninsula Water Management District* (1997) 60 Cal. App. 4th 1109).

Review Periods

In General. The minimum public review period for a draft EIR is 30 days, and the maximum is generally sixty days. When a draft EIR is sent to the SCH for review, the public review period must be at least forty-five days unless a shorter period (of not less than thirty days) is approved by the SCH. When the SCH review period is longer than the public review period established by the lead agency, the lead agency must adhere to the review period approved by the SCH (Pub. Res. Code §§ 21091, 15087, 15105). Any agency or member of the public may request an extension of the draft EIR comment period. Although the lead agency is not required to extend the comment period beyond that required by CEQA, in practice the lead agency will extend the comment period if a reasonable request is made.

Requests for Shortened Review. OPR establishes criteria for granting shortened review periods for draft EIRs (and negative declarations) requiring SCH review. Requests must be made by the lead agency's decision-making body or its designee. Shorter review periods are not available for projects of statewide, regional, or areawide significance. The lead agency must submit with its request for shortened review the approval of those responsible and trustee agencies that will need to review the draft EIR. Approval of a shortened review period must be shown in the notice that the draft EIR (or negative declaration) is available for review (Pub. Res. Code § 21091; Guidelines § 15105; Guidelines Appendix K).

Impacts to significant historic resources must be considered in an EIR.

Preparation of a Final EIR

Contents of Final EIR

The final EIR must include a list of persons, agencies, and organizations commenting on the draft EIR; copies of comments received during public review of the draft EIR; and the lead agency's response to those comments. This includes comments received by e-mail. The responses may take the form of a revision to the draft EIR or may be a separate action in the final EIR (Guidelines § 15132). The final EIR may take the form of a re-publication of the entire draft EIR, with changes made in the final EIR. However, in most instances, the lead agency chooses to incorporate the information in the draft EIR by reference and to only publish an "errata" document showing the particular changes made as part of the final EIR.

Response to Comments

The lead agency must prepare a final EIR responding to all environmental comments received on the draft EIR, including e-mail comments, and certify the final EIR before approving the project. The responses to comments in the final EIR must include good faith, well-reasoned, written responses to all comments received on the draft EIR during its review period. As discussed above, the lead

> **Practice Tip: Beware of Differing Review Periods**
>
> Make sure the publication or mailing of public notice coincides with the submittal of the draft EIR to the SCH for review. If they do not coincide, be aware that the 45-day review period will begin on the latter of the two dates so that the affected segment of the reviewing entities (whether state agencies relying on the SCH or others relying on local notice) will receive their full 45 days to review and comment on the draft EIR (Guidelines § 15105).

agency must also consider any late comments received after the review period before approving a project. Guidelines §§ 15088, 15132.

In responding to comments, CEQA does not require a lead agency to conduct every test or perform all research, study, or experimentation recommended or demanded by commenters. Rather, a lead agency need only respond to significant environmental issues and does not need to provide all information requested by reviewers, as long as a good faith effort at full disclosure is made in the EIR. Guidelines §§ 15088, 15204.

For example, if the lead agency has studied the traffic impacts of a project using a particular computer model with a particular set of assumptions, it need not reevaluate those impacts using another computer model, just because a commenter makes that suggestion. However, in this situation, the lead agency should explain the reason why it used the particular approach and why that approach constituted a good-faith effort at full disclosure.

The lead agency must also provide a copy of its responses to any public agency that submitted comments at least ten days prior to certifying the final EIR. Pub. Res. Code § 21092.5(a); Guidelines § 15088(b). In practice, before project approval, some agencies also provide at least a short public review period. Guidelines § 15089(b). *See* chapter 5 for further discussion of the contents of a final EIR.

Recirculation of a Draft EIR

When Recirculation Is Required. If "significant new information" is added to the EIR after the close of the public comment period on the draft EIR but before certification of the final EIR, the lead agency must provide a second public review period and recirculate the draft EIR for comments. Under the Guidelines, recirculation is required when new, significant information identifies:

- A significant, new environmental impact resulting from the project or from a new mitigation measure proposed to be implemented
- A substantial increase in the severity of an environmental impact, unless mitigation measures are adopted that reduce the impact to a level of insignificance
- A feasible project alternative or mitigation measure, considerably different from others previously analyzed, that clearly would lessen the environmental impacts of the project but that the project's proponents decline to adopt
- That the draft EIR was so fundamentally and basically inadequate and conclusory in nature that meaningful public review and comment were precluded

(Guidelines § 15088.5(a)).

> **Practice Tip: Shortened Review**
>
> Plan in advance if you intend to request a shortened review. First, review Appendix K and Guidelines § 15206 to determine if your project will qualify. Then, contact the SCH to identify the applicable, responsible, and trustee agencies whose approval will be needed. Finally, contact each of these agencies and obtain their approval of the shortened review period.

Recirculation of a draft EIR is not required where the new information merely clarifies, amplifies, or makes minor modifications to an adequate EIR (Guidelines § 15088.5(b)).

The decision not to recirculate an EIR must be supported by substantial evidence in the administrative record Guidelines § 15088.5(e)). Given the rules on recirculation of an EIR, if a lead agency decides not to recirculate a draft EIR after receiving public comments, it should clearly explain in the final EIR that recirculation of the draft was not necessary. This explanation should indicate that all the comments received merely clarified, amplified, or made insignificant modifications to the draft EIR.

Recirculation of an EIR is subject to the same public notice and consultation requirements that applied to the original draft EIR (Guidelines § 15088.5(d)). Although an additional notice of preparation is not required, many lead agencies issue a "supplemental NOP" to give additional notice and assist in scoping the recirculated draft EIR. The lead agency must send notice of the recirculated draft EIR (NOA and NOC) to every agency, person, or organization that commented on the original draft EIR (Guidelines § 15088.5(f)).

What to Include in a Recirculated EIR

Recirculating an EIR can result in a lead agency receiving more than one set of comments from reviewers. To avoid confusion of which comments are subject to formal response, the CEQA Guidelines provide two approaches a lead agency can follow to handle the recirculation.

- **When the EIR is substantially revised.** When the EIR is substantially revised and the entire document is recirculated, the lead agency may require that reviewers submit new comments and need not respond to those comments received during the earlier circulation period. In this situation, the lead agency must advise reviewers, either in the text of the revised EIR, or by an attachment, that new comments must be submitted.

  Additionally, the lead agency must directly notify every entity that commented on the prior draft EIR that new comments must be submitted.

  After recirculation, the lead agency need only respond to those comments submitted in response to the recirculated, revised EIR. Although the original comments are part of the administrative record, the lead agency need not respond to them in the final EIR (Guidelines § 15088.5(f)(1)).
- **When the EIR is partially revised.** When the EIR is only partially revised, the lead agency may recirculate only the revised chapters or portions. In that situation, the lead agency may request that reviewers limit their comments to the revised chapters or portions. The request to limit the scope of comments must be included either within the text of the revised EIR or in an attachment to it.

  In responding to comments on a partial recirculation, the lead agency must respond to both sets of comments on the unrevised portion of the EIR, but may limit its responses to the second set of comments on the revised portions (Guidelines § 15085.5(f)(2)).

When recirculating a revised EIR, in whole or in part, the lead agency must include, in the revision or as an attachment, a summary of the revisions made to the previously circulated EIR (Guidelines § 15088.5(g)).

Practice Tip: Responding to Opinions

In practice, many people use the EIR public review period to voice their opinions about the merits of a project. Given CEQA's objective of enhancing public participation, this is an appropriate time for people to present their views. The lead agency is not, however, obligated to prepare detailed responses to such comments. Nevertheless, the practice has developed to merely respond with the phrase "comment noted" or a variation thereof. While nothing in CEQA prohibits the use of this phrase, it is not advisable to use it without further explanation because its meaning is uncertain, especially to the person submitting the comment. Thus, better language would serve the same purpose, but could explain why a more detailed response is not provided. For example, agencies may want to use the following language to respond to opinions about the project:

> Section 15088 of the CEQA Guidelines only requires detailed responses when a comment raises significant environmental issues. This comment relates to the merits of the project—not to the environmental issues analyzed in the EIR. Thus, no changes to the document are necessary. The comment will, however, become part of the administrative record and will be considered by the decision makers. Thank you for participating in the CEQA process.

Recirculation of a Draft EIR Is Required When . . .

- A significant new environmental impact may result from the project or from a new mitigation measure proposed to be implemented
- A substantial increase in the severity of an environmental impact will occur unless mitigation measures are adopted that reduce the impact to a level of insignificance
- A feasible project alternative or mitigation measure considerably different from others previously analyzed, but that the project's proponents decline to adopt, would clearly lessen the project's environmental impacts
- The draft EIR was so fundamentally and basically inadequate and conclusory in nature that meaningful public review and comment were precluded

Practice Tip: Avoiding Recirculation

When reviewing comments on the draft EIR and responding to those comments, keep in mind the requirements for recirculation. If the comment introduces new information, but the lead agency believes that recirculation is not necessary or required (the information is not "significant"), it should explain its reasons for reaching that conclusion in the responses to comments. This is particularly important when a comment asserts that there is a new or more severe impact and suggests a new mitigation measure—or suggests a new project alternative.

Consideration and Certification of a Final EIR

Consideration

A decision-making body is required to read and consider the information in an EIR before making a decision. The lead agency's administrative record on the proposed project must show that the lead agency reviewed and considered the final EIR before acting on a project (Guidelines § 15090; *see* chapter 8 "Agency Decision-making").

Certification

Before approving the project, the lead agency must certify that the final EIR was prepared in compliance with CEQA and was presented to the lead agency's decision-making body, which reviewed and considered the final EIR before approving the project (Guidelines § 15090). In addition, the lead agency must certify that the EIR reflects its own independent judgment (Pub. Res. Code § 21082.1(c)(3)). Responsible agencies are not required under CEQA to make any additional certifications regarding the preparation or adequacy of the final EIR (Guidelines § 15096). The lead agency is not required to certify an EIR for a project that the agency has decided to deny or otherwise disapprove (Public Resources Code § 21080(b)(5)).

The decision-making body of the lead agency certifies the EIR. This may be elected officials, an advisory body (e.g., a planning commission) or staff (e.g., a planning director) depending on the type of project. When a final EIR is certified by a nonelected decision-making body, certification must be appealable to the agency's elected decision-making body (Pub. Res. Code § 21151(c); Guidelines § 15090(b)). Certification must be made by a majority of the decision-making body—a tie vote does not constitute certification of the EIR (*see Vedanta Society of Southern California v. California Quartet, Ltd.* (2000) 84 Cal. App. 4th 517).

Prior to certifying the final EIR for any project involving the purchase of a school site or the construction of a new elementary or secondary school by a school district, the lead agency must make the determination of whether the site is currently or was formerly a hazardous waste disposal site or solid waste disposal site and, if so, whether the wastes have been removed (Pub. Res. Code § 21151.8(a); Guidelines § 15186). In certain large projects, the lead agency must disclose, at the time it makes a decision on the proposed project, whether or not the projected water supplies presented in the EIR will be sufficient to satisfy the demands of the proposed project (Pub. Res. Code § 21151.9; *see* Impacts on Public Water Systems and Water Supply Assessments, Chapter 7).

Time Limits

CEQA provides that for private projects, the EIR must be completed and certified within one year of the time at which the application was determined complete. While this time limit is sometimes ignored in practice, the court in *Sunset Drive Corp v. City of Redlands* (1999) 73 Cal. App. 4th

215 held that the city's four-year delay in completing and certifying an EIR was a violation of CEQA. The court ordered the city to complete the EIR, stating that an agency has a statutory duty to comply with CEQA's time limit, however, *Schellinger Brothers v. City of Sebastopol* (2010), 179 Cal. App. 4th 1245 stated the CEQA one-year requirement was not fixed "in cement."

Comments Received after EIR Certification

When a public hearing is conducted to consider project approval (as occurs with most projects), new environmental comments can be made and must be accepted by the lead agency until the close of public testimony in that hearing. In those instances when the final EIR was certified before the close of public testimony on the project, the lead agency must also consider those comments it receives after certification of the final EIR (*Bakersfield Citizens for Local Control v. City of Bakersfield* (2004); 124 Cal. App. 4th 1184).

Therefore, a lead agency should respond to any substantive comment and include it in the final environmental document, even if received after the close of the review period. If the final document has already been prepared, the lead agency should include the late comment in its staff report or provide some other response on the record to demonstrate that the comment was not ignored.

> **Final EIR Certification Requirements**
>
> Before approving a project, a lead agency must certify that:
>
> - The final EIR has been completed in compliance with CEQA.
> - The final EIR was reviewed and considered by the decision-making body prior to approving the project.
> - The final EIR represents the lead agency's independent judgment and analysis.
>
> If certification is by a nonelected body, an appeal to the elected body must be allowed. However, the lead agency may wish to certify the EIR, notwithstanding project denial, to enable the use of information contained in responses to comments and other elements of the final EIR.

Judicial Standards for EIR Content Adequacy

If no legal action or proceeding alleging that the lead agency violated CEQA requirements is commenced before the expiration of the statute of limitations, the CEQA document shall be conclusively presumed to comply with CEQA (Pub. Res. Code § 21167.2).

Judicial review of the content of EIRs typically incorporates the "rule of reason" standard to assess whether the lead agency has complied with the requirements of CEQA. The courts do not hold an agency to a standard of absolute perfection, but rather require only that an EIR show that an agency has made an objective, good-faith effort at full disclosure (Guidelines § 15151). In reviewing an EIR for adequacy, courts will make sure that all required contents are included, and that conclusions are supported by substantial evidence in the record before the lead agency. Courts will assess whether the lead agency applied an objective, good-faith effort toward full disclosure. Disagreement among experts regarding conclusions in the EIR is acceptable, and perfection is not required. Also, exhaustive treatment of issues is not required in an EIR. Minor technical defects identified in an EIR are not necessarily fatal (Guidelines § 15151).

The scope of judicial review does not extend to the correctness of an EIR's conclusions, but only to the EIR's sufficiency as an informative document for decision makers and the public (Guidelines § 15003(i)). The court will review the administrative record to determine whether substantial evidence supports the lead agency's conclusions (*see* Chapter 10 for more information regarding CEQA litigation).

> **Practice Tip: Conducting Project Hearings**
>
> If comments are submitted at the public hearing on the project, it can be worthwhile to call for a recess in order to examine the submittal and quickly determine if it seems to bring up substantive new points that were not received in previous comments and addressed in either the final EIR or the staff report. If the comment brings up new points, they should be pointed out to the decisionmakers at the end of recess. Substantive new comments may necessitate delaying a final decision until they can be fully analyzed for decisionmakers and a detailed response is prepared. Agencies ignore "eleventh hour" comments at their own peril.

Tips for Successful Compliance

This chapter discussed the required contents of an EIR, including the project description, environmental setting, environmental impacts, alternatives, and mitigation measures. The following are some tips for ensuring that an EIR meets these requirements:

- **Make sure all required contents are included**—For a CEQA document to be adequate, it must include all of elements required by CEQA and the CEQA Guidelines.
- **Develop a clear, concise, and stable project description including a statement of project objectives**—An adequate project description is essential to preparing an adequate EIR.
- **Evaluate direct, indirect, growth-inducing, and cumulative impacts that are reasonably foreseeable**—Agencies must evaluate all "reasonably foreseeable" impacts, but need not engage in speculation or the analysis of worst-case scenarios.
- **Use the correct baseline for impact analysis**—The normal baseline for determining the impact of the proposed project's "existing conditions"; use of alternative baselines must be justified and carefully explained.
- **Identify the "significance" of each impact**—An EIR must identify the "significance" of each impact and explain why it is or is not significant.
- **Include and evaluate a reasonable range of alternatives**—Alternatives should be screened and either included in the EIR or eliminated based three main factors: meeting project objectives, avoiding impacts, and feasibility.
- **Don't overlook the "no-project" alternative**—The no-project alternative and its impacts serve as important reference for comparison. Keep in mind that in most situations, the no-project alternative is not the baseline for analysis.
- **Develop adequate and feasible mitigation measures**—An EIR must identify adequate and feasible measures to avoid, minimize, rectify, reduce, or compensate for each significant impact. If there are no feasible measures, explain why.

Chapter 7

EIR Preparation: Contents

Overall Purposes and Requirements for a Draft EIR

Since CEQA's inception, the EIR has been known as the "heart of CEQA" (*County of Inyo v. Yorty* (1973) 32 Cal. App. 3d 795). When a project may have significant effects, the EIR fulfills the central role in the CEQA process—objectively disclosing environmental effects and ways to reduce or avoid them. "Its purpose is to inform the public and its responsible officials of the environmental consequences of their decisions before they are made. Thus, the EIR 'protects not only the environment but also informed self government'" (*Citizens of Goleta Valley v. Board of Supervisors* (1990) 52 Cal. 3d 553).

This chapter discusses the content requirements of a draft EIR, focusing on the project description, environmental setting, environmental impacts, alternatives, mitigation measures, and monitoring. (Except for discussion of alternatives, these topics and the guidance related to EIR content should also be applied to the content of the initial study supporting the ND or MND.) CEQA requires that a draft EIR include a table of contents or index, a summary (including areas of known controversy), a description of the project, environmental setting, significant environmental impacts, alternatives, and mitigation measures. Draft EIRs for certain projects must also present the significant irreversible changes (for EIRs on plans, policies, ordinances, LAFCO actions, and joint NEPA documents) associated with the project, organizations and persons consulted, and the list of preparers of the draft EIR.

Required Contents of a Draft EIR

- Table of contents or index
- Summary of discussion contained in the draft EIR
- Project description
- Environmental setting
- Presentation of the significant environmental effects of the project (including direct, indirect, short-term, long-term, cumulative, and unavoidable impacts)
- Areas of known controversy
- Alternatives to the proposed project, including the no-project alternative and identification of the environmentally superior alternative
- Mitigation measures for significant environmental effects
- Growth-inducing impacts
- Expected significant irreversible changes due to the proposed project (required only for EIRs on plans, policies, ordinances, LAFCO actions, and EIR/EISs)

General Rules

Format and Scope of a Draft EIR

CEQA requires that each lead agency develop a standard format for EIR preparation, whenever feasible (Pub. Res. Code § 21100(a)). Regardless of the format used by an agency, every EIR must include all the required contents set forth in CEQA and the Guidelines (Pub. Res. Code § 21100; Guidelines §§ 15084(a),

Public access to environmentally important areas have both positive and adverse impacts on the environment.

15120, 15160). An EIR should be organized to best fit the decision-making process for which it is prepared.

Style and Page Limits

An EIR must be written in plain language that is easily understandable by decisionmakers and the public. Highly technical data should be summarized in the EIR, and the technical study itself should be placed in an appendix. The use of graphics, maps, and diagrams is also particularly helpful in making an EIR more readable.

According to CEQA Guidelines, an EIR should be no longer than 150 pages for a normal project and no longer than 300 pages for an unusually complex project (Guidelines §§ 15140, 15141, 15147). In practice, however, many EIRs exceed these page limits because of the need to ensure that the documents adequately cover all significant issues and contain the adequate supporting data to equate to substantial evidence. Because there are no page limits for the appendices to an EIR, these documents can create many additional volumes of material as part of the EIR.

Emphasis

An EIR should focus on the project's *significant* environmental effects. Discussions should be proportional to the severity and probability of these effects. Further, EIRs should be analytic rather than encyclopedic and should avoid long discussions of the environmental setting when they are not necessary to the impact evaluation (Guidelines §§ 15006(o), 15143). The lead agency may limit discussion of other (nonsignificant) effects to a brief explanation of why those effects are not potentially significant (Pub. Res. Code § 21002).1. In practice, however, many lead agencies include presentation of complete analyses of the full range of environmental resources, even if the EIR determines the effects of the action to be less than significant. The fear of litigation often causes lead agencies to prepare EIRs that go beyond the minimum legal requirement for analysis of environmental effects.

Forecasting and Speculation

An agency must use its best efforts to predict the reasonably foreseeable environmental impacts that could occur with project implementation. However, an EIR need not speculate on impacts that are not foreseeable. After thorough investigation, if it finds that an impact is too speculative to evaluate, an agency should note this conclusion and proceed. The distinction between foreseeable prediction and mere speculation is discussed further under "Indirect Impacts" on page 00 (Guidelines §§ 15144, 15145). CEQA does not require a "worst-case" analysis, but merely what is reasonably foreseeable.

Level of Specificity

The specificity required in an EIR should correspond to the specificity of the underlying activity being evaluated. For example, an EIR prepared for a development project is typically more specific than one prepared for a zoning ordinance or general plan (Guidelines § 15146.

Citations, Consultations, and List of Preparers

An EIR must cite all documents used in its preparation (Guidelines § 15148). The lead agency is required to make all documents cited in the EIR available for public review (Pub. Res. Code § 21092(b)). Lead agencies should take great care in managing the reference information cited in an EIR at the time of preparing the draft document. It is often difficult to retrace the steps of the document preparers after the fact, as the administrative record is prepared at the end of the EIR process (*see* Chapter 10 for more information on the administrative record).

The EIR must identify all federal, state, or local agencies; other organizations; and private individuals consulted in preparation of the document. The EIR is required to identify the persons, firm, or agency that actually prepared it, by contract or other authorization (Guidelines § 15129).

Incorporation by Reference

An EIR may incorporate portions or all of any publicly available document, including, but not limited to, EIRs prepared for other projects. The EIR should explicitly state that the lead agency is utilizing the incorporation by reference tool. The relevant portions of the incorporated document must be summarized or described briefly, its relationship to the EIR must be summarized, and the EIR must state where the document is available for public inspection (Guidelines § 15150). When a lead agency relies on tiering, the information from the first-tier EIR is generally incorporated by reference in the subsequent tier documents (Guidelines § 15152).

Practice Tip: Incorporation by Reference

Simply stating that a document is incorporated by reference is not sufficient. Be sure to include a summary of the document being incorporated. The summary should highlight the conclusions or discussions pertinent to the project at hand.

Restrictions on Disclosure of Certain Information

Although an EIR is a disclosure document, some information may be is subject to disclosure restrictions (Guidelines § 15120(d)). Specifically, an EIR (or any other document prepared under CEQA) should exclude from the public review version of the document any of the following:

- "Trade secrets" (as defined by Govt. Code § 6254.7)
- Information about the specific location of archaeological sites or sacred lands
- Any other information not subject to public disclosure under the California Public Records Act

(Govt. Code § 6254).

This information, where relevant, still must be considered as part of the agency's administrative record in making the appropriate findings in the CEQA process.

The are currently no national security or homeland security exceptions to what must be disclosed in an EIR. Thus, agencies may not rely on these concepts to avoid disclosing information about a project's description, location, or impacts.

Practice Tips: EIR Summaries

Practitioners should keep in mind that many reviewers of the EIR will not get beyond the summary. Or, they will rely on the summary to find those portions of the EIR and its conclusions that are of most interest to them. The summary should present its information clearly and concisely so that it is easy to reference. Tables identifying impacts and mitigation measures, as well as comparing the project alternatives, can help to organize the information presented.

When preparing an EIR, it can be helpful to prepare the summary last so that it accurately reflects the conclusions and mitigation measures identified in the rest of the EIR. Preparing the summary too early can result in preliminary draft results mistakenly carried over into the public draft.

The Draft EIR Project Description Should Include ...

- Project objectives
- Project location
  - Local map
  - Regional map
  - Identification of site boundaries
- Project characteristics
  - Project concept
  - Proposed buildings
  - Construction activities
  - Build-out assumptions
  - Conceptual drawings
  - Supporting public services
- Reasonably foreseeable future phases
- Required approvals or permits
- Agencies using the EIR

Table of Contents or Index

The EIR is required to contain at least a table of contents or an index to assist readers in finding particular resource analyses and issues (Guidelines § 15122). Most EIRs rely on a table of contents.

Summary

According to the CEQA Guidelines, the EIR's summary should be clear, concise, and normally no longer than fifteen pages. While this page limit may be impractical for complex projects, it represents the goal of making the summary a concise review of the findings and conclusions of the EIR. The summary must identify each significant effect; proposed mitigation measures; areas of known controversy, including issues raised by agencies and the public; and unresolved issues (Guidelines § 15123). For practical purposes, the summary should be written and formatted in a manner that will facilitate preparation of CEQA findings on significant impacts (*see* Chapter 8). The summary should specifically identify which impacts are significant, what specific mitigation measures have been recommended to reduce each significant impact, and whether each significant impact will be reduced to a less-than-significant level following mitigation. A matrix format is often useful for conveying this information.

Project Description

In General

The project description is one of the most important components of an EIR because it forms the basis for the remainder of the document. The courts have held that an inadequate project description may taint the entire EIR. The Guidelines require that the EIR's project description include a discussion of the project objectives. The project description must also include a discussion of project location, including presentation of a local and regional map and identification of site boundaries. When discussing project characteristics, the project description should include the project concept, proposed buildings and facilities, construction activities, build-out assumptions, conceptual drawings, supporting public services, and reasonably foreseeable future phases. Additionally, The project description must include a list of the required approvals for the project, including agencies using the EIR and required permits and the related environmental review and consultation requirements (Guidelines § 15124).

The project description is not required to supply extensive detail beyond that needed for evaluation and review of the environmental impacts (Guidelines § 15124(b)). Writing the project description is often considered one of the most challenging aspects of EIR preparation because lead agencies often begin the EIR process before having complete knowledge about a project and its characteristics. However, an accurate, complete, and stable project description is essential to preparing an adequate EIR. To avoid problems, the lead agency should write a detailed project description as early as possible (preferably before it distributes the notice of preparation) to enable technical environmental analysts and reviewing agencies to fully understand the project being evaluated or reviewed.

Statement of Objectives

The Guidelines require that the project description contain a clearly written statement of objectives, including the underlying fundamental purposes of the project (Guidelines § 15124(b)). The project's objectives are vital to understanding why the project is proposed. The statement of objectives is important in helping the lead agency select a reasonable range of alternatives to evaluate in the EIR and will aid the decisionmakers in preparing findings and a statement of overriding considerations, if necessary (*see* Chapter 8).

Project Location

The project description should include a discussion of the precise location and boundaries of the proposed project. This information should be presented on a detailed local map, preferably topographic. The location of the project site should also be presented on a regional map (Guidelines § 15124(a)). The environmental features of the project site and surrounding area should be discussed under the environmental setting section of the EIR (*see* discussion below).

Project Characteristics

The project description should include a narrative explaining the project concept and, if relevant, proposed buildings and facilities, construction activities, build-out activities and assumptions, diagrams and conceptual drawings, and proposed supporting public services (Guidelines § 15124(c)). The description of characteristics should discuss all actions necessary to achieve the project objectives, including the proposal for secondary support facilities.

Scope of Project

When an individual project is part of a larger project, the EIR project description and impact analysis must address the larger project (i.e., the "whole of the action"). An agency may not segment a larger project into pieces (i.e., "piecemeal" a project), thereby avoiding an analysis of the cumulative impacts of the larger project (Guidelines § 15165).

An EIR must describe and analyze "reasonably foreseeable future phases" of a project (except certain highway projects), if the larger project is a reasonably foreseeable consequence of the initial project and the future project will be significant because it will likely change the scope or nature of the initial project or its environmental effects. The discussion of "Project Segmenting" in Chapter 2 is also relevant to writing the project description in an EIR. The rule against project segmenting applies even if the lead agency has not yet formally approved the larger future project and it is impossible to predict precisely the future project's environmental effects, as long as these effects can be discussed generally (*Laurel Heights Improvement Association v. Regents of University of California* (1988) 47 Cal. 3d 376. For more information on project segmenting and tiering, *see* Chapter 3).

Practice Tip: Whose Project Objectives?

The statement of project objectives is supposed to represent those of the lead agency. Sometimes a private project applicant will have his or her own objectives that are not necessarily the same as the lead agency's. In these situations, the lead agency is under no obligation to use the proponent's objective as it own and should write the project objectives in such a way that explains the underlying need for the project from the standpoint of public need. The objectives should not apply to that applicant's project and it is the lead agency's objectives that form the basis for determining the appropriate range of alternatives to be analyzed in the EIR. For example, if a residential developer has the stated objective of "to build high-quality homes with views of the valley," the lead agency might want to frame the objective as "to provide housing opportunities for residents of the community consistent with the housing element of the city's general plan."

Approvals Required

The project description must describe how the lead and responsible agencies intend to use the EIR, and must include a list of the agencies that expect to use the EIR in their decisionmaking and a list of the approvals for which the EIR will be used. It must also include a list of the related environmental review and consultation needs required by federal, state, or local laws, regulations, or policies. To the fullest extent possible, the lead agency should integrate CEQA review with these requirements (Guidelines § 15124(d)). It is recommended that at the draft EIR stage, the presentation of required approvals include all potential permitting and consultation requirements for the proposed project and alternatives. The lead agency can use the review process of the draft EIR to finalize the list for the final EIR (*see* Chapter 9 for a discussion of the integration of CEQA with other requirements).

> **Practice Tip: Approval Requirements**
>
> Identifying the approvals that will be required helps the EIR preparers to identify the responsible agencies that must be consulted during the EIR review process. Preparers should consider the permit requirements of those other agencies when deciding on the scope of the EIR's impact analysis. This will assist in the integration of the other agency survey, impact analysis, and mitigation requirements into the EIR contents.

Environmental Setting and Baseline

The EIR is required to include a description of the physical environmental conditions in the vicinity of the project from both a local and regional perspective, as it exists at the time the NOP is published or, if no NOP is published, at the time the environmental analysis is commenced. This discussion should integrate an historic perspective if relevant. For example, the "setting" in a river riparian system during a drought would not fully represent the resources for an appropriate impact analysis unless accompanied by a description of the resources under more typical hydrologic counditions.

The environmental setting should be no longer than necessary to support an analysis of the significant environmental effects of the proposed project and its alternatives. Guidelines § 15125. If applicable, the EIR must include a statement indicating that the project is located on a toxic site listed by the California Environmental Protection Agency (Cal-EPA). Pub. Res. Code § 21092.6(a).

> **Practice Tip: Settings May Differ**
>
> Although the Guidelines refer to an environmental setting as if one rule should apply to all resource areas, in reality the various environmental issues discussed in the EIR can have different settings. For example, the air quality setting may be the regional air basin, while the water quality setting is a local watershed with different geographic boundaries. This is particularly true for cumulative impacts. Each impact section in the EIR should describe the environmental setting that forms the context for the analysis of that issue.

The environmental setting will normally constitute the baseline physical conditions by which a lead agency determines whether an impact is significant (*see* Chapter 3 for detailed discussion of baseline and Table 3-2). Actions considered new projects typically apply the existing conditions rule for determining baseline, even if previous illegal actions contributed to the current deteriorated condition (*see* for example, *Riverwatch v. County of San Diego* (1999) 76 Cal. App. 4th 1428; *Kenneth F. Fat v. County of Sacramento* (2002) 97 Cal App. 4th 1270). By implication, the Guidelines allow the lead agency to use a different baseline than that described above in "non-normal" circumstances. The lead agency should, however, explain its rationale for choosing a different baseline and must include substantial evidence to support its choice of baseline. For example, a baseline defined by average conditions or highest past use might be appropriate if existing conditions vary seasonally (*see* for example *Fairview Neighbors v. County of Ventura* (1999) to Cal. App. 4th 238).

The lead agency should tread cautiously when using a baseline that equates to a future condition that may be allowable under current permits but is not based on current activities. As the California Supreme Court stated in *Communities for a Better Environment v. South Coast Air Quality Management District* (2010) 48

Cal. App. 4th 310, an approach using hypothetical allowable conditions as the baseline results in 'illusory' comparisons that 'can only mislead the public as to the reality of the impacts and subvert full consideration of the actual environmental impacts,' a result at direct odds with CEQA's intent (*citations omitted*)." In the same case, the California Supreme Court acknowledged however that "neither CEQA nor the CEQA Guidelines mandates a uniform, inflexible rule for determination of the existing conditions baseline. Rather an agency enjoys the discretion to decide, in the first instance, exactly how the existing physical conditions without the project can most realistically be measured, subject to review . . . for support by substantial evidence."

If a project constitutes a *modification* to a previously approved (but not yet built) project that was subject to CEQA analysis (either by EIR or Neg Dec), then the baseline may be adjusted to assume that the originally approved project currently exists. For example, in *Temecula Band of Luiseño Mission Indians v. Rancho California Water District* (1996) 43 Cal. App. 4th 425, Supplemental EIR to measure incremental effects of a pipeline realignment project was upheld realignment was considered a modification of the previously approved pipeline project, which was included as part of the baseline conditions (*see* also *Benton v. Board of Supervisors* (1991) 226 Cal. App. 3d 1467)

Regional Setting and Planning Context

Knowledge of the regional setting is critical to the assessment of environmental impacts. Special emphasis should be placed on resources that are rare or unique to that region. The EIR must demonstrate that the project's significant effects were adequately investigated and discussed and must permit the significant effects to be considered in the full environmental context (Guidelines § 15125(c)).

The EIR must identify the policy and planning context in which the project is proposed. Specifically, it must discuss any inconsistencies between the proposed project and any applicable general plans and regional plans. When a proposed project is compared with an adopted plan, the analysis must examine the impacts on the existing physical conditions at the time the notice of preparation is published rather than the possible future conditions of plan buildout (Guidelines § 15125(e)). When preparing an EIR for a plan for the reuse of a military base, special rules apply with regard to the baseline (*see* Guidelines § 15229).

In practice, one of the most common criticisms of the CEQA process is the inclusion of voluminous and unnecessary background data in the section of an EIR dealing with the environmental setting. The Guidelines state that the EIR should include only enough setting information necessary to provide a meaningful context for the discussions of environmental impacts, alternatives, and mitigation measures, and lead agencies should minimize the settings discussion to only the relevant information (Guidelines § 15125). Highly detailed and technical background reports should be summarized in the setting and included—in full—in technical appendices. To ensure a proper balance between setting and impact evaluation, some EIR preparers recommend writing the

Environmental Setting

Failure to adequately describe the environmental setting can result in an inadequate impact analysis, a confusing analysis and, ultimately, the invalidation of the EIR by a court. In *Cadiz Land Company v. Rail Cycle, LP, et al* (2000) 83 Cal. App. 4th 74, the court held inadequate the County of San Bernardino's EIR for a proposed landfill in the Mojave Desert. The court found that the EIR failed to include a detailed description of the large groundwater aquifer beneath the project site. Without a detailed description of the extent of the aquifer, the EIR could not properly assess the significance of the landfill's impacts on groundwater or the extent of mitigation needed. In the *Save Our Peninsula Committee v. Monterey County Board of Supervisors* (2008) 87 Cal App. 4th 99, failure to describe the existing level of water use under normal conditions (the applicant had been extracting unusually large amounts of water during well testing) led to an inadequate analysis of project impacts.

For updated material on this topic, please see the 2013 Addendum at www.solano.com

impact section first and then writing the setting section to match the evaluation of impacts.

The rules and practices described for defining the environmental setting should be applied to the preparation of initial studies and negative declarations as well as to EIRs.

Significant Irreversible Changes

Uses of nonrenewable resources during the initial and continued phases of the project may be irreversible since a large commitment of such resources makes removal or nonuse thereafter unlikely. Therefore, for EIRs on plans, policies, ordinances, LAFCO actions, and joint NEPA documents, the EIR must analyze and justify the extent to which the proposed project will commit nonrenewable resources to uses that future generations will probably be unable to reverse (e.g.,construction of access to previously inaccessible areas or use of nonrenewable fuel resources for construction). The focus should be on both primary and, particularly, secondary impacts that generally commit future generations to similar uses and on the irreversible damage that could result from environmental accidents associated with the project (Pub. Res. Code § 21100(a); Guidelines §§ 15126(c), 15126.2(c), 15127).

Environmental Impacts

General

An EIR must identify and focus on the potentially significant environmental effects of all phases of the proposed project, including planning, acquisition, development, operation, and maintenance of the proposed project (Guidelines § 15126). In assessing the impacts of a proposed project, the lead agency should limit its examination to changes in the existing physical conditions (i.e., baseline) in the affected area as they exist at the time the NOP is published (Guidelines § 15126.2).

The impact of the proposed project must be clearly identified and described, giving due attention to both short-term and long-term effects. The EIR must present all direct and reasonably foreseeable indirect effects, although the EIR does not necessarily need to categorize an impact as "direct" or "indirect." The discussion should include, but not be limited to, relevant specifics of the area; the resources involved; physical alterations to ecological systems, changes induced in population distribution and concentration; the human use of the land, health, and safety problems caused by physical changes; and aspects of the resource base such as water, historic resources, scenic quality, and public services.

The specific issues evaluated in an EIR will vary from project to project, depending on the nature of the project and its location. Thus, a lead agency should utilize the scoping process to determine which impacts must be evaluated in an EIR. Additionally, an EIR should include a discussion of any environmental impacts determined to be "significant" or "potentially significant" on the initial study checklist found in Appendix G, or similar checklist developed by the lead agency.

Identifying Impact Significance

- **Less Than Significant**—the environmental effect of the proposed project does not reach the threshold of significance
- **Less Than Significant with Mitigation Incorporate**—the environmental effect of the proposed project reaches the threshold of significance, but feasible mitigation measures are available to reduce the impact to a less-than-significant level
- **Significant and Unavoidable**—the environmental effect of the proposed project reaches the threshold of significance, but no feasible mitigation is available to reduce the impact to a less than significant level
- **Beneficial**—the environmental effect of the proposed project will improve the environment regardless of the threshold of significance

An EIR should also analyze any significant environmental effects the project might cause by bringing development and people into the area affected (Guidelines § 15126.2(a)). For example, an EIR on a subdivision astride an active earthquake fault should identify as a significant effect the seismic hazard to future occupants of the subdivision. The subdivision would have the effect of attracting people to the location and exposing them to the hazards found there (Guidelines § 15126.2(a). See, however, *Baird v. County of Contra Costa* (1995) 32 Cal App. 4th 1464 and *South Orange County Wastewater Authority v. City of Dana Point* (2011) 196 Cal. App. 4th 1604 and *Ballona Wetlands Trust v. City of Los Angeles* (2011) 201 Cal. App. 4th 656 for the proposition that a project is only responsible for analyzing a project impact on the environment and not the existing environment's impact on a project.

Significance Determination

An EIR must identify the significance of each impact. In general, the EIR should define the threshold of significance for each impact and explain the criteria used to judge whether an impact is above or below that threshold (Guidelines § 15064(f)) (*see* Figure 7-1). As stated previously, determining whether a project may have a significant effect on the environment should be based on scientific and factual data; however, an ironclad definition of "significant effect" is not possible because the significance of an activity may vary with the setting (Guidelines § 15064(b)).

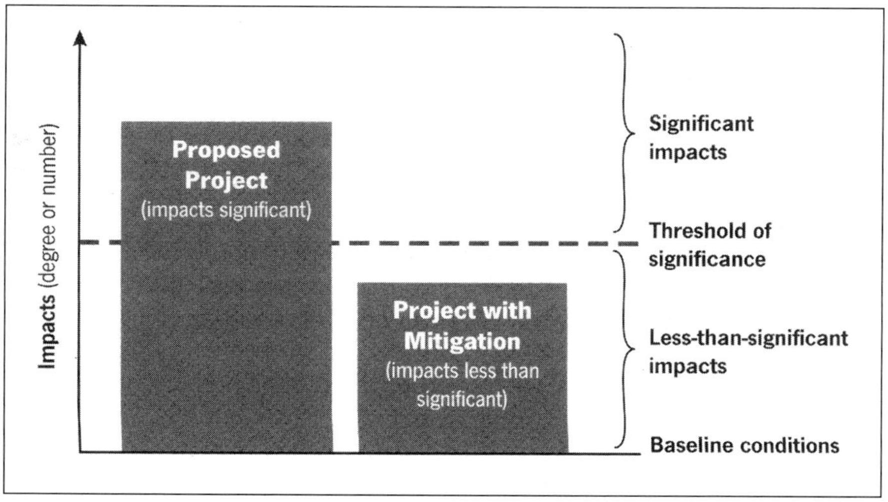

Figure 7-1
Determining the Significance of Impacts

Identifying Impacts of Significance: Avoid Unclear Modifiers

In preparing the impact analysis, the lead agency should avoid using unclear terminology that may confuse the reader. Using modifiers such as "somewhat," "potentially," "very," "major," "minor," or "partially" for impacts does not provide sufficient information as to whether the lead agency determines the impact to be significant. For example, an impact should not be described as "potentially significant" because the reader is not given a clear indication on the lead agency's conclusion. Instead, the lead agency should state that the impact is significant because of the potential for it to occur.

Determining Thresholds of Significance. The tools used to make significance determinations for an EIR are the same as those available to the lead agency during preparation of an initial study to determine if possibility exists of a significant effect on the environment. Guidance includes CEQA's Mandatory Findings of Significance, Appendix G of the Guidelines (the model initial study checklist), Agency Regulatory Standards, consultation with other agencies, and the lead agency's specific thresholds of significance (*see* Chapter 3, Determining Whether Effects Are Potentially Significant.

> **California Supreme Court Rules on When EIR Should Include Foreseeable Future Actions: *Laurel Heights Improvement Association of San Francisco v. Regents of the University of California* (1988) 47 Cal 3d 376**
>
> In 1988, the California Supreme Court aided CEQA practitioners in determining the scope of an EIR through its ruling on the adequacy of the University of California's EIR prepared for the expansion of the School of Pharmacy's biomedical research operations and the creation of a new research facility in a residential and commercial area of San Francisco. A citizens association brought suit to set aside the Regents of the University of California's decision to certify the EIR for the research facility.
>
> The University prepared an EIR for the initial research operations, set in 100,000 square feet of a 354,000-square-foot building. Although there was potential that the University would expand into the remainder of the building in the next five years, the University's EIR did not consider the expansion because no formal proposal had been approved.
>
> The State Supreme Court held the EIR inadequate for not including the assessment of the full use of the research facility. The court rejected the argument that an EIR need not analyze future actions that were not yet formally approved. The court stated that evidence in the record indicated the University's ultimate plans to expand into the entire research facility. Because the expansion was reasonably foreseeable and was likely to change the scope of the proposed project's environmental effects, the EIR should have disclosed the environmental effects that were likely to result from this expansion.

Lead agencies may use the relationship of the environmental effect of the proposed project to an established regulatory or legislative standard to assess the significance of the environmental effect. However, if a conflict exists between standards, or if substantial evidence in the record indicates that the standard is inappropriate, the EIR should explain why one is used rather than another.

Disagreement among Experts. When experts disagree on impact significance in an EIR, the lead agency need only summarize the main points of disagreement and explain its choice of expert opinions (Guidelines §§ 15064(f)(7), 15151). This explanation needs to be based on substantial evidence in the record. Disagreement among experts concerning the significance of a proposed project's environmental effect does not require the lead agency to follow the evidence concluding an impact is significant nor will a disagreement among experts make an EIR inadequate, so long as the disagreement is explained (CEQA Guidelines Section 15151). This is in contrast to the "fair argument" test used when a lead agency is deciding whether to prepare an EIR or a negative declaration.

Presentation of Impact Significance. In describing the significance of impacts, the lead agency should identify whether the impacts are "less than significant" (where the environmental effect of the proposed project does not reach the threshold of significance); "less than significant with mitigation incorporated" (where the environmental effect of the proposed project reaches the threshold of significance, but feasible mitigation measures are available to reduce the impact to a less-than-significant level); "significant and unavoidable" (where the environmental effect of the proposed project reaches the threshold of significance, but no feasible mitigation is available to reduce the impact to a less-than-significant level); or "beneficial" (where the environmental effect of the proposed project will improve the environment regardless of the threshold of significance) (Guidelines §§ 15126, 15126.2). It is not advisable for the lead agency to label an impact should not be described as "potentially significant" because the reader is not given a clear indication on the lead agency's conclusion. Instead, the lead agency should state that the impact is significant because of the potential for it to occur.

When unavoidable impacts would result from the project, the EIR should explain their implications and the reasons why the project is being proposed notwithstanding these impacts (Guidelines § 15126.2(b)). As discussed in Chapter 8, this determines if the project will still be approved with a statement of overriding considerations.

Types of Impacts

CEQA requires the lead agency to evaluate the environmental effect of a proposed project, considering the direct physical change in the environment as well as the reasonably foreseeable indirect physical changes in the environment that may be caused by the project. However, CEQA does not necessarily require that an EIR (or initial study) differentiate between direct and indirect impacts, as long as they are all addressed in the EIR or initial study (Guidelines §§ 15064(d), 15126.2(a)).

Types of Impacts to Be Included in an EIR

- Direct
- Reasonably Foreseeable Indirect
- Cumulative
- Short-Term
- Long-Term
- Social and Economic with Resulting Physical Effects

Direct Impacts. Direct impacts, also referred to as primary effects, are those caused by the project and occur at the same time and place (Guidelines § 15358). For example, a *direct effect* would be the ground-disturbing activities that occur when a project site is graded and otherwise prepared for construction of the project.

Indirect Impacts. Indirect impacts, also referred to as secondary effects, are those caused by a project that may occur either later in time or at some distance from the project site but that are still reasonably foreseeable (Guidelines § 15358). These impacts may not be immediately related to the project but which are caused individually. For example, *indirect effects* would be the air, noise, and traffic impacts eventually resulting from the occupation of a proposed housing project. An indirect effect need only be considered if it is a reasonably foreseeable impact that may be caused by the project. Speculative impacts are not reasonably foreseeable and should not be considered (Guidelines § 15064(d)(3)).

Impact of the Environment on Projects

In some circumstances, the impacts of the environment on a proposed project are important concerns to the lead agency and the public. For example, a proposed project could expose the future structures and residents to risks of earthquakes floods, landslides, wildfires, or other natural hazards. For decades, these types of hazards have been routinely evaluated as indirect impacts of projects. Then in 1995, in the case of *Baird v. Contra Costa County* (1995) 32 Cal. App.4th 1464, an appellate court held that the risk of exposing future residents of a project to pre-existing toxic contamination was not an environmental impact under CEQA and did not, therefore, trigger the need to prepare an EIR. According to the court, "to require an EIR in the present context, where the proposed project is challenged on the basis of preexisting environmental conditions rather than an adverse change in the environment, would impose a requirement beyond those stated in CEQA or its guidelines, and is thus prohibited." Despite the court's holding, most CEQA practitioners considered the Baird decision to be an anomaly based on the unique facts of case and it was generally ignored.

In fact, in response to that decision, the Resource Agency amended section 15126.2(a) of the state CEQA Guidelines to specifically clarify CEQA's application in light of the holding. That section provides, in part, that:

> . . . The EIR shall also analyze any significant environmental effects a project might cause by bringing development and people into the area. For example, an EIR on a subdivision astride an active fault line should identify as a significant effect the seismic hazard to future occupants of the subdivision. The subdivision would have the effect of attracting people to the location and exposing them to the hazards found there. Similarly, the EIR should evaluate any potential significant impacts of locating development

Growth-Inducing Impacts of Public Facilities

Growth-Inducing Impacts of Public Facilities. Growth-inducing impacts continue to be one of the most misunderstood and misapplied requirements of CEQA, despite the relatively clear language in the CEQA Guidelines. It is especially troublesome to agencies responsible for proposing and carrying out infrastructure projects. Some agencies avoid discussing growth-inducing impacts for fear that their projects will somehow become publicly tainted or branded in an unfavorable light. Similarly, some agencies use the phrase "growth accommodating" rather than "growth-inducing" to avoid such stigma. However, the CEQA Guidelines attempt to avoid this problem by declaring the "neutrality" of induced growth:

> It must not be assumed that growth in any areas is necessarily beneficial, detrimental or of little significance to the environment.

Section 15126.2(d) of the CEQA Guidelines requires an EIR to:

> ...discuss the ways in which a proposed project would foster economic or population growth, or the construction of additional housing, either directly or indirectly, in the surrounding environment. Included in this are projects, which would remove obstacles to population growth.

That section also requires an EIR to:

> ...discuss the characteristics of a project which may encourage and facilitate other activities that could significantly affect the environment, either individually or cumulatively.

The guidelines use the example of a major expansion of a waste water treatment plant, however, the concept would apply equally to the expansion of most types of public facilities, including transportation and water projects.

In view of the language in the Guidelines, there is little doubt that most public facilities and infrastructure projects have some potential for inducing future economic growth. The question whether growth would, in fact, be induced by a particular project, and the extent (e.g., "significance") of that growth, would depend on the specific facts and circumstances. For example, if a proposed public facility was sized exactly to alleviate an existing problem and no more, induced growth may be minimal. On the other hand, if a project is "oversized" to allow for future capacity, then the induced growth may be quite significant.

Applying the above principles to a proposed bridge replacement, such a project would certainly have the potential to be growth inducing. In fact, the objectives of a bridge enlargement project might include both alleviating current bottlenecks in traffic and anticipating the growth of future transportation activities. With regard to this latter objective, the existing bridge could be viewed as an "obstacle to growth," so replacement with a larger, more modern bridge, would "remove" that obstacle. Thus, the future increases in traffic on the bridge would, in part, represent induced growth. As far as the specific nature, extent, and "significance" of such induced growth, the lead agency would first have to conduct the necessary technical studies to quantify existing, proposed, and future scenarios regarding bridge capacity.

---

in other areas susceptible to hazardous conditions (e.g. floodplains, coastlines, wildfire risk areas) as identified in authoritative hazard maps, risk assessments or in land use plans addressing such hazard areas.

The amended guidelines also added several questions to the Initial Study Checklist (Appendix G) that addressed environmental hazards. These regulatory changes bolstered the common practice of evaluating environmental hazards in CEQA documents.

In 2011, however, two additional court decisions concurred with the Baird reasoning and raise the issue of whether CEQA contains a specific requirement to evaluate impacts of the environment on the project. In *South Orange County Wastewater Authority v. City of Dana Point* (2011) 196 Cal. App. 4th 1604, the court held that pre-existing noise and odor impacts from a waste treatment plant on people living in nearby future land developments were not issues contemplated by CEQA. In reaching its decision, the court concluded that the language in Guidelines section 15126.2 is inconsistent with the CEQA statute. The court noted rather dismissively that: "The Legislature did not enact CEQA to protect people from the environment. Other statutes, ordinances, and regulations fulfill that function. [citations]"

Another court reached the same conclusion in *Ballona Wetlands Trust v City of Los Angeles* (2011) 201 Cal. App. 4th 656. In that decision, which dealt with the adequacy of an EIR, the court held that the future impacts from sea level rise were not required to be evaluated under CEQA. The court offered the following statements about the necessity to consider the environment's impacts on a project:

- "the purpose of an EIR is to identify the significant effects of a project on the environment, not the significant effects of the environment on the project";
- "Identifying the effects on the project and its users of locating the project in a particular environmental setting is neither consistent with CEQA's legislative purpose nor required by the CEQA statutes"; and
- "Although the Guidelines ordinarily are entitled to great weight, a Guidelines provision that is unauthorized under CEQA is invalid."

The *Ballona* court then went a step further, not only opining that a portion of Section 15126.2 reaches beyond CEQA's intent, but that the Initial Study questions in Appendix G of the Guidelines dealing with existing hazards are also invalid.

Based on these two decisions as well as the Baird case, the Guidelines' requirement to evaluate the impacts of the environment on a project appears to be questionable. This has two important ramifications for CEQA practice: 1) any impacts of the environment on a project, by themselves, would not trigger an EIR, and 2) when an agency prepares an EIR, it generally would not have to evaluate the impacts of the environment on the project. One exception to this latter rule is when the project would exacerbate the existing environmental risk. For example, if a housing development on a steep hillside involved excavation that would increase the likelihood of landslides, then the risk of future landslides that could be caused by the project should be evaluated in the EIR. Similarly, if locating a residential development within a high wildfire hazard area would increase the risk of wildfire, then the impact on wildfire risk should be evaluated. A second exception is the effects of greenhouse gases on a project, as required by Public Resources Code Section 21083.05. The Ballona decision did not consider this CEQA provision, despite the link between sea level rise and climate change resulting from greenhouse gas emissions.

CEQA may require an agency to consider how growth may encroach upon preservation areas.

Although an agency is not required to evaluate impacts of the environment on a project, no court has prohibited an agency from examining such impacts as optional studies. Thus, if an agency wants to evaluate various impacts of the environment on a project, such as dam failure, tsunami run-up or wild fire, it may do so. When this is done, however, the agency would not be required to identify the significance of those impacts, identify mitigation measures for them, and adopt findings for those impacts when it approves a project.

For updated material on this topic, please see the 2013 Addendum at www.solano.com

Short- and Long-Term Impacts. Short-term impacts are those of a limited duration, such as the impacts that would typically occur during the construction of a project. Long-term impacts are those of greater duration, including those that would endure for the life of a project and beyond. The Guidelines do not provide a specific definition for dividing duration between short- and long-term impacts. No matter how they are characterized, these impacts should be analyzed in the EIR. Effects may be significant even though they are short-term. Similarly, effects that occur during construction of a project may be significant even though they will terminate when construction is completed. Thus, for example, impacts from truck traffic, equipment noise, and air emissions that occur during construction must be evaluated in an EIR—even if they are of limited duration.

A Project Would Result in Growth-Inducing Impacts if it . . .

- Fosters economic or population growth or additional housing
- Removes obstacles to growth
- Taxes community services or facilities to such an extent that new services or facilities would be necessary
- Encourages or facilitates other activities that cause significant environmental effects

Growth-Inducing Impacts

The EIR must discuss how the proposed project, if implemented, could induce growth where it is reasonably foreseeable to occur. Although identified separately from indirect effects, growth inducement should be characterized as a type of secondary, or indirect, project impact. A project may be growth-inducing if it directly or indirectly fosters economic or population growth or the construction of additional housing, removes obstacles to population growth, taxes community service facilities to the extent that the construction of new facilities would be necessary, or encourages or facilitates other activities that cause significant environmental effects. A project EIR need not evaluate general growth within a community if that growth is not caused, in part, by the project being evaluated (Guidelines § 15126.2(d)).

In practice, the evaluation of growth-inducing impacts is often treated in a far too cursory manner. Although the Guidelines do not specify any particular level of analysis, to ensure adequate treatment of such impacts, a lead agency should consider the following approach:

- Describe how the project might induce growth
- Estimate the amount, location, and timeframe of growth that could occur as a result of the project
- Determine the possible environmental effects from growth
- Determine the significance of these impacts and mitigation measures to reduce significant impacts to a less-than-significant level

The best time to evaluate growth-inducing impacts is in a first-tier EIR, such as a program EIR or master EIR prepared for plans, programs, policies, or ordinances. If the impacts of future growth are adequately evaluated in a first-tier document, then second-tier, or focused, EIRs on specific projects may be able to incorporate the prior discussions by reference, thereby avoiding repetitive analysis.

Some agencies avoid use of the term "growth inducing" because it has a negative connotation, substituting instead the phrase "growth accommodating." Although the impacts of induced growth clearly must be discussed in an EIR, the Guidelines also indicate that growth should not be assumed either beneficial or detrimental (Guidelines § 15126.2(d)). Agencies should therefore spend less time worrying about the terminology and devote greater effort to ensuring that the impacts of induced growth are properly evaluated.

List past, present, and "reasonably foreseeable" future projects producing related impacts, including those outside the control of the Lead Agency

Factors to consider

- **Location of other projects**
- **Jurisdiction of other projects**
- **Types of other projects**
- **Size of other projects**

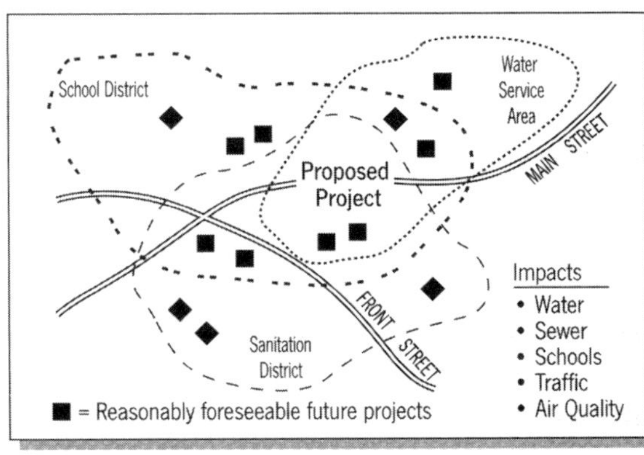

Figure 7-2 Cumulative Impacts: List Approach

Cumulative Impacts

Cumulative impacts refer to two or more individual impacts that, when considered together, are significant or that compound or increase significant environmental impacts. The cumulative impact of several projects is the change in the environment that results from the incremental impact of the project when added to other, closely related past, present, or reasonably foreseeable probable future projects. Cumulative impacts can result from individually minor but collectively significant projects taking place over a period of time (Guidelines § 15355).

An EIR must discuss the cumulative impacts to which a project would contribute and determine whether the project's incremental contribution to that effect is cumulatively considerable (*see* Chapter 3.) When a lead agency is examining a project with an incremental effect that is not "cumulatively considerable," the agency need not consider that effect significant, but must briefly describe its basis for concluding that the incremental effect is not cumulatively considerable (Guidelines §§ 15064(i), 15130(a)). Simply because the project may result in a small impact, or its individual impact is insignificant, does not mean that the project does not make a considerable contribution to a cumulative effect. As a cumulative impact becomes more acute, small individual contributions may be cumulatively considerable. Therefore, even a "de minimis" contribution may be considerable under the right circumstances (*Communities for a Better Environment, et al. v. California Resources Agency* (2002) 103 Cal. App. 4th 98). Accordingly, EIR preparers should avoid using a ratio approach (i.e., the project contributes only one percent of the overall impact and is therefore not a considerable contribution to the cumulative impact) to determining whether a project's contribution is considerable (*Communities for a Better Environment, et al. v. California Resources Agency* (2002) 103 Cal. App. 4th 98).

An EIR may determine that a project's contribution of a significant cumulative impact will be offset so as not to be "cumulatively considerable," or that the larger significant cumulative impact can be mitigated to a less-than-significant level and thus is not significant. For example, a project's contribution is not cumulatively considerable where the project is required to implement or fund its fair share of mitigation measures designed to alleviate the cumulative impact (Guidelines §§ 15130(a)(1), (2), (3)). This may include, for example, traffic impact fees that are part of "a reasonable plan for mitigation" that is tied "to the actual mitigation of the impacts of increased traffic" (*Save Our Peninsula Committee v. Monterey County Board of Supervisors* (2001) 87 Cal. App. 4th 99).

In contrast to the initial study stage of CEQA, at the EIR stage a lead agency must prepare a more detailed evaluation of cumulative impacts. The EIR must contain a reasonable analysis of the project's contribution in the context of the significant cumulative impacts. The EIR's cumulative impact analysis must identify related projects through a "list" or "projection" approach (or a combination of the two), summarize effects of the related projects, and reasonably analyze the cumulative contribution of the proposed project and recommend mitigation measures for that contribution (Guidelines § 15130(b)).

The discussion of cumulative impacts must reflect their severity and likelihood of occurring, but the discussion need not be as detailed as the discussion of

"Probable Future Projects" Should Include:

- Private projects requiring agency approval for an application that has been received at the time the NOP is released, unless a project has been abandoned by the applicant
- Public projects for which money has been budgeted or included in an adopted capital improvement program, general plan, regional transportation plan, or other similar plan
- Projects included in a summary of projects in a general plan or similar plan
- Projects anticipated as later phases of a previously approved project

An EIR Cumulative Impact Analysis Must . . .

- Identify the cumulative significant effect to which the project would contribute.
- Reasonably analyze the proposed project's contribution to the cumulative effect
- Identify other projects that contribute to that effect through a "list" or "projection" approach
- Identify mitigation measures for the project's contribution to the significant cumulative impact, including implementing or funding its fair share of mitigation measures designed to alleviate the cumulative impact
- Conclude whether the project's contribution is or is not "cumulatively considerable"

a project's direct effects. The discussion should focus on the cumulative impact to which the identified other projects contribute rather than the attributes of the other projects that do not contribute to the cumulative impact. For example if another project contributes only to the cumulative water supply problem, its impacts on air quality need not be discussed (Guidelines §§ 15064(i), 15130(b)).

In determining the significance of a cumulative impact, the lead agency's analysis should focus on whether the project's incremental contribution to cumulative impacts is considerable. As with growth-inducing impacts, the best time to evaluate cumulative impacts is in a first-tier EIR, such as a program EIR or master EIR prepared for plans, programs, policies, or ordinances; however, using the list or projection approach in an EIR may be appropriate if no first-tier analysis was performed or if the analysis does not include the proposed project within its assessment of projected cumulative impacts.

List Approach. Under the list approach, the lead agency must identify all past, present, and probable future projects that could contribute to a significant cumulative environmental impact. If necessary, these projects must include those that may be outside the lead agency's control (Guidelines 15130(b)).

When EIR preparers utilize the list approach, factors to consider in determining whether to include a related project include the nature of each environmental resource examined, the location of the project, and its type. Location may be important, for example, when water supply impacts are at issue since projects outside the watershed would probably not contribute to a cumulative effect. The type of project may be important, for example, when the impact is specialized, such as a particular air pollutant or mode of traffic (Guidelines § 15130(b)). When utilizing the list approach, the lead agency should define the geographic scope of the area affected by the cumulative effect, which will most likely vary by resource topic, and provide a reasonable explanation for the geographic limitation used (*see* Figure 7-2, page 146). The geographic scope would typically extend to the area in which the cumulative effect is reasonably foreseeable.

The list of probable future projects should include all of the following, as well as any other reasonably foreseeable future projects: an application that has been received at the time the NOP is released; public projects for which money has been budgeted or included in an adopted capital improvement program, general plan, regional transportation plan, or other similar plan; and projects from a summary of projects in a general plan or similar plan and those projects anticipated as later phases of a previously approved project.

In practice, when EIR preparers rely on the list approach to evaluate cumulative impacts, several practical issues are frequently encountered in developing adequate lists. First, EIR preparers should be aware that project lists may differ for each resource (water-type projects for effects related to fish may differ from traffic-type projects for effects related to traffic, air, and noise). The California Supreme Court, in *Ebbetts Pass Forest Watch v. California Department of Forestry and Fire Protection* (2008) 43 Cal. 4th 936, acknowledged that the area subject to cumulative impact analysis may differ from resource to resource. Although that decision dealt with CDF's certified regulatory program, the principles set forth in it are applicable to CEQA in general (*see also Environmental Protection and Information Center v. California Department of Forestry and Fire Protection* (2008) 44 Cal. 4th 459).

Second, EIR preparers must recognize that related-project lists are constantly changing. Although this may lead to frustration, minor changes in a list will not cause an EIR to be inadequate if the lead agency can demonstrate that a good-faith effort was made to address cumulative impacts. To enhance the adequacy of the EIR, an agency should clearly explain how it is evaluating the cumulative impacts of each subject and how it developed its related-project list.

Projection Approach. In lieu of using the list approach, a lead agency may base the cumulative impact analysis on a summary of projections contained in an adopted general plan or related planning document, or in a prior environmental document that has been adopted or certified (Pub. Res. Code § 21100(d)). In using this approach, the lead agency must be certain that the adopted plan actually described or evaluated regional or areawide conditions contributing to the cumulative impact (Guidelines § 15130(b)(1)). However, the projections approach may not adequately characterize the cumulative impact if there are proposals for major contributing projects that were not analyzed in the projections (*Bakersfield Citizens for Local Control v. City of Bakersfield* (2004) 124 Cal. App. 4th 1184). Therefore, most agencies may prefer to take a combined approach, utilizing the projections of a planning document with updated information from a list of additional projects to consider within the cumulative impacts analysis.

Evaluation of the Cumulative Effects—General Rules. Regardless of whether the lead agency uses the list approach or the projection approach, certain general rules apply to the evaluation of cumulative impacts. The analysis must include a summary of the expected environmental effects to be produced by those projects, with specific reference to additional information stating where that information is available. Additionally, the cumulative impact assessment must include a reasonable analysis of the relevant projects and must examine reasonable, feasible options for mitigating or avoiding the project's contribution to the cumulative impacts. With some projects, the only feasible mitigation for cumulative impacts may involve the adoption of ordinances or regulations rather than the imposition of conditions on a project-by-project basis (Guidelines §§ 15130(b)(2), (3)(c)).

Previously approved land use documents such as general plans, specific plans, and local coastal plans may be used in the cumulative impact analysis. A pertinent discussion of cumulative impacts contained in one or more previously certified EIRs may be incorporated by reference pursuant to the provisions for "tiering," master EIRs, and program EIRs. No further cumulative impacts analysis is required when a project is consistent with a general, specific, master, or comparable programmatic plan where the lead agency determines that the regional or areawide cumulative impacts of the project have already been adequately addressed in a certified EIR for that plan (Guidelines § 15130(d)).

Further, if a cumulative impact was adequately addressed in a prior EIR for a community plan, zoning action, or general plan, and the project is consistent with that plan or action, then an EIR for such a project should not further analyze that cumulative impact (Guidelines § 15130(e)). It must, however, document that the cumulative impact was previously addressed in the prior EIR and remains adequate for this later project.

CEQA vs. NEPA: Environmental Justice

Environmental justice—the consideration of whether a proposed action might result in a disproportionately high-adverse environmental impact on low-income or minority populations—is an issue of concern for projects subject to NEPA. Executive Order 12898, signed by President Clinton in 1994, requires federal agencies to consider environmental justice for federal projects that are subject to NEPA. CEQA, however, does not require the consideration of environmental justice. Rather than incorporating environmental justice into the environmental analysis process, California has chosen to address environmental justice by providing low-income and minority communities greater access to and information about environmental regulations. The Governor's Office of Planning and Research is the statewide coordinator for environmental justice efforts by state agencies. The 2003 edition of the General Plan Guidelines encourages cities and counties to consider environmental justice when preparing their general plans. CalEPA has adopted environmental justice policies for its component departments so that residents will be informed of and encouraged to participate in regulatory actions that could affect their neighborhood.

Although not required by CEQA, environmental justice would be required when a state or local agency prepares a joint document with a federal agency.

A more detailed discussion of the federal requirements for evaluating environmental justice is found in Chapter 9.

Economic and Social Effects

Effects analyzed under CEQA must be related to a physical change in the environment (Guidelines § 15358(b)). Economic and social effects are not considered environmental effects under CEQA unless they relate to physical changes. These effects need to be considered in EIRs only if they would lead to an environmental effect. For example, an EIR is required to analyze the economic effect on existing businesses from construction of a large shopping mall if the mall would result in "urban decay," as manifested in long-term vacancies and the physical deterioration of structures (*see*, for example, *Bakersfield Citizens for Local Control v. City of Bakersfield* (2004) 124 Cal. App. 4th 1184). When not related to a physical change in the environment, the evaluation of economic or social effects is generally treated as optional; agencies may, but are not required to, evaluate them, and sometimes do include an analysis of economic or social effects of the proposed project (Guidelines § 15131).

Environmental Justice

Environmental Justice–the consideration of whether a proposed action might result in a disproportionately high or adverse environmental impact on low-income or minority populations–is not required in CEQA documents. It is, however, an issue of concern for projects subject to the National Environmental Policy Act. Executive Order 12898, signed by President Clinton in 1994, and its implementing rules and regulations require federal agencies to consider environmental justice for federal projects that are subject to NEPA.

When a joint NEPA/CEQA document is prepared, it must evaluate environmental justice because of the NEPA requirements (*see* Chapter 9 for a discussion of joint documents). In addition, several state and local agencies (such as Cal EPA and the Port of Los Angeles) have proactively committed to addressing environmental justice issues within their CEQA processes.

Resource Topics and Impact Assessment Methodology

CEQA requires the lead agency to assess the possible effects on the "environment," which is defined as the "physical conditions which exist with the area ... and includes both natural and man-made conditions" (Guidelines § 15360). Although neither a specific mandate nor a limitation, lead agencies should start with the list of resource topics outlined in Appendix G as a guide in defining the physical environment for analysis in an EIR. For most environmental impacts that are included in an EIR, neither CEQA nor the CEQA guidelines prescribe any particular method by which impacts must be evaluated. On the contrary, the choice of methodology lies with the discretion of the lead agency. Thus, agencies are free to develop or utilize any methodology regarding assessment of the environmental effects of a proposed project. In deciding how to evaluate impacts, agencies must consider the facts and circumstances surrounding the specific project, including any requests received, during scoping, for using particular methods of analysis. So long as reasonable methods are utilized, the courts will typically defer to the judgment of the lead agency. Nor does CEQA require any particular qualifications of expertise for EIR preparation.

However, some lead agencies have adopted regulatory requirements or developed manuals setting forth how they will undertake environmental analysis for CEQA purposes. If an agency's regulations or manuals provide for a particular method of impact analysis, they must be followed. For example, in one case a county's general plan required traffic impact to be evaluated using a particular model. Instead, the county utilized a different traffic model and, when challenged, the court found the analysis of traffic inadequate (*Endangered Habitats League v. County of Orange* (2005) 131 Cal. App. 4th 777).

Additionally, some regulatory agencies have developed specific protocols for evaluating impacts in order to comply with other environmental laws and regulations. For example, both the federal and state Endangered Species Acts have detail protocols for conducting Biological Assessments. CEQA, on the other hand, does not require an EIR to use any particular protocols. Thus, lead agencies should comply with more specific protocols to achieve compliance both with other environmental law and CEQA, thereby avoiding duplication and delay.

CEQA generally requires agencies to use reasonable methods of analysis, not necessarily the best and latest methods. Thus, agencies (and their consultants) should be aware of the state-of-the art analysis tool in each respective impact area that might be included in EIRs and should be prepared to explain why they are not using them. For example, in a case dealing with a proposed airport expansion, the failure of the lead agency to use a new model for evaluating toxic air emissions developed by the state Air Resources Board led the court to declare the EIR inadequate. In that case, the lead agency ignored requests received during scoping to use the latest models and failed to explain why it was doing so (*Berkeley Keep Jets Over the Bay Committee v. Board of Port Commissioners* (2001) 91 Cal. App. 4th 1344).

Topics for Which CEQA Does Provide Guidance

CEQA does specifically provide guidance on the analysis of impacts for some resources, such as for impacts on agricultural land, archaeological and historic resources, public water systems, and related greenhouse gas emissions and climate change. CEQA also specifies analytical considerations for projects within airport planning areas and school-related facilities. These are discussed next.

Impacts on Agricultural Land

CEQA includes a policy statement that the conversion of agricultural lands to nonagricultural uses threatens the long-term health of the state's agricultural industry and that CEQA should play an important role in the preservation of

Practice Tip: Regional Information Centers

The State Office of Historic Preservation contracts with regional Information Centers that maintain lists of historical resources, including identified archaeological finds. Contact the pertinent Information Center to arrange for a records search when beginning the impact analysis for historic resources.

Local historical societies often have information about locally significant or locally listed resources, and can be a good source for that information.

agricultural land. Therefore, CEQA encourages agencies to make wise and efficient land use decisions by adopting and using the Land Evaluation and Site Assessment (LESA) criteria developed by the U.S. Natural Resources Conservation Service to implement the federal Farmland Protection Policy Act (Chapter 812, Statutes of 1993).

To assist lead agencies in accomplishing this objective, the California Department of Conservation has prepared a state version of LESA (Pub. Res. Code § 21095(b)). The state LESA system is intended to be modified by lead agencies and adopted as a decision-making methodology for assessing the potential environmental impact of state and local projects on agricultural land (Pub. Res. Code § 21061.2). The Department of Conservation developed the model system in 1997. However, lead agencies that lack the time or resources to modify the state model for their own use may want to use the federal LESA system, which is routinely used under NEPA, to evaluate the effects of projects on agricultural resources.

The LESA system requires agencies to systematically quantify and evaluate the effect of their activities on farmland. In addition to the traditional emphasis on soil classification, the LESA procedures require that agencies assign a numeric rating to a variety of other factors affecting the viability of agricultural operations that are threatened by nonagricultural land uses. Based on this valuation, the lead agency determines whether the conversion of the agricultural land is considered significant.

Historical Resources

In determining if there is a significant impact to an historic resource, there is a two-part test: (1) Is the resource "historically significant" and (2) Would the project cause a "substantial adverse change" in the significance of the resource? The term "historic resource" is given a broad definition with three categories of significance (Guidelines § 15064.5(a)). The California Office of Historic Preservation has prepared a guidebook, "CEQA and Historical Resources," which provides a detailed discussion of how CEQA relates to the protection of historic resources. It's available online at www.ohp.parks.ca.gov.

California Register of Historical Resources. An historic resource is deemed significant if it is a resource listed in—or determined to be eligible for listing in—the California Register of Historical Resources. An historic resource is eligible if it:

- Is associated with events that have made a significant contribution to the broad patterns of California's history and cultural heritage
- Is associated with the lives of persons important in our past
- Embodies the distinctive characteristics of a type, period, region, or method of construction, or represents the work of an important creative individual, or possesses high artistic value
- Has yielded, or may be likely to yield, information about prehistory or history

Historic resources on or eligible for inclusion in the National Register of Historic Places fall within this definition.

Practice Tip: Consultation with Tribes

The archaeologist working on the project may contact affected Native American tribes and individuals during the archaeological impact analysis to elicit their input. Names and contact information for tribal representatives can be obtained from the Native American Heritage Commission in Sacramento.

Locally Designated Historic Resources. Historic resources included in a local register of historical resources or identified as significant in an historical resource survey meeting certain requirements shall be presumed historically or culturally significant. Public agencies must treat such resources as significant unless a preponderance of the evidence demonstrates that they are not historically or culturally significant.

Other Historically Significant Resources. Any object, building, structure, site, area, place, record, or manuscript that a lead agency determines historically significant in the architectural, engineering, scientific, economic, agricultural, educational, social, political, military, or cultural annals of California may be considered an historic resource—even if not formally listed—provided the lead agency's determination is supported by substantial evidence in light of the whole record. The reports prepared by consulting historians or archeologists often contain the substantial evidence to support the significance of the resources.

Substantial adverse change to a significant historical resource is a significant effect under CEQA.

Substantial Adverse Changes to Historic Resources. A project with an effect that may cause a "substantial adverse change" in the significance of an historical resource is a project that may have a significant effect on the environment. "Substantial adverse change" means physical demolition, destruction, relocation, or alteration in the resource, such that the resource is "materially impaired." The significance of an historical resource is considered materially impaired when a project demolishes or materially alters the physical characteristics that justify the determination of its significance (Guidelines § 15064.5(b)).

Consultation with the State Historic Preservation Officer (SHPO) is only required for federal agencies in compliance with Section 106 of the National Historic Preservation Act not required by CEQA. SHPO consultation is not required for state or local agencies as a part of CEQA, except where the state lead agency proposes an action affecting state-owned historical resources. Consultation should be coordinated in a timely manner with the preparation of the environmental document (Guidelines § 15064.5(b)(5)).

Archaeological Resources

The rules relating to historic resources were adopted after those relating specifically to archeological resources, and they are defined broadly to include archeological resources. Although many practitioners use the rules related to historical resources to address archaeological resources, the archeological resource rules have not been repealed and must also be considered when such resources may be affected by a proposed project.

When a project will have an impact on an archaeological site, a lead agency must first determine whether the site falls within the definition of an historical resource as described above. If the archaeological site meets the definition of an historical resource, then it may be treated like any other historical resource.

If an archaeological site does not fall within the definition of an historical resource, but does meet the definition of a "unique archaeological resource" (Pub. Res. Code 21083.2), then the site may be treated in accordance with the

CA Supreme Court reviews CEQA's Water Supply Assessment Requirements: *Vineyard Area Citizens for Responsible Growth, Inc. v. City of Rancho Cordova* (2007) 40 Cal. 4th 412

Introduction and background. In *Vineyard Area Citizens for Responsible Growth, Inc. v. City of Rancho Cordova* (2007) 40 Cal. 4th 412, the California Supreme Court elucidated some of the most important principles regarding how agencies should evaluate water supply impacts for land development projects. The case involved an EIR for a large, 6,000-acre, master-planned community known as Sunrise-Douglas that would include more than 22,000 residential units and a future population of approximately 60,000 people. The project included both a *Community Plan* for the entire area, and a Specific Plan for the near-term development of 2,600 acres (9,886 residential units, as well as commercial development and public facilities).

Water Supply Analysis

Project demand. According to the EIR, the average water demand for the Specific Plan area at full build-out was estimated to be 8,539 acre-feet annually (afa). Demand in the remainder of the Community Plan Area was estimated at 13,564 afa with a total of about 22,564.

Short-term water supply. In evaluating short-term water supply, the EIR relied on both groundwater and surface water supplies. Initially, groundwater of approximately 5,527 afa would be provided from a newly developed well field estimated to have a safe yield of approximately 10,000 afa. The EIR further indicated that not all of the water in the well field would be available to this project, but that additional project water needs would later be met from surface water diverted from the American River provided by the Sacramento Court Water Agency. Well field water and river water would be provided to the project under a "conjunctive use" program with the well field providing more water in wet years and surface supplies predominating in dry years. The water agency has an existing contract with the federal Bureau of Reclamation for 15,000 afa for use in that geographic area.

Long-term water supply. In evaluating long-term water supply, the EIR relied to a great extent on a prior multi-agency water planning process known as the Water Forum. The Water Forum produced a long-term agreement and a Program EIR for providing up to 78,000 afa over a twenty-five- to thirty-year period. The Water Forum EIR, which included a variety of alternative programs, analyzed the impacts of the participants' planned increases in surface water diversions from the American River. Unfortunately, the Water Forum Agreement was not finalized at the time the current EIR attempted to tier from it, and did not provide Sunrise-Douglas plan area with any firm commitment to future water. Further, the Water Forum EIR was not formally incorporated by reference into the project EIR.

Supreme Court's Principles for Water Supply Analysis. Before addressing the adequacy of the short- and long-term water supplies evaluation for the Sunrise-Douglas project, the Supreme Court surveyed all of the relevant appellate court decisions dealing with water supply under CEQA. Based on this review, the court elucidated four general principles for analytical adequacy under CEQA:

1. CEQA's informational purposes are not satisfied by an EIR that simply ignores or assumes a solution to the problem of supplying water to a proposed land use project. Rather, decision makers and the public must be presented with sufficient facts to evaluate the pros and cons of supplying the amount of water that the project will need.
2. An adequate environmental impact analysis for a large project, to be built and occupied over a number of years, cannot be limited to the water supply for the first stage or the first few years. While tiering may be used to defer the analysis of certain details of the later phases of long-term projects, simply stating that information will be provided in the future does not satisfy CEQA's demand for meaningful information. Rather, an EIR for a planned land use project must assume that all phases of the project will eventually be built and will need water and must analyze, to the extent reasonably possible, the impacts of providing water to the entire project.
3. The future water supplies identified and analyzed must bear a likelihood of actually proving available; speculative sources and unrealistic allocations (e.g. "paper water") are insufficient bases for decision making under CEQA. Rather, an EIR for a land use project must address the impacts of likely future water sources, and the discussion must include a reasoned analysis of the circumstances affecting the likelihood of the water's availability.
4. Even if a full discussion leaves some uncertainty regarding actual availability of the anticipated future water sources, CEQA requires some discussion of possible replacement sources or alternatives to use of the anticipated water, and of the environmental consequences of those contingencies.

Despite these relatively strict analysis principles, the Supreme Court pointed out that the burden of identifying likely water sources for a project varies with the stage of project approval involved.

According to the court, "the degree of confidence involved for approval of a conceptual plan is much lower than for issuance of building permits." Additionally, the Supreme Court pointed out that none of the prior Court of Appeals decisions suggests that a guaranteed water supply and delivery facilities is necessary for an EIR to be adequate. Neither, according to the court, do the two 2001 water supply bills (SB 221 and SB 610) require assurances regarding long-term future waters supplies at an early phase of planning for large land development projects. SB 221 requires a "written verification" of an adequate water supply prior to approval of a subdivision map for certain large residential projects (Gov. Code Sec. 66455.3 and 66473.7). SB 610 requires that a water supply assessment from the applicable public water supplier be included in the CEQA document (Pub. Res. Code 21151.9; Water Code 10910(a)-(c)). In view of these two laws, the Supreme Court announced the principle that water supplies must be identified with increasing detail as land use planning and water supply planning move from general phases to more specific phases. (But as the court noted, compliance with these two water supply laws was not specifically at issue in this case.)

The court further pronounced that the ultimate question under CEQA is not whether an EIR actually establishes a likely source of water, but whether it adequately addresses the reasonably foreseeable impacts of supplying water to the project. Thus, even in the face of uncertainties regarding long-term land use and water planning, an EIR will satisfy CEQA if it:

- Acknowledges the degree of uncertainty involved
- Discusses the reasonably foreseeable alternatives—including alternative water sources
- Discusses the option of curtailing development if sufficient water is not available for later phases,
- Discloses the significant foreseeable environmental effects of each alternative, and
- Identifies mitigation measures that minimize each adverse impact

However, the court reminded agencies that even after preparing an EIR that met these requirements, the lead agency would have to make findings as to mitigation measures and alternatives and, if appropriate, a statement of overriding consideration.

The court also pointed out that, in meeting these demands of CEQA, an agency need not "reinvent the water planning wheel." Rather, it may, as appropriate, rely on information on an adopted Urban Water Master Plan in achieving CEQA requirements, assuming that the individual project's demand was included in the overall water plan. Thus, the amount of new analysis may be limited, if prior information can be properly incorporated by reference.

special provisions for such resources, including the optional time and cost limitations for implementing mitigation. An archaeological resource will be "unique" if it:

- Is associated with an event or person of recognized significance in California or American history or recognized scientific importance in prehistory
- Can provide information of demonstrable public interest and is useful in addressing scientifically consequential and reasonable research questions
- Has a special or particular quality such as oldest, best example, largest, or last surviving example of its kind

(Pub. Res. Code § 21083.2).

In practice, most archaeological resources that meet the definition of "unique" will also meet the definition of an "historical resource."

If an archaeological site is neither a unique archaeological resource nor an historical resource, any effect to it shall not be considered significant. The environmental document must include an explanation supporting such conclusion and no further consideration is necessary (Guidelines § 15064.5(c)).

Guidelines § 15126.4(b) discusses mitigation measures for impacts on historical resources, including archaeological resources. See the discussion under Mitigation Measures for more information.

Native American Human Remains. When an environmental document identifies the existence of—or the probable likelihood of—Native American human remains within a project site, the lead agency shall work with the most likely descendant as designated by the Native American Heritage Commission, and special rules apply (Guidelines § 15064.5(d)).

Accidental Discovery of Resources. As a part of its CEQA procedures, a lead agency should make provisions for historical or archaeological resources accidentally discovered during construction. Special rules apply in those situations (Guidelines § 15064.5(e)).

In preparing an EIR, any information about the specific location of archaeological sites and sacred lands must not be included in the document circulated for public review (Guidelines § 15120(d)).

Impacts on Public Water Systems and Water Supply Assessments

Although many types and sizes of projects will result in water supply impacts that must be evaluated, special requirements apply for evaluating the impacts of certain large projects on public water systems (Pub. Res. Code § 21151.9; Water Code Part 2.10, Division 6, § 10910; Guidelines § 15155). The public water systems subject to these requirements are limited to those with 3,000 or more domestic water connections (or that would have 3,000 or more connections including the project) or to public water systems with fewer than 5,000 connections where the project would

DWR Guidebook Assists Lead Agencies in Conducting Water Supply Assessments

Water supply assessments must be performed for certain types of large projects. The Department of Water Resources has developed a Guidebook to assist water suppliers, cities, and counties in integrating water and land use planning and meeting the requirements of Senate Bill 610 and Senate Bill 221 of 2001. Guidance is also provided by CEQA Guidelines § 15155.

In preparing the 134-page Guidebook, DWR sought the views of dozens of water-related interest groups and agencies. It provides detailed advice as to how to address key issues and answer important questions relating to the preparation of an adequate water supply assessment, including:

- When Does SB 610 apply to a proposed development?
- Who will prepare the SB 610 assessment?
- Determining if a previous assessment has already been prepared that includes the proposed project
- Determining if there is a current Urban Water Management Plan
- What information should be included in an assessment?
- Documenting wholesale water supplies
- Documenting supply If groundwater is the water source
- Documenting project demand
- Detailing existing and planned future uses
- Documenting dry-year(s) supply
- Determining the sufficiency or insufficiency or water supply for the proposed project
- What must be done if water supply is determined to be insufficient?

The guidebook is an invaluable resource for meeting the requirements of SB 610 and SB 221. It is available online at: www.owue.water.ca.gov/Guidebook_101003.pdf.

increase by ten percent or more the number of existing service connections. When lead agencies fail to comply with these requirements, they forego an opportunity to improve land use and water supply planning, and they make their environmental document vulnerable to legal challenge.

Whenever a lead agency prepares a draft EIR (or a negative declaration or a mitigated negative declaration) for these large projects, it must identify the public water system that will serve the project and must request from the public water supplier a detailed assessment of the water system's available supplies and whether the projected water demand associated with the project can be accommodated.

The projects subject to this provision are:

- Residential projects of more than 500 dwelling units
- Shopping centers and businesses that would employ more than 1,000 people or have more than 500,000 square feet of floor space
- Commercial office buildings where more than 1,000 persons would be employed or that would have more than 250,000 square feet of floor space
- Hotels or motels with more than 500 rooms
- Industrial, manufacturing, processing plant, or industrial park projects that would employ more than 1,000 persons, occupy more than forty acres, or have more than 650,000 square feet of floor space
- Mixed-use projects that would demand an amount of water equal to or greater than the amount required by a housing project of 500 dwelling units

Pursuant to the Water Code, a public water supplier must prepare an assessment indicating whether its total projected water supplies for the next twenty years will meet the projected water demand of the proposed project, in addition to the other planned future uses of water. The governing body of the public water system must approve the assessment at one of its official meetings no later than ninety days after the date on which the request for the assessment was received. If the public water system fails to submit the assessment to the lead agency in a timely manner, the lead agency may bring suit against the water agency. Where there is no public water system that would supply a qualifying project, the responsibility for preparing the detailed water supply assessment falls to the lead agency.

Practice Tip: Analysis of Water Supply Impacts

Analysis of water supply is always required under CEQA. While the special requirements described above apply to large projects, do not assume that smaller projects do not need an analysis of their impacts on water supply. There may be indirect impacts from even a small project's need for water supply.

A Ten-Step Approach to Water Supply Analysis in CEQA Documents

The impacts of water supply are not exclusive to only certain types of projects. All EIRs must examine impacts on water supply even if the formal SB 610 WSA is not triggered.The Supreme Court in the *Vineyard* case explained how CEQA fundamental principles should guide CEQA water supply analysis for development projects. However, the court did not necessarily set forth out a clear road map for compliance. The following is a practical ten-step approach to assist CEQA practitioners in complying with the decision that established general CEQA principals. Thus lead agencies should attempt to follow these steps regardless of whether a formal Water Supply Assessment is triggered:

Table 7-1 CEQA Decisions Dealing with Water Supply	
	Water Supply Analysis Found Inadequate
Stanislaus Natural Heritage v. Stanislaus County (1996) 48 Cal App. 4th 182	Programmatic EIR prepared for a large master-planned community was inadequate because it failed to evaluate water supply impacts, but rather deferred such evaluation to subsequent tier EIRs.
County of Amador v. El Dorado County Water Agency (1999) 76 Cal. App. 4th 931	An EIR for the development of new water supplies was inadequate because it was "predicated" on population projections in a draft general plan that had not been adopted and was subsequently held to be inadequate by another court.
Planning and Conservation League v. Department of Water Resources (2000) 83 Cal.App.4th 892	Programmatic EIR prepared for a multi-agency water agreement ("Monterey Agreement") was inadequate because it failed to properly evaluate a realistic no-project alternative and because the wrong lead agency (Central Coast Water Agency rather than State Department of Water Resources) prepared the document.
Cadiz Land Company, Inc. v. Rail Cycle, L.P.(2000) 83 Cal. App. 4th 74	EIR for a proposed landfill in the desert was inadequate where it failed to discuss the volume and size of an existing groundwater aquifer underlying the proposed project. Without an adequate description of the environmental setting, the impact and mitigation discussions in an EIR cannot be adequate.
Save Our Peninsula Committee v. Monterey County Board of Supervisors(2001) 87 Cal. App. 4th 99	EIR for a proposed residential project was inadequate because county used wrong environmental baseline for evaluation of water supply impacts and related mitigation measures.
Napa Citizens for Honest Government v. Napa County Board of Supervisors(2001) 91 Cal. App. 4th 342	EIR for Airport Industrial Area Specific Plan was inadequate because it failed to describe secondary sources of water supply in the event the primary designated sources were not available.
Friends of the Santa Clara River v. Castaic Lake Water Agency (2002) 95 Cal. App. 4th 1373	EIR prepared for water purchase agreement was inadequate in its evaluation of water supply because it tiered the water supply analysis off a programmatic EIR that had been declared inadequate by another court.
Santa Clarita Organization for Planning and the Environment v. County of Los Angeles (2003) 106 Cal. App. 4th 715	EIR prepared for 2,545 unit residential development was inadequate because it did not present an accurate description or analysis of available water supply to serve the project. Specifically, it failed to analyze and disclose the differences between legal water entitlements and actual supply.
Friends of the Eel River v. Sonoma County Water Agency (2003) 108 Cal. App. 4th 859	EIR on water diversion project was inadequate for failure to properly consider cumulative impacts of reduction in the Russian River water levels that would result from the proposed project together with potential reductions of Eel River water transfers that could foreseeably occur from the FERC licensing proceeding.
Vineyard Area Citizens for Reasonable Growth, Inc. v. City of Rancho Cordova (2007) 40 Cal. 4th 412	Water supply assessment for large specific plan inadequately disclosed long-term water supplies and impacts of obtaining those supplies. See sidebar on Vineyard Decision.
	Water Supply Analysis Upheld
Santa Clarita Organization for Planning the Environment v. County of Los Angeles (2007) 157 Cal. App. 4th 149	Water supply assessment adequately disclosed available water supplies and discussed reliability in light of concerns over supplies from the Kern-Cost????? transfer.
Watsonville Pilots Assoc. v. City of Watsonville (2010) 183 Cal. App. 4th 1059	Water supply assessment disclosed future demand and supply, as well as limitations on meeting future demand under the proposed general plan update. The court found that the analysis adequately disclosed future shortages and was not required to specifically resolve the overdraft problem.

Step 1: Determine reasonably foreseeable development scenarios, both near-term and at project build-out.

- The EIR should forecast likely population, housing, and land use—both near-term and at ultimate project build-out. The level of detail of later phases may be less than that for earlier phases.

Step 2: Determine the water demands necessary to serve both near-term development and project build-out.

- The EIR should calculate potential water usage for the entire project, based on established water use factors from reliable sources such as the retail or wholesale water supplier, or the Department of Water Resources.
- If demand projections differ due to conflicting data from different agencies, or different assumptions about future water conservation, then the lead agency should acknowledge and explain those differences.

Step 3: Rely on Urban Water Management Plan (UWMP) or SB 610 Water Supply Assessment (WSA), if available.

- A UWMP prepared for the water supplier, or an SB 610 WSA prepared for certain large projects, may contain much of the information needed to prepare an adequate CEQA water supply analysis.
- The lead agency has a duty under CEQA to independently review this information and change it if necessary. Also, UWMPs and WSAs are not required to address the environmental impacts of developing alternative water sources, so this information needs to be developed for the EIR (see Steps 8 and 9).

Step 4: Identify likely (reasonably foreseeable) near-term and long-term water supply sources and, if necessary, alternative sources.

- If adequate supplies do not currently exist, the EIR must identify future sources and explain what actions would be necessary to develop them.
- The EIR should also address the likelihood of the sources becoming available. If there is uncertainty about the availability of future water supply sources, this uncertainty should be acknowledged.
- Agencies may not conclude that future water sources are "remote and speculative" to avoid dealing with the future supplies necessary to serve the project.

Step 5: Identify the likely (reasonably foreseeable) yields of future water from the sources in Step 3.

- If potential future water supply quantities differ due to conflicting data from various courses, then the lead agency should acknowledge and explain the differences.
- The EIR should distinguish between "paper water" and water that is likely to be available.
- The EIR should address the risks of climate change reducing the yields of future water supply sources and how these risks would be managed.

Step 6: Determine cumulative demands on the water supply system.

- Determine whether proposed water supplies (or alternatives) are sufficient to serve the proposed project, together with other reasonably foreseeable future development in the water supplier's service area.
- Cumulative demand on the water should be developed based on either of CEQA's acceptable approaches: the list method or the projection method (e.g., projections in an UWMP).

A water supply assessment must rely on actual suppliers, not "paper water."

Step 7: Compare both near-term and long-term demand to near-term and long-term supply options, respectively, to determine water supply sufficiency.

- If uncertainty exists about particular sources, acknowledge and explain the uncertainty and identify additional contingent sources if the proposed sources become unavailable. Absolute guarantees of water supply availability, for example, signed contracts, are not required.
- The level of certainty about water supply sufficiency can be lower for project build-out than for near-term development.
- Discuss the option of curtailing development if sufficient water is not available for later phases. (This by itself, however, is not mitigation.)

Step 8: Evaluate the environmental impacts of developing future sources of water.

- The EIR must identify the impacts of developing future water sources (e.g., impacts of groundwater use on groundwater overdraft and stream flows).
- Tiering or incorporation by reference may be used to streamline CEQA compliance if an earlier CEQA document evaluated these impacts. The EIR must explicitly state it is tiering or incorporating by reference another document and summarize the information relied on to reach EIR conclusions.
- Analysis of impacts of developing long-term water supplies may not be deferred to second-tier CEQA documents.

Step 9: Identify mitigation measures for any significant environmental impacts of developing future water supplies.

- Mitigation measures must be developed that assume the project will be approved in its entirety and proposed water supply sources developed.
- Curtailing development until impacts are mitigated does not constitute adequate mitigation for the impacts related to water supply; rather, proceed to Step 10.

Step 10: Adopt findings and Statement of Overriding Considerations if necessary.

- The lead agency must adopt CEQA findings about significant water supply impacts and significant impacts of developing water supplies. CEQA findings of water supply sufficiency should be coordinated with SB 610's similar requirements for water supply sufficiency findings.
- If there are unavoidable impacts, the agency must adopt a State of Overriding Considerations. If sufficient water supplies are not identified in the EIR, approving a project may be difficult to justify.

The lead agency must include the water supply analysis in the EIR. Also, at the time it makes a decision on the project, the lead agency must determine whether the projected water supplies will be sufficient to satisfy the demands of the proposed project, in addition to existing and planned future uses. If the lead agency determines that water supplies will not be sufficient, it must include that determination in its findings for the project.

Greenhouse Gas and Climate Change Impacts

There is broad scientific consensus that humans are changing the chemical composition of our atmosphere. Activities such as fossil fuel combustion, deforestation, and other changes in land use are resulting in the accumulation of trace greenhouse gases (GHGs) such as carbon dioxide (CO_2) in the atmosphere. The increase in GHG emissions is resulting in an increase in the earth's average surface temperature. This, in turn, is affecting weather patterns, average sea level, ocean acidification, chemical reaction rates, precipitation rates, and so on, in a manner commonly referred to as *climate change*. To highlight the scope of this change, the Intergovernmental Panel on Climate Change has predicted that the average global temperature rise between 1990 and 2100 could be as great as 5.8°C (10.4°F), which could have massive deleterious impacts on natural and human environments.

Specific GHG Guidelines

- Determine Significance
- Environmental Setting
- Discussion of Impacts
- Mitigation Measures

The passage of the California Global Warming Solutions Act of 2006 (AB 32) ushered in a new era for environmental impact analysis under CEQA. Since the enactment of that law, the pace of legislation and regulatory developments has rapidly brought GHG and climate change impacts to the forefront of CEQA practice. Although AB 32 did not specifically discuss CEQA, its passage signaled a "green light" for evaluating greenhouse gas and climate change impacts in CEQA documents. Prior to 2007, many lead agencies were skeptical of evaluating GHG climate change impacts, too often relying on CEQA's "remote and speculative" rule as a reason to leave these important impacts out of CEQA documents. However, the Act's policy statements, together with advances in scientific research, new federal and California case law, and local government actions to address the problem, there is little doubt that climate change should be treated as a reasonably foreseeable impact under CEQA.

Recognizing the lack of a CEQA-specific provision in the Global Warming Solutions Act, the legislature enacted SB 97 in 2008. SB 97, specifically requires OPR to recommend and the Natural Resources Agency to adopt revisions to the CEQA Guidelines "for the mitigation of greenhouse gas emissions or the effects of greenhouse gas emissions." (Pub. Res. code §21083.05) In response to that legislation, OPR first issued interim guidance during the summer of 2008 in the form of a technical advisory entitled *CEQA and Climate Change: Addressing Climate Change Through California Environmental Quality Act (CEQA) Review*. In April 2009, OPR transmitted to the Natural Resources Agency proposed SB 97 CEQA Guidelines amendments addressing the evaluation of GHG impacts. The Natural Resources Agency adopted these amendments on December 30, 2009 and became effective March 18, 2010.

The amended CEQA Guidelines recognize that projects in California are contributing to global climate change and that GHG impacts must be evaluated in CEQA documents. Although the Guidelines require that lead agencies evaluate GHG impacts, they do not introduce any dramatic new requirements that change the way CEQA is implemented, nor do they provide a quantitative threshold of significance for GHG emissions. Here are the key aspects of the Guidelines amendments on GHGs, by section:

> **Specific GHG Guidelines**
>
> - Cumulative Effect
> - Projects Consistent with Community Plan or Zoning
> - Tiering and Streamlining Analysis of GHG Emissions
> - Definition of GHGs
> - Appendix F: Energy Conservation

15064. Determining Significance.
The amendment expands the list of examples of approved plans and mitigation programs that can be considered when determining whether a project may make a considerable contribution to a cumulative impact. The new examples include: habitat conservation plan, natural communities conservation plan, and "plans or regulations for the reduction of greenhouse gas emissions." The amendment also suggests that the lead agency explain how the plan or program will ensure that the project's incremental contribution is not considerable.

15064.4. Determining the Significance of Impacts from Greenhouse Gas Emissions.
This new section provides that a lead agency "should make a good-faith effort, based to the extent possible on scientific and factual data, to describe, calculate or estimate the amount of greenhouse gas emissions resulting from a project." The lead agency has the discretion to decide whether to either use an appropriate model or methodology to quantify the emissions, or to rely on a qualitative analysis or performance-based standards.

This section provides a list of considerations for assessing greenhouse gas emissions impacts. They include the increase or reduction in GHG emissions resulting from the project in comparison to baseline conditions; whether the emissions exceed an adopted threshold of significance; and the extent to which the project complies with plans for the reduction of GHG emissions.

15125. Environmental Setting.
The Guidelines require an EIR to discuss inconsistencies between the project and applicable general plans and regional plans. The amendment adds "regional blueprint plans" and "plans for the reduction of greenhouse gas emissions" to air quality maintenance plans, water quality control plans, regional transportation plans, regional conservation plans, and HCP/NCCPs.

15126.2. Consideration and Discussion of Significant Environmental Impacts.
The amendment adds a cross reference to Section 15127 and its limitation on the need to discuss significant irreversible changes in certain

types of EIRs. It also advises that the EIR should evaluate the impacts of locating development in areas susceptible to hazardous conditions, such as wildfire and flooding, "as identified in authoritative hazard maps, risk assessments or in land use plans addressing such hazards areas." This change is not related to GHG emissions alone, but would include such related hazards as sea level rise.

15126.4. Consideration and Discussion of Mitigation Measures Proposed to Minimize Significant Effects.

The amendment adds subsection (c) that discusses mitigation measures for GHG emissions. The subsection reminds agencies that mitigation measures must be feasible and are subject to monitoring or reporting. Suggested mitigation measures include:

(1) Measures in an adopted plan or program that will be required as part of the decision
(2) Reduction in emissions resulting from project design features
(3) Off-site measures, including offsets
(4) Measures that would sequester GHGs
(5) Long-range development plan (a new term not defined in the amendments) where the project is a general plan, or plan for the reduction of greenhouse gas emissions, specific measures included in the plan that will be implemented on a project-by-project basis.

Under item (5), the amendment provides that integrating the specific measures or policies found in an adopted ordinance or regulation that reduces GHG emissions can also be considered mitigation.

15130. Discussion of Cumulative Impacts.

The Guidelines provide that the analysis of cumulative impacts can employ either a list or projections approach. The amendment provides that the projection may be part of "an adopted local, regional or statewide plan, or related planning document, that describes or evaluates conditions contributing to the cumulative effect." It also expands the list of items that may be used in a projections approach from a general plan or related planning document to also include a regional transportation plan, plan for the reduction of greenhouse gas emissions, and the certified environmental document for any of these plans. The amendment also states that the projections "may be supplemented with additional information such as a regional modeling program."

15150. Incorporation by Reference.

The amendment clarifies that a description of the effects of GHG emissions on the environment is something that may be incorporated into an EIR or Negative Declaration by reference.

15183. Projects Consistent with a Community Plan or Zoning. This section of the Guidelines describes a method of streamlining the analysis of later site-specific projects consistent with a general plan, community plan, or zoning action for which an EIR was prepared. Under the Guidelines, a project-specific effect does not trigger further environmental analysis unless it is "peculiar to the project." Uniformly applied development policies or standards that mitigate project impacts can be cited as the reason why a project-specific effect is not "peculiar." The amendment adds "requirements for reducing greenhouse gas emissions, as set forth in an adopted land use plan, policy or regulation," to the list of uniformly applied policies and standards.

15183.5. Tiering and Streamlining the Analysis of Greenhouse Gas Emissions.

This new section specifies that the effects of GHG emissions may be analyzed and mitigated at a programmatic level, with later project-specific environmental documents tiering from that prior review. The amendment cites tiering under Section 15152; staged EIRs under Section 15167; program EIRs under Section 15168; Master EIRs under Section 15175 et seq.; specific plan EIRs under Section 15182, and EIRs for general plans, community plans, or zoning actions under Section 15183 as acceptable means of applying this programmatic approach.

When an agency has chosen to analyze and mitigate GHG emissions in a plan for the reduction of GHG emissions or similar document, that plan may be used as the basis for cumulative impact analysis. A project that conforms to that plan may be determined to have a less than considerable contribution to GHG emissions. The environmental document that relies on the plan must show that its provisions will apply to the project and any requirements specified by the plan will be applied to the project. The language in this section is careful to leave the determination open to a "fair argument" that would require preparation of an EIR.

The amendment lists the following as the elements of a GHG emissions reduction plan:

(1) A quantification of existing and projected GHG emissions from activities within a defined geographic area

(2) A threshold, based on substantial evidence, below which the GHG emissions contribution of a covered activity would be less than considerable

(3) An identification and analysis of GHG emissions arising from the specific actions or categories of actions to be covered by the plan

A Ten-Step Approach to Evaluating Climate Change Impacts

The following is a recommended ten-step approach for the consideration of GHG/climate change impacts under CEQA. These recommendations take into consideration OPR's technical advisory and the amendments to the CEQA Guidelines. They are broken down to conform to the main elements of a CEQA document.

Environmental Setting

Step 1—Describe the existing global context in which climate change impacts are occurring and are expected to continue to occur in the future.

Step 2—Summarize the relevant state laws that address climate change (*e.g.*, California Global Warming Solutions Act).

Step 3—Establish baseline: describe any relevant statewide and/or regional GHG inventories to which the project will contribute (e.g., County General Plan).

Environmental Impacts

Step 4—Quantify the project's direct and indirect GHG emissions and convert the GHG emissions into carbon equivalents using an established "carbon calculator."

Step 5—Compare the project's GHG emissions to existing baseline conditions.

Step 6—Discuss whether the project would enhance or impede the attainment of state GHG reduction targets under AB 32 and how it relates to relevant general plan policies or other local programs. Present appropriate significance threshold based on state, regional, or other guiding evidence. Assess whether the project's contribution to the baseline GHG levels would be "considerable."

Step 7—If found to be a considerable contribution to baseline GHG levels, describe the cumulative, global climate change impacts to which the project would contribute. This description may include how the project would add to the current impacts of climate change. (This may be the same information as in Step 1).

Step 8—Describe how the effects of greenhouse gas emissions would affect the proposed project and identify mitigation measures. (Pub. Res. Code Section 21083.05)

Alternatives

Step 9—Include alternatives that would meet the project objectives but would also reduce GHG emissions.

Mitigation Measures

Step 10—Identify mitigation measures that would reduce GHG emissions, including both project design or operational changes and/or potential compensatory mitigation (e.g., carbon offsets, sequestering).

(4) Measures, including performance standards, that would collectively achieve the specified emissions level if implemented on a project-by-project basis (this level of achievement must be supported by substantial evidence)
(5) A mechanism to monitor the plan's implementation and require any amendments needed to reach the specified emissions levels
(6) Adoption of the plan in a public process following environmental review

In a bow to consistency with the CEQA exemptions created under SB 375, the amendment provides that a qualifying infill project or "transit priority project" need not analyze the global warming impacts of car and light truck traffic associated with that project. The project must still consider GHG emissions from other sources.

15364.5. Greenhouse Gas.
This new section adds a definition of GHG to the Guidelines. Six gases or classes of gas are identified: carbon dioxide, methane, nitrous oxide, hydrofluorocarbons, perfluorocarbons, and sulfur hexafluoride.

Appendix F. Energy Conservation.
The amendments emphasize the need to consider a project's use of energy. The references to "lifetime costs" and "lifecycle" in the prior version of Appendix F have been deleted. The amendments provide that the lead agency may consider the extent to which the energy source serving the project has undergone environmental review.

Appendix G. Initial Study Checklist.
A new checklist item has been added for "Greenhouse Gas Emissions." It asks whether the project may directly or indirectly have a significant effect due to its GHG emissions and whether the project would conflict with any applicable plan, policy, or regulation intended to reduce GHGs.

Unfortunately, the amended CEQA Guidelines do not address all of the issues that can arise in dealing with GHG and climate change impacts. The following issues still need further clarification.

- **Baseline**—what is the appropriate baseline for impact analysis and for making significance determinations? Although the CEQA Guidelines indicate that existing conditions should normally be the baseline, some agencies are using a future scenario referred to as the "business as usual" baseline under which no future reductions of GHGs are achieved. If a lead agency uses "business as usual" as the baseline for impact analysis instead of using existing conditions it should be clear in its justification on why it is appropriate. The business as usual baseline maybe is more fittingly considered as the no-project alternative.

- **Indirect life cycle impacts**—CEQA requires the evaluation of both direct and reasonably foreseeable, indirect impacts. Clearly, GHG emissions are reasonably foreseeable from most projects. An unanswered question, is: when are "*life cycle*" impacts reasonably foreseeable and when they can be considered remote and speculative? "Life cycle" can refer to the totality of inputs and outputs of a project. For example, in evaluating the GHG impacts from a manufacturing facility, inputs might include the GHG emissions related to the construction materials used to build the facility as well as the production and shipping of raw materials to the facility. Outputs might include the shipping and delivery of products made in the plant.

CEQA's impact analysis must assess construction impacts related to reparian and historic resources, as well as contribution of greenhouse gases.

- **Threshold of "significance"**—Under CEQA, the question of when a project's contribution to a cumulative impact is "*significant*" is one of the more troublesome issues facing practitioners. Although the CEQA Guidelines use the phrase "cumulatively considerable," that, too, is an elusive concept that must be determined by lead agencies on a case-by-case basis. The issue is particularly problematic in evaluating GHG impacts because of the global nature of the problem and the characteristic lengthy lifespan of GHGs released to the atmosphere. Although the CEQA Guidelines amendments encourage the use of thresholds to evaluate GHG emissions, they do not provide such thresholds (§ 15064.4). In the absence of statewide thresholds, some air quality management and air pollutions control districts are developing their own thresholds for projects within their air basins. Future plans for the reductions of GHG emissions will likely include thresholds. In the absence of their own thresholds, lead agencies should use the thresholds, if any, adopted by their air district. Keep in mind that the "fair argument" is not trumped by a threshold if substantial evidence exists that the project may result in a cumulatively considerable GHG contribution even when it meets the air district's threshold.

- **Compensatory Mitigation**—Compensation is a well- established category of mitigation allowed under CEQA. Air quality off-sets, wetland banks, and fee-based traffic improvement programs are some common examples. However, this type of mitigation has typically been limited to localized or regional compensation. Since greenhouse gas impacts contribute to a global problem, theoretically compensatory mitigation could occur anywhere on earth. This gives rise to several unanswered questions: 1) Should there be geographic limits on GHG mitigation? 2) If not, how would more far-flung mitigation programs, such as those located in other nations or with no specific identified site, be verified and enforced? 3) Are there established national or international "carbon dioxide banks" that can be used for CEQA purposes? It is advisable for lead agencies using compensation to offset GHG impacts limit themselves to transparent and enforceable measures to ensure the adequacy of mitigation under CEQA.

GHG and Impacts of Climate Change on the Project. In addition to evaluating and mitigating a project's GHG impacts, CEQA documents should evaluate the effects of greenhouse gas emissions on a project, when relevant (Pub. Res. Code § 21083.05). Although this is not specifically addressed in the 2010 CEQA Guidelines amendments. CEQA documents should include mitigation measures, sometime referred to as "adaptation" measures for such impacts. The impacts of greenhouse gas emissions include, but are not limited to:

- Sea level rise and its effects on ecosystems and human settlements
- Changes in rainfall and snow pack
- Frequency and severity of extreme weather events, including flooding
- Drought and the effects on agriculture
- Frequency/severity of air quality problems
- Habitat change, species migration, and extinctions
- Increased potential for wildfire

One source of maps illustrating potential impacts under low and high GHG future scenarios is the California Energy Commission's Cal-Adapt Website (http://cal-adapt.org/). In 2011, this website offered charts and maps of local climate snapshots related to temperature change, snowpack, precipitation, sea level rise, and wildfire risk.

The relevance of these climate change impacts and the extent to which they are evaluated in a CEQA document will vary from location to location and from project to project. A CEQA document is not required to analyze impacts that are speculative and for which there is insufficient data to support a reasonable forecast (State CEQA Guidelines §§ 15144 and 15145). State and federal agencies with jurisdiction over these resources are developing policies and methods for evaluating climate change impacts and should, therefore, be consulted during the scoping phase of CEQA document preparation.

Projects within Airport Comprehensive Land Use Plan Areas and Military Facility Flight Path

In preparing EIRs on projects within the jurisdiction of an airport comprehensive land use plan or within two nautical miles of a public or public use airport, the lead agency must evaluate the impacts on safety and noise by using the handbook prepared by the California Department of Transportation, Division of Aeronautics (Pub. Res. Code § 21096; Guidelines § 15154). The current edition of the "California Airport Land Use Planning Handbook" is available online at: www.dot.ca.gov/hq/planning/aeronaut/htmfile/landuse.html.

The lead agency must also consider the project's effects on military aviation when the U.S. Department of Defense or a military branch has notified the lead agency and provided it with the specific boundaries of a low-level flight path, military impact zone, or special use airspace, and the project meets any of the following criteria:

- The project includes a general plan amendment
- The project is of statewide, regional, or areawide significance

- The project is required to be referred to the airport land use commission

CEQA provides that while a project's effect on military activities may cause, or be associated with, adverse environmental effects, the project's effect or potential effect does not itself constitute an adverse effect (Public Resources Code § 21098).

Projects Involving Schools

Special requirements apply to certain school projects and projects near schools to ensure that potential health impacts resulting from exposure to hazardous materials, wastes, and substances will be carefully examined and disclosed in an EIR (or in a negative declaration) (Guidelines § 15186). Specifically, for any project located within one-quarter mile of a school that is expected to involve the construction or alteration of a facility that emit hazardous material above certain limits, the lead agency must consult with the affected school district during preparation of the document and notify the district within thirty days prior to certification.

When a project involves a school district's purchase of a school site or construction of a secondary or elementary school, the EIR must disclose:

- Any sites of current or former hazardous waste disposal and their status
- Records of any hazardous substance releases
- Any buried or above ground pipelines that carry hazardous substances
- A site within 500 feet of the edge of the closest traffic lane of a freeway or other busy traffic corridor (i.e., roadways with traffic in excess of 50,000 vehicles per day in a rural area or 100,000 vehicles per day in an urban area)

(Pub. Res. Code § 21151.8(a)).

The lead agency must also consult with and notify the appropriate air pollution control district or air quality management district. When the lead agency is the school district, it must also consult with the appropriate hazardous materials management agency to identify both permitted and nonpermitted facilities within that agency's and air district's authority that could emit hazardous emissions or handle hazardous or acutely hazardous materials, substances, or waste. Facilities include, but are not limited to free-

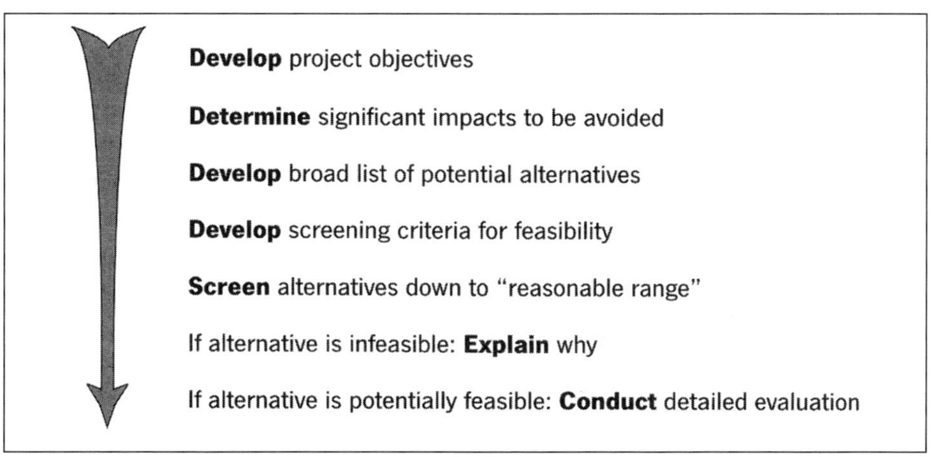

Figure 7-3 Alternatives Screening Process

Figure 7-4
Alternatives Screening Process

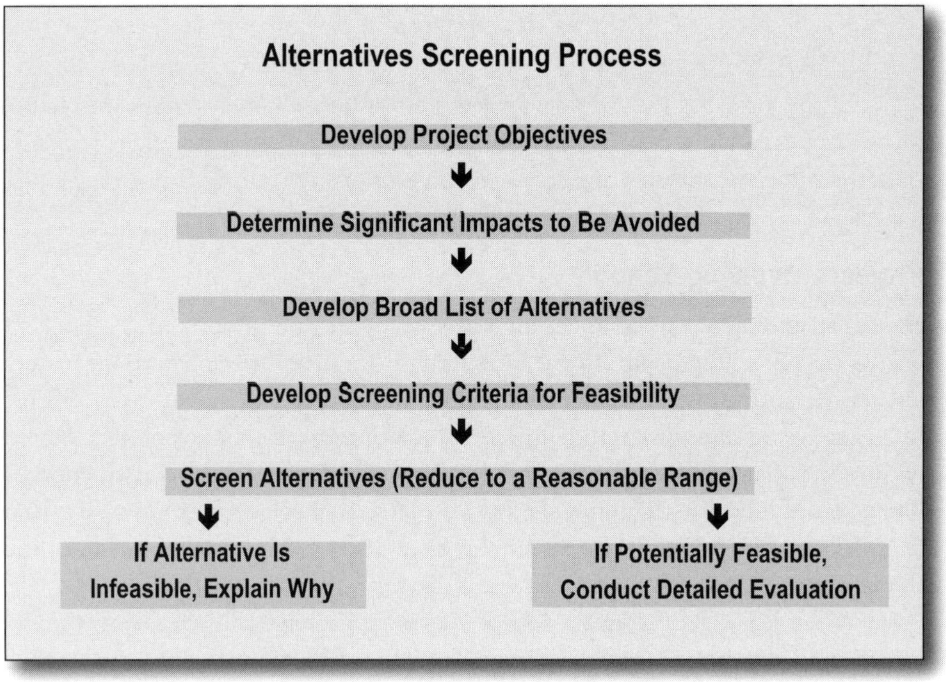

ways and busy traffic corridors, large agricultural operations, and railyards within one-quarter mile of the proposed school site.

In preparing findings for the project, the school board must find that no hazardous facilities are present or, if such facilities exist, that:

- No health risks from the facilities will endanger the public health of persons attending or working at the school.
- Corrective action will mitigate all hazardous air emissions before the school is occupied.
- For a school site with a boundary within 500 feet of a freeway or busy traffic corridor, the school board determines that through air quality modeling and after considering mitigation measures, the air quality at the proposed site is such that neither short- nor long-term exposure poses significant health risks to pupils.

Alternatively, if the facilities or other pollution sources specified above do exist, but the conditions described above cannot be met, and the school district is unable to locate a suitable alternative site due to a severe shortage of sites that meet Education Code school site criteria, the school board may only approve the school site upon:

- Preparing an EIR
- Making a finding describing the inability to avoid the impacts and the shortage of suitable other sites
- Adopting a statement of overriding considerations

These CEQA Guidelines provisions involving school facilities are very specific and include various cross references to the California Health and Safety Code (Pub. Res. Code § 21151.8; Guidelines § 15186).

California Supreme Court Rules When an Offsite Alternatives Needs to Be Analyzed in an EIR in: *Citizens of Goleta Valley v. Board of Supervisors* (1990) 52 Cal. App. 3d 553:

The California Supreme Court clarified the circumstances under which public agencies may evaluate alternative sites in EIRs. This case involved a decade-long struggle over the Hyatt Corporation's attempt to develop a coastal resort hotel in Goleta, a community in Santa Barbara County. After the Court of Appeal held that the EIR prepared for the coastal resort hotel was deficient in that it failed to examine any alternative sites for the proposed project (*see Citizens of Goleta Valley v. Board of Supervisors* (*Goleta I*) (1988) 197 Cal. App. 3d 1167), Santa Barbara County prepared a supplemental EIR (SEIR) analyzing the potential for developing alternative sites. This SEIR analyzed a single alternative site rather than a range of sites. Although the appellate court again declared the EIR inadequate in that it did not evaluate a reasonable range of alternatives and did not explain why other ostensibly feasible alternatives were eliminated from consideration (*see Citizens of Goleta Valley v. Board of Supervisors* (*Goleta II*) (1989) 214 Cal. App. 3d 264), the California Supreme Court reversed, holding that the SEIR was legally sufficient and that substantial evidence supported the county's decision approving the project.

The county's draft SEIR contained a brief discussion of an alternative site on the Santa Barbara coast the county believed could feasibly accommodate a resort hotel of the scale proposed for the project. In comments on the draft SEIR, the county was requested to include more detail about this alternative site and to discuss any other feasible alternative sites (including other coastal and specific inland sites). The final SEIR included an expanded discussion of the alternate coastal site but rejected it because of anticipated environmental impacts and the fact that the site was not zoned for this use and was not available to the project proponents. The final SEIR justified not analyzing other coastal sites by referencing a staff report separately prepared that concluded no other sites along the coast could accommodate a resort hotel. The final SEIR justified not analyzing inland sites because coastal access was an essential aspect of the proposed project objectives. During the hearings on the final SEIR, the county was requested to analyze seven additional alternative sites; although the county did not revise the final SEIR, in its findings on the project, the county specifically addressed the feasibility of and rejected the seven additional alternatives.

In upholding the SEIR, the high court stated that the range of alternatives, governed by the "rule of reason," should offer "substantial environmental advantages over the proposed project" and are "feasibly accomplished in a successful manner considering economic, environmental, social, and technical factors." The Court emphasized that there is no "categorical legal imperative" as to the scope of alternatives and that each case "must be evaluated on its facts" to determine whether the purposes of CEQA have been achieved. The Court stated that generally the EIR should set forth the reasons for rejecting certain alternatives as infeasible but added that such reasons may be found elsewhere in the administrative record. For specific alternative sites brought to the lead agency's attention after the public review process, the lead agency must consider them but may address them "by means of administrative findings, rather than by commissioning a supplemental EIR."

The Court stated also that an EIR was "not ordinarily an occasion for the reconsideration or overhaul of fundamental land use policy;" however, the Court recognized that although an alternative may require a legislative change (*e.g.,* general plan amendment or zoning change), that should not preclude it from consideration in an EIR. The Court held that adopted regional and local plans may be relied on by a lead agency in determining the infeasibility of alternative sites. The Court identified certain circumstances under which the inclusion of alternative sites would be appropriate, including the project being a public project (because of the power of eminent domain); the project proponent owning or controlling, having the ability to purchase or lease, or having access to feasible alternative sites; or two or more developers seeking approval for the same type of development at different locations. The Court also noted that the existence of alternative sites outside the lead agency's jurisdiction does not necessarily preclude them from consideration in an EIR.

The Department of Toxic Substances Control publishes an advisory document on the relationship between CEQA requirements and those of Education Code sections 17210.1 and 17213.1 requiring preliminary endangerment assessments (PEA) for school acquisition and construction. It offers alternatives for undertaking PEA review in conjunction with or separate from CEQA review. "Fact Sheet #3 Update on School Site Environmental Review

Figure 7-5
Developing a Reasonable Range of Alternatives

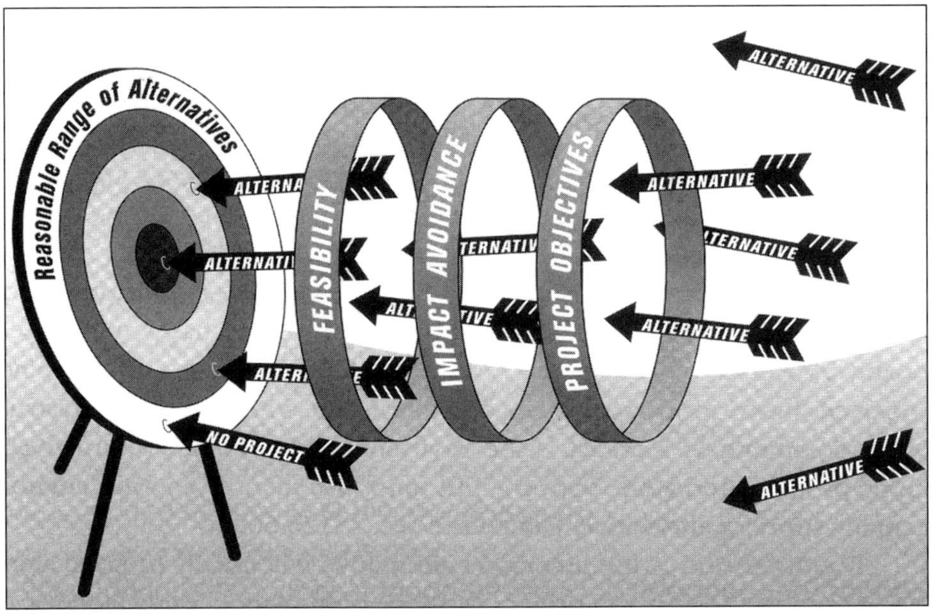

Process" (November 2001) is available at www.dtsc.ca.gov/schools/upload/smp_schools_FS_AB972.pdf

Alternatives

In General

A draft EIR must describe a reasonable range of alternatives to the project or project location that could feasibly attain most of the basic project objectives and would avoid or substantially lessen any of the significant environmental impacts of the proposed project. Additionally, the no-project alternative (page 176) must also be analyzed in a draft EIR, even though it may not share any of the project's objectives or offer a substantial lessening of the project's significant environmental impacts (Guidelines §§ 15126.6(a)).

There is no ironclad rule governing the nature or scope of the alternatives to be discussed other than the "rule of reason." The discussion of alternatives must focus on those alternatives that are capable of avoiding or substantially lessening the significant environmental effects of the proposed project, even if the alternative could impede to some degree the attainment of all the project objectives or would be more costly (Guidelines § 15126.6(b)).

The EIR must briefly explain why any other alternatives considered for inclusion in the EIR were rejected (Guidelines § 15126.6(c)).

The treatment of alternatives in an EIR should be based on the following methodology:

- Describe the project objectives.
- Conduct a preliminary assessment of the project's potential significant environmental effects.
- Develop screening criteria for feasibility of alternatives.
- Select a reasonable range of alternatives that:

CA Supreme Court Rules on CEQA Requirements for EIR Reasonable Range of Alternatives: *In re: Bay-Delta Programmatic Environmental Impact Report Coordinated Proceedings* (2008) 43 Cal.4th 1143.

In this case, consolidated from a number of CEQA challenges to the program EIS/EIR that was certified for the CalFed project in 2000, the CA Supreme Court reviewed the adequacy of alternatives considered in the long-range, joint federal and state strategy for balancing water transfer with environmental and habitat issues within the Sacramento-San Joaquin River Delta.

The Court of Appeal had held that CALFED's Bay Delta Programmatic EIR was inadequate because it (1) eliminated the alternative of reducing water exports from the Delta as a means to control growth (2) did not fully describe sources of water and the impacts of taking that water for use in the program and (3) inadequately described the proposed "Environmental Water Account." The Supreme Court reversed on all of these points and upheld the adequacy of the CALFED Programmatic EIR.

CALFED identified four fundamental objectives of the program (paraphrased here): 1) improve ecosystem quality and functions; 2) reduce the mismatch between Bay-Delta water supplies and the beneficial uses dependent on the Bay-Delta system; 3) provide good water quality for all beneficial uses; and 4) reduce the vulnerability of Delta functions to catastrophic levee failures. Alternatives must meet most or all of the project objectives and be feasible. An EIR need not examine every possible alternative. Analysis is guided by the "rule of reason" and whether the alternative feasibly meets project objectives. This decision adds a further consideration: Does the alternative achieve the project's "underlying fundamental purpose?" Here, CALFED had defined the fundamental purpose of this program "to develop and implement a long-term comprehensive plan that will restore ecological health and improve water management for beneficial uses of the Bay-Delta system." Further, the program "was established to reduce the conflicts and provide a solution that competing interests could support."

Based on years of conflicts over solutions to the Bay-Delta's problems, CALFED determined that its four primary objectives had to be addressed concurrently in an integrated manner if the project was to be successful and therefore feasible. A reduced export alternative would not meet the water supply reliability objective. Opponents argued that the reduced water supply alternative could meet reliability objectives for the Delta and points north. The Court held that the underlying purpose of CALFED project is to encompass all beneficial uses of Delta water and "cannot be achieved by an alternative that benefits some groups of water users at the expense of the others." Therefore, CALFED properly exercised its discretion when it declined to further study the reduced export alternative in the final PEIS/EIR.

The Court further held that although a lead agency cannot give a project's purpose an artificially narrow definition in order to limit the available alternatives, it "may structure its analysis around a reasonable definition of underlying purpose and need not study alternatives that cannot achieve that basic goal." Here, the determination that an integrated solution was necessary and that the water supply objective could not be met by the reduced exports alternative was supported by substantial evidence and supported by the rule of reason. CALFED adequately made the case that an integrated approach, where all the objectives would need to be met in order to solve the problems of the Bay-Delta system, made a reduced export alternative infeasible.

The Court found that the Court of Appeal had failed to sufficiently distinguish between the Bay-Delta's baseline environmental setting and the impacts caused by the proposed program. As a result, the Court of Appeal's request for a reduced export alternative attempted to solve the Bay-Delta's existing environmental problems (as detailed in the setting of the PEIS/EIR), but didn't address the impacts of the CALFED program. Those problems "would continue to exist even if there were no CALFED program" and therefore were not impacts that would determine the required range of alternatives.

  - Meet most or all of the project objectives
  - Substantially avoid or lessen the proposed project's significant environmental effects
  - Are feasible based on specific economic, social, legal, or technical considerations
- Explain why other alternatives have been rejected from evaluation.
- Provide meaningful evaluation and analysis of the environmental effects of the reasonable range of alternatives and the no-project alternative in comparison with environmental effects of the proposed project.
- Identify the environmentally superior alternative.

The EIR's range of alternatives must include those that would avoid or substantially lessen one or more of the project's significant environmental impacts.

Selection of Range of Alternatives

Rule of Reason. The range of alternatives required in an EIR is governed by a "rule of reason" that requires an EIR to set forth only those alternatives necessary to permit a reasoned choice. An EIR need not consider every conceivable alternative to a project.

Rather, the alternatives must be limited to ones that meet most of the project objectives, are ostensibly feasible, and would avoid or substantially lessen at least one of the significant environmental effects of the project. Of those alternatives, the EIR need only examine in detail the ones that the lead agency determines could feasibly attain most of the basic objectives of the project, although the lead agency must identify a fundamental objective that all alternatives must meet. The range of reasonable alternatives must be selected and discussed in a manner to foster meaningful public participation and informed decisionmaking (Guidelines § 15126.6(f)). The process of screening alternatives is illustrated in Figure 7-3 (page 167) and Figure 7-4 (page 168).

The EIR must briefly describe the rationale for selection and rejection of alternatives and the information the lead agency relied on in making the selection. It should also identify any alternatives that were considered by the lead agency but were rejected as infeasible during the scoping process and briefly explain the reasons for their exclusion. Additional information explaining the choice of alternatives should be included in the administrative record (but not necessarily in the EIR itself). Alternatives may be eliminated from detailed consideration in the EIR if they fail to meet most of the basic project objectives, are infeasible, or do not avoid any significant environmental effects (Guidelines § 15126.6(c)). The EIR is not required to undertake a detailed or final analysis of the feasibility of an alternative before the alternative can be included in the EIR. That the alternative is potentially feasible is sufficient to include it in the EIR. Final feasibility will be determined when the lead agency decisionmakers adopt the project's CEQA findings. See, for example, *Sierra Club v. County of Napa* (2004) 121 Cal. App. 4th 1490; *San Franciscans Upholding the Downtown Plan v. City and County of San Francisco* (2002) 102 Cal. App. 4th 656.

Importance of a Clear Statement of Project Objectives. In developing a range of alternatives, a lead agency should focus on those alternatives that meet most or all of the project objectives (Guidelines § 15126.6(a)). Thus, clearly written project objectives will help in the development of a reasonable range of alternatives. The statement of objectives should include the underlying, fundamental, purpose of the project (Guidelines § 15124(b)).

When defining the project objectives, a distinction should be made between the action (the project) and the goal of the action (the objective). If the term "objective" is viewed in this manner, even a private project (e.g., a housing development) can be described as having a public objective (e.g.,providing housing for the community). A lead agency may narrow the range of alternatives to be evaluated by defining a relatively narrow objective. For example, an EIR for a bay-oriented aquarium need not evaluate alternatives that do not include siting the project near the bay, which was one of the stated objectives of the project. Although the lead agency should not describe the objective so narrowly as to preclude appropriate alternatives, one court has found an EIR that contained only one alternative (other than the no-project alternative) to be adequate because of the very explicit and narrow project objective (*Marin Municipal Water District v. K.G. Land Corporation* (1991) 235 Cal. App. 3d 1652). On the other hand, if the project has multiple objectives, every alternative need not satisfy every objective. It is sufficient if each alternative meets most of the project's objectives (*City of Carmel-by-the-Sea v. United States Department of Transportation* (9th Cir. 1997) 123 Fed. 3d 1142).

Feasibility. No single factor establishes a fixed limit on the scope of reasonable alternatives. In determining whether alternatives are feasible, lead agencies are guided by the general definition of feasibility found in CEQA: "capable of being accomplished in a successful manner within a reasonable period of time, taking into account economic, environmental, legal, social, and technological factors" (Guidelines § 15364). In addition, the lead agency may consider site suitability, economic viability, availability of infrastructure, general plan consistency, other regulatory limitations, jurisdictional boundaries, and proponent's control over alternative sites in determining the range of alternatives to be evaluated in an EIR (Guidelines § 15126.6(f)). All of the alternatives selected for evaluation in the EIR (except the no-project alternative) must be potentially feasible. The final feasibility will be determined when EIR findings are made after the project is approved (*Sierra Club v. County of Napa* (2004) 121 Cal. App. 4th 1490; *San Franciscans Upholding the Downtown Plan v. City and County of San Francisco* (2002) 102 Cal. App. 4th 656).

Alternative Locations. Alternative locations need not be evaluated in every case. A key question in determining whether to evaluate alternative locations is whether any of the significant environmental effects of the project would be avoided or substantially lessened by putting the project in another location. Only locations that would avoid or substantially lessen any significant effects need be

CA Supreme Court Rules on a Lead Agency's Responsibility to Mitigate: *City of Marina et al. v. Board of Trustees of the California State University* (2006) 39 Cal. 4th 341

The City of Marina and the Fort Ord Reuse Authority (FORA) challenged the CEQA findings and statement of overriding considerations made by California State University Monterey Bay (CSU) for its Master Plan EIR. The EIR disclosed that the planned campus expansion to accommodate 25,000 students on a portion of the former Fort Ord would have a number of significant effects. In its CEQA findings, CSU concluded that improvements to roads and fire protection were the sole responsibility of FORA (although CSU is contributing for water, drainage, and wastewater costs); CSU could not legally contribute its share to off-site facilities that would mitigate the traffic and fire safety impacts of CSU; and the planned expansion offers overriding benefits. CSU cited the restrictions established under Government Code Section 54999 *et seq.* (the "San Marcos legislation"), which limits school payments to local agencies for public utilities services. In its opposing arguments, FORA asserted that CEQA required CSU to mitigate the impacts of its project and to contribute its fair share of the cost of mitigating cumulative effects.

The Supreme Court agreed with FORA. CEQA obligates CSU to mitigate the impacts of its project (including off-site impacts) unless it is infeasible to do so. The Court found that the "plain language of the California Constitution does not support the Trustee's position that voluntary mitigation payments are impermissible." The Trustees incorrectly interpreted the decision in *San Marcos Water District v. San Marcos Unified School District* (1986) 42 Cal. 3d 154 and the subsequent San Marcos legislation. That decision addressed only compulsory charges imposed by one public entity on another. Here, the situation involves the discretionary payment made by a public agency that voluntarily chooses that method of discharging its CEQA duty to mitigate a project's environmental effects. The question then becomes whether the method of mitigation is feasible.

The Court found that nothing in San Marcos "can fairly be read as addressing, much less narrowing, a public agency's obligations under CEQA." It therefore, does not affect the feasibility of voluntarily paying for off-site improvements. Paying to mitigate CSU's environmental effects is not an unlawful gift of public funds.

As part of the planning for Fort Ord's reuse, FORA had identified approximately $249.2 million in infrastructure improvements that will be needed over the life of the Reuse Plan. FORA assumed that CSU would pay its fair share of these costs, but did not establish a tax, fee, or charge on CSU. CSU attempted to argue that the mitigation is infeasible because CSU cannot guarantee that FORA will actually implement the infrastructure improvements identified in the Reuse Plan.

The Court found no reason to doubt that FORA would meet its obligations. FORA has identified infrastructure needs and has a variety of methods by which it can finance those improvements. In addition, payment of fees to satisfy a cumulative environmental impact is authorized under CEQA. FORA is not solely responsible for paying for the infrastructure improvements. In fact, its cooperation provides CSU with the opportunity to pay their fair share of the mitigation.

Because the Court found that mitigation is feasible, it invalidated CSU's statement of overriding considerations. The Court also vacated the findings certifying the EIR.

For Each Significant Impact, the Lead Agency Must . . .

- Discuss whether the measure avoids or substantially reduces the significant environmental effect
- Distinguish measures proposed by project proponents
- Identify responsibility of implementation for each measure
- Discuss the basis for selecting a particular measure (when several measures are available)
- Discuss significant impacts associated with implementation of each mitigation measure
- Consider special limits for archaeological resources, school facilities, housing units, and public water systems

Mitigation Is Defined as:

- Avoiding the impact
- Minimizing the impact
- Rectifying the impace
- Reducing or eliminating the impact over time
- Compensating for the impact

evaluated in the EIR. If the lead agency determines that no feasible alternative locations exist, it must disclose the reasons for this conclusion in the EIR. When alternative locations are evaluated in an EIR, to the extent possible, they should rely on previous documents (e.g., plan, policy, or program level EIRs) that have already analyzed a range of reasonable alternative locations. Guidelines § 15126.6(f).

Relationship to Comprehensive Planning. Alternative locations for projects are best evaluated in program or master EIRs prepared for plans, programs, or policies. A project-level EIR should not ordinarily be an occasion for the reconsideration or overhaul of fundamental land use policy. However, the fact that an alternative site may require a legislative change (e.g., general plan amendment or rezoning) does not necessarily exclude it from consideration in an EIR.

Adopted regional and local plans may be relied on when the feasibility of alternative sites is being determined and may result in eliminated of those sites from detailed discussion in an EIR. At the same time, if they have been identified in adopted plans, feasible alternative sites may be included in an EIR. The inconsistency of an alternative site with an adopted plan may be a factor in its being determined to be infeasible.(Guidelines § 15126.6(f)(2)).

Rationale for Rejecting Alternatives. The lead agency may, as part of the scoping process, make an initial determination as to which alternatives are potentially feasible and merit in-depth consideration—and which do not. Although an EIR should generally set forth the alternatives that the lead agency considered and rejected as infeasible during the scoping process, and the reasons for their rejection, such explanations may be found elsewhere in the administrative record. Thus, the entire administrative record, and not merely the EIR, may be studied to assess the degree of discussion any particular alternative deserves, based on its feasibility and the stage in the decision-making process at which it is brought to the attention of the lead agency. Alternatives brought to the lead agency's attention after the public review period must also be considered, but the lead agency may address these alternatives by means of administrative findings, rather than in a supplemental EIR (*Citizens of Goleta Valley v. Board of Supervisors* (1990) 52 Cal. App. 3d 553).

Alternatives that are remote or speculative, or the effects of which cannot be reasonably predicted, need not be considered. However, alternatives may not be rejected merely because they are beyond an agency's authority, would require new implementing legislation, or would be too costly (Guidelines § 15126(f)(2)).

An EIR must analyze alternatives even if mitigation measures can reduce the impacts of the proposed project to less-than-significant levels. If it concludes that no feasible alternatives exist, an EIR must present the reasons why alternatives were rejected in sufficient detail to enable meaningful public review. The lead agency's responsibility to provide an adequate analysis of alternatives does not depend on project opponents first showing that feasible alternatives exist.

Ultimately, when the lead agency prepares EIR findings at the time of project approval, they must determine whether each of the alternatives analyzed in the EIR is feasible (Guidelines § 15091). The lead agency is not required to determine the ultimate feasibility of the alternatives until that time, and the

Details of Mitigation Plans May Be Deferred in an EIR

The issue of "deferred mitigation" is a topic of considerable uncertainty to many CEQA practitioners. The fundamental questions are: How specific does mitigation have to be in a CEQA document? What details, if any, can be deferred to the future?

To understand the concept of deferred mitigation, one must first understand how CEQA defines "mitigation." According to the CEQA Guidelines, "mitigation" includes any of the following:

- Avoiding the impact altogether by not taking an action or part of an action
- Minimizing the impact by limiting the degree or magnitude of the action
- Rectifying the impact by repairing, rehabilitating, or restoring the affected environment
- Reducing or eliminating the impact over time by preservation or maintenance actions
- Compensating for the impact by providing replacement or substitute resources or environments

While these terms are called a definition, they are actually conceptual categories representing a broad range of potential solutions to environmental problems. The common denominator in all of these definitional concepts is that a mitigation measure is supposed to actually solve an identified environmental problem by keeping or bringing impacts below the level of significance. Despite the wide latitude provided by the Guideline categories, some agencies do not take mitigation seriously and develop measures that do not actually solve problems. One of the most common mistakes agencies make is to "defer" mitigation to the future, rather than identify it in the EIR or mitigated negative declaration, as CEQA requires.

In practice, deferred mitigation takes several forms. First, some agencies, in the name of mitigation, defer essential environmental studies to the future rather than including them conducting them during preparation of an EIR or mitigated declaration. A second form of deferral is when the environmental document only describes mitigation measure in a very general, conceptual fashion, but the details are deferred to the future. A third type of deferral is when the agency identifies a "menu" of possible mitigation measures but fails to describe them in sufficient detail to ensure that the selection of one or more of the measures will reduce the impact. Over the years, the courts have been presented with the issue of deferred mitigation numerous times to the point where patterns of appropriate and inappropriate CEQA behavior have emerged.

The most important principle in this area of CEQA practice is that deferral is *impermissible* when the CEQA document is a mitigated negative declaration. When an agency concludes that a proposed project will have no significant impacts, it must be virtually certain of that conclusion. Such certainty is not possible if relevant information about the affected environment and the impacts to it are deferred to the future. Thus, the only legitimate use of deferred mitigation would be in the context of an EIR. However, even when an EIR is prepared, *deferred mitigation* should be the exception not the rule. Deferral should only be considered when there is some legitimate reason why the agency cannot develop a specific mitigation measure at the time it prepares the EIR. For example, a project with the potential to impact endangered plants that will not bloom for many months after EIR preparation, or the case of a program EIR where site-specific development plans will not be available until sometime in the future.

To support the concept of deferral, the mitigation measure must meet three basic elements: First, the agency must commit itself to the mitigation. In other words, it must identify and adopt mitigation. Second, the agency must establish performance standards for what the end result of mitigation must achieve (some agencies call this the *desired future condition*). Third, the agency must provide a range of feasible mitigation options from which the applicant or agency staffs can choose to achieve the stated performance standards (*Sacramento Old City Assoc. v. City Council of Sacramento* (1991) 229 Cal. App. 3d 1011).

The courts have discussed the question of how much detail is necessary in an EIR's discussion of mitigation measures. The courts have allowed agencies to include a generalized discussion of mitigation in an EIR, with details deferred to future environmental analysis or implementation of the measures themselves. In *Dry Creek Citizen's Coalition v. County of Tulare* (1999) 70 Cal. App. 4th 20, the court upheld the county's mitigation detail in an EIR for a sand and gravel mine, stating that a general description of the technical aspects of the project's design features to mitigate impacts was sufficient to understand the environmental impacts. The mitigation measures were not required to include full technical specifications. In *Riverwatch v. County of San Diego* (1999) 76 Cal. App. 4th 1428, the court upheld the county's description of mitigation in an EIR for a rock quarry (but disapproved the EIR on other grounds), stating that including the details on the mitigation for a road (road improvements were in the planning stage) was "not meaningfully possible" at the time.

draft EIR and possibly final EIR may include alternatives that are ultimately found to be infeasible during the preparation of the findings (*see*, for example, *San Franciscans Upholding the Downtown Plan v. City and County of San Francisco* (2002) 102 Cal. App. 4th 656).

Evaluation and Comparison of Alternatives

The EIR must include sufficient information about each alternative to allow meaningful evaluation, analysis, and comparison with the proposed project.

Figure 7-6
Types of Mitigation

Mitigation Action	Explanation
Avoid	Avoid the impact altogether by not taking certain actions or parts of actions
Minimize	Minimize impacts by limiting the degree or magnitude of the action and its implementation
Rectify	Rectify the impact by repairing, rehabilitating, or restoring the affected environment
Reduce or Eliminate	Reduce or eliminate the impact over time by through preservation and maintenance during the life of the action
Compensate	Compensate for the impact by replacing or providing substitute resources or environments

While CEQA does not require that alternatives be evaluated in equal level of detail, the EIR must evaluate the comparative merits of the alternatives. A matrix displaying the major characteristics and impacts of each alternative may be used to summarize the comparison. When possible, the comparison should rely on quantitative factors. Generalized qualitative factors (e.g., "Alternative A is better than Alternative B") may not be adequate. However, the discussion of environmental effects of alternatives may be in less detail than the discussion of the impacts of the project as proposed (Guidelines § 15126.6(d)).

No-Project Alternative

The EIR must always evaluate and analyze the impacts of the no-project alternative. The purpose of evaluating the no-project alternative is to allow decisionmakers to compare the impacts of approving the project with the impacts of not approving the project. However, the no-project alternative is not the baseline for determining whether the proposed project's impacts are significant

Figure 7-7
Adequacy of Mitigation Measures

Adequate

- Avoid
- Minimize
- Rectify
- Reduce over time
- Compensate

Questionable

- Provide funding for
- Monitor or report
- Comply with existing regulations or ordinances
- Preserve already existing natural area

Inadequate

- Consult with
- Submit for review
- Coordinate with
- Study further
- Inform
- Encourage/discourage
- Facilitate
- Strive to

unless it is identical to the existing environmental setting analysis that establishes the baseline (Guidelines §§ 15125, 15126.6(e)).

The no-project analysis must discuss the existing conditions at the time the notice of preparation is published as well as what would be reasonably expected to occur in the foreseeable future if the project were not approved, based on current plans and consistency with available infrastructure and community services.

The discussion of the no-project alternative will usually proceed along one of two lines. When the project is the revision of an existing land use or

Court Requires EIR for Demolition of Historic Building and Declares Mitigation Measures Inadequate: *League for Protection of Oakland's Architectural and Historical Resources v. City of Oakland* (1997) 52 Cal App. 4th 60

In a decision with potentially far reaching implications for practices of historical resource protection under CEQA, the court of appeals held that demolition of an identified historic structure was, in and of itself, a significant environmental impact. The court also held that some of the most common methods of mitigating impacts to historic buildings were not adequate under CEQA. This case involved the proposed demolition of the old Montgomery Ward building in one of Oakland's warehouse districts. The City of Oakland had identified the building as an historic structure in its general plan, although it was not listed either on the national or state listings of historic buildings. A developer proposed to demolish the building to construct a new one. In response to this proposal, the city prepared a mitigated negative declaration. The proposed mitigation for the loss of the building consisted of the following measures, which until this decision, were commonly used throughout California:

- Prepare an historic resource documentation report to provide historic material for the city's archives
- Conduct a historic building survey to further document the historic structure
- Design the new building to reflect the historic elements of the old building
- Display a plaque or marker commemorating the building
- Consult with a qualified archaeologist to monitor excavation for discovery of any possible cultural elements

The court first found that the historic building was a "significant" historical resource even though it was on neither the state nor federal listing of historic structures. On the question of whether a historic resource is "significant," the court established three possible criteria:

- Mandatory significance—an historical resource must be considered significant if it is on or eligible for listing on the National Register of Historic Places or the California Register of Historic Resources
- Presumptive significance—an historical resource is presumed to be significant if it is listed on a local register of historical resources unless the preponderance of the evidence demonstrates otherwise
- Discretionary significance—an historical resource may still be considered significant even it is not on a federal, state, or local list if substantial evidence demonstrates it's significance

Having found that the Montgomery Ward building was significant, the court also held that the proposed package of mitigation measures was not adequate under CEQA. The court concluded that, even taken together, this package of mitigation measures would not reduce the effects of the building's demolition to a less than significant level.

Figure 7-8
Five Questions for Effective Mitigation Measures

Question	Requirement
WHY	State the objective of the mitigation measure and why it is recommended
WHAT	Explain the specifics of the mitigation measure and how it will be designated and implemented Identify measurable performance standards by which the success of the mitigation can be determined Provide for contingent mitigation if monitoring reveals that the success standards are not satisfied
WHO	Identify the agency, organization, or individual responsible for implementing the measure
WHERE	Identify the specific location of the mitigation measure
WHEN	Develop a schedule for implementation

regulatory plan, policy, or ongoing operation, the no-project alternative will be the continuation of the plan, policy, or operation into the future (not necessarily the plan at full build-out). If, on the other hand, the project is an individual development project on identifiable location, the no-project alternative should evaluate the environmental effects of the property remaining in its exiting state. If, however, other future uses of the land are reasonably foreseeable, such uses should also be discussed as possible no-project scenarios and the project should be compared to them also (Guidelines § 15126.6(e)(3)).

The description of the no-project alternative must provide a realistic view of the situation that would result if the project does not occur. And, the EIR must provide more than a cursory analysis of the no-project alternative (*see*, for example, *Planning and Conservation League v. Department of Water Resources* (2000) 83 Cal. App. 4th 892) where the EIR for the State Water Project water allocations was overturned because the No Project Alternative failed to represent foreseeable future actions under existing regulations.

Identifying the Environmentally Superior Alternative

When the no-project alternative is the environmentally superior alternative (that is, on balance, the alternative with the least significant effect), the EIR must also identify the environmentally superior of the other alternatives (Guidelines § 15126.6(e)). Typically, most lead agencies do not treat the project itself as an alternative and if appropriate looks to the alternatives to identify one as environmentally superior. It is sometimes difficult to compare

Mitigation Measure Evaluation Checklist: Developing Adequate and Successful Mitigation Measures

Definitional Factors	**Does the measure clearly:**
	Avoid the impact? Reduce the impact? Rectify the impact? Eliminate the impact over time? Compensate for the impact?
Specificity Factors	
	Why is that particular measure recommended? *What* is specifically being proposed? What are the success criteria? What contingency measures will be required if initial success is not achieved? *Where* - will the mitigation occur? *Who* is responsible for implementation? *When* will the mitigation occur? Does the measure contain vague or uncertain language that is (e.g. "to the extent feasible"?)
Feasibility Factors	
	Economic Feasibility • Does the proponent have the money to implement the measure? *Technical feasibility* •Is the technology available to implement the measure? *Legal Feasibility* • Does the agency have the legal authority to require implementation? • Has a proper "nexus" been established? • Is the mitigation measure "roughly proportional" to the impact? *Social feasibility* Is the mitigation measure acceptable to affected parties (e.g. neighbors, the community) *Political feasibility* • Is the measure acceptable to decision makers? • Are they likely to require it? • How will it read in the local newspaper?
Monitoring	
	Can the measure be monitored for: • Implementation? • Success?
Proponent Concurrence (Required for Mitigated Negative Declarations)	
	Has the proponent (applicant or agency) agreed to implement the measure?

Table 7-2.
Deferred mitigation:

What the Courts Have Allowed and Disallowed

Inadequate Deferred Mitigation Measure

Measure: Hydrologic impacts of sewer treatment plant

- Applicant shall have a civil engineer with a hydrology background or a hydrologist who concludes that adjacent sewage disposal systems and surface and ground water hydrology will not be adversely affected by the proposed sewage facility.
- Said study shall be subject to review and approval by the County Planning Commission and County Division of Environmental Health.
- Applicant shall have a study prepared by a civil engineer that evaluates potential effects of the proposed development on soil stability, erosion, sediment transport, and the flooding of downslope properties and that contains recommended measures to minimize such impacts.
- Said study shall be subject to review and approval by planning and building services.
- Mitigation measures recommended by the studies shall be incorporated as requirements of this use permit.

Inadequate to support a Negative Declaration because deferred studies, in the name of mitigation violates CEQA where there is evidence that the deferred mitigation is infeasible
Sundstrom v. County of Mendocino (1988) 202 Cal. App. 3d 296

Measure: Biological impacts from construction

- Project applicant shall conduct future biological studies and adopt mitigation measures recommended in such studies.

Inadequate to support a negative declaration because it deferred essential studies to the future
Gentry v. City of Murrieta (1995) 36 Cal. App. 4th 1359

Measure: Construction impacts (noise, supply depots, staging area) Before grading occurs, developer must

- Prepare an acoustical analysis describing exterior noise environment.
- Include preliminary mitigation recommendations.
- Submit analysis to city building permit division for review.
- Place stockpiles and staging areas "as far away as practical."

Inadequate because it deferred essential studies and did not describe performance standards
Endangered Habitat League, Inc v. County of Orange (2005) 131 Cal. App. 4th 777

Measure: Biological impacts—vernal pools and burrowing owl prior to construction

- Developer must prepare management plans and submit them to the USFWS and DFG for review.
- Conform to the future management plans.

Inadequate because there were no performance standards identified that would guide the content and outcome of the management plans
San Joaquin Raptor Rescue Center v. County of Merced (2007) 149 Cal. App. 4th 645

Adequate Deferred Mitigation Measure

Measure: Biological Impacts from construction (Foothill Mariposa Lily and Western Spadefoot Toad)—project applicant shall

- Perform pre-construction studies for presence of species.
- Commit to specific measures if those studies reveal potential impacts.
- Mitigate pursuant to a proposed NCCP/HCP.

Adequate because specify of commitment to mitigate and both study and mitigation performance standards established
Defend the Bay v. City of Irvine (2004) 119 Cal. App. 4th 1261

Measure: Increase in construction vehicle traffic—applicant must develop a construction vehicle plan that

- Assures public safety
- Restricts daily trips
- Limits or avoids peak hour trips
- Sets up clearly marked no passing zones
- Uses flaggers at site entrances

Adequate because parameters were established
Endangered Habitat League, Inc. v. County of Orange (2005) 131 Cal. App.4th777

Measure: Wildfire risks Prior to issuance of grading permit applicant must prepare and submit a *fuel modification plan* that:

- Complies with Orange County Fire Authority guidelines
- Is approved by Orange County Fire authority

Adequate because it is tied to established guidelines
Endangered Habitat League, Inc v. County of Orange (2005) 131 Cal. App.4th 777

Measure: Gnatcatcher impacts from construction—developer shall either

- Preserve similar habitat on-site or off-site, or
- Obtain habitat loss permits from relevant agencies

Adequate because alternative methods were proposed
Endangered Habitat League, Inc v. County of Orange (2005) 131 Cal. App.4th 777

Measure: Loss of trees from construction—developer shall either:

- seek approval for replanting trees off-site, or
- Prepare tree restoration, main, and monitoring plan that includes
    - Contract with certified arborist for least 10 years
    - Periodic reports on tree restoration

Adequate because included best management practice detail
Endangered Habitat League, Inc v. County of Orange (2005) 131 Cal. App.4th 777.

Measure: Water quality degradation from runoff—developer must prepare a water quality plan to reduce storm water runoff that

- Incorporates "best management practices" including four traps and filters for trash; biological matter; nutrients and microbes; and oil and gas
- Imposes water quality restrictions on homeowners in CC&Rs

Adequate because it relied on established practices and contained parameters
Endangered Habitat League, Inc v. County of Orange (2005) 131 Cal. App.4th 777

Measure: Parking impacts from expansion of convention center—city shall achieve "parking utilization rate of 90% by some combination of the following:

- Limit the size of "short-term" weekday events
- Promote regional/national conventions
- Provide satellite parking
- Restrict event schedules
- Promote alternative transportation modes for attendees (e.g. special buses etc)
- Construct additional parking (at specific designated locations)

Adequate because city committed to a specific level of mitigation and developed a "menu" of options to achieve it
Sacramento Old City Association v. City of Sacramento (1991) 229 Cal. App. 3d 1001

Mitigation monitoring is required for all measures made a condition of approval for EIRs and MNDs.

alternatives to conclude which is environmentally superior when the alternatives impact different resources, in effect, comparing "apples to oranges." Therefore, some agencies may have several alternatives identified as "superior" for different resource impacts. The lead agency is not obligated to adopt the environmentally superior alternative as long as it finds, after approving the project, that the environmentally superior alternative is ultimately infeasible. This finding is part of the findings required under Guidelines § 15091. (*see* Chapter 8.)

Mitigation Measures

In General

In general, CEQA requires that, for each significant impact identified in the EIR, the EIR must discuss identify measures to either avoid or substantially reduce the significant environmental effect (Guidelines 15126.4(a)). Mitigation measures must be made a part of the project approval, unless infeasible.

In practice, the EIR preparer should include all measures that it considers to be potentially feasible, even though the ultimate determination of feasibility is not made until the decisionmakers prepare findings later in the project approval process. A measure brought to the attention of the lead agency staff should not be left out of the EIR unless it is infeasible on its face. Even in that case, the lead agency should explain why it is infeasible (*Los Angeles Unified School District v. City of Los Angeles* (1997) 58 Cal. App. 4th 1019).

The EIR must distinguish between the measures proposed by the project proponents to be included in the project from other measures proposed by the lead, responsible, or trustee agency that are not included but could reasonably be expected to reduce the adverse impacts. Where several measures are available to mitigate an impact, each should be discussed and the basis for selecting a particular measure should be identified (Guidelines § 15126.4(a)).

The Guidelines provide for five categories of mitigation—measures that avoid, minimize, rectify, reduce or eliminate, or compensate for the significant environmental effect of the proposed project (Guidelines § 15370; *see* Figure 7-6 on page 176). A mitigation measure must fall into one of the five categories.

Drafting Adequate Mitigation Measures

Adequacy and Feasibility. To be considered adequate, mitigation measures should be specific, potentially feasible actions that will actually improve the adverse environmental conditions caused by the proposed project. A mitigation measure is considered feasible if it is capable of being accomplished in a successful manner within a reasonable period of time, taking into consideration economic, environmental, legal, social, and technological factors (Guidelines § 15364). Mitigation measures should be measurable to allow monitoring of their implementation. Mitigation measures consisting only of further studies, or consultation with regulatory agencies that are not tied to a specific action plan, may not be adequate and should, therefore, be avoided (*see* Figure 7-7, page 176). See, for example, *Sundstrom v. County of Mendocino* (1998) 202 Cal. App. 3d 296) (MND overturned for relying on deferred mitigation). It may be appropriate, however, for a lead agency to list alternative mitigation measures in an EIR if the agency commits to mitigating the impacts and if the measures are tied to measurable performance standards. See, discussion of deferred mitigation below.

While a lead agency should attempt to apply mitigation consistently, CEQA does not mandate that the same mitigation measures be applied to similar projects. For example, historically applied ratios (e.g., 3:1 wetland replacement) may not be applicable to future projects with different circumstances.

Effective Mitigation Measures. In practice, drafting an effective mitigation measure involves clearly explaining its objectives—specifically, how it will be implemented, who is responsible for its implementation, where it will occur, and when it will occur. In drafting or reviewing mitigation measures, a lead agency may use the five factors found in CEQA's definition of mitigation as a test of a measure's adequacy. If they are not specific, mitigation measures are less likely to be implemented, effective, and capable of being monitored.

> **Judicial Criteria for Analyzing the Adequacy of an EIR**
>
> - All required contents must be included.
> - The lead agency should make an objective, good-faith effort toward full disclosure.
> - Disagreement among experts is acceptable.
> - Perfection is not required.
> - Exhaustive treatment of issues is not required.
> - Minor technical defects are not necessarily fatal.

Analysis of Impacts of Mitigation

The EIR must discuss the environmental "side effects" of implementation of the mitigation measures, if any, in addition to those caused by the proposed project. For example, if road widening is a mitigation for traffic impacts, the EIR must examine whether the widening would result in any significant effects and disclose them. Although the Guidelines provide that the discussion of a mitigation measure's significant effects may be less detailed than those of the proposed project, most lead agencies include the impact analysis of mitigation in the same detail to remove the potential for triggering a subsequent or supplemental document (Guidelines § 15126.4(a)).

Deferred Mitigation

In general, formulation of mitigation measures should not be deferred until some future time. However, a mitigation measure may be adequate even though the specifics of its design may not be developed until after issuance of the EIR and project approval. Mitigation measures may allow for future choices as to the detail of how they will be accomplished if they also contain specific performance standards that would assure that the significant effect of the project is indeed reduced. For example, if a mitigation measure for wildlife habitat loss is to create replacement habitat, the detailed design of the new habitat may be deferred to the future so long as the EIR includes performance standards such as types of vegetation to be used, timing of implementation, and contingency plans if the replanting is not successful. However, the possibility of secondary impacts of the development of mitigation lands should be identified if potential exists for impacts on the mitigation site. Additionally, if the activity being evaluated in the EIR is a plan or program, the mitigation measures will typically consist of policy statements included in the program that will serve to guide project-specific mitigation in the future (Guidelines § 15126.4(a)). Further, full technical design may not need to be included in the measure if it is adequately described otherwise (*Dry Creek Citizen's Coalition v. County of Tulare* (1999) 70 Cal. App. 4th 20) or if details are not meaningfully possible to include at the time of the EIR (*Riverwatch v. County of San Diego* (1999) 76 Cal. App. 4th 1428).

Adaptive Management as Part of Mitigation. If periodic monitoring is added to the three elements of acceptable deferred mitigation, then the concept of deferred mitigation is quite similar to the ecological concept of "adaptive management." Adaptive management, frequently used by land management and environmental protection agencies is based on the idea that the mitigation measures should be adapted over time depending on how well they are actually working to achieve the *desired future condition*. Adaptive management typically relies on a six-step process:

1. Assess the problem (e.g., environmental impacts).
2. Design mitigation measures.
3. Implement mitigation measures.
4. Monitor mitigation measures.
5. Evaluate to determine if desired results are being achieved.
6. Adjust the mitigation, as necessary, to ensure desired results will be achieved.

An increasing number of environmental professionals feel that such adaptive approaches to environmental problems are preferable to a "one-size-fits all solution." For more information, see discussion on page 188 on *Relationship of Mitigation Monitoring to Adaptive Management.*

To assist practitioners in developing adequate, feasible, and effective mitigation measures, the Mitigation Measure Evaluation Checklist may be a useful tool. Table 7-2 summarizes some examples of what the courts have found to be adequate and inadequate regarding deferred mitigation. In the cases in which the courts found deferred mitigation to be inadequate, the common feature was the improper deferral of the essential impact studies that should have been performed during the CEQA process, in addition to the complete deferral of any mitigation. Thus, if an agency is tempted to support a negative declaration, or a mitigated negative declaration, with mitigation such as "prepare a study . . ."—that agency might as well wave a big red flag over the document.

On the other hand, the courts have been more lenient toward agencies that prepare EIRs and then make a good faith effort to avoid or reduce the impact—even if those efforts are a bit short on specifics—as long as the three key ingredients are present: 1) performance standards, 2) menu of mitigation options, and 3) a com- mitment to mitigation. Note that simply committing to prepare a future management plan may not be sufficient to meet this test. In describing the management plan, the mitigation measure must set out the objectives to be met, the basic methods of meeting them, and performance standards that will ensure that the objectives are met.

Authority to Mitigate Impacts

Subject to the limitations discussed below, CEQA gives a public agency the authority to require feasible changes in any or all activities involved in a project to substantially lessen or avoid significant effects on the environment (Guidelines § 15041). An agency does not, however, have unlimited authority to impose mitigation measures. CEQA does not grant an agency any new powers. When imposing mitigation measures, the agency must work within its existing powers.

Limitations on Mitigation. CEQA contains both general and specific limitations on an agency's authority to mitigate impacts. As discussed in chapter 4, in mitigating a project's significant environmental effects, an agency may exercise only those express or implied powers provided by law, aside from those provided by CEQA. Where another law grants an agency discretionary powers, CEQA authorizes its use (Guidelines § 15040). However, if under other law, an agency lacks the legal authority to impose those mitigation measures for a significant environmental impact, CEQA does not provide that authority.

If the lead agency determines that a mitigation measure cannot be legally imposed, the measure may be screened out as infeasible. The EIR should reference that fact and briefly explain the reasons underlying the lead agency's determination (Guidelines § 15126.4(a)). However if the measure can and should be legally imposed by another agency, the lead agency should identify this in the EIR and make its findings accordingly.

Constitutional Limitations. The U.S. Constitution limits an agency's authority to impose conditions on project applicants to those situations where there is a clear "nexus" between the impact and the mitigation measure; otherwise, the agency may be accused of "taking" private property without "just compensation" (*Nollan v. California Coastal Commission* (1988) 107 S. Ct. 3141). Thus, the mitigation proposed for a project must relate directly to the impacts caused. Additionally, "rough proportionality" must exist between the environmental problems caused by a development project and the mitigation measure imposed on the project applicant (*Dolan v. City of Tigard* (1994) 512 U.S. 374; CEQA Guidelines §§ 15041, 15126.4).

Limitations Applicable to Particular Environmental Resources

For some subjects, CEQA imposes limitations on the nature and extent of mitigation that an agency may impose. Such limitations have been established for impacts to historical resources, archeological resources, schools, housing density, and oak woodlands.

Historical Resources. A lead agency must identify any potentially feasible measures to mitigate significant adverse changes in the significance of an historical resource. Any adopted mitigation measures must be made fully enforceable through permits, conditions, agreements, or other measures (Guideline §§ 15064.5(b)(3–5)).

Mitigation measures that do not truly reduce or avoid an adverse impact to significant historical resources are inadequate under CEQA. The courts have held that demolition of a significant historic resource, as defined under CEQA Guidelines § 15064.5, cannot be mitigated to a less than significant level (*League for Protection of Oakland's Architectural and Historical Resources v. City of Oakland* (1997) 52 Cal. App. 4th 60). In other words, measures such as placing a historical marker on a site, writing a report documenting the resource, or consulting with a historic society do not mitigate the demolition of a historic structure.

> **Practice Tip:**
> **Detail of Mitigation Measures vs. Monitoring Program**
>
> Avoid confusing the contents of the mitigation measure with the purpose and contents of the mitigation monitoring or reporting program. Mitigation measures commonly include monitoring requirements to ensure the effectiveness of mitigation over time (for example, biological restoration may need to be monitored to ensure that plantings meet survival criteria and replanting is undertaken when necessary). These requirements must be included in the mitigation measure itself and should not be assigned solely to the mitigation monitoring or reporting program.
>
> Remember that mitigation measures and mitigation monitoring or reporting programs do not have the same purpose. The purpose of the mitigation measure is to reduce, avoid, or otherwise limit the project's potential impacts through fully enforceable requirements. The purpose of the mitigation monitoring or reporting program is simply to ensure that the mitigation measure is implemented.

> **Public Policy Objectives Served by Monitoring**
>
> - To ensure implementation of mitigation measures during project implementation
> - To provide feedback to agency staff and decisionmakers about the effectiveness of their actions
> - To provide learning opportunities for improving mitigation measures on future projects
> - To identify the need for enforcement action before irreversible environmental damage occurs

Generally, a project that seeks to improve an historical resource in accordance with either of the following publications will be considered as mitigated to a level of less than significant:

- Secretary of Interior's *Standards for the Treatment of Historic Properties with Guidelines for Preserving, Rehabilitating, Restoring, and Reconstructing Historic Buildings*
- Secretary of Interior's *Standards for Rehabilitation and Guidelines for Rehabilitating Historic Buildings*

(Guidelines § 15064.5(b)(3)).

Archaeological Resources. Public agencies should, whenever possible, seek to avoid damaging effects to any archaeological resources. Preservation in place to maintain the relationship between the artifacts and the archaeological context is the preferred manner of mitigating impacts to archaeological sites. Preservation may be accomplished by:

- Planning construction to avoid archaeological sites
- Incorporating sites within parks, greenspace, or other open space
- Covering the sites with a layer of chemically stable soil
- Deeding the site into a permanent conservation easement

When in-place mitigation is not feasible, the CEQA document must explain why. In those situations, data recovery through excavation may be necessary. A data recovery plan, which makes provisions for adequately recovering the scientifically consequential information about the site, must be prepared and adopted prior to any excavation being undertaken. Such studies must be deposited with the California Historical Resources Regional Information Center. If an artifact must be removed during project excavation or testing, curation of the artifact may be an appropriate mitigation. Special rules apply to any archaeological sites known to contain human remains (Health and Safety Code § 7050.5; Guidelines § 15126.4(b)).

Data recovery is not required if the lead agency determines that testing or studies already completed have adequately recovered the necessary data, provided that the data have already been documented in another EIR and are available for review at the California Historical Resource Regional Information Center (Guidelines § 15126.4(b)).

CEQA may limit a public agency's ability to mitigate the impacts on unique archaeological resources by authorizing optinal cost limitations on the amount of mitigation that can be required of project applicants. These limitations are discussed in CEQA but, in practice, are rarely used (Pub. Res. Code § 21082.2).

School Impacts

State law prohibits a local agency from either denying approval of a land use project because of inadequate school facilities or imposing school impact mitigation measures other than fees specifically designated by statute. For residential and commercial developments, mitigation for schools—imposed as impact fees—is statutorily limited (Govt. Code § 65995). The fee limits are adjusted for inflation every two years; The Leroy F. Greene School Facilities Act of 1998 (SB 50) and bond procedures under Proposition 1A of 1998 regulate school facilities financing and mitigation of land use approvals by setting fee caps, removing application denial authority, and setting the CEQA standard for full and complete school facilities mitigation. These were effectively extended by the passage of school bonds under Proposition 1D in November 2006.

Mandatory Employee Trip Reduction Program

Health & Safety Code Section 40717.9 prohibits the lead agency from requiring the applicant to implement an "employee trip reduction" program, unless such program is otherwise required by federal law.

Reductions in Housing Density

In accordance with state laws, requiring a reduction in the density of a housing development project as a condition of approval is only permissible if the project would have a specific adverse impact on health or safety that cannot be mitigated except by lowering of the density (Govt. Code § 65589.5. Pub. Res. Code § 21159.26).

Oak Woodland (Required for Counties Only)

Where the project would have a significant impact on oak woodlands and a county is the lead agency, CEQA requires that the EIR include one or more of the following specific mitigation measures:

- Conserving oaks through the use of conservation easements
- Planting and maintaining an appropriate number of trees either on-site or in restoration of a former oak woodlands (tree planting is limited to half the mitigation requirement)
- Contributing funds to the Oak Woodlands Conservation Fund for the purpose of purchasing conservation easements
- Other mitigation measures developed by the county (this element of "required" mitigation gives the county lead agency the discretion to substitute different mitigation than prescribed above, as long as substantial evidence supports the conclusion that it is equivalent or better than the enumerated measures)

The oak woodlands requirement does not apply to any of the following:

- Projects undertaken pursuant to an NCCP that includes oaks as a covered species or that conserves oak habitats consistent with the bill
- Affordable housing projects for lower income households
- Conversion of oak woodlands on agricultural land "that includes land that is used to produce or process plant and animal products for commercial purposes"
- Projects undertaken pursuant to a certified regulatory program

(Pub. Res. Code § 21083.4).

Monitoring ensures the implementation of the mitigation measures.

Mitigation Reporting and Monitoring

Where the lead agency requires implementation of mitigation as a condition of approval, it is required to adopt a mitigation monitoring or reporting program when it prepares its findings on significant effects identified in an EIR (or when adopting a negative declaration that contains mitigation measures). Such a program must address how it will monitor all of the mitigation measures that were adopted or made conditions of project approval (Pub. Res. Code § 21081.6(a); Guidelines §§ 15091(d), 15097). Although not required to be included in the draft (or final) EIR, a lead agency may choose to include the draft mitigation monitoring program in the draft EIR to obtain public comment. The monitoring program is implemented to ensure that the mitigation measures and project revisions identified in the EIR (or negative declaration) are implemented (*see* Chapter 8 for a full discussion of this requirement).

Relationship of Mitigation Monitoring to Adaptive Management

Monitoring can incorporate the important concept of adaptive management. Adaptive Management, frequently used by land management and environmental protection agencies, is based on the idea that the mitigation measures should be adapted over time depending on how well they are actually working to achieve specified performance standards. Adaptive management typically relies on a four-step process consisting of:

1. Develop the management approach or mitigation measure with desired or future condition and performance standards included
2. Implement the mitigation measure
3. Monitor to determine what is actually happening to the resource and if the desired results are being achieved or not
4. Adjust the mitigation, if necessary, to ensure that desired results will be achieved

Many environmental professionals feel that such adaptive approaches are preferable to a "one-size-fits all solution" to environmental problems.

Mitigation Monitoring Programs: Practical Experience

Monitoring the Success of Mitigation. Monitoring the success of a mitigation measure—although not required by CEQA unless success monitoring is already included in a mitigation measure—may be included in a mitigation monitoring program. Descriptions of monitoring approaches should be, but are not required to be, included in the EIR to ensure that mitigation measures are capable of being monitored, to take advantage of the technical expertise of the EIR preparer, and to allow for public review.

Incorporation into a Draft EIR. Although the project-specific monitoring program is not required to be included in the EIR or negative declaration, in practice, many agencies are including monitoring programs with the documents that are circulated for public review so that members of the public, responsible agencies, and others can review them before they are adopted. Including the monitoring program in the environmental documents is also recommended to ensure that mitigation measures will be specific enough to be monitored effectively (drafting the mitigation measure with monitoring in mind may ensure that the measure is written in a way to provide for effective monitoring).

Phased Monitoring Programs. Generally, agencies implement the mitigation monitoring requirement in two phases. First, many agencies voluntarily adopt jurisdiction-wide, comprehensive monitoring programs in which the basic framework for monitoring is established for all projects. Second, they develop detailed, project-specific monitoring plans as individual projects are approved.

At its discretion, an agency may adopt standardized policies and requirements to guide individually adopted monitoring or reporting programs. Such a jurisdiction-wide program may include, but is not limited to:

- The relative responsibilities of various departments within the agency
- The role, if any, of project proponents
- Agency guidelines for preparing monitoring or reporting programs
- General standards for determining project compliance with the mitigation measures
- Enforcement procedures for noncompliance, including provisions for administrative appeals
- Processes for informing staff and decision makers of the relative success of mitigation measures and using those results to improve future mitigation measures

(Guidelines section 15097(e)).

In practice, the components of a project-specific monitoring program typically include the following:

- A description of specific performance standards
- A master mitigation checklist
- Identification of project-specific monitoring activities:
  - Assignment of responsibilities
  - Development of schedule
  - Specific reporting requirements
  - Field visit verification reports
  - Applicant compliance reports

Future of Mitigation Monitoring. Minimum requirements under CEQA is for monitoring law is not a remedy for all problems arising under CEQA's overall objective to mitigate or avoid all significant effects of the proposed project where feasible. In addition to being overly general and providing agencies with few specific details on what a monitoring program should entail, the law requires agencies to monitor only the implementation of mitigation measures; the success of those measures is only an optional component (Guidelines § 15097(e)(6)). For example, if a mitigation measure recommends that trees be replanted the agency's responsibility is only to monitor the planting, and not necessarily to determine whether the trees survive. For the law truly to meet the objective of successful mitigation, agencies should write much more specific mitigation measures that include measurable performance standards by which success can be determined.

Contents of a Final EIR

After the public review period, the lead agency must prepare a final EIR (Guidelines §§ 15089, 15132). As discussed in chapter 6, a final EIR is required to include the draft EIR, or a revision of the draft EIR, copies or a summary of comments and recommendations received during public review of the draft EIR, a list of persons and entities commenting on the draft EIR, lead agency responses to the comments received on the draft EIR, and any other information added by the lead agency.

The responses to comments in the final EIR must demonstrate good faith and a well-reasoned analysis, and may not be conclusory (Pub. Res. Code § 21091(d); Guidelines § 15088(b)). When responding to comments, the lead agency need only respond to significant environmental issues and does not need to provide all information requested by reviewers (Guidelines § 15204(a)). To respond to the comments, the lead agency may revise portions of or the entire draft EIR, add new material to the draft EIR, or both. These changes may be a separate section of the final EIR (Guidelines § 15088(c)). However, changes to the draft EIR considered to be "significant new information" or substantial changes may require the lead agency to recirculate the EIR (*see* Preparation of a Final EIR in Chapter 6).

Chapter 8

Agency Decisionmaking and Post-Decision CEQA Compliance

Taking Action on Projects for Which an EIR Was Prepared

Lead and Responsible Agency Authority

In General. As discussed in Chapter 6, after an EIR is prepared, the lead agency must certify that the EIR was prepared in compliance with CEQA and was presented to the decisionmakers that reviewed and considered it prior to approving the project. In addition, the lead agency must certify that the EIR reflects the independent judgment of the lead agency (Guidelines § 15090).

CEQA gives lead and responsible agencies a broad range of authority to deal with a project after the lead agency certifies an EIR. In reaction to the EIR, a lead or responsible agency may either disapprove a project because it may cause significant environmental effects, require changes in a project as part of project approval, reduce or avoid a significant environmental effect, or possibly approve a project despite its significant and unavoidable environmental effects, if the proper findings and statement of overriding considerations are adopted (Guidelines §§ 15042, 15043).

> **When Acting on a Project, a Lead Agency May . . .**
>
> - Disapprove a project because it has significant environmental effects
> - Require changes in a project to reduce or avoid a significant environmental effect
> - Approve a project despite its significant environmental effects, if the proper findings and a statement of overriding considerations are adopted; an agency need not select the most environmentally superior alternative

Limitations on Authority. As discussed in Chapter 7, an agency does not have unlimited authority to impose mitigation measures or alternatives discussed in an EIR that would reduce the environmental effects of the proposed project to a less than significant level. Rather, a public agency is subject to both general and specific limitations on its authority. In mitigating or avoiding a project's significant environmental effects, an agency may exercise only those express or implied powers provided by law, regulation, or ordinance aside from those provided by CEQA. Where another law grants an agency discretionary powers, CEQA authorizes its use for the mitigation of significant impacts (Guidelines § 15040). For example, in *Friends of Davis v. City of Davis* (2000) 83 Cal. App. 4th 1004, the court held that CEQA did not give the city authority to regulate the specific occupants of a proposed commercial development when the city's design review ordinance was limited to regulating the exterior appearance of such buildings.

In addition, for projects where an agency wants to impose conditions or exactions, the U.S. Constitution limits its authority to those situations where there is a clear nexus between the impact and the mitigation measure; otherwise, the exercise of government authority may be considered a taking of private property without just compensation (*Nollan v. California Coastal Commission* (1988) 107 S. Ct. 3141). Thus, the mitigation proposed for a project must relate directly to the impacts caused. For example, if a proposed private development project would result in significant air quality impacts, the agency would be allowed to require the applicant to pay for air quality mitigation. However, the agency would not be able to require mitigation to solve water quality problems not caused by the project.

In addition to the required nexus, the U.S. Supreme court held that there must be rough proportionality between the environmental problems caused by a development project and the mitigation measure imposed on the project applicant (*Dolan v. City of Tigard* (1994) 512 U.S. 854). While the court held that there was no precise mathematical formula for determining rough proportionality, some form of individualized determination is required (Guidelines §§ 15041, 15126.4(a)(4)).

One method for a lead agency to determine that the rough proportionality test is satisfied would be to calculate an applicant's pro rata share of a problem and impose no more than a pro rata share of the solution on the applicant by way of mitigation. Thus, for example, if an applicant's project is contributing ten percent of the traffic on a roadway, then the applicant may be required to pay for only ten percent of the mitigation. The EIR (or negative declaration) should be used to document such a determination of "rough proportionality" (for a detailed discussion of limitations on agency authority to impose mitigation, *see Exactions and Impact Fees in California* by Abbott, et al., Solano Press Books, 2012).

In addition to the general limitations discussed above, CEQA sets forth certain specific limits on the authority of an agency to mitigate impacts to archaeological and historic resources, schools, housing, and public water systems (*see* Chapter 7 for further information regarding the limitations of lead agencies on requiring mitigation).

Findings

In General. To support the decision to approve a project for which an EIR was prepared, lead and responsible agencies must prepare written findings of fact for each significant environmental impact identified in the EIR, including those that would be reduced below the level of significance by mitigation measures (Guidelines §§ 15091, 15096(h)). A statement of overriding considerations (*see* next section) does not substitute for the requirement to prepare findings (Guidelines § 15091(f)).

Findings are a sometimes misunderstood aspect of CEQA implementation. Simply stated, a finding is a written statement made by the decision-making body of the lead or responsible agency that explains how it dealt with each significant impact and alternative in the EIR. Each finding must contain an ultimate conclusion regarding each significant impact, substantial evidence supporting the conclusion, and an explanation of how the substantial evidence supports the conclusion (Guidelines § 15091). Findings "bridge the gap" between the decision and the substantial evidence that supports the decision. When findings are absent from the administrative record, the court will generally overturn the agency's action (*see*, for example, *Protect Our Water; et al. v. County of Merced* (2003) 110 Cal. App. 4th 362).

Specifically, the agencies must make one of three possible findings for each significant impact identified in the EIR:

- The project has been changed (including adoption of mitigation measures) to avoid or substantially reduce the magnitude of the impact.
- Changes to the project are within another agency's jurisdiction, and the other agency has or should mitigate the impact.
- Specific economic, social, legal, technical, or other considerations, such as employment opportunities for highly trained workers, make the mitigation measure or alternative infeasible.

(Guidelines § 15091).

For Each Significant Impact, an Agency Must Make One or More of the Following Findings . . .

- Changes in the project have been made, including adoption of mitigation measures,) to avoid or substantially reduce the magnitude of the impact. (The agency must ensure that adopted mitigation measures are fully enforceable through permit conditions, agreements, or other measures.)
- Changes to the project are within another agency's jurisdiction and have been—or should be—adopted.
- Specific economic, social, legal, technical, or other considerations make mitigation measures or alternatives infeasible.

A responsible agency, in granting subsequent approvals for a project studied in an EIR, cannot rely on the lead agency's findings but must make its own findings for each significant effect identified in the EIR that relates to its action (Guidelines § 15096(h) (*see* Figure 8-1 below).

Timing. Findings are made at the time a project is approved. In practice, tentative findings, often written by agency legal or planning staff, are presented to the decision-making body with the project staff report and recommendation. However, the agency's decision-making body cannot delegate the adoption of findings. Thus, if the decision-making body makes a decision inconsistent with the tentative findings, those findings must be rewritten to conform to the decision before

Figure 8-1
CEQA Decision-Making Pyramid

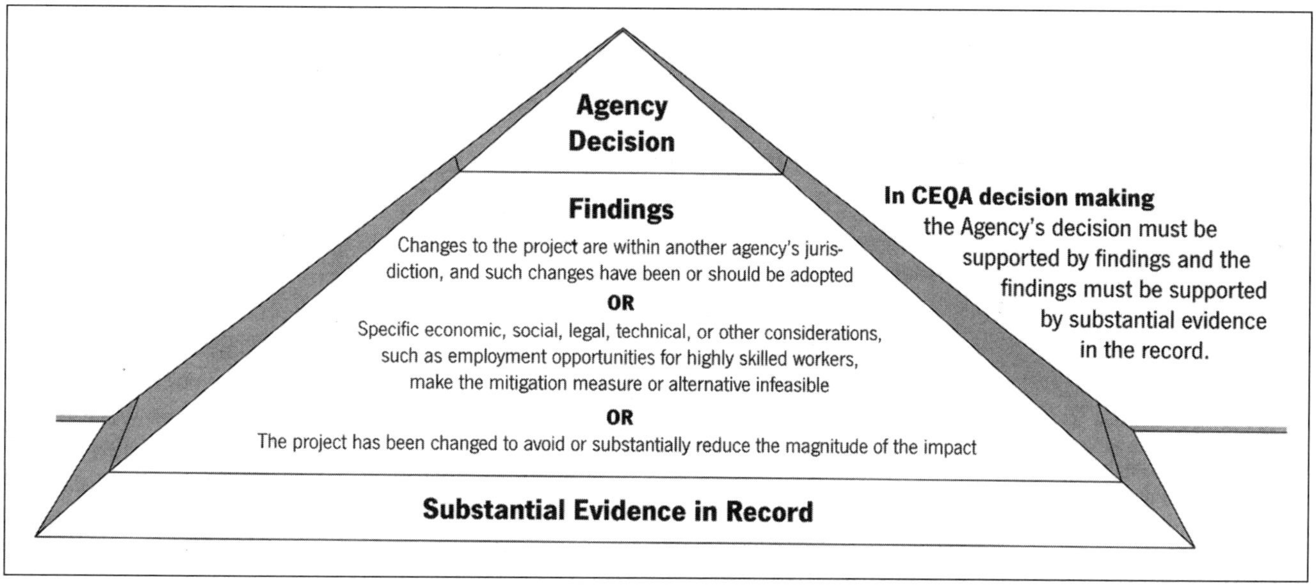

Examples of Findings

The following are examples of each of the different possible findings. These examples are for illustrative purposes only, the precise language must be tailored to fit the facts and circumstances of each project. Since findings are legal documents, they should be prepared or reviewed by agency legal counsel before adoption by the decision-making body.

A mitigation measure is feasible:

The City Council hereby finds that requiring the project applicant to protect oak trees during construction and landscaping, in accordance with the specification set forth in the EIR, is a feasible mitigation measure and has, therefore, been adopted. Therefore, the City Council further finds that changes or alternatives have been required in, or incorporated into, the project which would avoid or substantially lessen the significant environment effect, as identified in the final EIR.

Another agency will mitigate the impact:

The City Council hereby finds that it does not have the legal authority to require the project applicant to mitigate the impact on the state highway. Rather, this impact will be mitigated through a separate agreement between the applicant and the State Department of Transportation. Therefore, the City Council further finds that such changes or alterations are within the responsibility and jurisdiction of another public agency and have been or should be adopted by that agency.

An impact is not feasible to mitigate:

The City Council hereby finds that widening the roadway to mitigate the traffic impacts is not feasible for technical and economic reasons. First, inadequate land is available for the widening without the necessity to condemn adjacent buildings—which is against the current policy of the city. Second, the cost of the roadway widening is not included in the city's public facilities plan and, therefore, the city has no ability to fund the improvements in the foreseeable future. The substantial evidence to support these conclusions is found in the traffic technical appendix in the EIR and in the city's Public Facility Improvement Plan.

An alternative is not feasible:

The City Council hereby finds that the "all residential alternative" is legally and economically infeasible for the following reasons. First, it is not consistent with the policy of the City General Plan requiring all projects to be mixed use. Second, the "all residential alternative" would not generate sufficient funds for the city to offset the cost of providing public services to the project." The data to support the substantial evidence to support these conclusions is found in the Land Use and Public Facilities sections of the EIR.

Example of a Statement of Overriding Considerations

The City Council hereby finds that, for the reasons set forth below, the economic, social, and other considerations of the project outweigh the unavoidable traffic and air quality impacts identified in the findings. First, the need for housing, as identified in the housing element of the general plan, is of paramount importance to the city. Second, the commercial aspects of the project will enable the city to achieve its plans for revitalization of the central business district. Third, the commercial base of the project will enhance the tax base, create more jobs, and provide diverse shopping opportunities for residents of the city. The data to support these overridding factors are found in the "Population, Employment, and Housing" section of the EIR and in the deographic data submitted by the project applicant.

adoption. The findings become part of the project's administrative record and are available to the public, but they do not have to be circulated for public review prior to adoption.

Drafting Findings. In drafting findings, agency decisionmakers and their staff should remember that one of the stated objectives of CEQA is public accountability. Therefore, the findings should be presented in a clear, well-organized manner that enables the reader to understand how the agency addressed every significant impact and alternative.

Infeasibility of Mitigation Measures or Alternatives. If it finds a mitigation measure or an alternative infeasible, the lead or responsible agency must explain the specific reasons for rejecting the identified mitigation measure or alternative in its findings (Guidelines § 15091(a)(3)). A mitigation measure or alternative is considered feasible if it can be accomplished successfully within a reasonable period of time and take into account economic, environmental, legal, social, and technological factors as well as considerations for employment of highly trained workers (Pub. Res. Code § 21081(c)). When economics is used as a factor to support a finding of infeasibility, the agency must support the finding with specific data that shows the additional cost or lost profits are great enough to make it impractical to proceed with the project. The fact that an alternative may be more expensive than the project does not necessarily make it infeasible.

The findings must be supported by substantial evidence in the record before the lead agency. This may include information, such as an economic or technical study, that is not necessarily a part of the EIR itself (*see Sierra Club v. County of Napa* (2004) 121 Cal. App. 4th 1490 and *San Franciscans Upholding the Downtown Plan v. City and County of San Francisco* (2002) 102 Cal. App. 4th 656). This information may be supplied by the applicant, but it must be independently reviewed by the lead agency based on its own investigation as to the validity of the applicant's assertions regarding an alternative's infeasibility (*see Preservation Action Council v. City of San Jose, et al.* (2006) 141 Cal. App. 4th 1336). If the lead agency wants to make a finding that an alternative is economically infeasible based on the applicant's assertions, information regarding investment backed interests as well as costs of the proposed project may be necessary to use as a reference point for comparing costs of other alternatives (*see Uphold Our Heritage v. Town of Woodside* (2007) 147 Cal. App. 4th 587).

Statement of Overriding Considerations

If the lead agency decides to approve a project with unavoidable, adverse environmental impacts, it must prepare a statement of overriding considerations (Pub. Res. Code § 21081; Guidelines § 15093). Unavoidable impacts are those that cannot be mitigated to below the level of significance. The statement of overriding considerations must explain in detail why the benefits of the proposed project outweigh the unavoidable, adverse environmental impacts and why the agency is willing to accept such impacts. The statement of overriding considerations must be adopted at the time the agency adopts its findings, but it is a separate, legally distinct requirement.

In this way, CEQA requires decisionmakers to balance the benefits of a proposed project against unavoidable environmental risks in determining whether to approve the project. The statement setting forth the specific overriding social, economic, legal, technical, or other beneficial project aspects supporting the agency's decision must be based on substantial evidence in the final EIR or elsewhere in the record (*see* Figure 8-2 below). A statement of overriding considerations must be included in the record of project approval and must be mentioned in the notice of determination (*see* discussion in the following section) (Guidelines § 15093(c)).

Drafting Statements of Overriding Considerations

Typically, the statement of overriding considerations begins with a summary of the unavoidable impacts and then lists specific social, economic, or other factors that justify approving the project despite these impacts. As with findings, a statement of overriding considerations should clearly enable the reader to understand the rationale for the agency's decision and must be supported by substantial evidence. In practice, there should be only one statement of overriding considerations even though there may be multiple findings under Guidelines section 15091 (*see* the sidebar for an example of a statement of overriding consideration).

Figure 8-2
Balancing Environmental Damage against Social, Economic and Other Factors

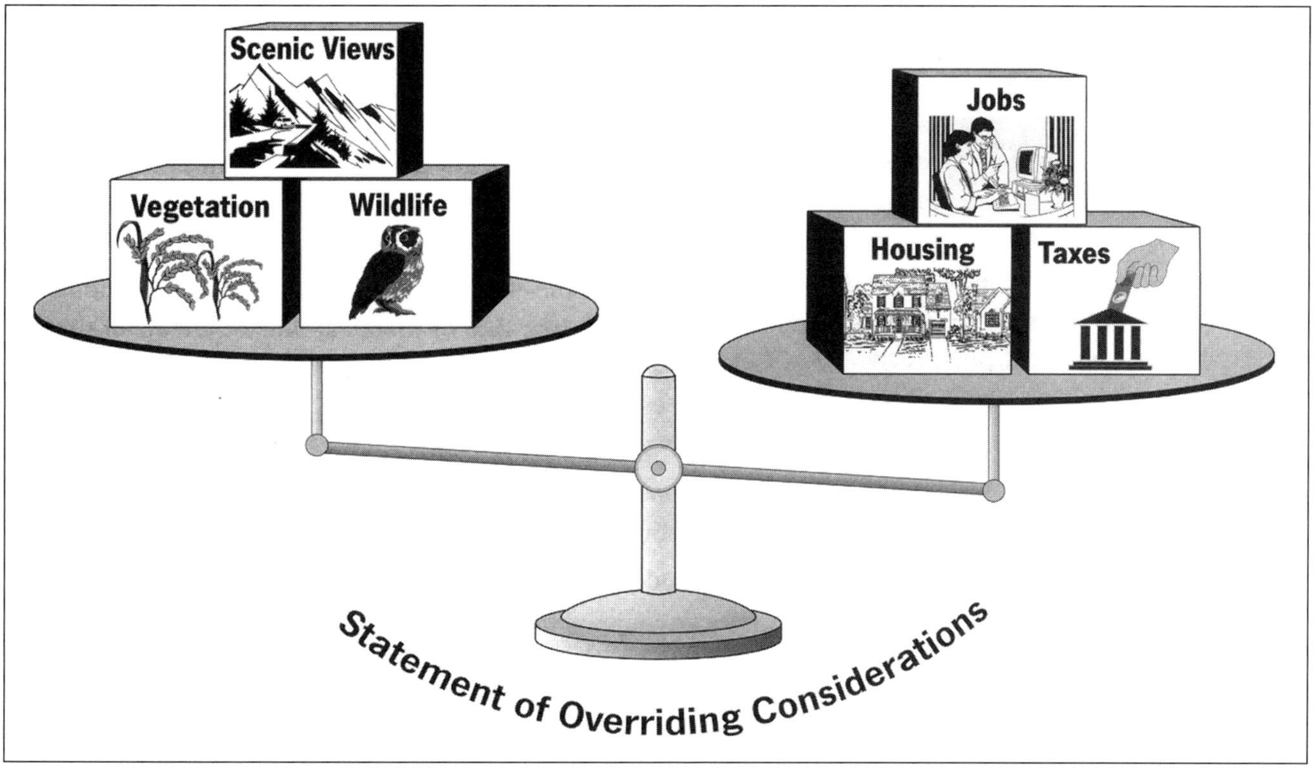

Mitigation Reporting or Monitoring

When it makes findings on significant effects identified in an EIR (or adopts a negative declaration containing mitigation measures) at project approval, an agency must also adopt a program for reporting or monitoring mitigation measures that were adopted or made conditions of project approval (Pub. Res. Code § 21081.6(a); Guidelines §§ 15091(d), 15097). The reporting or monitoring program must ensure compliance with mitigation measures during project implementation (*see* Figure 8-3 below).

Figure 8-3
Mitigation Monitoring and Reporting Requirements

Trigger	• Agency adopts a Mitigated Negative Declaration • Agency makes finding after adopting an EIR
CEQA Requirement	• Agency must adopt a "reporting or monitoring" program for changes in the project adopted or made as conditions of approval to mitigate or avoid significant effects
Provisions for Mitigation Measures	• Mitigation measures must be made express conditions of project approval • Agencies with jurisdiction by law over natural resources must provide the Lead Agency with performance standards for mitigation measures • Agencies with jurisdiction by law over natural resources may be required to prepare monitoring programs if their recommended mitigation measures are adopted by the Lead Agency • Responsible agencies and agencies with jurisdiction over natural resources must identify mitigation performance objectives
Payment for Monitoring Program	• CEQA authorizes levy fees to pay for monitoring program

The mitigation monitoring or reporting program need not be included in the draft EIR; however, to obtain public comment some lead agencies choose to include draft mitigation monitoring programs in the draft EIR. The monitoring program is implemented to ensure that the mitigation measures and project revisions identified in the EIR (or negative declaration) are implemented. Therefore, the monitoring program must include all changes in the proposed project—either adopted by the project proponent or made conditions of approval by the lead or responsible agency—that would mitigate or avoid each significant environmental effect identified in the EIR (Guidelines § 15097). CEQA authorizes the lead agency to levy fees to pay for the monitoring program.

The reporting or monitoring program must ensure compliance with mitigation measures during project implementation. CEQA only requires monitoring to determine if mitigation measures have been implemented. Thus, if an agency wants its monitoring program to evaluate the success of mitigation, it should incorporate success criteria and performance standards into the mitigation measure.

Therefore, monitoring may provide feedback to agency staff and decision-makers about the effectiveness of their actions and learning opportunities for improving mitigation measures on future projects and identify the need for enforcement action before irreversible environmental damage occurs.

A public agency may delegate its reporting or monitoring responsibilities to another public agency or to a private entity that accepts the delegation. However, until the mitigation measures have been completed, the lead agency remains responsible for ensuring that the implementation of the measures occurs in accordance with the program (Guidelines § 15097(a)).

Where the project consists of the adoption of a general plan, specific plan, or other plan-level document, the monitoring plan shall apply to any policies in the plan designed to mitigate environmental effects. The monitoring plan may consist of policies included in such plan-level documents (Guidelines § 15097(b)).

Differences between Monitoring and Reporting

A public agency may choose whether its program will monitor mitigation, report on mitigation, or both. However, there is often no clear distinction between reporting and monitoring, and the program best suited to ensuring compliance in any given project will usually involve elements of both (Guidelines § 15097(c)).

Reporting. Reporting generally consists of a written compliance review that is presented to the decision-making body or authorized staff person. A report may be required at various stages of a project. Reporting is suited to projects that have readily measurable or quantitative mitigation measures or that already involve regular review under some other law or ordinance. For example, a report may be required upon final occupancy for a project whose mitigation measures were confirmed by a building inspection (Guidelines § 15097(c)(1)).

Good practice encourages "success monitoring" not just to report that an important resource was avoided in the short term but that the mitigation measure achieved its ultimate objectives.

Monitoring. Monitoring is generally an ongoing process of project oversight, often involving site visits, and is suited to projects with complex mitigation that exceeds the local agency's expertise, is expected to be implemented over a period of time, or requires careful implementation to assure compliance. Wetland restoration or archaeological recovery activities are examples of such mitigation measures (Guidelines § 15097(c)(2)).

Coordination between Lead and Responsible Agencies

Generally, lead and responsible agencies will adopt separate and different monitoring and reporting programs for the same project. This often occurs because the agencies have adopted and are responsible for different mitigation measures, have made their decision on the project at different times, or have their own expertise. Although lead and responsible agencies have the discretion to choose their own approach to monitoring and reporting, they should coordinate their mitigation monitoring programs where possible (Guidelines § 15097(d)).

Possible Procedures to Ensure Mitigation Requirement Compliance

- "Stop work" orders
- Denial of building occupancy permits
- Revocation of project approval
- Misdemeanor criminal sanctions
- Performance bonds

Role of Responsible Agencies and Agencies with Jurisdiction over Natural Resources

Before the close of the public review period for the draft EIR (or mitigated negative declaration), a responsible agency (or agencies with jurisdiction by law over natural resources) must provide the lead agency with detailed performance standards for mitigation measures subject to their jurisdiction. Any mitigation measures submitted to the lead agency must be limited to those that mitigate impacts subject to that agency's jurisdiction (Pub. Res. Code § 21080.6(c)). That agency may be required to prepare a monitoring program for the recommended mitigation measures that are adopted by the lead agency (Guidelines § 15097(f)).

When a project is of statewide, regional, or areawide importance, any transportation information generated by a required monitoring or reporting program must be submitted to both the transportation planning agency in the region where the project is located and to Caltrans. Caltrans and the transportation planning agency must adopt guidelines for the submittal of such information (Guidelines § 15097(g)).

Contents of a Notice of Determination

- Project name
- Project description
- Project location
- Date of project approval
- Statement that the EIR was prepared and certified
- Summary of project's significant effects
- Whether mitigation measures were made conditions of project approval
- Whether findings were made and a Statement of Overriding Considerations adopted
- Address where final EIR may be reviewed

Enforcement of Mitigation Measures

CEQA does not give an agency additional authority to remedy violations of mitigation requirements. Most public agencies, however, have considerable authority under other state laws or local ordinances to ensure compliance. These other legal enforcement procedures may be used to remedy violations of mitigation requirements discovered by monitoring. Such enforcement provisions may include "stop work" orders, denial of building occupancy permits, revocation of project approval, misdemeanor criminal sanctions and performance bonds.

Notice of Determination

In General. A lead agency must file a notice of determination after deciding to approve a project for which an EIR is prepared. No notice of determination is required if the agency decides to disapprove the project. The notice of determination must include the project name, description, location, lead agency's name, and the date of project approval. It also must summarize the project's significant impacts and state whether mitigation measures were made conditions of approval, findings were prepared, a mitigation monitoring or reporting program was adopted, and a statement of overriding considerations was adopted. The notice must state that the final EIR is available for public review and disclose the location where the final EIR and record of project approval is available for review (Guidelines § 15094; Guidelines Appendix D).

Notice of Determination Filing and Posting Time Periods

- Lead agency files with county clerk and/or OPR within five days
- County clerk posts notice within 24 hours
- Notice kept posted for 30 days
- Notice retained for 12 months

Filing and Posting. Within five days of project approval, if the lead agency is a local agency, the notice of determination must be filed with the county clerk (or several county clerks if the project is located in more than one county) and, if any state agency discretionary approval is involved, with OPR. The county clerk must post the notice within twenty-four hours of receipt (Pub. Res. Code §§ 21092.3,

21152(a)(c); Guidelines § 15094). If the lead agency is a state agency, the notice of determination must be filed with OPR. The notice must be posted during regular business hours for thirty calendar days and retained in the agency files for at least twelve months (Pub. Res. Code §§ 21108,21152; Guidelines § 15094). The first day of posting does not count towards the thirty (*Latinos Unidos de Napa v. City of Napa* (2011) 196 Cal. App. 4th 1154). The notice must also be sent to anyone previously requesting notice (Pub. Res. Code § 21092.2).

A Department of Fish and Game (DFG) review fee must be paid at the time the notice of determination is filed. The fee is adjusted annually. Contact the State Clearinghouse or DFG reginal office for the current amount.

Statute of Limitations. Posting the notice of determination starts a thirty-day statute of limitations period for parties intending to challenge the lead agency's decision under CEQA (Pub. Res. Code § 21167(c); Guidelines § 15094(f)). If more than one notice is filed for the same project, the thirty-day period begins on the day the last notice is posted.

Lead Agency Disposition of a Final EIR

After project approval, the lead agency must: 1) file the final EIR with the planning agency of any city or county where significant effects may occur; 2) include the final EIR in any regular project report used for project review or budgeting; 3) retain the final EIR as a public record for a reasonable time; and 4) require the project applicant to provide copies of the final EIR to responsible agencies (Guidelines § 15095. Pub. Res. Code § 21105).

Responsible Agency Consideration

CEQA envisions that only one EIR (or ND or MND) will be prepared for any given project. With the exceptions listed below, this EIR will be used by both the lead agency and responsible agencies when considering whether to approve the project.

Each responsible agency is required to:

- Use the final EIR, prepared by the lead agency.
- Reach a separate decision on the proposed project.
- Make its own CEQA findings for each significant impact identified in the EIR.
- Adopt a statement of overriding considerations, if necessary.
- Adopt a mitigation monitoring and reporting program.

The actions of the lead and responsible agencies are separate. A responsible agency is not required to approve a project that has been approved by the lead agency; however, subject to the provisions below, the responsible agency must use the lead agency's CEQA document in its decision-making process. It should be noted that many responsible agencies have supplemental authority to require measures to offset particular resource effects within their jurisdiction through separate authorizing legislation; for example, DFG may require additional measures outside of the CEQA process in order for the project to comply with specific Fish and Game Code requirements.

If a responsible agency believes that an EIR is not adequate for its own use, its options are limited. The responsible agency must resort to litigation and file a CEQA court challenge against the lead agency (assuming the 30-day statute of limitations period has not elapsed). Otherwise, it is deemed to have waived objections to the final EIR and must proceed to use the final EIR in project decision making. The responsible agency may cause the preparation of a new CEQA document in very limited instances. A responsible agency may assume the lead agency role if:

- It successfully challenges the lead agency's document.
- A subsequent or supplemental EIR is required per the requirements of CEQA Guidelines Section 15162 (*see* below), and the responsible agency still has discretionary authority over the project.
- The previous lead agency failed to prepare any CEQA document (e.g. found the project exempt).
- The previous lead agency failed to notify and consult with the responsible agency.

(Guidelines § 15096)

Given the limited options a responsible agency has in preparing additional CEQA documentation, it is in the responsible agency's best interests to work closely with the lead agency in every phase of the EIR preparation process to ensure that the EIR meets the responsible agency's needs.

CEQA Compliance after a Project Is Approved:

Subsequent EIR and Supplemental EIR

In General. Typically, only one EIR is prepared for a project. However, project design and planning are often dynamic, resulting in the need to change the project or for an agency to respond to changing circumstances. Whether occurring in between agency discretionary approvals or triggering additional discretionary approvals that must be granted after a project's initial approval, CEQA provides for the preparation of supplemental documentation when certain conditions arise.

Specifically, an agency must prepare a subsequent or supplemental EIR for a project if 1) the agency has continuing discretionary authority over the project (Guidelines § 15162(c) and 2) it determines—on the basis of substantial evidence in light of the whole record—that:

- Substantial changes proposed in the project will require major revisions to the previous EIR because of the involvement of new significant environmental effects or a substantial increase in the severity of previously identified effects.
- Substantial changes occur with respect to the circumstances under which the project is undertaken that will require major revision of a previous EIR because of the involvement of new significant environmental effects or a substantial increase in the severity of previously identified effects.

- New information of substantial importance that was not known or could not have been known without the exercise of reasonable diligence at the time the previous EIR was certified shows any of the following:
  - The project will have one or more significant effects not discussed in the previous EIR.
  - Significant effects previously examined will be substantially more severe than shown in the previous EIR.
  - Mitigation measures or alternatives previously found not to be feasible would, in fact, be feasible and substantially reduce one or more significant effects of the project, but the project proponents decline to adopt them.
  - Mitigation measures or alternatives considerably different from those analyzed in the previous document would substantially reduce one or more significant effects, but the project proponents decline to adopt them.

(Guidelines § 15162(a)).

The courts have traditionally looked upon Pub. Res. Code § 21166 (the foundation for Guidelines § 15162) as a restriction on the need to prepare an additional EIR for a project. A subsequent or supplemental EIR need only address those EIR topics that, for the reasons listed above, require "major revisions to the original EIR." Topics adequately addressed in the original EIR do not need to be analyzed again. When an original EIR has been certified, in-depth review of the project is assumed to have already occurred and the question now before the agency is whether circumstances have changed enough to justify repeating a portion of the CEQA process. CEQA provides no expiration date on which documents can no longer be used in agency decision making (with the exception of a Master EIR). The courts have upheld the use of original CEQA documents of from nine to eighteen years in age (*see Snarled Traffic Obstructs Progress v. City and County of San Francisco* (1999) 74 Cal. App. 4th 793 [nine-year-old Negative Declaration reused]; *Citizens for Responsible Equitable Environmental Development v. City of San Diego Redevelopment Agency, et al.* (2005) 134 Cal. App. 4th 598 [twelve-year-old EIR reused]; *Mani Brothers Real Estate Group v. City of Los Angeles* (2007) 153 Cal. App. 4th 1385 [addendum could be based on an eighteen-year-old program EIR). However, as time passes, and the project or circumstances change, or substantial new information becomes available indicating a new or more severe impact than those analyzed in the original program EIR, the chances increase that a subsequent or supplemental EIR may be required.

The use of subsequent and supplemental EIRs is intended to be limited to projects that are essentially the same as the project for which the original EIR was prepared. *Sierra Club v. County of Sonoma* (1992) 6 Cal. App. 4th 1307. This might include, for example, a revised tentative subdivision map, reconsideration of a conditional use permit, later activities under a prior approval, or later phases of a multiphase project. If the later action is not part of and consistent with the project as analyzed in the original EIR, or if it is outside the

A Subsequent or Supplemental EIR Is Required When . . .

- Substantial changes are proposed in the project that will require major revisions to the previous EIR because of the involvement of new significant environmental effects or a substantial increase in the severity of previously identified effects.
- Substantial changes occur with respect to the circumstances under which the project is undertaken that will require major revision of a previous EIR because of the involvement of new significant environmental effects or a substantial increase in the severity of previously identified effects.
- New information of substantial importance that was not known or could not have been known without the exercise of reasonable diligence at the time the previous EIR was certified shows any of the following:
  - The project will have one or more significant effects not discussed in the previous EIR.
  - Significant effects previously examined will be substantially more severe than shown in the previous EIR.
  - Mitigation measures or alternatives previously found not to be feasible would, in fact, be feasible and substantially reduce one or more significant effects of the project, but the project proponents decline to adopt them.
  - Mitigation measures or alternatives considerably different from those analyzed in the previous document would substantially reduce one or more significant effects, but the project proponents decline to adopt them.

geographic area of the original project, then a subsequent or supplemental EIR is inappropriate. In either of those cases, separate CEQA compliance is required.

For updated material on this topic, please see the 2013 Addendum at www.solano.com

A subsequent or supplemental EIR is subject to the same notice and public review requirements as the original EIR—from the notice of availability of the draft supplemental or subsequent EIR through the notice of determination after the revised project approval—and is required to state whether the previous document is available for review (Guidelines § 15162(d)). However, a new notice of preparation is not required, but it may be desirable in some situations.

An initial study approach may be used to determine if the changes or new information lead to significant environmental effects. However, no initial study is necessary when determining whether or not a subsequent or supplemental EIR will be required, as long as substantial evidence exists that supports the agency's determination (*Friends of Davis v. City of Davis* (2000) 83 Cal. App. 4th 1004). If the conditions or the project have changed—but not enough to trigger a subsequent or supplemental EIR—the agency must either prepare a subsequent negative declaration or addendum to the EIR (Guidelines § 15162(b)).

If the project was approved by the lead agency before the occurrence of the conditions that trigger a subsequent or supplemental EIR, then the subsequent document must be prepared by the responsible agency that grants the next discretionary approval for the project (Guidelines § 15162(c)).

Differences between Subsequent EIR and Supplemental EIR. According to the Guidelines, a subsequent EIR is prepared if the previous EIR requires major revisions (Guidelines § 15162), whereas a supplemental EIR may be prepared if the triggers under section 15162 are met but the revisions are not considered major (Guidelines § 15163). For example, if sufficient important changes have occurred since the original EIR was certified to warrant revisiting practically every part of that EIR, then a subsequent EIR is appropriate. If, on the other hand, only one or two impact sections need to be updated, then a supplemental EIR would suffice. In practice, the two document titles are somewhat interchangeable, although the supplemental EIR must be considered in conjunction with the original EIR before the project may be approved, and findings must be made relative to all significant effects, whereas the subsequent EIR basically replaces the original EIR (Guidelines §§ 15162, 15163(c)).

Addendum to an EIR

An agency prepares an addendum to the previously certified EIR when the lead or responsible agency retains some discretion over the project implementation and some changes or additions are necessary to the project, or other circumstances arise regarding the impact analysis—but none of the conditions triggering a subsequent EIR, negative declaration, or supplemental EIR have occurred (Guidelines § 15164(a)). An addendum should be prepared if only minor technical changes or additions are necessary (Guidelines § 15164(b)). An addendum need not be circulated for public review (Guidelines § 15164(c)). The decision-making body is required to consider the addendum with the prior final EIR or negative declaration before making a decision on the project (Guidelines § 15164(d)). A brief explanation of the decision not to prepare a subsequent EIR should be included in the addendum, in the findings, or elsewhere in the record. The explanation must be supported by substantial evidence in the administrative record (Guidelines § 15164(e)). The agency should file a notice of determination after the discretionary action has occurred.

Standard of Judicial Review

In reviewing an agency's refusal to prepare a subsequent or supplemental EIR, the courts do not use the fair argument standard used for determining if an EIR should have been prepared initially, but instead employ a more deferential, traditional "substantial evidence," standard. The agency's decision will be supported as long as it is based on substantial evidence in the record—even if opposing substantial evidence exists. If an agency makes substantial changes to a project and prepares an addendum with a new notice of determination, a thirty-day statute of limitations would apply to the decision not to prepare a subsequent or supplemental EIR. If no notice of determination is filed, a 180-day statute of limitations period starts when a project opponent knew—or reasonably should have known—of the changes.

Changing or Eliminating Mitigation Measures

After an EIR has been certified, any agency using that EIR is obligated to apply the mitigation measures identified as being their responsibility by the findings adopted under Guidelines § 15091. These mitigation measures would also be identified in the mitigation monitoring or reporting program adopted by the agency.

A mitigation measure may be changed or deleted if the agency has found the measure to be impractical or unworkable. The agency must provide a legitimate reason and support that reasoning with substantial evidence. A previously adopted mitigation measure cannot be deleted without demonstrating that it is no longer feasible to implement (*see Napa Citizens for Honest Government v. Napa County Board of Supervisors* (2001) 91 Cal. App. 4th 342). Deletion of a mitigation measure requires preparation and certification of a supplemental EIR that includes the supporting evidence (*see Lincoln Place Tenants Association v. City of Los Angeles* (2005) 130 Cal. App. 4th 1491).

Tips for Successful Compliance

This chapter addressed agency decision making and post-decision requirements. The following are some tips for making this part of CEQA successful:

- **Adopt appropriate findings**—Findings and, when necessary, the Statement of Overriding Consideration are important documents that explain an agency's decision and the rationale for making it. They must be supported by substantial evidence.
- **Adopt a mitigation monitoring program**—A mitigation monitoring and reporting program is essential to the successful implementation mitigation measures.

Feasible mitigation must be capable of being accomplished in a successful manner within a reasonable period of time, taking into consideration economic, environmental, legal, social, and technological factores.

- **Make mitigation measures enforceable**—Decision makers are required to make mitigation measures enforceable either as permit conditions or agency commitments.
- **Prepare and justify the use of subsequent documents, when necessary**—Under certain circumstances, CEQA documents must be redone to reflect changes in projects or circumstances or when new significant information arises.

Chapter 9

Integration of CEQA with Other Environmental Laws

The Concept of Integration

Many projects that are subject to CEQA are also subject to other state and federal environmental laws. CEQA requires that the project description in an EIR include a list of all permits and other approvals required to implement the project as well as a list of related environmental review and consultation requirements required by federal, state, or local laws, regulations, or policies. CEQA Guidelines also state that "to the fullest extent possible, the lead agency should integrate CEQA review with these related environmental review and consultation requirements" (Guidelines §§ 15124(d)(a)(B), (C)).

This means that when a lead agency prepares an EIR for a project, it must determine which federal, state, and local environmental requirements apply to the project, and it must attempt to consolidate any environmental analysis requirements of those other laws into it. While not specifically stated in the Guidelines, the requirement to integrate with other laws should also be followed with negative declarations and mitigated negative declarations. Thus, a general knowledge of these laws and how they relate to CEQA is important for successful implementation.

Integration with NEPA

Background and Implementation of NEPA

The National Environmental Policy Act was signed into law on January 1, 1970, in response to an overwhelming national sentiment that federal agencies should take the lead in providing greater protection for the environment. NEPA established an environmental review process that served as a model for California's CEQA.

NEPA applies only to federal agencies and their proposed actions, while CEQA applies only to California state and local agencies and their proposed projects. This section compares and contrasts NEPA and CEQA and briefly reviews how they can be integrated. Those interested in detailed information

Figure 9-1
CEQA and NEPA:
Parallel Processes

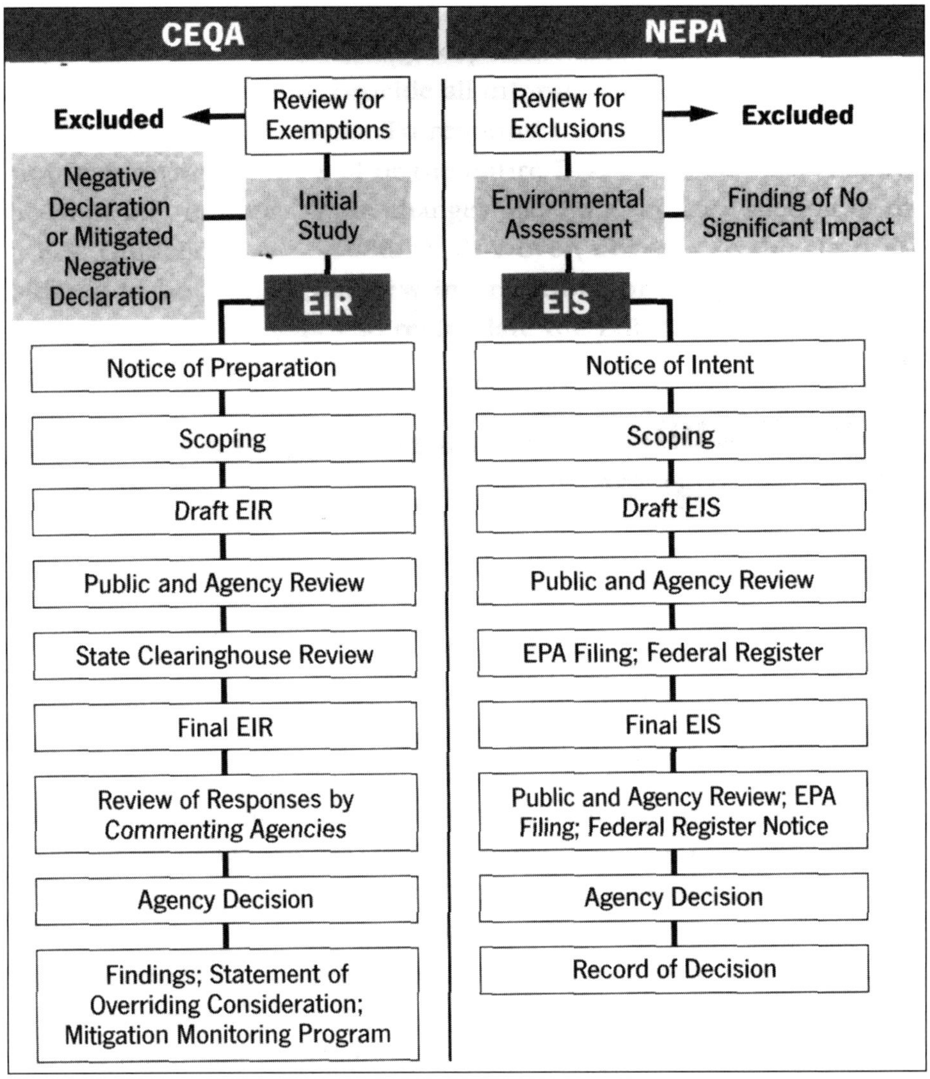

about NEPA should refer to *The NEPA Book: A Step-by-Step Guide on How to Comply With the National Environmental Policy Act,* published by Solano Press Books. Additional NEPA references are listed in the Suggested Reading section of this book.

Under NEPA, all federal agencies are authorized and directed, to the fullest extent possible, to carry out their regulations, policies, and programs in accordance with NEPA's policies of environmental protection (42 U.S.C. 4332; 40 C.F.R. 1500.2). To ensure the policies are achieved, NEPA requires that every federal agency prepare an environmental impact statement (EIS) for proposed legislation or other "major federal actions significantly affecting the quality of the human environment" (42 U.S.C. 4332; 40 C.F.R. 1501).

As presented in NEPA and CEQA's NEPA regulations (40 C.F.R. 1500 et seq.), the overall environmental review process under NEPA is similar to CEQA, and involves three key phases:

- Review of a project for categorical exclusions or other exemptions (generally equivalent to CEQA's statutory and categorical exemptions)

- Preparation of an environmental assessment (equivalent to CEQA's initial study) to determine whether the possibility exists of significant environmental effects
- Preparation of an EIS (equivalent to CEQA's EIR) or finding of no significant impact (FONSI) (equivalent to CEQA's negative declaration or mitigated negative declaration)

The similarities and differences between NEPA and CEQA are discussed in the section beginning on page 202.

NEPA-Related Information on the Internet

Most information related to federal agency NEPA compliance can be found on the Internet. Many federal agencies have adopted their own NEPA regulations and procedures and maintain their own NEPA websites. They are listed on CEQA's NEPANET. Two websites of particular interest are described here.

Council on Environmental Quality. The Council on Environmental Quality (CEQ), within the Executive Office of the President, is responsible for the implementation of NEPA, including adopting NEPA regulations and providing advice and assistance to federal agencies on NEPA compliance. The CEQ's home page includes a website of NEPA-related resources on the law, regulations, CEQ publications, and links to federal agency NEPA resources. Users may reach it at: http:ceq.hss.doe.gov/.

U.S. Environmental Protection Agency—Office of Federal Activities. The Environmental Protection Agency's Office of Federal Activities (OFA) is required to review and comment on all environmental impact statements. OFA's home page provides a broad variety of NEPA-related information, including a complete listing of EISs submitted to EPA for review and EPA's comments on those documents. Users may reach the OFA home page at www.epa.gov/compliance/nepa.

CEQA Projects Subject to NEPA

CEQA applies to California agencies; NEPA applies to federal agencies. Some projects require approvals from both California and federal agencies. The CEQA Guidelines contain a separate section for projects that are also subject to NEPA (Guidelines §§ 15220–15229). A project subject to CEQA will also be subject to NEPA when: it is either jointly carried out by a federal agency; requires a federal discretionary permit, entitlement, authorization, or federal funding; or occurs on federal land.

A Project Is Subject to NEPA If It:

- Is proposed to be undertaken by a federal agency
- Requires a federal permit, lease, entitlement, or authorization
- Will receive federal funding
- Occurs on federal land
- Otherwise includes a federal action

Joint Environmental Reviews

When a project is subject to both CEQA and NEPA, state and local agencies are encouraged to cooperate with federal agencies—to the fullest extent possible—through such measures as joint planning, research, hearings, and preparation of environmental documents (Guidelines § 15226).

If a lead agency finds that an EIS or FONSI for a project would not be prepared by the federal agency by the time the lead agency would need to

Overlapping regulatory requirements for resources such as wetlands may trigger the need for joint environmental review under CEQA and NEPA.

consider an EIR or negative declaration, the lead agency should try to prepare a combined EIR/EIS or negative declaration/FONSI. To avoid the need for the federal agency to prepare a separate document for the same project, the lead agency must obtain the federal agreement for the preparation of the joint document. This involvement is necessary because federal law generally prohibits a federal agency from using an EIR prepared by a state agency unless the federal agency was involved in the preparation of the document.

Use of NEPA Documents to Satisfy CEQA

In General. State and local agencies are encouraged to use NEPA documents to replace CEQA documents if the NEPA process is proceeding faster than the CEQA process and the NEPA document complies with CEQA (Guidelines § 15221). Because NEPA differs from CEQA in some respects, and possibly less stringent environmental review requirements (see discussion on page 219), it is rare that the already prepared NEPA document will meet the requirements of CEQA without some additional elements. The Guidelines acknowledge that NEPA does not specifically require separate discussion of mitigation measures or growth inducing impacts and that "these points of analysis will need to be added, supplemented, or identified before the EIS can be used as an EIR" (Guidelines § 15221(b)). The Guidelines are silent as to what form this document must take and what notice and circulation requirements are necessary. To be conservative, lead agencies may wish to issue an addendum-like document to complete the administrative record.

The state or local agency may use the NEPA document without recirculation if the NEPA document is circulated as broadly as required by CEQA, and if the agency gives notice that it intends to use the NEPA document (Guidelines § 15225). The Guidelines are silent as to whether the notice should be equivalent to a draft EIR or if the lead agency may merely adopt findings based on the EIS and move to project approval. To be conservative, lead agencies may wish to treat the EIS as draft EIR, circulate it for review like any draft EIR, accept comments on the analysis, and issue a separate final EIR. When a state or local lead agency intends to use an EIS as an EIR, it must consult with the federal lead agency for the EIS and notify that agency of any scoping meetings for the proposed project (Public Resources Code § 21083.7).

When a scoping meeting has been held under NEPA and the noticing of that meeting complies with the requirements of CEQA, the scoping meeting can meet the requirements of both CEQA and NEPA. (Pub. Res. Code § 21083.9; Guidelines § 15082(c)).

Special Rules for Military Bases. For approvals related to a local military base reuse plan (prepared as a general plan or amendment, specific plan, redevelopment plan, or other plan), the lead agency is authorized to use the EIS on the military base closure as the basis for preparing an EIR under CEQA (Pub. Res. Code § 21083.8.1; Guidelines § 15229; *see* OPR's CEQA Technical Advice Series report, *CEQA, NEPA, and Base Closure: Recipes for Streamlining Environmental Review* (March 1996)).

Joint Environmental Documents

State and local agencies are encouraged to prepare a joint EIR/EIS or negative declaration/FONSI (Guidelines § 15222). The two laws establish essentially similar processes (*see* Figure 9-1 on page 206). Sometimes a federal agency will prepare an environmental assessment on a project (rather than an EIS) even though the state or local agency prepares an EIR. While a joint EA/EIR might seem odd to some state or local agencies, this may be appropriate because of the difference in the concept of significant impacts under CEQA and NEPA. NEPA does not have the "fair argument" standard that drives the preparation of EIRs under CEQA. As a result, an EIS may not be triggered by the level of evidence of an impact that triggers an EIR.

In practice, several recommendations may facilitate state and local agency interaction with federal lead agencies when preparing joint CEQA/NEPA documents. First, a written memorandum of understanding (MOU) between the two lead agencies should spell out the roles and responsibilities of each agency; expected schedule; other expectations regarding the preparation of the environmental document (including assumptions regarding impact analysis), and dispute resolution procedures. Second, because NEPA and CEQA are somewhat different with regard to procedural and content requirements (*see* Figure 9-2, page 210), the agencies should agree at the outset to apply whichever requirements are more stringent. Third, the scope and content of the EIR/EIS, and the respective responsibilities for reviewing interim drafts, should be clearly spelled out.

Some agencies so routinely prepare joint state/federal documents that they have developed special procedures for achieving integration. For example, under the provisions of The Safe, Accountable, Flexible, Efficient Transportation Equity Act: A Legacy for Users (SAFETEA-LU), the responsibility for implementing NEPA for federally funded surface transportation projects has been delegated from the U.S. Department of Transportation to the California Department of Transportation. Under the delegation, Caltrans completely takes over the Federal Highway Administration's (FHWA) responsibilities under NEPA, as well as other federal environmental laws such as the Endangered Species Act and Section 106 of the National Historic Preservation Act. This pilot program offers the opportunity to test a streamlined environmental process that takes over the federal responsibility. Thus, for projects subject to the delegation, Caltrans serves as both the federal Lead Agency under NEPA and the state Lead Agency under CEQA and prepares joint documents that satisfy both laws. The rules and procedures under which Caltrans implements NEPA and CEQA are found in Chapter 38 of the *Caltrans Standard Environmental Reference*. California is the only state to participate in the delegation pilot project under SAFETEA-LU. *Caltrans Standard Environmental Reference* is an online resource for information about Caltrans' procedures regarding environmental analysis. It is key to preparing analysis documents the Caltrans way, and Chapter 37 of the Reference describes Caltrans' approach to joint CEQA/NEPA documents. Caltrans' Standard Environmental Reference can be found online at: www.dot.ca.gov/ser/index.htm.

Difference	Subject Area	CEQA	NEPA
Substantive Differences	Agency Decision on Project	Agencies must mitigate project impacts when feasible	Agencies need not mitigate project impacts, even if feasible, unless required by agency regulations
Procedural Differences	Public Notice and Review	Public Notice required for Negative Declarations	Public Notice not always required for FONSIs
		Public Notice required for Draft EIRs	Notice in Federal Register required for Draft EIS
		Public Notice and review not required for Final EIRs but Commenting Agencies must receive responses prior to the Final EIR	Notice in Federal Register and 30-day review required for Final EIS
	Time Limits	Non-agency projects subject to the Permit Streamlining Act	No time limits for preparation of environmental documents
	Agency Decision to Prepare EIR or EIS	Agencies must prepare if "fair argument" can be made that project may have significant impact	Agencies must prepare only if there is substantial evidence that project may have significant impact
	Statutes of Limitation	CEQA provides short statute of limitation for legal challenges	NEPA contains no specific statute of limitation
Document Content Differences	Decision Document	"Findings" must explain whether each impact has been mitigated and if each has not, why	"Record of Decision" need only explain why the decision was made
	Alternatives Analysis	EIR must compare alternatives, but may evaluate them in less detail than the proposed project	EIS must treat alternatives in relatively similar level of detail

Figure 9-2
Major Differences between CEQA and NEPA

Using CEQA Documents to Satisfy NEPA

There is no express provision in NEPA or the CEQ's NEPA Regulations that authorizes a federal agency to use a CEQA document to comply with NEPA. Rather, in the case of an EIS, NEPA requires the document to be prepared by or under contract to the federal lead agency. A narrow exception exists, allowing a federal agency only to use an EIR to satisfy NEPA if a state agency with statewide jurisdiction prepares the EIR for a federal grant project and the federal agency actively participates in the environmental review process (40 C.F.R. 1506.2). This provision would typically apply only to Caltrans in the federal-aid highway program and HUD approved local housing projects.

In practice, however, federal agencies typically utilize CEQA documents as important background information to prepare NEPA documents. To ensure that the procedural requirements of NEPA are met, the federal agency, in using a CEQA document for NEPA compliance, should make sure the record shows that there was independent review of the CEQA document. The record should also reflect that the federal agency is preparing its own NEPA document based on the CEQA document (and not that the NEPA document is replaced by the CEQA document).

Similarities and Differences between CEQA and NEPA

In general, CEQA and NEPA contain many similar terms and concepts (*see* Figure 9-3, page 213); yet, despite their similarities, they also have several important differences (*see* Figure 9-2, page 210). Both laws require the preparation of a detailed environmental study to evaluate the environmental effects of proposed governmental activities. Both laws establish multistep procedures for evaluating projects and preparing environmental impact documents. Generally, the differences between CEQA and NEPA may be classified into categories of terminology, procedures, environmental document content, and substantive mandates to protect the environment.

Terminology

Proposal for Action. NEPA defines a federal undertaking as a "proposal for action" (42 U.S.C. § 4332(2)(C)), whereas CEQA uses the term "project" (Pub. Res. Code § 21080). As with CEQA's definition of "project," an "action" under NEPA includes policies, rules, regulations, plans, programs, and specific projects, including private undertakings requiring federal agency permits or regulatory decisions (40 C.F.R. § 1508.18; Guidelines § 15378). Continuing or ongoing activities of federal agencies may also be considered actions under NEPA. A proposal for action exists at the stage of planning when a federal agency has a goal and is actively preparing to make a decision furthering that goal (40 C.F.R. § 1508.23).

CEQA, NEPA, and other laws use similar terminology with different meaning and it is important that this be clearly identified in the joint environmental review.

Lead Agency. The term and concept of "lead agency" are essentially the same under NEPA and CEQA. NEPA regulations define it as the agency that has primary responsibility for preparing an EIS (40 C.F.R. § 1508.16). The Guidelines define "lead agency" as the agency carrying out the project or having the greatest responsibility for supervising or approving a project (Guidelines § 15051). Although the Guidelines contain a more elaborate definition of "lead agency," the concept is essentially the same.

Both NEPA and CEQA provide similar procedures and criteria for resolving lead agency disputes. Lead agency disputes may be submitted to the CEQ under NEPA and to OPR under CEQA (40 C.F.R. § 1501.5(e); Guidelines §§ 16000–16041). It is more common to have more than one federal agency act as co-leads in the NEPA process.

Cooperating Agency. Under NEPA, agencies other than the lead agency that are involved in EIS preparation are referred to as "cooperating agencies." The concept of a cooperating agency under NEPA is broader than that of a "responsible agency" under CEQA. A NEPA cooperating agency is any federal agency other than the lead agency with jurisdiction over the project by law, or with special expertise regarding the impacts of the action (40 C.F.R. § 1508.5). CEQ directive has expanded that list to include any state or local agencies, or federally recognized tribes that have special expertise regarding the impacts of the action (CEQ's Memoranda: *Designation of Non-Federal Agencies to be Cooperating Agencies in Implementing the Procedural Requirements of NEPA* 1999). Under CEQA, responsible agencies are only those state or local agencies that issue permits or provide funding for the project (Guidelines § 15381). Under NEPA, a cooperating agency is expected to participate in the preparation of the EIS when requested to do so by a lead agency; under CEQA, a responsible agency generally serves in a more passive commenting role (40 C.F.R. § 1501.6; Guidelines § 15096).

Categorical Exclusion. A "categorical exclusion" is NEPA's equivalent to a categorical exemption under CEQA (Guidelines § 15354). Each federal agency, in its NEPA-implementing regulations, has identified certain types of proposed federal actions that it has determined would not have a significant effect on the environment. These actions are categorically excluded from the requirement to prepare further NEPA environmental documentation. A categorical exclusion will not apply if any "extraordinary circumstances" (as opposed to CEQA's "exceptions") designated by the federal agency exist (40 C.F.R. § 1508.4).

Practitioners should be aware that the range of federal actions that have been categorically excluded is very broad. Unlike the Guidelines, which list 33 standard classes of exemptions to which all state and local agencies must adhere (Guidelines §§ 15300–15333), each federal agency has identified its own list of categorical exclusions that differ substantially from agency to agency. Thus, a careful reading of a particular agency's NEPA regulations is necessary to determine which proposed actions are categorically excluded.

Another difference from CEQA is that some federal agencies' NEPA regulations establish a checklist through which compliance with related laws will be reviewed, and possibly mitigation measures incorporated, before a categorical exclusion may be adopted. Unlike CEQA, which does not allow the use of mitigated categorical exemptions, compliance with related laws may effectively result in a mitigated categorical exclusion (although it is not labeled as such).

Environmental Assessment. An "environmental assessment" is the NEPA analog to an initial study under CEQA (Guidelines § 15063). After determining that a proposed action is not categorically excluded, a federal agency generally prepares an environmental assessment. Like a CEQA initial study, an environmental assessment has several purposes. It helps the federal agency determine whether an EIS is required by briefly evaluating whether a proposed action may have significant environmental effects. If an agency decides that an EIS is not required, the environmental assessment provides the documentation to support a FONSI (discussed below). When an agency decides an EIS must be prepared, the environmental assessment helps determine the scope and content of the EIS. An environmental assessment is a formally recognized part of the NEPA process and should be distinguished from informal studies that are often referred to as environmental assessments (40 C.F.R. §§ 1501.4(b), 1508.9).

The required contents of an environmental assessment are similar to those of an initial study. One difference, however, is that when there are unresolved issues relating to natural resources, an environmental assessment must discuss alternatives to a proposed action, whereas an initial study is not required to dis-

CEQA Term	Correlated NEPA Term
Lead Agency	Lead Agency
Responsible Agency	Cooperating Agency
Categorical Exemption	Categorical Exclusion
Initial Study	Environmental Assessment
Negative Declaration	Finding of No Significant Impact
Environmental Impact Report	Environmental Impact Statement
Notice of Preparation	Notice of Intent
Findings	Record of Decision

Figure 9-3
Similarities in Terminology between CEQA and NEPA

cuss alternatives. Although some flexibility exists within this requirement, in practice most federal agencies include a discussion of alternatives in the EA. The section explores the differences in legal standards for determining whether to prepare an EIS as opposed to an EIR (40 C.F.R. § 1508.9(b); Guidelines § 15063(d)). Unlike under CEQA, there is no uniformly recommended checklist comparable to the initial study checklist found in the state CEQA Guidelines. Thus, in practice, each federal agency (and sometimes staff members within a particular federal agency) has its own unique format and approach to preparing an EA.

Finding of No Significant Impact. A FONSI is NEPA's equivalent to CEQA's negative declaration (Guidelines §§ 15070–15075). A FONSI is a public document that briefly describes why an action that is otherwise not excluded from NEPA will not have any significant environmental effect and why the action will not require an EIS. A federal agency preparing an environmental assessment must prepare a FONSI if it decides not to prepare an EIS (40 C.F.R. §§ 1501.4(e), 1508.13). Like a negative declaration, which must be supported by an initial study, a FONSI must be supported by an environmental assessment (40 C.F.R. § 1508.13).

A federal agency may prepare a "mitigated FONSI" when an environmental assessment indicates that environmental effects of a proposed action are potentially significant but that, with mitigation, they may be reduced or avoided. CEQ and federal courts have approved the use of FONSIs where mitigation was added to the proposed action to demonstrate the agency had taken a "hard look" at the possibility of significant effects on the quality of the human environment. In practice, federal agencies go through the process of adding mitigation to support the FONSI, and simply calling the final document a FONSI (that includes mitigation commitments) (*see* CEQ guidance document "Appropriate Use of Mitigation and Monitoring and Clarifying Appropriate Use of Mitigated Finding of No Significant Impact, 76 Fed. Reg. 3843, January 20, 2011).

Environmental Impact Statement. The purpose of an EIS prepared under NEPA is essentially the same as an EIR prepared under CEQA. Both are disclosure documents designed to ensure that the environmental factors are taken into consideration in government decisionmaking. Like CEQA, NEPA requires a federal lead agency to prepare an EIS in draft and final stages (40 C.F.R. §§ 1502.9, 1508.11; Guidelines §§ 15084–15089).

Notice of Intent. A notice of intent serves the same functional purpose as an NOP under CEQA (Guidelines § 15082); the notice of intent is the first formal step in EIS preparation. As soon as practical after its decision to prepare an EIS but before the scoping process begins, a federal lead agency must publish a notice of intent in the Federal Register. A notice of intent must briefly describe the proposed federal action and alternatives, the agency's scoping process and the opportunity to participate in scoping meetings, and the name and address of persons to contact within the lead agency regarding the EIS (40 C.F.R. §§ 1501.7, 1508.22).

Record of Decision. A record of decision is analogous to the certification, project approval, findings, mitigation monitoring and reporting program, and statements of overriding considerations under CEQA. The record of decision is a written record explaining why the federal agency has taken a particular course of action based on the EIS it has prepared. It must include:

- A statement explaining the decision
- An explanation of other alternatives that were considered and rejected
- A description of social, economic, and environmental factors considered by the agency in making its decision
- A summary of any mitigation measures that were adopted and an explanation for any that were not adopted
- A monitoring and enforcement program for any adopted mitigation measures

(40 C.F.R. § 1505.2).

Unlike findings under CEQA, NEPA does not require that a record of decision expressly find each unadopted mitigation measure to be infeasible.

Procedures

Role of Agency NEPA Regulations. In California, CEQA and the Guidelines set forth universal requirements to which all state and local agencies must adhere. Although each state and local agency is required to adopt its own CEQA procedures that are consistent with the Guidelines, in practice, most of these procedures vary little from agency to agency.

Under NEPA, the Council has adopted regulations that, like CEQA, require federal agencies to adopt their own regulations tailored to their unique situations (40 C.F.R. § 1507.3(a)). However, unlike CEQA, CEQ's regulations are very general and the NEPA regulations of each federal agency often contain significant differences in practice and interpretation from agency to agency. Thus, practitioners must become familiar not only with CEQ's NEPA Regulations, but also with those NEPA regulations adopted by any particular agency with which they deal. Additionally, some federal agencies have prepared detailed procedural manuals or handbooks for NEPA compliance. The CEQ NEPAnet website contains a thorough listing of other agency NEPA websites.

Public Review of FONSIs. CEQA requires all state and local agencies to adhere to the same public notice and review requirements for negative declarations; the content of such notices and time periods for review (minimum twenty days) are standardized (Pub. Res. Code § 21091(b)). Although the NEPA regulations require federal agencies to provide notice of the availability of FONSIs in some instances, practice concerning public review of FONSIs differs substantially from agency to agency; there are no standard requirements for the content of public notices, and only certain actions require a minimum thirty-day public review. Specifically, NEPA requires a FONSI to be made available for a thirty-day period if the proposal is unusual or precedent setting, or is similar to one normally requiring an EIS. Additionally, CEQ advises agencies to make a FONSI available for thirty days in borderline situations in which there is a reasonable argument that an EIS should have been prepared, if the proposal is controversial, or if the proposal is located in a floodplain or wetland. Several federal agencies provide a public review period for most FONSIs (*see* Council on Environmental Quality, "Memorandum: Forty Most Asked Questions Concerning CEQ's NEPA Regulations," 46 Fed. Reg. 18026 (March 23, 1981)).

Scoping. Although scoping is used under both NEPA and CEQA to determine the focus and content of an EIS or EIR, it is a more formalized process under NEPA. NEPA requires a formal scoping process for each EIS. 40 C.F.R. §§ 1501.7(a), (b). Additionally, the Council has issued formal guidance to assist federal agencies in the scoping process. Council on Environmental Quality, "Memorandum: Scoping Guidance" (April 30, 1981). Under CEQA, scoping may differ considerably from agency to agency.

Public Notice and Review Requirements for an EIS. After preparing a draft EIS, a federal lead agency must request comments from other federal agencies, project applicants, Native American tribes, state and local agencies, and the general public (40 C.F.R. § 1503.1(a)). As with FONSIs, the specific requirements for giving public notice of the availability of draft EISs differ considerably from agency to agency; each federal agency's regulations must be consulted to determine the specifics. All federal agencies send their EISs for filing and review to EPA (42 U.S.C. § 7609). In addition to conducting reviews of EISs, EPA files a notice of the availability of the EIS in the Federal Register (40 C.F.R. § 1506.10(a)).

The requirement for a federal lead agency to obtain the comments of other federal agencies is similar to that under CEQA. A federal agency preparing an EIS in California must also send the draft document to OPR for state agency review. OPR serves as the state's single point of contact for review of NEPA documents under Presidential Executive Order 12372 (July 14, 1982) and Guidelines § 15205(b)(4).

EPA Review of Draft EISs. EPA's Office of Federal Activities (40 C.F.R. § 1.37(a)) reviews and rates all EISs for adequacy and to determine whether the proposed action is environmentally damaging.

Under CEQA, OPR—through the SCH—distributes EIRs to other agencies for review, but no formal system exists for OPR review and rating of EIRs.

Notice Requirements for a Final EIS. CEQA does not require public notice and review of a final EIR before the agency may act on the proposed project, although some agencies provide such notice. The only provision for review of a final EIR is the requirement that a lead agency send other agencies any responses to their comments prior to certifying an EIR (Pub. Res. Code § 21092.5). Under NEPA, however, a final EIS must be given similar public review, typically for thirty days, and notice as the draft EIS, including filing with EPA and notification in the Federal Register (40 C.F.R. §§ 1502.19, 1506.10(a)). The final EIS integrates the comments, responses, and related revisions into a single, revised document.

Time Limits. For environmental documents prepared on "development projects," CEQA and the Permit Streamlining Act (Govt. Code §§ 65920–65963.1) impose mandatory time limits for completing EIRs or negative declarations and approving projects (Govt. Code § 65950; Guidelines §§ 15107, 15108). NEPA contains no such standardized time limits.

Although the NEPA Regulations contain minimum review periods for the Federal Register notice of draft EISs (forty-five days) and final EISs (thirty days), they do not require completion of the entire EIS preparation process within specified periods (40 C.F.R. § 1506.10). There is a provision allowing time limits to be established for preparing an EIS (40 C.F.R. § 1501.8); however, in practice, few time limits are established.

Statutes of Limitation. CEQA imposes very short limitation periods for initiating litigation challenging agency action—thirty days if a notice of determination is filed, 180 days if no notice of determination is filed, and thirty-five days if a notice of exemption is filed (Pub. Res. Code § 21167). NEPA, on the other hand, has no statute of limitations, however, actions challenging federal agencies under NEPA are typically brought under the Administrative Procedures Act, which contains a general six-year statute of limitations. Additionally, some courts have relied on the common law equitable defense of "laches" under which excessive delays in filing may result in dismissal at the discretion of the court. Thus, federal agencies are subject to longer periods of potential legal vulnerability under NEPA than state or local agencies under CEQA.

Pursuant to the Safe, Accountable, Flexible, Efficient Transportation Equity Act: A Legacy for Users (SAFETEA-LU) enacted in 2005, certain highway and public transit projects undertaken or funded by the U.S. Department of Transportation are subject to a 180-day statute of limitations on NEPA challenges. This is currently the only NEPA statute of limitations, and it does not apply to any other types of projects subject to NEPA.

Legal Standard for Determining Whether to Prepare an EIS. Under CEQA, a lead agency must prepare an EIR if it is presented with a fair argument, based on substantial evidence, that a project may have a significant effect on the environment. A significant effect on the environment is defined as a "substantial or potentially substantial adverse change in any of the physical conditions in the area affected by the project."

Under NEPA, a federal agency must prepare an EIS for any "proposals for legislation and other major federal actions significantly affecting the quality of the human environment" (42 U.S.C. § 4332(2)(C)). "Significantly" is defined by the twin factors of "context" and "intensity" (40 C.F.R. 1508.27). "Context" means the seeing in which a project is proposed and may include the local area, region, nation, or even globe, depending on the environmental resource being evaluated. "Intensity" means the severity of the impact and is defined by ten factors (*see* sidebar).

In determining whether to prepare an EIS or a FONSI, the federal lead agency must consider all of these factors, to the extent that they are relevant to the action being evaluated.

Although the relevant CEQA and NEPA definitions are similar, the courts have applied very different standards of review to agency determinations of significance. Under CEQA, the "fair argument" standard of review has been interpreted by the California courts as a very low threshold for EIR preparation; by this standard, virtually any factual information showing potentially significant impacts can support a fair argument that significant impacts may occur.

Under NEPA, however, the federal courts generally rely on an "arbitrary and capricious" standard when reviewing agency decisions not to prepare an EIS. This standard is far more deferential to agency decisions. Thus, challenging a federal agency's decision that impacts are not significant is considerably more difficult as long as the agency has not acted arbitrarily.

These different legal standards are part of the reason that more EIRs are prepared by state and local agencies in California each year than the total number of EISs prepared by federal agencies nationwide. The difference in the legal standard explains why federal agencies will sometimes prepare an EA/FONSI on the same project that triggers an EIR under CEQA.

"Intensity": the Severity of the Impact Is Defined by Ten Factors

1. A significant effect may exist even if on balance the effects of a federal action would be beneficial
2. The degree to which the proposed actions affect public health or safely
3. Unique characteristics of the geographic area
4. The degree to which the effects are likely highly controversial
5. The degree to which the possible effects are highly uncertain or involve unique or unknown risks
6. The degree to which the action may establish a precedent for future actions with significant effects
7. Whether the action would contribute to cumulatively significant impacts
8. The degree to which the action may adversely affect historic or cultural resources
9. The degree to which the action may adversely affect an endangered or threatened species or its habitat
10. Whether the action threatens a violation of federal, state, or local laws or requirements for the protection of the environment

Environmental Document Content

In general, an EIS prepared under NEPA is similar to an EIR prepared under CEQA. Both documents must include a description of the proposed activity, the environmental setting, an analysis of significant environmental impacts (direct, indirect, and cumulative), and a discussion of mitigation measures to reduce or avoid those impacts (40 C.F.R. §§ 1502.11–1502.25; Guidelines §§ 15120–15132). "Mitigation" is defined exactly the same under NEPA and CEQA (40 C.F.R. § 1508.20; Guidelines § 15370). One difference is that CEQA requires an EIR to identify whether or not an impact is significant, whereas many federal agencies avoid using of the word "significant" in the EIS itself, using it only to determine if an EIS was necessary.

Technical impact analysis of topical issues, such as construction impacts, generally does not differ between NEPA and CEQA.

The technical impact analysis of topical issues (e.g., biology and air quality) generally does not differ between NEPA and CEQA because neither the law nor its implementing regulations prescribe any particular type or level of analysis. Rather, the practices of each federal agency and the facts and circumstances of each proposed action determine the scope and content of the documents. However, as discussed in the section under Integration of NEPA on page 219, federal permitting requirements or other laws may dictate specific analysis requirements or protocols and may need to be completed before the final EIS is adopted.

There are, however, several key differences in document content between the two laws as discussed below.

Analysis of Alternatives. The most important difference in document content between an EIS and an EIR is the treatment of alternatives. Although both NEPA and CEQA require that the documents evaluate a "reasonable range" of alternatives, NEPA requires that an EIS rigorously evaluate and compare all reasonable alternatives to provide a clear basis for choice of options. Although no particular level of treatment is required, the degree of analysis devoted to each alternative must be substantially similar to that devoted to the proposed action (40 C.F.R. § 1502.14). In practice, most federal agencies conduct an equal analysis of each alternative in an EIS.

This standard differs from CEQA, which does not require substantially equal treatment of alternatives. Rather, under CEQA, the analysis of the proposed project is often evaluated at a greater level of detail than that of the alternatives. Although CEQA allows this, it nevertheless requires a meaningful comparison of the impacts of the alternatives (Guidelines § 15126.6(d)).

Incomplete or Unavailable Information. Another difference between an EIS and an EIR is the treatment given to incomplete or unavailable information. Before 1986, the NEPA regulations required federal agencies confronted with incomplete or unavailable information to conduct a "worst-case analysis." In 1986, CEQ revoked the worst-case analysis requirement because it often resulted in expensive and unreasonable technical studies and analyses. Under the new regulations, when information is incomplete or unavailable, it must be obtained if costs are not unreasonable. If the costs are exorbitant, the agency must state that the information is incomplete or unavailable, state the relevance of the information to evaluating reasonably foreseeable impacts, summarize the credible scientific evidence that exists about the topic, and evaluate the impacts based on scientifically accepted methods (40 C.F.R. § 1502.22).

Under CEQA, drafting an EIR generally involves some degree of forecasting those impacts that are reasonably foreseeable. Although forecasting the unforeseeable is not possible, an agency must use its best efforts to discover and disclose all it reasonably can about an issue (Guidelines § 15144). However, if after thorough investigation a lead agency finds that a particular impact is too speculative for evaluation, the agency should note its conclusion and terminate discussion of the impact (Guidelines § 15145). In practice, this standard enables a state or local agency to cut off discussion of speculative impacts more easily than a federal agency can under NEPA.

Socioeconomic Impacts. NEPA and CEQA differ with regard to the requirement to evaluate social and economic impacts. Under NEPA, the definition of "human environment" states that economic or social effects alone are not intended to require preparation of an EIS. However, when an EIS is prepared, the economic and social effects must be discussed if they are interrelated to the natural or physical environmental effects (40 C.F.R. § 1508.14). The definition of the term "effects" also includes economic and social factors (40 C.F.R. § 1508.8). In addition, under Executive Order 12898, federal agencies are obligated to consider environmental justice in their NEPA analyses. This examines whether the action will result in a disproportionately adverse effect on low-income or minority populations.

Under CEQA, economic and social changes resulting from a project are not treated as significant effects on the environment (Guidelines § 15064(f)). Effects analyzed in an EIR must be related to a physical change in the environment (Guidelines § 15358(b)). However, economic or social changes may be used to determine that a physical change is significant. If a physical change in the environment will result in economic and social changes, which in turn have secondary physical effects, those effects may be evaluated in an EIR (Guidelines § 15064(f)).

Integration of NEPA Document Preparation with Other Federal Environmental Laws. One of the most complex aspects of EIS preparation is the requirement that federal agencies integrate NEPA with other federal environmental review and consultation requirements. Generally, proposed federal actions that trigger review under NEPA also require compliance with a variety of other federal environmental laws. Each federal agency has an obligation to identify and list in the EIS all other federal environmental requirements that may be applicable to the proposed action. Additionally, NEPA, like CEQA, requires that, to the fullest extent possible, agencies integrate the NEPA process with the review processes established by these other laws (40 C.F.R. § 1502.25(a)).

Each proposed federal action will trigger a different set of related environmental requirements, depending on the type of activity being proposed and its location. (*See* Figures 9-4, page 221, and 9-5, pages 222-223). For example, the replacement of an historic bridge across a navigable river could trigger the need for U.S. Army Corps of Engineers permits under section 404 of the Clean Water Act (33 U.S.C. § 1344), consultation with the U.S. Fish and Wildlife Service under section 7 of the federal Endangered Species Act (16 U.S.C. § 1536), and review of historic resources under section 106 of the National Historic Preservation Act (16 U.S.C. § 470(f)). Under this example, the review, consultation, evaluation, and documentation requirements of these other laws should be completed during EIS preparation, and the results should be incorporated into the EIS. Such integration of environmental review requirements is designed to avoid duplication and delay.

Although similar integration of state and local environmental review is encouraged and often occurs under CEQA, its integration mandate is much weaker than NEPA's and is generally easier to handle because fewer agencies are involved. When a joint EIS/EIR is prepared, the complexities of integration are compounded.

> **Socio-Economic Impact**
>
> NEPA's requirement to consider socioeconomic impacts is broader than CEQA's. In practice, federal agencies generally include more economic and social information in EISs than state or local agencies include in EIRs.

Coordinated Environmental Review Requirements

A goal of "one project, one document" should be adopted to minimize the need for costly duplicative environmental reviews by many agencies. Key federal agency environmental review requirements that often are relevant include but are not limited to:

- **U.S. Fish and Wildlife Service:** Section 7 consultation or section 10 incidental take permit and habitat conservation plan, pursuant to the federal Endangered Species Act. 16 U.S.C. 1536
- **U.S. Army Corps of Engineers:** Section 404 permit, including section 404(b)(1) alternatives analysis, for discharges of dredged or fill material into wetlands and waters of the United States pursuant to the federal Clean Water Act. 33 U.S.C. 1344
- **Advisory Council on Historic Preservation and State Historic Preservation Office:** Section 106 consultation, pursuant to the National Historic Preservation Act. 16 U.S.C. 470
- **U.S. Environmental Protection Agency and State Air Quality Management Districts:** conformity analysis, pursuant to the federal Clean Air Act. 42 U.S.C. 7401

Figure 9-4 presents an approach to integrating CEQA and NEPA with the key federal agency environmental review requirements and public involvement. Figure 9-5 presents a comprehensive overview of the federal and state environmental compliance requirements for CEQA/NEPA projects.

Substantive Mandates to Protect the Environment

Although NEPA and CEQA contain similar requirements to evaluate impacts and identify mitigation measures, CEQA's statutory mandate to protect the environment is stronger. While neither law requires that the environment be protected in all cases, CEQA expressly requires state and local agencies to avoid or mitigate significant environmental impacts whenever feasible (Guidelines §§ 15021, 15091). NEPA, on the other hand, allows federal agencies to disregard mitigation measures or alternatives even if they are feasible (*Robertson v. Methow Valley Citizens Council* (1989) 490 U.S. 332). Although a record of decision must generally explain the federal agency's reason for taking a proposed action, it does not require that each rejected mitigation measure be found infeasible as is the case with CEQA findings (40 C.F.R. § 1505.2).

In practice, NEPA has, however, become more mitigation driven over time. The greater emphasis on mitigation has been encouraged by the increase in the use of EA/FONSIs, rather than EISs for NEPA compliance. When a federal agency adopts a FONSI, it must conclude that all of the impacts are not significant or have been mitigated so that they are no longer significant. This legal requirement essentially requires impacts to be mitigated, which is not required when an EIS is prepared. In addition, many federal agencies have, in their own

Figure 9-4: Approach to Integrating Environmental Review Requirements

Requirement	Scoping Process	Draft Document	Final Document	Decision Making
NEPA	Notice of Intent	Draft EIS	Final EIS	Lead Agency issues a Record of Decision
CEQA	Notice of Preparation	Draft EIR	Final EIR	Notice of Determination
Endangered Species Act Sec. 7	Request species list	Biological Assessment	Biological Opinion	
Clean Water Act Sec. 404	Define objectives; Screen alternatives; Submit permit application	Draft Sec. 404(b)(1) analysis	Final Sec. 404(b)(1) analysis	USACE issues Sec. 4 permit (after Sec. 401 certification of waiver)
National Historic Preservation Act Sec. 106	Identify and evaluate historic and archaeological properties	Draft effects assessment	Memorandum of Agreement	
Clean Air Act Conformity (non-transportation project)	Determine whether the conformity requirement applies	Preliminary analysis (comparison to *de minimis* levels)	Detailed modeling analysis if necessary	Federal agency issues conformity determination
Public involvement	Scoping meetings	Public comment; Public hearing	Public comment	

NEPA regulations, added provisions that do require impacts to be mitigated for certain types of projects.

Evaluating Environmental Justice under NEPA

"Environmental justice" refers to "the fair treatment and meaningful involvement of all people regardless of race, color, national origin, or income with respect to the development, implementation, and enforcement of environmental laws, regulations, and policies. Fair treatment means that no group of people, including a racial, ethnic, or a socioeconomic group, should bear a disproportionate share of the negative environmental consequences resulting from industrial, municipal, and commercial operations or the execution of federal, state, local, and tribal programs and policies. Meaningful involvement means that: (1) potentially affected community residents have an appropriate opportunity to participate in decisions about a proposed activity that will affect their environment and/or health; (2) the public's contribution can influence the regulatory agency's decision; (3) the concerns of all participants involved will be considered in the decision-making process; and (4) the decisionmakers seek out and facilitate the involvement of those potentially affected."

This concept was propelled into the public policy spotlight at the national level in 1994 when President Clinton signed Executive Order 12898, entitled *Federal Actions to Address Environmental Justice in Minority Populations and Low-*

Figure 9-5. Environmental Review Requirements That May Require Integration

Regulated Activity and Resource	Implementing Agency	Regulatory Authority
Activities affecting species listed as "endangered" and "threatened"	U.S. Fish and Wildlife Service National Marine Fisheries Service	Sections 7 and 10, Endangered Species Act (16 USC 1536, 1538, 1539)
	California Department of Fish and Game	California Endangered Species Act (Fish and Game Code sec. 2081)
Activities affecting general fish and wildlife concerns	U.S. Fish and Wildlife Service National Marine Fisheries Service California Department of Fish and Game	Fish and Wildlife Coordination Act (16 USC 661-666)
Discharge of dredged or fill material into "waters of the United States" (including wetlands) or construction in "navigable waters" or activities within a floodplain	U.S. Army Corps of Engineers	Section 404, Clean Water Act (33 USC 1344) Section 10, Rivers and Harbors Act of 1899 (33 USC 403)
	Federal Lead Agency	Executive Order 11990, Protection of Wetlands Executive Order 11988, Floodplain Management
	California Department of Fish and Game	Streambed Alteration Agreement (Calif. Fish and Game Code secs 1600-1608)
Activities affecting clean air standards	California Air Quality Management Districts	Section 176, Clean Air Act (42 USC 7506)
Activities affecting cultural resources	Federal Lead Agency (The Advisory Council on Historic Preservation/State Historic Preservation Officer have oversight responsibilities relative to implementation of the National Historic Preservation Act)	National Historic Preservation Act (16 USC 470) American Indian Religious Freedom Act (42 USC 1996) Native American Graves Protection and Repatriation Act (25 USC 3001) Antiquities Act (16 USC 431) Archaeological Resources Protection Act (16 USC 470)
	State Lead Agency	State laws governing treatment of Native American remains: • Calif. Pub. Res. Code, secs. 5097.94, 5097.98, and 5097.99 • Calif. Health and Safety Code sec. 7050.5
Transportation or other activities affecting recreation areas and parks and historic sites	U.S. Federal Highway Administration	Section 4(f), Department of Transportation Act of 1966 (49 USC 303)
	Caltrans	FHWA NEPA delegation
Activities affecting agricultural land	Natural Resources Conservation Service	Farmland Protection Policy Act (7 USC 4201) Food Security Act (16 USC 3811)
	California Department of Conservation	California Land Conservation Act of 1965 (Williamson Act) (Govt. Code sec. 51200)
Activities involving hazardous materials or hazardous waste	U.S. Environmental Protection Agency	Comprehensive Environmental Response, Compensation and Liability Act (43 USC 9601) Superfund Amendments and Reauthorization Act (42 USC 9601) Resource Conservation Recovery Act (42 USC 692) Toxic Substances Control Act (15 USC 2601)
(continued next page)	California Environmental Protection Agency	Hazardous Waste Control Law (Calif. Health and Safety Code sec. 25100 et seq.)

Figure 9-5 (continued)

Regulated Activity and Resource	Implementing Agency	Regulatory Authority
Activities within the coastal zone	National Oceanic and Atmospheric Administration	Coastal Zone Management Act (16 USC 1451)
	California Coastal Commission	California Coastal Act (Pub. Res. Code sec. 30000 et seq.)
	City or County	Local Coastal Programs
Activities affecting wild and scenic rivers	U.S. Forest Service U.S. Bureau of Land Management U.S. Fish and Wildlife Service National Park Service	National Wild and Scenic Rivers Act (16 USC 1271)
	California Resources Agency	California Wild and Scenic Rivers Act (Pub. Res. Code sec. 5093.50 et seq.)
Activities affecting minority and low-income populations	Federal Lead Agency	Executive Order 12898, Federal Actions to Address Environmental Justice in Minority Populations and Low-Income Populations
Activities involving water quality	California State Water Resources Control Board/Regional Water Quality Control Boards	Section 401, Clean Water Act (33 USC 1341) Section 402, Clean Water Act (33 USC 1342) Porter-Cologne Water Quality Control Act (Division 7, California Water Code)
Activities affecting water rights	California State Water Resources Control Board	State Water Rights Law (Calif. Water Code sec. 1000 et seq.)
Activities affecting submerged lands and tidelands	California State Lands Commission	California Pub. Res. Code sec. 60001 et seq.
Activities involving dams or reservoirs	California Department of Water Resources, Division of Safety of Dams	California Water Code, sec. 6000 et seq.
Activities affecting designated wilderness areas	U.S. Bureau of Land Management	Federal Land Policy and Management Act of 1976 (43 USC 1701)
	U.S. Bureau of Land Management U.S. Forest Service National Park Service	Wilderness Act of 1964 (16 USC 1131)
	California Resources Agency	California Wilderness Act (Pub. Res. Code sec. 5093.30 et seq.)
Mining operations	CEQA Lead Agency	Surface Mining and Reclamation Act of 1975 (Calif. Pub. Res. Code sec. 2710)
	U.S. Bureau of Land Management	General Mining Law of 1872 (30 USC 22) Surface Mining Control and Reclamation Act of 1977 (30 USC 1201)
Activities involving timber harvests on private land	California Department of Forestry and Fire Protection	Z-Berg-Nejedly Forest Practice Act (Calif. Pub. Res. Code sec. 4511 et seq.)
Activities affecting federal forests	U.S. Bureau of Land Management	Federal Land Policy and Management Act of 1976 (43 USC 1701)
	U.S. Forest Service	National Forest Management Act of 1976 (16 USC 1600) Multiple-Use and Sustained-Yield Act of 1960 (16 USC 528) Organic Administration Act of 1897 (16 USC 473)
Management of grazing land	U.S. Bureau of Land Management U.S. Forest Service	Taylor Grazing Act of 1934 (43 USC 315)

Income Populations. Executive Order 12898 emphasized that existing federal laws provided federal agencies with the authority to address environmental justice, including–but not limited to–Title VI of the Civil Rights Act of 1964 and NEPA.

The Executive Order was followed by an advisory memorandum from the CEQ, which clearly required federal agencies to consider environmental justice in the implementation of NEPA. (See CEQ *Environmental Justice: Guidance Under the National Environmental Policy Act*, 10 December 1997,) Today, every federal agency has an environmental justice policy and agency-specific requirements to evaluate environmental justice under NEPA.

Application to NEPA

In the context of NEPA, environmental justice has both procedural and substantive components. From a procedural perspective, federal agencies are required to affirmatively reach out to low-income and minority communities at all phases of the NEPA process, including scoping, document preparation, public notice and review, and decision making. From a substantive perspective, federal agencies are required in their NEPA documents to address the fundamental question: *Would the proposed action result in a disproportionately high or adverse environmental impact on low-income or minority populations as compared to the general population?* To answer this question, federal agencies must develop and consider the socioeconomic factors about people who would be adversely affected by the physical environmental impacts of proposed federal actions. At the time that the CEQ released its Environmental Justice Guidance for NEPA, it also released NEPA Guidance for Federal Agencies on Key Terms in E.O. 12898, which offers key definitions, now generally accepted definitions, that are useful for environmental review of projects.

Environmental Justice in California

Government Code § 65040.12(c) establishes the Governor's Office of Planning and Research (OPR) as the coordinator for environmental justice programs for state agencies. Under this law, and with OPR's oversight, every state agency is supposed to consider environmental justice in carrying out their respective programs. The California definition of "environmental justice" is very similar to the federal definition: "the fair treatment of people of all races, cultures, and incomes with respect to the development, adoption, implementation and enforcement of environmental laws."

In addition, the 2003 edition of the state General Plan Guidelines, which assists cities and counties in preparing their general plans, contains suggestions for addressing environmental justice in the general plan. These include outreach to affected communities and land use compatibility.

Application to CEQA

Unlike NEPA, CEQA does not require the evaluation of environmental justice impacts. CEQA documents typically disclose the potential environmental impacts on residents, regardless of their income level or ethnic identity. The evaluation of environmental justice impacts under CEQA is strictly optional at the discretion of the lead agency.

Environmental Justice in Joint NEPA/CEQA Documents

One of the fundamental principles of preparing joint CEQA/NEPA documents is that the combined document should satisfy whichever legal requirement is the most stringent for each particular issue. Thus, since environmental justice must be evaluated under NEPA, when state and local agencies prepare a joint CEQA/NEPA document, the federal lead agency's rules for evaluating it must be followed. In practice, this means that CEQA practitioners must have some understanding of the concept of environmental justice and both the procedural and substantive requirements for addressing it.

Tips for Successful Compliance

This chapter discussed the importance of integrating CEQA with other federal and state environmental laws, and NEPA in particular. The following are some tips for successfully integrating CEQA with other laws:

- **Identify all applicable federal and state laws**—A critical first step to integrating NEPA with other environmental laws is to identify such laws and how they apply to the project. Each federal agency should be consulted to determine if and what type of NEPA compliance will be necessary for implementation of the proposed project.
- **Learn the difference and similarities between CEQA and NEPA**—Although CEQA and NEPA are fundamentally similar, some important differences must be addressed when integrating them. Variations exist in NEPA procedures between federal agencies, and practitioners should have knowledge of the relevant federal agency's NEPA requirements.
- **Prepare joint CEQA/NEPA documents when possible**—Both the CEQA Guidelines and the CEQ's NEPA regulations encourage the preparation of joint documents a way to avoid duplication and delay. Joint documents require close cooperation between the CEQA and NEPA lead agencies in order to be successful.
- **Develop a coordinated approach to compliance with other laws**—Once a lead agency identifies other environmental laws to be integrated, it should develop and implement a comprehensive strategy to achieving integration.

When a project is subject to both CEQA and NEPA, state and federal agencies are encouraged to prepare a joint environmental review to satisfy compliance with both laws.

Chapter 10
CEQA Litigation

The Role of Litigation
Legal Enforcement

CEQA is most often enforced through litigation brought by private citizens, organizations, and public agencies. The California Attorney General is also empowered to bring suit to enforce CEQA compliance. Although they have oversight responsibilities, neither OPR nor the Natural Resources Agency has authority to enforce the requirements of CEQA.

The courts have played a major role in extending CEQA's applicability and effect and, in general, have interpreted CEQA's statutory provisions liberally. Of particular importance in CEQA's early judicial development is the California Supreme Court's statement in *Friends of Mammoth v. Board of Supervisors of Mono County* (1972) 8 Cal. 3d. 247 that CEQA "is to be interpreted to afford the fullest possible protection to the environment within the reasonable scope of the statutory language." Overall, the Supreme Court's interpretation of legislative intent has strongly influenced lower court decisions throughout CEQA's history. For a complete discussion of CEQA and CEQA case law and litigation issues, see *Guide to the California Environmental Quality Act* by Michael H. Remy, Tina A. Thomas, James G. Moose, and Whitman F. Manley, published by Solano Press Books (2007).

The tendency of the courts to construe CEQA liberally led the legislature to amend the law in 1993 to provide some limits on court interpretations. The legislature declared its intent that courts, consistent with generally accepted rules of statutory interpretation, shall not interpret either CEQA or the Guidelines in a manner that imposes procedural or substantive requirements beyond those explicitly stated in CEQA or the Guidelines (Pub. Res. Code § 21083.1).

Effect of Potential for Litigation on CEQA Compliance

As stated in Chapter 1, lead agencies must be mindful of the legal and political risks inherent in taking shortcuts when deciding whether to comply with CEQA and which CEQA document to prepare. Generally, the risk of being challenged in court and potentially losing the challenge increases as less time and effort is devoted to preparing the CEQA document (*see* Figure 1-3 on page 8). Although litigation has been a major factor in CEQA "enforcement," a study by the Association of Bay Area Governments (ABAG) indicated that fewer than one percent of project applications subject to CEQA are actually litigated. That same study, based on a survey of local planning directors, indicated that the outcome of most CEQA judicial decisions favored the public agency (*see* Chapter 8). Thus, while CEQA litigation has not been a serious obstacle to economic development, the threat of potential litigation is a very real factor that often influences the type of document prepared and the content of that document.

Typical Issues and Trends in Litigation

> **Typical Issues and Trends in Litigation**
>
> - Definition of a Project and Examptions.
> - Failure to Prepare an EIR.
> - Adequacy of an EIR.
> - Procedural Requirements.

The judicial history of CEQA is marked by hundreds of published Supreme Court and appellate court decisions with several noticeable trends. Some of the most litigated aspects of CEQA are discussed here:

Definition of a Project and Exemptions. First, beginning with *Friends of Mammoth,* numerous court decisions have dealt with the applicability of CEQA to various types of activities and the question of whether statutory or categorical exemptions were appropriate.

Failure to Prepare an EIR. A second subject of considerable litigation has been use of the "fair argument" standard relative to negative declarations. While the legislature intended that there be a low threshold for triggering an EIR, in practice the negative declaration or mitigated negative declaration has become the most frequently prepared form of CEQA documentation. The judicial message has been clear, however—an agency choosing not to prepare an EIR does so at its own risk, unless the negative declaration is clearly justified and documented and no substantial evidence exists that the project may result in a significant effect. Since the 1993 CEQA amendments defining "substantial evidence" to consist of facts and expert opinion based on facts, the courts have upheld negative declarations and mitigated negative declarations where substantial evidence was lacking to support a fair argument.

Adequacy of an EIR. A third line of cases has established the parameters of an adequate EIR. In evaluating EIR adequacy, the courts have established a "rule of reason" now embodied in the Guidelines (Guidelines § 15151). As a result of this standard, challenges to the adequacy of EIRs are difficult to win. However, four notable exceptions have occurred: challenges to inadequate project descriptions, water supply analysis, alternatives analysis, and cumulative impacts analysis. Thus, current litigation on the adequacy of EIRs typically focuses on these four areas.

As discussed in Chapter 7, the courts do not hold an agency to a standard of perfection, but rather require only that an EIR show that an agency has made an objective, good-faith effort at full disclosure (Guidelines §§ 15003(i), 15151). Courts generally look to see that all required contents are included and accept that experts may disagree. Courts will examine whether substantial evidence exists within the administrative record that supports the agency's conclusions. Thus, given a choice between several methods of analysis, the courts will generally defer to the expertise of the lead agency when supported by substantial evidence. Nor do they require that the EIR have an exhaustive treatment of the environmental issues. Courts also will not hold an EIR as inadequate for minor technical defects. The scope of judicial review does not extend to the correctness of an EIR's conclusions, but only to the EIR's sufficiency as an informative document for decisionmakers and the public.

Procedural Requirements. The fourth trend in judicial interpretation has been an emphasis on strict procedural compliance. Many times, appellate courts have reversed agency decisions based on procedural violations, declaring them to be prejudicial abuses of discretion (The cases on inadequate findings are one example.) Even seemingly minor transgressions, such as failing to consult with responsible or trustee agencies, or failure to send the proper documents to the State Clearinghouse, have been the downfall of some agencies in litigation. Since CEQA is essentially a procedural law, it should not be surprising that the courts have required procedural accuracy.

Statute of Limitations

When deciding whether or not to pursue litigation through CEQA, parties must be mindful of CEQA's strict statutes of limitation. The statutes of limitation cut off the right of a party to file a court action, challenging approval of the project. Parties wishing to challenge agency approval of a project under CEQA must seek court review within the following time periods:

- 35 days after an agency has filed and posted a notice of exemption (NOE)
- 30 days after an agency has filed and posted a notice of determination (NOD) (for either a negative declaration or EIR)
- 180 days after an agency decides to carry out or approve a project, or 180 days from commencement of a project for projects without formal decision (when no NOE or NOD has been filed)

(Guidelines § 15112(c)).

If an agency substantially changes a project after completing an EIR without preparing a subsequent or supplemental EIR (with no addendum and NOD), the 180-day limitation period begins when a petitioner knows—or should have known—of the project changes.

The California Supreme Court has emphasized the importance of filing and NOE or NOD in opinions that reveal the strictness of CEQA's statute of limitations (*see Committee for Green Foothills v. Santa Clara County Board of Supervisors* (2010) 48 Cal. 4th 32; *Stockton Citizens for Sensible Planning v. City of Stockton* (2010) 48 Cal. 4th 481).

CEQA's Statutes of Limitations

- 35 days after an agency has filed and posted a notice of exemption
- 30 days after an agency has filed and posted a notice of determination (for either a negative declaration or an EIR)
- 180 days after an agency decides to carry out or approve a project, or 180 days from commencement of a project for projects without a formal decision (when no notice of exemption or notice of determination has been filed)

Overview of the CEQA Litigation Process

The following sections summarize the current legal procedures under CEQA and provide a general framework for nonlawyers who need to understand the fundamentals of CEQA litigation. These requirements are subject to change and readers should refer to the current version of the Public Resources Code for the most up-to-date legal procedures for CEQA litigation.

Procedural Pretrial Requirements

CEQA contains the following special pretrial procedural requirements that must be strictly adhered to in order to pursue a lawsuit under CEQA:

- Petition for writ of mandate
- Notice to the lead agency of commencement of action
- Petition for writ of mandate filed with the court
- Notice to the agency to prepare the administrative record
- Service to the defendant agency
- Service of pleadings to the State Attorney General
- Motion requesting a hearing (within ninety days of filing a petition)
- Briefing schedule established by the court (within thirty days of motion requesting hearing)

Materials Included in the Administrative Record

- Project application and all supplementary materials
- The CEQA document and all material related to its preparation
- All staff reports about the proposed project
- Project public hearing records
- Correspondence, including e-mails, related to the proposed project
- All public notices
- Written comments about the project
- Proposed decisions and findings about the project
- Documents about to prior versions of the project that were considered or approved
- All other documents relating to the agency decision on the project
- Project-related material in the possession of both responsible and lead agencies

Special Considerations

Petition for a Writ of Mandate. A party seeking to challenge an action under CEQA must file a petition for a writ of mandate. The petition for a writ of mandate is a request that the court issue an order requiring the lead agency to do something to remedy the perceived infraction, typically to correct the CEQA violation.

Notice of Commencement of an Action. A petitioner must serve the public agency with notice of the commencement of a CEQA lawsuit and must file proof of service of such notice with the initial pleading submitted to the court (Pub. Res. Code § 21167.5). A petitioner must furnish copies of the pleadings to the State Attorney General (Pub. Res. Code § 21167.7).

The petitioner must name as a real party in interest any recipient of an approval that is the subject of the lawsuit. They must serve the petition on that real party in interest within twenty business days of serving the public agency (Pub. Res. Code § 21167.6.5).

The public agency must provide the petitioner with a list of responsible agencies and agencies having jurisdiction over a natural resource affected by the project within ten business days of being served with a complaint. The petitioner must provide those agencies with notice of the legal action within fifteen days of receiving the list (Pub. Res. Code § 21167.6.5).

Request for Administrative Record. Within ten days after filing a CEQA action with the court, the petitioner must also personally serve the public agency with the complaint or petition and request that the agency prepare the record of administrative proceedings related to the action (Pub. Res. Code § 21167.6). The public agency must prepare and certify the administrative record within sixty days (Pub. Res. Code § 21167.6(b)). If the public agency fails to prepare and certify the record within the prescribed time limit, the petitioner may move for sanctions, and the court may, upon that motion, grant appropriate sanctions (Pub. Res. Code § 21167.6(d)).

For purposes of judicial review in CEQA litigation, the public agency is required to include in the administrative record the project application and all supplementary materials, all staff reports regarding the proposed project, project public hearing records, all public notices, written comments received regarding the project, proposed decisions and findings on the project, and any other documents relating to the agency decision on the project (Pub. Res. Code § 21167.6).

Pretrial Settlement. CEQA provides detailed procedures for pretrial settlement, including requiring pretrial settlement conferences. As a part of these procedures, the public agency must file a notice with the court no later than twenty days after filing a petition or complaint setting forth the time and place at which all the parties shall meet to attempt to settle the litigation. The meeting must be scheduled within forty-five days of the date of the service of petition or complaint (Pub. Res. Code § 21167.8).

Optional Mediation Procedures. Within five business days of the filing of an NOE or NOD, a petitioner intending to bring suit against a public agency may file with the agency and real party in interest, if applicable, a notice requesting mediation. The public agency would have five business days to respond if it wishes to engage in mediation. Mediation would proceed before litigation ensues. This provision expires January 1, 2006 (Pub. Res. Code § 21167.10).

Request for a Hearing. The petitioner must file a motion requesting a hearing within ninety days of filing the petition (Pub. Res. Code § 2167.4). Upon filing a request for hearing by the petitioner or upon application by any party, the court is required to establish a briefing schedule and hearing date. Unless there is good cause to do otherwise, the briefing must be completed within ninety days of filing the request, and the hearing must be held within thirty days thereafter. The parties to the suit may stipulate to a different briefing schedule or hearing date if the court approves that stipulation (Pub. Res. Code § 21167.4(c)). Failure to meet either of these schedules can result in dismissal of the case. The petitioner must serve notice of the request for a hearing on all parties to the litigation at the time of filing the request (Pub. Res. Code § 21167.4(b)). The hearing must be requested within ninety days, but need not be scheduled by the court within that time period (*Leavitt v. County of Madera* (2004) 123 Cal. App. 4th 1502; *Association for Sensible Development at Northstar v. Placer County* (2004) 122 Cal. App. 4th 1289).

The Administrative Record

The completeness of the administrative record is critical in CEQA litigation. In *Protect Our Water, et al. v. County of Merced* (2003) 110 Cal.App.4th 362, the Court of Appeals overturned a county's approval of a surface mining project for which an EIR was prepared when the administrative record was highly disorganized. The court vented its frustration in no uncertain terms:

> "When practicing appellate law, there are at least three immutable rules: first, take great care to prepare a complete record; second, if it is not in the record, it did not happen; and third, when in doubt, refer back to rules one and two. In this case, the parties totally missed the appellate mark by failing to provide an adequate record for review . . ."

The court went on:

> "The administrative record is large—14 binder-sized volumes. It reads as if its preparers randomly pulled out documents and threw them into binders, failing to organize them either chronologically or by subject matter. Key findings required under CEQA are impossible to find—let alone sufficient to enable us to determine whether they are supported by substantial evidence."

Finally, the court concluded in frustration:

> "We publish not because the merits of this case warrant public proclamation but because we have observed a pattern of CEQA cases with poorly prepared records making review difficult, if not impossible. We iterate to anyone who will listen: CEQA has very specific requirements regarding what findings must be in the record. Do not ignore the requirements or, like these parties, you will find yourself in the unenviable position of having your judgment reversed and being forced to start over at great public and personal expense."

Calendar Preference. Both trial and appellate courts are required to give CEQA actions calendar preference over other civil actions (Pub. Res. Code § 21167.1). To expedite the litigation process the courts must regulate the briefing schedule so that, to the extent feasible, a hearing on appeal commences within one year of the date the appeal is filed (Pub. Res. Code § 21167.1(a)). To further ensure that actions or proceedings challenging CEQA compliance are heard and determined quickly in the lower courts, the superior courts in all counties with a population of more than 200,000 must designate one or more judges to develop expertise in CEQA and related land use and environmental laws so that those judges will be available to hear—and quickly resolve—CEQA actions (Pub. Res. Code § 21167.1(b)).

Typical Defenses

Procedural Defenses

The procedural defenses commonly asserted during CEQA litigation include: filing after the statute of limitations, lack of standing, lack of substantial evidence, and failure of the petitioner to exhaust their administrative remedies.

Standing. CEQA does not have strict standing rules. Parties may sue under CEQA if they are property owners, taxpayers, or voters within the area affected by the project. The party must show a clear, present, and beneficial right to performance of the duty that the agency allegedly failed to perform (Code Civ. Proc. § 1086). Because courts, in practice, usually apply liberal standards for standing in CEQA cases, standing has generally not been a problem for would-be CEQA litigants and has even been extended to corporations with primarily commercial interests (*Save the Plastic Bag Coalition v. City of Manhattan Beach* (2011) 52 Cal. 4th 155).

Exhaustion of Administrative Remedies. A CEQA lawsuit may not be filed unless the alleged CEQA violations were raised orally or in writing during the public comment period or before the close of the public hearing and the issuing of the notice of determination, as long as an agency properly provided an opportunity for the public to comment (Pub. Res. Code § 21177). This includes projects for which a notice of exemption was filed. (*Tomlinson v. County of Alameda* (2012) __ Cal. 4th __) Courts disagree on the specificity with which objections must be stated during the administrative proceedings. Objections need not be raised before a lower administrative agency (e.g., a planning commission), provided they are raised before the decision-making body (e.g., a board of supervisors). If a party submits comments after the public review period provided by CEQA, but before the project decision is made, the exhaustion doctrine will nevertheless be satisfied, even though the lead agency is not required to formally respond to the comments in the final EIR (*see Galante Vineyards v. Monterey Peninsula Water District* (1997) 60 Cal. App. 4th 1109).

The primary purpose of this doctrine is to ensure that public agencies are given the opportunity to receive and respond to particular environmental or procedural issues during the administrative review process in hopes of avoiding a legal challenge. To ensure that the agency has been given the opportunity to respond to objections, the specific issues pertaining to the litigation must have been raised during the administrative process; however, the issues do not have to be personally raised by the petitioner, as long as someone else presented the objections to the agency (Pub. Res. Code § 21177(a)). The petitioner must have objected to the agency's approval of the project sometime during the administrative process, during the public comment period, or before the close of the public hearing and the issuing of the notice of determination (Pub. Res. Code § 21177(b)). It should be noted that the requirement of lead agencies to allow for appeals of CEQA decisions to the elected decisionmaking body for cities and counties means this must be taken advantage of in order to exhaust administrative remedies.

Typical Procedural Defenses

- Filing after the statute of limitations has run out
- Lack of standing
- Failing to exhaust administrative remedies
- lack of substantial evidence

Lack of Substantial Evidence. "Substantial evidence" is defined as, "Fact, a reasonable assumption predicted upon fact, or expert opinion supported by fact" (Pub. Res. Code § 21080(e); Guidelines § 15384). A challenge to an exemption or Negative Declaration based on a "fair argument" will not be sustained absent substantial evidence in the administrative record (*Wollmer v. City of Berkeley* (2011) 193 Cal. App. 4th 1329; *Porterville Citizens for Responsible Hillside Development v. City of Porterville* (2007) 157 Cal. App. 4th 885).

Substantive Defenses

As stated in the previous section, agencies are not held to a standard of perfection; therefore, the agency's substantive defense focuses on whether the agency has made an objective, good-faith attempt at full disclosure (Guidelines §§ 15003(i), 15151). The agency's defense should include the fact that all required procedures have been followed and contents of the CEQA document are adequate. Challengers to the agency action based on an EIR will generally not be successful if the challenge centers around the fact that experts disagree in regard to significance determinations or the adequacy of mitigation. However, as noted in the next section, the standard is different when the agency decision based on a categorical exemption or negative declaration is challenged.

Judicial Standards of Review

Review is by "administrative mandamus" if the challenged agency decision is based on an evidentiary hearing; otherwise, review is by traditional "mandamus" (Pub. Res. Code §§ 21168, 21168.5). Under either proceeding, a court may overturn an agency decision only if the agency did not proceed as required by law or if the decision was not supported by substantial evidence (*Western States Petroleum Association v. The Superior Court of Los Angeles County* (1995) 9 Cal. 4th 559). In either case, the court generally may not receive evidence outside the administrative record.

Reviewing courts generally defer to the agencies' substantive judgments while requiring strict compliance with the procedural aspects of CEQA. Courts cannot overturn agencies' discretionary decisions and substitute their own opinions as to what constitutes appropriate public policy. In this regard, the courts cannot pass judgment on the correctness of the EIR's environmental conclusions, but only on its sufficiency as an informative document.

Special Standard of Review

A special standard favorable to the petitioner—the "fair argument" standard—is used when a court reviews an agency decision to adopt a categorical exemption or a negative declaration. However, when reviewing the contents of an EIR for adequacy, the courts employ the "rule of reason" standard of review. The scope of judicial review focuses on whether the EIR's conclusions are supported by substantial evidence.

Remedies

Remedies in General

The court reviewing the CEQA challenge is required to address each of the alleged grounds for noncompliance (Pub. Res. Code § 21005). A court finding a CEQA violation may 1) void the agency action (or portions of the action if severable), 2) suspend all agency and relevant project actions that could have environmental impacts until CEQA compliance is achieved, and 3) order the agency to comply with CEQA.

CEQA is enforced through litigation.

The court must issue a peremptory writ of mandate specifying what actions are needed to comply with CEQA. A court may limit the writ of mandate to include only specific project activities that are out of compliance with CEQA if it determines that the project is severable, that severance would not prejudice CEQA compliance, and that the remainder of the project is in compliance (Pub. Res. Code § 21168.9(a)(1)). The trial court must retain continuing jurisdiction over the agency's proceedings until determining that the agency has complied with CEQA (Pub. Res. Code § 21168.9). Monetary damages for CEQA violations are not available.

Injunctions

The court will not proactively enjoin an action from proceeding in light of an aging CEQA challenge. Plaintiffs need to specifically request an injunction. In deciding whether to grant an injunction, the court will consider whether an injunction is necessary to further CEQA's primary purpose of protecting the environment, and whether the injunction would unduly prejudice the agency or the public. A court may only enjoin project implementation upon finding that a specific activity will prejudice the consideration or implementation of a particular mitigation measure or alternative (Pub. Res. Code § 21168.9(a)(2)). Thus, sometimes the court might find a CEQA violation, but the project proponent had decided to proceed with the project anyway. Such a proponent does so at his or her own risk, as courts will not accept a defense of mootness because the project is already built, and a remedy ordering project removal could be appropriate (*Woodward Park Homeowners Assoc. v. City of Fresno* (2000) 77 Ca. App. 4th 880).

Other CEQA Litigation Issues

Effect of Ongoing Litigation on Responsible Agencies

If a CEQA lawsuit has been filed and an injunction has been granted against the lead agency, a decision by a responsible agency will be conditional; however, the agency is required to act on the project within mandated time limits. If an interim injunction has not been granted, the responsible agency must assume lead agency CEQA compliance and act on the project within mandated time limits (Guidelines § 15233).

Possible Court-Ordered Remedies for CEQA Violations

- Void the agency action.
- Suspend all agency and relevant project actions that could have environmental impacts until CEQA compliance is achieved.
- Order the agency to comply with CEQA.

Appeals

CEQA contains specific provisions to expedite the judicial appeals process (Pub. Res. Code § 21167.6).

Attorneys' Fees

Awards of attorneys' fees may be authorized by the court in CEQA cases if the action resulted in enforcement of an important public right affecting the public interest, significant benefit would be conferred on the public or a large class, and necessity and financial burden of private enforcement of CEQA make the award appropriate (Code Civ. Proc. § 1021.5).

Courts tend to be sympathetic to requests for attorneys' fees by successful CEQA plaintiffs. However, it is up to the discretion of the court to grant the fees.

Summary of California Supreme Court Decisions

Early California Supreme Court decisions generally supported the challengers to state and local agencies. The court consistently held that public agencies should interpret CEQA "so as to afford the fullest protection of the environment within the reasonable scope of the statutory language" (*Friends of Mammoth v. Board of Supervisors of Mono County* (1972) 8 Cal. 3d 247, 104 Cal. Rptr. 76). The court's early pro-CEQA attitude has been an important factor in ensuring proper implementation of CEQA by public agencies throughout California.

Since the early 1990s, the Supreme Court has demonstrated a tendency to side with agencies and has taken a less expansive view of CEQA. Additionally, a 1993 CEQA amendment specifically instructed the courts not to add requirements beyond CEQA and the Guidelines (Pub. Res. Code § 21083). The following summaries present some of the California Supreme Court's key CEQA decisions. For a complete treatment of published CEQA court decisions, see *Guide to the California Environmental Quality Act* by Remy, Thomas, Moose, and Manley, Solano Press Books.

Friends of Mammoth v. Board of Supervisors of Mono County **(1972) 8 Cal. 3d 247, 104 Cal. Rptr. 76.** The Mono County Board of Supervisors violated CEQA by not complying with the law prior to approving a conditional use permit for a private development project. The court determined that the legislature intended CEQA to apply not only to public agency actions that directly affect the physical environment, but also to permit approvals of private actions that indirectly affect the environment.

No Oil, Inc. v. City of Los Angeles **(1975) 13 Cal. 3d 68, 118 Cal. Rptr. 34.** The City of Los Angeles violated CEQA by not preparing an EIR before enacting an ordinance allowing oil drilling within the city limits. The court held that an EIR is required if substantial evidence is produced that could support a fair argument that the project may have a significant effect on the environment. The court cautioned lead agencies that, to be significant, a potential impact need not be momentous or of a permanent or long enduring nature, but can range from not trivial to appreciable to important as well as momentous.

Bozung v. Local Agency Formation Commission **(1975) 13 Cal. 3d 263, 118 Cal. Rptr. 249.** The Ventura County LAFCO violated CEQA by not preparing an EIR on an annexation of a property to a city. The court held that annexation was the first step in the project approval process and, because the property was clearly destined to be developed, its environmental impacts could be evaluated.

Laurel Heights Improvement Association of San Francisco v. Regents of the University of California **(1988) 47 Cal. 3d 376, 253 Cal. Rptr. 426.** The EIR of the Regents of the University of California on the decision to occupy an existing building to be used for biomedical research was inadequate. The court held that the Regents' EIR should have analyzed reasonably foreseeable (although tentative) future phases of the project as well as alternative sites.

Citizens of Goleta Valley et al. v. Board of Supervisors **(1990) 52 Cal. 3d 553, 276 Cal. Rptr. 410.** Santa Barbara County properly excluded alternative sites for a coastal resort hotel from consideration in an EIR because the sites were not within the applicant's control, could require a local coastal plan/general plan amendment, and were outside the lead agency's permitting jurisdiction.

Laurel Heights Improvement Association of San Francisco v. Regents of the University of California **(1993) 6 Cal. 4th 1112.** Recirculation of a draft EIR for public comment is required where significant new information is added to the EIR after the close of the public comment period but before certification. The new information is significant when it results in a new or more severe impact or when it consists of a new mitigation measure or alternative that could reduce the significance of an impact. Information that merely clarifies or amplifies the draft EIR is not significant.

Western States Petroleum Association v. The Superior Court of Los Angeles County **(1995) 9 Cal. 4th 559.** In a challenge to the adoption of California Air Resources Board air quality regulations, the court held that, in a traditional mandamus proceeding under CEQA, the parties are severely limited as to submitting evidence that was not a part of the administrative record.

Friends of Sierra Madre v. City of Sierra Madre **(2001) 25 Cal. 4th 165.** The Sierra Madre City Council placed on the ballot for citywide election an amendment to its historic preservation ordinance. The amendment would have removed numerous historic properties from the list of historic properties. The court held that CEQA compliance is required when a project is proposed and placed in the ballot by a public agency. It is not required when an ordinance qualifies for the ballot by voter petition. An ordinance approved by voters after being placed on the ballot by the city is invalid without CEQA compliance.

***People ex rel Department of Conservation v. County of El Dorado* (2005) 36 Cal. 4th 971.** The Department of Conservation sued the county for failure to prepare an EIR on the preparation of a mine reclamation plan under the Surface Mining and Reclamation Act (SMARA). The county questioned the Department director's authority to challenge its action. The court held that the director was authorized by law to review the county's reclamation plan and take appropriate action. Thus, the director had standing to bring the CEQA challenge.

***City of Marina et al. v. Board of Trustees of the California State University* (2006) 39 Cal. 4th 341.** Marina and the Fort Ord Reuse Authority (FORA) challenged the CEQA findings and statement of overriding considerations made by California State University Monterey Bay (CSU) for its master plan EIR. The EIR disclosed that the planned campus expansion to accommodate 25,000 students would have a number of significant effects. In its CEQA findings, CSU concluded that improvements to roads and fire protection were the sole responsibility of FORA (although CSU was contributing for water, drainage, and wastewater costs); CSU could not legally contribute its share to off-site facilities that would mitigate the traffic and fire safety impacts of CSU; and the planned expansion offered overriding benefits. CSU cited the restrictions established under Government Code section 54999 et seq. (the "*San Marcos* legislation") that limits school payments to local agencies for public utilities services.

The Supreme Court ruled that CEQA obligated CSU to mitigate the impacts of its project (including off-site impacts) unless it is infeasible to do so. The court found that the "plain language of the California Constitution does not support the Trustee's position that voluntary mitigation payments are impermissible." Paying to mitigate CSU's environmental effects was not an unlawful gift of public funds.

The court found no reason to doubt that FORA would meet its obligations for traffic improvements. FORA had identified infrastructure needs and had a variety of methods by which it could finance those improvements. In addition, payment of fees to satisfy a cumulative environmental impact was authorized under CEQA. FORA was not solely responsible for paying for the infrastructure improvements. In fact, its cooperation provided CSU with the opportunity to pay their fair share of the mitigation.

***Vineyard Area Citizens for Responsible Growth, Inc. v. City of Rancho Cordova* (2007), 40 Cal. 4th 412.** In 2002, Sacramento County approved the Sunrise-Douglas Community Plan and SunRidge Specific Plan for the eventual development of more than 22,000 residences and related urban uses on approximately 6,000 rural acres near Rancho Cordova. The EIR prepared for the project was challenged by Vineyard Area Citizens on the grounds that it failed to identify the actual source of much of the water needed to meet long-term demand and that new information regarding the impact of the project's groundwater draw on water flows and fish habitat in the Cosumnes River required recirculation of the EIR before its certification.

The court held that the analysis of water supply was inadequate because it failed to provide readers with an adequate description of long-term water sources, as briefly mentioned in the challenged EIR and as discussed at greater length in a prior EIR for the "Water Forum" process. The EIR for the land use plans failed to formally incorporate by reference information from the Water Forum EIR, and contained numerical information at odds with parallel sets of water demand and water supply numbers in the Water Forum EIR. The EIR was also inadequate because the lead agency failed to recirculate it after identifying possible significant biological impacts on the Cosumnes River due to groundwater pumping associated with short-term water supply. The court also ruled that a mitigation measure providing for the curtailment of development should water sources not materialize or be delayed is an appropriate tool under CEQA but is not a substitute for an adequate impact analysis.

Muzzy Ranch Co. v. Solano County Airport Land Use Commission **(2007) 41 Cal. 4th 372.** Muzzy Ranch sued the County Airport Land Use Commission (ALUC) over its adoption of the Travis Air Force Base airport land use compatibility plan (TALUP) without preparation of a CEQA document. The court upheld the Commission's approval and reasoned that although the approval was a project under CEQA in setting fourth land use decisions, much like a general plan, the administrative record as a whole demonstrated that Commission had reached the correct result in finding that no detailed environmental analysis was warranted under CEQA's general exemption. The court found that the record reflects that the TALUP's restriction on land use simply incorporates the county's existing general plan and zoning restrictions. Therefore, "any potential displacement the TALUP might otherwise have effected *already* has been caused by the existing land use policies and zoning regulations to which the TALUP is keyed" (emphasis added). There is no reason to assume that local agencies will change their policies in the future to permit increased development within Compatibility Zone C.

Ebbetts Pass Forest Watch, et. al. v. California Department of Forestry and Fire Protection **(2008) 43 Cal. 4th 936.** Forest Watch sued CDF over the department's approval of three Timber Harvest Plans (THPs) in Tuolumne County. The Court held that a functional equivalent program such as a THP is subject to the CEQA standard of review. The Court examined the cumulative impact analyses and responses to comments contained in the THP at issue, and found that the analyses and responses properly considered the effects of the THPs on the Pacific fisher and spotted owl along the Sierra Nevada range, including National Forest lands. The THP's analysis of herbicide use was sufficient given that site-specific herbicide use over the life of the THP was not reasonably foreseeable.

In re: *Bay-Delta Programmatic Environmental Impact Report Coordinated Proceedings* (2008) 43 Cal.4th 1143. This case consolidated a number of CEQA challenges to the program EIS/EIR that was certified for the CalFed project in 2000 that considered the long-range, joint federal and state strategy for balancing water transfer with environmental and habitat issues within the

Sacramento-San Joaquin River Delta. The Court upheld the EIR's alternatives analysis, stating that the underlying purpose of CalFed project is to encompass all beneficial uses of Delta water and "cannot be achieved by an alternative that benefits some groups of water users at the expense of the others." Therefore, CalFed properly exercised its discretion when it declined to further study the reduced export alternative in the final PEIS/EIR. In addition, the Court held that the PEIS/EIR is a "first-tier program EIR" that is not required to "identify with certainty [the] particular sources of water for second-tier projects that will be further analyzed before implementation during later stages of the program." Similarly, the secondary effects of obtaining water from potential sources may be analyzed in general terms in the first-tier document.

***Save Tara v. City of West Hollywood* (2008) 45 Cal. 4th 116.** The City of West Hollywood approved an agreement with a developer for the reuse and redevelopment of a large historic home. The agreement would convey the property to the developer, provide the developer a substantial loan, and allow the construction of thirty-five units of housing on the site. While the agreement stated that all CEQA requirements be satisfied at some future time, it also gave the city manager authority to waive those requirements. The agreement would allow the developer to receive final approval of a grant from the federal Housing and Urban Development department (HUD) that would provide funding for the project. The court first held that the city's certification of a Final EIR completed subsequent to the trial court decision did not render the case moot.

The court set out two considerations important to the timing of EIR preparation in finding the city's actions violated CEQA:"1) that CEQA not be interpreted to require an EIR before the project is well enough defined to allow for meaningful environmental evaluation and 2) that CEQA not be interpreted as allowing an EIR to be delayed beyond the time when it can, as a practical matter, serve its intended function of informing and guiding decision makers."

***Environmental Protection and Information Center v. California Department of Forestry and Fire Protection* (2008) 44 Cal. 4th 459.** This case is concerned with the Headwaters Forest, Pacific Lumber's proposed "sustained yield plan" (SYP) for timber operations on the forest, and the state and federal Endangered Species Act incidental take permits. The Supreme Court held that an incidental take permit under the California ESA cannot contain a "no surprises" clause that would effectively prohibit future mitigation measures in response to changed circumstances. In addition, the court held that the EIS/EIR contained sufficient evidence to support its conclusion that the SYP would have a less than significant impact on wildlife. Because the project also included an HCP, the purpose of which was to mitigate the effects of the SYP, there was no need for findings to be made under CEQA Guidelines section 15091. Further, the court upheld CDF's projections approach to cumulative impact analysis. Although there was no particular "general plan or related planning document" on which to base the EIS/EIR's cumulative impact analysis, the court found that the EIS/EIR "contains within itself a great deal of information concerning current conditions of critical species and their habitat equivalent to what would be contained in general plans or similar planning documents."

Sunset Skyranch Pilots Assoc. v. County of Sacramento **(Dec. 28, 2009) 47 Cal. 4th 902.** The County of Sacramento denied the conditional use permit that would have allowed Sunset Skyranch, a small private airport, to remain in operation. Notwithstanding the possibility of indirect physical effects on the environment, the county cited Public Resources Code section 21080(b)(5), the statutory exemption that allows denial of a project without preparing a CEQA analysis, in determining that no CEQA analysis would be prepared. The court upheld the county's exemption, stating that "In many cases, disapproval of a proposed project could have possible environmental impacts associated with alternative courses of action. Yet the legislature has determined for reasons of policy to exempt project disapprovals from environmental review under CEQA. Our state legislators evidently concluded that public agencies should not be forced to commit their resources to the costly and time-consuming environmental review process for proposed private development projects slated for rejection, whatever the reason for agency disapproval. This court does not sit in judgment of the legislature's wisdom in balancing such competing public policies."

Committee for Green Foothills v. Santa Clara County Board of Supervisors **(2010) 48 Cal. 4th 32.** Stanford University had previously submitted an application to Santa Clara County for a community plan allowing Stanford to add buildings to its campus that the county approved under a program EIR, which included as mitigation easements for two trail alignments. The county prepared a supplemental EIR analyzing three potential routes for the first trail. The County filed a notice of determination (NOD) for approval of the alignment of the first trail; four days later, the county filed a second NOD for approval of the alignment of the two segments of the second trail. After 171 days after the county posted the revised NOD, and the Committee for Green Foothills filed a petition for writ of mandate. The California Supreme Court ruled that the plaintiffs had not satisfied the statute of limitations, holding that the filing of a valid notice of determination (NOD) triggers a thirty-day statute of limitations for all challenges pursuant to the California Environmental Quality Act (CEQA) to the determination announced in the notice, regardless of the nature of the alleged CEQA violation. The principle applies not merely to NODs reflecting the agency's determination that a project is exempt or to adopt a negative declaration or certify an EIR; it also applies to an agency's determinations regarding whether or not to perform supplemental review or whether or not an activity is within the scope of a program EIR.

Communities for a Better Environment v. South Coast Air Quality Management District **(2010) 48 Cal. 4th 310.** The Air District prepared a negative declaration for an existing facility that was proposing modifications to refine a different type of diesel fuel. The Air District used the previously permitted emissions as the baseline for the impact analysis, although the existing air emission operations were not nearly as high as the permitted level. In addition, evidence showed that the refinery could not feasibly ever reach the permitted level of emissions. The court overturned the Air District's CEQA document noting that CEQA's "general rule" related to baseline is that it "must be the existing physical conditions in the affected area, [reflecting] the real conditions on the ground, rather than the level of development or activity that could or should have been present according to a plan or regulation." The court concluded that reliance on a hypothetical future baseline was improper.

***Stockton Citizens for Sensible Planning v. City of Stockton* (2010) 48 Cal. 4th 481.** The City of Stockton certified a Master EIR and approved a master plan for the 653-acre "Spanos Park West" mixed-use project. The city subsequently certified a supplemental EIR and approved changes to the plan; part of the site was designated for a business park and zoned "mixed use." The developer subsequently informed the city that it wanted to construct a supercenter on two of the parcels in the mixed-use area that the city manager "approved" this change in a letter stating that the project substantially complied with the master plan and the city filed a "notice of exemption" concerning the approval. The petitioners filed a CEQA challenge over five months after the NOE was filed. The court ruled in favor of the city, holding that CEQA's statute of limitations barred plaintiffs from bringing the action and ruling that the posting of a NOE announcing staff-level approval of a proposed supercenter triggered a thirty-five-day statute of limitations to challenge that approval. A lawsuit filed more than thirty-five days after posting the NOE was time-barred, regardless of the merits of the underlying challenge.

***Save the Plastic Bag Coalition v. City of Manhattan Beach* (2011)52 Cal. 4th 155.** The city adopted an ordinance in 2008 prohibiting retail establishments, restaurants, and other "vendors" from providing plastic carry-out bags to customers. The city adopted a negative declaration for the ordinance. The Coalition sued, both the trial and Appeal Courts decided in their favor, and appeal followed.

The Supreme Court considered two questions in this case: 1) does a coalition of plastic bag manufacturers have standing to bring a CEQA case, and 2) was an EIR required? In the first instance, the court held that the Coalition had standing to bring this lawsuit. In doing so, it disapproved of the holding in *Waste Management of Alameda County, Inc. v. County of Alameda* (2007) 79 Cal. App. 4th 1223 (landfill operator lacked standing to bring a CEQA suit against an agency over the approval of a competing landfill) that corporations be routinely subject to heightened scrutiny when they file citizen suits. The plastic bag manufacturers would be affected by the city's ordinance and "a plaintiff's commercial interests [are] not an impediment to its standing." Further, "the fact that a corporation is not technically a 'citizen' for most purposes (citation) does not necessarily affect its standing to pursue a 'citizen suit.'"

On the second point, the Coalition had cited a number of life cycle studies in arguing to the city that an EIR was required before the ordinance could be approved. The city's Negative Declaration concluded that the ordinance, applicable as it was to a small city with a limited number of affected vendors, would not result in a significant impact. The court upheld the Negative Declaration, stating simply that "[s}ubstantial evidence and common sense support the city's determination that its ordinance would have no significant environmental effect." While the record was undisputed that paper bags have more negative lifecycle impacts, CEQA "does not demand an exhaustive comparative analysis of *relative* environmental detriments for every alternative course of action" (emphasis in original). Instead, it requires the lead agency to consider "only those aspects of a project likely to have *significant* environmental effects" (emphasis in original) within the area affected by the proposed project. Considering the actual scale of impacts resulting from the city's bag ban, rather than global impacts of paper and plastic bags, the court concluded that the city acted within its discretion to determine that the bag ban would not have a significant effect on the environment.

***Tomlinson v. County of Alameda* (June 14, 2012) __ Cal.4th __**. This case revolved around a project approved on the basis of a categorical exemption. The county argued that the plaintiff had not exhausted their administrative remedies on the key issues raised in their lawsuit. The Supreme Court disagreed.

Public Resources Code Section 21177(a) governs the exhaustion of administrative remedies. It "requires either (1) a public comment period provided by CEQA (the public comment provision) or (2) an opportunity for public comment at public hearings before issuance of a notice of determination (the public hearing provision)." The Court of Appeal correctly found that because an exemption was used the first situation did not exist. However, it was mistaken in concluding that because no notice of determination was filed, the second situation did not apply. The Supreme Court found that:

> . . . if no such notice is filed, the public hearing provision nonetheless applies. In that situation, the challenging party is still required to exhaust its administrative remedies by presenting its objections to the project to the pertinent public agency, so long as it is given the opportunity to do so at a public hearing held *before the project is approved*. When, as in this case, a party is given such an opportunity, and it fails to raise a particular objection to the project, it may not raise that objection in court, because it has not satisfied the exhaustion requirement of section 21177's subdivision (a). (emphasis in original)

The existence of a public hearing defines the application of Section 21177(a), not the filing of a notice of determination.

Tips for Successful Compliance

This chapter covered the role of litigation in enforcing CEQA and an overview of the litigation process. The following are some tips related to CEQA litigation:

- **Comply with CEQA to avoid litigation**—Although CEQA litigation always looms as a possibility, in practice, the risk of litigation can be avoided by properly complying with the law and avoiding the temptation to take unnecessary shortcuts.
- **Be mindful of the statutes of limitations**—Agencies can greatly reduce their exposure to litigation by filing notices of determination, which have the effect of shorting the periods during which litigation can be filed.
- **Adhere strictly to litigation procedures**—When litigation occurs, the parties involved must adhere strictly to the highly technical procedures governing CEQA litigation.
- **Prepare full and complete administrative records**—Since judicial review of CEQA actions is based on the administrative record, a full and complete record is essential to CEQA litigation.
- **Keep in mind the consequences of litigation**—For public agencies, the consequences of losing a CEQA challenge is typically a writ from the court to properly comply with CEQA before the underlying project can be approved.

Litigation challenging CEQA compliance may occur, especially when a project is in a sensitive area or is particularly controversial.

Litigation happens, so be prepared for it.

Chapter 11

Is CEQA Effective?

Have CEQA's Objectives Been Achieved?

Since its enactment in 1970, CEQA has become an important legal and regulatory institution in California. The procedural process introduced by CEQA has completely transformed the way state and local officials conduct their planning and make their decisions. The EIR and negative declaration have become the best tools available to alert citizens about the impacts of impending projects and to provide them the opportunities to effectively participate in government activities. Yet, despite the fundamental changes brought about by CEQA, it remains controversial because it is sometimes used by project opponents to delay or stop projects and because of the cost it adds to project planning. Although CEQA's supporters praise its benefits and its detractors decry its costs, relatively little empirical evidence is available about its overall effectiveness.

The governor and legislature established CEQA's key objectives in the 1970s.

While agency officials, developers, attorneys, and environmentalists have all pondered CEQA's effectiveness at various times over the past forty years, there is no simple answer to the question of whether CEQA's objectives have been achieved. One reason for the difficulty in answering the question is because of CEQA's six diverse objectives:

- To disclose to decisionmakers and the public the significant environmental effects of government decisions before they are made
- To identify ways to avoid or reduce environmental damage
- To prevent environmental damage by requiring implementation of feasible alternatives or mitigation measures
- To disclose to the public the reasons why agencies sometime approve projects despite their environmental damage
- To foster interagency coordination in the review of projects
- To enhance public participation in the planning process

Because CEQA applies to all types of state and local agencies and to most of the projects they approve or carry out, any serious evaluation of its effectiveness will vary depending on which objective is evaluated, the type of agency involved, and the nature of the projects studied.

While almost everyone involved in the CEQA process has strong opinions about the advantages and disadvantages of the law, relatively few independent studies have been conducted that evaluate CEQA's effectiveness. Several studies of CEQA were conducted in the 1970s and 1980s, and, while academics and others researchers may find these older studies interesting, the results are dated. However, since 1990, a series of newer studies have shed considerable light on CEQA practice and local government attitudes about CEQA's effectiveness.

Association of Bay Area Governments CEQA Study (1991)

In 1991, the Association of Bay Area Governments conducted a comprehensive study of CEQA implementation by local governments in the San Francisco Bay Area. ABAG surveyed all city and county planning directors and city and county attorneys in the San Francisco Bay Area and approximately 275 private CEQA consultants.

The study was one of the first in the state to provide data on how many environmental studies are typically conducted under CEQA in each jurisdiction. Bay Area planning directors reported receiving an average of sixty-five project applications that were subject to CEQA each year. Of the 65 applications, respondents report an average of four EIRs were prepared. The remaining projects were processed either as negative declarations or were determined exempt from CEQA.

With regard to meeting CEQA's objectives, the survey found that most local governments felt they were fairly well achieved. Respondents identified six issue areas where considerable uncertainty clouded CEQA's implementation:

- Alternatives analysis
- Cumulative impact requirements
- Recirculation requirements when new information is added to a document
- Lack of thresholds of significance
- Definition of "substantial evidence"
- Mitigation monitoring requirements

The survey also revealed that the greatest dissatisfaction with CEQA was the poor relationship between the environmental review and the ultimate project decision.

One of the most interesting aspects of the study was the data relating to CEQA litigation. Although some critics complain that litigation drives the CEQA process, the survey disclosed that the actual numbers of CEQA lawsuits is quite small. According to the city attorneys and county counsels responding, fewer than one percent of project applications were the object of litigation. Further, it showed that of those subject to litigation, a majority (76 percent) were decided in favor of the public agency being challenged. Thus, the survey reflects a relatively low level of CEQA litigation activity and demonstrates that CEQA challenges are generally not successful. Nevertheless, over half of the respondents believed that legal defensibility, rather than improved information disclosure, drives the preparation of most EIRs. ABAG concluded that, while the actual level of litigation is relatively low, the perceived threat of litigation is very influential in determining the type of environmental document prepared (e.g., EIR versus negative declaration versus categorical exemption) and the scope and content of the documents (*see* Association of Bay Area Governments, *CEQA Process and Practices,* Oakland, California, 1991).

California Planning Department Survey (1992)

In the first and only truly comprehensive statewide study of CEQA's effectiveness, a researcher from the University of Illinois concluded that most professional planners feel that CEQA has done a fairly good job of accomplishing its stated objectives. Robert Olshansky, formerly of the University of California, Berkeley, surveyed planning departments throughout California to determine attitudes regarding CEQA implementation. To ensure its professional acceptability, the survey was reviewed by representatives of the Governor's Office of Planning and Research, the California Chapter of the American Planning Association, and the California Association of Environmental Professionals. After this independent review, the survey was mailed to all cities and counties in the state. Of the 500 departments that received the questionnaires, 350, or seventy percent responded. This rate of return was considered excellent for such a survey.

Like the ABAG effort, the study revealed some interesting statistical data regarding CEQA implementation; for example, at that time, cities and counties prepared only an average of 2.4 environmental impact reports per year (this was less than the average of 4 in the Bay Area). Of greater interest, however, were the attitudinal responses of planning officials regarding the accomplishment of CEQA's objectives. Respondents were asked to rate how successful CEQA has been in accomplishing each of its stated objectives. Respondents ranked CEQA functions on a scale of one to eight, with one being the best score.

The study confirmed that professional planners felt CEQA had been fairly successful at accomplishing most of its intended objectives. It is notable, however, that according to local planners, CEQA was more successful in achieving environmental protection than it was in achieving government procedural reform. See *The California Environmental Quality Act: Implications for Local Land Use Planning* by Robert B. Olshansky, Department of Urban and Regional Planning, University of Illinois, Champaign-Urbana, Illinois, 1991. Unfortunately, Professor Olahansky's study remains as the only comprehensive, academic evaluation of CEQA effectiveness, although it was partially updated in 1995 by the California Policy Center at the University of California, Berkeley (*see* next section).

Bay Area Mitigation Monitoring Study (1993)

In this effort, a private researcher in the San Francisco Bay Area conducted a limited study that focused only on the effectiveness of the mitigation monitoring requirements of CEQA that were added to the law in the late 1980s. That study, which was also based on a survey of local government planning departments in the 17-county area of Northern California, concluded that CEQA's mitigation monitoring requirements have been generally ineffective in accomplishing its objectives of improving mitigation practices (*see* "Bay Area Mitigation Monitoring," page 247.) Specifically, the study revealed that formal programs for mitigation monitoring remained the exception rather than the rule and that the extent monitoring varied dramatically jurisdictions (*see* "Mitigation Monitoring Programs" by Dominic Roques, *The Environmental Monitor*, published by California Association of Environmental Professionals, Fall 1993).

State Bar CEQA Review Committee (1994–1995)

In 1995, the Environmental Law Section of the State Bar of California completed a comprehensive legal evaluation of CEQA. The study was initiated in response to strongly voiced requests by state bar members and other professionals to conduct a careful legal review of CEQA. To accomplish this, the Executive Committee of the Environmental Law Section appointed a select CEQA review committee consisting of attorneys who represent a diverse group of clients affected by CEQA, including government agencies, citizens' groups, developers, and industry interests. The committee developed a list of fourteen key issues and solicited input about these issues from more than 2,500 members of the Environmental Law Section, interested agencies, bar associations, and others.

In arriving at its recommendations, the committee reached consensus that the overall intent and underlying policies of CEQA were fundamentally sound, but various areas needed improvement. Under each of these issue areas, the committee conducted a detailed analysis of the statutory provisions, the CEQA Guidelines, and relevant case law. Additionally, for each problem, detailed recommendations for improving CEQA were presented. The following were problem areas addressed in the report:

- **Timing of environmental review**—particularly the lack of clear rules for deferring analysis to future stages of decisionmaking
- **Tiering**—the lack of clear rules about when to use it and how it works
- **Thresholds of significance**—the lack of standards for making significance determinations
- **Mitigation measures**—the need for clarification regarding specificity, enforceability, feasibility, effectiveness, and monitoring
- **Alternatives**—the lack of clear rules regarding the selection of a reasonable range of alternatives
- **Cumulative impacts**—particularly the problems that occur when a project contributes a small increment to an already existing significant environmental problem
- **Public review and participation**—specifically relating to translation of EIRs into other languages, the submittal of late comments, and the lack of required public hearings

- **Model guidance and documents**—the lack of regular, informal guidance from the Resources Agency
- **Statewide indexing of EIRs**—the need for the Resources Agency to create an EIR data bank from documents filed with the State Clearinghouse so that such data may be accessed by future EIR preparers
- **Compliance with other applicable environmental laws**—the fact that CEQA is poorly integrated with other environmental laws and regulations
- **Certified regulatory programs**—the need for greater clarity with regard to these programs
- **Findings and integration of environmental review into agency decisions**—the lack of clarity over how these procedures should work in practice
- **Revisiting CEQA documents**—the need to revise or clarify the test for when a previously circulated CEQA document must be revised and recirculated
- **CEQA litigation**—the study identified several different problems with CEQA litigation

After evaluating each of these issue areas in detail, the Environmental Law Section's report provided an affirmative answer to the two more fundamental questions established by the committee at the outset: 1) given CEQA's policy objectives, the CEQA process can be restructured to improve environmental decisions and to provide greater certainty to all parties regarding the adequacy of CEQA compliance; and 2) given CEQA's general procedural framework, the CEQA process can be made more cost-effective and less time-consuming (Environmental Law Section, State Bar of California *The California Environmental Policy Act: Assessment and Recommendations, Final Report*, Sacramento, California, 1995).

California Policy Seminar CEQA Study (1995)

In 1995, the California Policy Seminar, a joint program of the University of California and state government, undertook a comprehensive survey of CEQA practice at the local government level. This study was directed by Professor John Landis of U.C. Berkeley and was essentially a continuation of the work done by Olshansky in 1991. The research was based on detailed evaluation of local CEQA practices in fourteen selected communities throughout California. The communities were chosen to represent the fullest possible range of local governments.

For each of the selected communities, the research team first determined the total level of CEQA reviews, the number of EIRs and negative declarations, and the frequency of CEQA litigation. Against this background, the researchers then compared and contrasted local practices with regard to all aspects of the environmental review process. The study not only includes empirical data about the environmental review process in each community, but also the opinions of various local officials and others about the effectiveness of CEQA as well as case studies of specific projects. The study also compares practices in California to those in other states with laws similar to CEQA.

While the study concluded that most local government planners generally feel that CEQA's general objectives have been achieved, it identified eight specific problems areas with the law's implementation:

- State and regional agencies do not play a predictable role in local CEQA reviews.

- Within local agencies, environmental review is often uncertain and inconsistent.
- CEQA review cannot effectively mitigate cumulative impacts.
- Alternatives analysis is generally inadequate and inconsistent.
- CEQA lacks incentives for timely dispute resolution.
- The State Clearinghouse does not provide a meaningful role in CEQA.
- There are too few incentives and too little funding for advance planning.
- There is a lack of consistent data with which to conduct environmental review.

For each of these identified problem areas, the study recommended proposed solutions.

The study concluded with an evaluation of common "myths" about CEQA and recommendations for change.

Myth 1. CEQA applies to a much broader range of projects than similar laws in other states. The study revealed that CEQA did apply to more types of projects than similar laws in the other sixteen states with environmental impact assessment requirements, but that the complexity or extent of environmental review was relatively similar from state to state.

Studies have found that typical CEQA review is properly integrated with other forms of federal, state, regional and local planning and environmenta regulations.

Myth 2. CEQA encourages the unnecessary writing of EIRs, often for projects that should not require them. The study revealed quite the contrary. The vast majority of initial studies result in negative declarations, not EIRs. Nearly a quarter of the communities responding reported that they did not initiate a single EIR in 1990. Another twenty-two percent reported preparing only one EIR that year. On average, agencies prepared twenty negative declarations for every EIR.

Myth 3. EIRs are unnecessarily costly and time-consuming and add little substantive information to the decision-making process. The study revealed that while there are occasional EIR "horror stories," the average cost of an EIR in 1990 was only $38,124. Further, most EIRs are completed in less than one year and many in less than six months. These numbers support the conclusion that a typical EIR is neither excessively costly nor time-consuming. With regard to usefulness, while no quantitative data exists on this issue, nearly ninety percent of the planning directors responding believed CEQA was successful in providing a thorough analysis of environmental impacts.

Myth 4. CEQA reviews are usually associated with litigation. The study results were consistent with the findings in the ABAG research that litigation is relatively rare under CEQA. Most communities reported no CEQA litigation in the years between 1986 and 1990. The average number of lawsuits was one for every 354 initial studies and one for every eighteen draft EIRs, respectively.

Myth 5. The costs and uncertainties associated with CEQA discourage businesses from relocating or expanding in California. The study provided insufficient evidence to support this assertion. The only evidence the researchers found was anecdotal information from several other studies of the effects of government regulation on California's businesses. While CEQA may contribute to what some perceive as "overregulation," the study concluded that it is difficult to hold CEQA solely responsible for delays and difficulties in project reviews.

Myth 6. CEQA review is poorly integrated with other forms of federal, state, regional, and local planning and environmental regulations. Case studies provided ample evidence of the truth of this assertion. The study revealed problems with integrating CEQA with other local planning activities. It also demonstrated problems integrating local CEQA activities with state and regional environmental regulations.

Myth 7. While valuable in theory, in practice, the evaluation of alternatives, cumulative impacts, and growth-inducing impacts are usually incomplete, poorly done, and confusing. As with Myth 6, the study provided strong support for this assertion. With regard to alternatives, the study revealed that time and budget constraints cause most agencies to evaluate alternatives on only a cursory basis. With regard to cumulative and growth-inducing impacts, it revealed that there is often a lack of data and a deficiency in analytical models with which to evaluate the impacts. Further, most respondents felt that, even with a thorough analysis, agencies can do little to mitigate these problems (*see* "Fixing CEQA:Options and Opportunities for Reforming the California Environmental Quality Act," California Policy Seminar, University of California, Berkeley, 1995).

CEQA: Making It Work Better (1997) by the Legislative Analyst's Office

This study, conducted by the Legislative Analyst's Office, was prepared in response to concerns expressed by California's business community that CEQA has had a detrimental effect on economic development in the state. In particular, the business community was concerned about the complexity and unpredictability of the CEQA process, the costs of compliance, and the ease of making legal challenges that impede development.

The study concluded that some of these problems exist, but their extent is unclear. It also found that little information exists about the cost-effectiveness of public agency mitigation measures. Furthermore, the study found that CEQA has become a substitute for general, long-term planning in some jurisdictions even though it is not well-suited for the job.

The study responded to some of the concerns about CEQA with a series of recommendations that fall into three broad categories:

- Measures to make the process more efficient, thereby making it less costly and time-consuming for project developers and public agencies
- Measures to make mitigation of environmental impacts more cost-effective
- Measures to improve the resolution of CEQA disputes

According to the study, these recommendations, if adopted, would address the concerns identified by the business community and would make CEQA work harder at achieving its goals.

CEQA's Objective	Relative Score	Accomplishment
Ensuring thorough analysis of environmental impacts	2.39	most successful
Causing the adoption of mitigation measures	3.26	
Informing the public about environmental impacts	3.59	
Protecting the environment	3.63	
Coordinating public agency review	4.90	
Facilitating citizen participation	5.04	
Making local officials accountable for their decisions	5.33	least successful

Environmental Mitigation Monitoring and Reporting under CEQA (2000) by the Association of Environmental Professionals

This report revealed the results of a 1999 survey of cities and counties conducted by private environmental consultants. Its basic finding was that public agencies are improving their compliance with CEQA's mitigation monitoring and reporting requirements. According to the report, while monitoring has been successfully incorporated into day-to-day CEQA practice, inconsistent implementation still exists among jurisdictions and from project to project. Public agencies reported that they were understaffed and underfunded relative to their monitoring needs.

The Determination of Thresholds of Environmental Significance in the Application of the California Environmental Quality Act (2001), Commissioned by the Governor's Office of Planning and Research

Researchers from California State University Northridge undertook a random survey of 500 lead agencies at the state, county, and local level on a series of questions regarding the agencies' adoption and use of thresholds of significance. The questionnaire asked whether the agency had adopted thresholds, whether the thresholds relied on adopted agency standards, and what the agency's opinions were regarding the use of thresholds.

The 185 agencies that responded to the survey included 112 cities, 31 counties, and 33 state agencies. Only six of these agencies reported that they had adopted thresholds of significance. Two major themes appeared from the responses—the respondents wanted more support from the state to help prepare thresholds, and they did not want to return to the pre-1998 State CEQA Guidelines, which made no provision for thresholds.

The researchers concluded that current thresholds are not particularly clear or easy to defend; experience in developing thresholds seems to give agencies greater confidence in thresholds; strong interest exists in developing a database of existing thresholds; and agencies want to retain the ability to develop their own thresholds (as opposed to thresholds mandated by the state) due to site-specific issues.

The researchers recommended the following steps to increase the use of thresholds:

- Use the internet to improve training and provide a database of thresholds.
- Seek out ways to improve interagency dialogue about thresholds.
- Include reference to a statewide database on thresholds of significance in the State CEQA Guidelines.

None of these recommendations have been implemented.

Better Protection of Fish and Wildlife: Improving Fish and Game's CEQA Review (2002) by the Legislative Analyst's Office

The California Department of Fish and Game (DFG), as both a responsible and trustee agency under CEQA, receives from 8,000 to 13,000 CEQA documents for review each year. Unique among agencies, DFG collects fees to help fund its review of these documents.

The LAO interviewed a number of interested parties in the CEQA process, including lead agencies, developers, environmental organizations, and DFG to determine whether DFG's review of CEQA documents is effective in protecting California's fish and wildlife. The LAO also reviewed DFG's comments on specific CEQA projects to consider their effectiveness.

The LAO found that DFG's CEQA review program fell short in the following areas:

- No formalized process exists for prioritizing workloads.
- A standard protocol is not in place regarding the extent or level of detail of comments.
- DFG is not involved early enough in the CEQA process to affect project design.
- DFG seldom follows up on its comments by taking part in the project approval process (i.e., hearing attendance).
- DFG does not check on the effectiveness of the mitigation measures that it recommends.
- DFG does not have reliable data on its management of its CEQA review responsibilities.

Further, LAO found that DFG's program for the collection and administration of CEQA review fees was weak. Specifically, the "de minimis" exemption from fee payment is not consistently applied by lead agencies, some lead agencies believe that the fees are inequitable, and DFG does not conduct an annual review or fee adjustment as required by statute.

The LAO recommended that the legislature direct DFG to establish clear workload priorities, standardize the type of information provided to lead agencies in its comments, improve data management to allow tracking of reviews within DFG, assess the effectiveness of mitigation measures by studying a representative sample, and re-examine the fee structure. As of this writing, the legislature has not adopted any of these recommendations.

Are "Certified Regulatory Programs" Functionally Equivalent to CEQA? (2002) by the California Research Bureau

Pursuant to CEQA, the Secretary of the Resources Agency has certified 16 regulatory programs of state agencies as the functional equivalent of CEQA. Of those, twelve were certified prior to 1982. None have been re-examined to determine whether they continue to meet CEQA's requirements.

This study reviewed the certified regulatory program for timber harvest plans (Department of Forestry and Fire Protection); Rulemaking by the Department of Fish and Game; water quality plan adoption by the State Water Resources Control Board and Regional Boards; and registration, evaluation, and classification of pesticides by the Department of Pesticide Regulation for conformity to current CEQA requirements. The CRB compared these programs to 17 basic CEQA goals and requirements relating to informing decisionmakers and the public of a project's potential environmental impacts, identifying ways to reduce impacts, preventing significant impacts, and disclosing the reasons for public approval of the programs.

The study concluded that none of these programs met all of CEQA's basic goals and requirements. The Department of Pesticide Regulation's program met ten of the seventeen; the others nine of the seventeen. Common shortcomings were in the areas of project description, public disclosure, criteria for identifying impacts, alternatives analysis, mitigation measures and enforcement, and consultation with other agencies.

The CRB's recommendations for improvement included requiring more documentation and disclosure of environmental effects, and adding more CEQA-like requirements to the programs. The study also recommended that the Secretary for Resources review the certified programs occasionally to ensure they continue to comply with CEQA's basic goals and requirements.

In 2002, responding to this report's recommendations, Governor Davis signed SB 1393 (Chapter 1121, Statutes of 2002) directing the Secretary for Resources to develop a protocol for the review of certified regulatory programs. The protocol was released in 2004. Apparently, additional authority would need to be granted by the legislature for the Secretary for Resources to review and recertify programs absent a request by the affected agency.

CEQA Reform: Issues and Options (2005) by the Public Policy Institute of California

This paper is an overview of the most controversial issues surrounding CEQA. It was prepared for the CEQA Improvement Advisory Group, a broad-based committee convened by the California Resources Agency to draft proposals for legislative changes to CEQA. The Resources Agency was particularly interested in ways that CEQA might be amended to simplify and encourage infill development. This includes means by which NIMBY opposition to needed housing might be reduced.

The paper offers a brief history of CEQA and past reform efforts. It also describes the past studies and reports that have been done. Despite these past studies and statutory changes, many of the issues identified more than a decade ago still remain unresolved.

The authors (Elisa Barbour and Michael Teitz) suggest that a regional model, such as the "smart growth" plans proposed by several Councils of Government and the Natural Communities Conservation Planning approach, may be worth examining as a means of more effectively addressing cumulative impacts as well as providing standard significance thresholds and mitigation measures.

The report concludes that "CEQA reform should be part of a wider discussion and more comprehensive set of solutions to growth concerns." And that "without an effective state framework, even concerted regional and local smart growth efforts may be prone to failure."

Everyday Heroes Protect the Air We Breathe, the Water We Drink, and the Natural Areas We Prize: Thirty-Five Years of the California Environmental Quality Act (2005) by the Planning and Conservation League, Planning and Conservation League Foundation, and California League of Conservation Voters

This is primarily a celebration of CEQA's victories, large and small, rather than a study of its effectiveness. It was prepared in anticipation of proposals to change CEQA that, in the opinion of the Leagues, might reduce its strength as a "general, catch-all environmental law" and its empowerment of residents to affect the course of projects.

The seventy-five success stories described in this report offer anecdotal evidence of the power of CEQA to protect the environment. They focus on situations where potentially damaging projects were abandoned or substantially revised due to their potential environmental effects. CEQA's disclosure of significant environmental impacts increased community awareness of the projects' impacts. These case studies also show how CEQA can be used by residents and community groups to effectively challenge and improve projects.

CEQA and Affordable Housing Exemptions: A Policy Analysis (2006) by Ethan Elkind and Edward Stone

Two students at the UCLA School of Law investigated the use and usefulness of CEQA's statutory exemptions and the Class 32 Categorical exemption for infill development. They released their report in 2006.

Using OPR's annual *Book of Lists* survey as a starting point, they contacted those agencies that had indicated they used either of these exemptions as well as a selected group of experienced, affordable housing builders. Their initial contacts revealed that the statutory exemptions were seldomly used in practice; many local planners either didn't know about the statutory exemptions or were unaware of the amendments made to the exemptions in 2002; and that local attitudes toward affordable housing projects (friendly/not friendly) were as important in determining whether an exemption might be successfully employed as were the provisions of the exemptions and characteristics of the project.

Their research found that neither of these types of exemptions provided developers with "hard" exemptions that would allow them to avoid the CEQA process. The qualifiers contained in the statutory exemptions, including both the extensive list of limitations and the "soft" trigger for full CEQA review, limited its use. The categorical exemption was the most commonly used, but it is not available to projects in unincorporated areas. It was the more straightforward and understandable of the two options. Planners who "are friendly to infill and affordable housing" tend to rely on the Class 32 exemption.

Many planners and affordable housing developers were unaware of the statutory exemptions (Pub. Res. Code § 21159.20). When familiar with the exemption, they found it difficult to qualify for and did not trust that it would protect them from future neighborhood opposition. Many developers instead rely on previous EIRs as a means of avoiding site-specific CEQA analysis.

This report offered several recommendations:

- **Take no action**—see how things develop as the statutory exemptions become more well known and understood.
- **Promote awareness of the exemptions**—OPR could prepare an annual newsletter explaining the exemptions.
- **Encourage more zoning for multifamily housing**—either completely exempt rezoning and general plans for multifamily development from CEQA or offer local jurisdictions financial incentives to rezone more land for multifamily development.
- **Streamline the statutory exemptions**—remove some of the qualifiers; create more focused exemptions, such as infill development near transit centers; or create a streamlined EIR for infill development.
- **Codify a modified version of the Class 32 categorical exemption**—place this exemption into statute and "harden" it so that it is an absolute exemption.

Conclusion

Taken together, these studies reveal considerable common ground about the CEQA's effectiveness. Most observers agree that CEQA is an important part of California's scheme for protecting the environment and is anchored by a strong legal foundation and based on sound public policy. Considerable agreement also exists that CEQA is misunderstood by many of its critics and poorly implemented by some agencies. Clearly, a wide gulf lies between the myths surrounding CEQA and the reality of how it is carried out. For example, the studies concluded that agencies are not burdened by excessive numbers of EIRs. Nor are projects typically held up by CEQA-related litigation. Yet, countless anecdotal accounts exist of CEQA-based litigation being used to delay worthwhile projects.

On the other hand, there is considerable agreement that many aspects of CEQA practice are cumbersome and should be streamlined. For example, the nature of CEQA analyses undertaken for infill housing projects consistent with adopted plans is one area worthy of discussion (although the parties disagree on the degree to which change is needed). Agencies are also not always performing to the best of their abilities—either through insufficient funding or bureaucratic inertia. The studies have also revealed that, while reforms are needed, neither the state legislature nor the two oversight agencies (OPR and the Resources Agency) have been successful in achieving reform. Some observers have noted that there is a need for greater legislative and regulatory oversight and, in particular, a need for further guidance about how to implement the law successfully.

Hopefully these research efforts will encourage the Legislature, the Resources Agency, and OPR to continue the quest to streamline CEQA without removing its fundamental policies and procedures. Further, even in the absence of legislative or regulatory change, the agencies implementing CEQA can likely learn from these studies and make their own improvements to their CEQA practices. With modest and thoughtful improvements at all levels, CEQA should remain the bedrock of California's environmental laws for years to come.

CEQA balances development and the protection of sensitive resources.

Appendix 1

The California Environmental Quality Act

Public Resources Code, Division 13, Sections 21000-21177

Table of Contents

The California Environmental Quality Act

Public Resources Code, Division 13, Sections 21000-21177

Chapter 1. Policy

21000. The Legislature finds and declares as follows:

(a) The maintenance of a quality environment for the people of this state now and in the future is a matter of statewide concern.

(b) It is necessary to provide a high-quality environment that at all times is healthful and pleasing to the senses and intellect of man.

(c) There is a need to understand the relationship between the maintenance of high-quality ecological systems and the general welfare of the people of the state, including their enjoyment of the natural resources of the state.

(d) The capacity of the environment is limited, and it is the intent of the Legislature that the government of the state take immediate steps to identify any critical thresholds for the health and safety of the people of the state and take all coordinated actions necessary to prevent such thresholds being reached.

(e) Every citizen has a responsibility to contribute to the preservation and enhancement of the environment.

(f) The interrelationship of policies and practices in the management of natural resources and waste disposal requires systematic and concerted efforts by public and private interests to enhance environmental quality and to control environmental pollution.

(g) It is the intent of the Legislature that all agencies of the state government which regulate activities of private individuals, corporations, and public agencies which are found to affect the quality of the environment, shall regulate such activities so that major consideration is given to preventing environmental damage, while providing a decent home and satisfying living environment for every Californian.

21001. The Legislature further finds and declares that it is the policy of the state to:

(a) Develop and maintain a high-quality environment now and in the future, and take all action necessary to protect, rehabilitate, and enhance the environmental quality of the state.

(b) Take all action necessary to provide the people of this state with clean air and water, enjoyment of aesthetic, natural, scenic, and historic environmental qualities, and freedom from excessive noise.

(c) Prevent the elimination of fish or wildlife species due to man's activities, insure that fish and wildlife populations do not drop below self-prepetuating levels, and preserve for future generations representations of all plant and animal communities and examples of the major periods of California history.

(d) Ensure that the long-term protection of the environment, consistent with the provision of a decent home and suitable living environment for every Californian, shall be the guiding criterion in public decisions.

(e) Create and maintain conditions under which man and nature can exist in productive harmony to fulfill the social and economic requirements of present and future generations.

(f) Require governmental agencies at all levels to develop standards and procedures necessary to protect environmental quality.

(g) Require governmental agencies at all levels to consider qualitative factors as well as economic and technical factors and long-term benefits and costs, in addition to short-term benefits and costs and to consider alternatives to proposed actions affecting the environment.

21001.1. The Legislature further finds and declares that it is the policy of the state that projects to be carried out by public agencies be subject to the same level of review and consideration under this division as that of private projects required to be approved by public agencies.

21002. The Legislature finds and declares that it is the policy of the state that public agencies should not approve projects as proposed if there are feasible alternatives or feasible mitigation measures available which would substantially lessen the significant environmental effects of such projects, and that the procedures required by this division are intended to assist public agencies in systematically identifying both the significant effects of proposed projects and the feasible alternatives or feasible mitigation measures which will avoid or substantially lessen such significant effects. The Legislature further finds and declares that in the event specific economic, social, or other conditions make infeasible such project alternatives or such mitigation measures, individual projects may be approved in spite of one or more significant effects thereof.

21002.1. In order to achieve the objectives set forth in Section 21002, the Legislature hereby finds and declares that the following policy shall apply to the use of environmental impact reports prepared pursuant to this division:

(a) The purpose of an environmental impact report is to identify the significant effects on the environment of a project, to identify alternatives to the project, and to indicate the manner in which those significant effects can be mitigated or avoided.

(b) Each public agency shall mitigate or avoid the significant effects on the environment of projects that it carries out or approves whenever it is feasible to do so.

(c) If economic, social, or other conditions make it infeasible to mitigate one or more significant effects on the environment of a project, the project may nonetheless be carried out or approved at the discretion of a public agency if the project is otherwise permissible under applicable laws and regulations.

(d) In applying the policies of subdivisions (b) and (c) to individual projects, the responsibility of the lead agency shall differ from that of a responsible agency. The lead agency shall be responsible for considering the effects, both individual and collective, of all activities involved in a project. A responsible agency shall be responsible for considering only the effects of those activities involved in a project which it is required by law to carry out or approve. This subdivision applies only to decisions by a public agency to carry out or approve a project and does not otherwise affect the scope of the comments that the public agency may wish to make pursuant to Section 21104 or 21153.

(e) To provide more meaningful public disclosure, reduce the time and cost required to prepare an environmental impact report, and focus on potentially significant effects on the environment of a proposed project, lead agencies shall, in accordance with Section 21100, focus the discussion in the environmental impact report on those potential effects on the environment of a proposed project which the lead agency has determined are or may be significant. Lead agencies may limit discussion on other effects to a brief explanation as to why those effects are not potentially significant.

21003. The Legislature further finds and declares that it is the policy of the state that:

(a) Local agencies integrate the requirements of this division with planning and environmental review procedures otherwise required by law or by local practice so that all those procedures, to the maximum feasible extent, run concurrently, rather than consecutively.

(b) Documents prepared pursuant to this division be organized and written in a manner that will be meaningful and useful to decisionmakers and to the public.

(c) Environmental impact reports omit unnecessary descriptions of projects and emphasize feasible mitigation measures and feasible alternatives to projects.
(d) Information developed in individual environmental impact reports be incorporated into a data base which can be used to reduce delay and duplication in preparation of subsequent environmental impact reports.
(e) Information developed in environmental impact reports and negative declarations be incorporated into a data base which may be used to make subsequent or supplemental environmental determinations.
(f) All persons and public agencies involved in the environmental review process be responsible for carrying out the process in the most efficient, expeditious manner in order to conserve the available financial, governmental, physical, and social resources with the objective that those resources may be better applied toward the mitigation of actual significant effects on the environment.

21003.1. The Legislature further finds and declares it is the policy of the state that:
(a) Comments from the public and public agencies on the environmental effects of a project shall be made to lead agencies as soon as possible in the review of environmental documents, including, but not limited to, draft environmental impact reports and negative declarations, in order to allow the lead agencies to identify, at the earliest possible time in the environmental review process, potential significant effects of a project, alternatives, and mitigation measures which would substantially reduce the effects.
(b) Information relevant to the significant effects of a project, alternatives, and mitigation measures which substantially reduce the effects shall be made available as soon as possible by lead agencies, other public agencies, and interested persons and organizations.
(c) Nothing in subdivisions (a) or (b) reduces or otherwise limits public review or comment periods currently prescribed either by statute or in guidelines prepared and adopted pursuant to Section 21083 for environmental documents, including, but not limited to, draft environmental impact reports and negative declarations.

21004. In mitigating or avoiding a significant effect of a project on the environment, a public agency may exercise only those express or implied powers provided by law other than this division. However, a public agency may use discretionary powers provided by such other law for the purpose of mitigating or avoiding a significant effect on the environment subject to the express or implied constraints or limitations that may be provided by law.

21005.
(a) The Legislature finds and declares that it is the policy of the state that noncompliance with the information disclosure provisions of this division which precludes relevant information from being presented to the public agency, or noncompliance with substantive requirements of this division, may constitute a prejudicial abuse of discretion within the meaning of Sections 21168 and 21168.5, regardless of whether a different outcome would have resulted if the public agency had complied with those provisions.
(b) It is the intent of the Legislature that, in undertaking judicial review pursuant to Sections 21168 and 21168.5, courts shall continue to follow the established principle that there is no presumption that error is prejudicial.
(c) It is further the intent of the Legislature that any court, which finds, or, in the process of reviewing a previous court finding, finds, that a public agency has taken an action without compliance with this division, shall specifically address each of the alleged grounds for noncompliance.

21006. The Legislature finds and declares that this division is an integral part of any public agency's decisionmaking process, including, but not limited to, the issuance of permits, licenses, certificates, or other entitlements required for activities undertaken pursuant to federal statutes containing specific waivers of sovereign immunity.

Chapter 2. Short Title

21050. This division shall be known and may be cited as the California Environmental Quality Act.

Chapter 2.5 Definitions

21060. Unless the context otherwise requires, the definitions in this chapter govern the construction of this division.

21060.1.
(a) "Agricultural land" means prime farmland, farmland of statewide importance, or unique farmland, as defined by the United States Department of Agriculture land inventory and monitoring criteria, as modified for California.
(b) In those areas of the state where lands have not been surveyed for the classifications specified in subdivision (a), "agricultural land" means land that meets the requirements of "prime agricultural land" as defined in paragraph (1), (2), (3), or (4) of subdivision
(c) of Section 51201 of the Government Code.

21060.3. "Emergency" means a sudden, unexpected occurrence, involving a clear and imminent danger, demanding immediate action to prevent or mitigate loss of, or damage to, life, health, property, or essential public services. "Emergency" includes such occurrences as fire, flood, earthquake, or other soil or geologic movements, as well as such occurrences as riot, accident, or sabotage.

21060.5. "Environment" means the physical conditions which exist within the area which will be affected by a proposed project, including land, air, water, minerals, flora, fauna, noise, objects of historic or aesthetic significance.

21061. "Environmental impact report" means a detailed statement setting forth the matters specified in Sections 21100 and 21100.1; provided that information or data which is relevant to such a statement and is a matter of public record or is generally available to the public need not be repeated in its entirety in such statement, but may be specifically cited as the source for conclusions stated therein; and provided further that such information or data shall be briefly described, that its relationship to the environmental impact report shall be indicated, and that the source thereof shall be reasonably available for inspection at a public place or public building. An environmental impact report also includes any comments which are obtained pursuant to Section 21104 or 21153, or which are required to be obtained pursuant to this division.
An environmental impact report is an informational document which, when its preparation is required by this division, shall be considered by every public agency prior to its approval or disapproval of a project. The purpose of an environmental impact report is to provide public agencies and the public in general with detailed information about the effect which a proposed project is likely to have on the environment; to list ways in which the significant effects of such a project might be minimized; and to indicate alternatives to such a project.
In order to facilitate the use of environmental impact reports, public agencies shall require that such reports contain an index or table of contents and a summary. Failure to include such index, table of contents, or summary shall not constitute a cause of action pursuant to Section 21167.

21061.1. "Feasible" means capable of being accomplished in a successful manner within a reasonable period of time, taking into account economic, environmental, social, and technological factors.

21061.2. "Land evaluation and site assessment" means a decisionmaking methodology for assessing the potential environmental impact of state and local projects on agricultural land.

21061.3. "Infill site" means a site in an urbanized area that meets either of the following criteria:
(a) The site has not been previously developed for urban uses and both of the following apply:
   (1) The site is immediately adjacent to parcels that are developed with qualified urban uses, or at least 75 percent of the perimeter of the site adjoins parcels that are developed with qualified urban uses, and the remaining 25 percent of the site adjoins parcels that have previously been developed for qualified urban uses.
   (2) No parcel within the site has been created within the past 10 years unless the parcel was created as a result of the plan of a redevelopment agency.
(b) The site has been previously developed for qualified urban uses.

21062. "Local agency" means any public agency other than a state agency, board, or commission. For purposes of this division a redevelopment agency and a local agency formation commission are local agencies, and neither is a state agency, board, or commission.

21063. "Public agency" includes any state agency, board, or commission, any county, city and county, city, regional agency, public district, redevelopment agency, or other political subdivision.

21064. "Negative declaration" means a written statement briefly describing the reasons that a proposed project will not have a significant effect on the environment and does not require the preparation of an environmental impact report.

21064.3. "Major transit stop" means a site containing an existing rail transit station, a ferry terminal served by either a bus or rail transit service, or the intersection of two or more major bus routes with a frequency of service interval of 15 minutes or less during the morning and afternoon peak commute periods.

21064.5. "Mitigated negative declaration" means a negative declaration prepared for a project when the initial study has identified potentially significant effects on the environment, but
(a) revisions in the project plans or proposals made by, or agreed to by, the applicant before the proposed negative declaration and initial study are released for public review would avoid the effects or mitigate the effects to a point where clearly no significant effect on the environment would occur, and (2) there

is no substantial evidence in light of the whole record before the public agency that the project, as revised, may have a significant effect on the environment.

21065. "Project" means an activity which may cause either a direct physical change in the environment, or a reasonably foreseeable indirect physical change in the environment, and which is any of the following:
(a) An activity directly undertaken by any public agency.
(b) An activity undertaken by a person which is supported, in whole or in part, through contracts, grants, subsidies, loans, or other forms of assistance from one or more public agencies.
(c) An activity that involves the issuance to a person of a lease, permit, license, certificate, or other entitlement for use by one or more public agencies.

21065.3. "Project-specific effect" means all the direct or indirect environmental effects of a project other than cumulative effects and growth-inducing effects.

21065.5. "Geothermal exploratory project" means a project as defined in Section 21065 composed of not more than six wells and associated drilling and testing equipment, whose chief and original purpose is to evaluate the presence and characteristics of geothermal resources prior to commencement of a geothermal field development project as defined in Section 65928.5 of the Government Code. Wells included within a geothermal exploratory project must be located at least one-half mile from geothermal development wells which are capable of producing geothermal resources in commercial quantities.

21066. "Person" includes any person, firm, association, organization, partnership, business, trust, corporation, limited liability company, company, district, county, city and county, city, town, the state, and any of the agencies and political subdivisions of those entities, and, to the extent permitted by federal law, the United States, or any of its agencies or political subdivisions.

21067. "Lead agency" means the public agency which has the principal responsibility for carrying out or approving a project which may have a significant effect upon the environment.

21068. "Significant effect on the environment" means a substantial, or potentially substantial, adverse change in the environment.

21068.5. "Tiering" or "tier" means the coverage of general matters and environmental effects in an environmental impact report prepared for a policy, plan, program or ordinance followed by narrower or site-specific environmental impact reports which incorporate by reference the discussion in any prior environmental impact report and which concentrate on the environmental effects which (a) are capable of being mitigated, or (b) were not analyzed as significant effects on the environment in the prior environmental impact report.

21069. "Responsible agency" means a public agency, other than the lead agency, which has responsibility for carrying out or approving a project.

21070. "Trustee agency" means a state agency that has jurisdiction by law over natural resources affected by a project, that are held in trust for the people of the State of California.

21071. "Urbanized area" means either of the following:
(a) An incorporated city that meets either of the following criteria:
 (1) Has a population of at least 100,000 persons.
 (2) Has a population of less than 100,000 persons if the population of that city and not more than two contiguous incorporated cities combined equals at least 100,000 persons.
(b) An unincorporated area that satisfies the criteria in both paragraph (1) and (2) of the following criteria:
 (1) Is either of the following:
  (A) Completely surrounded by one or more incorporated cities, and both of the following criteria are met:
   (i) The population of the unincorporated area and the population of the surrounding incorporated city or cities equals not less than 100,000 persons.
   (ii) The population density of the unincorporated area at least equals the population density of the surrounding city or cities.
  (B) Located within an urban growth boundary and has an existing residential population of at least 5,000 persons per square mile. For purposes of this subparagraph, an "urban growth boundary" means a provision of a locally adopted general plan that allows urban uses on one side of the boundary and prohibits urban uses on the other side.
 (2) The board of supervisors with jurisdiction over the unincorporated area has previously taken both of the following actions:
  (A) Issued a finding that the general plan, zoning ordinance, and related policies and programs applicable to the unincorporated area are consistent with principles that encourage compact development in a manner that does both of the following:
   (i) Promotes efficient transportation systems, economic growth, affordable housing, energy efficiency, and an appropriate balance of jobs and housing.
   (ii) Protects the environment, open space, and agricultural areas.
  (B) Submitted a draft finding to the Office of Planning and Research at least 30 days prior to issuing a final finding, and allowed the office 30 days to submit comments on the draft findings to the board of supervisors.

21072. "Qualified urban use" means any residential, commercial, public institutional, transit or transportation passenger facility, or retail use, or any combination of those uses.

Chapter 2.6. General

21080.
(a) Except as otherwise provided in this division, this division shall apply to discretionary projects proposed to be carried out or approved by public agencies, including, but not limited to, the enactment and amendment of zoning ordinances, the issuance of zoning variances, the issuance of conditional use permits, and the approval of tentative subdivision maps unless the project is exempt from this division.
(b) This division does not apply to any of the following activities:
 (1) Ministerial projects proposed to be carried out or approved by public agencies.
 (2) Emergency repairs to public service facilities necessary to maintain service.
 (3) Projects undertaken, carried out, or approved by a public agency to maintain, repair, restore, demolish, or replace property or facilities damaged or destroyed as a result of a disaster in a disaster-stricken area in which a state of emergency has been proclaimed by the governor pursuant to Chapter 7 (commencing with Section 8550) of Division 1 of Title 2 of the Government Code.
 (4) Specific actions necessary to prevent or mitigate an emergency.
 (5) Projects which a public agency rejects or disapproves.
 (6) Actions undertaken by a public agency relating to any thermal power plant site or facility, including the expenditure, obligation, or encumbrance of funds by a public agency for planning, engineering, or design purposes, or for the conditional sale or purchase of equipment, fuel, water (except groundwater), steam, or power for a thermal power plant, if the power plant site and related facility will be the subject of an environmental impact report, negative declaration, or other document, prepared pursuant to a regulatory program certified pursuant to Section 21080.5, which will be prepared by the State Energy Resources Conservation and Development Commission, by the Public Utilities Commission, or by the city or county in which the power plant and related facility would be located if the environmental impact report, negative declaration, or document includes the environmental impact, if any, of the action described in this paragraph.
 (7) Activities or approvals necessary to the bidding for, hosting or staging of, and funding or carrying out of, an Olympic games under the authority of the International Olympic Committee, except for the construction of facilities necessary for the Olympic games.
 (8) The establishment, modification, structuring, restructuring, or approval of rates, tolls, fares, or other charges by public agencies which the public agency finds are for the purpose of (A) meeting operating expenses, including employee wage rates and fringe benefits, (B) purchasing or leasing supplies, equipment, or materials, (C) meeting financial reserve needs and requirements, (D) obtaining funds for capital projects necessary to maintain service within existing service areas, or (E) obtaining funds necessary to maintain those intracity transfers as are authorized by city charter. The public agency shall incorporate written findings in the record of any proceeding in which an exemption under this paragraph is claimed setting forth with specificity the basis for the claim of exemption.
 (9) All classes of projects designated pursuant to Section 21084.
 (10) A project for the institution or increase of passenger or commuter services on rail or highway rights-of-way already in use, including modernization of existing stations and parking facilities.
 (11) A project for the institution or increase of passenger or commuter service on high-occupancy vehicle lanes already in use, including the modernization of existing stations and parking facilities.
 (12) Facility extensions not to exceed four miles in length which are required for the transfer of passengers from or to exclusive public mass transit guideway or busway public transit services.
 (13) A project for the development of a regional transportation improvement program, the state transportation improvement program, or a congestion management program prepared pursuant to Section 65089 of the Government Code.
 (14) Any project or portion thereof located in another state which will be subject to environmental

impact review pursuant to the National Environmental Policy Act of 1969 (42 U.S.C. Sec. 4321 et seq.) or similar state laws of that state. Any emissions or discharges that would have a significant effect on the environment in this state are subject to this division.

(15) Projects undertaken by a local agency to implement a rule or regulation imposed by a state agency, board, or commission under a certified regulatory program pursuant to Section 21080.5. Any site-specific effect of the project which was not analyzed as a significant effect on the environment in the plan or other written documentation required by Section 21080.5 is subject to this division.

(16) The selection, credit, and transfer of emission credits by the South Coast Air Quality Management District pursuant to Section 40440.14 of the Health and Safety Code, until the repeal of that section on January 1, 2012, or a later date.

(c) If a lead agency determines that a proposed project, not otherwise exempt from this division, would not have a significant effect on the environment, the lead agency shall adopt a negative declaration to that effect. The negative declaration shall be prepared for the proposed project in either of the following circumstances:

(1) There is no substantial evidence, in light of the whole record before the lead agency, that the project may have a significant effect on the environment.

(2) An initial study identifies potentially significant effects on the environment, but (A) revisions in the project plans or proposals made by, or agreed to by, the applicant before the proposed negative declaration and initial study are released for public review would avoid the effects or mitigate the effects to a point where clearly no significant effect on the environment would occur, and (B) there is no substantial evidence, in light of the whole record before the lead agency, that the project, as revised, may have a significant effect on the environment.

(d) If there is substantial evidence, in light of the whole record before the lead agency, that the project may have a significant effect on the environment, an environmental impact report shall be prepared.

(e) (1) For the purposes of this section and this division, substantial evidence includes fact, a reasonable assumption predicated upon fact, or expert opinion supported by fact.

(2) Substantial evidence is not argument, speculation, unsubstantiated opinion or narrative, evidence that is clearly inaccurate or erroneous, or evidence of social or economic impacts that do not contribute to, or are not caused by, physical impacts on the environment.

(f) As a result of the public review process for a mitigated negative declaration, including administrative decisions and public hearings, the lead agency may conclude that certain mitigation measures identified pursuant to paragraph (2) of subdivision (c) are infeasible or otherwise undesirable. In those circumstances, the lead agency, prior to approving the project, may delete those mitigation measures and substitute for them other mitigation measures that the lead agency finds, after holding a public hearing on the matter, are equivalent or more effective in mitigating significant effects on the environment to a less than significant level and that do not cause any potentially significant effect on the environment. If those new mitigation measures are made conditions of project approval or are otherwise made part of the project approval, the deletion of the former measures and the substitution of the new mitigation measures shall not constitute an action or circumstance requiring recirculation of the mitigated negative declaration.

(g) Nothing in this section shall preclude a project applicant or any other person from challenging, in an administrative or judicial proceeding, the legality of a condition of project approval imposed by the lead agency. If, however, any condition of project approval set aside by either an administrative body or court was necessary to avoid or lessen the likelihood of the occurrence of a significant effect on the environment, the lead agency's approval of the negative declaration and project shall be invalid and a new environmental review process shall be conducted before the project can be reapproved, unless the lead agency substitutes a new condition that the lead agency finds, after holding a public hearing on the matter, is equivalent to, or more effective in, lessening or avoiding significant effects on the environment and that does not cause any potentially significant effect on the environment.

21080.01. This division shall not apply to any activity or approval necessary for the reopening and operation of the California Men's Colony West Facility in San Luis Obispo County.

21080.02. This division shall not apply to any activity or approval necessary for or incidental to planning, design, site acquisition, construction, operation, or maintenance of the new prison facility at or in the vicinity of Corcoran in Kings County as authorized by the act that enacted this section.

21080.03. This division shall not apply to any activity or approval necessary for or incidental to the location, development, construction, operation, or maintenance of the prison in the County of Kings, authorized by Section 9 of Chapter 958 of the Statutes of 1983, as amended, and of the prison in the County of Amador (Ione), authorized by Chapter 957 of the Statutes of 1983, as amended.

21080.04. (a) Notwithstanding paragraph (10) of subdivision (b) of Section 21080, this division applies to a project for the institution of passenger rail service on a line paralleling State Highway 29 and running from Rocktram to Krug in the Napa Valley. With respect to that project, and for the purposes of this division, the Public Utilities Commission is the lead agency.

(b) It is the intent of the Legislature in enacting this section to abrogate the decision of the California Supreme Court "that Section 21080, subdivision (b)(11), exempts Wine Train's institution of passenger service on the Rocktram-Krug line from the requirements of CEQA" in Napa Valley Wine Train, Inc. v. Public Utilities Com., 50 Cal. 3d 370.

(c) Nothing in this section is intended to affect or apply to, or to confer jurisdiction upon the Public Utilities Commission with respect to, any other project involving rail service.

21080.05. This division does not apply to a project by a public agency to lease or purchase the rail right-of-way used for the San Francisco Peninsula commute service between San Francisco and San Jose, together with all branch and spur lines, including the Dumbarton and Vasona lines.

21080.07. This division shall not apply to any activity or approval necessary for or incidental to planning, design, site acquisition, construction, operation, or maintenance of the new prison facilities located in any of the following places:

(a) The County of Riverside.

(b) The County of Del Norte.

21080.09. (a) For purposes of this section, the following definitions apply:

(1) "Public higher education" has the same meaning as specified in Section 66010 of the Education Code.

(2) "Long range development plan" means a physical development and land use plan to meet the academic and institutional objectives for a particular campus or medical center of public higher education.

(b) The selection of a location for a particular campus and the approval of a long range development plan are subject to this division and require the preparation of an environmental impact report. Environmental effects relating to changes in enrollment levels shall be considered for each campus or medical center of public higher education in the environmental impact report prepared for the long range development plan for the campus or medical center.

(c) The approval of a project on a particular campus or medical center of public higher education is subject to this division and may be addressed, subject to the other provisions of this division, in a tiered environmental analysis based upon a long range development plan environmental impact report.

(d) Compliance with this section satisfies the obligations of public higher education pursuant to this division to consider the environmental impact of academic and enrollment plans as they affect campuses or medical centers, provided that any such plans shall become effective for a campus or medical center only after the environmental effects of those plans have been analyzed as required by this division in a long range development plan environmental impact report or tiered analysis based upon that environmental impact report for that campus or medical center, and addressed as required by this division.

21080.1. (a) The lead agency shall be responsible for determining whether an environmental impact report, a negative declaration, or a mitigated negative declaration shall be required for any project which is subject to this division. That determination shall be final and conclusive on all persons, including responsible agencies, unless challenged as provided in Section 21167.

(b) In the case of a project described in subdivision (c) of Section 21065, the lead agency shall, upon the request of a potential applicant, provide for consultation prior to the filing of the application regarding the range of actions, potential alternatives, mitigation measures, and any potential and significant effects on the environment of the project.

21080.2. In the case of a project described in subdivision (c) of Section 21065, the determination required by Section 21080.1 shall be made within 30 days from the date on which an application for a project has been received and accepted as complete by the lead agency. This period may be extended 15 days upon the consent of the lead agency and the project applicant.

21080.3. (a) Prior to determining whether a negative declaration or environmental impact report is required for a project, the lead agency shall consult with all responsible agencies and trustee agencies. Prior to that required consultation, the lead agency may informally contact any of those agencies.

(b) In order to expedite the requirements of subdivision (a), the Office of Planning and Research, upon request of a lead agency, shall assist the lead agency in determining the various responsible agencies and trustee agencies, for a proposed project. In the case of a project described in subdivision (c) of Section 21065, the request may also be made by the project applicant.

21080.4. (a) If a lead agency determines that an environmental impact report is required for a project, the lead agency shall immediately send notice of that determination by certified mail or an equivalent procedure to each responsible agency, the Office of Planning and Research, and those public agencies having jurisdiction by law over natural resources affected by the project that are held in trust for the people of the State of California. Upon receipt of the notice, each responsible agency, the office, and each public agency having jurisdiction by law over natural resources affected by the project that are held in trust for the people of the State of California shall specify to the lead agency the scope and content of the environmental information that is germane to the statutory responsibilities of that responsible agency, the office, or the public agency in connection with the proposed project and which, pursuant to the requirements of this division, shall be included in the environmental impact report. The information shall be specified in writing and shall be communicated to the lead agency by certified mail or equivalent procedure not later than 30 days after the date of receipt of the notice of the lead agency's determination. The lead agency shall request similar guidance from appropriate federal agencies.

(b) To expedite the requirements of subdivision (a), the lead agency, any responsible agency, the Office of Planning and Research, or a public agency having jurisdiction by law over natural resources affected by the project that are held in trust for the people of the State of California, may request one or more meetings between representatives of those agencies and the office for the purpose of assisting the lead agency to determine the scope and content of the environmental information that any of those responsible agencies, the office, or the public agencies may require. In the case of a project described in subdivision (c) of Section 21065, the request may also be made by the project applicant. The meetings shall be convened by the lead agency as soon as possible, but not later than 30 days after the date that the meeting was requested.

(c) To expedite the requirements of subdivision (a), the Office of Planning and Research, upon request of a lead agency, shall assist the lead agency in determining the various responsible agencies, public agencies having jurisdiction by law over natural resources affected by the project that are held in trust for the people of the State of California, and any federal agencies that have responsibility for carrying out or approving a proposed project. In the case of a project described in subdivision (c) of Section 21065, that request may also be made by the project applicant.

(d) With respect to the Department of Transportation, and with respect to any state agency that is a responsible agency or a public agency having jurisdiction by law over natural resources affected by the project that are held in trust for the people of the State of California, subject to the requirements of subdivision (a), the Office of Planning and Research shall ensure that the information required by subdivision (a) is transmitted to the lead agency, and that affected agencies are notified regarding meetings to be held upon request pursuant to subdivision (b), within the required time period.

21080.5. (a) Except as provided in Section 21158.1, when the regulatory program of a state agency requires a plan or other written documentation containing environmental information and complying with paragraph (3) of subdivision (d) to be submitted in support of an activity listed in subdivision (b), the plan or other written documentation may be submitted in lieu of the environmental impact report required by this division if the Secretary of the Resources Agency has certified the regulatory program pursuant to this section.

(b) This section applies only to regulatory programs or portions thereof that involve either of the following:

(1) The issuance to a person of a lease, permit, license, certificate, or other entitlement for use.

(2) The adoption or approval of standards, rules, regulations, or plans for use in the regulatory program.

(c) A regulatory program certified pursuant to this section is exempt from Chapter 3 (commencing with Section 21100), Chapter 4 (commencing with Section 21150), and Section 21167, except as provided in Article 2 (commencing with Section 21157) of Chapter 4.5.

(d) To qualify for certification pursuant to this section, a regulatory program shall require the utilization of an interdisciplinary approach that will ensure the integrated use of the natural and social sciences in decisionmaking and that shall meet all of the following criteria:

(1) The enabling legislation of the regulatory program does both of the following:

(A) Includes protection of the environment among its principal purposes.

(B) Contains authority for the administering agency to adopt rules and regulations for the protection of the environment, guided by standards set forth in the enabling legislation.

(2) The rules and regulations adopted by the administering agency for the regulatory program do all of the following:

(A) Require that an activity will not be approved or adopted as proposed if there are feasible alternatives or feasible mitigation measures available that would substantially lessen a significant adverse effect that the activity may have on the environment.

(B) Include guidelines for the orderly evaluation of proposed activities and the preparation of the plan or other written documentation in a manner consistent with the environmental protection purposes of the regulatory program.

(C) Require the administering agency to consult with all public agencies that have jurisdiction, by law, with respect to the proposed activity.

(D) Require that final action on the proposed activity include the written responses of the issuing authority to significant environmental points raised during the evaluation process.

(E) Require the filing of a notice of the decision by the administering agency on the proposed activity with the Secretary of the Resources Agency. Those notices shall be available for public inspection, and a list of the notices shall be posted on a weekly basis in the Office of the Resources Agency. Each list shall remain posted for a period of 30 days.

(F) Require notice of the filing of the plan or other written documentation to be made to the public and to a person who requests, in writing, notification. The notification shall be made in a manner that will provide the public or a person requesting notification with sufficient time to review and comment on the filing.

(3) The plan or other written documentation required by the regulatory program does both of the following:

(A) Includes a description of the proposed activity with alternatives to the activity, and mitigation measures to minimize any significant adverse effect on the environment of the activity.

(B) Is available for a reasonable time for review and comment by other public agencies and the general public.

(e) (1) The Secretary of the Resources Agency shall certify a regulatory program that the secretary determines meets all the qualifications for certification set forth in this section, and withdraw certification on determination that the regulatory program has been altered so that it no longer meets those qualifications. Certification and withdrawal of certification shall occur only after compliance with Chapter 3.5 (commencing with Section 11340) of Part 1 of Division 3 of Title 2 of the Government Code.

(2) In determining whether or not a regulatory program meets the qualifications for certification set forth in this section, the inquiry of the secretary shall extend only to the question of whether the regulatory program meets the generic requirements of subdivision (d). The inquiry may not extend to individual decisions to be reached under the regulatory program, including the nature of specific alternatives or mitigation measures that might be proposed to lessen any significant adverse effect on the environment of the activity.

(3) If the secretary determines that the regulatory program submitted for certification does not meet the qualifications for certification set forth in this section, the secretary shall adopt findings setting forth the reasons for the determination.

(f) After a regulatory program has been certified pursuant to this section, a proposed change in the program that could affect compliance with the qualifications for certification specified in subdivision (d) may be submitted to the Secretary of the Resources Agency for review and comment. The scope of the secretary's review shall extend only to the question of whether the regulatory program meets the generic requirements of subdivision (d). The review may not extend to individual decisions to be reached under the regulatory program, including specific alternatives or mitigation measures that might be proposed to lessen any significant adverse effect on the environment of the activity. The secretary shall have 30 days from the date of receipt of the proposed change to notify the state agency whether the proposed change will alter the regulatory program so that it no longer meets the qualification for certification established in this section and will result in a withdrawal of certification as provided in this section.

(g) An action or proceeding to attack, review, set aside, void, or annul a determination or decision of a state agency approving or adopting a proposed activity under a regulatory program that has been certified pursuant to this section on the basis that the plan or other written documentation prepared pursuant to paragraph (3) of subdivision (d) does not comply with this section shall be commenced not later than

30 days from the date of the filing of notice of the approval or adoption of the activity.

(h) (1) An action or proceeding to attack, review, set aside, void, or annul a determination of the Secretary of the Resources Agency to certify a regulatory program pursuant to this section on the basis that the regulatory program does not comply with this section shall be commenced within 30 days from the date of certification by the secretary.
   (2) In an action brought pursuant to paragraph (1), the inquiry shall extend only to whether there was a prejudicial abuse of discretion by the secretary. Abuse of discretion is established if the secretary has not proceeded in a manner required by law or if the determination is not supported by substantial evidence.

(i) For purposes of this section, a county agricultural commissioner is a state agency.

(j) For purposes of this section, an air quality management district or air pollution control district is a state agency, except that the approval, if any, by a district of a nonattainment area plan is subject to this section only if, and to the extent that, the approval adopts or amends rules or regulations.

(k) (1) The secretary, by July 1, 2004, shall develop a protocol for reviewing the prospective application of certified regulatory programs to evaluate the consistency of those programs with the requirements of this division. Following the completion of the development of the protocol, the secretary shall provide a report to the Senate Committee on Environmental Quality and the Assembly Committee on Natural Resources regarding the need for a grant of additional statutory authority authorizing the secretary to undertake a review of the certified regulatory programs.
   (2) The secretary shall provide a significant opportunity for public participation in developing the protocol described in paragraph (1) including, but not limited to, at least two public meetings with interested parties. A notice of each meeting shall be provided at least 10 days prior to the meeting to a person who files a written request for a notice with the agency.

21080.8. This division does not apply to the conversion of an existing rental mobile home park to a resident initiated subdivision, cooperative, or condominium for mobilehomes if the conversion will not result in an expansion of or change in existing use of the property.

21080.9. This division shall not apply to activities and approvals by any local government, as defined in Section 30109, or any state university or college, as defined in Section 30119, as necessary for the preparation and adoption of a local coastal program or long-range land use development plan pursuant to Division 20 (commencing with Section 30000); provided, however, that certification of a local coastal program or long-range land use development plan by the California Coastal Commission pursuant to Chapter 6 (commencing with Section 30500) of Division 20 shall be subject to the requirements of this division. For the purpose of Section 21080.5, a certified local coastal program or long-range land use development plan constitutes a plan for use in the California Coastal Commission's regulatory program.

21080.10. This division does not apply to any of the following:

(a) An extension of time, granted pursuant to Section 65361 of the Government Code, for the preparation and adoption of one or more elements of a city or county general plan.

(b) Actions taken by the Department of Housing and Community Development or the California Housing Finance Agency to provide financial assistance or insurance for the development and construction of residential housing for persons and families of low or moderate income, as defined in Section 50093 of the Health and Safety Code, if the project that is the subject of the application for financial assistance or insurance will be reviewed pursuant to this division by another public agency.

21080.11. This division shall not apply to settlements of title and boundary problems by the State Lands Commission and to exchanges or leases in connection with those settlements.

21080.12. (a) This division does not apply to the repair of critical levees of the State Plan for Flood Control specified pursuant to Section 8361 of the Water Code within an existing levee footprint to meet standards of public health and safety funded pursuant to Section 5096.821, except as otherwise provided in Section 15300.2 of Title 14 of the California Code of Regulations.

(b) For purposes of undertaking urgent levee repairs, the lead agency shall do all of the following:
   (1) Conduct outreach efforts in the vicinity of the project to ensure public awareness of the proposed repair work prior to approval of the project.
   (2) To the extent feasible, comply with standard construction practices, including, but not limited to, any rules, guidelines, or regulations adopted by the applicable air district for construction equipment and for control of particulate matter emissions.
   (3) To the extent feasible, use equipment powered by emulsified diesel fuel, electricity, natural gas, or ultralow sulfur diesel as an alternative to conventional diesel-powered construction equipment.

(c) This section shall remain in effect only until July 1, 2016, and as of that date is repealed, unless a later enacted statute, that is enacted before July 1, 2016, deletes or extends that date.

21080.13. This division shall not apply to any railroad grade separation project which eliminates an existing grade crossing or which reconstructs an existing grade separation.

21080.17. This division does not apply to the adoption of an ordinance by a city or county to implement the provisions of Section 65852.1 or Section 65852.2 of the Government Code.

21080.18. This division does not apply to the closing of any public school in which kindergarten or any of grades 1 through 12 is maintained or the transfer of students from that public school to another school if the only physical changes involved are categorically exempt under Chapter 3 (commencing with Section 15000) of Division 6 of Title 14 of the California Administrative Code.

21080.19. This division does not apply to a project for restriping of streets or highways to relieve traffic congestion.

21080.21. This division does not apply to any project of less than one mile in length within a public street or highway or any other public right-of-way for the installation of a new pipeline or the maintenance, repair, restoration, reconditioning, relocation, replacement, removal, or demolition of an existing pipeline. For purposes of this section, "pipeline" includes subsurface facilities but does not include any surface facility related to the operation of the underground facility.

21080.22. (a) This division does not apply to activities and approvals by a local government necessary for the preparation of general plan amendments pursuant to Section 29763, except that the approval of general plan amendments by the Delta Protection Commission is subject to the requirements of this division.

(b) For purposes of Section 21080.5, a general plan amendment is a plan required by the regulatory program of the Delta Protection Commission.

21080.23. (a) This division does not apply to any project which consists of the inspection, maintenance, repair, restoration, reconditioning, relocation, replacement, or removal of an existing pipeline, as defined in subdivision (a) of Section 51010.5 of the Government Code, or any valve, flange, meter, or other piece of equipment that is directly attached to the pipeline, if the project meets all of the following conditions:
   (1) (A) The project is less than eight miles in length.
      (B) Notwithstanding subparagraph (A), actual construction and excavation activities undertaken to achieve the maintenance, repair, restoration, reconditioning, relocation, replacement, or removal of an existing pipeline are not undertaken over a length of more than one-half mile at any one time.
   (2) The project consists of a section of pipeline that is not less than eight miles from any section of pipeline that has been subject to an exemption pursuant to this section in the past 12 months.
   (3) The project is not solely for the purpose of excavating soil that is contaminated by hazardous materials, and, to the extent not otherwise expressly required by law, the party undertaking the project immediately informs the lead agency of the discovery of contaminated soil.
   (4) To the extent not otherwise expressly required by law, the person undertaking the project has, in advance of undertaking the project, prepared a plan that will result in notification of the appropriate agencies so that they may take action, if determined to be necessary, to provide for the emergency evacuation of members of the public who may be located in close proximity to the project.
   (5) Project activities are undertaken within an existing right-of-way and the right-of-way is restored to its condition prior to the project.
   (6) The project applicant agrees to comply with all conditions otherwise authorized by law, imposed by the city or county planning department as part of any local agency permit process, that are required to mitigate potential impacts of the proposed project, and to otherwise comply with the Keene-Nejedly California Wetlands Preservation Act (Chapter 7 (commencing with Section 5810) of Division 5), the California Endangered Species Act (Chapter 1.5 (commencing with Section 2050) of Division 3 of the Fish and Game Code), and other applicable state laws, and with all applicable federal laws.

(b) If a project meets all of the requirements of subdivision (a), the person undertaking the project shall do all of the following:
   (1) Notify, in writing, any affected public agency, including, but not limited to, any public agency having permit, land use, environmental, public health protection, or emergency response authority of the exemption of the project from this division by subdivision (a).

(2) Provide notice to the public in the affected area in a manner consistent with paragraph (3) of subdivision (b) of Section 21092.
(3) In the case of private rights-of-way over private property, receive from the underlying property owner permission for access to the property.
(4) Comply with all conditions otherwise authorized by law, imposed by the city or county planning department as part of any local agency permit process, that are required to mitigate potential impacts of the proposed project, and otherwise comply with the Keene-Nejedly California Wetlands Preservation Act (Chapter 7 (commencing with Section 5810) of Division 5), the California Endangered Species Act (Chapter 1.5 (commencing with Section 2050) of Division 3 of the Fish and Game Code), and other applicable state laws, and with all applicable federal laws.

(c) Prior to January 1, 1999, this section shall not apply to ARCO Pipeline Company's crude oil pipelines designated as Crude Oil Line 1, from Tejon Station south to its terminus, and Crude Oil Line 90.
(d) This section does not apply to either of the following:
(1) A project in which the diameter of the pipeline is increased.
(2) A project undertaken within the boundaries of an oil refinery.

21080.23.5. (a) For purposes of Section 21080.23, "pipeline" also means a pipeline located in Fresno, Kern, Kings, or Tulare County, that is used to transport biogas, and meeting the requirements of Section 21080.23 and all local, state, and federal laws.
(b) For purposes of this section, "biogas" means natural gas that meets the requirements of Section 2292.5 of Title 13 of the California Code of Regulations and is derived from anaerobic digestion of dairy animal waste.
(c) This section shall remain in effect only until January 1, 2013, and as of that date is repealed, unless a later enacted statute, that is enacted before January 1, 2013, deletes or extends that date.

21080.24. (a) This division does not apply to the issuance, modification, amendment, or renewal of a permit by an air pollution control district or air quality management district pursuant to Title V, as defined in Section 39053.3 of the Health and Safety Code, or pursuant to a district Title V program established pursuant to Sections 42301.10, 42301.11, and 42301.12 of the Health and Safety Code, unless the issuance, modification, amendment, or renewal authorizes a physical or operational change to a source or facility.
(b) Nothing in this section is intended to result in the application of this division to a physical or operational change that, prior to January 1, 1995, was not subject to this division.

21080.26. This division does not apply to minor alterations to utilities made for the purposes of complying with Sections 4026.7 and 4026.8 of the Health and Safety Code or regulations adopted thereunder.

21080.29. (a) A project located in Los Angeles County that is approved by a public agency before the effective date of the act adding this section is not in violation of any requirement of this division by reason of the failure to construct a roadway across the property transferred to the state pursuant to subdivision (c) and to construct a bridge over the adjacent Ballona Channel in Los Angeles County, otherwise required as a mitigation measure pursuant to this division, if all of the following conditions apply:
(1) The improvements specified in this subdivision are not constructed, due in whole or in part, to the project owner's or developer's relinquishment of easement rights to construct those improvements.
(2) The easement rights in paragraph (1) are relinquished in connection with the State of California, acting by and through the Wildlife Conservation Board of the Department of Fish and Game, acquiring a wetlands project that is a minimum of 400 acres in size and located within the coastal zone.

(b) Where those easement rights have been relinquished, any municipal ordinance or regulation adopted by a charter city or a general law city shall be inapplicable to the extent that the ordinance or regulation requires construction of the transportation improvements specified in subdivision (a), or would otherwise require reprocessing or resubmittal of a permit or approval, including, but not limited to, a final recorded map, a vesting tentative map, or a tentative map, as a result of the transportation improvements specified in subdivision (a) not being constructed.
(c) (1) If the Wildlife Conservation Board of the Department of Fish and Game acquires property within the coastal zone that is a minimum of 400 acres in size pursuant to a purchase and sale agreement with Playa Capital Company, LLC, the Controller shall direct the trustee under the Amendment to Declaration of Trust entered into on or about December 11, 1984, by First Nationwide Savings, as trustee, Summa Corporation, as trustor, and the Controller, as beneficiary, known as the HRH Inheritance Tax Security Trust, to convey title to the trust estate of the trust, including real property commonly known as Playa Vista Area C, to the State of California acting by and through the Wildlife Conservation Board of the Department of Fish and Game for conservation, restoration, or recreation purposes only, with the right to transfer the property for those uses to any other agency of the State of California.
(2) This subdivision shall constitute the enabling legislation required by the Amendment to Declaration of Trust to empower the Controller to direct the trustee to convey title to the trust estate under the HRH Inheritance Tax Security Trust to the State of California or an agency thereof.
(3) The conveyance of the trust estate to the Wildlife Conservation Board pursuant to this subdivision shall supersede any duty or obligation imposed upon the Controller under the Probate Code or the Revenue and Taxation Code with respect to the disposition or application of the net proceeds of the trust estate.

21080.32. (a) This section shall only apply to publicly owned transit agencies, but shall not apply to any publicly owned transit agency created pursuant to Section 130050.2 of the Public Utilities Code.
(b) Except as provided in subdivision (c), and in accordance with subdivision (d), this division does not apply to actions taken on or after July 1, 1995, by a publicly owned transit agency to implement budget reductions caused by the failure of agency revenues to adequately fund agency programs and facilities.
(c) This section does not apply to any action to reduce or eliminate a transit service, facility, program, or activity that was approved or adopted as a mitigation measure in any environmental document authorized by this division or the National Environmental Policy Act (42 U.S.C. Sec. 4321 et seq.) or to any state or federal requirement that is imposed for the protection of the environment.
(d) (1) This section applies only to actions taken after the publicly owned transit agency has made a finding that there is a fiscal emergency caused by the failure of agency revenues to adequately fund agency programs and facilities, and after the publicly owned transit agency has held a public hearing to consider those actions. A publicly owned transit agency that has held such a hearing shall respond within 30 days at a regular public meeting to suggestions made by the public at the initial public hearing. Those actions shall be limited to projects defined in subdivision (a) or (b) of Section 21065 which initiate or increase fees, rates, or charges charged for any existing public service, program, or activity; or reduce or eliminate the availability of an existing publicly owned transit service, facility, program, or activity.
(2) For purposes of this subdivision, "fiscal emergency," when applied to a publicly owned transit agency, means that the agency is projected to have negative working capital within one year from the date that the agency makes the finding that there is a fiscal emergency pursuant to this section. Working capital shall be determined by adding together all unrestricted cash, unrestricted short-term investments, and unrestricted short-term accounts receivable and then subtracting unrestricted accounts payable. Employee retirement funds, including Internal Revenue Code Section 457 deferred compensation plans and Section 401(k) plans, health insurance reserves, bond payment reserves, workers' compensation reserves, and insurance reserves, shall not be factored into the formula for working capital.

21080.33. This division does not apply to any emergency project undertaken, carried out, or approved by a public agency to maintain, repair, or restore an existing highway, as defined in Section 360 of the Vehicle Code, except for a highway designated as an official state scenic highway pursuant to Section 262 of the Streets and Highways Code, within the existing right-of-way of the highway, damaged as a result of fire, flood, storm, earthquake, land subsidence, gradual earth movement, or landslide, within one year of the damage. This section does not exempt from this division any project undertaken, carried out, or approved by a public agency to expand or widen a highway damaged by fire, flood, storm, earthquake, land subsidence, gradual earth movement, or landslide.

21080.35.[1] For the purposes of Section 21069, the phrase "carrying out or approving a project" shall include the carrying out or approval of a plan for a project that expands or enlarges an existing publicly owned airport by any political subdivision, as described in Section 21661.6 of the Public Utilities Code.

21080.35.1
a) Except as provided in subdivision (d), this division does not apply to the installation of a solar energy system on the roof of an existing building or at an existing parking lot.
b) For the purposes of this section, the following terms mean the following:

[1]Section 21080.35, as added by SB 226, was mislabeled and codified under the same number as an existing code section with unrelated content. AB 226 does not amend the existing language of Section 21080.35.

(1) "Existing parking lot" means an area designated and used for parking of vehicles as of the time of the application for the solar energy system and for at least the previous two years.
(2) "Solar energy system" includes all associated equipment. Associated equipment consists of parts and materials that enable the generation and use of solar electricity or solar-heated water, including any monitoring and control, safety, conversion, and emergency responder equipment necessary to connect to the customer's electrical service or plumbing and any equipment, as well as any equipment necessary to connect the energy generated to the electrical grid, whether that connection is onsite or on an adjacent parcel of the building and separated only by an improved right-of-way. "Associated equipment" does not include a substation.

(c) (1) Associated equipment shall be located on the same parcel of the building, except that associated equipment necessary to connect the energy generated to the electrical grid may be located immediately adjacent to the parcel of the building or immediately adjacent to the parcel of the building and separated only by an improved right-of-way.
(2) Associated equipment shall not occupy more than 500 square feet of ground surface and the site of the associated equipment shall not contain plants protected by the Native Plant Protection Act (Chapter 10 (commencing with Section 1900) of Division 2 of the Fish and Game Code).

(d) This section does not apply if the associated equipment would otherwise require one of the following:
(1) An individual federal permit pursuant to Section 401 or 404 of the federal Clean Water Act (33 U.S.C. Sec. 1341 or 1344) or waste discharge requirements pursuant to the Porter-Cologne Water Quality Control Act (Division 7 (commencing with Section 13000) of the Water Code).
(2) An individual take permit for species protected under the federal Endangered Species Act of 1973 (16 U.S.C. Sec. 1531 et seq.) or the California Endangered Species Act (Chapter 1.5 (commencing with Section 2050) of Division 3 of the Fish and Game Code).
(3) A streambed alteration permit pursuant to Chapter 6 (commencing with Section 1600) of Division 2 of the Fish and Game Code.

(e) This section does not apply if the installation of a solar energy system at an existing parking lot involves either of the following:
(1) The removal of a tree required to be planted, maintained, or protected pursuant to local, state, or federal requirements, unless the tree dies and there is no requirement to replace the tree.
(2) The removal of a native tree over 25 years old.

(f) This section does not apply to any transmission or distribution facility or connection.

21080.42. (a) The following transportation projects are exempt from this division:
(1) U.S. Highway 101 interchange modification, adding southbound auxiliary lane and southbound mixed flow lane, from Interstate 280 to Yerba Buena Road, in Santa Clara County.
(2) Construct north- and southbound high-occupancy vehicle lanes on I-805 from I-5 to Carroll Canyon Road, including construction of north-facing direct access ramps in San Diego County.
(3) State Route 99, Los Molinas rehabilitation and traffic calming, from Orange Street to Tehama Vine Road, in Tehama County.
(4) State Route 99, Island Park widening project, adding one mixed flow lane in each direction, from Ashlan Avenue to Grantlund Avenue, in Fresno County.
(5) State Route 99 median widening, adding one mixed flow lane in each direction, from State Route 120 west to 0.4 miles north of Arch Road, in Manteca in San Joaquin County.
(6) State Route 12 pavement rehabilitation and shoulder widening in San Joaquin County on Bouldin Island.
(7) State Route 91 widening, adding one mixed flow lane in each direction, from State Route 55 to Weir Canyon Road in Orange County.
(8) U.S. Highway 101 pavement rehabilitation and shoulder widening in San Luis Obispo County.

(b) An exemption provided pursuant to subdivision (a) shall not apply to a transportation project if, on or after February 1, 2009, a lead agency changes the scope of that project from the manner in which the project is described in subdivision (a).

21081. Pursuant to the policy stated in Sections 21002 and 21002.1, no public agency shall approve or carry out a project for which an environmental impact report has been certified which identifies one or more significant effects on the environment that would occur if the project is approved or carried out unless both of the following occur:

(a) The public agency makes one or more of the following findings with respect to each significant effect:
(1) Changes or alterations have been required in, or incorporated into, the project which mitigate or avoid the significant effects on the environment.
(2) Those changes or alterations are within the responsibility and jurisdiction of another public agency and have been, or can and should be, adopted by that other agency.
(3) Specific economic, legal, social, technological, or other considerations, including considerations for the provision of employment opportunities for highly trained workers, make infeasible the mitigation measures or alternatives identified in the environmental impact report.

(b) With respect to significant effects which were subject to a finding under paragraph (3) of subdivision (a), the public agency finds that specific overriding economic, legal, social, technological, or other benefits of the project outweigh the significant effects on the environment.

21081.2. (a) Except as provided in subdivision (c), if a residential project, not exceeding 100 units, with a minimum residential density of 20 units per acre and within one-half mile of a transit stop, on an infill site in an urbanized area is in compliance with the traffic, circulation, and transportation policies of the general plan, applicable community plan, applicable specific plan, and applicable ordinances of the city or county with jurisdiction over the area where the project is located, and the city or county requires that the mitigation measures approved in a previously certified project area environmental impact report applicable to the project be incorporated into the project, the city or county is not required to comply with subdivision (a) of Section 21081 with respect to the making of any findings regarding the impacts of the project on traffic at intersections, or on streets, highways, or freeways.

(b) Nothing in subdivision (a) restricts the authority of a city or county to adopt feasible mitigation measures with respect to the impacts of a project on pedestrian and bicycle safety.

(c) Subdivision (a) does not apply in any of the following circumstances:
(1) The application for a proposed project is made more than five years after certification of the project area environmental impact report applicable to the project.
(2) A major change has occurred within the project area after certification of the project area environmental impact report applicable to the project.
(3) The project area environmental impact report applicable to the project was certified with overriding considerations pursuant to subdivision (b) of Section 21081 to the significant impacts on the environment with respect to traffic or transportation.
(4) The proposed project covers more than four acres.

(d) A project shall not be divided into smaller projects in order to qualify pursuant to this section.

(e) Nothing in this section relieves a city or county from the requirement to analyze the project's effects on traffic at intersections, or on streets, highways, or freeways, or from making a determination that the project may have a significant effect on traffic.

(f) For the purposes of this section, "project area environmental impact report" means an environmental impact report certified on any of the following:
(1) A general plan.
(2) A revision or update to the general plan that includes at least the land use and circulation elements.
(3) An applicable community plan.
(4) An applicable specific plan.
(5) A housing element of the general plan, if the environmental impact report analyzed the environmental effects of the density of the proposed project.
(6) A zoning ordinance.

21081.5. In making the findings required by paragraph (3) of subdivision (a) of Section 21081, the public agency shall base its findings on substantial evidence in the record.

21081.6. (a) When making the findings required by paragraph (1) of subdivision (a) of Section 21081 or when adopting a mitigated negative declaration pursuant to paragraph (2) of subdivision (c) of Section 21080, the following requirements shall apply:
(1) The public agency shall adopt a reporting or monitoring program for the changes made to the project or conditions of project approval, adopted in order to mitigate or avoid significant effects on the environment. The reporting or monitoring program shall be designed to ensure compliance during project implementation. For those changes which have been required or incorporated into the project at the request of a responsible agency or a public agency having jurisdiction by law over natural resources affected by the project, that agency shall, if so requested by the lead agency or a responsible agency, prepare and submit a proposed reporting or monitoring program.
(2) The lead agency shall specify the location and custodian of the documents or other material which constitute the record of proceedings upon which its decision is based.

(b) A public agency shall provide that measures to mitigate or avoid significant effects on the environment are fully enforceable through permit conditions, agreements, or other measures. Conditions of project approval may be set forth in referenced documents which address required mitigation measures or, in the case of the adoption of a plan, policy, regulation, or other public project, by incorporating the mitigation measures into the plan, policy, regulation, or project design.

(c) Prior to the close of the public review period for a draft environmental impact report or mitigated negative declaration, a responsible agency, or a public agency having jurisdiction over natural resources affected by the project, shall either submit to the lead agency complete and detailed performance objectives for mitigation measures which would address the significant effects on the environment identified by the responsible agency or agency having jurisdiction over natural resources affected by the project, or refer the lead agency to appropriate, readily available guidelines or reference documents. Any mitigation measures submitted to a lead agency by a responsible agency or an agency having jurisdiction over natural resources affected by the project shall be limited to measures which mitigate impacts to resources which are subject to the statutory authority of, and definitions applicable to, that agency. Compliance or noncompliance by a responsible agency or agency having jurisdiction over natural resources affected by a project with that requirement shall not limit the authority of the responsible agency or agency having jurisdiction over natural resources affected by a project, or the authority of the lead agency, to approve, condition, or deny projects as provided by this division or any other provision of law.

21081.7. Transportation information resulting from the reporting or monitoring program required to be adopted by a public agency pursuant to Section 21081.6 shall be submitted to the transportation planning agency in the region where the project is located and to the Department of Transportation for a project of statewide, regional, or areawide significance according to criteria developed pursuant to Section 21083. The transportation planning agency and the Department of Transportation shall adopt guidelines for the submittal of those reporting or monitoring programs.

21082. All public agencies shall adopt by ordinance, resolution, rule, or regulation, objectives, criteria, and procedures for the evaluation of projects and the preparation of environmental impact reports and negative declarations pursuant to this division. A school district, or any other district, whose boundaries are coterminous with a city, county, or city and county, may utilize the objectives, criteria, and procedures of the city, county, or city and county, as may be applicable, in which case, the school district or other district need not adopt objectives, criteria, and procedures of its own. The objectives, criteria, and procedures shall be consistent with the provisions of this division and with the guidelines adopted by the Secretary of the Resources Agency pursuant to Section 21083. Such objectives, criteria, and procedures shall be adopted by each public agency no later than 60 days after the Secretary of the Resources Agency has adopted guidelines pursuant to Section 21083.

21082.1. (a) Any draft environmental impact report, environmental impact report, negative declaration, or mitigated negative declaration prepared pursuant to the requirements of this division shall be prepared directly by, or under contract to, a public agency.

(b) This section is not intended to prohibit, and shall not be construed as prohibiting, any person from submitting information or other comments to the public agency responsible for preparing an environmental impact report, draft environmental impact report, negative declaration, or mitigated negative declaration. The information or other comments may be submitted in any format, shall be considered by the public agency, and may be included, in whole or in part, in any report or declaration.

(c) The lead agency shall do all of the following:
  (1) Independently review and analyze any report or declaration required by this division.
  (2) Circulate draft documents that reflect its independent judgment.
  (3) As part of the adoption of a negative declaration or a mitigated negative declaration, or certification of an environmental impact report, find that the report or declaration reflects the independent judgment of the lead agency.
  (4) Submit a sufficient number of copies of the draft environmental impact report, proposed negative declaration, or proposed mitigated negative declaration, and a copy of the report or declaration in an electronic form as required by the guidelines adopted pursuant to Section 21083, to the State Clearinghouse for review and comment by state agencies, if any of the following apply:
    (A) A state agency is any of the following:
      (i) The lead agency.
      (ii) A responsible agency.
      (iii) A trustee agency.
    (B) A state agency otherwise has jurisdiction by law with respect to the project.
    (C) The proposed project is of sufficient statewide, regional, or areawide environmental significance as determined pursuant to the guidelines certified and adopted pursuant to Section 21083.

21082.2. (a) The lead agency shall determine whether a project may have a significant effect on the environment based on substantial evidence in light of the whole record.

(b) The existence of public controversy over the environmental effects of a project shall not require preparation of an environmental impact report if there is no substantial evidence in light of the whole record before the lead agency that the project may have a significant effect on the environment.

(c) Argument, speculation, unsubstantiated opinion or narrative, evidence which is clearly inaccurate or erroneous, or evidence of social or economic impacts which do not contribute to, or are not caused by, physical impacts on the environment, is not substantial evidence. Substantial evidence shall include facts, reasonable assumptions predicated upon facts, and expert opinion supported by facts.

(d) If there is substantial evidence, in light of the whole record before the lead agency, that a project may have a significant effect on the environment, an environmental impact report shall be prepared.

(e) Statements in an environmental impact report and comments with respect to an environmental impact report shall not be deemed determinative of whether the project may have a significant effect on the environment.

21083. (a) The Office of Planning and Research shall prepare and develop proposed guidelines for the implementation of this division by public agencies. The guidelines shall include objectives and criteria for the orderly evaluation of projects and the preparation of environmental impact reports and negative declarations in a manner consistent with this division.

(b) The guidelines shall specifically include criteria for public agencies to follow in determining whether or not a proposed project may have a "significant effect on the environment." The criteria shall require a finding that a project may have a "significant effect on the environment" if one or more of the following conditions exist:
  (1) A proposed project has the potential to degrade the quality of the environment, curtail the range of the environment, or to achieve short-term, to the disadvantage of long-term, environmental goals.
  (2) The possible effects of a project are individually limited but cumulatively considerable. As used in this paragraph, "cumulatively considerable" means that the incremental effects of an individual project are considerable when viewed in connection with the effects of past projects, the effects of other current projects, and the effects of probable future projects.
  (3) The environmental effects of a project will cause substantial adverse effects on human beings, either directly or indirectly.

(c) The guidelines shall include procedures for determining the lead agency pursuant to Section 21165.

(d) The guidelines shall include criteria for public agencies to use in determining when a proposed project is of sufficient statewide, regional, or areawide environmental significance that a draft environmental impact report, a proposed negative declaration, or a proposed mitigated negative declaration shall be submitted to appropriate state agencies, through the State Clearinghouse, for review and comment prior to completion of the environmental impact report, negative declaration, or mitigated negative declaration.

(e) The Office of Planning and Research shall develop and prepare the proposed guidelines as soon as possible and shall transmit them immediately to the Secretary of the Resources Agency. The Secretary of the Resources Agency shall certify and adopt the guidelines pursuant to Chapter 3.5 (commencing with Section 11340) of Part 1 of Division 3 of Title 2 of the Government Code, which shall become effective upon the filing thereof. However, the guidelines shall not be adopted without compliance with Sections 11346.4, 11346.5, and 11346.8 of the Government Code.

(f) The Office of Planning and Research shall, at least once every two years, review the guidelines adopted pursuant to this section and shall recommend proposed changes or amendments to the Secretary of the Resources Agency. The Secretary of the Resources Agency shall certify and adopt guidelines, and any amendments thereto, at least once every two years, pursuant to Chapter 3.5 (commencing with Section 11340) of Part 1 of Division 3 of Title 2 of the Government Code, which shall become effective upon the filing thereof. However, guidelines may not be adopted or amended without compliance with Sections 11346.4, 11346.5, and 11346.8 of the Government Code.

21083.05. (a) On or before July 1, 2009, the Office of Planning and Research shall prepare, develop, and transmit to the Resources Agency guidelines for the mitigation of greenhouse gas emissions or the effects of greenhouse gas emissions as required by this division, including, but not limited to, effects associated with transportation or energy consumption.

(b) On or before January 1, 2010, the Resources Agency shall certify and adopt guidelines prepared and developed by the Office of Planning and Research pursuant to subdivision (a).

(c) The Office of Planning and Research and the Resources Agency shall periodically update the guidelines to incorporate new information or criteria established by the State Air Resources Board pursuant to Division 25.5 (commencing with Section 38500) of the Health and Safety Code.

21083.1. It is the intent of the Legislature that courts, consistent with generally accepted rules of statutory interpretation, shall not interpret this division or the state guidelines adopted pursuant to Section 21083 in a manner which imposes procedural or substantive requirements beyond those explicitly stated in this division or in the state guidelines.

21083.2. (a) As part of the determination made pursuant to Section 21080.1, the lead agency shall determine whether the project may have a significant effect on archaeological resources. If the lead agency determines that the project may have a significant effect on unique archaeological resources, the environmental impact report shall address the issue of those resources. An environmental impact report, if otherwise necessary, shall not address the issue of nonunique archaeological resources. A negative declaration shall be issued with respect to a project if, but for the issue of nonunique archaeological resources, the negative declaration would be otherwise issued.

(b) If it can be demonstrated that a project will cause damage to a unique archaeological resource, the lead agency may require reasonable efforts to be made to permit any or all of these resources to be preserved in place or left in an undisturbed state. Examples of that treatment, in no order of preference, may include, but are not limited to, any of the following:
 (1) Planning construction to avoid archaeological sites.
 (2) Deeding archaeological sites into permanent conservation easements.
 (3) Capping or covering archaeological sites with a layer of soil before building on the sites.
 (4) Planning parks, greenspace, or other open space to incorporate archaeological sites.

(c) To the extent that unique archaeological resources are not preserved in place or not left in an undisturbed state, mitigation measures shall be required as provided in this subdivision. The project applicant shall provide a guarantee to the lead agency to pay one-half the estimated cost of mitigating the significant effects of the project on unique archaeological resources. In determining payment, the lead agency shall give due consideration to the in-kind value of project design or expenditures that are intended to permit any or all archaeological resources or California Native American culturally significant sites to be preserved in place or left in an undisturbed state. When a final decision is made to carry out or approve the project, the lead agency shall, if necessary, reduce the specified mitigation measures to those which can be funded with the money guaranteed by the project applicant plus the money voluntarily guaranteed by any other person or persons for those mitigation purposes. In order to allow time for interested persons to provide the funding guarantee referred to in this subdivision, a final decision to carry out or approve a project shall not occur sooner than 60 days after completion of the recommended special environmental impact report required by this section.

(d) Excavation as mitigation shall be restricted to those parts of the unique archaeological resource that would be damaged or destroyed by the project. Excavation as mitigation shall not be required for a unique archaeological resource if the lead agency determines that testing or studies already completed have adequately recovered the scientifically consequential information from and about the resource, if this determination is documented in the environmental impact report.

(e) In no event shall the amount paid by a project applicant for mitigation measures required pursuant to subdivision (c) exceed the following amounts:
 (1) An amount equal to one-half of 1 percent of the projected cost of the project for mitigation measures undertaken within the site boundaries of a commercial or industrial project.
 (2) An amount equal to three-fourths of 1 percent of the projected cost of the project for mitigation measures undertaken within the site boundaries of a housing project consisting of a single unit.
 (3) If a housing project consists of more than a single unit, an amount equal to three-fourths of 1 percent of the projected cost of the project for mitigation measures undertaken within the site boundaries of the project for the first unit plus the sum of the following:
  (A) Two hundred dollars ($200) per unit for any of the next 99 units.
  (B) One hundred fifty dollars ($150) per unit for any of the next 400 units.
  (C) One hundred dollars ($100) per unit in excess of 500 units.

(f) Unless special or unusual circumstances warrant an exception, the field excavation phase of an approved mitigation plan shall be completed within 90 days after final approval necessary to implement the physical development of the project or, if a phased project, in connection with the phased portion to which the specific mitigation measures are applicable. However, the project applicant may extend that period if he or she so elects. Nothing in this section shall nullify protections for Indian cemeteries under any other provision of law.

(g) As used in this section, "unique archaeological resource" means an archaeological artifact, object, or site about which it can be clearly demonstrated that, without merely adding to the current body of knowledge, there is a high probability that it meets any of the following criteria:
 (1) Contains information needed to answer important scientific research questions and that there is a demonstrable public interest in that information.
 (2) Has a special and particular quality such as being the oldest of its type or the best available example of its type.
 (3) Is directly associated with a scientifically recognized important prehistoric or historic event or person.

(h) As used in this section, "nonunique archaeological resource" means an archaeological artifact, object, or site which does not meet the criteria in subdivision (g). A nonunique archaeological resource need be given no further consideration, other than the simple recording of its existence by the lead agency if it so elects.

(i) As part of the objectives, criteria, and procedures required by Section 21082 or as part of conditions imposed for mitigation, a lead agency may make provisions for archaeological sites accidentally discovered during construction. These provisions may include an immediate evaluation of the find. If the find is determined to be a unique archaeological resource, contingency funding and a time allotment sufficient to allow recovering an archaeological sample or to employ one of the avoidance measures may be required under the provisions set forth in this section. Construction work may continue on other parts of the building site while archaeological mitigation takes place.

(j) This section does not apply to any project described in subdivision (a) or (b) of Section 21065 if the lead agency elects to comply with all other applicable provisions of this division. This section does not apply to any project described in subdivision (c) of Section 21065 if the applicant and the lead agency jointly elect to comply with all other applicable provisions of this division.

(k) Any additional costs to any local agency as a result of complying with this section with respect to a project of other than a public agency shall be borne by the project applicant.

(l) Nothing in this section is intended to affect or modify the requirements of Section 21084 or 21084.1.

21083.3. (a) If a parcel has been zoned to accommodate a particular density of development or has been designated in a community plan to accommodate a particular density of development and an environmental impact report was certified for that zoning or planning action, the application of this division to the approval of any subdivision map or other project that is consistent with the zoning or community plan shall be limited to effects upon the environment which are peculiar to the parcel or to the project and which were not addressed as significant effects in the prior environmental impact report, or which substantial new information shows will be more significant than described in the prior environmental impact report.

(b) If a development project is consistent with the general plan of a local agency and an environmental impact report was certified with respect to that general plan, the application of this division to the approval of that development project shall be limited to effects on the environment which are peculiar to the parcel or to the project and which were not addressed as significant effects in the prior environmental impact report, or which substantial new information shows will be more significant than described in the prior environmental impact report.

(c) Nothing in this section affects any requirement to analyze potentially significant offsite impacts and cumulative impacts of the project not discussed in the prior environmental impact report with respect to the general plan. However, all public agencies with authority to mitigate the significant effects shall undertake or require the undertaking of any feasible mitigation measures specified in the prior environmental impact report relevant to a significant effect which the project will have on the environment or, if not, then the provisions of this section shall have no application to that effect. The lead agency shall make a finding, at a public hearing, as to whether those mitigation measures will be undertaken.

(d) An effect of a project upon the environment shall not be considered peculiar to the parcel or to the project, for purposes of this section, if uniformly applied development policies or standards have been previously adopted by the city or county, with a finding based upon substantial evidence, which need not include an environmental impact report, that the development policies or standards will substantially mitigate that environmental effect when applied to future projects, unless substantial new information shows that the policies or standards will not substantially mitigate the environmental effect.

(e) Where a community plan is the basis for application of this section, any rezoning action consistent with the community plan shall be a project subject to exemption from this division in accordance with this section. As used in this section, "community plan" means a part of the general plan of a city or county which (1) applies to a defined geographic portion of the total area included in the general plan, (2) complies with Article 5 (commencing with Section 65300) of Chapter 3 of Division 1 of Title 7 of the Government Code by including or referencing each of the mandatory elements specified in Section 65302 of the Government Code, and (3) contains specific development policies adopted for the area included in the community plan and identifies measures to implement those policies, so that the policies which will apply to each parcel can be determined.

(f) No person shall have standing to bring an action or proceeding to attack, review, set aside, void, or annul a finding of a public agency made at a public hearing pursuant to subdivision (a) with respect to the conformity of the project to the mitigation measures identified in the prior environmental impact report for the zoning or planning action, unless he or she has participated in that public hearing. However, this subdivision shall not be applicable if the local agency failed to give public notice of the hearing as required by law. For purposes of this subdivision, a person has participated in the public hearing if he or she has either submitted oral or written testimony regarding the proposed determination, finding, or decision prior to the close of the hearing.

(g) Any community plan adopted prior to January 1, 1982, which does not comply with the definitional criteria specified in subdivision (e) may be amended to comply with that criteria, in which case the plan shall be deemed a "community plan" within the meaning of subdivision (e) if (1) an environmental impact report was certified for adoption of the plan, and (2) at the time of the conforming amendment, the environmental impact report has not been held inadequate by a court of this state and is not the subject of pending litigation challenging its adequacy.

21083.4. (a) For purposes of this section, "oak" means a native tree species in the genus Quercus, not designated as Group A or Group B commercial species pursuant to regulations adopted by the State Board of Forestry and Fire Protection pursuant to Section 4526, and that is 5 inches or more in diameter at breast height.

(b) As part of the determination made pursuant to Section 21080.1, a county shall determine whether a project within its jurisdiction may result in a conversion of oak woodlands that will have a significant effect on the environment. If a county determines that there may be a significant effect to oak woodlands, the county shall require one or more of the following oak woodlands mitigation alternatives to mitigate the significant effect of the conversion of oak woodlands:

(1) Conserve oak woodlands, through the use of conservation easements.

(2) (A) Plant an appropriate number of trees, including maintaining plantings and replacing dead or diseased trees.

(B) The requirement to maintain trees pursuant to this paragraph terminates seven years after the trees are planted.

(C) Mitigation pursuant to this paragraph shall not fulfill more than one-half of the mitigation requirement for the project.

(D) The requirements imposed pursuant to this paragraph also may be used to restore former oak woodlands.

(3) Contribute funds to the Oak Woodlands Conservation Fund, as established under subdivision (a) of Section 1363 of the Fish and Game Code, for the purpose of purchasing oak woodlands conservation easements, as specified under paragraph (1) of subdivision (d) of that section and the guidelines and criteria of the Wildlife Conservation Board. A project applicant that contributes funds under this paragraph shall not receive a grant from the Oak Woodlands Conservation Fund as part of the mitigation for the project.

(4) Other mitigation measures developed by the county.

(c) Notwithstanding subdivision (d) of Section 1363 of the Fish and Game Code, a county may use a grant awarded pursuant to the Oak Woodlands Conservation Act (Article 3.5 (commencing with Section 1360) of Chapter 4 of Division 2 of the Fish and Game Code) to prepare an oak conservation element for a general plan, an oak protection ordinance, or an oak woodlands management plan, or amendments thereto, that meets the requirements of this section.

(d) The following are exempt from this section:

(1) Projects undertaken pursuant to an approved Natural Community Conservation Plan or approved subarea plan within an approved Natural Community Conservation Plan that includes oaks as a covered species or that conserves oak habitat through natural community conservation preserve designation and implementation and mitigation measures that are consistent with this section.

(2) Affordable housing projects for lower income households, as defined pursuant to Section 50079.5 of the Health and Safety Code, that are located within an urbanized area, or within a sphere of influence as defined pursuant to Section 56076 of the Government Code.

(3) Conversion of oak woodlands on agricultural land that includes land that is used to produce or process plant and animal products for commercial purposes.

(4) Projects undertaken pursuant to Section 21080.5 of the Public Resources Code.

(e) (1) A lead agency that adopts, and a project that incorporates, one or more of the measures specified in this section to mitigate the significant effects to oaks and oak woodlands shall be deemed to be in compliance with this division only as it applies to effects on oaks and oak woodlands.

(2) The Legislature does not intend this section to modify requirements of this division, other than with regard to effects on oaks and oak woodlands.

(f) This section does not preclude the application of Section 21081 to a project.

(g) This section, and the regulations adopted pursuant to this section, shall not be construed as a limitation on the power of a public agency to comply with this division or any other provision of law.

21083.5. (a) The guidelines prepared and adopted pursuant to Section 21083 shall provide that, when an environmental impact statement has been, or will be, prepared for the same project pursuant to the requirements of the National Environmental Policy Act of 1969 (42 U.S.C. Sec. 4321 et seq.) and implementing regulations, or an environmental impact report has been, or will be, prepared for the same project pursuant to the requirements of the Tahoe Regional Planning Compact (Section 66801 of the Government Code) and implementing regulations, all or any part of that statement or report may be submitted in lieu of all or any part of an environmental impact report required by this division, if that statement or report, or the part which is used, complies with the requirements of this division and the guidelines adopted pursuant thereto.

(b) Notwithstanding subdivision (a), compliance with this division may be achieved for the adoption in a city or county general plan, without any additions or change, of all or any part of the regional plan prepared pursuant to the Tahoe Regional Planning Compact and implementing regulations by reviewing environmental documents prepared by the Tahoe Regional Planning Agency addressing the plan, providing an analysis pursuant to this division of any significant effect on the environment not addressed in the environmental documents, and proceeding in accordance with Section 21081. This subdivision does not exempt a city or county from complying with the public review and notice requirements of this division.

21083.6. In the event that a project requires both an environmental impact report prepared pursuant to the requirements of this division and an environmental impact statement prepared pursuant to the requirements of the National Environmental Policy Act of 1969, an applicant may request and the lead agency may waive the time limits established pursuant to Section 21100.2 or 21151.5 if it finds that additional time is required to prepare a combined environmental impact report environmental impact statement and that the time required to prepare such a combined document would be shorter than that required to prepare each document separately.

21083.7. (a) In the event that a project requires both an environmental impact report prepared pursuant to the requirements of this division and an environmental impact statement prepared pursuant to the requirements of the National Environmental Policy Act of 1969, the lead agency shall, whenever possible, use the environmental impact statement as such environmental impact report as provided in Section 21083.5.

(b) In order to implement this section, each lead agency to which this section is applicable shall do both of the following, as soon as possible:

(1) Consult with the federal agency required to prepare such environmental impact statement.

(2) Notify the federal agency required to prepare the environmental impact statement regarding any scoping meeting for the proposed project.

21083.8.1. (a) (1) For purposes of this section, "reuse plan" for a military base means an initial plan for the reuse of a military base adopted by a local government or a redevelopment agency in the form of a general plan, general plan amendment, specific plan, redevelopment plan, or other planning document, except that the reuse plan shall also consist of a statement of development policies, include a diagram or diagrams illustrating its provisions, and make the designation required in paragraph (2). "Military base" or "base" means a military base or reservation either closed or realigned by, or scheduled for closure or realignment by, the federal government.

(2) The reuse plan shall designate the proposed general distribution and general location of development intensity for housing, business, industry, open space, recreation, natural resources, public buildings and grounds, roads and other transportation facilities, infrastructure, and other categories of public and private uses of land.

(b) (1) When preparing and certifying an environmental impact report for a reuse plan, including when utilizing an environmental impact statement pursuant to Section 21083.5, the determination of whether the reuse plan may have a significant effect on the environment may be made in the context of the physical conditions that were present at the time that the federal decision became final for the closure or realignment of the base. The no project alternative analyzed in the environmental impact report shall discuss the existing conditions on the base, as they exist at the time that the environmental impact report is prepared, as well as what could be reasonably expected to occur in the foreseeable future if the reuse plan were not approved, based on current plans and consistent with available infrastructure and services.

(2) For purposes of this division, all public and private activities taken pursuant to, or in furtherance of, a reuse plan shall be deemed to be a single project. However, further environmental review of any such public or private activity shall be conducted if any of the events specified in Section 21166 have occurred.

(c) Prior to preparing an environmental impact report for which a lead agency chooses to utilize the provisions of this section, the lead agency shall do all of the following:

(1) Hold a public hearing at which is discussed the federal environmental impact statement prepared for, or in the process of being prepared for, the closure of the military base. The discussion shall include the significant effects on the environment examined in the environmental impact statement, potential methods of mitigating those effects, including feasible alternatives, and the mitigative effects of federal, state, and local laws applicable to future nonmilitary activities. Prior to the close of the hearing, the lead agency may specify the baseline conditions for the reuse plan environmental impact report prepared, or in the process of being prepared, for the closure of the base. The lead agency may specify particular physical conditions that it will examine in greater detail than were examined in the environmental impact statement. Notice of the hearing shall be given as provided in Section 21092. The hearing may be continued from time to time.

(2) Identify pertinent responsible agencies and trustee agencies and consult with those agencies prior to the public hearing as to the application of their regulatory policies and permitting standards to the proposed baseline for environmental analysis, as well as to the reuse plan and planned future nonmilitary land uses of the base. The affected agencies shall have not less than 30 days prior to the public hearing to review the proposed reuse plan and to submit their comments to the lead agency.

(3) At the close of the hearing, the lead agency shall state in writing how the lead agency intends to integrate the baseline for analysis with the reuse planning and environmental review process, taking into account the adopted environmental standards of the community, including, but not limited to, the applicable general plan, specific plan, and redevelopment plan, and including other applicable provisions of adopted congestion management plans, habitat conservation or natural communities conservation plans, integrated waste management plans, and county hazardous waste management plans.

(4) At the close of the hearing, the lead agency shall state, in writing, the specific economic or social reasons, including, but not limited to, new job creation, opportunities for employment of skilled workers, availability of low- and moderate-income housing, and economic continuity, which support the selection of the baseline.

(d) (1) Nothing in this section shall in any way limit the scope of a review or determination of significance of the presence of hazardous or toxic wastes, substances, or materials including, but not limited to, contaminated soils and groundwater, nor shall the regulation of hazardous or toxic wastes, substances, or materials be constrained by prior levels of activity that existed at the time that the federal agency decision to close the military base became final.

(2) This section does not apply to any project undertaken pursuant to Chapter 6.5 (commencing with Section 25100) of, or Chapter 6.8 (commencing with Section 25300) of, Division 20 of the Health and Safety Code, or pursuant to the Porter-Cologne Water Quality Control Act (Division 7 (commencing with Section 13000) of the Water Code).

(3) This section may apply to any reuse plan environmental impact report for which a notice of preparation pursuant to subdivision (a) of Section 21092 is issued within one year from the date that the federal record of decision was rendered for the military base closure or realignment and reuse, or prior to January 1, 1997, whichever is later, if the environmental impact report is completed and certified within five years from the date that the federal record of decision was rendered.

(e) All subsequent development at the military base shall be subject to all applicable federal, state, or local laws, including, but not limited to, those relating to air quality, water quality, traffic, threatened and endangered species, noise, and hazardous or toxic wastes, substances, or materials.

21083.9. (a) Notwithstanding Section 21080.4, 21104, or 21153, a lead agency shall call at least one scoping meeting for either of the following:

(1) A proposed project that may affect highways or other facilities under the jurisdiction of the Department of Transportation if the meeting is requested by the department. The lead agency shall call the scoping meeting as soon as possible, but not later than 30 days after receiving the request from the Department of Transportation.

(2) A project of statewide, regional, or areawide significance.

(b) The lead agency shall provide notice of at least one scoping meeting held pursuant to paragraph (2) of subdivision (a) to all of the following:

(1) A county or city that borders on a county or city within which the project is located, unless otherwise designated annually by agreement between the lead agency and the county or city.

(2) A responsible agency.

(3) A public agency that has jurisdiction by law with respect to the project.

(4) A transportation planning agency or public agency required to be consulted pursuant to Section 21092.4.

(5) An organization or individual who has filed a written request for the notice.

(c) For an entity, organization, or individual that is required to be provided notice of a lead agency public meeting, the requirement for notice of a scoping meeting pursuant to subdivision (b) may be met by including the notice of a scoping meeting in the public meeting notice.

(d) A scoping meeting that is held in the city or county within which the project is located pursuant to the National Environmental Policy Act (42 U.S.C. Sec. 4321 et seq.) and the regulations adopted pursuant to that act shall be deemed to satisfy the requirement that a scoping meeting be held for a project subject to paragraph (2) of subdivision (a) if the lead agency meets the notice requirements of subdivision (b) or subdivision (c).

(e) The referral of a proposed action to adopt or substantially amend a general plan to a city or county pursuant to paragraph (1) of subdivision (a) of Section 65352 of the Government Code may be conducted concurrently with the scoping meeting required pursuant to this section, and the city or county may submit its comments as provided pursuant to subdivision (b) of that section at the scoping meeting.

21084. (a) The guidelines prepared and adopted pursuant to Section 21083 shall include a list of classes of projects which have been determined not to have a significant effect on the environment and which shall be exempt from this division. In adopting the guidelines, the Secretary of the Resources Agency shall make a finding that the listed classes of projects referred to in this section do not have a significant effect on the environment.

(b) A project's greenhouse gas emissions shall not, in and of themselves, be deemed to cause an exemption adopted pursuant to subdivision (a) to be inapplicable if the project complies with all applicable regulations or requirements adopted to implement statewide, regional, or local plans consistent with Section 15183.5 of Title 14 of the California Code of Regulations.

(c) A project that may result in damage to scenic resources, including, but not limited to, trees, historic buildings, rock outcroppings, or similar resources, within a highway designated as an official state scenic highway, pursuant to Article 2.5 (commencing with Section 260) of Chapter 2 of Division 1 of the Streets and Highways Code, shall be exempted from this division pursuant to subdivision (a). This subdivision does not apply to improvements as mitigation for a project for which a negative declaration has been approved or an environmental impact report has been certified.

(d) A project located on a site which is included on any list compiled pursuant to Section 65962.5 of the Government Code shall not be exempted from this division pursuant to subdivision (a).

(e) The changes made to this section by Chapter 1212 of the Statutes of 1991 apply only to projects for which applications have not been deemed complete on or before January 1, 1992, pursuant to Section 65943 of the Government Code.

(f) A project that may cause a substantial adverse change in the significance of an historical resource, as specified in Section 21084.1, shall not be exempted from this division pursuant to subdivision (a).

21084.1. A project that may cause a substantial adverse change in the significance of an historical resource is a project that may have a significant effect on the environment. For purposes of this section, an historical resource is a resource listed in, or determined to be eligible for listing in, the California Register of Historical Resources. Historical resources included in a local register of historical resources, as defined in subdivision (k) of Section 5020.1, or deemed significant pursuant to criteria set forth in subdivision (g) of Section 5024.1, are presumed to be historically or culturally significant for purposes of this section, unless the preponderance of the evidence demonstrates that the resource is not historically or culturally significant. The fact that a resource is not listed in, or determined to be eligible for listing in, the California Register of Historical Resources, not included in a local register of historical resources, or not deemed significant pursuant to criteria set forth in subdivision (g) of Section 5024.1 shall not preclude a lead agency from determining whether the resource may be an historical resource for purposes of this section.

21086. (a) A public agency may, at any time, request the addition or deletion of a class of projects, to the list designated pursuant to Section 21084. That request shall be made in writing to the Office of Planning and Research and shall include information supporting the public agency's position that the class of projects does, or does not, have a significant effect on the environment.

(b) The Office of Planning and Research shall review each request and, as soon as possible, shall submit its recommendation to the Secretary of the Resources Agency. Following the receipt of that recommendation, the Secretary of the Resources Agency may add or delete the class of projects to the list of classes of projects designated pursuant to Section 21084 that are exempt from the requirements of this division.

(c) The addition or deletion of a class of projects, as provided in this section, to the list specified in Section 21084 shall constitute an amendment to the guidelines adopted pursuant to Section 21083 and shall be adopted in the manner prescribed in Sections 21083 and 21084.

21088. The Secretary of the Resources Agency shall provide for the timely distribution to all public agencies of the guidelines and any amendments or changes thereto. In addition, the Secretary of the Resources Agency may provide for publication of a bulletin to provide public notice of the guidelines, or any amendments or changes thereto, and of the completion of environmental impact reports prepared in compliance with this division.

21089. (a) A lead agency may charge and collect a reasonable fee from a person proposing a project subject to this division in order to recover the estimated costs incurred by the lead agency in preparing a negative declaration or an environmental impact report for the project and for procedures necessary to comply with this division on the project. Litigation expenses, costs, and fees incurred in actions alleging noncompliance with this division under Section 21167 are not recoverable under this section.

(b) The Department of Fish and Game may charge and collect filing fees, as provided in Section 711.4 of the Fish and Game Code. Notwithstanding Section 21080.1, a finding required under Section 21081, or a project approved under a certified regulatory program authorized pursuant to Section 21080.5 is not operative, vested, or final until the filing fees required pursuant to Section 711.4 of the Fish and Game Code are paid.

(c) (1) A public agency may charge and collect a reasonable fee from members of the public for a copy of an environmental document not to exceed the cost of reproducing the environmental document. A public agency may provide the environmental document in an electronic format as provided pursuant to Section 6253.9 of the Government Code.

(2) For purposes of this subdivision, "environmental document" means an initial study, negative declaration, mitigated negative declaration, draft and final environmental impact report, a document prepared as a substitute for an environmental impact report, negative declaration, or mitigated negative declaration under a program certified pursuant to Section 21080.5, and a document prepared under the federal National Environmental Policy Act of 1969 (42 U.S.C. Sec. 4321 et seq.) and used by a state or local agency in the place of the initial study, negative declaration, mitigated negative declaration, or an environmental impact report.

21090. (a) An environmental impact report for a redevelopment plan may be a master environmental impact report, program environmental impact report, or a project environmental impact report. Any environmental impact report for a redevelopment plan shall specify the type of environmental impact report that is prepared for the redevelopment plan.

(b) If the environmental impact report for a redevelopment plan is a project environmental impact report, all public and private activities or undertakings pursuant to, or in furtherance of, a redevelopment plan shall be deemed to be a single project. However, further environmental review of any public or private activity or undertaking pursuant to, or in furtherance of, a redevelopment plan for which a project environmental impact report has been certified shall be conducted if any of the events specified in Section 21166 have occurred.

21090.1. For all purposes of this division, a geothermal exploratory project shall be deemed to be separate and distinct from any subsequent geothermal field development project as defined in Section 65928.5 of the Government Code.

21091. (a) The public review period for a draft environmental impact report may not be less than 30 days. If the draft environmental impact report is submitted to the State Clearinghouse for review, the review period shall be at least 45 days, and the lead agency shall provide a sufficient number of copies of the document to the State Clearinghouse for review and comment by state agencies.

(b) The public review period for a proposed negative declaration or proposed mitigated negative declaration may not be less than 20 days. If the proposed negative declaration or proposed mitigated negative declaration is submitted to the State Clearinghouse for review, the review period shall be at least 30 days, and the lead agency shall provide a sufficient number of copies of the document to the State Clearinghouse for review and comment by state agencies.

(c) (1) Notwithstanding subdivisions (a) and (b), if a draft environmental impact report, proposed negative declaration, or proposed mitigated negative declaration is submitted to the State Clearinghouse for review and the period of review by the State Clearinghouse is longer than the public review period established pursuant to subdivision (a) or (b), whichever is applicable, the public review period shall be at least as long as the period of review and comment by state agencies as established by the State Clearinghouse.

(2) The public review period and the state agency review period may, but are not required to, begin and end at the same time. Day one of the state agency review period shall be the date that the State Clearinghouse distributes the document to state agencies.

(3) If the submittal of a CEQA document is determined by the State Clearinghouse to be complete, the State Clearinghouse shall distribute the document within three working days from the date of receipt. The State Clearinghouse shall specify the information that will be required in order to determine the completeness of the submittal of a CEQA document.

(d) (1) The lead agency shall consider comments it receives on a draft environmental impact report, proposed negative declaration, or proposed mitigated negative declaration if those comments are received within the public review period.

(2) (A) With respect to the consideration of comments received on a draft environmental impact report, the lead agency shall evaluate comments on environmental issues that are received from persons who have reviewed the draft and shall prepare a written response pursuant to subparagraph (B). The lead agency may also respond to comments that are received after the close of the public review period.

(B) The written response shall describe the disposition of each significant environmental issue that is raised by commenters. The responses shall be prepared consistent with Section 15088 of Title 14 of the California Code of Regulations, as those regulations existed on June 1, 1993.

(3) (A) With respect to the consideration of comments received on a draft environmental impact report, proposed negative declaration, proposed mitigated negative declaration, or notice pursuant to Section 21080.4, the lead agency shall accept comments via e-mail and shall treat e-mail comments as equivalent to written comments.

(B) Any law or regulation relating to written comments received on a draft environmental impact report, proposed negative declaration, proposed mitigated negative declaration, or notice received pursuant to Section 21080.4, shall also apply to e-mail comments received for those reasons.

(e) (1) Criteria for shorter review periods by the State Clearinghouse for documents that must be submitted to the State Clearinghouse shall be set forth in the written guidelines issued by the Office of Planning and Research and made available to the public.

(2) Those shortened review periods may not be less than 30 days for a draft environmental impact report and 20 days for a negative declaration.

(3) A request for a shortened review period shall only be made in writing by the decisionmaking body of the lead agency to the Office of Planning and Research. The decisionmaking body may designate by resolution or ordinance a person authorized to request a shortened review period. A designated person shall notify the decisionmaking body of this request.

(4) A request approved by the State Clearinghouse shall be consistent with the criteria set forth in the written guidelines of the Office of Planning and Research.

(5) A shortened review period may not be approved by the Office of Planning and Research for a proposed project of statewide, regional, or areawide environmental significance as determined pursuant to Section 21083.

(6) An approval of a shortened review period shall be given prior to, and reflected in, the public notice required pursuant to Section 21092.

(f) Prior to carrying out or approving a project for which a negative declaration has been adopted, the lead agency shall consider the negative declaration together with comments that were received and considered pursuant to paragraph (1) of subdivision (d).

21091.5. Notwithstanding subdivision (a) of Section 21091, or any other provision of this division, the public review period for a draft environmental impact report prepared for a proposed project involving the expansion or enlargement of a publicly owned airport requiring the acquisition of any tide and submerged lands or other lands subject to the public trust for commerce, navigation, or fisheries, or any interest therein, shall be not less than 120 days.

21092. (a) Any lead agency that is preparing an environmental impact report or a negative declaration or making a determination pursuant to subdivision (c) of Section 21157.1 shall provide public notice of that fact within a reasonable period of time prior to certification of the environmental impact report, adoption of the negative declaration, or making the determination pursuant to subdivision (c) of Section 21157.1.

(b) (1) The notice shall specify the period during which comments will be received on the draft environmental report or negative declaration, and shall include the date, time, and place of any public meetings or hearings on the proposed project, a brief description of the proposed project and its location, the significant effects on the environment, if any, anticipated as a result of the project, and the address where copies of the draft environmental impact report or negative declaration, and all documents referenced in the draft environmental impact report or negative declaration, are available for review, and a description of how the draft environmental impact report or negative declaration can be provided in an electronic format.

(2) This section shall not be construed in any manner that results in the invalidation of an action because of the alleged inadequacy of the notice content, provided that there has been substantial compliance with the notice content requirements of this section.

(3) The notice required by this section shall be given to the last known name and address of all organizations and individuals who have previously requested notice and shall also be given by at least one of the following procedures:

(A) Publication, no fewer times than required by Section 6061 of the Government Code, by the public agency in a newspaper of general circulation in the area affected by the proposed project. If more than one area will be affected, the notice shall be published in the newspaper of largest circulation from among the newspapers of general circulation in those areas.

(B) Posting of notice by the lead agency on- and off-site in the area where the project is to be located.

(C) Direct mailing to the owners and occupants of contiguous property shown on the latest equalized assessment roll.

(c) For any project involving the burning of municipal wastes, hazardous waste, or refuse-derived fuel, including, but not limited to, tires, meeting the qualifications of subdivision (d), notice shall be given to all organizations and individuals who have previously requested notice and shall also be given by at least the procedures specified in subparagraphs (A), (B), and (C) of paragraph (3) of subdivision (b). In addition, notification shall be given by direct mailing to the owners and occupants of property within one-fourth of a mile of any parcel or parcels on which is located a project subject to this subdivision.

(d) The notice requirements of subdivision (c) apply to both of the following:

(1) The construction of a new facility.

(2) The expansion of an existing facility which burns hazardous waste which would increase its permitted capacity by more than 10 percent. For purposes of this paragraph, the amount of expansion of an existing facility shall be calculated by comparing the proposed facility capacity with whichever of the following is applicable:

(A) The facility capacity approved in the facility's hazardous waste facilities permit pursuant to Section 25200 of the Health and Safety Code or its grant of interim status pursuant to Section 25200.5 of the Health and Safety Code, or the facility capacity authorized in any state or local agency permit allowing the construction or operation of a facility for the burning of hazardous waste, granted before January 1, 1990.

(B) The facility capacity authorized in the facility's original hazardous waste facilities permit, grant of interim status, or any state or local agency permit allowing the construction or operation of a facility for the burning of hazardous waste, granted on or after January 1, 1990.

(e) The notice requirements specified in subdivision (b) or (c) shall not preclude a public agency from providing additional notice by other means if the agency so desires, or from providing the public notice required by this section at the same time and in the same manner as public notice otherwise required by law for the project.

21092.1. When significant new information is added to an environmental impact report after notice has been given pursuant to Section 21092 and consultation has occurred pursuant to Sections 21104 and 21153, but prior to certification, the public agency shall give notice again pursuant to Section 21092, and consult again pursuant to Sections 21104 and 21153 before certifying the environmental impact report.

21092.2. The notices required pursuant to Sections 21080.4, 21083.9, 21092, 21108, and 21152 shall be mailed to every person who has filed a written request for notices with either the clerk of the governing body or, if there is no governing body, the director of the agency. If the agency offers to provide the notices by e-mail, upon filing a written request for notices, a person may request that the notices be provided to him or her by e-mail. The request may also be filed with any other person designated by the governing body or director to receive these requests. The agency may require requests for notices to be annually renewed. The public agency may charge a fee, except to other public agencies, that is reasonably related to the costs of providing this service. This section may not be construed in any manner that results in the invalidation of an action because of the failure of a person to receive a requested notice, provided that there has been substantial compliance with the requirements of this section.

21092.3. The notices required pursuant to Sections 21080.4 and 21092 for an environmental impact report shall be posted in the office of the county clerk of each county in which the project will be located and shall remain posted for a period of 30 days. The notice required pursuant to Section 21092 for a negative declaration shall be so posted for a period of 20 days, unless otherwise required by law to be posted for 30 days. The county clerk shall post the notices within 24 hours of receipt.

21092.4. (a) For a project of statewide, regional, or areawide significance, the lead agency shall consult with transportation planning agencies and public agencies that have transportation facilities within their jurisdictions that could be affected by the project. Consultation shall be conducted in the same manner as for responsible agencies pursuant to this division, and shall be for the purpose of the lead agency obtaining information concerning the project's effect on major local arterials, public transit, freeways, highways, overpasses, on-ramps, off-ramps, and rail transit service within the jurisdiction of a transportation planning agency or a public agency that is consulted by the lead agency. A transportation planning agency or public agency that provides information to the lead agency shall be notified of, and provided with copies of, environmental documents pertaining to the project.

(b) As used in this section, "transportation facilities" includes major local arterials and public transit within five miles of the project site and freeways, highways, overpasses, on-ramps, off-ramps, and rail transit service within 10 miles of the project site.

21092.5. (a) At least 10 days prior to certifying an environmental impact report, the lead agency shall provide a written proposed response to a public agency on comments made by that agency which conform with the requirements of this division. Proposed responses shall conform with the legal standards established for responses to comments on draft environmental impact reports. Copies of responses or the environmental document in which they are contained, prepared in conformance with other requirements of this division and the guidelines adopted pursuant to Section 21083, may be used to meet the requirements imposed by this section.

(b) The lead agency shall notify any public agency which comments on a negative declaration, of the public hearing or hearings, if any, on the project for which the negative declaration was prepared. If notice to the commenting public agency is provided pursuant to Section 21092, the notice shall satisfy the requirement of this subdivision.

(c) Nothing in this section requires the lead agency to respond to comments not received within the comment periods specified in this division, to reopen comment periods, or to delay acting on a negative declaration or environmental impact report.

21092.6. (a) The lead agency shall consult the lists compiled pursuant to Section 65962.5 of the Government Code to determine whether the project and any alternatives are located on a site which is included on any list. The lead agency shall indicate whether a site is on any list not already identified by the applicant. The lead agency shall specify the list and include the information in the statement required pursuant to subdivision (f) of Section 65962.5 of the Government Code, in the notice required pursuant to Section 21080.4, a negative declaration, and a draft environmental impact report. The requirement in this section to specify any list shall not be construed to limit compliance with this division.

(b) If a project or any alternatives are located on a site which is included on any of the lists compiled pursuant to Section 65962.5 of the Government

Code and the lead agency did not accurately specify or did not specify any list pursuant to subdivision (a), the California Environmental Protection Agency shall notify the lead agency specifying any list with the site when it receives notice pursuant to Section 21080.4, a negative declaration, and a draft environmental impact report. The California Environmental Protection Agency shall not be liable for failure to notify the lead agency pursuant to this subdivision.

(c) This section applies only to projects for which applications have not been deemed complete pursuant to Section 65943 of the Government Code on or before January 1, 1992.

21093. (a) The Legislature finds and declares that tiering of environmental impact reports will promote construction of needed housing and other development projects by (1) streamlining regulatory procedures, (2) avoiding repetitive discussions of the same issues in successive environmental impact reports, and (3) ensuring that environmental impact reports prepared for later projects which are consistent with a previously approved policy, plan, program, or ordinance concentrate upon environmental effects which may be mitigated or avoided in connection with the decision on each later project. The Legislature further finds and declares that tiering is appropriate when it helps a public agency to focus upon the issues ripe for decision at each level of environmental review and in order to exclude duplicative analysis of environmental effects examined in previous environmental impact reports.

(b) To achieve this purpose, environmental impact reports shall be tiered whenever feasible, as determined by the lead agency.

21094. (a) (1) If a prior environmental impact report has been prepared and certified for a program, plan, policy, or ordinance, the lead agency for a later project that meets the requirements of this section shall examine significant effects of the later project upon the environment by using a tiered environmental impact report, except that the report on the later project is not required to examine those effects that the lead agency determines were either of the following:

(A) Mitigated or avoided pursuant to paragraph (1) of subdivision (a) of Section 21081 as a result of the prior environmental impact report.

(B) Examined at a sufficient level of detail in the prior environmental impact report to enable those effects to be mitigated or avoided by site-specific revisions, the imposition of conditions, or by other means in connection with the approval of the later project.

(2) If a prior environmental impact report has been prepared and certified for a program, plan, policy, or ordinance, and the lead agency makes a finding of overriding consideration pursuant to subdivision (b) of Section 21081, the lead agency for a later project that uses a tiered environmental impact report from that program, plan, policy, or ordinance may incorporate by reference that finding of overriding consideration if all of the following conditions are met:

(A) The lead agency determines that the project's significant impacts on the environment are not greater than or different from those identified in the prior environmental impact report.

(B) The lead agency incorporates into the later project all the applicable mitigation measures identified by the prior environmental impact report.

(C) The prior finding of overriding considerations was not based on a determination that mitigation measures should be identified and approved in a subsequent environmental review.

(D) The prior environmental impact report was certified not more than three years before the date findings are made pursuant to Section 21081 for the later project.

(E) The lead agency has determined that the mitigation measures or alternatives found to be infeasible in the prior environmental impact report pursuant to paragraph (3) of subdivision (a) of Section 21081 remain infeasible based on the criteria set forth in that section.

(3) On and after January 1, 2016, a lead agency shall not take action pursuant to paragraph (2) with regard to incorporating by reference a prior finding of overriding consideration, and paragraph (2) shall become inoperative on January 1, 2016.

(b) This section applies only to a later project that the lead agency determines is all of the following:

(1) Consistent with the program, plan, policy, or ordinance for which an environmental impact report has been prepared and certified.

(2) Consistent with applicable local land use plans and zoning of the city, county, or city and county in which the later project would be located.

(3) Not subject to Section 21166.

(c) For purposes of compliance with this section, an initial study shall be prepared to assist the lead agency in making the determinations required by this section. The initial study shall analyze whether the later project may cause significant effects on the environment that were not examined in the prior environmental impact report.

(d) All public agencies that propose to carry out or approve the later project may utilize the prior environmental impact report and the environmental impact report on the later project to fulfill the requirements of Section 21081.

(e)(1) If a lead agency determines pursuant to this subdivision that a cumulative effect has been adequately addressed in a prior environmental impact report, that cumulative effect is not required to be examined in a later environmental impact report, mitigated negative declaration, or negative declaration for purposes of subparagraph (B) of paragraph (1) of subdivision (a).

(2) When assessing whether there is new significant cumulative effect, the lead agency shall consider whether the incremental effects of the project are cumulatively considerable.

(3)(A) For purposes of paragraph (2), if the lead agency determines the incremental effects of the project are significant when viewed in connection with the effects of past, present, and probable future projects, the incremental effects of a project are cumulatively considerable.

(B) If the lead agency determines incremental effects of a project are cumulatively considerable, the later environmental impact report, mitigated negative declaration, or negative declaration shall examine those effects.

(4) If the lead agency makes one of the following determinations, the cumulative effects of a project are adequately addressed for purposes of paragraph (1):

(A) The cumulative effect has been mitigated or avoided as a result of the prior environmental impact report and findings adopted pursuant to paragraph (1) of subdivision (a) of Section 21081 as a result of the prior environmental impact report.

(B) The cumulative effect has been examined at a sufficient level of detail in the prior environmental impact report to enable the effect to be mitigated or avoided by site-specific revisions, the imposition of conditions, or by other means in connection with the approval of the later project.

(f) If tiering is used pursuant to this section, an environmental impact report prepared for a later project shall refer to the prior environmental impact report and state where a copy of the prior environmental impact report may be examined.

(g) This section shall remain in effect only until January 1, 2016, and as of that date is repealed, unless a later enacted statute, that is enacted before January 1, 2016, deletes or extends that date.

21094. (a) Where a prior environmental impact report has been prepared and certified for a program, plan, policy, or ordinance, the lead agency for a later project that meets the requirements of this section shall examine significant effects of the later project upon the environment by using a tiered environmental impact report, except that the report on the later project is not required to examine those effects that the lead agency determines were either of the following:

(1) Mitigated or avoided pursuant to paragraph (1) of subdivision (a) of Section 21081 as a result of the prior environmental impact report.

(2) Examined at a sufficient level of detail in the prior environmental impact report to enable those effects to be mitigated or avoided by site-specific revisions, the imposition of conditions, or by other means in connection with the approval of the later project.

(b) This section applies only to a later project that the lead agency determines is all of the following:

(1) Consistent with the program, plan, policy, or ordinance for which an environmental impact report has been prepared and certified.

(2) Consistent with applicable local land use plans and zoning of the city, county, or city and county in which the later project would be located.

(3) Not subject to Section 21166.

(c) For purposes of compliance with this section, an initial study shall be prepared to assist the lead agency in making the determinations required by this section. The initial study shall analyze whether the later project may cause significant effects on the environment that were not examined in the prior environmental impact report.

(d) All public agencies that propose to carry out or approve the later project may utilize the prior environmental impact report and the environmental impact report on the later project to fulfill the requirements of Section 21081.

(e) When tiering is used pursuant to this section, an environmental impact report prepared for a later project shall refer to the prior environmental impact report and state where a copy of the prior environmental impact report may be examined.

(f) This section shall become operative on January 1, 2016.

21094.4.5.

(a)(1) If an environmental impact report was certified for a planning level decision of a city or county, the application of this division to the approval of an infill project shall be limited to the effects on the environment that (A) are specific to the project or to the project site and were not addressed as significant effects in the prior environmental impact report or (B) substantial new information shows the effects will be more significant than described in the prior environmental impact report. A lead agency's determination pursuant to this section shall be supported by substantial evidence.

(2) An effect of a project upon the environment shall not be considered a specific effect of the project or a significant effect that was not considered significant in a prior environmental impact report, or an effect that is more significant than was described in the prior environmental impact report if uniformly applicable development policies or standards adopted by the city, county, or the lead agency, would apply to the project and the lead agency makes a finding, based upon substantial evidence, that the development policies or standards will substantially mitigate that effect.

(b) If an infill project would result in significant effects that are specific to the project or the project site, or if the significant effects of the infill project were not addressed in the prior environmental impact report, or are more significant than the effects addressed in the prior environmental impact report, and if a mitigated negative declaration or a sustainable communities environmental assessment could not be otherwise adopted, an environmental impact report prepared for the project analyzing those effects shall be limited as follows:

(1) Alternative locations, densities, and building intensities to the project need not be considered.

(2) Growth inducing impacts of the project need not be considered.

(b) This section applies to an infill project that satisfies both of the following:

(1) The project satisfies any of the following:

(A) Is consistent with the general use designation, density, building intensity, and applicable policies specified for the project area in either a sustainable communities strategy or an alternative planning strategy for which the State Air Resources Board, pursuant to subparagraph (H) of paragraph (2) of subdivision (b) of Section 65080 of the Government Code, has accepted a metropolitan planning organization's determination that the sustainable communities strategy or the alternative planning strategy would, if implemented, achieve the greenhouse gas emission reduction targets.

(B) Consists of a small walkable community project located in an area designated by a city for that purpose.

(C) Is located within the boundaries of a metropolitan planning organization that has not yet adopted a sustainable communities strategy or alternative planning strategy, and the project has a residential density of at least 20 units per acre or a floor area ratio of at least 0.75.

(2) Satisfies all applicable statewide performance standards contained in the guidelines adopted pursuant to Section 21094.5.5.

(d) This section applies after the Secretary of the Natural Resources Agency adopts and certifies the guidelines establishing statewide standards pursuant to Section 21094.5.5.

(e) For the purposes of this section, the following terms mean the following:

(1) "Infill project" means a project that meets the following conditions:

(A) Consists of any one, or combination, of the following uses:

(i) Residential.

(ii) Retail or commercial, where no more than one-half of the project area is used for parking.

(iii) A transit station.

(iv) A school.

(v) A public office building.

(B) Is located within an urban area on a site that has been previously developed, or on a vacant site where at least 75 percent of the perimeter of the site adjoins, or is separated only by an improved public right-of-way from, parcels that are developed with qualified urban uses.

(2) "Planning level decision" means the enactment or amendment of a general plan, community plan, specific plan, or zoning code.

(3) "Prior environmental impact report" means the environmental impact report certified for a planning level decision, as supplemented by any subsequent or supplemental environmental impact reports, negative declarations, or addenda to those documents.

(4) "Small walkable community project" means a project that is in an incorporated city, which is not within the boundary of a metropolitan planning organization and that satisfies the following requirements:

(A) Has a project area of approximately one-quarter mile diameter of contiguous land completely within the existing incorporated boundaries of the city.

(B) Has a project area that includes a residential area adjacent to a retail downtown area.

(C) The project has a density of at least eight dwelling units per acre or a floor area ratio for retail or commercial use of not less than 0.50.

(5) "Urban area" includes either an incorporated city or an unincorporated area that is completely surrounded by one or more incorporated cities that meets both of the following criteria:

(A) The population of the unincorporated area and the population of the surrounding incorporated cities equal a population of 100,000 or more.

(B) The population density of the unincorporated area is equal to, or greater than, the population density of the surrounding cities.

21094.5.5.

(a) On or before July 1, 2012, the Office of Planning and Research shall prepare, develop, and transmit to the Natural Resources Agency for certification and adoption guidelines for the implementation of Section 21094.5 and the Secretary of the Natural Resources Agency, on or before January 1, 2013, shall certify and adopt the guidelines.

(b) The guidelines prepared pursuant to this section shall include statewide standards for infill projects that may be amended from time to time and promote all of the following:

(1) The implementation of the land use and transportation policies in the Sustainable Communities and Climate Protection Act of 2008 (Chapter 728 of the Statutes of 2008).

(2) The state planning priorities specified in Section 65041.1 of the Government Code and in the most recently adopted Environmental Goals and Policy Report issued by the Office of Planning and Research supporting infill development.

(3) The reduction of greenhouse gas emissions under the California Global Warming Solutions Act of 2006 (Division 25.5 (commencing with Section 38500) of the Health and Safety Code).

(4) The reduction in per capita water use pursuant to Section 10608.16 of the Water Code.

(5) The creation of a transit village development district consistent with Section 65460.1 of the Government Code.

(6) Substantial energy efficiency improvements, including improvements to projects related to transportation energy.

(7) Protection of public health, including the health of vulnerable populations from air or water pollution, or soil contamination.

(c) The standards for projects on infill sites shall be updated as frequently as necessary to ensure the protection of the environment.

21095. (a) The Resources Agency, in consultation with the Office of Planning and Research, shall develop an amendment to Appendix G of the state guidelines, for adoption pursuant to Section 21083, to provide lead agencies an optional methodology to ensure that significant effects on the environment of agricultural land conversions are quantitatively and consistently considered in the environmental review process.

(b) The Department of Conservation, in consultation with the United States Department of Agriculture pursuant to Section 658.6 of Title 7 of the Code of Federal Regulations, and in consultation with the Resources Agency and the Office of Planning and Research, shall develop a state model land evaluation and site assessment system, contingent upon the availability of funding from non-General Fund sources. The department shall seek funding for that purpose from non-General Fund sources, including, but not limited to, the United States Department of Agriculture.

(c) In lieu of developing an amendment to Appendix G of the state guidelines pursuant to subdivision (a), the Resources Agency may adopt the state model land evaluation and site assessment system developed pursuant to subdivision (b) as that amendment to Appendix G.

21096. (a) If a lead agency prepares an environmental impact report for a project situated within airport land use compatibility plan boundaries, or, if an airport land use compatibility plan has not been adopted, for a project within two nautical miles of a public airport or public use airport, the Airport Land Use Planning Handbook published by the Division of Aeronautics of the Department of Transportation, in compliance with Section 21674.5 of the Public Utilities Code and other documents, shall be utilized as technical resources to assist in the preparation of the environmental impact report as the report relates to airport-related safety hazards and noise problems.

(b) A lead agency shall not adopt a negative declaration for a project described in subdivision (a) unless the lead agency considers whether the project will result in a safety hazard or noise problem for persons using the airport or for persons residing or working in the project area.

21098. (a) For the purposes of this section, the following terms have the following meanings:

(1) "Low-level flight path" includes any flight path for any aircraft owned, maintained, or that is under the jurisdiction of the United States Department of Defense that flies lower than 1,500 feet above ground level, as indicated in the United States Department of Defense Flight Information

Publication, "Area Planning Military Training Routes: North and South America (AP/1B)" published by the United States National Imagery and Mapping Agency.

(2) "Military impact zone" includes any area, including airspace, that meets both of the following criteria:

(A) Is within two miles of a military installation, including, but not limited to, any base, military airport, camp, post, station, yard, center, homeport facility for a ship, or any other military activity center that is under the jurisdiction of the United States Department of Defense.

(B) Covers greater than 500 acres of unincorporated land, or greater than 100 acres of city incorporated land.

(3) "Military service" means any branch of the United States Armed Forces.

(4) "Special use airspace" means the land area underlying the airspace that is designated for training, research, development, or evaluation for a military service, as that land area is established by the United States Department of Defense Flight Information Publication, "Area Planning: Special Use Airspace: North and South America (AP/1A)" published by the United States National Imagery and Mapping Agency.

(b) If the United States Department of Defense or a military service notifies a lead agency of the contact office and address for the military service and the specific boundaries of a low-level flight path, military impact zone, or special use airspace, the lead agency shall submit notices, as required pursuant to Sections 21080.4 and 21092, to the military service if the project is within those boundaries and any of the following apply:

(1) The project includes a general plan amendment.

(2) The project is of statewide, regional, or areawide significance.

(3) The project is required to be referred to the airport land use commission, or appropriately designated body, pursuant to Article 3.5 (commencing with Section 21670) of Chapter 4 of Part 1 of Division 9 of the Public Utilities Code.

(c) The requirement to submit notices imposed by this section does not apply to any of the following:

(1) Response actions taken pursuant to Chapter 6.8 (commencing with Section 25300) of Division 20 of the Health and Safety Code.

(2) Response actions taken pursuant to Chapter 6.85 (commencing with Section 25396) of Division 20 of the Health and Safety Code.

(3) Sites subject to corrective action orders issued pursuant to Section 25187 of the Health and Safety Code.

(d) (1) The effect or potential effect that a project may have on military activities does not itself constitute an adverse effect on the environment for the purposes of this division.

(2) Notwithstanding paragraph (1), a project's impact on military activities may cause, or be associated with, adverse effects on the environment that are subject to the requirements of this division, including, but not limited to, Section 21081.

Chapter 3. State Agencies, Boards, and Commissions

21100. (a) All lead agencies shall prepare, or cause to be prepared by contract, and certify the completion of, an environmental impact report on any project which they propose to carry out or approve that may have a significant effect on the environment. Whenever feasible, a standard format shall be used for environmental impact reports.

(b) The environmental impact report shall include a detailed statement setting forth all of the following:

(1) All significant effects on the environment of the proposed project.

(2) In a separate section:

(A) Any significant effect on the environment that cannot be avoided if the project is implemented.

(B) Any significant effect on the environment that would be reversible if the project is implemented.

(3) Mitigation measures proposed to minimize significant effects on the environment, including, but not limited to, measures to reduce the wasteful, inefficient, and unnecessary consumption of energy.

(4) Alternatives to the proposed project.

(5) The growth-inducing impact of the proposed project.

(c) The report shall also contain a statement briefly indicating the reasons for determining that various effects on the environment of a project are not significant and consequently have not been discussed in detail in the environmental impact report.

(d) For purposes of this section, any significant effect on the environment shall be limited to substantial, or potentially substantial, adverse changes in physical conditions which exist within the area as defined in Section 21060.5.

(e) Previously approved land use documents, including, but notlimited to, general plans, specific plans, and local coastal plans, may be used in cumulative impact analysis.

21100.1. The information described in subparagraph (B) of paragraph (2) of subdivision (b) of Section 21100 shall be required only in environmental impact reports prepared in connection with the following:

(a) The adoption, amendment, or enactment of a plan, policy, or ordinance of a public agency.

(b) The adoption by a local agency formation commission of a resolution making determinations.

(c) A project which will be subject to the requirement for preparing an environmental impact statement pursuant to the requirements of the National Environmental Policy Act of 1969.

21100.2. (a) (1) For projects described in subdivision (c) of Section 21065, each state agency shall establish, by resolution or order, time limits that do not exceed the following:

(A) One year for completing and certifying environmental impact reports.

(B) One hundred eighty days for completing and adopting negative declarations.

(2) The time limits specified in paragraph (1) shall apply only to those circumstances in which the state agency is the lead agency for a project. These resolutions or orders may establish different time limits for different types or classes of projects, but all limits shall be measured from the date on which an application requesting approval of the project is received and accepted as complete by the state agency.

(3) No application for a project may be deemed incomplete for lack of a waiver of time periods prescribed in state regulations.

(4) The resolutions or orders required by this section may provide for a reasonable extension of the time period in the event that compelling circumstances justify additional time and the project applicant consents thereto.

(b) If a draft environmental impact report, environmental impact report, or focused environmental impact report is prepared under a contract to a state agency, the contract shall be executed within 45 days from the date on which the state agency sends a notice of preparation pursuant to Section 21080.4. The state agency may take longer to execute the contract if the project applicant and the state agency mutually agree to an extension of the time limit provided by this subdivision.

21101. In regard to any proposed federal project in this state which may have a significant effect on the environment and on which the state officially comments, the state officials responsible for such comments shall include in their report a detailed statement setting forth the matters specified in Section 21100 prior to transmitting the comments of the state to the federal government. No report shall be transmitted to the federal government unless it includes such a detailed statement as to the matters specified in Section 21100.

21102. No state agency, board, or commission shall request funds, nor shall any state agency, board, or commission which authorizes expenditures of funds, other than funds appropriated in the Budget Act, authorize funds for expenditure for any project, other than a project involving only feasibility or planning studies for possible future actions which the agency, board, or commission has not approved, adopted or funded, which may have a significant effect on the environment unless such request or authorization is accompanied by an environmental impact report.

Feasibility and planning studies exempted by this section from the preparation of an environmental impact report shall nevertheless include consideration of environmental factors.

21104. (a) Prior to completing an environmental impact report, the state lead agency shall consult with, and obtain comments from, each responsible agency, trustee agency, any public agency that has jurisdiction by law with respect to the project, and any city or county that borders on a city or county within which the project is located unless otherwise designated annually by agreement between the state lead agency and the city or county, and may consult with any person who has special expertise with respect to any environmental impact involved. In the case of a project described in subdivision (c) of Section 21065, the state lead agency shall, upon the request of the applicant, provide for early consultation to identify the range of actions, alternatives, mitigation measures, and significant effects to be analyzed in depth in the environmental impact report. The state lead agency may consult with persons identified by the applicant who the applicant believes will be concerned with the environmental effects of the project and may consult with members of the public who have made a written request to be consulted on the project. A request by the applicant for early consultation shall be made not later than 30 days after the determination required by Section 21080.1 with respect to the project.

(b) The state lead agency shall consult with, and obtain comments from, the State Air Resources Board in preparing an environmental impact report on a highway or freeway project, as to the air pollution impact of the potential vehicular use of the highway or freeway.

(c) A responsible agency or other public agency shall only make substantive comments regarding those activities involved in a project that are within an area of expertise of the agency or that are required to be carried out or approved by the agency. Those comments shall be supported by specific documentation.

21104.2. The state lead agency shall consult with, and obtain written findings from, the Department of Fish and Game in preparing an environmental impact report on a project, as to the impact of the roject on the continued existence of any endangered species or threatened species pursuant to Article 4 (commencing with Section 2090) of Chapter 1.5 of Division 3 of the Fish and Game Code.

21105. The state lead agency shall include the environmental impact report as a part of the regular project report used in the existing review and budgetary process. It shall be available to the Legislature. It shall also be available for inspection by any member of the general public, who may secure a copy thereof by paying for the actual cost of such a copy. It shall be filed by the state lead agency with the appropriate local planning agency of any city, county, or city and county which will be affected by the project.

21106. All state agencies, boards, and commissions shall request in their budgets the funds necessary to protect the environment in relation to problems caused by their activities.

21108. (a) Whenever a state agency approves or determines to carry out a project that is subject to this division, the state agency shall file notice of that approval or that determination with the office of Planning and Research. The notice shall identify the person or persons in subdivision (b) or (c) of Section 21065, as reflected in the agency's record of proceedings, and indicate the determination of the state agency whether the project will, or will not, have a significant effect on the environment and shall indicate whether an environmental impact report has been prepared pursuant to this division.

(b) Whenever a state agency determines that a project is not subject to this division pursuant to subdivision (b) of Section 21080 or Section 21172, and the state agency approves or determines to carry out the project, the state agency or the person specified in subdivision (b) or (c) of Section 21065 may file notice of the determination with the Office of Planning and Research. A notice filed pursuant to this subdivision shall identify the person or persons in subdivision (b) or (c) of Section 21065, as reflected in the agency's record of proceedings. A notice filed pursuant to this subdivision by a person specified in subdivision (b) or (c) of Section 21065 shall have a certificate of determination attached to it issued by the state agency responsible for making the determination that the project is not subject to this division pursuant to subdivision (b) of Section 21080 or pursuant to Section 21172. The certificate of determination may be in the form of a certified copy of an existing document or record of the state agency.

(c) All notices filed pursuant to this section shall be available for public inspection, and a list of these notices shall be posted on a weekly basis in the Office of Planning and Research. Each list shall remain posted for a period of 30 days. The Office of Planning and Research shall retain each notice for not less than 12 months.

Chapter 4. Local Agencies

21150. State agencies, boards, and commissions, responsible for allocating state or federal funds on a project-by-project basis to local agencies for any project which may have a significant effect on the environment, shall require from the responsible local governmental agency a detailed statement setting forth the matters specified in Section 21100 prior to the allocation of any funds other than funds solely for projects involving only feasibility or planning studies for possible future actions which the agency, board, or commission has not approved, adopted, or funded.

21151. (a) All local agencies shall prepare, or cause to be prepared by contract, and certify the completion of, an environmental impact report on any project that they intend to carry out or approve which may have a significant effect on the environment. When a report is required by Section 65402 of the Government Code, the environmental impact report may be submitted as a part of that report.

(b) For purposes of this section, any significant effect on the environment shall be limited to substantial, or potentially substantial, adverse changes in physical conditions which exist within the area as defined in Section 21060.5.

(c) If a nonelected decisionmaking body of a local lead agency certifies an environmental impact report, approves a negative declaration or mitigated negative declaration, or determines that a project is not subject to this division, that certification, approval, or determination may be appealed to the agency's elected decisionmaking body, if any.

21151.1. (a) Notwithstanding paragraph (6) of subdivision (b) of Section 21080, or Section 21080.5 or 21084, or any other provision of law, except as provided in this section, a lead agency shall prepare or cause to be prepared by contract, and certify the completion of, an environmental impact report or, if appropriate, a modification, addendum, or supplement to an existing environmental impact report, for a project involving any of the following:

(1) (A) The burning of municipal wastes, hazardous waste, or refuse-derived fuel, including, but not limited to, tires, if the project is either of the following:

(i) The construction of a new facility.

(ii) The expansion of an existing facility that burns hazardous waste that would increase its permitted capacity by more than 10 percent.

(B) This paragraph does not apply to a project exclusively burning hazardous waste, for which a final determination under Section 21080.1 has been made prior to July 14, 1989.

(2) The initial issuance of a hazardous waste facilities permit to a land disposal facility, as defined in subdivision (d) of Section 5199.1 of the Health and Safety Code.

(3) The initial issuance of a hazardous waste facilities permit pursuant to Section 25200 of the Health and Safety Code to an offsite large treatment facility, as defined pursuant to subdivision (d) of Section 25205.1 of the Health and Safety Code.

(4) A base reuse plan as defined in Section 21083.8.1. The Legislature hereby finds that no reimbursement is required pursuant to Section 6 of Article XIII B of the California Constitution for an environmental impact report for a base reuse plan if an environmental impact report is otherwise required for that base reuse plan pursuant to any other provision of this division.

(b) For purposes of clause (ii) of subparagraph (A) of paragraph (1) of subdivision (a), the amount of expansion of an existing facility shall be calculated by comparing the proposed facility capacity with whichever of the following is applicable:

(1) The facility capacity authorized in the facility's hazardous waste facilities permit pursuant to Section 25200 of the Health and Safety Code or its grant of interim status pursuant to Section 25200.5 of the Health and Safety Code, or the facility capacity authorized in a state or local agency permit allowing the construction or operation of a facility for the burning of hazardous waste, granted before January 1, 1990.

(2) The facility capacity authorized in the facility's original hazardous waste facilities permit, grant of interim status, or a state or local agency permit allowing the construction or operation of a facility for the burning of hazardous waste, granted on or after January 1, 1990.

(c) For purposes of paragraphs (2) and (3) of subdivision (a), the initial issuance of a hazardous waste facilities permit does not include the issuance of a closure or post-closure permit pursuant to Chapter 6.5 (commencing with Section 25100) of Division 20 of the Health and Safety Code.

(d) Paragraph (1) of subdivision (a) does not apply to a project that does any of the following:

(1) Exclusively burns digester gas produced from manure or any other solid or semisolid animal waste.

(2) Exclusively burns methane gas produced from a disposal site, as defined in Section 40122, that is used only for the disposal of solid waste, as defined in Section 40191.

(3) Exclusively burns forest, agricultural, wood, or other biomass wastes.

(4) Exclusively burns hazardous waste in an incineration unit that is transportable and that is either at a site for not longer than three years or is part of a remedial or removal action. For purposes of this paragraph, "transportable" means any equipment that performs a "treatment" as defined in Section 66216 of Title 22 of the California Code of Regulations, and that is transported on a vehicle as defined in Section 66230 of Title 22 of the California Code of Regulations, as those sections read on June 1, 1991.

(5) Exclusively burns refinery waste in a flare on the site of generation.

(6) Exclusively burns in a flare methane gas produced at a municipal sewage treatment plant.

(7) Exclusively burns hazardous waste, or exclusively burns hazardous waste as a supplemental fuel, as part of a research, development, or demonstration project that, consistent with federal regulations implementing the Resource Conservation and Recovery Act of 1976, as amended (42 U.S.C. Sec. 6901 et seq.), has been determined to be innovative and experimental by the Department of Toxic Substances Control and that is limited in type and quantity of waste to that necessary to determine the efficacy and performance capabilities of the technology or process. However, a facility that operated as a research, development, or demonstration project and for which an application is thereafter submitted for a hazardous waste facility permit for operation other than as a research, development, or demonstration project shall be considered a new facility for the burning of hazardous waste and shall be subject to subdivision (a) of Section 21151.1.

(8) Exclusively burns soils contaminated only with petroleum fuels or the vapors from these soils.

(9) Exclusively treats less than 3,000 pounds of hazardous waste per day in a thermal proces-

sing unit operated in the absence of open flame, and submits a worst-case health risk assessment of the technology to the Department of Toxic Substances Control for review and distribution to the interested public. This assessment shall be prepared in accordance with guidelines set forth in the Air Toxics Assessment Manual of the California Air Pollution Control Officers Association.

(10) Exclusively burns less than 1,200 pounds per day of medical waste, as defined in Section 117690 of the Health and Safety Code, on hospital sites.

(11) Exclusively burns chemicals and fuels as part of firefighter training.

(12) Exclusively conducts open burns of explosives subject to the requirements of the air pollution control district or air quality management district and in compliance with OSHA and Cal-OSHA regulations.

(13) Exclusively conducts onsite burning of less than 3,000 pounds per day of fumes directly from a manufacturing or commercial process.

(14) Exclusively conducts onsite burning of hazardous waste in an industrial furnace that recovers hydrogen chloride from the flue gas if the hydrogen chloride is subsequently sold, distributed in commerce, or used in a manufacturing process at the site where the hydrogen chloride is recovered, and the burning is in compliance with the requirements of the air pollution control district or air quality management district and the Department of Toxic Substances Control.

(e) Paragraph (1) of subdivision (a) does not apply to a project for which the State Energy Resources Conservation and Development Commission has assumed jurisdiction under Chapter 6 (commencing with Section 25500) of Division 15.

(f) Paragraphs (2) and (3) of subdivision (a) do not apply if the facility only manages hazardous waste that is identified or listed pursuant to Section 25140 or 25141 of the Health and Safety Code on or after January 1, 1992, but not before that date, or only conducts activities that are regulated pursuant to Chapter 6.5 (commencing with Section 25100) of Division 20 of the Health and Safety Code on or after January 1, 1992, but not before that date.

(g) This section does not exempt a project from any other requirement of this division.

(h) For purposes of this section, offsite facility means a facility that serves more than one generator of hazardous waste.

21151.2. To promote the safety of pupils and comprehensive community planning the governing board of each school district before acquiring title to property for a new school site or for an addition to a present school site, shall give the planning commission having jurisdiction notice in writing of the proposed acquisition. The planning commission shall investigate the proposed site and within 30 days after receipt of the notice shall submit to the governing board a written report of the investigation and its recommendations concerning acquisition of the site.

The governing board shall not acquire title to the property until the report of the planning commission has been received. If the report does not favor the acquisition of the property for a school site, or for an addition to a present school site, the governing board of the school district shall not acquire title to the property until 30 days after the commission's report is received.

21151.4. (a) An environmental impact report shall not be certified or a negative declaration shall not be approved for any project involving the construction or alteration of a facility within one-fourth of a mile of a school that might reasonably be anticipated to emit hazardous air emissions, or that would handle an extremely hazardous substance or a mixture containing extremely hazardous substances in a quantity equal to or greater than the state threshold quantity specified pursuant to subdivision (j) of Section 25532 of the Health and Safety Code, that may pose a health or safety hazard to persons who would attend or would be employed at the school, unless both of the following occur:

(1) The lead agency preparing the environmental impact report or negative declaration has consulted with the school district having jurisdiction regarding the potential impact of the project on the school.

(2) The school district has been given written notification of the project not less than 30 days prior to the proposed certification of the environmental impact report or approval of the negative declaration.

(b) As used in this section, the following definitions apply:

(1) "Extremely hazardous substance" means an extremely hazardous substance as defined pursuant to paragraph (2) of subdivision (g) of Section 25532 of the Health and Safety Code.

(2) "Hazardous air emissions" means emissions into the ambient air of air contaminants that have been identified as a toxic air contaminant by the State Air Resources Board or by the air pollution control officer for the jurisdiction in which the project is located. As determined by the air pollution control officer, hazardous air emissions also means emissions into the ambient air of a substance identified in subdivisions (a) to (f), inclusive, of Section 44321 of the Health and Safety Code.

21151.5. (a) (1) For projects described in subdivision (c) of Section 21065, each local agency shall establish, by ordinance or resolution, time limits that do not exceed the following:

(A) One year for completing and certifying environmental impact reports.

(B) One hundred eighty days for completing and adopting negative declarations.

(2) The time limits specified in paragraph (1) shall apply only to hose circumstances in which the local agency is the lead agency for a project. These ordinances or resolutions may establish different time limits for different types or classes of projects and different types of environmental impact reports, but all limits shall be measured from the date on which an application requesting approval of the project is received and accepted as complete by the local agency.

(3) No application for a project may be deemed incomplete for lack of a waiver of time periods prescribed by local ordinance or resolution.

(4) The ordinances or resolutions required by this section may provide for a reasonable extension of the time period in the event that compelling circumstances justify additional time and the project applicant consents thereto.

(b) If a draft environmental impact report, environmental impact report, or focused environmental impact report is prepared under a contract to a local agency, the contract shall be executed within 45 days from the date on which the local agency sends a notice of preparation pursuant to Section 21080.4. The local agency may take longer to execute the contract if the project applicant and the local agency mutually agree to an extension of the time limit provided by this subdivision.

21151.7. Notwithstanding any other provision of law, a lead agency shall prepare or cause to be prepared by contract, and certify the completion of, an environmental impact report for any open-pit mining operation that is subject to the permit requirements or reclamation plan requirements of the Surface Mining and Reclamation Act of 1975 (Chapter 9 (commencing with Section 2710) of Division 2) and utilizes a cyanide heap-leaching process for the purpose of producing gold or other metallic minerals.

21151.8. (a) An environmental impact report shall not be certified or a negative declaration shall not be approved for a project involving the purchase of a school site or the construction of a new elementary or secondary school by a school district unless all of the following occur:

(1) The environmental impact report or negative declaration includes information that is needed to determine if the property proposed to be purchased, or to be constructed upon, is any of the following:

(A) The site of a current or former hazardous waste disposal site or solid waste disposal site and, if so, whether the wastes have been removed.

(B) A hazardous substance release site identified by the Department of Toxic Substances Control in a current list adopted pursuant to Section 25356 of the Health and Safety Code for removal or remedial action pursuant to Chapter 6.8 (commencing with Section 25300) of Division 20 of the Health and Safety Code.

(C) A site that contains one or more pipelines, situated underground or aboveground, that carries hazardous substances, extremely hazardous substances, or hazardous wastes, unless the pipeline is a natural gas line that is used only to supply natural gas to that school or neighborhood, or other nearby schools.

(D) A site that is within 500 feet of the edge of the closest traffic lane of a freeway or other busy traffic corridor.

(2) (A) The school district, as the lead agency, in preparing the environmental impact report or negative declaration has notified in writing and consulted with the administering agency in which the proposed schoolsite is located, pursuant to Section 2735.3 of Title 19 of the California Code of Regulations, and with any air pollution control district or air quality management district having jurisdiction in the area, to identify both permitted and nonpermitted facilities within that district's authority, including, but not limited to, freeways and busy traffic corridors, large agricultural operations, and railyards, within one-fourth of a mile of the proposed schoolsite, that might reasonably be anticipated to emit hazardous emissions or handle hazardous or extremely hazardous substances or waste. The notification by the school district, as the lead agency, shall include a list of the locations for which information is sought.

(B) Each administering agency, air pollution control district, or air quality management district receiving written notification from a lead agency to identify facilities pursuant to subparagraph (A) shall provide the requested information and provide a written response to the lead agency within 30 days of receiving the notification. The environmental impact report or negative declaration shall be conclusively presumed to comply with subparagraph (A) as to the area of responsibility of an agency that does not respond within 30 days.

(C) If the school district, as a lead agency, has carried out the consultation required by subparagraph (A), the environmental impact report or the negative declaration shall be conclusively presumed to comply with subparagraph (A), notwithstanding any failure of the consultation to identify an existing facility or other pollution source specified in subparagraph (A).

(3) The governing board of the school district makes one of the following written findings:

(A) Consultation identified no facilities of this type or other significant pollution sources specified in paragraph (2).

(B) The facilities or other pollution sources specified in paragraph (2) exist, but one of the following conditions applies:

(i) The health risks from the facilities or other pollution sources do not and will not constitute an actual or potential endangerment of public health to persons who would attend or be employed at the proposed school.

(ii) Corrective measures required under an existing order by another agency having jurisdiction over the facilities or other pollution sources will, before the school is occupied, result in the mitigation of all chronic or accidental hazardous air emissions to levels that do not constitute an actual or potential endangerment of public health to persons who would attend or be employed at the proposed school. If the governing board makes a finding pursuant to this clause, it shall also make a subsequent finding, prior to occupancy of the school, that the emissions have been so mitigated.

(iii) For a schoolsite with a boundary that is within 500 feet of the edge of the closest traffic lane of a freeway or other busy traffic corridor, the governing board of the school district determines, through analysis pursuant to paragraph (2) of subdivision (b) of Section 44360 of the Health and Safety Code, based on appropriate air dispersion modeling, and after considering any potential mitigation measures, that the air quality at the proposed site is such that neither short-term nor long-term exposure poses significant health risks to pupils.

(C) The facilities or other pollution sources specified in paragraph (2) exist, but conditions in clause (i), (ii), or (iii) of subparagraph (B) cannot be met, and the school district is unable to locate an alternative site that is suitable due to a severe shortage of sites that meet the requirements in subdivision (a) of Section 17213 of the Education Code. If the governing board makes this finding, the governing board shall adopt a statement of overriding considerations pursuant to Section 15093 of Title 14 of the California Code of Regulations.

(b) As used in this section, the following definitions shall apply:

(1) "Hazardous substance" means any substance defined in Section 25316 of the Health and Safety Code.

(2) "Extremely hazardous substances" means an extremely hazardous substance as defined pursuant to paragraph (2) of subdivision (g) of Section 25532 of the Health and Safety Code.

(3) "Hazardous waste" means any waste defined in Section 25117 of the Health and Safety Code.

(4) "Hazardous waste disposal site" means any site defined in Section 25114 of the Health and Safety Code.

(5) "Hazardous air emissions" means emissions into the ambient air of air contaminants that have been identified as a toxic air contaminant by the State Air Resources Board or by the air pollution control officer for the jurisdiction in which the project is located. As determined by the air pollution control officer, hazardous air emissions also means emissions into the ambient air from any substances identified in subdivisions (a) to (f), inclusive, of Section 44321 of the Health and Safety Code.

(6) "Administering agency" means an agency authorized pursuant to Section 25502 of the Health and Safety Code to implement and enforce Chapter 6.95 (commencing with Section 25500) of Division 20 of the Health and Safety Code.

(7) "Handle" means handle as defined in Article 1 (commencing with Section 25500) of Chapter 6.95 of Division 20 of the Health and Safety Code.

(8) "Facilities" means any source with a potential to use, generate, emit, or discharge hazardous air pollutants, including, but not limited to, pollutants that meet the definition of a hazardous substance, and whose process or operation is identified as an emission source pursuant to the most recent list of source categories published by the California Air Resources Board.

(9) "Freeway or other busy traffic corridors" means those roadways that, on an average day, have traffic in excess of 50,000 vehicles in a rural area, as defined in Section 50101 of the Health and Safety Code, and 100,000 vehicles in an urban area, as defined in Section 50104.7 of the Health and Safety Code.

21151.9. Whenever a city or county determines that a project, as defined in Section 10912 of the Water Code, is subject to this division, it shall comply with Part 2.10 (commencing with Section 10910) of Division 6 of the Water Code.

21152. (a) Whenever a local agency approves or determines to carry out a project that is subject to this division, the local agency shall file notice of the approval or the determination within five working days after the approval or determination becomes final, with the county clerk of each county in which the project will be located. The notice shall identify the person or persons in subdivision (b) or (c) of Section 21065, as reflected in the agency's record of proceedings, and indicate the determination of the local agency whether the project will, or will not, have a significant effect on the environment and shall indicate whether an environmental impact report has been prepared pursuant to this division. The notice shall also include certification that the final environmental impact report, if one was prepared, together with comments and responses, is available to the general public.

(b) Whenever a local agency determines that a project is not subject to this division pursuant to subdivision (b) of Section 21080 or pursuant to Section 21172, and the local agency approves or determines to carry out the project, the local agency or the person specified in subdivision (b) or (c) of Section 21065 may file a notice of the determination with the county clerk of each county in which the project will be located. A notice filed pursuant to this subdivision shall identify the person or persons in subdivision (b) or (c) of Section 21065, as reflected in the agency's record of proceedings. A notice filed pursuant to this subdivision by a person specified in subdivision (b) or (c) of Section 21065 shall have a certificate of determination attached to it issued by the local agency responsible for making the determination that the project is not subject to this division pursuant to subdivision (b) of Section 21080 or Section 21172. The certificate of determination may be in the form of a certified copy of an existing document or record of the local agency.

(c) All notices filed pursuant to this section shall be available for public inspection, and shall be posted within 24 hours of receipt in the office of the county clerk. A notice shall remain posted for a period of 30 days. Thereafter, the clerk shall return the notice to the local agency with a notation of the period it was posted. The local agency shall retain the notice for not less than 12 months.

21152.1. (a) When a local agency determines that a project is not subject to this division pursuant to Section 21159.22, 21159.23, or 21159.24, and it approves or determines to carry out that project, he local agency or the person specified in subdivision (b) or (c) of Section 21065, shall file notice of the determination with the Office of Planning and Research.

(b) All notices filed pursuant to this section shall be available for public inspection, and a list of these notices shall be posted on a weekly basis in the Office of Planning and Research. Each list shall remain posted for a period of 30 days.

(c) Failure to file the notice required by this section does not affect the validity of a project.

(d) Nothing in this section affects the time limitations contained in Section 21167.

21153. (a) Prior to completing an environmental impact report, every local lead agency shall consult with, and obtain comments from, each responsible agency, trustee agency, any public agency that has jurisdiction by law with respect to the project, and any city or county that borders on a city or county within which the project is located unless otherwise designated annually by agreement between the local lead agency and the city or county, and may consult with any person who has special expertise with respect to any environmental impact involved. In the case of a project described in subdivision (c) of Section 21065, the local lead agency shall, upon the request of the project applicant, provide for early consultation to identify the range of actions, alternatives, mitigation measures, and significant effects to be analyzed in depth in the environmental impact report. The local lead agency may consult with persons identified by the project applicant who the applicant believes will be concerned with the environmental effects of the project and may consult with members of the public who have made written request to be consulted on the project. A request by the project applicant for early consultation shall be made not later than 30 days after the date that the determination required by Section 21080.1 was made with respect to the project. The local lead agency may charge and collect a fee from the project applicant in an amount that does not exceed the actual costs of the consultations.

(b) In the case of a project described in subdivision (a) of Section 21065, the lead agency may provide for early consultation to identify the range of actions, alternatives, mitigation measures, and significant effects to be analyzed in depth in the environmental impact report. At the request of the lead agency, the Office of Planning and Research shall ensure that each responsible agency, and any public agency that has jurisdiction by law with respect to the project, is notified regarding any early consultation.

(c) A responsible agency or other public agency shall only make substantive comments regarding those activities involved in a project that are within an area of expertise of the agency or that are required to be carried out or approved by the agency. Those comments shall be supported by specific documentation.

21154. Whenever any state agency, board, or commission issues an order which requires a local agency to carry out a project which may have a significant effect on the environment, any environmental impact report which the local agency may prepare shall be limited to consideration of those factors and alternatives which will not conflict with such order.

Chapter 4.2. Implementation of Sustainable Communities Strategy

21155. (a) This chapter applies only to a transit priority project that is consistent with the general use designation, density, building intensity, and applicable policies specified for the project area in either a sustainable communities strategy or an alternative planning strategy, for which the State Air Resources Board, pursuant to subparagraph (H) of paragraph (2) of subdivision (b) of Section 65080 of the Government Code, has accepted a metropolitan planning organization's determination that the sustainable communities strategy or the alternative planning strategy would, if implemented, achieve the greenhouse gas emission reduction targets.

(b) For purposes of this chapter, a transit priority project shall (1) contain at least 50 percent residential use, based on total building square footage and, if the project contains between 26 percent and 50 percent nonresidential uses, a floor area ratio of not less than 0.75; (2) provide a minimum net density of at least 20 dwelling units per acre; and (3) be within one-half mile of a major transit stop or high-quality transit corridor included in a regional transportation plan. A major transit stop is as defined in Section 21064.3, except that, for purposes of this section, it also includes major transit stops that are included in the applicable regional transportation plan. For purposes of this section, a high-quality transit corridor means a corridor with fixed route bus service with service intervals no longer than 15 minutes during peak commute hours. A project shall be considered to be within one-half mile of a major transit stop or high-quality transit corridor if all parcels within the project have no more than 25 percent of their area farther than one-half mile from the stop or corridor and if not more than 10 percent of the residential units or 100 units, whichever is less, in the project are farther than one-half mile from the stop or corridor.

21155.1. If the legislative body finds, after conducting a public hearing, that a transit priority project meets all of the requirements of subdivisions (a) and (b) and one of the requirements of subdivision (c), the transit priority project is declared to be a sustainable communities project and shall be exempt from this division.

(a) The transit priority project complies with all of the following environmental criteria:

(1) The transit priority project and other projects approved prior to the approval of the transit priority project but not yet built can be adequately served by existing utilities, and the transit priority project applicant has paid, or has committed to pay, all applicable in-lieu or development fees.

(2) (A) The site of the transit priority project does not contain wetlands or riparian areas and does not have significant value as a wildlife habitat, and the transit priority project does not harm any species protected by the federal Endangered Species Act of 1973 (16 U.S.C. Sec. 1531 et seq.), the Native Plant Protection Act (Chapter 10 (commencing with Section 1900) of Division 2 of the Fish and Game Code), or the California Endangered Species Act (Chapter 1.5 (commencing with Section 2050) of Division 3 of the Fish and Game Code), and the project does not cause the destruction or removal of any species protected by a local ordinance in effect at the time the application for the project was deemed complete.

(B) For the purposes of this paragraph, "wetlands" has the same meaning as in the United States Fish and Wildlife Service Manual, Part 660 FW 2 (June 21, 1993).

(C) For the purposes of this paragraph:

(i) "Riparian areas" means those areas transitional between terrestrial and aquatic ecosystems and that are distinguished by gradients in biophysical conditions, ecological processes, and biota. A riparian area is an area through which surface and subsurface hydrology connect waterbodies with their adjacent uplands. A riparian area includes those portions of terrestrial ecosystems that significantly influence exchanges of energy and matter with aquatic ecosystems. A riparian area is adjacent to perennial, intermittent, and ephemeral streams, lakes, and estuarine-marine shorelines.

(ii) "Wildlife habitat" means the ecological communities upon which wild animals, birds, plants, fish, amphibians, and invertebrates depend for their conservation and protection.

(iii) Habitat of "significant value" includes wildlife habitat of national, statewide, regional, or local importance; habitat for species protected by the federal Endangered Species Act of 1973 (16 U.S.C. Sec. 1531, et seq.), the California Endangered Species Act (Chapter 1.5 (commencing with Section 2050) of Division 3 of the Fish and Game Code), or the Native Plant Protection Act (Chapter 10 (commencing with Section 1900) of Division 2 of the Fish and Game Code); habitat identified as candidate, fully protected, sensitive, or species of special status by local, state, or federal agencies; or habitat essential to the movement of resident or migratory wildlife.

(3) The site of the transit priority project is not included on any list of facilities and sites compiled pursuant to Section 65962.5 of the Government Code.

(4) The site of the transit priority project is subject to a preliminary endangerment assessment prepared by a registered environmental assessor to determine the existence of any release of a hazardous substance on the site and to determine the potential for exposure of future occupants to significant health hazards from any nearby property or activity.

(A) If a release of a hazardous substance is found to exist on the site, the release shall be removed or any significant effects of the release shall be mitigated to a level of insignificance in compliance with state and federal requirements.

(B) If a potential for exposure to significant hazards from surrounding properties or activities is found to exist, the effects of the potential exposure shall be mitigated to a level of insignificance in compliance with state and federal requirements.

(5) The transit priority project does not have a significant effect on historical resources pursuant to Section 21084.1.

(6) The transit priority project site is not subject to any of the following:

(A) A wildland fire hazard, as determined by the Department of Forestry and Fire Protection, unless the applicable general plan or zoning ordinance contains provisions to mitigate the risk of a wildland fire hazard.

(B) An unusually high risk of fire or explosion from materials stored or used on nearby properties.

(C) Risk of a public health exposure at a level that would exceed the standards established by any state or federal agency.

(D) Seismic risk as a result of being within a delineated earthquake fault zone, as determined pursuant to Section 2622, or a seismic hazard zone, as determined pursuant to Section 2696, unless the applicable general plan or zoning ordinance contains provisions to mitigate the risk of an earthquake fault or seismic hazard zone.

(E) Landslide hazard, flood plain, flood way, or restriction zone, unless the applicable general plan or zoning ordinance contains provisions to mitigate the risk of a landslide or flood.

(7) The transit priority project site is not located on developed open space.

(A) For the purposes of this paragraph, "developed open space" means land that meets all of the following criteria:

(i) Is publicly owned, or financed in whole or in part by public funds.

(ii) Is generally open to, and available for use by, the public.

(iii) Is predominantly lacking in structural development other than structures associated with open spaces, including, but not limited to, playgrounds, swimming pools, ballfields, enclosed child play areas, and picnic facilities.

(B) For the purposes of this paragraph, "developed open space" includes land that has been designated for acquisition by a public agency for developed open space, but does not include lands acquired with public funds dedicated to the acquisition of land for housing purposes.

(8) The buildings in the transit priority project are 15 percent more energy efficient than required by

Chapter 6 of Title 24 of the California Code of Regulations and the buildings and landscaping are designed to achieve 25 percent less water usage than the average household use in the region.

(b) The transit priority project meets all of the following land use criteria:
  (1) The site of the transit priority project is not more than eight acres in total area.
  (2) The transit priority project does not contain more than 200 residential units.
  (3) The transit priority project does not result in any net loss in the number of affordable housing units within the project area.
  (4) The transit priority project does not include any single level building that exceeds 75,000 square feet.
  (5) Any applicable mitigation measures or performance standards or criteria set forth in the prior environmental impact reports, and adopted in findings, have been or will be incorporated into the transit priority project.
  (6) The transit priority project is determined not to conflict with nearby operating industrial uses.
  (7) The transit priority project is located within one-half mile of a rail transit station or a ferry terminal included in a regional transportation plan or within one-quarter mile of a high-quality transit corridor included in a regional transportation plan.

(c) The transit priority project meets at least one of the following three criteria:
  (1) The transit priority project meets both of the following:
    (A) At least 20 percent of the housing will be sold to families of moderate income, or not less than 10 percent of the housing will be rented to families of low income, or not less than 5 percent of the housing is rented to families of very low income.
    (B) The transit priority project developer provides sufficient legal commitments to the appropriate local agency to ensure the continued availability and use of the housing units for very low, low-, and moderate-income households at monthly housing costs with an affordable housing cost or affordable rent, as defined in Section 50052.5 or 50053 of the Health and Safety Code, respectively, for the period required by the applicable financing. Rental units shall be affordable for at least 55 years. Ownership units shall be subject to resale restrictions or equity sharing requirements for at least 30 years.
  (2) The transit priority project developer has paid or will pay in-lieu fees pursuant to a local ordinance in an amount sufficient to result in the development of an equivalent number of units that would otherwise be required pursuant to paragraph (1).
  (3) The transit priority project provides public open space equal to or greater than five acres per 1,000 residents of the project.

21155.2. (a) A transit priority project that has incorporated all feasible mitigation measures, performance standards, or criteria set forth in the prior applicable environmental impact reports and adopted in findings made pursuant to Section 21081, shall be eligible for either the provisions of subdivision (b) or (c).

(b) A transit priority project that satisfies the requirements of subdivision (a) may be reviewed through a sustainable communities environmental assessment as follows:
  (1) An initial study shall be prepared to identify all significant or potentially significant impacts of the transit priority project, other than those which do not need to be reviewed pursuant to Section 21159.28 based on substantial evidence in light of the whole record. The initial study shall identify any cumulative effects that have been adequately addressed and mitigated pursuant to the requirements of this division in prior applicable certified environmental impact reports. Where the lead agency determines that a cumulative effect has been adequately addressed and mitigated, that cumulative effect shall not be treated as cumulatively considerable for the purposes of this subdivision.
  (2) The sustainable communities environmental assessment shall contain measures that either avoid or mitigate to a level of insignificance all potentially significant or significant effects of the project required to be identified in the initial study.
  (3) A draft of the sustainable communities environmental assessment shall be circulated for public comment for a period of not less than 30 days. Notice shall be provided in the same manner as required for an environmental impact report pursuant to Section 21092.
  (4) Prior to acting on the sustainable communities environmental assessment, the lead agency shall consider all comments received.
  (5) A sustainable communities environmental assessment may be approved by the lead agency after conducting a public hearing, reviewing the comments received, and finding that:
    (A) All potentially significant or significant effects required to be identified in the initial study have been identified and analyzed.
    (B) With respect to each significant effect on the environment required to be identified in the initial study, either of the following apply:
      (i) Changes or alterations have been required in or incorporated into the project that avoid or mitigate the significant effects to a level of insignificance.
      (ii) Those changes or alterations are within the responsibility and jurisdiction of another public agency and have been, or can and should be, adopted by that other agency.
  (6) The legislative body of the lead agency shall conduct the public hearing or a planning commission may conduct the public hearing if local ordinances allow a direct appeal of approval of a document prepared pursuant to this division to the legislative body subject to a fee not to exceed five hundred dollars ($500).
  (7) The lead agency's decision to review and approve a transit priority project with a sustainable communities environmental assessment shall be reviewed under the substantial evidence standard.

(c) A transit priority project that satisfies the requirements of subdivision (a) may be reviewed by an environmental impact report that complies with all of the following:
  (1) An initial study shall be prepared to identify all significant or potentially significant effects of the transit priority project other than those that do not need to be reviewed pursuant to Section 21159.28 based upon substantial evidence in light of the whole record. The initial study shall identify any cumulative effects that have been adequately addressed and mitigated pursuant to the requirements of this division in prior applicable certified environmental impact reports. Where the lead agency determines that a cumulative effect has been adequately addressed and mitigated, that cumulative effect shall not be treated as cumulatively considerable for the purposes of this subdivision.
  (2) An environmental impact report prepared pursuant to this subdivision need only address the significant or potentially significant effects of the transit priority project on the environment identified pursuant to paragraph (1). It is not required to analyze off-site alternatives to the transit priority project. It shall otherwise comply with the requirements of this division.

21155.3. (a) The legislative body of a local jurisdiction may adopt traffic mitigation measures that would apply to transit priority projects. These measures shall be adopted or amended after a public hearing and may include requirements for the installation of traffic control improvements, street or road improvements, and contributions to road improvement or transit funds, transit passes for future residents, or other measures that will avoid or mitigate the traffic impacts of those transit priority projects.

(b) (1) A transit priority project that is seeking a discretionary approval is not required to comply with any additional mitigation measures required by paragraph (1) or (2) of subdivision (a) of Section 21081, for the traffic impacts of that project on intersections, streets, highways, freeways, or mass transit, if the local jurisdiction issuing that discretionary approval has adopted traffic mitigation measures in accordance with this section.
  (2) Paragraph (1) does not restrict the authority of a local jurisdiction to adopt feasible mitigation measures with respect to the effects of a project on public health or on pedestrian or bicycle safety.

(c) The legislative body shall review its traffic mitigation measures and update them as needed at least every five years.

Chapter 4.5. Streamlined Environmental Review

Article 1. Findings

21156. It is the intent of the Legislature in enacting this chapter that a master environmental impact report shall evaluate the cumulative impacts, growth inducing impacts, and irreversible significant effects on the environment of subsequent projects to the greatest extent feasible. The Legislature further intends that the environmental review of subsequent projects be substantially reduced to the extent that the project impacts have been reviewed and appropriate mitigation measures are set forth in a certified master environmental impact report.

Article 2. Master Environmental Impact Report

21157. (a) A master environmental impact report may be prepared for any one of the following projects:
  (1) A general plan, element, general plan amendment, or specific plan.
  (2) A project that consists of smaller individual projects that will be carried out in phases.
  (3) A rule or regulation that will be implemented by subsequent projects.
  (4) A project that will be carried out or approved pursuant to a development agreement.
  (5) A public or private project that will be carried out or approved pursuant to, or in furtherance of, a redevelopment plan.

(6) A state highway project or mass transit project that will be subject to multiple stages of review or approval.
(7) A regional transportation plan or congestion management plan.
(8) A plan proposed by a local agency for the reuse of a federal military base or reservation that has been closed or that is proposed for closure.
(9) Regulations adopted by the Fish and Game Commission for the regulation of hunting and fishing.
(10) A plan for district projects to be undertaken by a school district, that also complies with applicable school facilities requirements, including, but not limited to, the requirements of Chapter 12.5 (commencing with Section 17070.10) of Part 10 of, and Article 1 (commencing with Section 17210) of Chapter 1 of Part 10.5 of, Division 1 of Title 1 of the Education Code.

(b) When a lead agency prepares a master environmental impact report, the document shall include all of the following:
(1) A detailed statement as required by Section 21100.
(2) A description of anticipated subsequent projects that would be within the scope of the master environmental impact report, that contains sufficient information with regard to the kind, size, intensity, and location of the subsequent projects, including, but not limited to, all of the following:
(A) The specific type of project anticipated to be undertaken.
(B) The maximum and minimum intensity of any anticipated subsequent project, such as the number of residences in a residential development, and, with regard to a public works facility, its anticipated capacity and service area.
(C) The anticipated location and alternative locations for any development projects.
(D) A capital outlay or capital improvement program, or other scheduling or implementing device that governs the submission and approval of subsequent projects.
(3) A description of potential impacts of anticipated subsequent projects for which there is not sufficient information reasonably available to support a full assessment of potential impacts in the master environmental impact report. This description shall not be construed as a limitation on the impacts which may be considered in a focused environmental impact report.

(c) Lead agencies may develop and implement a fee program in accordance with applicable provisions of law to generate the revenue necessary to prepare a master environmental impact report.

21157.1. The preparation and certification of a master environmental impact report, if prepared and certified consistent with this division, may allow for the limited review of subsequent projects that were described in the master environmental impact report as being within the scope of the report, in accordance with the following requirements:
(a) The lead agency for a subsequent project shall be the lead agency or any responsible agency identified in the master environmental impact report.
(b) The lead agency shall prepare an initial study on any proposed subsequent project. This initial study shall analyze whether the subsequent project may cause any significant effect on the environment that was not examined in the master environmental impact report and whether the subsequent project was described in the master environmental impact report as being within the scope of the report.
(c) If the lead agency, based on the initial study, determines that a proposed subsequent project will have no additional significant effect on the environment, as defined in subdivision (d) of Section 21158, that was not identified in the master environmental impact report and that no new or additional mitigation measures or alternatives may be required, the lead agency shall make a written finding based upon the information contained in the initial study that the subsequent project is within the scope of the project covered by the master environmental impact report. No new environmental document nor findings pursuant to Section 21081 shall be required by this division. Prior to approving or carrying out the proposed subsequent project, the lead agency shall provide notice of this fact pursuant to Section 21092 and incorporate all feasible mitigation measures or feasible alternatives set forth in the master environmental impact report which are appropriate to the project. Whenever a lead agency approves or determines to carry out any subsequent project pursuant to this section, it shall file a notice pursuant to Section 21108 or 21152.
(d) Where a lead agency cannot make the findings required in subdivision (c), the lead agency shall prepare, pursuant to Section 21157.7, either a mitigated negative declaration or environmental impact report.

21157.5. (a) A proposed mitigated negative declaration shall be prepared for any proposed subsequent project if both of the following occur:
(1) An initial study has identified potentially new or additional significant effects on the environment that were not analyzed in the master environmental impact report.
(2) Feasible mitigation measures or alternatives will be incorporated to revise the proposed subsequent project, before the negative declaration is released for public review, in order to avoid the effects or mitigate the effects to a point where clearly no significant effect on the environment will occur.
(b) If there is substantial evidence in light of the whole record before the lead agency that the proposed subsequent project may have a significant effect on the environment and a mitigated negative declaration is not prepared, the lead agency shall prepare an environmental impact report or a focused environmental impact report pursuant to Section 21158.

21157.6. (a) The master environmental impact report shall not be used for the purposes of this chapter if either of the following has occurred:
(1) The certification of the master environmental impact report occurred more than five years prior to the filing of an application for the subsequent project.
(2) The filing of an application for the subsequent project occurs following the certification of the master environmental impact report, and the approval of a project that was not described in the master environmental impact report, may affect the adequacy of the environmental review in the master environmental impact report for any subsequent project.
(b) A master environmental impact report that was certified more than five years prior to the filing of an application for the subsequent project may be used for purposes of this chapter to review a subsequent project that was described in the master environmental impact report if the lead agency reviews the adequacy of the master environmental impact report and does either of the following:
(1) Finds that no substantial changes have occurred with respect to the circumstances under which the master environmental impact report was certified or that no new information, which was not known and could not have been known at the time that the master environmental impact report was certified as complete, has become available.
(2) Prepares an initial study and, pursuant to the findings of the initial study, does either of the following:
(A) Certifies a subsequent or supplemental environmental impact report that has been either incorporated into the previously certified master environmental impact report or references any deletions, additions, or any other modifications to the previously certified master environmental impact report.
(B) Approves a mitigated negative declaration that addresses substantial changes that have occurred with respect to the circumstances under which the master environmental impact report was certified or the new information that was not known and could not have been known at the time the master environmental impact report was certified.

21157.7. (a) For purposes of this section, a master environmental impact report is a document prepared in accordance with subdivision (c) for the projects described in subdivision (b) that, upon certification, is followed by review of subsequent projects as provided in Sections 21157.1 and 21157.5.
(b) A master environmental impact report may be prepared for a plan adopted by the Department of Transportation for improvements to regional segments of Highway 99 funded pursuant to subdivision (b) of Section 8879.23 of the Government Code, to streamline, coordinate, and improve environmental review.
(c) The report shall include all of the following:
(1) A detailed statement as required by Section 21100.
(2) A description of the anticipated highway improvements along Highway 99 that would be within the scope of the master environmental impact report, that contains sufficient information about all phases of the Highway 99 construction activities, including, but not limited to, all of the following:
(A) The specific types of improvements that will be undertaken.
(B) The anticipated location and alternative locations for any of the Highway 99 improvements, including overpasses, bridges, railroad crossings, and interchanges.
(C) A capital outlay or capital improvement program, or other scheduling or implementing device that governs the construction activities associated with the Highway 99 improvements.
(d) The Department of Transportation may communicate, coordinate, and consult with the Resources Agency, Wildlife Conservation Board, Department of Fish and Game, Department of Conservation, and other appropriate federal, state, or local governments, including interested stakeholders, to consider and implement mitigation requirements on a regional basis for the projects described in subdivision (b). This may include both of the following:

(1) Identification of priority areas for mitigation, using information from these agencies and departments as well as from other sources.
(2) Utilization of existing conservation programs of the agencies or departments identified in this subdivision, if mitigation under those programs for improvements under this section does not supplant mitigation for a project.

(e) The Department of Transportation may execute an agreement, memorandum of understanding, or other similar instrument to memorialize its understanding of any communication, coordination, or implementation activities with other state agencies for the purposes of meeting mitigation requirements on a regional basis.

(f) Notwithstanding any other provision of law, nothing in this section is intended to interfere with or prevent the existing authority of an agency or department to carry out its programs, projects, or responsibilities to identify, review, approve, deny, or implement any mitigation requirements, and nothing in this section shall be construed as a limitation on mitigation requirements for the project, or a limitation on compliance with requirements under this division or any other provision of law.

(g) Notwithstanding Section 21157.6, the master environmental impact report shall not be used for the purposes of this section, if the certification of the master environmental impact report occurred more than seven years prior to the filing of an application for the subsequent project.

Article 3. Focused Environmental Impact Report

21158. (a) A focused environmental impact report is an environmental impact report on a subsequent project identified in a master environmental impact report. A focused environmental impact report may be utilized only if the lead agency finds that the analysis in the master environmental impact report of cumulative impacts, growth inducing impacts, and irreversible significant effects on the environment is adequate for the subsequent project. The focused environmental impact report shall incorporate, by reference, the master environmental impact report and analyze only the subsequent project's additional significant effects on the environment, as defined in subdivision (d), and any new or additional mitigation measures or alternatives that were not identified and analyzed by the master environmental impact report.

(b) The focused environmental impact report need not examine those effects which the lead agency finds were one of the following:
(1) Mitigated or avoided pursuant to paragraph (1) of subdivision (a) of Section 21081 as a result of mitigation measures identified in the master environmental impact report which will be required as part of the approval of the subsequent project.
(2) Examined at a sufficient level of detail in the master environmental impact report to enable those significant environmental effects to be mitigated or avoided by specific revisions to the project, the imposition of conditions, or by other means in connection with the approval of the subsequent project.
(3) Subject to a finding pursuant to paragraph (2) of subdivision (a) of Section 21081.

(c) A focused environmental impact report on any subsequent project shall analyze any significant effects on the environment where substantial new or additional information shows that the adverse environmental impact may be more significant than was described in the master environmental impact report. The substantial new or additional information may also show that mitigation measures or alternatives identified in the master environmental impact report, which were previously determined to be infeasible, are feasible and will avoid or reduce the significant effects on the environment of the subsequent project to a level of insignificance.

(d) For purposes of this chapter, "additional significant effects on the environment" are those project specific effects on the environment which were not addressed as significant effects on the environment in the master environmental impact report.

(e) Nothing in this chapter is intended to limit or abridge the ability of a lead agency to focus upon the issues that are ripe for decision at each level of environmental review, or to exclude duplicative analysis of environmental effects examined in previous environmental impact reports pursuant to Section 21093.

21158.1. When a lead agency is required to prepare an environmental impact report pursuant to subdivision (d) of Section 21157.1 or is authorized to prepare a focused environmental impact report pursuant to Section 21158, the lead agency may not rely on subdivision (a) of Section 21080.5 for that purpose even though the lead agency's regulatory program is otherwise certified in accordance with Section 21080.5.

21158.5. (a) Where a project consists of multiple-family residential development of not more than 100 units or a residential and commercial or retail mixed-use development of not more than 100,000 square feet which complies with all of the following, a focused environmental impact report shall be prepared, notwithstanding that the project was not identified in a master environmental impact report:
(1) Is consistent with a general plan, specific plan, community plan, or zoning ordinance for which an environmental impact report was prepared within five years of the certification of the focused environmental impact report.
(2) The lead agency cannot make the finding described in subdivision (c) of Section 21157.1, a negative declaration or mitigated negative declaration cannot be prepared pursuant to Section 21080, 21157.5, or 21158, and Section 21166 does not apply.
(3) Meets one or more of the following conditions:
(A) The parcel on which the project is to be developed is surrounded by immediately contiguous urban development.
(B) The parcel on which the project is to be developed has been previously developed with urban uses.
(C) The parcel on which the project is to be developed is within one-half mile of an existing rail transit station.

(b) A focused environmental impact report prepared pursuant to this section shall be limited to a discussion of potentially significant effects on the environment specific to the project, or which substantial new information shows will be more significant than described in the prior environmental impact report. No discussion shall be required of alternatives to the project, cumulative impacts of the project, or the growth inducing impacts of the project.

Article 4. Expedited Environmental Review for Environmental Mandated Projects

21159. (a) An agency listed in Section 21159.4 shall perform, at the time of the adoption of a rule or regulation requiring the installation of pollution control equipment, or a performance standard or treatment requirement, including a rule or regulation that requires the installation of pollution control equipment or a performance standard or treatment requirement pursuant to the California Global Warming Solutions Act of 2006 (Division 25.5 (commencing with Section 38500) of the Health and Safety Code), an environmental analysis of the reasonably foreseeable methods of compliance. In the preparation of this analysis, the agency may utilize numerical ranges or averages where specific data is not available; however, the agency shall not be required to engage in speculation or conjecture. The environmental analysis shall, at minimum, include all of the following:
(1) An analysis of the reasonably foreseeable environmental impacts of the methods of compliance.
(2) An analysis of reasonably foreseeable feasible mitigation measures.
(3) An analysis of reasonably foreseeable alternative means of compliance with the rule or regulation.
(4) For a rule or regulation that requires the installation of pollution control equipment adopted pursuant to the California Global Warming Solutions Act of 2006 (Division 25.5 (commencing with Section 38500) of the Health and Safety Code), the analysis shall also include reasonably foreseeable greenhouse gas emission impacts of compliance with the rule or regulation.

(b) The preparation of an environmental impact report at the time of adopting a rule or regulation pursuant to this division shall be deemed to satisfy the requirements of this section.

(c) The environmental analysis shall take into account a reasonable range of environmental, economic, and technical factors, population and geographic areas, and specific sites.

(d) This section does not require the agency to conduct a project-level analysis.

(e) For purposes of this article, the term "performance standard" includes process or raw material changes or product reformulation.

(f) This section is not intended, and may not be used, to delay the adoption of any rule or regulation for which an analysis is required to be performed pursuant to this section.

21159.1. (a) A focused environmental impact report may be utilized if a project meets all of the following requirements:
(1) The project consists solely of the installation of either of the following:
(A) Pollution control equipment required by a rule or regulation of an agency listed in subdivision (a) of Section 21159.4 and other components necessary to complete the installation of that equipment.
(B) Pollution control equipment and other components necessary to complete the installation of that equipment that reduces greenhouse gases required by a rule or regulation of an agency listed in Section 21159.4 pursuant to the California Global Warming Solutions Act of 2006 (Division 25.5 (commencing with Section 38500) of the Health and Safety Code).
(2) The agency certified an environmental impact report on the rule or regulation or reviewed it pursuant to a certified regulatory program, and, in either case, the review included an assessment of growth inducing impacts and cumulative impacts of, and alternatives to, the project.
(3) The environmental review required by paragraph (2) was completed within five years of certification of the focused environmental impact report.

(4) An environmental impact report is not required pursuant to Section 21166.

(b) The discussion of significant effects on the environment in the focused environmental impact report shall be limited to project-specific potentially significant effects on the environment of the project that were not discussed in the environmental analysis of the rule or regulation required pursuant to subdivision (a) of Section 21159. A discussion of growth-inducing impacts or cumulative impacts shall not be required in the focused environmental impact report, and the discussion of alternatives shall be limited to a discussion of alternative means of compliance, if any, with the rule or regulation.

21159.2. (a) If a project consists solely of compliance with a performance standard or treatment requirement imposed by an agency listed in Section 21159.4, the lead agency for the compliance project shall, to the greatest extent feasible, utilize the environmental analysis required pursuant to subdivision (a) of Section 21159 in the preparation of a negative declaration, mitigated negative declaration, or environmental impact report on the compliance project or in otherwise fulfilling its responsibilities under this division. The use of numerical averages or ranges in an environmental analysis shall not relieve a lead agency of its obligations under this division to identify and evaluate the environmental effects of a compliance project.

(b) If the lead agency determines that an environmental impact report on the compliance project is required, the lead agency shall prepare an environmental impact report which addresses only the project-specific issues related to the compliance project or other issues that were not discussed in sufficient detail in the environmental analysis to enable the lead agency to fulfill its responsibilities under Section 21100 or 21151, as applicable. The mitigation measures imposed by the lead agency for the project shall relate only to the significant effects on the environment to be mitigated. The discussion of alternatives shall be limited to a discussion of alternative means of compliance, if any, with the rule or regulation.

21159.3. In the preparation of any environmental impact report pursuant to Section 21159.1 or 21159.2, the following deadlines shall apply:

(a) A lead agency shall determine whether an environmental impact report should be prepared within 30 days of its determination that the application for the project is complete.

(b) If the environmental impact report will be prepared under contract to the lead agency pursuant to Section 21082.1, the lead agency shall issue a request for proposals for preparation of the environmental impact report as soon as it has enough information to prepare a request for proposals, and in any event, not later than 30 days after the time for response to the notice of preparation has expired. The contract shall be awarded within 30 days of the response date for the request for proposals.

21159.4. (a) This article shall apply to all of the following agencies:

(1) The State Air Resources Board.
(2) A district as defined in Section 39025 of the Health and Safety Code.
(3) The State Water Resources Control Board.
(4) A California regional water quality control board.
(5) The Department of Toxic Substances Control.
(6) The Department of Resources Recycling and Recovery.

(b) This article shall apply to the State Energy Resources Conservation and Development Commission and the California Public Utilities Commission for rules and regulations requiring the installation of pollution control equipment adopted pursuant to the California Global Warming Solutions Act of 2006 (Division 25.5 (commencing with Section 38500) of the Health and Safety Code).

Article 5. Public Assistance Program

21159.9. The Office of Planning and Research shall implement, utilizing existing resources, a public assistance and information program, to ensure efficient and effective implementation of this division, to do all of the following:

(a) Establish a public education and training program for planners, developers, and other interested parties to assist them in implementing this division.

(b) Establish and maintain a data base to assist in the preparation of environmental documents.

(c) Establish and maintain a central repository for the collection, storage, retrieval, and dissemination of notices of exemption, notices of preparation, notices of determination, and notices of completion provided to the office, and make the notices available through the Internet. The office may coordinate with another state agency for that agency to make the notices available through the Internet.

(d) Commencing January 1, 2003, copies of any documents submitted in electronic format to the Office of Planning and Research pursuant to this division shall be furnished by the office to the California State Library. The California State Library shall be the repository for those electronic documents, which shall be made available for viewing by the general public upon request.

Article 6. Special Review of Housing Projects

21159.20. For the purposes of this article, the following terms have the following meanings:

(a) "Census-defined place" means a specific unincorporated land area within boundaries determined by the United States Census Bureau in the most recent decennial census.

(b) "Community-level environmental review" means either of the following:

(1) An environmental impact report certified on any of the following:
(A) A general plan.
(B) A revision or update to the general plan that includes at least the land use and circulation elements.
(C) An applicable community plan.
(D) An applicable specific plan.
(E) A housing element of the general plan, if the environmental impact report analyzed the environmental effects of the density of the proposed project.

(2) Pursuant to this division and the implementing guidelines adopted pursuant to this division that govern subsequent review following a program environmental impact report, or pursuant to Section 21157.1, 21157.5, or 21166, a negative declaration or mitigated negative declaration was adopted as a subsequent environmental review document, following and based upon an environmental impact report on any of the projects listed in subparagraphs (A), (C), or (D) of paragraph (1).

(c) "Low-income households" means households of persons and families of very low and low income, as defined in Sections 50093 and 50105 of the Health and Safety Code.

(d) "Low- and moderate-income households" means households of persons and families of low or moderate income, as defined in Section 50093 of the Health and Safety Code.

21159.21. A housing project qualifies for an exemption from this division pursuant to Section 21159.22, 21159.23, or 21159.24 if it meets the criteria in the applicable section and all of the following criteria:

(a) The project is consistent with any applicable general plan, specific plan, and local coastal program, including any mitigation measures required by a plan or program, as that plan or program existed on the date that the application was deemed complete and with any applicable zoning ordinance, as that zoning ordinance existed on the date that the application was deemed complete, except that a project shall not be deemed to be inconsistent with the zoning designation for the site if that zoning designation is inconsistent with the general plan only because the project site has not been rezoned to conform with a more recently adopted general plan.

(b) Community-level environmental review has been adopted or certified.

(c) The project and other projects approved prior to the approval of the project can be adequately served by existing utilities, and the project applicant has paid, or has committed to pay, all applicable in-lieu or development fees.

(d) The site of the project does not contain wetlands, does not have any value as a wildlife habitat, and the project does not harm any species protected by the federal Endangered Species Act of 1973 (16 U.S.C. Sec. 1531 et seq.) or by the Native Plant Protection Act (Chapter 10 (commencing with Section 1900) of Division 2 of the Fish and Game Code), the California Endangered Species Act (Chapter 1.5 (commencing with Section 2050) of Division 3 of the Fish and Game Code), and the project does not cause the destruction or removal of any species protected by a local ordinance in effect at the time the application for the project was deemed complete. For the purposes of this subdivision, "wetlands" has the same meaning as in Section 328.3 of Title 33 of the Code of Federal Regulations and "wildlife habitat" means the ecological communities upon which wild animals, birds, plants, fish, amphibians, and invertebrates depend for their conservation and protection.

(e) The site of the project is not included on any list of facilities and sites compiled pursuant to Section 65962.5 of the Government Code.

(f) The site of the project is subject to a preliminary endangerment assessment prepared by a registered environmental assessor to determine the existence of any release of a hazardous substance on the site and to determine the potential for exposure of future occupants to significant health hazards from any nearby property or activity.

(1) If a release of a hazardous substance is found to exist on the site, the release shall be removed, or any significant effects of the release shall be mitigated to a level of insignificance in compliance with state and federal requirements.

(2) If a potential for exposure to significant hazards from surrounding properties or activities is found to exist, the effects of the potential exposure shall be mitigated to a level of insignificance in compliance with state and federal requirements.

(g) The project does not have a significant effect on historical resources pursuant to Section 21084.1.

(h) The project site is not subject to any of the following:

(1) A wildland fire hazard, as determined by the Department of Forestry and Fire Protection, unless the applicable general plan or zoning ordinance contains provisions to mitigate the risk of a wildland fire hazard.

(2) An unusually high risk of fire or explosion from materials stored or used on nearby properties.

(3) Risk of a public health exposure at a level that would exceed the standards established by any state or federal agency.
(4) Within a delineated earthquake fault zone, as determined pursuant to Section 2622, or a seismic hazard zone, as determined pursuant to Section 2696, unless the applicable general plan or zoning ordinance contains provisions to mitigate the risk of an earthquake fault or seismic hazard zone.
(5) Landslide hazard, flood plain, flood way, or restriction zone, unless the applicable general plan or zoning ordinance contains provisions to mitigate the risk of a landslide or flood.

(i) (1) The project site is not located on developed open space.
(2) For the purposes of this subdivision, "developed open space" means land that meets all of the following criteria:
(A) Is publicly owned, or financed in whole or in part by public funds.
(B) Is generally open to, and available for use by, the public.
(C) Is predominantly lacking in structural development other than structures associated with open spaces, including, but not limited to, playgrounds, swimming pools, ballfields, enclosed child play areas, and picnic facilities.
(3) For the purposes of this subdivision, "developed open space" includes land that has been designated for acquisition by a public agency for developed open space, but does not include lands acquired by public funds dedicated to the acquisition of land for housing purposes.

(j) The project site is not located within the boundaries of a state conservancy.

21159.22. (a) This division does not apply to any development project that meets the requirements of subdivision (b), and meets either of the following criteria:
(1) Consists of the construction, conversion, or use of residential housing for agricultural employees, and meets all of the following criteria:
(A) Is affordable to lower income households, as defined in Section 50079.5 of the Health and Safety Code.
(B) Lacks public financial assistance.
(C) The developer of the development project provides sufficient legal commitments to the appropriate local agency to ensure the continued availability and use of the housing units for lower income households for a period of at least 15 years.
(2) Consists of the construction, conversion, or use of residential housing for agricultural employees and meets all of the following criteria:
(A) Is housing for very low, low-, or moderate-income households as defined in paragraph (2) of subdivision (h) of Section 65589.5 of the Government Code.
(B) Public financial assistance exists for the development project.
(C) The developer of the development project provides sufficient legal commitments to the appropriate local agency to ensure the continued availability and use of the housing units for low- and moderate-income households for a period of at least 15 years.

(b) (1) If the development project is proposed within incorporated city limits or within a census defined place with a minimum population density of at least 5,000 persons per square mile, it is located on a project site that is adjacent, on at least two sides, to land that has been developed, and consists of not more than 45 units, or is housing for a total of 45 or fewer agricultural employees if the housing consists of dormitories, barracks, or other group living facilities.
(2) If the development project is located on a project site zoned for general agricultural use, and consists of not more than 20 units, or is housing for a total of 20 or fewer agricultural employees if the housing consists of dormitories, barracks, or other group living facilities.
(3) The project satisfies the criteria in Section 21159.21.
(4) The development project is not more than five acres in area, except that a project site located in an area with a population density of at least 1,000 persons per square mile shall not be more than two acres in area.

(c) Notwithstanding subdivision (a), if a project satisfies the criteria described in subdivisions (a) and (b), but does not satisfy the criteria described in paragraph (1) of subdivision (b), this division does not apply to the project if the project meets all of the following criteria:
(1) Is located within either an incorporated city or a census-defined place.
(2) The population density of the incorporated city or census-defined place has a population density of at least 1,000 persons per square mile.
(3) The project site is adjacent on at least two sides to land that has been developed and the project consists of not more than 45 units, or the project consist of dormitories, barracks, or other group housing facilities for a total of 45 or fewer agricultural employees.

(d) Notwithstanding subdivision (c), this division shall apply to a project that meets the criteria described in subdivision (c) if a public agency that is carrying out or approving the project determines that there is a reasonable possibility that the project, if completed, would have a significant effect on the environment due to unusual circumstances or that the cumulative impacts of successive projects of the same type in the same area, over time, would be significant.

For the purposes of this section, "agricultural employee" has the same meaning as defined by subdivision (b) of Section 1140.4 of the Labor Code.

21159.23. (a) This division does not apply to any development project that consists of the construction, conversion, or use of residential housing consisting of 100 or fewer that is affordable to low-income households if both of the following criteria are met:
(1) The developer of the development project provides sufficient legal commitments to the appropriate local agency to ensure the continued availability and use of the housing units for lower income households, as defined in Section 50079.5 of the Health and Safety Code, for a period of at least 30 years, at monthly housing costs, as determined pursuant to Section 50053 of the Health and Safety Code.
(2) The development project meets all of the following requirements:
(A) The project satisfies the criteria described in Section 21159.21.
(B) The project site meets one of the following conditions:
(i) Has been previously developed for qualified urban uses.
(ii) The parcels immediately adjacent to the site are developed with qualified urban uses, or at least 75 percent of the perimeter of the site adjoins parcels that are developed with qualified urban uses and the remaining 25 percent of the perimeter of the site adjoins parcels that have previously been developed for qualified urban uses, and the site has not been developed for urban uses and no parcel within the site has been created within 10 years prior to the proposed development of the site.
(C) The project site is not more than five acres in area.
(D) The project site is located within an urbanized area or within a census-defined place with a population density of at least 5,000 persons per square mile or, if the project consists of 50 or fewer units, within an incorporated city with a population density of at least 2,500 persons per square mile and a total population of at least 25,000 persons.

(b) Notwithstanding subdivision (a), if a project satisfies all of the criteria described in subdivision (a) except subparagraph (D) of paragraph (2) of that subdivision, this division does not apply to the project if the project is located within either an incorporated city or a census defined place with a population density of at least 1,000 persons per square mile.

(c) Notwithstanding subdivision (b), this division applies to a project that meets the criteria of subdivision (b), if there is a reasonable possibility that the project would have a significant effect on the environment or the residents of the project due to unusual circumstances or due to the related or cumulative impacts of reasonably foreseeable projects in the vicinity of the project.

(d) For the purposes of this section, "residential" means a use consisting of either of the following:
(1) Residential units only.
(2) Residential units and primarily neighborhood-serving goods, services, or retail uses that do not exceed 15 percent of the total floor area of the project.

21159.24. (a) Except as provided in subdivision (b), this division does not apply to a project if all of the following criteria are met:
(1) The project is a residential project on an infill site.
(2) The project is located within an urbanized area.
(3) The project satisfies the criteria of Section 21159.21.
(4) Within five years of the date that the application for the project is deemed complete pursuant to Section 65943 of the Government Code, community-level environmental review was certified or adopted.
(5) The site of the project is not more than four acres in total area.
(6) The project does not contain more than 100 residential units.
(7) Either of the following criteria are met:
(A) (i) At least 10 percent of the housing is sold to families of moderate income, or not less than 10 percent of the housing is rented to families of low income, or not less than 5 percent of the housing is rented to families of very low income.
(ii) The project developer provides sufficient legal commitments to the appropriate local agency to ensure the continued availability and use of the housing units for very low, low-, and moderate-income households at monthly housing costs determined pursuant to paragraph (3) of subdivision (h) of Section 65589.5 of the Government Code.

(B) The project developer has paid or will pay in-lieu fees pursuant to a local ordinance in an amount sufficient to result in the development of an equivalent number of units that would otherwise be required pursuant to subparagraph (A).
(8) The project is within one-half mile of a major transit stop.
(9) The project does not include any single level building that exceeds 100,000 square feet.
(10) The project promotes higher density infill housing. A project with a density of at least 20 units per acre shall be conclusively presumed to promote higher density infill housing. A project with a density of at least 10 units per acre and a density greater than the average density of the residential properties within 1,500 feet shall be presumed to promote higher density housing unless the preponderance of the evidence demonstrates otherwise.

(b) Notwithstanding subdivision (a), this division shall apply to a development project that meets the criteria described in subdivision (a), if any of the following occur:
(1) There is a reasonable possibility that the project will have a project-specific, significant effect on the environment due to unusual circumstances.
(2) Substantial changes with respect to the circumstances under which the project is being undertaken that are related to the project have occurred since community-level environmental review was certified or adopted.
(3) New information becomes available regarding the circumstances under which the project is being undertaken and that is related to the project, that was not known, and could not have been known, at the time that community-level environmental review was certified or adopted.

(c) If a project satisfies the criteria described in subdivision (a), but is not exempt from this division as a result of satisfying the criteria described in subdivision (b), the analysis of the environmental effects of the project in the environmental impact report or the negative declaration shall be limited to an analysis of the project-specific effect of the projects and any effects identified pursuant to paragraph (2) or (3) of subdivision (b).

(d) For the purposes of this section, "residential" means a use consisting of either of the following:
(1) Residential units only.
(2) Residential units and primarily neighborhood-serving goods, services, or retail uses that do not exceed 15 percent of the total floor area of the project.

21159.26. With respect to a project that includes a housing development, a public agency may not reduce the proposed number of housing units as a mitigation measure or project alternative for a particular significant effect on the environment if it determines that there is another feasible specific mitigation measure or project alternative that would provide a comparable level of mitigation. This section does not affect any other requirement regarding the residential density of that project.

21159.27. A project may not be divided into smaller projects to qualify for one or more exemptions pursuant to this article.

21159.28. (a) If a residential or mixed-use residential project is consistent with the use designation, density, building intensity, and applicable policies specified for the project area in either a sustainable communities strategy or an alternative planning strategy, for which the State Air Resources Board pursuant to subparagraph (I) of paragraph (2) of subdivision (b) of Section 65080 of the Government Code has accepted the metropolitan planning organization's determination that the sustainable communities strategy or the alternative planning strategy would, if implemented, achieve the greenhouse gas emission reduction targets and if the project incorporates the mitigation measures required by an applicable prior environmental document, then any findings or other determinations for an exemption, a negative declaration, a mitigated negative declaration, a sustainable communities environmental assessment, an environmental impact report, or addenda prepared or adopted for the project pursuant to this division shall not be required to reference, describe, or discuss (1) growth inducing impacts; or (2) any project specific or cumulative impacts from cars and light-duty truck trips generated by the project on global warming or the regional transportation network.

(b) Any environmental impact report prepared for a project described in subdivision (a) shall not be required to reference, describe, or discuss a reduced residential density alternative to address the effects of car and light-duty truck trips generated by the project.

(c) "Regional transportation network," for purposes of this section, means all existing and proposed transportation system improvements, including the state transportation system, that were included in the transportation and air quality conformity modeling, including congestion modeling, for the final regional transportation plan adopted by the metropolitan planning organization, but shall not include local streets and roads. Nothing in the foregoing relieves any project from a requirement to comply with any conditions, exactions, or fees for the mitigation of the project's impacts on the structure, safety, or operations of the regional transportation network or local streets and roads.

(d) A residential or mixed-use residential project is a project where at least 75 percent of the total building square footage of the project consists of residential use or a project that is a transit priority project as defined in Section 21155.

Article 5. Submission of Information

21160. Whenever any person applies to any public agency for a lease, permit, license, certificate, or other entitlement for use, the public agency may require that person to submit data and information which may be necessary to enable the public agency to determine whether the proposed project may have a significant effect on the environment or to prepare an environmental impact report.

If any or all of the information so submitted is a "trade secret" as defined in Section 6254.7 of the Government Code by those submitting that information, it shall not be included in the impact report or otherwise disclosed by any public agency. This section shall not be construed to prohibit the exchange of properly designated trade secrets between public agencies who have lawful jurisdiction over the preparation of the impact report.

21161. Whenever a public agency has completed an environmental impact report, it shall cause a notice of completion of that report to be filed with the Office of Planning and Research. The notice of completion shall briefly identify the project and shall indicate that an environmental impact report has been prepared. The notice of completion shall identify the project location by latitude and longitude. Failure to file the notice required by this section shall not affect the validity of a project.

21162. A copy of the notice of completion of an environmental impact report on a project shall be provided, by the State Clearinghouse, to any legislator in whose district the project has an environmental impact, if the legislator requests the notice and the State Clearinghouse has received it.

Article 6. Limitations

21165. (a) When a project is to be carried out or approved by two or more public agencies, the determination of whether the project may have a significant effect on the environment shall be made by the lead agency, and that agency shall prepare, or cause to be prepared by contract, the environmental impact report for the project, if a report is required by this division. In the event that a dispute arises as to which is the lead agency, any of the disputing public agencies, or in the case of a project described in subdivision (c) of Section 21065 the applicant for such project, may submit the question to the Office of Planning and Research, and the Office of Planning and Research shall designate, within 21 days of receiving the request, the lead agency, giving due consideration to the capacity of that agency to adequately fulfill the requirements of this division.

(b) For the purposes of this section, a "dispute" means a contested, active difference of opinion between two or more public agencies as to which of those agencies shall prepare any necessary environmental document. A dispute exists where each of those agencies claims that it either has or does not have the obligation to prepare that environmental document. The Office of Planning and Research shall not designate a lead agency in the absence of such a dispute.

21166. When an environmental impact report has been prepared for a project pursuant to this division, no subsequent or supplemental environmental impact report shall be required by the lead agency or by any responsible agency, unless one or more of the following events occurs:
(a) Substantial changes are proposed in the project which will require major revisions of the environmental impact report.
(b) Substantial changes occur with respect to the circumstances under which the project is being undertaken which will require major revisions in the environmental impact report.
(c) New information, which was not known and could not have been known at the time the environmental impact report was certified as complete, becomes available.

21166.1. The decision of a lead agency to prepare an environmental impact report with respect to environmental impacts within a geographic area or for a group of projects shall not be a basis for determining that an environmental document prepared for an individual project within that area or group is inadequate.

21167. An action or proceeding to attack, review, set aside, void, or annul the following acts or decisions of a public agency on the grounds of noncompliance with this division shall be commenced as follows:
(a) An action or proceeding alleging that a public agency is carrying out or has approved a project that may have a significant effect on the environment without having determined whether the project may have a significant effect on the environment shall be commenced within 180 days from the date of the public agency's decision to carry out or approve the project, or, if a project is undertaken without a formal

decision by the public agency, within 180 days from the date of commencement of the project.

(b) An action or proceeding alleging that a public agency has improperly determined whether a project may have a significant effect on the environment shall be commenced within 30 days from the date of the filing of the notice required by subdivision (a) of Section 21108 or subdivision (a) of Section 21152.

(c) An action or proceeding alleging that an environmental impact report does not comply with this division shall be commenced within 30 days from the date of the filing of the notice required by subdivision (a) of Section 21108 or subdivision (a) of Section 21152 by the lead agency.

(d) An action or proceeding alleging that a public agency has improperly determined that a project is not subject to this division pursuant to subdivision (b) of Section 21080 or Section 21172 shall be commenced within 35 days from the date of the filing by the public agency, or person specified in subdivision (b) or (c) of Section 21065, of the notice authorized by subdivision (b) of Section 21108 or subdivision (b) of Section 21152. If the notice has not been filed, the action or proceeding shall be commenced within 180 days from the date of the public agency's decision to carry out or approve the project, or, if a project is undertaken without a formal decision by the public agency, within 180 days from the date of commencement of the project.

(e) An action or proceeding alleging that another act or omission of a public agency does not comply with this division shall be commenced within 30 days from the date of the filing of the notice required by subdivision (a) of Section 21108 or subdivision (a) of Section 21152.

(f) If a person has made a written request to the public agency for a copy of the notice specified in Section 21108 or 21152 prior to the date on which the agency approves or determines to carry out the project, then not later than five days from the date of the agency's action, the public agency shall deposit a written copy of the notice addressed to that person in the United States mail, first class postage prepaid. The date upon which this notice is mailed shall not affect the time periods specified in subdivisions (b), (c), (d), and (e).

21167.1. (a) In all actions or proceedings brought pursuant to Sections 21167, 21168, and 21168.5, including the hearing of an action or proceeding on appeal from a decision of a lower court, all courts in which the action or proceeding is pending shall give the action or proceeding preference over all other civil actions, in the matter of setting the action or proceeding for hearing or trial, and in hearing or trying the action or proceeding, so that the action or proceeding shall be quickly heard and determined. The court shall regulate the briefing schedule so that, to the extent feasible, the court shall commence hearings on an appeal within one year of the date of the filing of the appeal.

(b) To ensure that actions or proceedings brought pursuant to Sections 21167, 21168, and 21168.5 may be quickly heard and determined in the lower courts, the superior courts in all counties with a population of more than 200,000 shall designate one or more judges to develop expertise in this division and related land use and environmental laws, so that those judges will be available to hear, and quickly resolve, actions or proceedings brought pursuant to Sections 21167, 21168, and 21168.5.

(c) In an action or proceeding filed pursuant to this chapter that is joined with any other cause of action, the court, upon a motion by any party, may grant severance of the actions. In determining whether to grant severance, the court shall consider such matters as judicial economy, administrative economy, and prejudice to any party.

21167.2. If no action or proceeding alleging that an environmental impact report does not comply with the provisions of this division is commenced during the period prescribed in subdivision (c) of Section 21167, the environmental impact report shall be conclusively presumed to comply with the provisions of this division for purposes of its use by responsible agencies, unless the provisions of Section 21166 are applicable.

21167.3. (a) If an action or proceeding alleging that an environmental impact report or a negative declaration does not comply with the provisions of this division is commenced during the period described in subdivision (b) or (c) of Section 21167, and if an injunction or stay is issued prohibiting the project from being carried out or approved pending final determination of the issue of such compliance, responsible agencies shall assume that the environmental impact report or the negative declaration for the project does comply with the provisions of this division and shall issue a conditional approval or disapproval of such project according to the timetable for agency action in Article 5 (commencing with Section 65950) of Chapter 4.5 of Division 1 of Title 7 of the Government Code. A conditional approval shall constitute permission to proceed with a project when and only when such action or proceeding results in a final determination that the environmental impact report or negative declaration does comply with the provisions of this division.

(b) In the event that an action or proceeding is commenced as described in subdivision (a) but no injunction or similar relief is sought and granted, responsible agencies shall assume that the environmental impact report or negative declaration for the project does comply with the provisions of this division and shall approve or disapprove the project according to the timetable for agency action in Article 5 (commencing with Section 65950) of Chapter 4.5 of Division 1 of Title 7 of the Government Code. Such approval shall constitute permission to proceed with the project at the applicant's risk pending final determination of such action or proceeding.

21167.4. (a) In any action or proceeding alleging noncompliance with this division, the petitioner shall request a hearing within 90 days from the date of filing the petition or shall be subject to dismissal on the court's own motion or on the motion of any party interested in the action or proceeding.

(b) The petitioner shall serve a notice of the request for a hearing on all parties at the time that the petitioner files the request for a hearing.

(c) Upon the filing of a request by the petitioner for a hearing and upon application by any party, the court shall establish a briefing schedule and a hearing date. In the absence of good cause, briefing shall be completed within 90 days from the date that the request for a hearing is filed, and the hearing, to the extent feasible, shall be held within 30 days thereafter. Good cause may include, but shall not be limited to, the conduct of discovery, determination of the completeness of the record of proceedings, the complexity of the issues, and the length of the record of proceedings and the timeliness of its production. The parties may stipulate to a briefing schedule or hearing date that differs from the schedule set forth in this subdivision if the stipulation is approved by the court.

(d) In an action or proceeding alleging noncompliance with this division, the Attorney General may file a motion with the court seeking an expedited schedule for resolution of the case upon the grounds that it would be in the public interest to do so. This subdivision does not affect the rights of any party under existing law to seek an expedited schedule for resolution of the case.

(e) This section shall remain in effect only until January 1, 2016, and as of that date is repealed, unless a later enacted statute, that is enacted before January 1, 2016, deletes or extends that date.

21167.4. (a) In any action or proceeding alleging noncompliance with this division, the petitioner shall request a hearing within 90 days from the date of filing the petition or shall be subject to dismissal on the court's own motion or on the motion of any party interested in the action or proceeding.

(b) The petitioner shall serve a notice of the request for a hearing on all parties at the time that the petitioner files the request for a hearing.

(c) Upon the filing of a request by the petitioner for a hearing and upon application by any party, the court shall establish a briefing schedule and a hearing date. In the absence of good cause, briefing shall be completed within 90 days from the date that the request for a hearing is filed, and the hearing, to the extent feasible, shall be held within 30 days thereafter. Good cause may include, but shall not be limited to, the conduct of discovery, determination of the completeness of the record of proceedings, the complexity of the issues, and the length of the record of proceedings and the timeliness of its production. The parties may stipulate to a briefing schedule or hearing date that differs from the schedule set forth in this subdivision if the stipulation is approved by the court.

(d) This section shall become operative on January 1, 2016.

21167.5. Proof of prior service by mail upon the public agency carrying out or approving the project of a written notice of the commencement of any action or proceeding described in Section 21167 identifying the project shall be filed concurrently with the initial pleading in such action or proceeding.

21167.6. Notwithstanding any other provision of law, in all actions or proceedings brought pursuant to Section 21167, except those involving the Public Utilities Commission, all of the following shall apply:

(a) At the time that the action or proceeding is filed, the plaintiff or petitioner shall file a request that the respondent public agency prepare the record of proceedings relating to the subject of the action or proceeding. The request, together with the complaint or petition, shall be served personally upon the public agency not later than 10 business days from the date that the action or proceeding was filed.

(b) (1) The public agency shall prepare and certify the record of proceedings not later than 60 days from the date that the request specified in subdivision (a) was served upon the public agency. Upon certification, the public agency shall lodge a copy of the record of proceedings with the court and shall serve on the parties notice that the record of proceedings has been certified and lodged with the court. The parties shall pay any reasonable costs or fees imposed for the preparation of the record of proceedings in conformance with any law or rule of court.

(2) The plaintiff or petitioner may elect to prepare the record of proceedings or the parties may agree to an alternative method of preparation of the record of proceedings, subject to certification of its accuracy by the public agency, within the time limit specified in this subdivision.

(c) The time limit established by subdivision (b) may be extended only upon the stipulation of all parties who have been properly served in the action or proceeding or upon order of the court. Extensions shall be liberally granted by the court when the size of the record of proceedings renders infeasible compliance with that time limit. There is no limit on the number of extensions that may be granted by the court, but no single extension shall exceed 60 days unless the court determines that a longer extension is in the public interest.
(d) If the public agency fails to prepare and certify the record within the time limit established in paragraph (1) of subdivision (b), or any continuances of that time limit, the plaintiff or petitioner may move for sanctions, and the court may, upon that motion, grant appropriate sanctions.
(e) The record of proceedings shall include, but is not limited to, all of the following items:
  (1) All project application materials.
  (2) All staff reports and related documents prepared by the respondent public agency with respect to its compliance with the substantive and procedural requirements of this division and with respect to the action on the project.
  (3) All staff reports and related documents prepared by the respondent public agency and written testimony or documents submitted by any person relevant to any findings or statement of overriding considerations adopted by the respondent agency pursuant to this division.
  (4) Any transcript or minutes of the proceedings at which the decisionmaking body of the respondent public agency heard testimony on, or considered any environmental document on, the project, and any transcript or minutes of proceedings before any advisory body to the respondent public agency that were presented to the decisionmaking body prior to action on the environmental documents or on the project.
  (5) All notices issued by the respondent public agency to comply with this division or with any other law governing the processing and approval of the project.
  (6) All written comments received in response to, or in connection with, environmental documents prepared for the project, including responses to the notice of preparation.
  (7) All written evidence or correspondence submitted to, or transferred from, the respondent public agency with respect to compliance with this division or with respect to the project.
  (8) Any proposed decisions or findings submitted to the decisionmaking body of the respondent public agency by its staff, or the project proponent, project opponents, or other persons.
  (9) The documentation of the final public agency decision, including the final environmental impact report, mitigated negative declaration, or negative declaration, and all documents, in addition to those referenced in paragraph (3), cited or relied on in the findings or in a statement of overriding considerations adopted pursuant to this division.
  (10) Any other written materials relevant to the respondent public agency's compliance with this division or to its decision on the merits of the project, including the initial study, any drafts of any environmental document, or portions thereof, that have been released for public review, and copies of studies or other documents relied upon in any environmental document prepared for the project and either made available to the public during the public review period or included in the respondent public agency's files on the project, and all internal agency communications, including staff notes and memoranda related to the project or to compliance with this division.
  (11) The full written record before any inferior administrative decisionmaking body whose decision was appealed to a superior administrative decisionmaking body prior to the filing of litigation.
(f) In preparing the record of proceedings, the party preparing the record shall strive to do so at reasonable cost in light of the scope of the record.
(g) The clerk of the superior court shall prepare and certify the clerk's transcript on appeal not later than 60 days from the date that the notice designating the papers or records to be included in the clerk's transcript was filed with the superior court, if the party or parties pay any costs or fees for the preparation of the clerk's transcript imposed in conformance with any law or rules of court. Nothing in this subdivision precludes an election to proceed by appendix, as provided in Rule 8.124 of the California Rules of Court.
(h) Extensions of the period for the filing of any brief on appeal may be allowed only by stipulation of the parties or by order of the court for good cause shown. Extensions for the filing of a brief on appeal shall be limited to one 30-day extension for the preparation of an opening brief, and one 30-day extension for the preparation of a responding brief, except that the court may grant a longer extension or additional extensions if it determines that there is a substantial likelihood of settlement that would avoid the necessity of completing the appeal.
(i) At the completion of the filing of briefs on appeal, the appellant shall notify the court of the completion of the filing of briefs, whereupon the clerk of the reviewing court shall set the appeal for hearing on the first available calendar date.

21167.6.5. (a) The petitioner or plaintiff shall name, as a real party in interest, the person or persons identified by the public agency in its notice filed pursuant to subdivision (a) or (b) of Section 21108 or Section 21152 or, if no notice is filed, the person or persons in subdivision (b) or (c) of Section 21065, as reflected in the agency's record of proceedings for the project that is the subject of an action or proceeding brought pursuant to Section 21167, 21168, or 21168.5, and shall serve the petition or complaint on that real party in interest, by personal service, mail facsimile, or any other method permitted by law, not later than 20 business days following service of the petition or complaint on the public agency.
(b) The public agency shall provide the petitioner or plaintiff, not later than 10 business days following service of the petition or complaint on the public agency, with a list of responsible agencies and any public agency having jurisdiction over a natural resource affected by the project.
(c) The petitioner or plaintiff shall provide the responsible agencies, and any public agency having jurisdiction over a natural resource affected by the project, with notice of the action or proceeding within 15 days of receipt of the list described in subdivision (b).
(d) Failure to name potential parties, other than those real parties in interest described in subdivision (a), is not grounds for dismissal pursuant to Section 389 of the Code of Civil Procedure.
(e) This section is not intended to affect an existing right of a party to intervene in the action.

21167.7. Every person who brings an action pursuant to Section 21167 shall comply with the requirements of Section 388 of the Code of Civil Procedure. Every such person shall also furnish pursuant to Section 388 of the Code of Civil Procedure a copy of any amended or supplemental pleading filed by such person in such action to the Attorney General. No relief, temporary or permanent, shall be granted until a copy of the pleading has been furnished to the Attorney General in accordance with such requirements.

21167.8. (a) Not later than 20 days from the date of service upon a public agency of a petition or complaint brought pursuant to Section 21167, the public agency shall file with the court a notice setting forth the time and place at which all parties shall meet and attempt to settle the litigation. The meeting shall be scheduled and held not later than 45 days from the date of service of the petition or complaint upon the public agency. The notice of the settlement meeting shall be served by mail upon the counsel for each party. If the public agency does not know the identity of counsel for any party, the notice shall be served by mail upon the party for whom counsel is not known.
(b) At the time and place specified in the notice filed with the court, the parties shall meet and confer regarding anticipated issues to be raised in the litigation and shall attempt in good faith to settle the litigation and the dispute which forms the basis of the litigation. The settlement meeting discussions shall be comprehensive in nature and shall focus on the legal issues raised by the parties concerning the project that is the subject of the litigation.
(c) The settlement meeting may be continued from time to time without postponing or otherwise delaying other applicable time limits in the litigation. The settlement meeting is intended to be conducted concurrently with any judicial proceedings.
(d) If the litigation is not settled, the court, in its discretion, may, or at the request of any party, shall, schedule a further settlement conference before a judge of the superior court. If the petition or complaint is later heard on its merits, the judge hearing the matter shall not be the same judge conducting the settlement conference, except in counties that have only one judge of the superior court.
(e) The failure of any party, who was notified pursuant to subdivision (a), to participate in the litigation settlement process, without good cause, may result in an imposition of sanctions by the court.
(f) Not later than 30 days from the date that notice of certification of the record of proceedings was filed and served in accordance with Section 21167.6, the petitioner or plaintiff shall file and serve on all other parties a statement of issues which the petitioner or plaintiff intends to raise in any brief or at any hearing or trial. Not later than 10 days from the date on which the respondent or real party in interest has been served with the statement of issues from the petitioner or plaintiff, each respondent and real party in interest shall file and serve on all other parties a statement of issues which that party intends to raise in any brief or at any hearing or trial.
(g) This section shall become operative on January 1, 2016.

21167.9. Any action brought in the superior court relating to this division may be subject to a mediation proceeding conducted pursuant to Chapter 9.3 (commencing with Section 66030) of Division 1 of Title 7 of the Government Code.

21167.10. (a) Within five business days of the filing of a notice required by subdivision (a) or (b) of Section 21108, or subdivision (a) or (b) of Section 21152 by the lead agency, a person wishing to bring an action or a proceeding pursuant to Section 21167, 21168, or 21168.5 may file with the lead agency and the real party in interest a notice requesting mediation.

(b) Within five business days of the receipt of the notice requesting mediation, a lead agency may respond to the person by accepting the request for mediation and proceed with mediation.

(c) The request for mediation is deemed denied if the lead agency fails to respond within five business days of receiving the request for mediation.

(d) The limitation periods provided pursuant to this chapter shall be tolled until the completion of the mediation conducted pursuant to this section.

(e) This section shall apply to notices that are filed on or after July 1, 2011.

(f) This section does not apply in cases where the lead agency has not filed the notice required by subdivision (a) or (b) of Section 21108, or subdivision (a) or (b) of Section 21152.

(g) (1) Except as set forth in paragraph (2), this section shall remain in effect only until January 1, 2016, and as of that date is repealed, unless a later enacted statute, that is enacted before January 1, 2016, deletes or extends that date.

(2) Notwithstanding paragraph (1), the tolling of the limitation periods provided pursuant to subdivision (d) shall apply if a mediation conducted pursuant to this section is completed on or after January 1, 2016.

21168. Any action or proceeding to attack, review, set aside, void or annul a determination, finding, or decision of a public agency, made as a result of a proceeding in which by law a hearing is required to be given, evidence is required to be taken and discretion in the determination of facts is vested in a public agency, on the grounds of noncompliance with the provisions of this division shall be in accordance with the provisions of Section 1094.5 of the Code of Civil Procedure.

In any such action, the court shall not exercise its independent judgment on the evidence but shall only determine whether the act or decision is supported by substantial evidence in the light of the whole record.

21168.5. In any action or proceeding, other than an action or proceeding under Section 21168, to attack, review, set aside, void or annul a determination, finding, or decision of a public agency on the grounds of noncompliance with this division, the inquiry shall extend only to whether there was a prejudicial abuse of discretion. Abuse of discretion is established if the agency has not proceeded in a manner required by law or if the determination or decision is not supported by substantial evidence.

21168.6. In any action or proceeding under Sections 21168 or 21168.5 against the Public Utilities Commission the writ of mandate shall lie only from the Supreme Court to such commission.

21168.6.5.

(a) For the purposes of this section, the following definitions shall apply:

(1) "Applicant" means a private entity or its affiliates that proposes the project and its successors, heirs, and assignees.

(2) "Initial project approval" means any actions, activities, ordinances, resolutions, agreements, approvals, determinations, findings, or decisions taken, adopted, or approved by the lead agency required to allow the applicant to commence the construction of the project, as determined by the lead agency.

(3) "Project" means a project that substantially conforms to the project description for the Convention Center Modernization and Farmers Field Project set forth in the notice of preparation released by the City of Los Angeles on March 17, 2011.

(4) "Stadium" means, except as the context indicates otherwise, the stadium built pursuant to the project for football and other spectator events.

(5) "Subsequent project approval" means any actions, activities, ordinances, resolutions, agreements, approvals, determinations, findings, or decisions by the lead agency required for, or in furtherance of, the project that are taken, adopted, or approved following the initial project approvals until the project obtains certificates of occupancy.

(6) "Trip ratio" means the total annual number of private automobiles arriving at the stadium for spectator events divided by the total annual number of spectators at the events.

(b) (1) This section does not apply to the project and shall become inoperative on the date of the release of the draft environmental impact report and is repealed on January 1 of the following year, if the applicant fails to notify the lead agency prior to the release of the draft environmental impact report for public comment that the applicant is electing to proceed pursuant to this section.

(2) The lead agency shall notify the Secretary of State if the applicant fails to notify the lead agency of its election to proceed pursuant to this section.

(c) (1) (A) Notwithstanding any other law, the procedures set forth in subdivision (d) shall apply to any action or proceeding brought to attack, review, set aside, void, or annul the certification of the environmental impact report for the project or the granting of any initial project approvals.

(B) Notwithstanding any other law, the procedures set forth in subdivision (j) shall apply to any action or proceeding brought to attack, review, set aside, void, or annul any subsequent project approvals.

(2) Notwithstanding any other law, the procedure set forth in subdivision (f) shall apply to the certification of the environmental impact report for the project and to any initial project approvals.

(d) (1) An action or proceeding to attack, set aside, void, or annul a determination, finding, or decision of the lead agency certifying the environmental impact report or granting one or more initial project approvals shall be commenced by filing a petition for a writ of mandate with the Second District Court of Appeal and shall be served on the respondent and the real party in interest within 30 days of the filing by the lead agency of the notice required by subdivision (a) of Section 21152.

(2) The petitioner shall file and serve the opening brief in support of the petition for writ of mandate within 40 days of the filing of the petition for a writ of mandate.

(3) The respondent and real party in interest shall file and serve any brief in opposition to the petition for writ of mandate within 25 days of the filing of the opening brief.

(4) The petitioner shall file and serve the reply brief within 20 days of the filing of the last opposition brief to the petitioner's opening brief.

(5) Except as provided in paragraph (6), parties to the action shall comply with all applicable California Rules of Court in the filing of the petition for writ of mandate and the briefs.

(6) (A) Rule 8.220 of the California Rules of Court shall not apply to the time periods set forth in paragraphs (2) to (4), inclusive.

(B) If a petitioner fails to file the opening brief pursuant to paragraph (2), the Court of Appeal shall dismiss the petition.

(C) If the respondents and real party in interest fail to file the brief in opposition pursuant to paragraph (3), the Court of Appeal shall decide the petition for writ of mandate based on the record, the opening brief, and any oral argument by the petitioner.

(7) Except upon a showing of extraordinary good cause, the Court of Appeal shall not grant any extensions of time to the deadlines specified in this subdivision. Any extension shall be limited to the minimum amount the Court of Appeal deems to be necessary.

(8) The Court of Appeal may, on its motion or upon request from a party, appoint a special master to assist the Court of Appeal in conducting the expedited judicial review required pursuant to this subdivision. If the Court of Appeal appoints a special master, the applicant shall pay all reasonable costs for the special master, not to exceed one hundred fifty thousand dollars ($150,000). If the Court of Appeal determines that the cost of the special master may exceed one hundred fifty thousand dollars ($150,000), it may request that additional funds be provided by the applicant and, if the applicant agrees to provide the funding, shall use the funds to pay the additional costs of the special master.

(9) The Court of Appeal shall hold a hearing and issue a decision on all petitions for writ of mandate filed pursuant to this subdivision within 60 days of the filing of the last timely reply brief.

(10) (A) A petition for review of the decision rendered by the Court of Appeal shall be filed with the Supreme Court and served on all parties to the petition for writ of mandate within 15 days of the decision.

(B) Any opposition to the petition for review shall be filed and served within 15 days of the filing of the petition for review.

(C) The Supreme Court shall render a decision on the petition for review within 30 days after the filing of the petition for review or within 15 days after the filing of the opposition to the petition for review, whichever is earlier.

(11) All briefs and notices filed pursuant to this subdivision shall be electronically served on parties pursuant to Rule 8.71 of the California Rules of Court. Each party to the petition shall provide an electronic service address at which the party agrees to accept the service.

(12) (A) No provision of law that is inconsistent or conflicts with this subdivision shall apply to a petition for a writ of mandate subject to this subdivision, including, but not limited to, any of the following:

(i) Section 21167.4.

(ii) Subdivisions (a) through (d), inclusive, and (g) through (i), inclusive, of Section 21167.6.

(iii) Subdivision (f) of Section 21167.8.

(iv) Section 21167.6.5.

(v) Sections 66031 through 66035, inclusive, of the Government Code.

(B) Except as provided in this section, including subparagraph (A), the requirements of this division are fully applicable to the project.

(e) (1) The draft and final environmental impact report shall include a notice in not less than 12-point type stating the following:

THIS EIR IS SUBJECT TO SECTION 21168.6.5 OF THE PUBLIC RESOURCES CODE, WHICH PROVIDES, AMONG OTHER THINGS, THAT THE LEAD AGENCY NEED NOT CONSIDER CERTAIN COMMENTS FILED AFTER THE CLOSE OF THE PUBLIC COMMENT PERIOD FOR THE DRAFT EIR. ANY JUDICIAL ACTION CHALLENGING THE CERTIFICATION OF THE EIR OR THE APPROVAL OF THE PROJECT DESCRIBED IN THE EIR IS SUBJECT TO THE PROCEDURES SET FORTH IN SECTION 21168.6.5 OF THE PUBLIC RESOURCES CODE AND MUST BE FILED WITH THE SECOND DISTRICT COURT OF APPEAL. A COPY OF SECTION 21168.6.5 OF THE PUBLIC RESOURCES CODE IS INCLUDED IN THE APPENDIX TO THIS EIR.

(2) The draft environmental impact report and final environmental impact report shall contain, as an appendix, the full text of this section.

(f) (1) Within 10 days after the release of the draft environmental impact report, the lead agency shall conduct an informational workshop to inform the public of the key analyses and conclusions of that report.

(2) Within 10 days before the close of the public comment period, the lead agency shall hold a public hearing to receive testimony on the draft environmental impact report. A transcript of the hearing shall be included as an appendix to the final environmental impact report.

(3) (A) Within five days following the close of the public comment period, a commenter on the draft environmental impact report may submit to the lead agency a written request for nonbinding mediation. The lead agency and applicant shall participate in nonbinding mediation with all commenters who submitted timely comments on the draft environmental impact report and who requested the mediation. Mediation conducted pursuant to this paragraph shall end no later than 35 days after the close of the public comment period.

(B) A request for mediation shall identify all areas of dispute raised in the comment submitted by the commenter that are to be mediated.

(C) The lead agency shall select one or more mediators who shall be retired judges or recognized experts with at least five years experience in land use and environmental law or science, or mediation. The applicant shall bear the costs of mediation.

(D) A mediation session shall be conducted on each area of dispute with the parties requesting mediation on that area of dispute.

(E) The lead agency shall adopt, as a condition of approval, any measures agreed upon by the lead agency, the applicant, and any commenter who requested mediation. A commenter who agrees to a measure pursuant to this subparagraph shall not raise the issue addressed by that measure as a basis for a petition for writ of mandate challenging the lead agency's decision to certify the environmental impact report or to grant one or more initial project approvals.

(4) The lead agency need not consider written comments submitted after the close of the public comment period, unless those comments address any of the following:

(A) New issues raised in the response to comments by the lead agency.

(B) New information released by the public agency subsequent to the release of the draft environmental impact report, such as new information set forth or embodied in a staff report, proposed permit, proposed resolution, ordinance, or similar documents.

(C) Changes made to the project after the close of the public comment period.

(D) Proposed conditions for approval, mitigation measures, or proposed findings required by Section 21081 or a proposed reporting and monitoring program required by paragraph (1) of subdivision (a) of Section 21081.6, where the lead agency releases those documents subsequent to the release of the draft environmental impact report.

(E) New information that was not reasonably known and could not have been reasonably known during the public comment period.

(5) (A) The lead agency shall file the notice required by subdivision (a) of Section 21152 within five days after the last initial project approval.

(B) If the notice required by subdivision (a) of Section 21152 is filed after June 1, 2013, this section shall become inoperative as of June 1, 2013, and is repealed as of January 1, 2014.

(C) In the event this section is repealed pursuant to subparagraph (B), the lead agency shall notify the Secretary of State.

(g) (1) For a petition for writ of mandate filed pursuant to this section, the lead agency shall prepare and certify the record of the proceedings in accordance with this subdivision and in accordance with Rule 3.1365 of the California Rules of Court. The applicant shall pay the lead agency for all costs of preparing and certifying the record of proceedings.

(2) No later than the date of the release of the draft environmental impact report, the lead agency shall make available to the public in a readily accessible electronic format the draft environmental impact report and all other documents submitted to or relied on by the lead agency in the preparation of the draft environmental impact report. A document prepared by the lead agency or submitted by the applicant after the date of the release of the draft environmental impact report that is a part of the record of the proceedings shall be made available to the public in a readily accessible electronic format within five business days after the document is prepared or received by the lead agency.

(3) The lead agency shall encourage written comments on the project to be submitted in a readily accessible electronic format, and shall make any such comment available to the public in a readily accessible electronic format within five days of its receipt.

(4) Within seven business days after the receipt of any comment that is not in an electronic format, the lead agency shall convert that comment into a readily accessible electronic format and make it available to the public in that format.

(5) The lead agency shall indicate in the record of the proceedings comments received that were not considered by the lead agency pursuant to paragraph (4) of subdivision (f) and need not include the content of the comments as a part of the record.

(6) Within five days after the filing of the notice required by subdivision (a) of Section 21152, the lead agency shall certify the record of the proceedings for the approval or determination and shall provide an electronic copy of the record to a party that has submitted a written request for a copy. The lead agency may charge and collect a reasonable fee for the electronic copy, which shall not exceed the reasonable cost of reproducing that copy.

(7) Within 10 days after being served with a petition for a writ of mandate pursuant to paragraph (1) of subdivision (d), the lead agency shall lodge a copy of the certified record of proceedings with the Court of Appeal.

(8) Any dispute over the content of the record of the proceedings shall be resolved by the Court of Appeal. Unless the Court of Appeal directs otherwise, a party disputing the content of the record shall file a motion to augment the record at the time it files its initial brief.

(9) The contents of the record of proceedings shall be as set forth in subdivision (e) of Section 21167.6.

(h) It is the intent of the Legislature that the project minimize traffic congestion and air quality impacts that may result from private automobile trips to the stadium through the requirements of this division as supplemented, pursuant to subdivision (i), by the implementation of measures that will do both of the following:

(1) Achieve and maintain carbon neutrality by reducing to zero the net emissions of greenhouse gases, as defined in subdivision (g) of Section 38505 of the Health and Safety Code, from private automobile trips to the stadium.

(2) Achieve and maintain a trip ratio that is no more than 90 percent of the trip ratio at any other stadium serving a team in the National Football League.

(i) (1) As a condition of approval of the project subject to this section, the lead agency shall require the applicant to implement measures that will meet the requirements of this division and paragraph (1) of subdivision (h) by the end of the first season during which a National Football League team has played at the stadium. To maximize public health, environmental, and employment benefits, the lead agency shall place the highest priority on feasible measures that will reduce greenhouse gas emissions on the stadium site and in the neighboring communities of the stadium. Offset credits shall be employed by the applicant only after feasible local emission reduction measures have been implemented. The applicant shall, to the extent feasible, place the highest priority on the purchase of offset credits that produce emission reductions within the city or the boundaries of the South Coast Air Quality Management District.

(2) To ensure that the stadium achieves a trip ratio that is no more than 90 percent of the trip ratio at any other stadium serving a team in the National Football League, the applicant shall implement the necessary measures as follows:

(A) Not later than the date of the certification of the environmental impact report for the project, the lead agency shall develop and adopt a protocol to implement this subdivision pursuant to this division and subdivision (h), including, but not limited to, criteria and guidelines that will be used to determine the trip ratio.

(B) Following the conclusion of the second, third, fourth, and fifth seasons during which a National Football League team has played at the stadium, the applicant shall prepare a report to the lead agency that describes the measures it has undertaken to reduce trips based on the protocol developed and adopted pursuant to subparagraph (A), the trip ratio at the stadium, and the results of those measures. The report shall also include a summary of publicly available data and other data gathered by the applicant regarding average vehicle ridership, nonpassenger automobile modes of arrival, and trip reduction measures undertaken at other stadiums serving a team in the National Football League.

(C) Following the lead agency's review of the report submitted allowing the fourth season, the lead agency shall determine whether adequate data is available to determine whether the trip ratio at stadium events is more than 90 percent of the trip ratio at any other stadiums serving a National Football League team. If the lead agency concludes that adequate data does not exist, the lead agency shall take necessary steps to collect, or cause to be collected, the data reasonably necessary to make the determination. The applicant shall pay the reasonable costs of collecting the data pursuant to subdivision (a) of Section 21089.

(D) Following the lead agency's review of the report submitted following the fifth season, the lead agency shall determine the trip ratio at stadium events and the lowest trip ratio at any other stadium serving a National Football League team. If the trip ratio at the stadium is more than 90 percent of the trip ratio at the other stadium with the lowest trip ratio, the lead agency shall, within six months following the receipt of the report, require the applicant to implement additional feasible measures that the lead agency determines pursuant to subparagraph (E) will be sufficient for the stadium to achieve the target specified in paragraph (2) of subdivision (h).

(E) Any trip reduction measure used at other stadiums serving a National Football League team shall be presumed to be feasible unless a preponderance of the evidence demonstrates that the measure is infeasible. The lead agency's decision whether to adopt any mitigation measures pursuant to subparagraph (D) other than those used at another stadium serving a National Football League team shall be governed by the substantial evidence test. This subparagraph does not require the applicant to bear the cost of improving the capacity or performance of transit facilities other than the following:
  (i) Temporarily expanding the capacity of a public transit line, as needed, to serve stadium events.
  (ii) Providing private charter buses or other similar services, as needed, to serve stadium events.
  (iii) Paying its fair share of the cost of measures that expand the capacity of a public fixed or light rail station that is used by spectators attending stadium events.

(F) Any action or proceeding to attack, review, set aside, void, or annul a determination, finding, or decision of the lead agency regarding the additional mitigation measures pursuant to subparagraph (D) shall be commenced within 30 days following the lead agency's filing of the notice required by subdivision (a) of Section 21152 and shall be governed by this division. The procedures set forth in subdivision (d) shall not apply to that action or proceeding. Notwithstanding any other law, compliance or noncompliance with this paragraph shall not result in the stadium being required to cease or limit operations.

(G) If the lead agency requires the applicant to implement additional measures pursuant to subparagraph (D), the applicant shall submit the report described in subparagraph (B) to the lead agency following the conclusion of each subsequent season until the lead agency determines that the applicant has achieved a trip ratio at the stadium that is not more than 90 percent of the trip ratio at any other stadium serving a National Football League team for two consecutive seasons or until the applicant submits the required report following the conclusion of the 10th season, whichever occurs earlier. Nothing in this subparagraph affects the ongoing obligations of the applicant pursuant to subdivision (h) and this subdivision.

(H) All obligations of the applicant set forth in this subdivision or imposed upon the applicant by the lead agency pursuant to this subdivision shall run with the land.

(3) This subdivision and subdivision (h) shall not serve as a basis for any action or proceeding to attack, set aside, void, or annul a determination, finding, or decision of the lead agency in certifying the environmental impact report for the project or in granting the initial or subsequent project approvals.

(4) The obligations imposed pursuant to this subdivision and subdivision (h) supplement, and do not replace, mitigation measures otherwise imposed on the project pursuant to this division.

(i) (1) An action or proceeding to attack, set aside, void, or annul a determination, finding, or decision of the lead agency granting a subsequent project approval shall be subject to the requirements of Chapter 6 (commencing with Section 21165).

(2) (A) In granting relief in an action or proceeding brought pursuant to this subdivision, the court shall not stay or enjoin the construction or operation of the project unless the court finds either of the following:
  (i) The continued construction or operation of the project presents an imminent threat to the public health and safety.
  (ii) The project site contains unforeseen important Native American artifacts or unforeseen important historical, archaeological, or ecological values that would be materially, permanently, and adversely affected by the continued construction or operation of the project.

(B) If the court finds that clause (i) or (ii) is satisfied, the court shall only enjoin those specific project activities that present an imminent threat to public health and safety or that materially, permanently, and adversely affect unforeseen important Native American artifacts or unforeseen important historical, archaeological, or ecological values.

(k) The provisions of this section are severable. If any provision of this section or its application is held invalid, that invalidity shall not affect other provisions or applications that can be given effect without the invalid provision or application.

21168.7. Sections 21168 and 21168.5 are declaratory of existing law with respect to the judicial review of determinations or decisions of public agencies made pursuant to this division.

21168.9. (a) If a court finds, as a result of a trial, hearing, or remand from an appellate court, that any determination, finding, or decision of a public agency has been made without compliance with this division, the court shall enter an order that includes one or more of the following:
  (1) A mandate that the determination, finding, or decision be voided by the public agency, in whole or in part.
  (2) If the court finds that a specific project activity or activities will prejudice the consideration or implementation of particular mitigation measures or alternatives to the project, a mandate that the public agency and any real parties in interest suspend any or all specific project activity or activities, pursuant to the determination, finding, or decision, that could result in an adverse change or alteration to the physical environment, until the public agency has taken any actions that may be necessary to bring the determination, finding, or decision into compliance with this division.
  (3) A mandate that the public agency take specific action as may be necessary to bring the determination, finding, or decision into compliance with this division.

(b) Any order pursuant to subdivision (a) shall include only those mandates which are necessary to achieve compliance with this division and only those specific project activities in noncompliance with this division. The order shall be made by the issuance of a peremptory writ of mandate specifying what action by the public agency is necessary to comply with this division. However, the order shall be limited to that portion of a determination, finding, or decision or the specific project activity or activities found to be in noncompliance only if a court finds that (1) the portion or specific project activity or activities are severable, (2) severance will not prejudice complete and full compliance with this division, and (3) the court has not found the remainder of the project to be in noncompliance with this division. The trial court shall retain jurisdiction over the public agency's proceedings by way of a return to the peremptory writ until the court has determined that the public agency has complied with this division.

(c) Nothing in this section authorizes a court to direct any public agency to exercise its discretion in any particular way. Except as expressly provided in this section, nothing in this section is intended to limit the equitable powers of the court.

21169. Any project defined in subdivision (c) of Section 21065 undertaken, carried out or approved on or before the effective date of this section and the issuance by any public agency of any lease, permit, license, certificate or other entitlement for use executed or issued on or before the effective date of this section notwithstanding a failure to comply with this division, if otherwise legal and valid, is hereby confirmed, validated and declared legally effective. Any project undertaken by a person which was supported in whole or part through contracts with one or more public agencies on or before the effective date of this section, notwithstanding a failure to comply with this division, if otherwise legal and valid, is hereby confirmed, validated and declared legally effective.

21169.11. (a) At any time after a petition has been filed pursuant to this division, but at least 30 days before the hearing on the merits, a party may file a motion requesting the court to impose a sanction for a frivolous claim made in the course of an action brought pursuant to this division.

(b) If the court determines that a claim is frivolous, the court may impose an appropriate sanction, in an amount up to ten thousand dollars ($10,000), upon the attorneys, law firms, or parties responsible for the violation.

(c) For purposes of this section, "frivolous" means totally and completely without merit.

(d) (1) This section shall remain in effect only until January 1, 2016, and as of that date is repealed, unless a later enacted statute, that is enacted before January 1, 2016, deletes or extends that date.

(2) Notwithstanding paragraph (1), the sanction provided pursuant to this section shall apply to an action filed on or before December 31, 2015.

21170. (a) Section 21169 shall not operate to confirm, validate or give legal effect to any project the legality of which was being contested in a judicial proceeding in which proceeding the pleadings, prior to the effective date of this section, alleged facts constituting a cause of action for, or raised the issue of, a violation of this division and which was pending and undetermined on the effective date of this section; provided, however, that Section 21169 shall operate to confirm, validate or give legal effect to any project to which this subdivision applies if, prior to the commencement of judicial proceedings and in good faith and in reliance upon the issuance by a public agency of any lease, permit, license, certificate or other entitlement for use, substantial construction has been performed and substantial liabilities for construction and necessary materials have been incurred.

(b) Section 21169 shall not operate to confirm, validate or give legal effect to any project which had been determined in any judicial proceeding, on or before the effective date of this section to be illegal, void or ineffective because of noncompliance with this division.

21171. This division, except for Section 21169, shall not apply to the issuance of any lease, permit, license, certificate or other entitlement for use for any project defined in subdivision (c) of Section 21065 or to any project undertaken by a person which is supported in whole or in part through contracts with one or more public agencies until the 121st day after the effective date of this section. This section shall not apply to any project to which Section 21170 is applicable or to any successor project which is the same as, or substantially identical to, such a project.

This section shall not prohibit or prevent a public agency, prior to the 121st day after the effective date of this section, from considering environmental factors in connection with the approval or disapproval of a project and from imposing reasonable fees in connection therewith.

21172. This division shall not apply to any project undertaken, carried out, or approved by a public agency to maintain, repair, restore, demolish or replace property or facilities damaged or destroyed as a result of a disaster in a disaster stricken area in which a state of emergency has been proclaimed by the Governor pursuant to Chapter 7 (commencing with Section 8550) of Division 1, Title 2 of the Government Code.

21172.5. Until the 121st day after the effective date of this section, any objectives, criteria and procedures adopted by public agencies in compliance with this division shall govern the evaluation of projects defined in subdivisions (a) and (b) of Section 21065 and the preparation of environmental impact reports on such projects when required by this division. Any environmental impact report which has been completed or on which substantial work has been performed on or before the 121st day after the effective date of this section, if otherwise legally sufficient, shall, when completed, be deemed to be in compliance with this division and no further environmental impact report shall be required except as provided in Section 21166.

21173. If any provision of this division or the application thereof to any person or circumstances is held invalid, such invalidity shall not affect other provisions or applications of this division which can be given effect without the invalid provision or application thereof, and to this end the provisions of this division are severable.

21174. No provision of this division is a limitation or restriction on the power or authority of any public agency in the enforcement or administration of any provision of law which it is specifically permitted or required to enforce or administer, including, but not limited to, the powers and authority granted to the California Coastal Commission pursuant to Division 20 (commencing with Section 30000). To the extent of any inconsistency or conflict between the provisions of the California Coastal Act of 1976 (Division 20 (commencing with Section 30000)) and the provisions of this division, the provisions of Division 20 (commencing with Section 30000) shall control.

21175. In the event that a local agency formation commission, acting pursuant to the provisions of Chapter 6.6 (commencing with Section 54773) of Part 1 of Division 2 of Title 5 of, or pursuant to Division 1 (commencing with Section 56000) of Title 6 of, the Government Code, has approved a project without complying with this division, such approval is hereby confirmed, validated, and declared legally effective notwithstanding the failure to comply with this division; provided, that such approval shall have occurred prior to February 7, 1975.

21176. (a) Section 21175 shall not operate to confirm, validate, or give legal effect to any project, the legality of which was being contested in a judicial proceeding in which proceeding the pleadings, prior to February 7, 1975, alleged facts constituting a cause of action for, or raised the issue of, a violation of this division, and which was pending and undetermined on February 7, 1975.

(b) Section 21175 shall not operate to confirm, validate, or give legal effect to any project which had been determined in any judicial proceeding, on or before the effective date of this section, to be illegal, void, or ineffective because of noncompliance with this division.

21177. (a) An action or proceeding shall not be brought pursuant to Section 21167 unless the alleged grounds for noncompliance with this division were presented to the public agency orally or in writing by any person during the public comment period provided by this division or prior to the close of the public hearing on the project before the issuance of the notice of determination.

(b) A person shall not maintain an action or proceeding unless that person objected to the approval of the project orally or in writing during the public comment period provided by this division or prior to the close of the public hearing on the project before the filing of the notice of determination pursuant to Sections 21108 and 21152.

(c) This section does not preclude any organization formed after the approval of a project from maintaining an action pursuant to Section 21167 if a member of that organization has complied with subdivisions (a) and (b). The grounds for noncompliance may have been presented directly by a member or by a member agreeing with or supporting the comments of another person.

(d) This section does not apply to the Attorney General.

(e) This section does not apply to any alleged grounds for noncompliance with this division for which there was no public hearing or other opportunity for members of the public to raise those objections orally or in writing prior to the approval of the project, or if the public agency failed to give the notice required by law.

(f) This section shall remain in effect only until January 1, 2016, and as of that date is repealed, unless a later enacted statute, that is enacted before January 1, 2016, deletes or extends that date.

Chapter 6.5: Jobs and Economic Improvement through Environmental Leadership Act of 2011

21178. The Legislature finds and declares all of the following:

(a) The overall unemployment rate in California is 12 percent, and in certain regions of the state that rate exceeds 13 percent.

(b) The California Environmental Quality Act (Division 13 (commencing with Section 21000) of the Public Resources Code) requires that the environmental impacts of development projects be identified and mitigated.

(c) The act also guarantees the public an opportunity to review and comment on the environmental impacts of a project and to participate meaningfully in the development of mitigation measures for potentially significant environmental impacts.

(d) There are large projects under consideration in various regions of the state that would replace old and outmoded facilities with new job-creating facilities to meet those regions' needs while also establishing new, cutting-edge environmental benefits to those regions.

(e) These projects are privately financed or financed from revenues generated from the projects themselves and do not require taxpayer financing.

(f) These projects further will generate thousands of full-time jobs during construction and thousands of additional permanent jobs once they are constructed and operating.

(g) These projects also present an unprecedented opportunity to implement nation-leading innovative measures that will significantly reduce traffic, air quality, and other significant environmental impacts, and fully mitigate the greenhouse gas emissions resulting from passenger vehicle trips attributed to the project.

(h) These pollution reductions will be the best in the nation compared to other comparable projects in the United States.

(i) The purpose of this act is to provide unique and unprecedented streamlining benefits under the California Environmental Quality Act for projects that provide the benefits described above for a limited period of time to put people to work as soon as possible.

21180. For the purposes of this chapter, the following terms shall have the following meanings:

(a) "Applicant" means a public or private entity or its affiliates, or a person or entity that undertakes a public works project, that proposes a project and its successors, heirs, and assignees.

(b) "Environmental leadership development project," "leadership project," or "project" means a project as described in Section 21065 that is one the following:

(1) A residential, retail, commercial, sports, cultural, entertainment, or recreational use project that is certified as LEED silver or better by the United States Green Building Council and, where applicable, that achieves a 10-percent greater standard for transportation efficiency than for comparable projects. These projects must be located on an infill site. For a project that is within a metropolitan planning organization for which a sustainable communities strategy or alternative planning strategy is in effect, the infill project shall be consistent with the general use designation, density, building intensity, and applicable policies specified for the project area in either a sustainable communities strategy or an alternative planning strategy, for which the State Air Resources Board, pursuant to subparagraph (H) of paragraph (2) of subdivision (b) of Section 65080 of the Government Code, has accepted a metropolitan planning organization's determination that the sustainable communities strategy or the alternative planning strategy would, if implemented, achieve the greenhouse gas emission reduction targets.

(2) A clean renewable energy project that generates electricity exclusively through wind or solar, but not including waste incineration or conversion.

(3) A clean energy manufacturing project that manufactures products, equipment, or components used for renewable energy generation, energy efficiency, or for the production of clean alternative fuel vehicles.

(c) "Transportation efficiency" means the number of vehicle trips by employees, visitors, or customers of the residential, retail, commercial, sports, cultural, entertainment, or recreational use project divided by the total number of employees, visitors, and customers.

21181. This chapter does not apply to a project if the applicant fails to notify a lead agency prior to the release of the draft environmental impact report for public comment that the applicant is electing to proceed pursuant to this chapter. The lead agency shall notify the Secretary of the Natural Resources Agency if the applicant fails to provide notification pursuant to this section.

21182. A person proposing to construct a leadership project may apply to the Governor for certification that the leadership project is eligible for streamlining provided by this chapter. The person shall supply evidence and materials that the Governor deems necessary to make a decision on the application. Any evidence or materials shall be made available to the public at least 15 days before the Governor certifies a project pursuant to this chapter.

21183. The Governor may certify a leadership project for streamlining pursuant to this chapter if all the following conditions are met:

(a) The project will result in a minimum investment of one hundred million dollars ($100,000,000) in California upon completion of construction.

(b) The project creates high-wage, highly skilled jobs that pay prevailing wages and living wages and provide construction jobs and permanent jobs for Californians, and helps reduce unemployment.

(c) The project does not result in any net additional emission of greenhouse gases, including greenhouse gas emissions from employee transportation, as determined by the State Air Resources Board pursuant to Division 25.5 (commencing with Section 38500) of the Health and Safety Code.

(d) The project applicant has entered into a binding and enforceable agreement that all mitigation measures required pursuant to this division to certify the project under this chapter shall be conditions of approval of the project, and those conditions will be fully enforceable by the lead agency or another agency designated by the lead agency. In the case of environmental mitigation measures, the applicant agrees, as an ongoing obligation, that those measures will be monitored and enforced by the lead agency for the life of the obligation.

(e) The project applicant agrees to pay the costs of the Court of Appeal in hearing and deciding any case, including payment of the costs for the appointment of a special master if deemed appropriate by the court, in a form and manner specified by the Judicial Council, as provided in the Rules of Court adopted by the Judicial Council pursuant to subdivision (f) of Section 21185.

(f) The project applicant agrees to pay the costs of preparing the administrative record for the project concurrent with review and consideration of the project pursuant to this division, in a form and manner specified by the lead agency for the project.

21184.

(a) The Governor may certify a project for streamlining pursuant to this chapter if it complies with the conditions specified in Section 21183.

(b) (1) Prior to certifying a project, the Governor shall make a determination that each of the conditions specified in Section 21183 has been met. These findings are not subject to judicial review.

(2) (A) If the Governor determines that a leadership project is eligible for streamlining pursuant to this chapter, he or she shall submit that determination, and any supporting information, to the Joint Legislative Budget Committee for review and concurrence or nonconcurrence.

(B) Within 30 days of receiving the determination, the Joint Legislative Budget Committee shall concur or nonconcur in writing on the determination.

(C) If the Joint Legislative Budget Committee fails to concur or nonconcur on a determination by the Governor within 30 days of the submittal, the leadership project is deemed to be certified.

(c) The Governor may issue guidelines regarding application and certification of projects pursuant to this chapter. Any guidelines issued pursuant to this subdivision are not subject to the rulemaking provisions of the Administrative Procedure Act (Chapter 3.5 (commencing with Section 11340) of Part 1 of Division 3 of Title 2 of the Government Code).

21185.

(a) Notwithstanding any other law, any action or proceeding alleging that a public agency or has approved or is undertaking a leadership project certified by the Governor in violation of this division shall be conducted in accordance with the following streamlining benefits:

(1) The action or proceeding shall be filed in the Court of Appeal with geographic jurisdiction over the project.

(2) Any party bringing such a claim shall also file concurrently any other claims alleging that a public agency has granted land use approvals for the leadership project in violation of the law. The Court of Appeal shall have original jurisdiction over all those claims.

(3) The Court of Appeal shall issue its decision in the case within 175 days of the filing of the petition.

(4) The court may appoint a master to assist the court in managing and processing the case.

(5) The court may grant extensions of time only for good cause shown and in order to promote the interests of justice.

(b) On or before July 1, 2012, the Judicial Council shall adopt Rules of Court to implement this chapter.

21186. Notwithstanding any other law, the preparation and certification of the administrative record for a leadership project certified by the Governor shall be performed in the following manner:

(a) The lead agency for the project shall prepare the administrative record pursuant to this division concurrently with the administrative process.

(b) All documents and other materials placed in the administrative record shall be posted on, and be downloadable from, an Internet Web site maintained by the lead agency commencing with the date of the release of the draft environmental impact report.

(c) The lead agency shall make available to the public in a readily accessible electronic format the draft environmental impact report and all other documents submitted to, or relied on by, the lead agency in the preparation of the draft environmental impact report.

(d) A document prepared by the lead agency or submitted by the applicant after the date of the release of the draft environmental impact report that is a part of the record of the proceedings shall be made available to the public in a readily accessible electronic format within five business days after the document is released or received by the lead agency.

(e) The lead agency shall encourage written comments on the project to be submitted in a readily accessible electronic format, and shall make any comment available to the public in a readily accessible electronic format within five days of its receipt.

(f) Within seven business days after the receipt of any comment that is not in an electronic format, the lead agency shall convert that comment into a readily accessible electronic format and make it available to the public in that format.

(g) The lead agency shall certify the final administrative record within five days of its approval of the project.

(h) Any dispute arising from the administrative record shall be resolved by the Court of Appeal pursuant to Section 21185.

21187. The draft and final environmental impact report shall include a notice in no less than 12-point type stating the following:

"THIS EIR IS SUBJECT TO CHAPTER 6.5 (COMMENCING WITH SECTION 21178) OF THE PUBLIC RESOURCES CODE, WHICH PROVIDES, AMONG OTHER THINGS, THAT ANY JUDICIAL ACTION CHALLENGING THE CERTIFICATION OF THE EIR OR THE APPROVAL OF THE PROJECT DESCRIBED IN THE EIR IS SUBJECT TO THE PROCEDURES SET FORTH IN SECTION 21178.2 OF THE PUBLIC RESOURCES CODE AND MUST BE FILED WITH THE COURT OF APPEAL. A COPY OF CHAPTER 6.5 OF THE PUBLIC RESOURCES CODE IS INCLUDED IN THE APPENDIX TO THIS EIR."

21188. The provisions of this chapter are severable. If any provision of this chapter or its application is held to be invalid, that invalidity shall not affect any other provision or application that can be given effect without the invalid provision or application.

21189. Except as otherwise provided expressly in this chapter, nothing in this chapter affects the duty of any party to comply with this division.

21189.1.

(a) If a lead agency fails to certify an environmental impact report for a leadership project subject to this chapter on or before June 1, 2014, this chapter shall not apply to that project. The lead agency shall notify the Secretary of the Natural Resources Agency by July 1, 2014, if an environmental impact report subject to this chapter has not been certified by that date.

(b) If, prior to June 1, 2014, a certification issued pursuant to this chapter has not been used or the time period during which an action or proceeding, for purposes of Section 21185, may be filed under this chapter has not elapsed, the certification expires and is no longer valid.

21189.2. The Judicial Council shall report to the Legislature on or before January 1, 2015, on the effects of this chapter, which shall include, but not be limited to, a description of the benefits, costs, and detriments of the certification of leadership projects pursuant to this chapter.

21189.3 This chapter shall remain in effect until January 1, 2015, and as of that date is repealed unless a later enacted statute extends or repeals that date.

The maintenance of a quality environment for the people of this state now and in the future is a mtter of statewide concern. (Pub. Res. Code Section 21000(a))

Appendix 2

Guidelines for Implementing the California Environmental Quality Act

California Code of Regulations, Title 14, Division 6
Chapter 3. Section 1500-15387 and Appendices A-K

Table of Contents, July 2011

Division 6. Resources Agency
Chapter 3. Guidelines for Implementation of the California Environmental Quality Act

Article 1. General

§ 15000. Authority.

The regulations contained in this chapter are prescribed by the Secretary for Resources to be followed by all state and local agencies in California in the implementation of the California Environmental Quality Act. These Guidelines have been developed by the Office of Planning and Research for adoption by the Secretary for Resources in accordance with Section 2108-3. Additional information may be obtained by writing:Secretary for Resources Room 1311, 1416 Ninth Street Sacramento, CA 95814. These Guidelines are binding on all public agencies in California.

Note: Authority cited: Section 21083, Public Resources Code. Reference: Sections 21082 and 21083, Public Resources Code; *City of Santa Ana v. City of Garden Grove* (1979), 100 Cal. App. 3d 521.

§ 15001. Short Title.

These Guidelines may be cited as the "State CEQA Guidelines." Existing references to the "State EIR Guidelines" shall be construed to be references to the "State CEQA Guidelines."

Note: Authority cited: Section 21083, Public Resources Code. Reference: Section 21083, Public Resources Code.

§ 15002. General Concepts.

(a) Basic Purposes of CEQA. The basic purposes of CEQA are to:
  (1) Inform governmental decision makers and the public about the potential, significant environmental effects of proposed activities.
  (2) Identify ways that environmental damage can be avoided or significantly reduced.
  (3) Prevent significant, avoidable damage to the environment by requiring changes in projects through the use of alternatives or mitigation measures when the governmental agency finds the changes to be feasible.
  (4) Disclose to the public the reasons why a governmental agency approved the project in the manner the agency chose if significant environmental effects are involved.

(b) Governmental Action. CEQA applies to governmental action. This action may involve:
  (1) Activities directly undertaken by a governmental agency,
  (2) Activities financed in whole or in part by a governmental agency, or
  (3) Private activities which require approval from a governmental agency.

(c) Private Action. Private action is not subject to CEQA unless the action involves governmental participation, financing, or approval.(d) Project. A "project" is an activity subject to CEQA. The term "project" has been interpreted to mean far more than the ordinary dictionary definition of the term. See Section 15378.(e) Time for Compliance. A governmental agency is required to comply with CEQA procedures when the agency proposes to carry out or approve the activity. See Section 15004.(f) Environmental Impact Reports and Negative Declarations. An environmental impact report (EIR) is the public document used by the governmental agency to analyze the significant environmental effects of a proposed project, to identify alternatives, and to disclose possible ways to reduce or avoid the possible environmental damage.
  (1) An EIR is prepared when the public agency finds substantial evidence that the project may have a significant effect on the environment. See Section 15064(a)(1).
  (2) When the agency finds that there is no substantial evidence that a project may have a significant environmental effect, the agency will prepare a "Negative Declaration" instead of an EIR. See Section 15070.

(g) Significant Effect on the Environment. A significant effect on the environment is defined as a substantial adverse change in the physical conditions which exist in the area affected by the proposed project. See Section 15382. Further, when an EIR identifies a significant effect, the government agency approving the project must make findings on whether the adverse environmental effects have been substantially reduced or if not, why not. See Section 15091.(h) Methods for Protecting the Environment. CEQA requires more than merely preparing environmental documents. The EIR by itself does not control the way in which a project can be built or carried out. Rather, when an EIR shows that a project could cause substantial adverse changes in the environment, the governmental agency must respond to the information by one or more of the following methods:
  (1) Changing a proposed project;
  (2) Imposing conditions on the approval of the project;
  (3) Adopting plans or ordinances to control a broader class of projects to avoid the adverse changes;
  (4) Choosing an alternative way of meeting the same need;
  (5) Disapproving the project;
  (6) Finding that changes in, or alterations, the project are not feasible.
  (7) Finding that the unavoidable, significant environmental damage is acceptable as provided in Section 15093.

(i) Discretionary Action. CEQA applies in situations where a governmental agency can use its judgment in deciding whether and how to carry out or approve a project. A project subject to such judgmental controls is called a "discretionary project." See Section 15357.
  (1) Where the law requires a governmental agency to act on a project in a set way without allowing the agency to use its own judgment, the project is called "ministerial," and CEQA does not apply. See Section 15369.
  (2) Whether an agency has discretionary or ministerial controls over a project depends on the authority granted by the law providing the controls over the activity. Similar projects may be subject to discretionary controls in one city or county and only ministerial controls in another. See Section 15268.

(j) Public Involvement. Under CEQA, an agency must solicit and respond to comments from the public and from other agencies concerned with the project. See Sections 15073, 15086, 15087 and 15088.(k) Three Step Process. An agency will normally take up to three separate steps in deciding which document to prepare for a project subject to CEQA.
  (1) In the first step the lead agency examines the project to determine whether the project is sub-

ject to CEQA at all. If the project is exempt, the process does not need to proceed any farther. The agency may prepare a notice of exemption. See Sections 15061 and 15062.

(2) If the project is not exempt, the lead agency takes the second step and conducts an initial study (Section 15063) to determine whether the project may have a significant effect on the environment. If the initial study shows that there is no substantial evidence that the project may have a significant effect, the lead agency prepares a negative declaration. See Sections 15070 et seq.

(3) If the initial study shows that the project may have a significant effect, the lead agency takes the third step and prepares an EIR. See Sections 15080 et seq.

(l) Certified Equivalent Programs. A number of environmental regulatory programs have been certified by the Secretary of the Resources Agency as involving essentially the same consideration of environmental issues as is provided by use of EIRs and negative declarations. Certified programs are exempt from preparing EIRs and negative declarations but use other documents instead. Certified programs are discussed in Article 17 and are listed in Section 15251.(m) This section is intended to present the general concepts of CEQA in a simplified and introductory manner. If there are any conflicts between the short statement of a concept in this section and the provisions of other sections of these guidelines, the other sections shall prevail.

Note: Authority cited: Section 21083, Public Resources Code. Reference: Sections 21000-21176, Public Resources Code; *No Oil, Inc. v. City of Los Angeles*, 13 Cal. 3d 68 (1974); *Running Fence Corp. v. Superior Court*, 15 Cal. App. 3d 400 (1975).

§ 15003. Policies.

In addition to the policies declared by the Legislature concerning environmental protection and administration of CEQA in Sections 21000, 21001, 21002, and 21002.1 of the Public Resources Code, the courts of this state have declared the following policies to be implicit in CEQA:(a) The EIR requirement is the heart of CEQA. (*County of Inyo v. Yorty*, 32 Cal. App. 3d 795.)(b) The EIR serves not only to protect the environment but also to demonstrate to the public that it is being protected. (*County of Inyo v. Yorty*, 32 Cal. App. 3d 795.)(c) The EIR is to inform other governmental agencies and the public generally of the environmental impact of a proposed project. (*No Oil, Inc. v. City of Los Angeles*, 13 C. 3d 68.)(d) The EIR is to demonstrate to an apprehensive citizenry that the agency has, in fact, analyzed and considered the ecological implications of its action. (*People ex rel. Department of Public Works v. Bosio*, 47 Cal. App. 3d 495.)(e) The EIR process will enable the public to determine the environmental and economic values of their elected and appointed officials thus allowing for appropriate action come election day should a majority of the voters disagree. (*People v. County of Kern*, 39 Cal. App. 3d 830.)(f) CEQA was intended to be interpreted in such a manner as to afford the fullest possible protection to the environment within the reasonable scope of the statutory language. (*Friends of Mammoth v. Board of Supervisors*, 8 Cal. 3d 247.)(g) The purpose of CEQA is not to generate paper, but to compel government at all levels to make decisions with environmental consequences in mind. (*Bozung v. LAFCO* (1975) 13 Cal.3d 263)(h) The lead agency must consider the whole of an action, not simply its constituent parts, when determining whether it will have a significant environmental effect. (*Citizens Assoc. For Sensible Development of Bishop Area v. County of Inyo* (1985) 172 Cal.App.3d 151)(i) CEQA does not require technical perfection in an EIR, but rather adequacy, completeness, and a good-faith effort at full disclosure. A court does not pass upon the correctness of an EIR's environmental conclusions, but only determines if the EIR is sufficient as an informational document. (*Kings County Farm Bureau v. City of Hanford* (1990) 221 Cal.App.3d 692)(j) CEQA requires that decisions be informed and balanced. It must not be subverted into an instrument for the oppression and delay of social, economic, or recreational development or advancement. (*Laurel Heights Improvement Assoc. v. Regents of U.C.* (1993) 6 Cal.4th 1112 and *Citizens of Goleta Valley v. Board of Supervisors* (1990) 52 Cal.3d 553)

Note: Authority cited: Section 21083, Public Resources Code. Reference: Sections 21000-21176, Public Resources Code.

§ 15004. Time of Preparation.

(a) Before granting any approval of a project subject to CEQA, every lead agency or responsible agency shall consider a final EIR or negative declaration or another document authorized by these guidelines to be used in the place of an EIR or negative declaration. See the definition of "approval" in Section 15352.(b) Choosing the precise time for CEQA compliance involves a balancing of competing factors. EIRs and negative declarations should be prepared as early as feasible in the planning process to enable environmental considerations to influence project program and design and yet late enough to provide meaningful information for environmental assessment.

(1) With public projects, at the earliest feasible time, project sponsors shall incorporate environmental considerations into project conceptualization, design, and planning. CEQA compliance should be completed prior to acquisition of a site for a public project.

(2) To implement the above principles, public agencies shall not undertake actions concerning the proposed public project that would have a significant adverse effect or limit the choice of alternatives or mitigation measures, before completion of CEQA compliance. For example, agencies shall not:

(A) Formally make a decision to proceed with the use of a site for facilities which would require CEQA review, regardless of whether the agency has made any final purchase of the site for these facilities, except that agencies may designate a preferred site for CEQA review and may enter into land acquisition agreements when the agency has conditioned the agency's future use of the site on CEQA compliance.

(B) Otherwise take any action which gives impetus to a planned or foreseeable project in a manner that forecloses alternatives or mitigation measures that would ordinarily be part of CEQA review of that public project.

(3) With private projects, the Lead Agency shall encourage the project proponent to incorporate environmental considerations into project conceptualization, design, and planning at the earliest feasible time.

(c) The environmental document preparation and review should be coordinated in a timely fashion with the existing planning, review, and project approval processes being used by each public agency. These procedures, to the maximum extent feasible, are to run concurrently, not consecutively. When the lead agency is a state agency, the environmental document shall be included as part of the regular project report if such a report is used in its existing review and budgetary process.

Note: Authority cited: Section 21083, Public Resources Code. Reference: Sections 21003, 21061 and 21105, Public Resources Code; *Friends of Mammoth v. Board of Supervisors* (1972) 8 Cal. 3d 247; *Mount Sutro Defense Committee v. Regents of the University of California* (1978) 77 Cal. App. 3d 20.

§ 15005. Terminology.

The following words are used to indicate whether a particular subject in the Guidelines is mandatory, advisory, or permissive:(a) "Must" or "shall" identifies a mandatory element which all public agencies are required to follow.(b) "Should" identifies guidance provided by the Secretary for Resources based on policy considerations contained in CEQA, in the legislative history of the statute, or in federal court decisions which California courts can be expected to follow. Public agencies are advised to follow this guidance in the absence of compelling, countervailing considerations.(c) "May" identifies a permissive element which is left fully to the discretion of the public agencies involved.

Note: Authority cited: Section 21083, Public Resources Code. Reference: Sections 21082 and 21083, Public Resources Code.

§ 15006. Reducing Delay and Paperwork.

Public agencies should reduce delay and paperwork by:(a) Integrating the CEQA process into early planning. (15004(c))(b) Ensuring the swift and fair resolution of lead agency disputes. (15053)(c) Identifying projects which fit within categorical exemptions and are therefore exempt from CEQA processing. (15300.4)(d) Using initial studies to identify significant environmental issues and to narrow the scope of EIRs. (15063)(e) Using a negative declaration when a project not otherwise exempt will not have a significant effect on the environment. (15070)(f) Using a previously prepared EIR when it adequately addresses the proposed project. (15153)(g) Consulting with state and local responsible agencies before and during preparation of an environmental impact report so that the document will meet the needs of all the agencies which will use it. (15083)(h) Urging applicants, either before or after the filing of an application, to revise projects to eliminate possible significant effects on the environment, thereby enabling the project to qualify for a negative declaration rather than an environmental impact report. (15063(c)(2))(i) Integrating CEQA requirements with other environmental review and consulting requirements. (Public Resources Code Section 21080.5)(j) Eliminating duplication with federal procedures by providing for joint preparation of environmental documents with federal agencies and by adopting completed federal NEPA documents. (15227)(k) Emphasizing consultation before an environmental impact report is prepared, rather than submitting adversary comments on a completed document. (15082(b))(l) Combining environmental documents with other documents such as general plans. (15166)(m) Eliminating repetitive discussions of the same issues by using environmental impact reports on programs, policies, or plans and tiering from reports of broad scope to those of narrower scope. (15152)(n) Reducing the length of environmental impact reports by means such as setting appropriate page limits. (15141)(o) Preparing analytic rather than encyclopedic environmental impact reports. (15142)(p) Mentioning only briefly issues other than significant ones in EIRs. (15143)(q) Writing environmental impact reports in plain language. (15140)(r) Following a clear format for environmental impact reports. (15120)(s) Emphasizing the portions of the environmental impact report that are useful to decision-makers and the public and reducing emphasis on background material. (15143)(t) Using incorporation by reference. (15150)(u) Making comments on environmental impact reports as specific as possible. (15204)

Note: Authority cited: Section 21083, Public Resources Code. Reference: Sections 21003 and 21083, Public Resources Code.

§ 15007. Amendments.

(a) These guidelines will be amended from time to time to match new developments relating to CEQA.(b) Amendments to the guidelines apply prospectively only. New requirements in amendments will apply to steps in the CEQA process not yet undertaken by the date when agencies must comply with the amendments.(c) If a document meets the content requirements in effect when the document is set out for public review, the document shall not need to be revised to conform to any new content requirements in guideline amendments taking effect before the document is finally approved.(d) Public agencies shall comply with new requirements in amendments to the guidelines beginning with the earlier of the following two dates:
   (1) The effective date of the agency's procedures amended to conform to the new guideline amendments; or
   (2) The 120th day after the effective date of the guideline amendments.
(e) Public agencies may implement any permissive or advisory elements of the guidelines beginning with the effective date of the guideline amendments.

Note: Authority cited: Section 21083, Public Resources Code. Reference: Sections 21082-21086, Public Resources Code; Stevens v. City of Glendale, 125 Cal. App. 3d 986.

Article 2. General Responsibilities

§ 15020. General.

Each public agency is responsible for complying with CEQA and these Guidelines. A public agency must meet its own responsibilities under CEQA and shall not rely on comments from other public agencies or private citizens as a substitute for work CEQA requires the lead agency to accomplish. For example, a lead agency is responsible for the adequacy of its environmental documents. The lead agency shall not knowingly release a deficient document hoping that public comments will correct defects in the document.

Note: Authority cited: Section 21083, Public Resources Code. Reference: Sections 21082, 21082.1, Public Resources Code; *Russian Hill Improvement Association v. Board of Permit Appeals* 44 Cal. App. 3d 158 (1975).

§ 15021. Duty to Minimize Environmental Damage and Balance Competing Public Objectives.

(a) CEQA establishes a duty for public agencies to avoid or minimize environmental damage where feasible.
   (1) In regulating public or private activities, agencies are required to give major consideration to preventing environmental damage.
   (2) A public agency should not approve a project as proposed if there are feasible alternatives or mitigation measures available that would substantially lessen any significant effects that the project would have on the environment.
(b) In deciding whether changes in a project are feasible, an agency may consider specific economic, environmental, legal, social, and technological factors.(c) The duty to prevent or minimize environmental damage is implemented through the findings required by Section 15091.(d) CEQA recognizes that in determining whether and how a project should be approved, a public agency has an obligation to balance a variety of public objectives, including economic, environmental, and social factors and in particular the goal of providing a decent home and satisfying living environment for every Californian. An agency shall prepare a statement of overriding considerations as described in Section 15093 to reflect the ultimate balancing of competing public objectives when the agency decides to approve a project that will cause one or more significant effects on the environment.

Note: Authority cited: Section 21083, Public Resources Code. Reference: Sections 21000, 21001, 21002, 21002.1 and 21081, Public Resources Code; *San Francisco Ecology Center v. City and County of San Francisco* (1975) 48 Cal. App. 3d 584; *Laurel Hills Homeowners Association v. City Council* (1978) 83 Cal. App. 3d 515.

§ 15022. Public Agency Implementing Procedures.

(a) Each public agency shall adopt objectives, criteria, and specific procedures consistent with CEQA and these Guidelines for administering its responsibilities under CEQA, including the orderly evaluation of projects and preparation of environmental documents. The implementing procedures should contain at least provisions for:
   (1) Identifying the activities that are exempt from CEQA. These procedures should contain:
      (A) Provisions for evaluating a proposed activity to determine if there is no possibility that the activity may have a significant effect on the environment.
      (B) A list of projects or permits over which the public agency has only ministerial authority.
      (C) A list of specific activities which the public agency has found to be within the categorical exemptions established by these guidelines.
   (2) Conducting initial studies.
   (3) Preparing negative declarations.
   (4) Preparing draft and final EIRs.
   (5) Consulting with and obtaining comments from other public agencies and members of the public with regard to the environmental effects of projects.
   (6) Assuring adequate opportunity and time for public review and comment on the Draft EIR or Negative Declaration.
   (7) Evaluating and responding to comments received on environmental documents.
   (8) Assigning responsibility for determining the adequacy of an EIR or negative declaration.
   (9) Reviewing and considering environmental documents by the person or decision making body who will approve or disapprove a project.
   (10) Filing documents required or authorized by CEQA and these Guidelines.
   (11) Providing adequate comments on environmental documents which are submitted to the public agency for review.
   (12) Assigning responsibility for specific functions to particular units of the public agency.
   (13) Providing time periods for performing functions under CEQA.
(b) Any district, including a school district, need not adopt objectives, criteria, and procedures of its own if it uses the objectives, criteria, and procedures of another public agency whose boundaries are coterminous with or entirely encompass the district.(c) Public agencies should revise their implementing procedures to conform to amendments to these guidelines within 120 days after the effective date of the amendments. During the period while the public agency is revising its procedures, the agency must conform to any statutory changes in the California Environmental Quality Act that have become effective regardless of whether the public agency has revised its formally adopted procedures to conform to the statutory changes.(d) In adopting procedures to implement CEQA, a public agency may adopt the State CEQA Guidelines through incorporation by reference. The agency may then adopt only those specific procedures or provisions described in subsection (a) which are necessary to tailor the general provisions of the guidelines to the specific operations of the agency. A public agency may also choose to adopt a complete set of procedures identifying in one document all the necessary requirements.

Note: Authority cited: Section 21083, Public Resources Code. Reference: Sections 21082, 21100.2 and 21151.5, Public Resources Code.

§ 15023. Office of Planning and Research (OPR).

(a) From time to time OPR shall review the State CEQA Guidelines and shall make recommendations for amendments to the Secretary for Resources.(b) OPR shall receive and evaluate proposals for adoption, amendment, or repeal of categorical exemptions and shall make recommendations on the proposals to the Secretary for Resources. People making suggestions concerning categorical exemptions shall submit their recommendations to OPR with supporting information to show that the class of projects in the proposal either will or will not have a significant effect on the environment.(c) The State Clearinghouse in the Office of Planning and Research shall be responsible for distributing environmental documents to State agencies, departments, boards, and commissions for review and comment.(d) Upon request of a Lead Agency or a project applicant, OPR shall provide assistance in identifying the various responsible agencies and any federal agencies which have responsibility for carrying out or approving a proposed project.(e) OPR shall ensure that state responsible agencies provide the necessary information to lead agencies in response to notices of preparation within at most 30 days after receiving a notice of preparation.(f) OPR shall resolve disputes as to which agency is the lead agency for a project.(g) OPR shall receive and file all notices of completion, determination, and exemption.(h) OPR shall establish and maintain a database for the collection, storage, retrieval, and dissemination of notices of exemption, notices of preparation, notices of determination, and notices of completion provided to the office. This database of notice information shall be available through the Internet.

Note: Authority cited: Section 21083, Public Resources Code. Reference: Sections 21080.4, 21083, 21086, 21087, 21108, 21159.9 and 21161, Public Resources Code.

§ 15024. Secretary for Resources.

(a) The Guidelines shall be adopted by the Secretary for Resources. The Secretary shall make a finding that each class of projects given a categorical exemption will not have a significant effect on the environment.(b) The Secretary may issue amendments to these Guidelines.(c) The Secretary shall certify state environmental regulatory programs which meet the standards for certification in Section 21080.5, Public Resources Code.(d) The Secretary shall receive and file notices required by certified state environmental regulatory programs.

Note: Authority cited: Section 21083, Public Resources Code. Reference: Sections 21080.5, 21083, 21084, 21086, 21088 and 21152, Public Resources Code.

§ 15025. Delegation of Responsibilities.

(a) A public agency may assign specific functions to its staff to assist in administering CEQA. Functions which may be delegated include but are not limited to:
   (1) Determining whether a project is exempt.
   (2) Conducting an initial study and deciding whether to prepare a draft EIR or negative declaration.
   (3) Preparing a negative declaration or EIR.
   (4) Determining that a negative declaration has been completed within a period of 180 days.
   (5) Preparing responses to comments on environmental documents.
   (6) Filing of notices.
(b) The decisionmaking body of a public agency shall not delegate the following functions:
   (1) Reviewing and considering a final EIR or approving a negative declaration prior to approving a project.
   (2) The making of findings as required by Sections 15091 and 15093.
(c) Where an advisory body such as a planning commission is required to make a recommendation on a project to the decisionmaking body, the advisory body shall also review and consider the EIR or negative declaration in draft or final form.

Note: Authority cited: Section 21083, Public Resources Code. Reference: Sections 21082, 21100.2 and 21151.5, Public Resources Code; Kleist v. City of Glendale (1976) 56 Cal. App. 3d 770.

Article 3. Authorities Granted to Public Agencies by CEQA

§ 15040. Authority Provided by CEQA.

(a) CEQA is intended to be used in conjunction with discretionary powers granted to public agencies by other laws.(b) CEQA does not grant an agency new powers independent of the powers granted to the agency by other laws.(c) Where another law grants an agency discretionary powers, CEQA supplements those discretionary powers by authorizing the agency to use the discretionary powers to mitigate or avoid significant effects on the environment when it is feasible to do so with respect to projects subject to the powers of the agency. Prior to January 1, 1983, CEQA provided implied authority for an agency to use its discretionary powers to mitigate or avoid significant effects on the environment. Effective January 1, 1983, CEQA provides express authority to do so.(d) The exercise of the discretionary powers may take forms that had not been expected before the enactment of CEQA, but the exercise must be within the scope of the power.(e) The exercise of discretionary powers for environmental protection shall be consistent with express or implied limitations provided by other laws.

Note: Authority cited: Section 21083, Public Resources Code. Reference: Sections 21000, 21001, 21002, 21002.1 and 21004, Public Resources Code; Section 4, Chapter 1438, Statutes of 1982; *Golden Gate Bridge, Etc., Dist. v. Muzzi* (1978) 83 Cal. App. 3d 707; E.D.F. v. Mathews, 410 F. Supp. 336, 339 (D.D.C., 1976); *Friends of Mammoth v. Board of Supervisors* (1972) 8 Cal. 3d 247; *Pinewood Investors v. City of Oxnard* (1982) 133 Cal. App. 3d 1030.

§ 15041. Authority to Mitigate.

Within the limitations described in Section 15040:

(a) A lead agency for a project has authority to require feasible changes in any or all activities involved in the project in order to substantially lessen or avoid significant effects on the environment, consistent with applicable constitutional requirements such as the "nexus" and "rough proportionality" standards established by case law (*Nollan v. California Coastal Commission* (1987) 483 U.S. 825, *Dolan v. City of Tigard* (1994) 512 U.S. 374, *Ehrlich v. City of Culver City* (1996) 12 Cal. 4th 854.).
(b) When a public agency acts as a responsible agency for a project, the agency shall have more limited authority than a lead agency. The responsible agency may require changes in a project to lessen or avoid only the effects, either direct or indirect, of that part of the project which the agency will be called on to carry out or approve.
(c) With respect to a project which includes housing development, a lead or responsible agency shall not reduce the proposed number of housing units as a mitigation measure or alternative to lessen a particular significant effect on the environment if that agency determines that there is another feasible, specific mitigation measure or alternative that would provide a comparable lessening of the significant effect.

Note: Authority cited: Section 21083, Public Resources Code. Reference: Sections 21002, 21002.1 and 21159.26, Public Resources Code; *Golden Gate Bridge, Etc., District v. Muzzi* (1978) 83 Cal. App. 3d 707; and *Laurel Hills Homeowners Assn. v. City Council of City of Los Angeles* (1978) 83 Cal.App.3d 515.

§ 15042. Authority to Disapprove Projects.

A public agency may disapprove a project if necessary in order to avoid one or more significant effects on the environment that would occur if the project were approved as proposed. A lead agency has broader authority to disapprove a project than does a responsible agency. A responsible agency may refuse to approve a project in order to avoid direct or indirect environmental effects of that part of the project which the responsible agency would be called on to carry out or approve. For example, an air quality management district acting as a responsible agency would not have authority to disapprove a project for water pollution effects that were unrelated to the air quality aspects of the project regulated by the district.

Note: Authority cited: Section 21083, Public Resources Code. Reference: Sections 21002 and 21002.1, Public Resources Code; *Friends of Mammoth v. Mono County*, 8 Cal. App. 3d 247; *San Diego Trust and Savings Bank v. Friends of Gill*, 121 Cal. App. 3d 203.

§ 15043. Authority to Approve Projects Despite Significant Effects.

A public agency may approve a project even though the project would cause a significant effect on the environment if the agency makes a fully informed and publicly disclosed decision that:

(a) There is no feasible way to lessen or avoid the significant effect (see Section 15091); and
(b) Specifically identified expected benefits from the project outweigh the policy of reducing or avoiding significant environmental impacts of the project. (See Section 15093.)

Note: Authority cited: Section 21083, Public Resources Code. Reference: Sections 21002 and 21002.1, Public Resources Code; *San Francisco Ecology Center v. City and County of San Francisco* (1975) 48 Cal. App. 3d 584; *San Diego Trust & Savings Bank v. Friends of Gill* (1981) 121 Cal. App. 3d 203.

§ 15044. Authority to Comment.

Any person or entity other than a responsible agency may submit comments to a lead agency concerning any environmental effects of a project being considered by the lead agency.

Note: Authority cited: Section 21083, Public Resources

Code. Reference: Sections 21000, 21001, 21002.1, 21104 and 21153, Public Resources Code.

§ 15045. Fees.

(a) For a project to be carried out by any person or entity other than the lead agency, the lead agency may charge and collect a reasonable fee from the person or entity proposing the project in order to recover the estimated costs incurred in preparing environmental documents and for procedures necessary to comply with CEQA on the project. Litigation expenses, costs and fees incurred in actions alleging noncompliance with CEQA are not recoverable under this section.

(b) Public agencies may charge and collect a reasonable fee from members of the public for a copy of an environmental document not to exceed the actual cost of reproducing a copy.

Note: Authority cited: Section 21083, Public Resources Code. Reference: Sections 21089 and 21105, Public Resources Code.

Article 4. Lead Agency

§ 15050. Lead Agency Concept.

(a) Where a project is to be carried out or approved by more than one public agency, one public agency shall be responsible for preparing an EIR or negative declaration for the project. This agency shall be called the lead agency.

(b) Except as provided in subdivision (c), the decisionmaking body of each responsible agency shall consider the lead agency's EIR or negative declaration prior to acting upon or approving the project. Each responsible agency shall certify that its decisionmaking body reviewed and considered the information contained in the EIR or negative declaration on the project.

(c) The determination of the lead agency of whether to prepare an EIR or a negative declaration shall be final and conclusive for all persons, including responsible agencies, unless:

  (1) The decision is successfully challenged as provided in Section 21167 of the Public Resources Code,

  (2) Circumstances or conditions change as provided in Section 15162, or

  (3) A responsible agency becomes a lead agency under Section 15052.

Note: Authority cited: Section 21083, Public Resources Code. Reference: Sections 21080.1, 21165 and 21167.2, Public Resources Code.

§ 15051. Criteria for Identifying the Lead Agency.

Where two or more public agencies will be involved with a project, the determination of which agency will be the lead agency shall be governed by the following criteria:

(a) If the project will be carried out by a public agency, that agency shall be the lead agency even if the project would be located within the jurisdiction of another public agency.

(b) If the project is to be carried out by a nongovernmental person or entity, the lead agency shall be the public agency with the greatest responsibility for supervising or approving the project as a whole.

  (1) The lead agency will normally be the agency with general governmental powers, such as a city or county, rather than an agency with a single or limited purpose such as an air pollution control district or a district which will provide a public service or public utility to the project.

  (2) Where a city prezones an area, the city will be the appropriate lead agency for any subsequent annexation of the area and should prepare the appropriate environmental document at the time of the prezoning. The local agency formation commission shall act as a responsible agency.

(c) Where more than one public agency equally meet the criteria in subdivision (b), the agency which will act first on the project in question shall be the lead agency.

(d) Where the provisions of subdivisions (a), (b), and (c) leave two or more public agencies with a substantial claim to be the lead agency, the public agencies may by agreement designate an agency as the lead agency. An agreement may also provide for cooperative efforts by two or more agencies by contract, joint exercise of powers, or similar devices.

Note: Authority cited: Section 21083, Public Resources Code. Reference: Section 21165, Public Resources Code.

§ 15051. Criteria for Identifying the Lead Agency.

Where two or more public agencies will be involved with a project, the determination of which agency will be the lead agency shall be governed by the following criteria:

(a) If the project will be carried out by a public agency, that agency shall be the lead agency even if the project would be located within the jurisdiction of another public agency.

(b) If the project is to be carried out by a nongovernmental person or entity, the lead agency shall be the public agency with the greatest responsibility for supervising or approving the project as a whole.

  (1) The lead agency will normally be the agency with general governmental powers, such as a city or county, rather than an agency with a single or limited purpose such as an air pollution control district or a district which will provide a public service or public utility to the project.

  (2) Where a city prezones an area, the city will be the appropriate lead agency for any subsequent annexation of the area and should prepare the appropriate environmental document at the time of the prezoning. The local agency formation commission shall act as a responsible agency.

(c) Where more than one public agency equally meet the criteria in subdivision (b), the agency which will act first on the project in question shall be the lead agency.

(d) Where the provisions of subdivisions (a), (b), and (c) leave two or more public agencies with a substantial claim to be the lead agency, the public agencies may by agreement designate an agency as the lead agency. An agreement may also provide for cooperative efforts by two or more agencies by contract, joint exercise of powers, or similar devices.

Note: Authority cited: Section 21083, Public Resources Code. Reference: Section 21165, Public Resources Code.

§ 15052. Shift in Lead Agency Designation.

(a) Where a responsible agency is called on to grant an approval for a project subject to CEQA for which another public agency was the appropriate lead agency, the responsible agency shall assume the role of the lead agency when any of the following conditions occur:

  (1) The lead agency did not prepare any environmental documents for the project, and the statute of limitations has expired for a challenge to the action of the appropriate lead agency.

  (2) The lead agency prepared environmental documents for the project, but the following conditions occur:

    (A) A subsequent EIR is required pursuant to Section 15162,

    (B) The lead agency has granted a final approval for the project, and

    (C) The statute of limitations for challenging the lead agency's action under CEQA has expired.

  (3) The lead agency prepared inadequate environmental documents without consulting with the responsible agency as required by Sections 15072 or 15082, and the statute of limitations has expired for a challenge to the action of the appropriate lead agency.

(b) When a responsible agency assumes the duties of a lead agency under this section, the time limits applicable to a lead agency shall apply to the actions of the agency assuming the lead agency duties.

Note: Authority cited: Section 21083, Public Resources Code. Reference: Section 21165, Public Resources Code.

§ 15053. Designation of Lead Agency by the Office of Planning and Research.

(a) If there is a dispute over which of several agencies should be the lead agency for a project, the disputing agencies should consult with each other in an effort to resolve the dispute prior to submitting it to the Office of Planning and Research. If an agreement cannot be reached, any of the disputing public agencies, or the applicant if a private project is involved, may submit the dispute to the Office of Planning and Research for resolution.

(b) For purposes of this section, a "dispute" means a contested, active difference of opinion between two or more public agencies as to which of those agencies shall prepare any necessary environmental document. A dispute exists where each of those agencies claims that it either has or does not have the obligation to prepare that environmental document.

(c) The Office of Planning and Research shall designate a lead agency within 21 days after receiving a completed request to resolve a dispute. The Office of Planning and Research shall not designate a lead agency in the absence of a dispute.

(d) Regulations adopted by the Office of Planning and Research for resolving lead agency disputes may be found in Title 14, California Code of Regulations, Sections 16000 et seq.(e) Designation of a lead agency by the Office of Planning and Research shall be based on consideration of the criteria in Section 15051 as well as the capacity of the agency to adequately fulfill the requirements of CEQA.

Note: Authority cited: Section 21083, Public Resources Code. Reference: Section 21165, Public Resources Code; and California Code of Regulations, Title 14, Sections 16000-16041.

Article 5. Preliminary Review of Projects and Conduct of Initial Study

§ 15060. Preliminary Review.

(a) A lead agency is allowed 30 days to review for completeness applications for permits or other entitlements for use. While conducting this review for completeness, the agency should be alert for environmental issues that might require preparation of an EIR or that may require additional explanation by the applicant. Accepting an application as complete does not limit the authority of the lead agency to require the applicant to submit additional information needed for environmental evaluation of the project. Requiring such additional information after the application is complete does not change the status of the application.(b) Except as provided in Section 15111, the lead agency shall begin the formal environmental evaluation of the project after accepting an application as complete and determining that the project is subject to CEQA.(c) Once an application is deemed complete, a lead agency must first determine whether an activity is subject to CEQA before conducting an initial study. An activity is not subject to CEQA if:
  (1) The activity does not involve the exercise of discretionary powers by a public agency;
  (2) The activity will not result in a direct or reasonably foreseeable indirect physical change in the environment; or
  (3) The activity is not a project as defined in Section 15378.

(d) If the lead agency can determine that an EIR will be clearly required for a project, the agency may skip further initial review of the project and begin work directly on the EIR process described in Article 9, commencing with Section 15080. In the absence of an initial study, the lead agency shall still focus the EIR on the significant effects of the project and indicate briefly its reasons for determining that other effects would not be significant or potentially significant.

Note: Authority cited: Section 21083, Public Resources Code. Reference: Sections 21080(b), 21080.2 and 21160, Public Resources Code.

§ 15060.5. Preapplication Consultation.

(a) For a potential project involving the issuance of a lease, permit, license, certificate, or other entitlement for use by one or more public agencies, the lead agency shall, upon the request of a potential applicant and prior to the filing of a formal application, provide for consultation with the potential applicant to consider the range of actions, potential alternatives, mitigation measures, and any potential significant effects on the environment of the potential project.

(b) The lead agency may include in the consultation one or more responsible agencies, trustee agencies, and other public agencies who in the opinion of the lead agency may have an interest in the proposed project. The lead agency may consult the Office of Permit Assistant in the Trade and Commerce Agency for help in identifying interested agencies.

Note: Authority cited: Section 21083, Public Resources Code. Reference: Section 21080.1, Public Resources Code.

§ 15061. Review for Exemption.

(a) Once a lead agency has determined that an activity is a project subject to CEQA, a lead agency shall determine whether the project is exempt from CEQA.(b) A project is exempt from CEQA if:
  (1) The project is exempt by statute (see, e.g. Article 18, commencing with Section 15260).
  (2) The project is exempt pursuant to a categorical exemption (see Article 19, commencing with Section 15300) and the application of that categorical exemption is not barred by one of the exceptions set forth in Section 15300.2.
  (3) The activity is covered by the general rule that CEQA applies only to projects which have the potential for causing a significant effect on the environment. Where it can be seen with certainty that there is no possibility that the activity in question may have a significant effect on the environment, the activity is not subject to CEQA.
  (4) The project will be rejected or disapproved by a public agency. (See Section 15270(b)).
  (5) The project is exempt pursuant to the provisions of Article 12.5 of this Chapter.

(c) Each public agency should include in its implementing procedures a listing of the projects often handled by the agency that the agency has determined to be exempt. This listing should be used in preliminary review.

(d) After determining that a project is exempt, the agency may prepare a notice of exemption as provided in Section 15062. Although the notice may be kept with the project application at this time, the notice shall not be filed with the Office of Planning and Research or the county clerk until the project has been approved.

(e) When a non-elected official or decisionmaking body of a local lead agency decides that a project is exempt from CEQA, and the public agency approves or determines to carry out the project, the decision that the project is exempt may be appealed to the local lead agency's elected decisionmaking body, if one exists. A local lead agency may establish procedures governing such appeals.

Note: Authority cited: Section 21083, Public Resources Code. Reference: Sections 21080(b), 21080.9, 21080.10, 21084, 21108(b), 21151, 21152(b) and 21159.21, Public Resources Code; *No Oil, Inc.v. City of Los Angeles* (1974) 13 Cal. 3d 68.

§ 15062. Notice of Exemption.

(a) When a public agency decides that a project is exempt from CEQA pursuant to Section 15061, and the public agency approves or determines to carry out the project, the agency may file a notice of exemption. The notice shall be filed, if at all, after approval of the project. Such a notice shall include:
  (1) A brief description of the project,
  (2) The location of the project (either by street address and cross street for a project in an urbanized area or by attaching a specific map, preferably a copy of a U.S.G.S. 15'or 7-1/2' topographical map identified by quadrangle name).
  (3) A finding that the project is exempt from CEQA, including a citation to the State Guidelines section or statute under which it is found to be exempt, and
  (4) A brief statement of reasons to support the finding.

(b) A notice of exemption may be filled out and may accompany the project application through the approval process. The notice shall not be filed with the county clerk or OPR until the project has been approved.(c) When a public agency approves an applicant's project, either the agency or the applicant may file a notice of exemption.
  (1) When a state agency files this notice, the notice of exemption shall be filed with the Office of Planning and Research. A form for this notice is provided in Appendix E. A list of all such notices shall be posted on a weekly basis at the Office of Planning and Research, 1400 Tenth Street, Sacramento, California. The list shall remain posted for at least 30 days. The Office of Planning and Research shall retain each notice for not less than 12 months.
  (2) When a local agency files this notice, the notice of exemption shall be filed with the county clerk of each county in which the project will be located. Copies of all such notices will be available for public inspection and such notices shall be posted within 24 hours of receipt in the office of the county clerk. Each notice shall remain posted for a period of 30 days. Thereafter, the clerk shall return the notice to the local agency with a notation of the period it was posted. The local agency shall retain the notice for not less than 12 months.
  (3) All public agencies are encouraged to make postings pursuant to this section available in electronic format on the Internet. Such electronic postings are in addition to the procedures required by these guidelines and the Public Resources Code.
  (4) When an applicant files this notice, special rules apply.
    (A) The notice filed by an applicant is filed in the same place as if it were filed by the agency granting the permit. If the permit was granted by a state agency, the notice is filed with the Office of Planning and Research. If the permit was granted by a local agency, the notice is filed with the county clerk of the county or counties in which the project will be located.
    (B) The notice of exemption filed by an applicant shall contain the information required in subdivision (a) together with a certified document issued by the public agency stating that the agency has found the project to be exempt. The certified document may be a certified copy of an existing document or record of the public agency.
    (C) A notice filed by an applicant is subject to the same posting and time requirements as a notice filed by a public agency.

(d) The filing of a Notice of Exemption and the posting on the list of notices start a 35 day statute of limitations period on legal challenges to the agency's decision that the project is exempt from CEQA. If a Notice of Exemption is not filed, a 180 day statute of limitations will apply.

(e) When a local agency determines that a project is not subject to CEQA under sections 15193, 15194, or 15195, and it approves or determines to carry out that project, the local agency or person seeking project approval shall file a notice with OPR identifying the section under which the exemption is claimed.

Note: Authority cited: Section 21083, Public Resources Code. Reference: Sections 21108, 21152 and 21152.1, Public Resources Code.

§ 15063. Initial Study.

(a) Following preliminary review, the lead agency shall conduct an initial study to determine if the project may have a significant effect on the environment. If the lead agency can determine that an EIR will clearly be required for the project, an initial study is not required but may still be desirable.
 (1) All phases of project planning, implementation, and operation must be considered in the initial study of the project.
 (2) To meet the requirements of this section, the lead agency may use an environmental assessment or a similar analysis prepared pursuant to the National Environmental Policy Act.
 (3) An initial study may rely upon expert opinion supported by facts, technical studies or other substantial evidence to document its findings. However, an initial study is neither intended nor required to include the level of detail included in an EIR.

(b) Results.
 (1) If the agency determines that there is substantial evidence that any aspect of the project, either individually or cumulatively, may cause a significant effect on the environment, regardless of whether the overall effect of the project is adverse or beneficial, the lead agency shall do one of the following:
  (A) Prepare an EIR or
  (B) Use a previously prepared EIR which the lead agency determines would adequately analyze the project at hand, or
  (C) Determine, pursuant to a program EIR, tiering, or another appropriate process, which of a project's effects were adequately examined by an earlier EIR or negative declaration. Another appropriate process may include, for example, a master EIR, a master environmental assessment, approval of housing and neighborhood commercial facilities in urban areas, approval of residential projects pursuant to a specific plan as described in section 15182, approval of residential projects consistent with a community plan, general plan or zoning as described in section 15183, or an environmental document prepared under a State certified regulatory program. The lead agency shall then ascertain which effects, if any, should be analyzed in a later EIR or negative declaration.
 (2) The lead agency shall prepare a negative declaration if there is no substantial evidence that the project or any of its aspects may cause a significant effect on the environment.

(c) Purposes. The purposes of an initial study are to:
 (1) Provide the lead agency with information to use as the basis for deciding whether to prepare an EIR or negative declaration;
 (2) Enable an applicant or lead agency to modify a project, mitigating adverse impacts before an EIR is prepared, thereby enabling the project to qualify for a negative declaration;
 (3) Assist the preparation of an EIR, if one is required, by:
  (A) Focusing the EIR on the effects determined to be significant,
  (B) Identifying the effects determined not to be significant,
  (C) Explaining the reasons for determining that potentially significant effects would not be significant, and
  (D) Identifying whether a program EIR, tiering, or another appropriate process can be used for analysis of the project's environmental effects.
 (4) Facilitate environmental assessment early in the design of a project;
 (5) Provide documentation of the factual basis for the finding in a negative declaration that a project will not have a significant effect on the environment;
 (6) Eliminate unnecessary EIRs;
 (7) Determine whether a previously prepared EIR could be used with the project.

(d) Contents. An initial study shall contain in brief form:
 (1) A description of the project including the location of the project;
 (2) An identification of the environmental setting;
 (3) An identification of environmental effects by use of a checklist, matrix, or other method, provided that entries on a checklist or other form are briefly explained to indicate that there is some evidence to support the entries. The brief explanation may be either through a narrative or a reference to another information source such as an attached map, photographs, or an earlier EIR or negative declaration. A reference to another document should include, where appropriate, a citation to the page or pages where the information is found.
 (4) A discussion of ways to mitigate the significant effects identified, if any;
 (5) An examination of whether the project would be consistent with existing zoning, plans, and other applicable land use controls;
 (6) The name of the person or persons who prepared or participated in the initial study.

(e) Submission of Data. If the project is to be carried out by a private person or private organization, the lead agency may require such person or organization to submit data and information which will enable the lead agency to prepare the initial study. Any person may submit any information in any form to assist a lead agency in preparing an initial study.(f) Format. Sample forms for an applicant's project description and a review form for use by the lead agency are contained in Appendices G and H. When used together, these forms would meet the requirements for an initial study, provided that the entries on the checklist are briefly explained pursuant to subdivision (d)(3). These forms are only suggested, and public agencies are free to devise their own format for an initial study. A previously prepared EIR may also be used as the initial study for a later project.(g) Consultation. As soon as a lead agency has determined that an initial study will be required for the project, the lead agency shall consult informally with all responsible agencies and all trustee agencies responsible for resources affected by the project to obtain the recommendations of those agencies as to whether an EIR or a negative declaration should be prepared. During or immediately after preparation of an initial study for a private project, the lead agency may consult with the applicant to determine if the applicant is willing to modify the project to reduce or avoid the significant effects identified in the initial study.

Note: Authority cited: Section 21083, Public Resources Code. Reference: Sections 21080(c), 21080.1, 21080.3, 21082.1, 21100 and 21151, Public Resources Code; *Gentry v. City of Murrieta* (1995) 36 Cal.App.4th 1359, *San Joaquin Raptor/Wildlife Rescue Center v. County of Stanislaus* (1994) 27 Cal.App.4th 713, *Leonoff v. Monterey County Board of Supervisors* (1990) 222 Cal.App.3d 1337.

§ 15064. Determining the Significance of the Environmental Effects Caused by a Project.

(a) Determining whether a project may have a significant effect plays a critical role in the CEQA process.
 (1) If there is substantial evidence, in light of the whole record before a lead agency, that a project may have a significant effect on the environment, the agency shall prepare a draft EIR.
 (2) When a final EIR identifies one or more significant effects, the lead agency and each responsible agency shall make a finding under Section 15091 for each significant effect and may need to make a statement of overriding considerations under Section 15093 for the project.

(b) The determination of whether a project may have a significant effect on the environment calls for careful judgment on the part of the public agency involved, based to the extent possible on scientific and factual data. An ironclad definition of significant effect is not always possible because the significance of an activity may vary with the setting. For example, an activity which may not be significant in an urban area may be significant in a rural area.

(c) In determining whether an effect will be adverse or beneficial, the lead agency shall consider the views held by members of the public in all areas affected as expressed in the whole record before the lead agency. Before requiring the preparation of an EIR, the lead agency must still determine whether environmental change itself might be substantial.

(d) In evaluating the significance of the environmental effect of a project, the lead agency shall consider direct physical changes in the environment which may be caused by the project and reasonably foreseeable indirect physical changes in the environment which may be caused by the project.
 (1) A direct physical change in the environment is a physical change in the environment which is

caused by and immediately related to the project. Examples of direct physical changes in the environment are the dust, noise, and traffic of heavy equipment that would result from construction of a sewage treatment plant and possible odors from operation of the plant.

(2) An indirect physical change in the environment is a physical change in the environment which is not immediately related to the project, but which is caused indirectly by the project. If a direct physical change in the environment in turn causes another change in the environment, then the other change is an indirect physical change in the environment. For example, the construction of a new sewage treatment plant may facilitate population growth in the service area due to the increase in sewage treatment capacity and may lead to an increase in air pollution.

(3) An indirect physical change is to be considered only if that change is a reasonably foreseeable impact which may be caused by the project. A change which is speculative or unlikely to occur is not reasonably foreseeable.

(e) Economic and social changes resulting from a project shall not be treated as significant effects on the environment. Economic or social changes may be used, however, to determine that a physical change shall be regarded as a significant effect on the environment. Where a physical change is caused by economic or social effects of a project, the physical change may be regarded as a significant effect in the same manner as any other physical change resulting from the project. Alternatively, economic and social effects of a physical change may be used to determine that the physical change is a significant effect on the environment. If the physical change causes adverse economic or social effects on people, those adverse effects may be used as a factor in determining whether the physical change is significant. For example, if a project would cause overcrowding of a public facility and the overcrowding causes an adverse effect on people, the overcrowding would be regarded as a significant effect.

(f) The decision as to whether a project may have one or more significant effects shall be based on substantial evidence in the record of the lead agency.

(1) If the lead agency determines there is substantial evidence in the record that the project may have a significant effect on the environment, the lead agency shall prepare an EIR (*Friends of B Street v. City of Hayward* (1980) 106 Cal. App. 3d 988). Said another way, if a lead agency is presented with a fair argument that a project may have a significant effect on the environment, the lead agency shall prepare an EIR even though it may also be presented with other substantial evidence that the project will not have a significant effect (No Oil, Inc. v. City of Los Angeles (1974) 13 Cal. 3d 68).

(2) If the lead agency determines there is substantial evidence in the record that the project may have a significant effect on the environment but the lead agency determines that revisions in the project plans or proposals made by, or agreed to by, the applicant would avoid the effects or mitigate the effects to a point where clearly no significant effect on the environment would occur and there is no substantial evidence in light of the whole record before the public agency that the project, as revised, may have a significant effect on the environment then a mitigated negative declaration shall be prepared.

(3) If the lead agency determines there is no substantial evidence that the project may have a significant effect on the environment, the lead agency shall prepare a negative declaration (*Friends of B Street v. City of Hayward* (1980) 106 Cal. App. 3d 988).

(4) The existence of public controversy over the environment effects of a project will not require preparation of an EIR if there is no substantial evidence before the agency that the project may have a significant effect on the environment.

(5) Argument, speculation, unsubstantiated opinion or narrative, or evidence that is clearly inaccurate or erroneous, or evidence that is not credible, shall not constitute substantial evidence. Substantial evidence shall include facts, reasonable assumptions predicated upon facts, and expert opinion supported by facts.

(6) Evidence of economic and social impacts that do not contribute to or are not caused by physical changes in the environment is not substantial evidence that the project may have a significant effect on the environment.

(7) The provisions of sections 15162, 15163, and 15164 apply when the project being analyzed is a change to, or further approval for, a project for which an EIR or negative declaration was previously certified or adopted (e.g. a tentative subdivision, conditional use permit). Under case law, the fair argument standard does not apply to determinations of significance pursuant to sections 15162, 15163, and 15164.

(g) After application of the principles set forth above in Section 15064(f), and in marginal cases where it is not clear whether there is substantial evidence that a project may have a significant effect on the environment, the lead agency shall be guided by the following principle: If there is disagreement among expert opinion supported by facts over the significance of an effect on the environment, the Lead Agency shall treat the effect as significant and shall prepare an EIR.

(h)(1) When assessing whether a cumulative effect requires an EIR, the lead agency shall consider whether the cumulative impact is significant and whether the effects of the project are cumulatively considerable. An EIR must be prepared if the cumulative impact may be significant and the project's incremental effect, though individually limited, is cumulatively considerable. "Cumulatively considerable" means that the incremental effects of an individual project are significant when viewed in connection with the effects of past projects, the effects of other current projects, and the effects of probable future projects.

(2) A lead agency may determine in an initial study that a project's contribution to a significant cumulative impact will be rendered less than cumulatively considerable and thus is not significant. When a project might contribute to a significant cumulative impact, but the contribution will be rendered less than cumulatively considerable through mitigation measures set forth in a mitigated negative declaration, the initial study shall briefly indicate and explain how the contribution has been rendered less than cumulatively considerable.

(3) A lead agency may determine that a project's incremental contribution to a cumulative effect is not cumulatively considerable if the project will comply with the requirements in a previously approved plan or mitigation program (including, but not limited to, water quality control plan, air quality attainment or maintenance plan, integrated waste management plan, habitat conservation plan, natural community conservation plan, plans or regulations for the reduction of greenhouse gas emissions) that provides specific requirements that will avoid or substantially lessen the cumulative problem within the geographic area in which the project is located. Such plans or programs must be specified in law or adopted by the public agency with jurisdiction over the affected resources through a public review process to implement, interpret, or make specific the law enforced or administered by the public agency. When relying on a plan, regulation or program, the lead agency should explain how implementing the particular requirements in the plan, regulation or program ensure that the project's incremental contribution to the cumulative effect is not cumulatively considerable. If there is substantial evidence that the possible effects of a particular project are still cumulatively considerable notwithstanding that the project complies with the specified plan or mitigation program addressing the cumulative problem, an EIR must be prepared for the project.

(4) The mere existence of significant cumulative impacts caused by other projects alone shall not constitute substantial evidence that the proposed project's incremental effects are cumulatively considerable.

Note: Authority cited: Sections 21083 and 21083.05, Public Resources Code. Reference: Sections 21003, 21065, 21068, 21080, 21082, 21082.1, 21082.2, 21083, 21083.05 and 21100, Public Resources Code; *No Oil, Inc. v. City of Los Angeles* (1974) 13 Cal.3d 68; *San Joaquin Raptor/Wildlife Center v. County of Stanislaus* (1996) 42 Cal.App.4th 608; *Gentry v. City of Murrieta* (1995) 36 Cal.App.4th 1359; *Laurel Heights Improvement Assn. v. Regents of the University of California* (1993)

§ 15064.4. Determining the Significance of Impacts from Greenhouse Gas Emissions.

(a) The determination of the significance of greenhouse gas emissions calls for a careful judgment by the lead agency consistent with the provisions in section 15064. A lead agency should make a good-faith effort, based to the extent possible on scientific and factual data, to describe, calculate or estimate the amount of greenhouse gas emissions resulting from a project. A lead agency shall have discretion to determine, in the context of a particular project, whether to:

(1) Use a model or methodology to quantify greenhouse gas emissions resulting from a project, and which model or methodology to use. The lead agency has discretion to select the model or methodology it considers most appropriate provided it supports its decision with substantial evidence. The lead agency should explain the limitations of the particular model or methodology selected for use; and/or

(2) Rely on a qualitative analysis or performance based standards.

(b) A lead agency should consider the following factors, among others, when assessing the significance of impacts from greenhouse gas emissions on the environment:

(1) The extent to which the project may increase or reduce greenhouse gas emissions as compared to the existing environmental setting;

(2) Whether the project emissions exceed a threshold of significance that the lead agency determines applies to the project.

(3) The extent to which the project complies with regulations or requirements adopted to implement a statewide, regional, or local plan for the reduction or mitigation of greenhouse gas emissions. Such requirements must be adopted by the relevant public agency through a public review process and must reduce or mitigate the project's incremental contribution of greenhouse gas emissions. If there is substantial evidence that the possible effects of a particular project are still cumulatively considerable notwithstanding compliance with the adopted regulations or requirements, an EIR must be prepared for the project.

Note: Authority cited: Sections 21083 and 21083.05, Public Resources Code. Reference: Sections 21001, 21002, 21003, 21065, 21068, 21080, 21082, 21082.1, 21082.2, 21083.05 and 21100, Public Resources Code; *Eureka Citizens for Responsible Govt. v. City of Eureka* (2007) 147 Cal.App.4th 357; *Mejia v. City of Los Angeles* (2005) 130 Cal.App.4th 322; *Protect the Historic Amador Waterways v. Amador Water Agency* (2004) 116 Cal.App.4th 1099; *Communities for a Better Environment v. California Resources Agency* (2002) 103 Cal.App.4th 98; *Berkeley Keep Jets Over the Bay Com. v. Board of Port Comm.* (2001) 91 Cal.App.4th 1344; and *City of Irvine v. Irvine Citizens Against Overdevelopment* (1994) 25 Cal.App.4th 868.

§ 15064.5. Determining the Significance of Impacts to Archaeological and Historical Resources.

(a) For purposes of this section, the term "historical resources" shall include the following:

(1) A resource listed in, or determined to be eligible by the State Historical Resources Commission, for listing in the California Register of Historical Resources (Pub. Res. Code §5024.1, Title 14 CCR, Section 4850 et seq.).

(2) A resource included in a local register of historical resources, as defined in section 5020.1(k) of the Public Resources Code or identified as significant in an historical resource survey meeting the requirements section 5024.1(g) of the Public Resources Code, shall be presumed to be historically or culturally significant. Public agencies must treat any such resource as significant unless the preponderance of evidence demonstrates that it is not historically or culturally significant.

(3) Any object, building, structure, site, area, place, record, or manuscript which a lead agency determines to be historically significant or significant in the architectural, engineering, scientific, economic, agricultural, educational, social, political, military, or cultural annals of California may be considered to be an historical resource, provided the lead agency's determination is supported by substantial evidence in light of the whole record. Generally, a resource shall be considered by the lead agency to be "historically significant" if the resource meets the criteria for listing on the California Register of Historical Resources (Pub. Res. Code, § 5024.1, Title 14 CCR, Section 4852) including the following:

(A) Is associated with events that have made a significant contribution to the broad patterns of California's history and cultural heritage;

(B) Is associated with the lives of persons important in our past;

(C) Embodies the distinctive characteristics of a type, period, region, or method of construction, or represents the work of an important creative individual, or possesses high artistic values; or

(D) Has yielded, or may be likely to yield, information important in prehistory or history.

(4) The fact that a resource is not listed in, or determined to be eligible for listing in the California Register of Historical Resources, not included in a local register of historical resources (pursuant to section 5020.1(k) of the Public Resources Code), or identified in an historical resources survey (meeting the criteria in section 5024.1(g) of the Public Resources Code) does not preclude a lead agency from determining that the resource may be an historical resource as defined in Public Resources Code sections 5020.1(j) or 5024.1.

(b) A project with an effect that may cause a substantial adverse change in the significance of an historical resource is a project that may have a significant effect on the environment.

(1) Substantial adverse change in the significance of an historical resource means physical demolition, destruction, relocation, or alteration of the resource or its immediate surroundings such that the significance of an historical resource would be materially impaired.

(2) The significance of an historical resource is materially impaired when a project:

(A) Demolishes or materially alters in an adverse manner those physical characteristics of an historical resource that convey its historical significance and that justify its inclusion in, or eligibility for, inclusion in the California Register of Historical Resources; or

(B) Demolishes or materially alters in an adverse manner those physical characteristics that account for its inclusion in a local register of historical resources pursuant to section 5020.1(k) of the Public Resources Code or its identification in an historical resources survey meeting the requirements of section 5024.1(g) of the Public Resources Code, unless the public agency reviewing the effects of the project establishes by a preponderance of evidence that the resource is not historically or culturally significant; or

(C) Demolishes or materially alters in an adverse manner those physical characteristics of a historical resource that convey its historical significance and that justify its eligibility for inclusion in the California Register of Historical Resources as determined by a lead agency for purposes of CEQA.

(3) Generally, a project that follows the Secretary of the Interior's Standards for the Treatment of Historic Properties with Guidelines for Preserving, Rehabilitating, Restoring, and Reconstructing Historic Buildings or the Secretary of the Interior's Standards for Rehabilitation and Guidelines for Rehabilitating Historic Buildings (1995), Weeks and Grimmer, shall be considered as mitigated to a level of less than a significant impact on the historical resource.

(4) A lead agency shall identify potentially feasible measures to mitigate significant adverse changes in the significance of an historical resource. The lead agency shall ensure that any adopted measures to mitigate or avoid significant adverse changes are fully enforceable through permit conditions, agreements, or other measures.

(5) When a project will affect state-owned historical resources, as described in Public Resources Code Section 5024, and the lead agency is a state agency, the lead agency shall consult with the State Historic Preservation Officer as provided in Public Resources Code Section 5024.5. Consultation should be coordinated in a timely fashion with the preparation of environmental documents.

(c) CEQA applies to effects on archaeological sites.

(1) When a project will impact an archaeological site, a lead agency shall first determine whether the site is an historical resource, as defined in subdivision (a).

(2) If a lead agency determines that the archaeological site is an historical resource, it shall refer to the provisions of Section 21084.1 of the Public Resources Code, and this section, Section 15126.4 of the Guidelines, and the limits contained in Section 21083.2 of the Public Resources Code do not apply.

(3) If an archaeological site does not meet the criteria defined in subdivision (a), but does meet the definition of a unique archeological resource in Section 21083.2 of the Public Resources Code, the site shall be treated in accordance with the provisions of section 21083.2. The time and cost limitations described in Public Resources Code Section 21083.2 (c-f) do not apply to surveys and site evaluation activities intended to de- termine whether the project location contains unique archaeological resources.

(4) If an archaeological resource is neither a unique archaeological nor an historical resource, the effects of the project on those resources shall not be considered a significant effect on the envi-

ronment. It shall be sufficient that both the resource and the effect on it are noted in the Initial Study or EIR, if one is prepared to address impacts on other resources, but they need not be considered further in the CEQA process.

(d) When an initial study identifies the existence of, or the probable likelihood, of Native American human remains within the project, a lead agency shall work with the appropriate Native Americans as identified by the Native American Heritage Commission as provided in Public Resources Code section 5097.98. The applicant may develop an agreement for treating or disposing of, with appropriate dignity, the human remains and any items associated with Native American burials with the appropriate Native Americans as identified by the Native American Heritage Commission." Action implementing such an agreement is exempt from:
  (1) The general prohibition on disinterring, disturbing, or removing human remains from any location other than a dedicated cemetery (Health and Safety Code Section 7050.5).
  (2) The requirements of CEQA and the Coastal Act.

(e) In the event of the accidental discovery or recognition of any human remains in any location other than a dedicated cemetery, the following steps should be taken:
  (1) There shall be no further excavation or disturbance of the site or any nearby area reasonably suspected to overlie adjacent human remains until:
    (A) The coroner of the county in which the remains are discovered must be contacted to determine that no investigation of the cause of death is required, and
    (B) If the coroner determines the remains to be Native American:
      1. The coroner shall contact the Native American Heritage Commission within 24 hours.
      2. The Native American Heritage Commission shall identify the person or persons it believes to be the most likely descended from the deceased Native American.
      3. The most likely descendent may make recommendations to the landowner or the person responsible for the excavation work, for means of treating or disposing of, with appropriate dignity, the human remains and any associated grave goods as provided in Public Resources Code section 5097.98, or
  (2) Where the following conditions occur, the landowner or his authorized representative shall rebury the Native American human remains and associated grave goods with appropriate dignity on the property in a location not subject to further subsurface disturbance.
    (A) The Native American Heritage Commission is unable to identify a most likely descendent or the most likely descendent failed to make a recommendation within 24 hours after being notified by the commission.
    (B) The descendant identified fails to make a recommendation; or
    (C) The landowner or his authorized representative rejects the recommendation of the descendant, and the mediation by the Native American Heritage Commission fails to provide measures acceptable to the landowner.

(f) As part of the objectives, criteria, and procedures required by Section 21082 of the Public Resources Code, a lead agency should make provisions for historical or unique archaeological resources accidentally discovered during construction. These provisions should include an immediate evaluation of the find by a qualified archaeologist. If the find is determined to be an historical or unique archaeological resource, contingency funding and a time allotment sufficient to allow for implementation of avoidance measures or appropriate mitigation should be available. Work could continue on other parts of the building site while historical or unique archaeological resource mitigation takes place.

Note: Authority cited: Section 21083, Public Resources Code. Reference: Sections 21083.2, 21084 and 21084.1, Public Resources Code; and *Citizens for Responsible Development in West Hollywood v. City of West Hollywood* (1995) 39 Cal.App.4th 490.

§ 15064.7. Thresholds of Significance.

(a) Each public agency is encouraged to develop and publish thresholds of significance that the agency uses in the determination of the significance of environmental effects. A threshold of significance is an identifiable quantitative, qualitative or performance level of a particular environmental effect, non-compliance with which means the effect will normally be determined to be significant by the agency and compliance with which means the effect normally will be determined to be less than significant.

(b) Thresholds of significance to be adopted for general use as part of the lead agency's environmental review process must be adopted by ordinance, resolution, rule, or regulation, and developed through a public review process and be supported by substantial evidence.

(c) When adopting thresholds of significance, a lead agency may consider thresholds of significance previously adopted or recommended by other public agencies or recommended by experts, provided the decision of the lead agency to adopt such thresholds is supported by substantial evidence.

Note: Authority cited: Section 21083, Public Resources Code. Reference: Sections 21000, 21082 and 21083, Public Resources Code.

§ 15065. Mandatory Findings of Significance.

(a) A lead agency shall find that a project may have a significant effect on the environment and thereby require an EIR to be prepared for the project where there is substantial evidence, in light of the whole record, that any of the following conditions may occur:
  (1) The project has the potential to substantially degrade the quality of the environment; substantially reduce the habitat of a fish or wildlife species; cause a fish or wildlife population to drop below self-sustaining levels; threaten to eliminate a plant or animal community; substantially reduce the number or restrict the range of an endangered, rare or threatened species; or eliminate important examples of the major periods of California history or prehistory.
  (2) The project has the potential to achieve short-term environmental goals to the disadvantage of long-term environmental goals.
  (3) The project has possible environmental effects that are individually limited but cumulatively considerable. "Cumulatively considerable" means that the incremental effects of an individual project are significant when viewed in connection with the effects of past projects, the effects of other current projects, and the effects of probable future projects.
  (4) The environmental effects of a project will cause substantial adverse effects on human beings, either directly or indirectly.

(b) (1) Where, prior to the commencement of public review of an environmental document, a project proponent agrees to mitigation measures or project modifications that would avoid any significant effect on the environment specified by subdivision (a) or would mitigate the significant effect to a point where clearly no significant effect on the environment would occur, a lead agency need not prepare an environmental impact report solely because, without mitigation, the environmental effects at issue would have been significant.
  (2) Furthermore, where a proposed project has the potential to substantially reduce the number or restrict the range of an endangered, rare or threatened species, the lead agency need not prepare an EIR solely because of such an effect, if:
    (A) the project proponent is bound to implement mitigation requirements relating to such species and habitat pursuant to an approved habitat conservation plan or natural community conservation plan;
    (B) the state or federal agency approved the habitat conservation plan or natural community conservation plan in reliance on an environmental impact report or environmental impact statement; and
    (C) 1. such requirements avoid any net loss of habitat and net reduction in number of the affected species, or
      2. such requirements preserve, restore, or enhance sufficient habitat to mitigate the reduction in habitat and number of the affected species to below a level of significance.

(c) Following the decision to prepare an EIR, if a lead agency determines that any of the conditions specified by subdivision (a) will occur, such a determination shall apply to:
  (1) the identification of effects to be analyzed in depth in the environmental impact report or the functional equivalent thereof,
  (2) the requirement to make detailed findings on the feasibility of alternatives or mitigation measures to substantially lessen or avoid the significant effects on the environment,
  (3) when found to be feasible, the making of changes in the project to substantially lessen or

avoid the significant effects on the environment, and

(4) where necessary, the requirement to adopt a statement of overriding considerations.

Note: Authority cited: Section 21083, Public Resources Code. Reference: Sections 21001(c) and 21083, Public Resources Code; *San Joaquin Raptor/Wildlife Center v. County of Stanislaus* (1996) 42 Cal.App.4th 608; *Los Angeles Unified School District v. City of Los Angeles* (1997) 58 Cal.App.4th 1019, 1024; and *Communities for a Better Environment v. California Resources Agency* (2002) 103 Cal.App.4th 98.

Article 6. Negative Declaration Process

§ 15070. Decision to Prepare a Negative or Mitigated Negative Declaration.

A public agency shall prepare or have prepared a proposed negative declaration or mitigated negative declaration for a project subject to CEQA when:

(a) The initial study shows that there is no substantial evidence, in light of the whole record before the agency, that the project may have a significant effect on the environment, or

(b) The initial study identifies potentially significant effects, but:

(1) Revisions in the project plans or proposals made by or agreed to by the applicant before a proposed mitigated negative declaration and initial study are released for public review would avoid the effects or mitigate the effects to a point where clearly no significant effects would occur, and

(2) There is no substantial evidence, in light of the whole record before the agency, that the project as revised may have a significant effect on the environment.

Note: Authority cited: Section 21083, Public Resources Code. Reference: Sections 21064, 21064.5, 21080(c) and 21082.1, Public Resources Code; *Friends of B Street v. City of Hayward* (1980) 106 Cal. App. 3d 988; *Running Fence Corp. v. Superior Court* (1975) 51 Cal. App. 3d 400.

§ 15071. Contents.

A negative declaration circulated for public review shall include:

(a) A brief description of the project, including a commonly used name for the project, if any;

(b) The location of the project, preferably shown on a map, and the name of the project proponent;

(c) A proposed finding that the project will not have a significant effect on the environment;

(d) An attached copy of the initial study documenting reasons to support the finding; and

(e) Mitigation measures, if any, included in the project to avoid potentially significant effects.

Note: Authority cited: Section 21083, Public Resources Code. Reference: Section 21080(c), Public Resources Code.

§ 15072. Notice of Intent to Adopt a Negative Declaration or Mitigated Negative Declaration.

(a) A lead agency shall provide a notice of intent to adopt a negative declaration or mitigated negative declaration to the public, responsible agencies, trustee agencies, and the county clerk of each county within which the proposed project is located, sufficiently prior to adoption by the lead agency of the negative declaration or mitigated negative declaration to allow the public and agencies the review period provided under Section 15105.(b) The lead agency shall mail a notice of intent to adopt a negative declaration or mitigated negative declaration to the last known name and address of all organizations and individuals who have previously requested such notice in writing and shall also give notice of intent to adopt a negative declaration or mitigated negative declaration by at least one of the following procedures to allow the public the review period provided under Section 15105:

(1) Publication at least one time by the lead agency in a newspaper of general circulation in the area affected by the proposed project. If more than one area is affected, the notice shall be published in the newspaper of largest circulation from among the newspapers of general circulation in those areas.

(2) Posting of notice by the lead agency on and off site in the area where the project is to be located.

(3) Direct mailing to the owners and occupants of property contiguous to the project. Owners of such property shall be identified as shown on the latest equalized assessment roll.

(c) The alternatives for providing notice specified in subdivision (b) shall not preclude a lead agency from providing additional notice by other means if the agency so desires, nor shall the requirements of this section preclude a lead agency from providing the public notice at the same time and in the same manner as public notice required by any other laws for the project.(d) The county clerk of each county within which the proposed project is located shall post such notices in the office of the county clerk within 24 hours of receipt for a period of at least 20 days.(e) For a project of statewide, regional, or areawide significance, the lead agency shall also provide notice to transportation planning agencies and public agencies which have transportation facilities within their jurisdictions which could be affected by the project as specified in Section 21092.4(a) of the Public Resources Code. "Transportation facilities" includes: major local arterials and public transit within five miles of the project site and freeways, highways and rail transit service within 10 miles of the project site.(f) If the United States Department of Defense or any branch of the United States Armed Forces has given a lead agency written notification of the specific boundaries of a low-level flight path, military impact zone, or special use airspace and provided the lead agency with written notification of the military contact office and address for the military service pursuant to subdivision (b) of Section 15190.5, then the lead agency shall include the specified military contact office in the list of organizations and individuals receiving a notice of intent to adopt a negative declaration or a mitigated negative declaration pursuant to this section for projects that meet the criteria set forth in subdivision (c) of Section 15190.5. The lead agency shall send the specified military contact office such notice of intent sufficiently prior to adoption by the lead agency of the negative declaration or mitigated negative declaration to allow the military service the review period provided under Section 15105.(g) A notice of intent to adopt a negative declaration or mitigated negative declaration shall specify the following:

(1) A brief description of the proposed project and its location.

(2) The starting and ending dates for the review period during which the lead agency will receive comments on the proposed negative declaration or mitigated negative declaration. This shall include starting and ending dates for the review period. If the review period has been is shortened pursuant to Section 15105, the notice shall include a statement to that effect.

(3) The date, time, and place of any scheduled public meetings or hearings to be held by the lead agency on the proposed project, when known to the lead agency at the time of notice.

(4) The address or addresses where copies of the proposed negative declaration or mitigated negative declaration including the revisions developed under Section 15070(b) and all documents referenced in the proposed negative declaration or mitigated negative declaration are available for review. This location or locations shall be readily accessible to the public during the lead agency's normal working hours.

(5) The presence of the site on any of the lists enumerated under Section 65962.5 of the Government Code including, but not limited to lists of hazardous waste facilities, land designated as hazardous waste property, and hazardous waste disposal sites, and the information in the Hazardous Waste and Substances Statement required under subdivision (f) of that section.

(6) Other information specifically required by statute or regulation for a particular project or type of project.

Note: Authority cited: Section 21083, Public Resources Code. Reference: Sections 21091, 21092, 21092.2, 21092.4, 21092.3, 21092.6, 21098 and 21151.8, Public Resources Code.

§ 15073. Public Review of a Proposed Negative Declaration or Mitigated Negative Declaration.

(a) The lead agency shall provide a public review period pursuant to Section 15105 of not less than 20 days. When a proposed negative declaration or mitigated negative declaration and initial study are submitted to the State Clearinghouse for review by state agencies, the public review period shall not be less than 30 days, unless a shorter period is approved by the State Clearinghouse under Section 15105(d).

(b) When a proposed negative declaration or mitigated negative declaration and initial study have been submitted to the State Clearinghouse for review by state agencies, the public review period shall be at least as long as the review period established by the State Clearinghouse. The public review period and the state agency review period may, but are not required to, begin and end at the same time. Day one of the state review period shall be the date that the State

Clearinghouse distributes the document to state agencies.

(c) A copy of the proposed negative declaration or mitigated negative declaration and the initial study shall be attached to the notice of intent to adopt the proposed declaration that is sent to every responsible agency and trustee agency concerned with the project and every other public agency with jurisdiction by law over resources affected by the project.

(d) Where one or more state agencies will be a responsible agency or a trustee agency or will exercise jurisdiction by law over natural resources affected by the project, or where the project is of statewide, regional, or areawide environmental significance, the lead agency shall send copies of the proposed negative declaration or mitigated negative declaration to the State Clearinghouse for distribution to the state agencies.

(e) The lead agency shall notify in writing any public agency which comments on a proposed negative declaration or mitigated negative declaration of any public hearing to be held for the project for which the document was prepared. A notice provided to a public agency pursuant to Section 15072 satisfies this requirement.

Note: Authority cited: Section 21083, Public Resources Code. Reference: Sections 21000(e), 21003(b), 21080(c), 21081.6, 21091 and 21092.5, Public Resources Code; *Plaggmier v. City of San Jose* (1980) 101 Cal. App. 3d 842.

§ 15073.5. Recirculation of a Negative Declaration Prior to Adoption.

(a) A lead agency is required to recirculate a negative declaration when the document must be substantially revised after public notice of its availability has previously been given pursuant to Section 15072, but prior to its adoption. Notice of recirculation shall comply with Sections 15072 and 15073.(b) A "substantial revision" of the negative declaration shall mean:

(1) A new, avoidable significant effect is identified and mitigation measures or project revisions must be added in order to reduce the effect to insignificance, or

(2) The lead agency determines that the proposed mitigation measures or project revisions will not reduce potential effects to less than significance and new measures or revisions must be required.

(c) Recirculation is not required under the following circumstances:

(1) Mitigation measures are replaced with equal or more effective measures pursuant to Section 15074.1.

(2) New project revisions are added in response to written or verbal comments on the project's effects identified in the proposed negative declaration which are not new avoidable significant effects.

(3) Measures or conditions of project approval are added after circulation of the negative declaration which are not required by CEQA, which do not create new significant environmental effects and are not necessary to mitigate an avoidable significant effect.

(4) New information is added to the negative declaration which merely clarifies, amplifies, or makes insignificant modifications to the negative declaration.

(d) If during the negative declaration process there is substantial evidence in light of the whole record, before the lead agency that the project, as revised, may have a significant effect on the environment which cannot be mitigated or avoided, the lead agency shall prepare a draft EIR and certify a final EIR prior to approving the project. It shall circulate the draft EIR for consultation and review pursuant to Sections 15086 and 15087, and advise reviewers in writing that a proposed negative declaration had previously been circulated for the project.

Note: Authority cited: Section 21083, Public Resources Code. Reference: Section 21080, Public Resources Code; *Gentry v. City of Murrieta* (1995) 36 Cal. App. 4th 1359; *Leonoff v. Monterey County Board of Supervisors* (1990) 222 Cal. App. 3d 1337; and *Long Beach Savings and Loan Assn. v. Long Beach Redevelopment Agency* (1986) 188 Cal. App. 3d 249.

§ 15074. Consideration and Adoption of a Negative Declaration or Mitigated Negative Declaration.

(a) Any advisory body of a public agency making a recommendation to the decisionmaking body shall consider the proposed negative declaration or mitigated negative declaration before making its recommendation.

(b) Prior to approving a project, the decisionmaking body of the lead agency shall consider the proposed negative declaration or mitigated negative declaration together with any comments received during the public review process. The decisionmaking body shall adopt the proposed negative declaration or mitigated negative declaration only if it finds on the basis of the whole record before it (including the initial study and any comments received), that there is no substantial evidence that the project will have a significant effect on the environment and that the negative declaration or mitigated negative declaration reflects the lead agency's independent judgment and analysis.

(c) When adopting a negative declaration or mitigated negative declaration, the lead agency shall specify the location and custodian of the documents or other material which constitute the record of proceedings upon which its decision is based.

(d) When adopting a mitigated negative declaration, the lead agency shall also adopt a program for reporting on or monitoring the changes which it has either required in the project or made a condition of approval to mitigate or avoid significant environmental effects.

(e) A lead agency shall not adopt a negative declaration or mitigated negative declaration for a project within the boundaries of a comprehensive airport land use plan or, if a comprehensive airport land use plan has not been adopted, for a project within two nautical miles of a public airport or public use airport, without first considering whether the project will result in a safety hazard or noise problem for persons using the airport or for persons residing or working in the project area.

(f) When a non-elected official or decisionmaking body of a local lead agency adopts a negative declaration or mitigated negative declaration, that adoption may be appealed to the agency's elected decisionmaking body, if one exists. For example, adoption of a negative declaration for a project by a city's planning commission may be appealed to the city council. A local lead agency may establish procedures governing such appeals.

Note: Authority cited: Section 21083, Public Resources Code. Reference: Sections 21080(c), 21081.6, 21082.1, 21096 and 21151, Public Resources Code; *Friends of B Street v. City of Hayward* (1980) 106 Cal. App. 3d 988.

§ 15074.1. Substitution of Mitigation Measures in a Proposed Mitigated Negative Declaration.

(a) As a result of the public review process for a proposed mitigated negative declaration, including any administrative decisions or public hearings conducted on the project prior to its approval, the lead agency may conclude that certain mitigation measures identified in the mitigated negative declaration are infeasible or otherwise undesirable. Prior to approving the project, the lead agency may, in accordance with this section, delete those mitigation measures and substitute for them other measures which the lead agency determines are equivalent or more effective.

(b) Prior to deleting and substituting for a mitigation measure, the lead agency shall do both of the following:

(1) Hold a public hearing on the matter. Where a public hearing is to be held in order to consider the project, the public hearing required by this section may be combined with that hearing. Where no public hearing would otherwise be held to consider the project, then a public hearing shall be required before a mitigation measure may be deleted and a new measure adopted in its place.

(2) Adopt a written finding that the new measure is equivalent or more effective in mitigating or avoiding potential significant effects and that it in itself will not cause any potentially significant effect on the environment.

(c) No recirculation of the proposed mitigated negative declaration pursuant to Section 15072 is required where the new mitigation measures are made conditions of, or are otherwise incorporated into, project approval in accordance with this section.

(d) "Equivalent or more effective" means that the new measure will avoid or reduce the significant effect to at least the same degree as, or to a greater degree than, the original measure and will create no more adverse effect of its own than would have the original measure.

Note: Authority cited: Section 21083, Public Resources Code. Reference: Section 21080(f), Public Resources Code.

§ 15075. Notice of Determination on a Project for Which a Proposed Negative or Mitigated Negative Declaration Has Been Approved.

(a) The lead agency shall file a notice of determination within five working days after deciding to carry out or approve the project. For projects with more than one phase, the lead agency shall file a notice of determination for each phase requiring a discretionary approval.

(b) The notice of determination shall include:
   (1) An identification of the project including the project title as identified on the proposed negative declaration, its location, and the State Clearinghouse identification number for the proposed negative declaration if the notice of determination is filed with the State Clearinghouse.
   (2) A brief description of the project.
   (3) The agency's name and the date on which the agency approved the project.
   (4) The determination of the agency that the project will not have a significant effect on the environment.
   (5) A statement that a negative declaration or a mitigated negative declaration was adopted pursuant to the provisions of CEQA.
   (6) A statement indicating whether mitigation measures were made a condition of the approval of the project, and whether a mitigation monitoring plan/program was adopted.
   (7) The address where a copy of the negative declaration or mitigated negative declaration may be examined.

(c) If the lead agency is a state agency, the lead agency shall file the notice of determination with the Office of Planning and Research within five working days after approval of the project by the lead agency.

(d) If the lead agency is a local agency, the local agency shall file the notice of determination with the county clerk of the county or counties in which the project will be located within five working days after approval of the project by the lead agency. If the project requires discretionary approval from any state agency, the local lead agency shall also, within five working days of this approval, file a copy of the notice of determination with the Office of Planning and Research.

(e) A notice of determination filed with the county clerk shall be available for public inspection and shall be posted by the county clerk within 24 hours of receipt for a period of at least 30 days. Thereafter, the clerk shall return the notice to the local lead agency with a notation of the period during which it was posted. The local lead agency shall retain the notice for not less than 12 months.

(f) A notice of determination filed with the Office of Planning and Research shall be available for public inspection and shall be posted for a period of at least 30 days. The Office of Planning and Research shall retain each notice for not less than 12 months.

(g) The filing of the notice of determination pursuant to subdivision (c) above for state agencies and the filing and posting of the notice of determination pursuant to subdivisions (d) and (e) above for local agencies, start a 30-day statute of limitations on court challenges to the approval under CEQA.

(h) A sample notice of determination is provided in Appendix D. Each public agency may devise its own form, but the minimum content requirements of subdivision (b) above shall be met.Public agencies are encouraged to make copies of all notices filed pursuant to this section available in electronic format on the Internet. Such electronic notices are in addition to the posting requirements of these guidelines and the Public Resources Code.

Note: Authority cited: Section 21083, Public Resources Code. Reference: Sections 21080(c), 21108(a) and (c), 21152(a) and (c) and 21167(b), Public Resources Code; *Citizens of Lake Murray Area Association v. City Council* (1982) 129 Cal. App. 3d 436.

Article 6.5. Statutory Exemptions [Repealed]

NO INFORMATION

Article 7. Eir Process

§ 15080. General.
To the extent possible, the EIR process should be combined with the existing planning, review, and project approval process used by each public agency.

Note: Authority cited: Section 21083, Public Resources Code. Reference: Sections 21003, 21061, 21100 and 21151, Public Resources Code.

§ 15081. Decision to Prepare an EIR.
The EIR process starts with the decision to prepare an EIR. This decision will be made either during preliminary review under Section 15060 or at the conclusion of an initial study after applying the standards described in Section 15064.

Note: Authority cited: Section 21083, Public Resources Code. Reference: Section 21100, Public Resources Code; *No Oil, Inc. v. City of Los Angeles* (1974) 13 Cal. 3d 68; *Friends of B Street v. City of Hayward* (1980) 106 Cal. App. 3d 988.

§ 15081.5. EIRs Required by Statute.

(a) A lead agency shall prepare or have prepared an EIR for the following types of projects. An initial study may be prepared to help identify the significant effects of the project.
   (1) The burning of municipal wastes, hazardous wastes, or refuse-derived fuel, including but not limited to tires, if the project is either:
      (A) The construction of a new facility; or
      (B) The expansion of an existing facility that burns hazardous waste that would increase its permitted capacity by more than 10 percent. This does not apply to any project exclusively burning hazardous waste for which a determination to prepare a negative declaration, or mitigated negative declaration or environmental impact report was made prior to July 14, 1989. The amount of expansion of an existing facility is calculated pursuant to subdivision (b) of Section 21151.1 of the Public Resources Code.
      (C) Subdivision (1) of the subdivision does not apply to:
         1. Projects for which the State Energy Resources Conservation and Development Commission has assumed jurisdiction pursuant to Chapter 6 (commencing with Section 25500) of Division 15 of the Public Resources Code.
         2. Any of the types of burn or thermal processing projects listed in subdivision (d) of Section 21151.1 of the Public Resources Code.
   (2) The initial issuance of a hazardous waste facilities permit to a land disposal facility, as defined in subdivision (d) of Section 25199.1 of the Health and Safety Code. Preparation of an EIR is not mandatory if the facility only manages hazardous waste which is identified or listed pursuant to Section 25140 or Section 25141 of the Health and Safety Code on or after January 1, 1992; or only conducts activities which are regulated pursuant to Chapter 6.5 (commencing with Section 25100) of Division 20 of the Health and Safety Code on or after January 1, 1992. "Initial issuance" does not include the issuance of a closure or postclosure permit pursuant to Chapter 6.5 (commencing with Section 25100) of Division 20 of the Health and Safety Code.
   (3) The initial issuance of a hazardous waste facility permit pursuant to Section 25200 of the Health and Safety Code to an off-site large treatment facility, as defined pursuant to subdivision (d) of Section 25205.1 of that code. Preparation of an EIR is not mandatory if the facility only manges hazardous waste which is identified or listed pursuant to Section 25140 or Section 25141 of the Health and Safety Code on or after January 1, 1992; or only conducts activities which are regulated pursuant to Chapter 6.5 (commencing with Section 25100) of Division 20 of the Health and Safety Code on or after January 1, 1992. "Initial issuance" does not include the issuance of a closure or postclosure permit pursuant to Chapter 6.5 (commencing with Section 25100) of Division 20 of the Health and Safety Code.
   (4) Any open pit mining operation which is subject to the permit requirements of the Surface Mining and Reclamation Act (beginning at Section 2710 of the Public Resources Code) and which utilizes a cyanide heap-leaching process for the purpose of extracting gold or other precious metals.
   (5) An initial base reuse plan as defined in Section 15229.

(b) A lead agency shall prepare or have prepared an EIR for the selection of a California Community College, California State University, University of California, or California Maritime Academy campus location and approval of a long range development plan for that campus.
   (1) The EIR for a long range development plan for a campus shall include an analysis of, among other significant impacts, those environmental effects relating to changes in enrollment levels.
   (2) Subsequent projects within the campus may be addressed in environmental analyses tiered on the EIR prepared for the long range development plan.

Note: Authority cited: Section 21083, Public Resources Code. Reference: Sections 21080.09, 21083.8.1, 21151.1 and 21151.7, Public Resources Code.

§ 15082. Notice of Preparation and Determination of Scope of EIR.

(a) Notice of Preparation. Immediately after deciding that an environmental impact report is required for a project, the lead agency shall send to the Office of Planning and Research and each responsible and trustee agency a notice of preparation stating that an environmental impact report will be prepared. This notice shall also be sent to every federal agency involved in approving or funding the project. If the United States Department of Defense or any branch of the United States Armed Forces has given the lead agency written notification of the specific boundaries of a low-level flight path, military impact zone, or special use airspace and provided the lead agency with written notification of the military contact office and address for the military service pursuant to subdivision (b) of Section 15190.5, then the lead agency shall include the specified military contact office in the list of organizations and individuals receiving a notice of preparation of an EIR pursuant to this section for projects that meet the criteria set forth in subdivision (c) of Section 15190.5.
   (1) The notice of preparation shall provide the responsible and trustee agencies and the Office of Planning and Research with sufficient information describing the project and the potential environmental effects to enable the responsible agencies to make a meaningful response. At a minimum, the information shall include:
      (A) Description of the project,
      (B) Location of the project (either by street address and cross street, for a project in an urbanized area, or by attaching a specific map, preferably a copy of a U.S.G.S. 15'or 7 1/2' topographical map identified by quadrangle name), and
      (C) Probable environmental effects of the project.
   (2) A sample notice of preparation is shown in Appendix I. Public agencies are free to devise their own formats for this notice. A copy of the initial study may be sent with the notice to supply the necessary information.
   (3) To send copies of the notice of preparation, the lead agency shall use either certified mail or any other method of transmittal that provides it with a record that the notice was received.
   (4) The lead agency may begin work on the draft EIR immediately without awaiting responses to the notice of preparation. The draft EIR in preparation may need to be revised or expanded to conform to responses to the notice of preparation. A lead agency shall not circulate a draft EIR for public review before the time period for responses to the notice of preparation has expired.

(b) Response to Notice of Preparation. Within 30 days after receiving the notice of preparation under subdivision (a), each responsible and trustee agency and the Office of Planning and Research shall provide the lead agency with specific detail about the scope and content of the environmental information related to the responsible or trustee agency's area of statutory responsibility that must be included in the draft EIR.
   (1) The response at a minimum shall identify:
      (A) The significant environmental issues and reasonable alternatives and mitigation measures that the responsible or trustee agency, or the Office of Planning and Research will need to have explored in the draft EIR; and
      (B) Whether the agency will be a responsible agency or trustee agency for the project.
   (2) If a responsible or trustee agency, or the Office of Planning and Research fails by the end of the 30-day period to provide the lead agency with either a response to the notice or a well-justified request for additional time, the lead agency may presume that none of those entities have a response to make.
   (3) A generalized list of concerns not related to the specific project shall not meet the requirements of this section for a response.

(c) Meetings. In order to expedite the consultation, the lead agency, a responsible agency, a trustee agency, the Office of Planning and Research, or a project applicant may request one or more meetings between representatives of the agencies involved to assist the lead agency in determining the scope and content of the environmental information that the responsible or trustee agency may require. Such meetings shall be convened by the lead agency as soon as possible, but no later than 30 days after the meetings were requested. On request, the Office of Planning and Research will assist in convening meetings that involve state agencies.
   (1) For projects of statewide, regional or areawide significance pursuant to Section 15206, the lead agency shall conduct at least one scoping meeting. A scoping meeting held pursuant to the National Environmental Policy Act, 42 USC 4321 et seq. (NEPA) in the city or county within which the project is located satisfies this requirement if the lead agency meets the notice requirements of subsection (c)(2) below.
   (2) The lead agency shall provide notice of the scoping meeting to all of the following:
      (A) any county or city that borders on a county or city within which the project is located, unless otherwise designated annually by agreement between the lead agency and the county or city;
      (B) any responsible agency
      (C) any public agency that has jurisdiction by law with respect to the project;
      (D) any organization or individual who has filed a written request for the notice.
   (3) A lead agency shall call at least one scoping meeting for a proposed project that may affect highways or other facilities under the jurisdiction of the Department of Transportation if the meeting is requested by the department. The lead agency shall call the scoping meeting as soon as possible but not later than 30 days after receiving the request from the Department of Transportation.

(d) The Office of Planning and Research. The Office of Planning and Research will ensure that the state responsible and trustee agencies reply to the lead agency within 30 days of receipt of the notice of preparation by the state responsible and trustee agencies.(e) Identification Number. When the notice of preparation is submitted to the State Clearinghouse, the state identification number issued by the Clearinghouse shall be the identification number for all subsequent environmental documents on the project. The identification number should be referenced on all subsequent correspondence regarding the project, specifically on the title page of the draft and final EIR and on the notice of determination.

Note: Authority cited: Section 21083, Public Resources Code. Reference: Sections 21083.9, 21080.4 and 21098, Public Resources Code.

§ 15083. Early Public Consultation.

Prior to completing the draft EIR, the lead agency may also consult directly with any person or organization it believes will be concerned with the environmental effects of the project. Many public agencies have found that early consultation solves many potential problems that would arise in more serious forms later in the review process. This early consultation may be called scoping. Scoping will be necessary when preparing an EIR/EIS jointly with a federal agency.

(a) Scoping has been helpful to agencies in identifying the range of actions, alternatives, mitigation measures, and significant effects to be analyzed in depth in an EIR and in eliminating from detailed study issues found not to be important.
(b) Scoping has been found to be an effective way to bring together and resolve the concerns of affected federal, state, and local agencies, the proponent of the action, and other interested persons including those who might not be in accord with the action on environmental grounds.
(c) Where scoping is used, it should be combined to the extent possible with consultation under Section 15082.

Note: Authority cited: Section 21083, Public Resources Code. Reference: Section 21082.1, Public Resources Code; Section 4, Chapter 480 of the Statutes of 1981; 40 Code of Federal Regulations, Part 1501.7.

§ 15083.5. City or County Consultation with Water Agencies. [Repealed]

Note: Authority cited: Section 21083, Public Resources Code. Reference: Section 21151.9.

§ 15084. Preparing the Draft EIR.

(a) The draft EIR shall be prepared directly by or under contract to the lead agency. The required contents of a draft EIR are discussed in Article 9 beginning with Section 15120.
(b) The lead agency may require the project applicant to supply data and information both to determine whether the project may have a significant effect on the environment and to assist the lead agency in preparing the draft EIR. The requested information should include an identification of other public agencies which will have jurisdiction by law over the project.
(c) Any person, including the applicant, may submit information or comments to the lead agency to assist

in the preparation of the draft EIR. The submittal may be presented in any format, including the form of a draft EIR. The lead agency must consider all information and comments received. The information or comments may be included in the draft EIR in whole or in part.

(d) The lead agency may choose one of the following arrangements or a combination of them for preparing a draft EIR.
  (1) Preparing the draft EIR directly with its own staff.
  (2) Contracting with another entity, public or private, to prepare the draft EIR.
  (3) Accepting a draft prepared by the applicant, a consultant retained by the applicant, or any other person.
  (4) Executing a third party contract or memorandum of understanding with the applicant to govern the preparation of a draft EIR by an independent contractor.
  (5) Using a previously prepared EIR.

(e) Before using a draft prepared by another person, the lead agency shall subject the draft to the agency's own review and analysis. The draft EIR which is sent out for public review must reflect the independent judgment of the lead agency. The lead agency is responsible for the adequacy and objectivity of the draft EIR.

Note: Authority cited: Section 21083, Public Resources Code. Reference: Section 21082.1, Public Resources Code.

§ 15085. Notice of Completion.

(a) As soon as the draft EIR is completed, a notice of completion must be filed with the Office of Planning and Research in a printed hard copy or in electronic form on a diskette or by electronic mail transmission.(b) The notice of completion shall include:
  (1) A brief description of the project,
  (2) The proposed location of the project (either by street address and cross street, for a project in an urbanized area, or by attaching a specific map, preferably a copy of a U.S.G.S. 15'or 7-1/2'topographical map identified by quadrangle name).
  (3) An address where copies of the draft EIR are available, and
  (4) The review period during which comments will be received on the draft EIR.

(c) A sample form for the notice of completion is included in Appendix L.

(d) Where the EIR will be reviewed through the state review process handled by the State Clearinghouse, the notice of completion cover form required by the State Clearinghouse will serve as the notice of completion (see Appendix C).

(e) Public agencies are encouraged to make copies of notices of completion filed pursuant to this section available in electronic format on the Internet.

Note: Authority cited: Section 21083, Public Resources Code. Reference: Section 21161, Public Resources Code.

§ 15086. Consultation Concerning Draft EIR.

(a) The lead agency shall consult with and request comments on the draft EIR from:
  (1) Responsible agencies,
  (2) Trustee agencies with resources affected by the project, and
  (3) Any other state, federal, and local agencies which have jurisdiction by law with respect to the project or which exercise authority over resources which may be affected by the project, including water agencies consulted pursuant to section 15083.5.
  (4) Any city or county which borders on a city or county within which the project is located.
  (5) For a project of statewide, regional, or areawide significance, the transportation planning agencies and public agencies which have transportation facilities within their jurisdictions which could be affected by the project. "Transportation facilities" includes: major local arterials and public transit within five miles of the project site, and freeways, highways and rail transit service within 10 miles of the project site.
  (6) For a state lead agency when the EIR is being prepared for a highway or freeway project, the California Air Resources Board as to the air pollution impact of the potential vehicular use of the highway or freeway and if a non-attainment area, the local air quality management district for a determination of conformity with the air quality management plan.
  (7) For a subdivision project located within one mile of a facility of the State Water Resources Development System, the California Department of Water Resources.

(b) The lead agency may consult directly with:
  (1) Any person who has special expertise with respect to any environmental impact involved,
  (2) Any member of the public who has filed a written request for notice with the lead agency or the clerk of the governing body.
  (3) Any person identified by the applicant whom the applicant believes will be concerned with the environmental effects of the project.

(c) A responsible agency or other public agency shall only make substantive comments regarding those activities involved in the project that are within an area of expertise of the agency or which are required to be carried out or approved by the responsible agency. Those comments shall be supported by specific documentation.

(d) Prior to the close of the public review period, a responsible agency or trustee agency which has identified what that agency considers to be significant environmental effects shall advise the lead agency of those effects. As to those effects relevant to its decision, if any, on the project, the responsible or trustee agency shall either submit to the lead agency complete and detailed performance objectives for mitigation measures addressing those effects or refer the lead agency to appropriate, readily available guidelines or reference documents concerning mitigation measures. If the responsible or trustee agency is not aware of mitigation measures that address identified effects, the responsible or trustee agency shall so state.

Note: Authority cited: Section 21083, Public Resources Code. Reference: Sections 21081.6, 21092.4, 21092.5, 21104 and 21153, Public Resources Code.

§ 15087. Public Review of Draft EIR.

(a) The lead agency shall provide public notice of the availability of a draft EIR at the same time as it sends a notice of completion to the Office of Planning and Research. If the United States Department of Defense or any branch of the United States Armed Forces has given the lead agency written notification of the specific boundaries of a low-level flight path, military impact zone, or special use airspace and provided the lead agency with written notification of the contact office and address for the military service pursuant to subdivision (b) of Section 15190.5, then the lead agency shall include the specified military contact office in the list of organizations and individuals receiving a notice of availability of a draft EIR pursuant to this section for projects that meet the criteria set forth in subdivision (c) of Section 15190.5. The public notice shall be given as provided under Section 15105 (a sample form is provided in Appendix L). Notice shall be mailed to the last known name and address of all organizations and individuals who have previously requested such notice in writing, and shall also be given by at least one of the following procedures:
  (1) Publication at least one time by the public agency in a newspaper of general circulation in the area affected by the proposed project. If more than one area is affected, the notice shall be published in the newspaper of largest circulation from among the newspapers of general circulation in those areas.
  (2) Posting of notice by the public agency on and off the site in the area where the project is to be located.
  (3) Direct mailing to the owners and occupants of property contiguous to the parcel or parcels on which the project is located. Owners of such property shall be identified as shown on the latest equalized assessment roll.

(b) The alternatives for providing notice specified in subdivision (a) shall not preclude a public agency from providing additional notice by other means if such agency so desires, nor shall the requirements of this section preclude a public agency from providing the public notice required by this section at the same time and in the same manner as public notice otherwise required by law for the project.

(c) The notice shall disclose the following:
  (1) A brief description of the proposed project and its location.
  (2) The starting and ending dates for the review period during which the lead agency will receive comments. If the review period is shortened, the notice shall disclose that fact.
  (3) The date, time, and place of any scheduled public meetings or hearings to be held by the lead agency on the proposed project when known to the lead agency at the time of notice.
  (4) A list of the significant environmental effects anticipated as a result of the project, to the extent which such effects are known to the lead agency at the time of the notice.
  (5) The address where copies of the EIR and all documents referenced in the EIR will be available for public review. This location shall be readily accessible to the public during the lead agency's normal working hours.

(6) The presence of the site on any of the lists of sites enumerated under Section 65962.5 of the Government Code including, but not limited to lists of hazardous waste facilities, land designated as hazardous waste property, hazardous waste disposal sites and others, and the information in the Hazardous Waste and Substances Statement required under subdivision (f) of that Section.

(d) The notice required under this section shall be posted in the office of the county clerk of each county in which the project will be located for a period of at least 30 days. The county clerk shall post such notices within 24 hours of receipt.

(e) In order to provide sufficient time for public review, the review period for a draft EIR shall be as provided in Section 15105. The review period shall be combined with the consultation required under Section 15086. When a draft EIR has been submitted to the State Clearinghouse, the public review period shall be at least as long as the review period established by the State Clearinghouse. The public review period and the state agency review period may, but are not required to, begin and end at the same time. Day one of the state review period shall be the date that the State Clearinghouse distributes the document to state agencies.

(f) Public agencies shall use the State Clearinghouse to distribute draft EIRs to state agencies for review and should use areawide clearinghouses to distribute the documents to regional and local agencies.

(g) To make copies of EIRs available to the public, lead agencies should furnish copies of draft EIRs to public library systems serving the area involved. Copies should also be available in offices of the lead agency.

(h) Public agencies should compile listings of other agencies, particularly local agencies, which have jurisdiction by law and/or special expertise with respect to various projects and project locations. Such listings should be a guide in determining which agencies should be consulted with regard to a particular project.

(i) Public hearings may be conducted on the environmental documents, either in separate proceedings or in conjunction with other proceedings of the public agency. Public hearings are encouraged, but not required as an element of the CEQA process.

Note: Authority cited: Section 21083, Public Resources Code. Reference: Sections 21091, 21092, 21092.2, 21092.3, 21092.6, 21098, 21104, 21152, 21153 and 21161, Public Resources Code.

§ 15088. Evaluation of and Response to Comments.

(a) The lead agency shall evaluate comments on environmental issues received from persons who reviewed the draft EIR and shall prepare a written response. The lead agency shall respond to comments received during the noticed comment period and any extensions and may respond to late comments.

(b) The lead agency shall provide a written proposed response to a public agency on comments made by that public agency at least 10 days prior to certifying an environmental impact report.

(c) The written response shall describe the disposition of significant environmental issues raised (e.g., revisions to the proposed project to mitigate anticipated impacts or objections). In particular, the major environmental issues raised when the lead agency's position is at variance with recommendations and objections raised in the comments must be addressed in detail giving reasons why specific comments and suggestions were not accepted. There must be good faith, reasoned analysis in response. Conclusory statements unsupported by factual information will not suffice.

(d) The response to comments may take the form of a revision to the draft EIR or may be a separate section in the final EIR. Where the response to comments makes important changes in the information contained in the text of the draft EIR, the lead agency should either:

(1) Revise the text in the body of the EIR, or

(2) Include marginal notes showing that the information is revised in the response to comments.

Note: Authority cited: Section 21083, Public Resources Code. Reference: Sections 21092.5, 21104 and 21153, Public Resources Code; *People v. County of Kern* (1974) 39 Cal. App. 3d 830; *Cleary v. County of Stanislaus* (1981) 118 Cal. App. 3d 348.

§ 15088.5. Recirculation of an EIR Prior to Certification.

(a) A lead agency is required to recirculate an EIR when significant new information is added to the EIR after public notice is given of the availability of the draft EIR for public review under Section 15087 but before certification. As used in this section, the term "information" can include changes in the project or environmental setting as well as additional data or other information. New information added to an EIR is not "significant" unless the EIR is changed in a way that deprives the public of a meaningful opportunity to comment upon a substantial adverse environmental effect of the project or a feasible way to mitigate or avoid such an effect (including a feasible project alternative) that the project's proponents have declined to implement. "Significant new information" requiring recirculation include, for example, a disclosure showing that:

(1) A new significant environmental impact would result from the project or from a new mitigation measure proposed to be implemented.

(2) A substantial increase in the severity of an environmental impact would result unless mitigation measures are adopted that reduce the impact to a level of insignificance.

(3) A feasible project alternative or mitigation measure considerably different from others previously analyzed would clearly lessen the significant environmental impacts of the project, but the project's proponents decline to adopt it.

(4) The draft EIR was so fundamentally and basically inadequate and conclusory in nature that meaningful public review and comment were precluded. (Mountain Lion Coalition v. Fish & Game Com.(1989) 214 Cal.App.3d 1043).

(b) Recirculation is not required where the new information added to the EIR merely clarifies or amplifies or makes insignificant modifications in an adequate EIR.

(c) If the revision is limited to a few chapters or portions of the EIR, the lead agency need only recirculate the chapters or portions that have been modified.

(d) Recirculation of an EIR requires notice pursuant to Section 15087, and consultation pursuant to Section 15086.

(e) A decision not to recirculate an EIR must be supported by substantial evidence in the administrative record.

(f) The lead agency shall evaluate and respond to comments as provided in Section 15088. Recirculating an EIR can result in the lead agency receiving more than one set of comments from reviewers. The following are two ways in which the lead agency may identify the set of comments to which it will respond. This dual approach avoids confusion over whether the lead agency must respond to comments which are duplicates or which are no longer pertinent due to revisions to the EIR. In no case shall the lead agency fail to respond to pertinent comments on significant environmental issues.

(1) When an EIR is substantially revised and the entire document is recirculated, the lead agency may require reviewers to submit new comments and, in such cases, need not respond to those comments received during the earlier circulation period. The lead agency shall advise reviewers, either in the text of the revised EIR or by an attachment to the revised EIR, that although part of the administrative record, the previous comments do not require a written response in the final EIR, and that new comments must be submitted for the revised EIR. The lead agency need only respond to those comments submitted in response to the recirculated revised EIR.

(2) When the EIR is revised only in part and the lead agency is recirculating only the revised chapters or portions of the EIR, the lead agency may request that reviewers limit their comments to the revised chapters or portions of the recirculated EIR. The lead agency need only respond to (i) comments received during the initial circulation period that relate to chapters or portions of the document that were not revised and recirculated, and (ii) comments received during the recirculation period that relate to the chapters or portions of the earlier EIR that were revised and recirculated. The lead agency's request that reviewers limit the scope of their comments shall be included either within the text of the revised EIR or by an attachment to the revised EIR.

(3) As part of providing notice of recirculation as required by Public Resources Code Section 21092.1, the lead agency shall send a notice of recirculation to every agency, person, or organization that commented on the prior EIR. The notice shall indicate, at a minimum, whether new comments may be submitted only on the recirculated portions of the EIR or on the entire EIR in order to be considered by the agency.

(g) When recirculating a revised EIR, either in whole or in part, the lead agency shall, in the revised EIR or by an attachment to the revised EIR, summarize the revisions made to the previously circulated draft EIR.

Note: Authority cited: Section 21083, Public Resources Code. Reference: Section 21092.1, Public Resources Code; *Laurel Heights Improvement Association v. Regents of the University of California* (1993) 6 Cal. 4th 1112.

§ 15089. Preparation of Final EIR.

(a) The lead agency shall prepare a final EIR before approving the project. The contents of a final EIR are specified in Section 15132 of these guidelines.

(b) Lead agencies may provide an opportunity for review of the final EIR by the public or by commenting agencies before approving the project. The review of a final EIR should focus on the responses to comments on the draft EIR.

Note: Authority cited: Section 21083, Public Resources Code. Reference: Sections 21100, 21105 and 21151, Public Resources Code; *City of Carmel-by-the-Sea v. Board of Supervisors* (1977) 71 Cal. App. 3d 84; State Administrative Manual, Section 1060.

§ 15090. Certification of the Final EIR.

(a) Prior to approving a project the lead agency shall certify that:
   (1) The final EIR has been completed in compliance with CEQA;
   (2) The final EIR was presented to the decision-making body of the lead agency and that the decisionmaking body reviewed and considered the information contained in the final EIR prior to approving the project; and
   (3) The final EIR reflects the lead agency's independent judgment and analysis.

(b) When an EIR is certified by a non-elected decision-making body within a local lead agency, that certification may be appealed to the local lead agency's elected decision-making body, if one exists. For example, certification of an EIR for a tentative subdivision map by a city's planning commission may be appealed to the city council. Each local lead agency shall provide for such appeals.

Note: Authority cited: Section 21083, Public Resources Code. Reference: Sections 21082.1, 21100 and 21151, Public Resources Code; *City of Carmel-by-the-Sea v. Board of Supervisors* (1977) 71 Cal. App. 3d 84; *Kleist v. City of Glendale* (1976) 56 Cal. App. 3d 770.

§ 15091. Findings.

(a) No public agency shall approve or carry out a project for which an EIR has been certified which identifies one or more significant environmental effects of the project unless the public agency makes one or more written findings for each of those significant effects, accompanied by a brief explanation of the rationale for each finding. The possible findings are:
   (1) Changes or alterations have been required in, or incorporated into, the project which avoid or substantially lessen the significant environmental effect as identified in the final EIR.
   (2) Such changes or alterations are within the responsibility and jurisdiction of another public agency and not the agency making the finding. Such changes have been adopted by such other agency or can and should be adopted by such other agency.
   (3) Specific economic, legal, social, technological, or other considerations, including provision of employment opportunities for highly trained workers, make infeasible the mitigation measures or project alternatives identified in the final EIR.

(b) The findings required by subdivision (a) shall be supported by substantial evidence in the record.

(c) The finding in subdivision (a)(2) shall not be made if the agency making the finding has concurrent jurisdiction with another agency to deal with identified feasible mitigation measures or alternatives. The finding in subdivision (a)(3) shall describe the specific reasons for rejecting identified mitigation measures and project alternatives.

(d) When making the findings required in subdivision (a)(1), the agency shall also adopt a program for reporting on or monitoring the changes which it has either required in the project or made a condition of approval to avoid or substantially lessen significant environmental effects. These measures must be fully enforceable through permit conditions, agreements, or other measures.

(e) The public agency shall specify the location and custodian of the documents or other material which constitute the record of the proceedings upon which its decision is based.(f) A statement made pursuant to Section 15093 does not substitute for the findings required by this section.

Note: Authority cited: Section 21083, Public Resources Code. Reference: Sections 21002, 21002.1, 21081 and 21081.6, Public Resources Code; *Laurel Hills Homeowners Association v. City Council* (1978) 83 Cal. App. 3d 515; *Cleary v. County of Stanislaus* (1981)118 Cal. App. 3d 348; *Sierra Club v. Contra Costa County* (1992) 10 Cal.App.4th 1212; *Citizens for Quality Growth v. City of Mount Shasta* (1988) 198 Cal.App.3d 433.

§ 15092. Approval.

(a) After considering the final EIR and in conjunction with making findings under Section 15091, the lead agency may decide whether or how to approve or carry out the project.

(b) A public agency shall not decide to approve or carry out a project for which an EIR was prepared unless either:
   (1) The project as approved will not have a significant effect on the environment, or
   (2) The agency has:
      (A) Eliminated or substantially lessened all significant effects on the environment where feasible as shown in findings under Section 15091, and
      (B) Determined that any remaining significant effects on the environment found to be unavoidable under Section 15091 are acceptable due to overriding concerns as described in Section 15093.
      (c) With respect to a project which includes housing development, the public agency shall not reduce the proposed number of housing units as a mitigation measure if it determines that there is another feasible specific mitigation measure available that will provide a comparable level of mitigation.

Note: Authority cited: Section 21083, Public Resources Code. Reference: Sections 21002, 21002.1, 21081 and 21159.26, Public Resources Code; *Friends of Mammoth v. Board of Supervisors* (1972) 8 Cal. App. 3d 247; *San Francisco Ecology Center v. City and County of San Francisco* (1975) 48 Cal. App. 3d 584; *City of Carmel-by-the-Sea v. Board of Supervisors* (1977) 71 Cal. App. 3d 84; *Laurel Hills Homeowners Association v. City Council* (1978) 83 Cal. App. 3d 515.

§ 15093. Statement of Overriding Considerations.

(a) CEQA requires the decision-making agency to balance, as applicable, the economic, legal, social, technological, or other benefits, including region-wide or statewide environmental benefits, of a proposed project against its unavoidable environmental risks when determining whether to approve the project. If the specific economic, legal, social, technological, or other benefits, including region-wide or statewide environmental benefits, of a proposal project outweigh the unavoidable adverse environmental effects, the adverse environmental effects may be considered "acceptable."

(b) When the lead agency approves a project which will result in the occurrence of significant effects which are identified in the final EIR but are not avoided or substantially lessened, the agency shall state in writing the specific reasons to support its action based on the final EIR and/or other information in the record. The statement of overriding considerations shall be supported by substantial evidence in the record.

(c) If an agency makes a statement of overriding considerations, the statement should be included in the record of the project approval and should be mentioned in the notice of determination. This statement does not substitute for, and shall be in addition to, findings required pursuant to Section 15091.

Note: Authority cited: Sections 21083 and 21083.05, Public Resources Code. Reference: Sections 21002 and 21081, Public Resources Code; *San Francisco Ecology Center v. City and County of San Francisco* (1975) 48 Cal. App. 3d 584; *City of Carmel-by-the-Sea v. Board of Supervisors* (1977) 71 Cal. App. 3d 84; *Sierra Club v. Contra Costa County* (1992) 10 Cal. App. 4th 1212; *Citizens for Quality Growth v. City of Mount Shasta* (1988) 198 Cal.MApp. 3d 433; and *City of Marina v. Board of Trustees of Cal. State Univ.* (2006) 39 Cal. 4th 341.

§ 15094. Notice of Determination.

(a) The lead agency shall file a notice of determination within five working days after deciding to carry out or approve the project.

(b) The notice of determination shall include:
   (1) An identification of the project including the project title as identified on the draft EIR, and the location of the project (either by street address and cross street for a project in an urbanized area or by attaching a specific map, preferably a copy of a U.S.G.S. 15'or 7-1/2' topographical map identified by quadrangle name). If the notice of determination is filed with the State Clearinghouse, the State Clearinghouse identification number for the draft EIR shall be provided.
   (2) A brief description of the project.

(3) The lead agency's name and the date on which the agency approved the project. If a responsible agency files the notice of determination pursuant to Section 15096(i), the responsible agency's name and date of approval shall also be identified.
(4) The determination of the agency whether the project in its approved form will have a significant effect on the environment.
(5) A statement that an EIR was prepared and certified pursuant to the provisions of CEQA.
(6) Whether mitigation measures were made a condition of the approval of the project, and whether a mitigation monitoring plan/program was adopted.
(7) Whether findings were made pursuant to Section 15091.
(8) Whether a statement of overriding considerations was adopted for the project.
(9) The address where a copy of the final EIR and the record of project approval may be examined.

(c) If the lead agency is a state agency, the lead agency shall file the notice of determination with the Office of Planning and Research within five working days after approval of the project by the lead agency.
(d) If the lead agency is a local agency, the local lead agency shall file the notice of determination with the county clerk of the county or counties in which the project will be located, within five working days after approval of the project by the lead agency. If the project requires discretionary approval from any state agency, the local lead agency shall also, within five working days of this approval, file a copy of the notice of determination with the Office of Planning and Research.
(e) A notice of determination filed with the county clerk shall be available for public inspection and shall be posted within 24 hours of receipt for a period of at least 30 days. Thereafter, the clerk shall return the notice to the local lead agency with a notation of the period during which it was posted. The local lead agency shall retain the notice for not less than 12 months.
(f) A notice of determination filed with the Office of Planning and Research shall be available for public inspection and shall be posted for a period of at least 30 days. The Office of Planning and Research shall retain each notice for not less than 12 months.
(g) The filing of the notice of determination pursuant to subdivision (c) above for state agencies and the filing and posting of the notice of determination pursuant to subdivisions (d) and (e) above for local agencies, start a 30-day statute of limitations on court challenges to the approval under CEQA.
(h) A sample notice of determination is provided in Appendix D. Each public agency may devise its own form, but any such form shall include, at a minimum, the information required by subdivision (b). Public agencies are encouraged to make copies of all notices filed pursuant to this section available in electronic format on the Internet. Such electronic notices are in addition to the posting requirements of the Guidelines and the Public Resources Code.

Note: Authority cited: Section 21083, Public Resources Code. Reference: Sections 21108, 21152 and 21167, Public Resources Code; *Citizens of Lake Murray Area Association v. City Council* (1982) 129 Cal. App. 3d 436.

§ 15095. Disposition of a Final EIR.

The lead agency shall:

(a) File a copy of the final EIR with the appropriate planning agency of any city, county, or city and county where significant effects on the environment may occur.
(b) Include the final EIR as part of the regular project report which is used in the existing project review and budgetary process if such a report is used.
(c) Retain one or more copies of the final EIR as public records for a reasonable period of time.
(d) Require the applicant to provide a copy of the certified, final EIR to each responsible agency.

Note: Authority cited: Section 21083, Public Resources Code. Reference: Sections 21105, 21151 and 21165, Public Resources Code; *County of Inyo v. Yorty* (1973) 32 Cal. App. 3d 795.

§ 15096. Process for a Responsible Agency.

(a) General. A responsible agency complies with CEQA by considering the EIR or negative declaration prepared by the lead agency and by reaching its own conclusions on whether and how to approve the project involved. This section identifies the special duties a public agency will have when acting as a responsible agency.
(b) Response to Consultation. A responsible agency shall respond to consultation by the lead agency in order to assist the lead agency in preparing adequate environmental documents for the project. By this means, the responsible agency will ensure that the documents it will use will comply with CEQA.
(1) In response to consultation, a responsible agency shall explain its reasons for recommending whether the lead agency should prepare an EIR or negative declaration for a project. Where the responsible agency disagrees with the lead agency's proposal to prepare a negative declaration for a project, the responsible agency should identify the significant environmental effects which it believes could result from the project and recommend either that an EIR be prepared or that the project be modified to eliminate the significant effects.
(2) As soon as possible, but not longer than 30 days after receiving a notice of preparation from the lead agency, the responsible agency shall send a written reply by certified mail or any other method which provides the agency with a record showing that the notice was received. The reply shall specify the scope and content of the environmental information which would be germane to the responsible agency's statutory responsibilities in connection with the proposed project. The lead agency shall include this information in the EIR.

(c) Meetings. The responsible agency shall designate employees or representatives to attend meetings requested by the lead agency to discuss the scope and content of the EIR.
(d) Comments on Draft EIRs and Negative Declarations. A responsible agency should review and comment on draft EIRs and negative declarations for projects which the responsible agency would later be asked to approve. Comments should focus on any shortcomings in the EIR, the appropriateness of using a negative declaration, or on additional alternatives or mitigation measures which the EIR should include. The comments shall be limited to those project activities which are within the agency's area of expertise or which are required to be carried out or approved by the agency or which will be subject to the exercise of powers by the agency. Comments shall be as specific as possible and supported by either oral or written documentation.
(e) Decision on Adequacy of EIR or Negative Declaration. If a responsible agency believes that the final EIR or negative declaration prepared by the lead agency is not adequate for use by the responsible agency, the responsible agency must either:
(1) Take the issue to court within 30 days after the lead agency files a notice of determination;
(2) Be deemed to have waived any objection to the adequacy of the EIR or negative declaration;
(3) Prepare a subsequent EIR if permissible under Section 15162; or
(4) Assume the lead agency role as provided in Section 15052(a)(3).

(f) Consider the EIR or Negative Declaration. Prior to reaching a decision on the project, the responsible agency must consider the environmental effects of the project as shown in the EIR or negative declaration. A subsequent or supplemental EIR can be prepared only as provided in Sections 15162 or 15163.(g) Adoption of Alternatives or Mitigation Measures.
(1) When considering alternatives and mitigation measures, a responsible agency is more limited than a lead agency. A responsible agency has responsibility for mitigating or avoiding only the direct or indirect environmental effects of those parts of the project which it decides to carry out, finance, or approve.
(2) When an EIR has been prepared for a project, the Responsible Agency shall not approve the project as proposed if the agency finds any feasible alternative or feasible mitigation measures within its powers that would substantially lessen or avoid any significant effect the project would have on the environment. With respect to a project which includes housing development, the responsible agency shall not reduce the proposed number of housing units as a mitigation measure if it determines that there is another feasible specific mitigation measure available that will provide a comparable level of mitigation.

(h) Findings. The responsible agency shall make the findings required by Section 15091 for each significant effect of the project and shall make the findings in Section 15093 if necessary.
(i) Notice of Determination. The responsible agency should file a notice of determination in the same manner as a lead agency under Section 15075 or 15094 except that the responsible agency does not need to state that the EIR or negative declaration complies with CEQA. The responsible agency should state that it considered the EIR or negative declaration as prepared by a lead agency.

Note: Authority cited: Section 21083, Public Resources Code. Reference: Sections 21165, 21080.1, 21080.3,

21080.4, 21082.1 and 21002.1(b) and (d), Public Resources Code.

§ 15097. Mitigation Monitoring or Reporting.

(a) This section applies when a public agency has made the findings required under paragraph (1) of subdivision (a) of Section 15091 relative to an EIR or adopted a mitigated negative declaration in conjunction with approving a project. In order to ensure that the mitigation measures and project revisions identified in the EIR or negative declaration are implemented, the public agency shall adopt a program for monitoring or reporting on the revisions which it has required in the project and the measures it has imposed to mitigate or avoid significant environmental effects. A public agency may delegate reporting or monitoring responsibilities to another public agency or to a private entity which accepts the delegation; however, until mitigation measures have been completed the lead agency remains responsible for ensuring that implementation of the mitigation measures occurs in accordance with the program.

(b) Where the project at issue is the adoption of a general plan, specific plan, community plan or other plan-level document (zoning, ordinance, regulation, policy), the monitoring plan shall apply to policies and any other portion of the plan that is a mitigation measure or adopted alternative. The monitoring plan may consist of policies included in plan-level documents. The annual report on general plan status required pursuant to the Government Code is one example of a reporting program for adoption of a city or county general plan.

(c) The public agency may choose whether its program will monitor mitigation, report on mitigation, or both. "Reporting" generally consists of a written compliance review that is presented to the decision making body or authorized staff person. A report may be required at various stages during project implementation or upon completion of the mitigation measure. "Monitoring" is generally an ongoing or periodic process of project oversight. There is often no clear distinction between monitoring and reporting and the program best suited to ensuring compliance in any given instance will usually involve elements of both. The choice of program may be guided by the following:
   (1) Reporting is suited to projects which have readily measurable or quantitative mitigation measures or which already involve regular review. For example, a report may be required upon issuance of final occupancy to a project whose mitigation measures were confirmed by building inspection.
   (2) Monitoring is suited to projects with complex mitigation measures, such as wetlands restoration or archeological protection, which may exceed the expertise of the local agency to oversee, are expected to be implemented over a period of time, or require careful implementation to assure compliance.
   (3) Reporting and monitoring are suited to all but the most simple projects. Monitoring ensures that project compliance is checked on a regular basis during and, if necessary after, implementation. Reporting ensures that the approving agency is informed of compliance with mitigation requirements.

(d) Lead and responsible agencies should coordinate their mitigation monitoring or reporting programs where possible. Generally, lead and responsible agencies for a given project will adopt separate and different monitoring or reporting programs. This occurs because of any of the following reasons: the agencies have adopted and are responsible for reporting on or monitoring different mitigation measures; the agencies are deciding on the project at different times; each agency has the discretion to choose its own approach to monitoring or reporting; and each agency has its own special expertise.

(e) At its discretion, an agency may adopt standardized policies and requirements to guide individually adopted monitoring or reporting programs. Standardized policies and requirements may describe, but are not limited to:
   (1) The relative responsibilities of various departments within the agency for various aspects of monitoring or reporting, including lead responsibility for administering typical programs and support responsibilities.
   (2) The responsibilities of the project proponent.
   (3) Agency guidelines for preparing monitoring or reporting programs.
   (4) General standards for determining project compliance with the mitigation measures or revisions and related conditions of approval.
   (5) Enforcement procedures for noncompliance, including provisions for administrative appeal.
   (6) Process for informing staff and decision makers of the relative success of mitigation measures and using those results to improve future mitigation measures.

(f) Where a trustee agency, in timely commenting upon a draft EIR or a proposed mitigated negative declaration, proposes mitigation measures or project revisions for incorporation into a project, that agency, at the same time, shall prepare and submit to the lead or responsible agency a draft monitoring or reporting program for those measures or revisions. The lead or responsible agency may use this information in preparing its monitoring or reporting program.

(g) When a project is of statewide, regional, or areawide importance, any transportation information generated by a required monitoring or reporting program shall be submitted to the transportation planning agency in the region where the project is located and to the California Department of Transportation. Each transportation planning agency and the California Department of Transportation shall adopt guidelines for the submittal of such information.

Note: Authority: Section 21083, Public Resources Code. References: Sections 21081.6 and 21081.7, Public Resources Code.

Article 8. Time Limits

§ 15100. General.

(a) Public agencies shall adopt time limits to govern their implementation of CEQA consistent with this article.

(b) Public agencies should carry out their responsibilities for preparing and reviewing EIRs within a reasonable period of time. The requirement for the preparation of an EIR should not cause undue delays in the processing of applications for permits or other entitlements to use.

Note: Authority cited: Section 21083, Public Resources Code. Reference: Sections 21000-21176, Public Resources Code.

§ 15101. Review of Application for Completeness.

A lead agency or responsible agency shall determine whether an application for a permit or other entitlement for use is complete within 30 days from the receipt of the application except as provided in Section 15111. If no written determination of the completeness of the application is made within that period, the application will be deemed complete on the 30th day.

Note: Authority cited: Section 21083, Public Resources Code. Reference: Section 21083, Public Resources Code; and Section 65943, Government Code.

§ 15102. Initial Study.

The lead agency shall determine within 30 days after accepting an application as complete whether it intends to prepare an EIR or a negative declaration or use a previously prepared EIR or negative declaration except as provided in Section 15111. The 30 day period may be extended 15 days upon the consent of the lead agency and the project applicant.

Note: Authority cited: Section 21083, Public Resources Code. Reference: Section 21080.2, Public Resources Code.

§ 15103. Response to Notice of Preparation.

Responsible and Trustee Agencies, and the Office of Planning and Research shall provide a response to a Notice of Preparation to the Lead Agency within 30 days after receipt of the notice. If they fail to reply within the 30 days with either a response or a well justified request for additional time, the lead agency may assume that none of those entitles have a response to make and may ignore a late response.

Note: Authority cited: Section 21083, Public Resources Code. Reference: Section 21080.4, Public Resources Code.

§ 15104. Convening of Meetings.

The lead agency shall convene a meeting with agency representatives to discuss the scope and content of the environmental information a responsible agency will need in the EIR as soon as possible but no later than 30 days after receiving a request for the meeting. The meeting may be requested by the lead agency, a responsible agency, a trustee agency, the Office of Planning and Research, or by the project applicant.

Note: Authority cited: Section 21083, Public Resources Code. Reference: Section 21080.4, Public Resources Code.

§ 15105. Public Review Period for a Draft EIR or a Proposed Negative Declaration or Mitigated Negative Declaration.

(a) The public review period for a draft EIR shall not be less than 30 days nor should it be longer than 60 days except in unusual circumstances. When a draft

EIR is submitted to the State Clearinghouse for review by state agencies, the public review period shall not be less than 45 days, unless a shorter period, not less than 30 days, is approved by the State Clearinghouse.

(b) The public review period for a proposed negative declaration or mitigated negative declaration shall be not less than 20 days. When a proposed negative declaration or mitigated negative declaration is submitted to the State Clearinghouse for review by state agencies, the public review period shall not be less than 30 days, unless a shorter period, not less than 20 days, is approved by the State Clearinghouse.

(c) If a draft EIR or proposed negative declaration or mitigated negative declaration has been submitted to the State Clearinghouse for review by state agencies, the public review period shall be at least as long as the review period established by the State Clearinghouse. The public review period and the state agency review period may, but are not required to, begin and end at the same time. Day one of the state review period shall be the date that the State Clearinghouse distributes the document to state agencies.

(d) A shortened Clearinghouse review period may be granted in accordance with the provisions of Appendix K and the following principles:
  (1) A shortened review shall not be granted for any proposed project of statewide, areawide, or regional environmental significance.
  (2) Requests for shortened review periods shall be submitted to the Clearinghouse in writing by the decision-making body of the lead agency, or a representative authorized by ordinance, resolution, or delegation of the decision-making body.
  (3) The lead agency has contacted responsible and trustee agencies and they have agreed to the shortened review period.

(e) The State Clearinghouse shall distribute a draft EIR or proposed negative declaration or mitigated negative declaration within three working days after the date of receipt if the submittal is determined by the State Clearinghouse to be complete.

Note: Authority cited: Section 21083, Public Resources Code. Reference: Sections 21091 and 21092, Public Resources Code;*People v. County of Kern* (1974) 39 Cal. App. 3d 830.

§ 15106. Review by State Agencies.

Note: Authority cited: Sections 21083 and 21087, Public Recources Code. Reference: Sections 21104 and 21153, Public Resources Code.

§ 15107. Completion of Negative Declaration for Certain Private Projects.

With private projects involving the issuance of a lease, permit, license, certificate, or other entitlement for use by one or more public agencies, the negative declaration must be completed and approved within 180 days from the date when the lead agency accepted the application as complete.

Note: Authority cited: Section 21083, Public Resources Code. Reference: Sections 21100.2 and 21151.5, Public Resources Code.

§ 15108. Completion and Certification of EIR.

With a private project, the lead agency shall complete and certify the final EIR as provided in Section 15090 within one year after the date when the lead agency accepted the application as complete. Lead agency procedures may provide that the one-year time limit may be extended once for a period of not more than 90 days upon consent of the lead agency and the applicant.

Note: Authority cited: Section 21083, Public Resources Code. Reference: Sections 21100.2 and 21151.5, Public Resources Code; and Government Code Section 65950.

§ 15109. Suspension of Time Periods.

An unreasonable delay by an applicant in meeting requests by the lead agency necessary for the preparation of a negative declaration or an EIR shall suspend the running of the time periods described in Sections 15107 and 15108 for the period of the unreasonable delay. Alternatively, an agency may disapprove a project application where there is unreasonable delay in meeting requests. The agency may allow a renewed application to start at the same point in the process where the application was when it was disapproved.

Note: Authority cited: Section 21083, Public Resources Code. Reference: Sections 21100.2 and 21151.5, *Public Resources Code; Carmel Valley View, Ltd. v. Maggini*, 91 Cal. App. 3d 318.

§ 15110. Projects with Federal Involvement.

(a) At the request of an applicant, the lead agency may waive the one-year time limit for completing and certifying a final EIR or the 105-day period for completing a negative declaration if:
  (1) The project will be subject to CEQA and to the National Environmental Policy Act,
  (2) Additional time will be required to prepare a combined EIR-EIS or combined negative declaration-finding of no significant impact as provided in Section 15221, and
  (3) The time required to prepare the combined document will be shorter than the time required to prepare the documents separately.

(b) The time limits for taking final action on a permit for a development project may also be waived where a combined EIR-EIS will be prepared.

(c) The time limits for processing permits for development projects under Government Code Sections 65950-65960 shall not apply if federal statutes or regulations require time schedules which exceed the state time limits. In this event, any state agencies involved shall make a final decision on the project within the federal time limits.

Note: Authority cited: Section 21083, Public Resources Code. Reference: Sections 21083.6 and 21083.7, Public Resources Code; Sections 65951 and 65954, Government Code; Public Law 91-190 as amended, 42 U.S.C.A. 4321-4347.

§ 15111. Projects with Short Time Periods for Approval.

(a) A few statutes or ordinances require agencies to make decisions on permits within time limits that are so short that review of the project under CEQA would be difficult. To enable the lead agency to comply with both the permit statute and CEQA, the lead agency shall deem an application for a project not received for filing under the permit statute or ordinance until such time as progress toward completing the environmental documentation required by CEQA is sufficient to enable the lead agency to finish the CEQA process within the short permit time limit. This section will apply where all of the following conditions are met:
  (1) The enabling legislation for a program, other than Chapter 4.5 (commencing with Section 65920) of Division 1 of Title 7 of the Government Code, requires the lead agency to take action on an application within a specified period of time that is six months or less, and
  (2) The enabling legislation provides that the project will become approved by operation of law if the lead agency fails to take any action within such specified time period, and
  (3) The project involves the issuance of a lease, permit, license, certificate, or other entitlement for use.

(b) Examples of time periods subject to this section include but are not limited to:
  (1) Action on a timber harvesting plan by the Director of Forestry within 15 days pursuant to Section 4582.7 of the Public Resources Code,
  (2) Action on a permit by the San Francisco Bay Conservation and Development Commission within 90 days pursuant to Section 66632(f) of the Government Code, and
  (3) Action on an oil and gas permit by the Division of Oil and Gas within 10 days pursuant to Sections 3203 or 3724 of the Public Resources Code.

(c) In any case described in this section, the environmental document shall be completed or certified and the decision on the project shall be made within the period established under the Permit Streamlining Act (Government Code Sections 65920, et seq.).

Note: Authority cited: Section 21083, Public Resources Code. Reference: Sections 21100.2 and 21151.5, Public Resources Code; *N.R.D.C. v. Arcata National Corp.* (1976) 59 Cal. App. 3d 959.

§ 15112. Statutes of Limitations.

(a) CEQA provides unusually short statutes of limitations on filing court challenges to the approval of projects under the act.

(b) The statute of limitations periods are not public review periods or waiting periods for the person whose project has been approved. The project sponsor may proceed to carry out the project as soon as the necessary permits have been granted. The statute of limitations cuts off the right of another person to file a court action challenging approval of the project after the specified time period has expired.

(c) The statute of limitations periods under CEQA are as follows:
  (1) Where the public agency filed a notice of determination in compliance with Sections 15075 or 15094, 30 days after the filing of the notice and the posting on a list of such notices.
  (2) Where the public agency filed a notice of exemption in compliance with Section 15062, 35

days after the filing of the notice and the posting on a list of such notices.

(3) Where a certified state regulatory agency files a notice of decision in compliance with Public Resources Code Section 21080.5(d)(2)(E), 30 days after the filing of the notice.

(4) Where the Secretary for Resources certifies a state environmental regulatory agency under Public Resources Code Section 21080.5, the certification may be challenged only during the 30 days following the certification decision.

(5) Where none of the other statute of limitations periods in this section apply, 180 days after either:

(A) The public agency's decision to carry out or approve the project, or

(B) Commencement of the project if the project is undertaken without a formal decision by the public agency.

Note: Authority cited: Section 21083, Public Resources Code. Reference: Sections 21167, 21167.3 and 21080.5, Public Resources Code; *Kriebel v. City Council*, 112 Cal. App. 3d 693; *Citizens of Lake Murray Area Association v. City Council* (1982) 129 Cal. App. 3d 436.

Article 9. Contents of Environmental Impact Reports

§ 15120. General.

(a) Environmental Impact Reports shall contain the information outlined in this article, but the format of the document may be varied. Each element must be covered, and when these elements are not separated into distinct sections, the document shall state where in the document each element is discussed.

(b) The EIR may be prepared as a separate document, as part of a general plan, or as part of a project report. If prepared as a part of the project report, it must still contain one separate and distinguishable section providing either analysis of all the subjects required in an EIR or as a minimum, a table showing where each of the subjects is discussed. When the lead agency is a state agency, the EIR shall be included as part of the regular project report if such a report is used in the agency's existing review and budgetary process.

(c) Draft EIRs shall contain the information required by Sections 15122 through 15131. Final EIRs shall contain the same information and the subjects described in Section 15132.

(d) No document prepared pursuant to this article that is available for public examination shall include a "trade secret" as defined in Section 6254.7 of the Government Code, information about the location of archaeological sites and sacred lands, or any other information that is subject to the disclosure restrictions of Section 6254 of the Government Code.

Note: Authority cited: Section 21083, Public Resources Code. Reference: Sections 21100, 21105 and 21160, Public Resources Code.

§ 15121. Informational Document.

(a) An EIR is an informational document which will inform public agency decisionmakers and the public generally of the significant environmental effect of a project, identify possible ways to minimize the significant effects, and describe reasonable alternatives to the project. The public agency shall consider the information in the EIR along with other information which may be presented to the agency.

(b) While the information in the EIR does not control the agency's ultimate discretion on the project, the agency must respond to each significant effect identified in the EIR by making findings under Section 15091 and if necessary by making a statement of overriding considerations under Section 15093.

(c) The information in an EIR may constitute substantial evidence in the record to support the agency's action on the project if its decision is later challenged in court.

Note: Authority cited: Section 21083, Public Resources Code. Reference: Section 21061, Public Resources Code; *Carmel Valley View, Ltd. v. Board of Supervisors* (1976) 58 Cal. App. 3d 817.

§ 15122. Table of Contents or Index.

An EIR shall contain at least a table of contents or an index to assist readers in finding the analysis of different subjects and issues.

Note: Authority cited: Section 21083, Public Resources Code. Reference: Section 21061, Public Resources Code.

§ 15123. Summary.

(a) An EIR shall contain a brief summary of the proposed actions and its consequences. The language of the summary should be as clear and simple as reasonably practical.

(b) The summary shall identify:

(1) Each significant effect with proposed mitigation measures and alternatives that would reduce or avoid that effect;

(2) Areas of controversy known to the lead agency including issues raised by agencies and the public; and

(3) Issues to be resolved including the choice among alternatives and whether or how to mitigate the significant effects.

(c) The summary should normally not exceed 15 pages.

Note: Authority cited: Section 21083, Public Resources Code. Reference: Section 21061, Public Resources Code.

§ 15124. Project Description.

The description of the project shall contain the following information but should not supply extensive detail beyond that needed for evaluation and review of the environmental impact.

(a) The precise location and boundaries of the proposed project shall be shown on a detailed map, preferably topographic. The location of the project shall also appear on a regional map.

(b) A statement of the objectives sought by the proposed project. A clearly written statement of objectives will help the lead agency develop a reasonable range of alternatives to evaluate in the EIR and will aid the decision makers in preparing findings or a statement of overriding considerations, if necessary. The statement of objectives should include the underlying purpose of the project.

(c) A general description of the project's technical, economic, and environmental characteristics, considering the principal engineering proposals if any and supporting public service facilities.(d) A statement briefly describing the intended uses of the EIR.

(1) This statement shall include, to the extent that the information is known to the lead agency,

(A) A list of the agencies that are expected to use the EIR in their decision-making, and

(B) A list of permits and other approvals required to implement the project.

(C) A list of related environmental review and consultation requirements required by federal, state, or local laws, regulations, or policies. To the fullest extent possible, the lead agency should integrate CEQA review with these related environmental review and consultation requirements.

(2) If a public agency must make more than one decision on a project, all its decisions subject to CEQA should be listed, preferably in the order in which they will occur. On request, the Office of Planning and Research will provide assistance in identifying state permits for a project.

Note: Authority cited: Section 21083, Public Resources Code. Reference: Sections 21080.3, 21080.4, 21165, 21166 and 21167.2, Public Resources Code; County of Inyo v. City of Los Angeles(1977) 71 Cal. App. 3d 185.

§ 15125. Environmental Setting.

(a) An EIR must include a description of the physical environmental conditions in the vicinity of the project, as they exist at the time the notice of preparation is published, or if no notice of preparation is published, at the time environmental analysis is commenced, from both a local and regional perspective. This environmental setting will normally constitute the baseline physical conditions by which a lead agency determines whether an impact is significant. The description of the environmental setting shall be no longer than is necessary to an understanding of the significant effects of the proposed project and its alternatives.

(b) When preparing an EIR for a plan for the reuse of a military base, lead agencies should refer to the special application of the principle of baseline conditions for determining significant impacts contained in Section 15229.

(c) Knowledge of the regional setting is critical to the assessment of environmental impacts. Special emphasis should be placed on environmental resources that are rare or unique to that region and would be affected by the project. The EIR must demonstrate that the significant environmental impacts of the proposed project were adequately investigated and discussed and it must permit the significant effects of the project to be considered in the full environmental context.

(d) The EIR shall discuss any inconsistencies between the proposed project and applicable general plans, specific plans and regional plans. Such regional plans include, but are not limited to, the applicable air quality attainment or maintenance plan or State Implementation Plan, area-wide waste treatment and water quality control plans, regional transportation plans, regional housing allocation plans, regional blueprint plans, plans for the reduction of greenhouse gas emissions, habitat conservation plans, natural community conservation plans and regional land use plans for the protection of the coastal zone, Lake Tahoe Basin, San Francisco Bay, and Santa Monica Mountains.

(e) Where a proposed project is compared with an adopted plan, the analysis shall examine the existing physical conditions at the time the notice of preparation is published, or if no notice of preparation is published, at the time environmental analysis is commenced as well as the potential future conditions discussed in the plan.

Note: Authority cited: Sections 21083 and 21083.05, Public Resources Code. Reference: Sections 21060.5, 21061 and 21100, Public Resources Code; *E.P.I.C. v. County of El Dorado* (1982) 131 Cal. App. 3d 350; *San Joaquin Raptor/Wildlife Rescue Center v. County of Stanislaus* (1994) 27 Cal. App. 4th 713; *Bloom v. McGurk* (1994) 26 Cal. App. 4th 1307.

§ 15126. Consideration and Discussion of Environmental Impacts.

All phases of a project must be considered when evaluating its impact on the environment: planning, acquisition, development, and operation. The subjects listed below shall be discussed as directed in Sections 15126.2, 15126.4 and 15126.6, preferably in separate sections or paragraphs of the EIR. If they are not discussed separately, the EIR shall include a table showing where each of the subjects is discussed.

(a) Significant Environmental Effects of the Proposed Project.
(b) Significant Environmental Effects Which Cannot be Avoided if the Proposed Project is Implemented.
(c) Significant Irreversible Environmental Changes Which Would be Involved in the Proposed Project Should it be Implemented.
(d) Growth-Inducing Impact of the Proposed Project.
(e) The Mitigation Measures Proposed to Minimize the Significant Effects.
(f) Alternatives to the Proposed Project.

Note: Authority cited: Section 21083, Public Resources Code. Reference: Sections 21002, 21003, 21100 and 21081.6, Public Resources Code; *Citizens of Goleta Valley v. Board of Supervisors* (1990) 52 Cal. 3d 553; *Laurel Heights Improvement Association v. Regents of the University of California* (1988) 47 Cal. 3d 376; *Gentry v. City of Murrieta* (1995) 36 Cal. App. 4th 1359; and *Laurel Heights Improvement Association v. Regents of the University of California* (1993) 6 Cal. 4th 1112.

§ 15126.2. Consideration and Discussion of Significant Environmental Impacts.

(a) The Significant Environmental Effects of the Proposed Project. An EIR shall identify and focus on the significant environmental effects of the proposed project. In assessing the impact of a proposed project on the environment, the lead agency should normally limit its examination to changes in the existing physical conditions in the affected area as they exist at the time the notice of preparation is published, or where no notice of preparation is published, at the time environmental analysis is commenced. Direct and indirect significant effects of the project on the environment shall be clearly identified and described, giving due consideration to both the short-term and long-term effects. The discussion should include relevant specifics of the area, the resources involved, physical changes, alterations to ecological systems, and changes induced in population distribution, population concentration, the human use of the land (including commercial and residential development), health and safety problems caused by the physical changes, and other aspects of the resource base such as water, historical resources, scenic quality, and public services. The EIR shall also analyze any significant environmental effects the project might cause by bringing development and people into the area affected. For example, an EIR on a subdivision astride an active fault line should identify as a significant effect the seismic hazard to future occupants of the subdivision. The subdivision would have the effect of attracting people to the location and exposing them to the hazards found there. Similarly, the EIR should evaluate any potentially significant impacts of locating development in other areas susceptible to hazardous conditions (e.g., floodplains, coastlines, wildfire risk areas) as identified in authoritative hazard maps, risk assessments or in land use plans addressing such hazards areas.

(b) Significant Environmental Effects Which Cannot be Avoided if the Proposed Project is Implemented. Describe any significant impacts, including those which can be mitigated but not reduced to a level of insignificance. Where there are impacts that cannot be alleviated without imposing an alternative design, their implications and the reasons why the project is being proposed, notwithstanding their effect, should be described.

(c) Significant Irreversible Environmental Changes Which Would be Caused by the Proposed Project Should it be Implemented. Uses of nonrenewable resources during the initial and continued phases of the project may be irreversible since a large commitment of such resources makes removal or nonuse thereafter unlikely. Primary impacts and, particularly, secondary impacts (such as highway improvement which provides access to a previously inaccessible area) generally commit future generations to similar uses. Also irreversible damage can result from environmental accidents associated with the project. Irretrievable commitments of resources should be evaluated to assure that such current consumption is justified. (See Public Resources Code section 21100.1 and Title 14, California Code of Regulations, section 15127 for limitations to applicability of this requirement.)

(d) Growth-Inducing Impact of the Proposed Project. Discuss the ways in which the proposed project could foster economic or population growth, or the construction of additional housing, either directly or indirectly, in the surrounding environment. Included in this are projects which would remove obstacles to population growth (a major expansion of a waste water treatment plant might, for example, allow for more construction in service areas). Increases in the population may tax existing community service facilities, requiring construction of new facilities that could cause significant environmental effects. Also discuss the characteristic of some projects which may encourage and facilitate other activities that could significantly affect the environment, either individually or cumulatively. It must not be assumed that growth in any area is necessarily beneficial, detrimental, or of little significance to the environment.

Note: Authority cited: Sections 21083 and 21083.05, Public Resources Code. Reference: Sections 21002, 21003 and 21100, Public Resources Code; *Citizens of Goleta Valley v. Board of Supervisors* (1990) 52 Cal. 3d 553; *Laurel Heights Improvement Association v. Regents of the University of California* (1988) 47 Cal. 3d 376; *Gentry v. City of Murrieta* (1995) 36 Cal. App. 4th 1359; *Laurel Heights Improvement Association v. Regents of the University of California* (1993) 6 Cal. 4th 1112; and *Goleta Union School Dist. v. Regents of the Univ. of Calif* (1995) 37 Cal. App. 4th 1025.

§ 15126.4. Consideration and Discussion of Mitigation Measures Proposed to Minimize Significant Effects.

(a) Mitigation Measures in General.
 (1) An EIR shall describe feasible measures which could minimize significant adverse impacts, including where relevant, inefficient and unnecessary consumption of energy.
  (A) The discussion of mitigation measures shall distinguish between the measures which are proposed by project proponents to be included in the project and other measures proposed by the lead, responsible or trustee agency or other persons which are not included but the lead agency determines could reasonably be expected to reduce adverse impacts if required as conditions of approving the project. This discussion shall identify mitigation measures for each significant environmental effect identified in the EIR.
  (B) Where several measures are available to mitigate an impact, each should be discussed and the basis for selecting a particular measure should be identified. Formulation of mitigation measures should not be deferred until some future time. However, measures may specify performance standards which would mitigate the significant effect of the project and which may be accomplished in more than one specified way.
  (C) Energy conservation measures, as well as other appropriate mitigation measures, shall be discussed when relevant. Examples of energy conservation measures are provided in Appendix F.
  (D) If a mitigation measure would cause one or more significant effects in addition to those that would be caused by the project as proposed, the effects of the mitigation measure shall be discussed but in less detail than the significant effects of the project as proposed. (*Stevens v. City of Glendale* (1981) 125 Cal.App.3d 986.)
 (2) Mitigation measures must be fully enforceable through permit conditions, agreements, or other

legally-binding instruments. In the case of the adoption of a plan, policy, regulation, or other public project, mitigation measures can be incorporated into the plan, policy, regulation, or project design.

(3) Mitigation measures are not required for effects which are not found to be significant.

(4) Mitigation measures must be consistent with all applicable constitutional requirements, including the following:

(A) There must be an essential nexus (i.e. connection) between the mitigation measure and a legitimate governmental interest. *Nollan v. California Coastal Commission*, 483 U.S. 825 (1987); and

(B) The mitigation measure must be "roughly proportional" to the impacts of the project. *Dolan v. City of Tigard*, 512 U.S. 374 (1994). Where the mitigation measure is an ad hoc exaction, it must be "roughly proportional" to the impacts of the project. *Ehrlich v. City of Culver City* (1996) 12 Cal.4th 854.

(5) If the lead agency determines that a mitigation measure cannot be legally imposed, the measure need not be proposed or analyzed. Instead, the EIR may simply reference that fact and briefly explain the reasons underlying the lead agency's determination.

(b) Mitigation Measures Related to Impacts on Historical Resources.

(1) Where maintenance, repair, stabilization, rehabilitation, restoration, preservation, conservation or reconstruction of the historical resource will be conducted in a manner consistent with the Secretary of the Interior's Standards for the Treatment of Historic Properties with Guidelines for Preserving, Rehabilitating, Restoring, and Reconstructing Historic Buildings (1995), Weeks and Grimmer, the project's impact on the historical resource shall generally be considered mitigated below a level of significance and thus is not significant.

(2) In some circumstances, documentation of an historical resource, by way of historic narrative, photographs or architectural drawings, as mitigation for the effects of demolition of the resource will not mitigate the effects to a point where clearly no significant effect on the environment would occur.

(3) Public agencies should, whenever feasible, seek to avoid damaging effects on any historical resource of an archaeological nature. The following factors shall be considered and discussed in an EIR for a project involving such an archaeological site:

(A) Preservation in place is the preferred manner of mitigating impacts to archaeological sites. Preservation in place maintains the relationship between artifacts and the archaeological context. Preservation may also avoid conflict with religious or cultural values of groups associated with the site.

(B) Preservation in place may be accomplished by, but is not limited to, the following:

1. Planning construction to avoid archaeological sites;
2. Incorporation of sites within parks, greenspace, or other open space;
3. Covering the archaeological sites with a layer of chemically stable soil before building tennis courts, parking lots, or similar facilities on the site.
4. Deeding the site into a permanent conservation easement.

(C) When data recovery through excavation is the only feasible mitigation, a data recovery plan, which makes provision for adequately recovering the scientifically consequential information from and about the historical resource, shall be prepared and adopted prior to any excavation being undertaken. Such studies shall be deposited with the California Historical Resources Regional Information Center. Archaeological sites known to contain human remains shall be treated in accordance with the provisions of Section 7050.5 Health and Safety Code. If an artifact must be removed during project excavation or testing, curation may be an appropriate mitigation.

(D) Data recovery shall not be required for an historical resource if the lead agency determines that testing or studies already completed have adequately recovered the scientifically consequential information from and about the archaeological or historical resource, provided that the determination is documented in the EIR and that the studies are deposited with the California Historical Resources Regional Information Center.

(c) Mitigation Measures Related to Greenhouse Gas Emissions.Consistent with section 15126.4(a), lead agencies shall consider feasible means, supported by substantial evidence and subject to monitoring or reporting, of mitigating the significant effects of greenhouse gas emissions. Measures to mitigate the significant effects of greenhouse gas emissions may include, among others:

(1) Measures in an existing plan or mitigation program for the reduction of emissions that are required as part of the lead agency's decision;

(2) Reductions in emissions resulting from a project through implementation of project features, project design, or other measures, such as those described in Appendix F;

(3) Off-site measures, including offsets that are not otherwise required, to mitigate a project's emissions;

(4) Measures that sequester greenhouse gases;

(5) In the case of the adoption of a plan, such as a general plan, long range development plan, or plans for the reduction of greenhouse gas emissions, mitigation may include the identification of specific measures that may be implemented on a project-by-project basis. Mitigation may also include the incorporation of specific measures or policies found in an adopted ordinance or regulation that reduces the cumulative effect of emissions.

Note: Authority: Sections 21083 and 21083.05, Public Resources Code. Reference: Sections 5020.5, 21002, 21003, 21083.05, 21084.1 and 21100, Public Resources Code; *Citizens of Goleta Valley v. Board of Supervisors* (1990) 52 Cal. 3d 553; *Laurel Heights Improvement Association v. Regents of the University of California* (1988) 47 Cal. 3d 376; *Gentry v. City of Murrieta* (1995) 36 Cal. App. 4th 1359; *Laurel Heights Improvement Association v. Regents of the University of California* (1993) 6 Cal. 4th 1112; *Sacramento Old City Assn. v. City Council of Sacramento* (1991) 229 Cal. App. 3d 1011; *San Franciscans Upholding the Downtown Plan v. City & Co. of San Francisco* (2002) 102 Cal. App. 4th 656; *Ass'n of Irritated Residents v. County of Madera* (2003) 107 Cal. App. 4th 1383; and *Environmental Council of Sacramento v. City of Sacramento* (2006) 142 Cal. App. 4th 1018.

§ 15126.6. Consideration and Discussion of Alternatives to the Proposed Project.

(a) Alternatives to the Proposed Project. An EIR shall describe a range of reasonable alternatives to the project, or to the location of the project, which would feasibly attain most of the basic objectives of the project but would avoid or substantially lessen any of the significant effects of the project, and evaluate the comparative merits of the alternatives. An EIR need not consider every conceivable alternative to a project. Rather it must consider a reasonable range of potentially feasible alternatives that will foster informed decisionmaking and public participation. An EIR is not required to consider alternatives which are infeasible. The lead agency is responsible for selecting a range of project alternatives for examination and must publicly disclose its reasoning for selecting those alternatives. There is no ironclad rule governing the nature or scope of the alternatives to be discussed other than the rule of reason. (*Citizens of Goleta Valley v. Board of Supervisors* (1990) 52 Cal. 3d 553 and *Laurel Heights Improvement Association v. Regents of the University of California* (1988) 47 Cal. 3d 376).

(b) Purpose. Because an EIR must identify ways to mitigate or avoid the significant effects that a project may have on the environment (Public Resources Code Section 21002.1), the discussion of alternatives shall focus on alternatives to the project or its location which are capable of avoiding or substantially lessening any significant effects of the project, even if these alternatives would impede to some degree the attainment of the project objectives, or would be more costly.

(c) Selection of a range of reasonable alternatives. The range of potential alternatives to the proposed project shall include those that could feasibly accomplish most of the basic objectives of the project and could avoid or substantially lessen one or more of the significant effects. The EIR should briefly describe the rationale for selecting the alternatives to be discussed. The EIR should also identify any alternatives that were considered by the lead agency but were rejected as infeasible during the scoping process and briefly explain the reasons underlying the lead agency's determination. Additional information explaining the choice of alternatives may be included in the administrative record. Among the factors that may be used to eliminate alternatives from detailed consideration in an EIR are:(i) failure to meet most of the basic project objectives, (ii) infeasibility, or (iii) inability to avoid significant environmental impacts.

(d) Evaluation of alternatives. The EIR shall include sufficient information about each alternative to allow meaningful evaluation, analysis, and comparison with the proposed project. A matrix displaying the major characteristics and significant environmental effects of each alternative may be used to summarize the comparison. If an alternative would cause one or more significant effects in addition to those that would be caused by the project as proposed, the significant effects of the alternative shall be discussed, but in less detail than the significant effects of the project as proposed. (*County of Inyo v. City of Los Angeles* (1981) 124 Cal. App. 3d 1).

(e) "No project" alternative.

(1) The specific alternative of "no project" shall also be evaluated along with its impact. The purpose of describing and analyzing a no project alternative is to allow decisionmakers to compare the impacts of approving the proposed project with the impacts of not approving the proposed project. The no project alternative analysis is not the baseline for determining whether the proposed project's environmental impacts may be significant, unless it is identical to the existing environmental setting analysis which does establish that baseline (see Section 15125).

(2) The "no project" analysis shall discuss the existing conditions at the time the notice of preparation is published, or if no notice of preparation is published, at the time environmental analysis is commenced, as well as what would be reasonably expected to occur in the foreseeable future if the project were not approved, based on current plans and consistent with available infrastructure and community services. If the environmentally superior alternative is the "no project" alternative, the EIR shall also identify an environmentally superior alternative among the other alternatives.

(3) A discussion of the "no project" alternative will usually proceed along one of two lines:

(A) When the project is the revision of an existing land use or regulatory plan, policy or ongoing operation, the "no project" alternative will be the continuation of the existing plan, policy or operation into the future. Typically this is a situation where other projects initiated under the existing plan will continue while the new plan is developed. Thus, the projected impacts of the proposed plan or alternative plans would be compared to the impacts that would occur under the existing plan.

(B) If the project is other than a land use or regulatory plan, for example a development project on identifiable property, the "no project" alternative is the circumstance under which the project does not proceed. Here the discussion would compare the environmental effects of the property remaining in its existing state against environmental effects which would occur if the project is approved. If disapproval of the project under consideration would result in predictable actions by others, such as the proposal of some other project, this "no project" consequence should be discussed. In certain instances, the no project alternative means "no build" wherein the existing environmental setting is maintained. However, where failure to proceed with the project will not result in preservation of existing environmental conditions, the analysis should identify the practical result of the project's non-approval and not create and analyze a set of artificial assumptions that would be required to preserve the existing physical environment.

(C) After defining the no project alternative using one of these approaches, the lead agency should proceed to analyze the impacts of the no project alternative by projecting what would reasonably be expected to occur in the foreseeable future if the project were not approved, based on current plans and consistent with available infrastructure and community services.

(f) Rule of reason. The range of alternatives required in an EIR is governed by a "rule of reason" that requires the EIR to set forth only those alternatives necessary to permit a reasoned choice. The alternatives shall be limited to ones that would avoid or substantially lessen any of the significant effects of the project. Of those alternatives, the EIR need examine in detail only the ones that the lead agency determines could feasibly attain most of the basic objectives of the project. The range of feasible alternatives shall be selected and discussed in a manner to foster meaningful public participation and informed decision making.

(1) Feasibility. Among the factors that may be taken into account when addressing the feasibility of alternatives are site suitability, economic viability, availability of infrastructure, general plan consistency, other plans or regulatory limitations, jurisdictional boundaries (projects with a regionally significant impact should consider the regional context), and whether the proponent can reasonably acquire, control or otherwise have access to the alternative site (or the site is already owned by the proponent). No one of these factors establishes a fixed limit on the scope of reasonable alternatives. (*Citizens of Goleta Valley v. Board of Supervisors* (1990) 52 Cal. 3d 553; see *Save Our Residential Environment v. City of West Hollywood* (1992) 9 Cal. App. 4th 1745, 1753, fn. 1).

(2) Alternative locations.

(A) Key question. The key question and first step in analysis is whether any of the significant effects of the project would be avoided or substantially lessened by putting the project in another location. Only locations that would avoid or substantially lessen any of the significant effects of the project need be considered for inclusion in the EIR.

(B) None feasible. If the lead agency concludes that no feasible alternative locations exist, it must disclose the reasons for this conclusion, and should include the reasons in the EIR. For example, in some cases there may be no feasible alternative locations for a geothermal plant or mining project which must be in close proximity to natural resources at a given location.

(C) Limited new analysis required. Where a previous document has sufficiently analyzed a range of reasonable alternative locations and environmental impacts for projects with the same basic purpose, the lead agency should review the previous document. The EIR may rely on the previous document to help it assess the feasibility of potential project alternatives to the extent the circumstances remain substantially the same as they relate to the alternative. (*Citizens of Goleta Valley v. Board of Supervisors* (1990) 52 Cal. 3d 553, 573).

(3) An EIR need not consider an alternative whose effect cannot be reasonably ascertained and whose implementation is remote and speculative. (*Residents Ad Hoc Stadium Committee v. Board of Trustees* (1979) 89 Cal. App. 3d 274).

Note: Authority cited: Section 21083, Public Resources Code. Reference: Sections 21002, 21002.1, 21003 and 21100, Public Resources Code; *Citizens of Goleta Valley v. Board of Supervisors* (1990) 52 Cal. 3d 553; *Laurel Heights Improvement Association v. Regents of the University of California* (1988) 47 Cal. 3d 376; *Gentry v. City of Murrieta* (1995) 36 Cal. App. 4th 1359; and *Laurel Heights Improvement Association v. Regents of the University of California* (1993) 6 Cal.4th 1112.

§ 15127. Limitations on Discussion of Environmental Impact.

The information required by Section 15126.2(c) concerning irreversible changes, need be included only in EIRs prepared in connection with any of the following activities:

(a) The adoption, amendment, or enactment of a plan, policy, or ordinance of a public agency;

(b) The adoption by a local agency formation commission of a resolution making determinations; or

(c) A project which will be subject to the requirement for preparing an environmental impact statement pursuant to the requirements of the National Environmental Policy Act of 1969, 42 U.S.C. 4321-4347.

Note: Authority cited: Section 21083, Public Resources Code. Reference: Section 21100.1, Public Resources Code.

§ 15128. Effects Not Found to Be Significant.

An EIR shall contain a statement briefly indicating the reasons that various possible significant effects of a project were determined not to be significant and were therefore not discussed in detail in the EIR. Such a statement may be contained in an attached copy of an initial study.

Note: Authority cited: Section 21083, Public Resources Code. Reference: Section 21100, Public Resources Code.

§ 15129. Organizations and Persons Consulted.

The EIR shall identify all federal, state, or local agencies, other organizations, and private individuals consulted in preparing the draft EIR, and the persons, firm, or agency preparing the draft EIR, by contract or other authorization.

Note: Authority cited: Section 21083, Public Resources Code. Reference: Sections 21104 and 21153, Public Resources Code.

§ 15130. Discussion of Cumulative Impacts.

(a) An EIR shall discuss cumulative impacts of a project when the project's incremental effect is cumulatively considerable, as defined in section 15065(a)(3). Where a lead agency is examining a project with an incremental effect that is not "cumulatively considerable," a lead agency need not consider that effect significant, but shall briefly describe its basis for concluding that the incremental effect is not cumulatively considerable.

(1) As defined in Section 15355, a cumulative impact consists of an impact which is created as a result of the combination of the project evaluated in the EIR together with other projects causing related impacts. An EIR should not discuss impacts which do not result in part from the project evaluated in the EIR.

(2) When the combined cumulative impact associated with the project's incremental effect and the effects of other projects is not significant, the EIR shall briefly indicate why the cumulative impact is not significant and is not discussed in further detail in the EIR. A lead agency shall identify facts and analysis supporting the lead agency's conclusion that the cumulative impact is less than significant.

(3) An EIR may determine that a project's contribution to a significant cumulative impact will be rendered less than cumulatively considerable and thus is not significant. A project's contribution is less than cumulatively considerable if the project is required to implement or fund its fair share of a mitigation measure or measures designed to alleviate the cumulative impact. The lead agency shall identify facts and analysis supporting its conclusion that the contribution will be rendered less than cumulatively considerable.

(b) The discussion of cumulative impacts shall reflect the severity of the impacts and their likelihood of occurrence, but the discussion need not provide as great detail as is provided for the effects attributable to the project alone. The discussion should be guided by the standards of practicality and reasonableness, and should focus on the cumulative impact to which the identified other projects contribute rather than the attributes of other projects which do not contribute to the cumulative impact. The following elements are necessary to an adequate discussion of significant cumulative impacts:

(1) Either:

(A) A list of past, present, and probable future projects producing related or cumulative impacts, including, if necessary, those projects outside the control of the agency, or

(B) A summary of projections contained in an adopted local, regional or statewide plan, or related planning document, that describes or evaluates conditions contributing to the cumulative effect. Such plans may include: a general plan, regional transportation plan, or plans for the reduction of greenhouse gas emissions. A summary of projections may also be contained in an adopted or certified prior environmental document for such a plan. Such projections may be supplemented with additional information such as a regional modeling program. Any such document shall be referenced and made available to the public at a location specified by the lead agency.

(2) When utilizing a list, as suggested in paragraph (1) of subdivision (b), factors to consider when determining whether to include a related project should include the nature of each environmental resource being examined, the location of the project and its type. Location may be important, for example, when water quality impacts are at issue since projects outside the watershed would probably not contribute to a cumulative effect. Project type may be important, for example, when the impact is specialized, such as a particular air pollutant or mode of traffic.

(3) Lead agencies should define the geographic scope of the area affected by the cumulative effect and provide a reasonable explanation for the geographic limitation used.

(4) A summary of the expected environmental effects to be produced by those projects with specific reference to additional information stating where that information is available, and

(5) A reasonable analysis of the cumulative impacts of the relevant projects. An EIR shall examine reasonable, feasible options for mitigating or avoiding the project's contribution to any significant cumulative effects.

(c) With some projects, the only feasible mitigation for cumulative impacts may involve the adoption of ordinances or regulations rather than the imposition of conditions on a project-by-project basis.

(d) Previously approved land use documents, including, but not limited to, general plans, specific plans, regional transportation plans, plans for the reduction of greenhouse gas emissions, and local coastal plans may be used in cumulative impact analysis. A pertinent discussion of cumulative impacts contained in one or more previously certified EIRs may be incorporated by reference pursuant to the provisions for tiering and program EIRs. No further cumulative impacts analysis is required when a project is consistent with a general, specific, master or comparable programmatic plan where the lead agency determines that the regional or areawide cumulative impacts of the proposed project have already been adequately addressed, as defined in section 15152(f), in a certified EIR for that plan.

(e) If a cumulative impact was adequately addressed in a prior EIR for a community plan, zoning action, or general plan, and the project is consistent with that plan or action, then an EIR for such a project should not further analyze that cumulative impact, as provided in Section15183(j).

Note: Authority cited: Sections 21083 and 21083.05, Public Resources Code. Reference: Sections 21003(d), 21083(b), 21093, 21094 and 21100, Public Resources Code; *Whitman v. Board of Supervisors* (1979) 88 Cal. App. 3d 397; *San Franciscans for Reasonable Growth v. City and County of San Francisco* (1984) 151 Cal. App. 3d 61; *Kings County Farm Bureau v. City of Hanford* (1990) 221 Cal. App. 3d 692; *Laurel Heights Homeowners Association v. Regents of the University of California* (1988) 47 Cal. 3d 376; *Sierra Club v. Gilroy* (1990) 220 Cal. App. 3d 30; *Citizens to Preserve the Ojai v. County of Ventura* (1985) 176 Cal. App. 3d 421; *Concerned Citizens of South Cent. Los Angeles v. Los Angeles Unified Sch. Dist.* (1994) 24 Cal. App. 4th 826; *Las Virgenes Homeowners Fed'n v. County of Los Angeles* (1986) 177 Cal. App. 3d 300; *San Joaquin Raptor/Wildlife Rescue Ctr v. County of Stanislaus* (1994) 27 Cal. App. 4th 713; *Fort Mojave Indian Tribe v. Cal. Dept. of Health Services* (1995) 38 Cal. App. 4th 1574; *Santa Monica Chamber of Commerce v. City of Santa Monica* (2002) 101 Cal. App. 4th 786; *Communities for a Better Environment v. California Resources Agency* (2002) 103 Cal. App. 4th 98; *and Ass'n of Irritated Residents v. County of Madera* (2003) 107 Cal. App. 4th 1383.

§ 15131. Economic and Social Effects.

Economic or social information may be included in an EIR or may be presented in whatever form the agency desires.

(a) Economic or social effects of a project shall not be treated as significant effects on the environment. An EIR may trace a chain of cause and effect from a proposed decision on a project through anticipated economic or social changes resulting from the project to physical changes caused in turn by the economic or social changes. The intermediate economic or social changes need not be analyzed in any detail greater than necessary to trace the chain of cause and effect. The focus of the analysis shall be on the physical changes.

(b) Economic or social effects of a project may be used to determine the significance of physical changes caused by the project. For example, if the construction of a new freeway or rail line divides an existing community, the construction would be the physical change, but the social effect on the community would be the basis for determining that the effect would be significant. As an additional example, if the construction of a road and the resulting increase in noise in an area disturbed existing religious practices in the area, the disturbance of the religious practices could be used to determine that the construction and use of the road and the resulting noise would be significant effects on the environment. The religious practices would need to be analyzed only to the extent to show that the increase in traffic and noise would conflict with the religious practices. Where an EIR uses economic or social effects to determine that a physical change is significant, the EIR shall explain the reason for determining that the effect is significant.

(c) Economic, social, and particularly housing factors shall be considered by public agencies together with technological and environmental factors in deciding whether changes in a project are feasible to reduce or avoid the significant effects on the environment identified in the EIR. If information on these factors is not contained in the EIR, the information must be added to the record in some other manner to allow the agency to consider the factors in reaching a decision on the project.

Note: Authority cited: Section 21083, Public Resources Code. Reference: Sections 21001(e) and (g), 21002, 21002.1, 21060.5, 21080.1, 21083(c) and 21100, Public Resources Code.

§ 15132. Contents of Final Environmental Impact Report.

The final EIR shall consist of:

(a) The Draft EIR or a revision of the draft.

(b) Comments and recommendations received on the Draft EIR either verbatim or in summary.

(c) A list of persons, organizations, and public agencies commenting on the Draft EIR.

(d) The responses of the Lead Agency to significant environmental points raised in the review and consultation process.

(e) Any other information added by the lead agency.

Note: Authority cited: Section 21083, Public Resources Code. Reference: Section 21100, Public Resources Code.

Article 10. Considerations in Preparing EIRs and Negative Declarations

§ 15140. Writing.

EIRs shall be written in plain language and may use appropriate graphics so that decisionmakers and the public can rapidly understand the documents.

Note: Authority cited: Section 21083, Public Resources Code. Reference: Sections 21003 and 21100, Public Resources Code.

§ 15141. Page Limits.

The text of draft EIRs should normally be less than 150 pages and for proposals of unusual scope or complexity should normally be less than 300 pages.

Note: Authority cited: Section 21083, Public Resources Code. Reference: Section 21100, Public Resources Code.

§ 15142. Interdisciplinary Approach.

An EIR shall be prepared using an interdisciplinary approach which will ensure the integrated use of the natural and social sciences and the consideration of qualitative as well as quantitative factors. The interdisciplinary analysis shall be conducted by competent individuals, but no single discipline shall be designated or required to undertake this evaluation.

Note: Authority cited: Section 21083, Public Resources Code. Reference: Sections 21000, 21001 and 21100, Public Resources Code.

§ 15143. Emphasis.

The EIR shall focus on the significant effects on the environment. The significant effects should be discussed with emphasis in proportion to their severity and probability of occurrence. Effects dismissed in an Initial Study as clearly insignificant and unlikely to occur need not be discussed further in the EIR unless the Lead Agency subsequently receives information inconsistent with the finding in the Initial Study. A copy of the Initial Study may be attached to the EIR to provide the basis for limiting the impacts discussed.

Note: Authority cited: Section 21083, Public Resources Code. Reference: Sections 21003, 21061 and 21100, Public Resources Code.

§ 15144. Forecasting.

Drafting an EIR or preparing a negative declaration necessarily involves some degree of forecasting. While foreseeing the unforeseeable is not possible, an agency must use its best efforts to find out and disclose all that it reasonably can.

Note: Authority cited: Section 21083, Public Resources Code. Reference: Sections 21003, 21061 and 21100, Public Resources Code.

§ 15145. Speculation.

If, after thorough investigation, a lead agency finds that a particular impact is too speculative for evaluation, the agency should note its conclusion and terminate discussion of the impact.

Note: Authority cited: Section 21083, Public Resources Code. Reference: Sections 21003, 21061 and 21100, Public Resources Code; *Topanga Beach Renters Association v. Department of General Services* (1976) 58 Cal. App. 3d 712.

§ 15146. Degree of Specificity.

The degree of specificity required in an EIR will correspond to the degree of specificity involved in the underlying activity which is described in the EIR.

(a) An EIR on a construction project will necessarily be more detailed in the specific effects of the project than will be an EIR on the adoption of a local general plan or comprehensive zoning ordinance because the effects of the construction can be predicted with greater accuracy.

(b) An EIR on a project such as the adoption or amendment of a comprehensive zoning ordinance or a local general plan should focus on the secondary effects that can be expected to follow from the adoption, or amendment, but the EIR need not be as detailed as an EIR on the specific construction projects that might follow.

Note: Authority cited: Section 21083, Public Resources Code. Reference: Sections 21003, 21061 and 21100, Public Resources Code.

§ 15147. Technical Detail.

The information contained in an EIR shall include summarized technical data, maps, plot plans, diagrams, and similar relevant information sufficient to permit full assessment of significant environmental impacts by reviewing agencies and members of the public. Placement of highly technical and specialized analysis and data in the body of an EIR should be avoided through inclusion of supporting information and analyses as appendices to the main body of the EIR. Appendices to the EIR may be prepared in volumes separate from the basic EIR document, but shall be readily available for public examination and shall be submitted to all clearinghouses which assist in public review.

Note: Authority cited: Section 21083, Public Resources Code. Reference: Sections 21003, 21061 and 21100, Public Resources Code.

§ 15148. Citation.

Preparation of EIRs is dependent upon information from many sources, including engineering project reports and many scientific documents relating to environmental features. These documents should be cited but not included in the EIR. The EIR shall cite all documents used in its preparation including, where possible, the page and section number of any technical reports which were used as the basis for any statements in the EIR.

Note: Authority cited: Section 21083, Public Resources Code. Reference: Sections 21003, 21061 and 21100, Public Resources Code.

§ 15149. Use of Registered Professionals in Preparing EIRs.

(a) A number of statutes provide that certain professional services can be provided to the public only by individuals who have been registered by a registration board established under California law. Such statutory restrictions apply to a number of professions including but not limited to engineering, land surveying, forestry, geology, and geophysics.

(b) In its intended usage, an EIR is not a technical document that can be prepared only by a registered professional. The EIR serves as a public disclosure document explaining the effects of the proposed project on the environment, alternatives to the project, and ways to minimize adverse effects and to increase beneficial effects. As a result of information in the EIR, the lead agency should establish requirements or conditions on project design, construction, or operation in order to protect or enhance the environment. State statutes may provide that only registered professionals can prepare technical studies which will be used in or which will control the detailed design, construction, or operation of the proposed project and which will be prepared in support of an EIR.

Note: Authority cited: Section 21083, Public Resources Code. Reference: Sections 21003, 21061 and 21100, Public Resources Code.

§ 15150. Incorporation by Reference.

(a) An EIR or negative declaration may incorporate by reference all or portions of another document which is a matter of public record or is generally available to the public. Where all or part of another document is incorporated by reference, the incorporated language shall be considered to be set forth in full as part of the text of the EIR or negative declaration.

(b) Where part of another document is incorporated by reference, such other document shall be made available to the public for inspection at a public place or public building. The EIR or negative declaration shall state where the incorporated documents will be available for inspection. At a minimum, the incorporated document shall be made available to the public in an office of the lead agency in the county where the project would be carried out or in one or more public buildings such as county offices or public libraries if the lead agency does not have an office in the county.

(c) Where an EIR or negative declaration uses incorporation by reference, the incorporated part of the referenced document shall be briefly summarized where possible or briefly described if the data or information cannot be summarized. The relationship between the incorporated part of the referenced document and the EIR shall be described.

(d) Where an agency incorporates information from an EIR that has previously been reviewed through the state review system, the state identification number of the incorporated document should be included in the summary or designation described in subdivision (c).

(e) Examples of materials that may be incorporated by reference include but are not limited to:
   (1) A description of the environmental setting from another EIR.
   (2) A description of the air pollution problems prepared by an air pollution control agency concerning a process involved in the project.
   (3) A description of the city or county general plan that applies to the location of the project.
   (4) A description of the effects of greenhouse gas emissions on the environment.

(f) Incorporation by reference is most appropriate for including long, descriptive, or technical materials that provide general background but do not contribute directly to the analysis of the problem at hand.

Note: Authority cited: Sections 21083 and 21083.05, Public Resources Code. Reference: Sections 21003, 21061, 21083.05 and 21100, Public Resources Code.

§ 15151. Standards for Adequacy of an EIR.

An EIR should be prepared with a sufficient degree of analysis to provide decisionmakers with information which enables them to make a decision which intelligently takes account of environmental consequences. An evaluation of the environmental effects of a proposed project need not be exhaustive, but the sufficiency of an EIR is to be reviewed in the light of what is reasonably feasible. Disagreement among experts does not make an EIR inadequate, but the EIR should summarize the main points of disagreement among the experts. The courts have looked not for perfection but for adequacy, completeness, and a good faith effort at full disclosure.

Note: Authority cited: Section 21083, Public Resources Code. Reference: Sections 21061 and 21100, Public Resources Code; *San Francisco Ecology Center v. City and County of San Francisco*, 48 Cal. App. 3d 584 (1975).

§ 15152. Tiering.

(a) "Tiering" refers to using the analysis of general matters contained in a broader EIR (such as one prepared for a general plan or policy statement) with later EIRs and negative declarations on narrower projects; incorporating by reference the general discussions from the broader EIR; and concentrating the later EIR or negative declaration solely on the issues specific to the later project.

(b) Agencies are encouraged to tier the environmental analyses which they prepare for separate but related projects including general plans, zoning changes, and development projects. This approach can eliminate repetitive discussions of the same issues and focus the later EIR or negative declaration on the actual issues ripe for decision at each level of environmental review. Tiering is appropriate when the sequence of analysis is from an EIR prepared for a general plan, policy, or program to an EIR or negative declaration for another plan, policy, or program of lesser scope, or to a site-specific EIR or negative declaration. Tiering does not excuse the lead agency from adequately analyzing reasonably foreseeable significant environmental effects of the project and does not justify deferring such analysis to a later tier EIR or negative declaration. However, the level of detail contained in a first tier EIR need not be greater than that of the program, plan, policy, or ordinance being analyzed.

(c) Where a lead agency is using the tiering process in connection with an EIR for a large-scale planning approval, such as a general plan or component thereof (e.g., an area plan or community plan), the development of detailed, site-specific information may not be feasible but can be deferred, in many instances, until such time as the lead agency prepares a future environmental document in connection with a project of a more limited geographical scale, as long as deferral does not prevent adequate identification of significant effects of the planning approval at hand.

(d) Where an EIR has been prepared and certified for a program, plan, policy, or ordinance consistent with the requirements of this section, any lead agency for a later project pursuant to or consistent with the program, plan, policy, or ordinance should limit the EIR or negative declaration on the later project to effects which:
   (1) Were not examined as significant effects on the environment in the prior EIR; or
   (2) Are susceptible to substantial reduction or avoidance by the choice of specific revisions in the project, by the imposition of conditions, or other means.

(e) Tiering under this section shall be limited to situations where the project is consistent with the general plan and zoning of the city or county in which the project is located, except that a project requiring a rezone to achieve or maintain conformity with a general plan may be subject to tiering.

(f) A later EIR shall be required when the initial study or other analysis finds that the later project may cause significant effects on the environment that were not adequately addressed in the prior EIR. A negative declaration shall be required when the provisions of Section 15070 are met.
   (1) Where a lead agency determines that a cumulative effect has been adequately addressed in the prior EIR, that effect is not treated as significant for purposes of the later EIR or negative declaration, and need not be discussed in detail.
   (2) When assessing whether there is a new significant cumulative effect, the lead agency shall consider whether the incremental effects of the project would be considerable when viewed in the context of past, present, and probable future projects. At this point, the question is not whether there is a significant cumulative impact, but whether the effects of the project are cumulatively considerable. For a discussion on how to assess whether project impacts are cumulatively considerable, see Section 15064(i).
   (3) Significant environmental effects have been "adequately addressed" if the lead agency determines that:
      (A) they have been mitigated or avoided as a result of the prior environmental impact report and findings adopted in connection with that prior environmental report; or
      (B) they have been examined at a sufficient level of detail in the prior environmental impact report to enable those effects to be mitigated or avoided by site specific revisions, the imposition of conditions, or by other means in connection with the approval of the later project.

(g) When tiering is used, the later EIRs or negative declarations shall refer to the prior EIR and state where a copy of the prior EIR may be examined. The later EIR or negative declaration should state that the lead agency is using the tiering concept and that it is being tiered with the earlier EIR.

(h) There are various types of EIRs that may be used in a tiering situation. These include, but are not limited to, the following:
   (1) General plan EIR (Section 15166).
   (2) Staged EIR (Section 15167).
   (3) Program EIR (Section 15168).
   (4) Master EIR (Section 15175).
   (5) Multiple-family residential development/residential and commercial or retail mixed-use development (Section 15179.5).
   (6) Redevelopment project (Section 15180).
   (7) Projects consistent with community plan, general plan, or zoning (Section 15183).

Note: Authority cited: Section 21083, Public Resources Code. Reference: Sections 21003, 21061, 21093, 21094, 21100 and 21151, Public Resources Code; Stanislaus Natural Heritage Project, *Sierra Club v. County of Stanislaus* (1996) 48 Cal. App. 4th 182; *Al Larson Boat Shop, Inc. v. Board of Harbor Commissioners* (1993) 18 Cal. App. 4th 729; and *Sierra Club v. County of Sonoma* (1992) 6 Cal. App. 4th 1307.

§ 15153. Use of an EIR from an Earlier Project.

(a) The lead agency may employ a single EIR to describe more than one project, if such projects are essentially the same in terms of environmental impact. Further, the lead agency may use an earlier EIR prepared in connection with an earlier project to apply to a later project, if the circumstances of the projects are essentially the same.

(b) When a lead agency proposes to use an EIR from an earlier project as the EIR for a separate, later project, the lead agency shall use the following procedures:
   (1) The lead agency shall review the proposed project with an initial study, using incorporation by reference if necessary, to determine whether the EIR would adequately describe:
      (A) The general environmental setting of the project,

(B) The significant environmental impacts of the project, and
(C) Alternatives and mitigation measures related to each significant effect.
(2) If the lead agency believes that the EIR would meet the requirements of subdivision (1), it shall provide public review as provided in Section 15087 stating that it plans to use the previously prepared EIR as the draft EIR for this project. The notice shall include as a minimum:
(A) An identification of the project with a brief description;
(B) A statement that the agency plans to use a certain EIR prepared for a previous project as the EIR for this project;
(C) A listing of places where copies of the EIR may be examined; and
(D) A statement that the key issues involving the EIR are whether the EIR should be used for this project and whether there are any additional, reasonable alternatives or mitigation measures that should be considered as ways of avoiding or reducing the significant effects of the project.
(3) The lead agency shall prepare responses to comments received during the review period.
(4) Before approving the project, the decisionmaker in the lead agency shall:
(A) Consider the information in the EIR including comments received during the review period and responses to those comments,
(B) Decide either on its own or on a staff recommendation whether the EIR is adequate for the project at hand, and
(C) Make or require certification to be made as described in Section 15090.
(D) Make findings as provided in Sections 15091 and 15093 as necessary.
(5) After making a decision on the project, the lead agency shall file a notice of determination.
(c) An EIR prepared for an earlier project may also be used as part of an initial study to document a finding that a later project will not have a significant effect. In this situation a negative declaration will be prepared.
(d) An EIR prepared for an earlier project shall not be used as the EIR for a later project if any of the conditions described in Section 15162 would require preparation of a subsequent or supplemental EIR.

Note: Authority cited: Section 21083, Public Resources Code. Reference: Sections 21100, 21151 and 21166, Public Resources Code.

§ 15154. Projects Near Airports.
(a) When a lead agency prepares an EIR for a project within the boundaries of a comprehensive airport land use plan or, if a comprehensive airport land use plan has not been adopted for a project within two nautical miles of a public airport or public use airport, the agency shall utilize the Airport Land Use Planning Handbook published by Caltrans' Division of Aeronautics to assist in the preparation of the EIR relative to potential airport-related safety hazards and noise problems.
(b) A lead agency shall not adopt a negative declaration or mitigated negative declaration for a project described in subdivision (a) unless the lead agency considers whether the project will result in a safety hazard or noise problem for persons using the airport or for persons residing or working in the project area.

Note: Authority cited: Section 21083, Public Resources Code. Reference: Section 21096, Public Resources Code.

§ 15155. City or County Consultation with Water Agencies.
(a) The following definitions are applicable to this section.
(1) A "water-demand project" means:
(A) A residential development of more than 500 dwelling units.
(B) A shopping center or business establishment employing more than 1,000 persons or having more than 500,000 square feet of floor space.
(C) A commercial office building employing more than 1,000 persons or having more than 250,000 square feet of floor space.
(D) A hotel or motel, or both, having more than 500 rooms.
(E) An industrial, manufacturing, or processing plant, or industrial park planned to house more than 1,000 persons, occupying more than 40 acres of land, or having more than 650,000 square feet of floor area.
(F) A mixed-use project that includes one or more of the projects specified in subdivisions (a)(1)(A), (a)(1)(B), (a)(1)(C), (a)(1)(D), (a)(1)(E), and (a)(1)(G) of this section.
(G) A project that would demand an amount of water equivalent to, or greater than, the amount of water required by a 500 dwelling unit project.
(H) For public water systems with fewer than 5,000 service connections, a project that meets the following criteria:
1. A proposed residential, business, commercial, hotel or motel, or industrial development that would account for an increase of 10 percent or more in the number of a public water system's existing service connections; or
2. A mixed-use project that would demand an amount of water equivalent to, or greater than, the amount of water required by residential development that would represent an increase of 10 percent or more in the number of the public water system's existing service connections.
(2) "Public water system" means a system for the provision of piped water to the public for human consumption that has 3000 or more service connections. A public water system includes all of the following:
(A) Any collection, treatment, storage, and distribution facility under control of the operator of the system which is used primarily in connection with the system.
(B) Any collection or pretreatment storage facility not under the control of the operator that is used primarily in connection with the system.
(C) Any person who treats water on behalf of one or more public water systems for the purpose of rendering it safe for human consumption.
(3) "Water acquisition plans" means any plans for acquiring additional water supplies prepared by the public water system or a city or county lead agency pursuant to subdivision (a) of section 10911 of the Water Code.
(4) "Water assessment" means the water supply assessment that must be prepared by the governing body of a public water system, or the city or county lead agency, pursuant to and in compliance with sections 10910 to 10915 of the Water Code, and that includes, without limitation, the elements of the assessment required to comply with subdivisions (d), (e), (f), and (g) of section 10910 of the Water Code.
(5) "City or county lead agency" means a city or county, acting as lead agency, for purposes of certifying or approving an environmental impact report, a negative declaration, or a mitigated negative declaration for a water-demand project.
(b) Subject to section 15155, subdivision (d) below, at the time a city or county lead agency determines whether an environmental impact report, a negative declaration, or a mitigated negative declaration, or any supplement thereto, is required for the water-demand project, the city or county lead agency shall take the following steps:
(1) The city or county lead agency shall identify any water system that either:
(A) is a public water system that may supply water to the water-demand project, or
(B) that may become such a public water system as a result of supplying water to the water-demand project. The city or county lead agency shall request the governing body of each such public water system to determine whether the projected water demand associated with a water-demand project was included in the most recently adopted urban water management plan adopted pursuant to Part 2.6 (commencing with section 10610) of the Water Code, and to prepare a water assessment approved at a regular or special meeting of that governing body.
(2) If the city or county lead agency is not able to identify any public water system that may supply water for the water-demand project, the city or county lead agency shall prepare a water assessment after consulting with any entity serving domestic water supplies whose service area includes the site of the water-demand project, the local agency formation commission, and the governing body of any public water system adjacent to the site of the water-demand project. The governing body of the city or county lead agency must approve the water assessment prepared pursuant to this section at a regular or special meeting.
(c) The city or county lead agency shall grant any reasonable request for an extension of time that is

made by the governing body of a public water system preparing the water assessment, provided that the request for an extension of time is made within 90 days after the date on which the governing body of the public water system received the request to prepare a water assessment. If the governing body of the public water system fails to request and receive an extension of time, or fails to submit the water assessment notwithstanding the 30-day extension, the city or county lead agency may seek a writ of mandamus to compel the governing body of the public water system to comply with the requirements of Part 2.10 of Division 6 (commencing with section 10910) of the Water Code relating to the submission of the water assessment.

(d) If a water-demand project has been the subject of a water assessment, no additional water assessment shall be required for subsequent water-demand projects that were included in such larger water-demand project if all of the following criteria are met:
  (1) The entity completing the water assessment had concluded that its water supplies are sufficient to meet the projected water demand associated with the larger water-demand project, in addition to the existing and planned future uses, including, but not limited to, agricultural and industrial uses; and
  (2) None of the following changes has occurred since the completion of the water assessment for the larger water-demand project:
    (A) Changes in the larger water-demand project that result in a substantial increase in water demand for the water-demand project.
    (B) Changes in the circumstances or conditions substantially affecting the ability of the public water system or the water supplying city or county identified in the water assessment to provide a sufficient supply of water for the water demand project.
    (C) Significant new information becomes available which was not known and could not have been known at the time when the entity had reached the conclusion in subdivision (d)(1).

(e) The city or county lead agency shall include the water assessment, and any water acquisition plan in the EIR, negative declaration, or mitigated negative declaration, or any supplement thereto, prepared for the water-demand project, and may include an evaluation of the water assessment and water acquisition plan information within such environmental document. The city or county lead agency shall determine, based on the entire record, whether projected water supplies will be sufficient to satisfy the demands of the project, in addition to existing and planned future uses. If a city or county lead agency determines that water supplies will not be sufficient, the city or county lead agency shall include that determination in its findings for the water-demand project.

Note: Authority cited: Section 21083, Public Resources Code. Reference: Section 21151.9, Public Resources Code; and Sections 10910-10915, Water Code.

Article 11. Types of EIRs

§ 15160. General.

This article describes a number of examples of variations in EIRs as the documents are tailored to different situations and intended uses. These variations are not exclusive. Lead agencies may use other variations consistent with the guidelines to meet the needs of other circumstances. All EIRs must meet the content requirements discussed in Article 9 beginning with Section 15120.

Note: Authority cited: Section 21083, Public Resources Code. Reference: Sections 21061, 21100 and 21151, Public Resources Code.

§ 15161. Project EIR.

The most common type of EIR examines the environmental impacts of a specific development project. This type of EIR should focus primarily on the changes in the environment that would result from the development project. The EIR shall examine all phases of the project including planning, construction, and operation.

Note: Authority cited: Section 21083, Public Resources Code. Reference: Sections 21061, 21100 and 21151, Public Resources Code.

§ 15162. Subsequent EIRs and Negative Declarations.

(a) When an EIR has been certified or a negative declaration adopted for a project, no subsequent EIR shall be prepared for that project unless the lead agency determines, on the basis of substantial evidence in the light of the whole record, one or more of the following:
  (1) Substantial changes are proposed in the project which will require major revisions of the previous EIR or negative declaration due to the involvement of new significant environmental effects or a substantial increase in the severity of previously identified significant effects;
  (2) Substantial changes occur with respect to the circumstances under which the project is undertaken which will require major revisions of the previous EIR or negative declaration due to the involvement of new significant environmental effects or a substantial increase in the severity of previously identified significant effects; or
  (3) New information of substantial importance, which was not known and could not have been known with the exercise of reasonable diligence at the time the previous EIR was certified as complete or the negative declaration was adopted, shows any of the following:
    (A) The project will have one or more significant effects not discussed in the previous EIR or negative declaration;
    (B) Significant effects previously examined will be substantially more severe than shown in the previous EIR;
    (C) Mitigation measures or alternatives previously found not to be feasible would in fact be feasible and would substantially reduce one or more significant effects of the project, but the project proponents decline to adopt the mitigation measure or alternative; or
    (D) Mitigation measures or alternatives which are considerably different from those analyzed in the previous EIR would substantially reduce one or more significant effects on the environment, but the project proponents decline to adopt the mitigation measure or alternative.

(b) If changes to a project or its circumstances occur or new information becomes available after adoption of a negative declaration, the lead agency shall prepare a subsequent EIR if required under subdivision (a). Otherwise the lead agency shall determine whether to prepare a subsequent negative declaration, an addendum, or no further documentation.

(c) Once a project has been approved, the lead agency's role in project approval is completed, unless further discretionary approval on that project is required. Information appearing after an approval does not require reopening of that approval. If after the project is approved, any of the conditions described in subdivision (a) occurs, a subsequent EIR or negative declaration shall only be prepared by the public agency which grants the next discretionary approval for the project, if any. In this situation no other responsible agency shall grant an approval for the project until the subsequent EIR has been certified or subsequent negative declaration adopted.

(d) A subsequent EIR or subsequent negative declaration shall be given the same notice and public review as required under Section 15087 or Section 15072. A subsequent EIR or negative declaration shall state where the previous document is available and can be reviewed.

Note: Authority cited: Section 21083, Public Resources Code. Reference: Section 21166, Public Resources Code; *Bowman v. City of Petaluma* (1986) 185 Cal. App. 3d 1065; *Benton v. Board of Supervisors* (1991) 226 Cal. App. 3d 1467; and *Fort Mojave Indian Tribe v. California Department of Health Services et al.* (1995) 38 Cal. App. 4th 1574.

§ 15163. Supplement to an EIR.

(a) The lead or responsible agency may choose to prepare a supplement to an EIR rather than a subsequent EIR if:
  (1) Any of the conditions described in Section 15162 would require the preparation of a subsequent EIR, and
  (2) Only minor additions or changes would be necessary to make the previous EIR adequately apply to the project in the changed situation.

(b) The supplement to the EIR need contain only the information necessary to make the previous EIR adequate for the project as revised.

(c) A supplement to an EIR shall be given the same kind of notice and public review as is given to a draft EIR under Section 15087.

(d) A supplement to an EIR may be circulated by itself without recirculating the previous draft or final EIR.

(e) When the agency decides whether to approve the project, the decision-making body shall consider the previous EIR as revised by the supplemental EIR. A finding under Section 15091 shall be made for each significant effect shown in the previous EIR as revised.

Note: Authority cited: Section 21083, Public Resources Code. Reference: Section 21166, Public Resources Code.

§ 15164. Addendum to an EIR or Negative Declaration.

(a) The lead agency or a responsible agency shall prepare an addendum to a previously certified EIR if some changes or additions are necessary but none of the conditions described in Section 15162 calling for preparation of a subsequent EIR have occurred.

(b) An addendum to an adopted negative declaration may be prepared if only minor technical changes or additions are necessary or none of the conditions described in Section 15162 calling for the preparation of a subsequent EIR or negative declaration have occurred.

(c) An addendum need not be circulated for public review but can be included in or attached to the final EIR or adopted negative declaration.

(d) The decision-making body shall consider the addendum with the final EIR or adopted negative declaration prior to making a decision on the project.

(e) A brief explanation of the decision not to prepare a subsequent EIR pursuant to Section 15162 should be included in an addendum to an EIR, the lead agency's required findings on the project, or elsewhere in the record. The explanation must be supported by substantial evidence.

Note: Authority cited: Section 21083, Public Resources Code. Reference: Section 21166, Public Resources Code; *Bowman v. City of Petaluma* (1986) 185 Cal. App. 3d 1065; and *Benton v. Board of Supervisors* (1991) 226 Cal. App. 3d 1467. Resources Code.

§ 15165. Multiple and Phased Projects.

Where individual projects are, or a phased project is, to be undertaken and where the total undertaking comprises a project with significant environmental effect, the lead agency shall prepare a single program EIR for the ultimate project as described in Section 15168. Where an individual project is a necessary precedent for action on a larger project, or commits the lead agency to a larger project, with significant environmental effect, an EIR must address itself to the scope of the larger project. Where one project is one of several similar projects of a public agency, but is not deemed a part of a larger undertaking or a larger project, the agency may prepare one EIR for all projects, or one for each project, but shall in either case comment upon the cumulative effect.

Note: Authority cited: Section 21083, Public Resources Code. Reference: Sections 21061, 21100 and 21151, Public Resources Code; *Whitman v. Board of Supervisors*, 88 Cal. App. 3d 397 (1979).

§ 15166. EIR As Part of a General Plan.

(a) The requirements for preparing an EIR on a local general plan, element, or amendment thereof will be satisfied by using the general plan, or element document, as the EIR and no separate EIR will be required, if:

 (1) the general plan addresses all the points required to be in an EIR by Article 9 of these guidelines and

 (2) the document contains a special section or a cover sheet identifying where the general plan document addresses each of the points required.

(b) Where an EIR rather than a negative declaration has been prepared for a general plan, element, or amendment thereto, the EIR shall be forwarded to the State Clearinghouse for review. The requirement shall apply regardless of whether the EIR is prepared as a separate document or as a part of the general plan or element document.

Note: Authority cited: Section 21083, Public Resources Code. Reference: Sections 21003, 21061, 21083, 21100, 21104, 21151 and 21152, Public Resources Code.

§ 15167. Staged EIR.

(a) Where a large capital project will require a number of discretionary approvals from government agencies and one of the approvals will occur more than two years before construction will begin, a staged EIR may be prepared covering the entire project in a general form. The staged EIR shall evaluate the proposal in light of current and contemplated plans and produce an informed estimate of the environmental consequences of the entire project. The aspect of the project before the public agency for approval shall be discussed with a greater degree of specificity.

(b) When a staged EIR has been prepared, a supplement to the EIR shall be prepared when a later approval is required for the project, and the information available at the time of the later approval would permit consideration of additional environmental impacts, mitigation measures, or reasonable alternatives to the project.

(c) Where a statute such as the Warren-Alquist Energy Resources Conservation and Development Act provides that a specific agency shall be the lead agency for a project and requires the lead agency to prepare an EIR, a responsible agency which must grant an approval for the project before the lead agency has completed the EIR may prepare and consider a staged EIR.(d) An agency requested to prepare a staged EIR may decline to act as the lead agency if it determines, among other factors, that:

 (1) Another agency would be the appropriate lead agency; and

 (2) There is no compelling need to prepare a staged EIR and grant an approval for the project before the appropriate lead agency will take its action on the project.

Note: Authority cited: Section 21083, Public Resources Code. Reference: Section 21003, Public Resources Code.

§ 15168. Program EIR.

(a) General. A program EIR is an EIR which may be prepared on a series of actions that can be characterized as one large project and are related either:

 (1) Geographically,

 (2) As logical parts in the chain of contemplated actions,

 (3) In connection with issuance of rules, regulations, plans, or other general criteria to govern the conduct of a continuing program, or

 (4) As individual activities carried out under the same authorizing statutory or regulatory authority and having generally similar environmental effects which can be mitigated in similar ways.

(b) Advantages. Use of a program EIR can provide the following advantages. The program EIR can:

 (1) Provide an occasion for a more exhaustive consideration of effects and alternatives than would be practical in an EIR on an individual action,

 (2) Ensure consideration of cumulative impacts that might be slighted in a case-by-case analysis,

 (3) Avoid duplicative reconsideration of basic policy considerations,

 (4) Allow the lead agency to consider broad policy alternatives and program wide mitigation measures at an early time when the agency has greater flexibility to deal with basic problems or cumulative impacts,

 (5) Allow reduction in paperwork.

(c) Use With Later Activities. Subsequent activities in the program must be examined in the light of the program EIR to determine whether an additional environmental document must be prepared.

 (1) If a later activity would have effects that were not examined in the program EIR, a new initial study would need to be prepared leading to either an EIR or a negative declaration.

 (2) If the agency finds that pursuant to Section 15162, no new effects could occur or no new mitigation measures would be required, the agency can approve the activity as being within the scope of the project covered by the program EIR, and no new environmental document would be required.

 (3) An agency shall incorporate feasible mitigation measures and alternatives developed in the program EIR into subsequent actions in the program.

 (4) Where the subsequent activities involve site specific operations, the agency should use a written checklist or similar device to document the evaluation of the site and the activity to determine whether the environmental effects of the operation were covered in the program EIR.

 (5) A program EIR will be most helpful in dealing with subsequent activities if it deals with the effects of the program as specifically and comprehensively as possible. With a good and detailed analysis of the program, many subsequent activities could be found to be within the scope of the project described in the program EIR, and no further environmental documents would be required.

(d) Use With Subsequent EIRS and Negative Declarations. A program EIR can be used to simplify the task of preparing environmental documents on later parts of the program. The program EIR can:

 (1) Provide the basis in an initial study for determining whether the later activity may have any significant effects.

 (2) Be incorporated by reference to deal with regional influences, secondary effects, cumulative impacts, broad alternatives, and other factors that apply to the program as a whole.

 (3) Focus an EIR on a subsequent project to permit discussion solely of new effects which had not been considered before.

(e) Notice With Later Activities. When a law other than CEQA requires public notice when the agency later proposes to carry out or approve an activity within the program and to rely on the program EIR for CEQA compliance, the notice for the activity shall include a statement that:
   (1) This activity is within the scope of the program approved earlier, and
   (2) The program EIR adequately describes the activity for the purposes of CEQA.

Note: Authority cited: Section 21083, Public Resources Code. Reference: Section 21003, Public Resources Code; *County of Inyo v. Yorty*, 32 Cal. App. 3d 795 (1973).

§ 15169. Master Environmental Assessment.

(a) General. A public agency may prepare a master environmental assessment, inventory, or data base for all, or a portion of, the territory subject to its control in order to provide information which may be used or referenced in EIRs or negative declarations. Neither the content, the format, nor the procedures to be used to develop a master environmental assessment are prescribed by these guidelines. The descriptions contained in this section are advisory. A master environmental assessment is suggested solely as an approach to identify and organize environmental information for a region or area of the state.
(b) Contents. A master environmental assessment may contain an inventory of the physical and biological characteristics of the area for which it is prepared and may contain such additional data and information as the public agency determines is useful or necessary to describe environmental characteristics of the area. It may include identification of existing levels of quality and supply of air and water, capacities and levels of use of existing services and facilities, and generalized incremental effects of different categories of development projects by type, scale, and location.
(c) Preparation.
   (1) A master environmental assessment or inventory may be prepared in many possible ways. For example, a master environmental assessment may be prepared as a special, comprehensive study of the area involved, as part of the EIR on a general plan, or as a data base accumulated by indexing EIRs prepared for individual projects or programs in the area involved.
   (2) The information contained in a master environmental assessment should be reviewed periodically and revised as needed so that it is accurate and current.
   (3) When advantageous to do so, master environmental assessments may be prepared through a joint exercise of powers agreement with neighboring local agencies or with the assistance of the appropriate Council of Governments.
(d) Uses.
   (1) A master environmental assessment can identify the environmental characteristics and constraints of an area. This information can be used to influence the design and location of individual projects.
   (2) A master environmental assessment may provide information agencies can use in initial studies to decide whether certain environmental effects are likely to occur and whether certain effects will be significant.
   (3) A master environmental assessment can provide a central source of current information for use in preparing individual EIRs and negative declarations.
   (4) Relevant portions of a master environmental assessment can be referenced and summarized in EIRs and negative declarations.
   (5) A master environmental assessment can assist in identifying long range, areawide, and cumulative impacts of individual projects proposed in the area covered by the assessment.
   (6) A master environmental assessment can assist a city or county in formulating a general plan or any element of such a plan by identifying environmental characteristics and constraints that need to be addressed in the general plan.
   (7) A master environmental assessment can serve as a reference document to assist public agencies which review other environmental documents dealing with activities in the area covered by the assessment. The public agency preparing the assessment should forward a completed copy to each agency which will review projects in the area.

Note: Authority cited: Section 21083, Public Resources Code. Reference: Section 21003, Public Resources Code.

§ 15170. Joint EIR-EIS.

A lead agency under CEQA may work with a federal agency to prepare a joint document which will meet the requirements of both CEQA and NEPA. Use of such a joint document is described in Article 14, beginning with Section 15220.

Note: Authority cited: Section 21083, Public Resources Code. Reference: Sections 21083.5 and 21083.7, Public Resources Code.

Article 11.5. Master Environmental Impact Report

§ 15175. Master EIR.

(a) The Master EIR procedure is an alternative to preparing a project EIR, staged EIR, or program EIR for certain projects which will form the basis for later decision making. It is intended to streamline the later environmental review of projects or approval included within the project, plan or program analyzed in the Master EIR. Accordingly, a Master EIR shall, to the greatest extent feasible, evaluate the cumulative impacts, growth inducing impacts, and irreversible significant effects on the environment of subsequent projects.
(b) A lead agency may prepare a Master EIR for any of the following classes of projects:
   (1) A general plan, general plan update, general plan element, general plan amendment, or specific plan.
   (2) Public or private projects that will be carried out or approved pursuant to, or in furtherance of, a redevelopment plan.
   (3) A project that consists of smaller individual projects which will be carried out in phases.
   (4) A rule or regulation which will be implemented by later projects.
   (5) Projects that will be carried out or approved pursuant to a development agreement.
   (6) A state highway project or mass transit project which will be subject to multiple stages of review or approval.
   (7) A plan proposed by a local agency, including a joint powers authority, for the reuse of a federal military base or reservation that has been closed or is proposed for closure by the federal government.
   (8) A regional transportation plan or congestion management plan.
   (9) Regulations adopted by the California Department of Fish and Game for the regulation of hunting and fishing.
(c) A lead agency may develop and implement a fee program in accordance with applicable provisions of law to generate the revenue necessary to prepare a Master EIR.

Note: Authority cited: Section 21083, Public Resources Code. Reference: Sections 21156, 21157 and 21089, Public Resources Code.

§ 15176. Contents of a Master EIR.

A lead agency shall include in a Master EIR all of the following:

(a) A detailed discussion as required by Section 15126.
(b) A description of anticipated subsequent projects that are within the scope of the Master EIR, including information with regard to the kind, size, intensity, and location of the subsequent projects, including, but not limited to all of the following:
   (1) The specific type of project anticipated to be undertaken such as a single family development, office-commercial development, sewer line installation or other activities.
   (2) The maximum and minimum intensity of any anticipated subsequent project, such as the number of residences in a residential development, and with regard to a public works facility, its anticipated capacity and service area.
   (3) The anticipated location for any subsequent development projects, and, consistent with the rule of reason set forth in Section 15126.6(f), alternative locations for any such projects.
   (4) A capital outlay or capital improvement program, or other scheduling or implementing device that governs the submission and approval of subsequent projects, or an explanation as to why practical planning considerations render it impractical to identify any such program or scheduling or other device at the time of preparing the Master EIR.
(c) A description of potential impacts of anticipated projects for which there is not sufficient information reasonably available to support a full assessment of potential impacts in the Master EIR. This description shall not be construed as a limitation on the impacts which may be considered in a focused EIR.

(d) Where a Master EIR is prepared in connection with a project identified in subdivision (b)(1) of section 15175, the anticipated subsequent projects included within a Master EIR may consist of later planning approvals, including parcel-specific approvals, consistent with the overall planning decision (e.g., general plan, or specific plan, or redevelopment plan) for which the Master EIR has been prepared. Such subsequent projects shall be adequately described for purposes of subdivision (b) or of this section (15176) if the Master EIR and any other documents embodying or relating to the overall planning decision identify the land use designations and the permissible densities and intensities of use for the affected parcel(s). The proponents of such subsequent projects shall not be precluded from relying on the Master EIR solely because that document did not specifically identify or list, by name, the subsequent project as ultimately proposed for approval.

Note: Authority cited: Section 21083, Public Resources Code. Reference: Section 21157, Public Resources Code.

§ 15177. Subsequent Projects Within the Scope of the MEIR.

(a) After a Master EIR has been prepared and certified, subsequent projects which the lead agency determines as being within the scope of the Master EIR will be subject to only limited environmental review.

(b) Except as provided in subdivision (2) of this subdivision, neither a new environmental document nor the preparation of findings pursuant to section 15091 shall be required of a subsequent project when all of the following requirements are met:

  (1) The lead agency for the subsequent project is the lead agency or any responsible agency identified in the Master EIR.

  (2) The lead agency for the subsequent project prepares an initial study on the proposal. The initial study shall analyze whether the subsequent project was described in the Master EIR and whether the subsequent project may cause any additional significant effect on the environment which was not previously examined in the Master EIR.

  (3) The lead agency for the subsequent project determines, on the basis of written findings, that no additional significant environmental effect will result from the proposal, no new additional mitigation measures or alternatives may be required, and that the project is within the scope of the Master EIR. "Additional significant environmental effect" means any project-specific effect which was not addressed as a significant effect in the Master EIR.

(c) Whether a subsequent project is within the scope of the Master EIR is a question of fact to be determined by the lead agency based upon a review of the initial study to determine whether there are additional significant effects or new additional mitigation measures or alternatives required for the subsequent project that are not already discussed in the Master EIR.

(d) Prior to approval of the proposed subsequent project, the lead agency shall incorporate all feasible mitigation measures or feasible alternatives appropriate to the project as set forth in the Master EIR and provide notice in the manner required by Section 15087.

(e) When the lead agency approves a project pursuant to this section, the lead agency shall file a notice in the manner required by Section 15075.

Note: Authority cited: Section 21083, Public Resources Code. Reference: Sections 21157, 21157.6 and 21158, Public Resources Code.

§ 15178. Subsequent Projects Identified in the MEIR.

(a) When a proposed subsequent project is identified in the Master EIR, but the lead agency cannot make a determination pursuant to Section 15177 that the subsequent project is within the scope of the Master EIR, and the lead agency determines that the cumulative impacts, growth inducing impacts and irreversible significant effects analysis in the Master EIR is adequate for the subsequent project, the lead agency shall prepare a mitigated negative declaration or a focused EIR if, after preparing an initial study, the lead agency determines that the project may result in new or additional significant effects. Whether the cumulative impacts, growth inducing impacts and irreversible significant effects analyses are adequate is a question of fact to be determined by the lead agency based upon a review of the proposed subsequent project in light of the Master EIR.

(b) A lead agency shall prepare a mitigated negative declaration for any proposed subsequent project if both of the following occur:

  (1) The initial study prepared pursuant to Section 15177 has identified potentially new or additional significant environmental effects that were not analyzed in the Master EIR; and

  (2) Feasible mitigation measures or alternatives will be incorporated to revise the subsequent project before the negative declaration is released for public review pursuant to Section 15073 in order to avoid or mitigate the identified effects to a level of insignificance.

(c) A lead agency shall prepare a focused EIR if the subsequent project may have a significant effect on the environment and a mitigated negative declaration pursuant to subdivision (b) of this section cannot be prepared.

  (1) The focused EIR shall incorporate by reference the Master EIR and analyze only the subsequent project's additional significant environmental effects and any new or additional mitigation measures or alternatives that were not identified and analyzed by the Master EIR. "Additional significant environmental effects" are those project-specific effects on the environment which were not addressed as significant in the Master EIR.

  (2) A focused EIR need not examine those effects which the lead agency, prior to public release of the focused EIR, finds, on the basis of the initial study, related documents, and commitments from the proponent of a subsequent project, have been mitigated in one of the following manners:

    (A) Mitigated or avoided as a result of mitigation measures identified in the Master EIR which the lead agency will require as part of the approval of the subsequent project;

    (B) Examined at a sufficient level of detail in the Master EIR to enable those significant effects to be mitigated or avoided by specific revisions to the project, the imposition of conditions of approval, or by other means in connection with approval of the subsequent project; or

    (C) The mitigation or avoidance of which is the responsibility of and within the jurisdiction of another public agency and is, or can and should be, undertaken by that agency.

  (3) The lead agency's findings pursuant to subdivision (2) shall be included in the focused EIR prior to public release pursuant to Section 15087.

  (4) A focused EIR prepared pursuant to this section shall analyze any significant environmental effects when:

    (A) Substantial new or additional information shows that the adverse environmental effect may be more significant that was described in the Master EIR; or

    (B) Substantial new or additional information shows that mitigation measures or alternatives which were previously determined to be infeasible are feasible and will avoid or reduce the significant effects of the subsequent project to a level of insignificance.

(d) A lead agency shall file a notice of determination shall be filed pursuant to Section 15075 if a project has been approved for which a mitigated negative declaration has been prepared pursuant to this section and a notice of determination shall be filed pursuant to Section 15094 if a project has been approved for which a focused EIR has been prepared pursuant to this section.

(e) When a lead agency determines that the cumulative impacts, growth inducing impacts and irreversible significant effects analysis in the Master EIR is inadequate for the subsequent project, the subsequent project is no longer eligible for the limited environmental review available under the Master EIR process and shall be reviewed according to Article 7 (commencing with Section 15080) of these guidelines. The lead agency shall tier the project specific EIR upon the Master EIR to the extent feasible under Section 15152.

Note: Authority cited: Section 21083, Public Resources Code. Reference: Sections 21081(a)(2), 21157.5 and 21158, Public Resources Code.

§ 15179. Limitations on the Use of the Master EIR.

(a) The certified Master EIR shall not be used for a subsequent project described in the Master EIR in accordance with this article if either:

  (1) The Master EIR was certified more than five years prior to the filing of an application for a subsequent project except as set forth in subsection (b) below, or

  (2) After the certification of the Master EIR, a project not described in the certified Master EIR as an anticipated subsequent project is approved and the approved project may affect the adequacy of the Master EIR for any subsequent project that was described in the Master EIR.

(b) A Master EIR that was certified more than five years prior to the filing of an application for a subsequent project described in the Master EIR may be used in accordance with this article to review such a subsequent project if the lead agency reviews the adequacy of the Master EIR and takes either of the following steps:
   (1) Finds that no substantial changes have occurred with respect to the circumstances under which the Master EIR was certified, or that there is no new available information which was not known and could not have been known at the time the Master EIR was certified; or
   (2) Prepares an initial study and, pursuant to the findings of the initial study, does either (A) or (B) below:
      (A) certifies subsequent or supplemental EIR that updates or revises the Master EIR and which either:
         1. is incorporated into the previously certified Master EIR,
         2. references any deletions, additions or other modifications to the previously certified Master EIR;
      (B) approves a mitigated negative declaration that addresses substantial changes that have occurred with respect to the circumstances under which the Master EIR was certified or the new information that was not known and could not have been known at the time the Master EIR was certified.

Note: Authority cited: Section 21083, Public Resources Code. Reference: Section 21157.6, Public Resources Code.

§ 15179.5. Focused EIRs and Small Projects.

(a) When a project is a multiple family residential development of 100 units or less or is a residential and commercial or retail mixed-use commercial development of not more then 100,000 square feet, whether or not the project is identified in the Master EIR, a focused EIR shall be prepared pursuant to this section when the following conditions are met:
   (1) The project is consistent with a general plan, specific plan, community plan, or zoning ordinance for which an EIR was prepared within five years of certification of the focused EIR; and
   (2) The parcel on which the project is to be developed is either:
      (A) Surrounded by immediately contiguous urban development;
      (B) Previously developed with urban uses; or
      (C) Within one-half mile of an existing rail transit station.
(b) A focused environmental impact report prepared pursuant to this section shall be limited to a discussion of potentially significant effects on the environment specific to the project, or which substantial new information shows will be more significant than described in the prior environmental impact report. No discussion shall be required of alternatives to the project, cumulative impacts of the project, or the growth inducing impacts of the project.
(c) This section does not apply where the lead agency can make a finding pursuant to Section 15177 that the subsequent project is within the scope of the Master EIR, where the lead agency can prepare a mitigated negative declaration or focused EIR pursuant to Section 15178, or where, pursuant to Section 15162 or Section 15163, the environmental impact report referenced in subdivision (a)(1) of this section must be updated through the preparation of a subsequent environmental impact report or a supplemental environmental impact report.

Note: Authority cited: Section 21083, Public Resources Code. Reference: Section 21158.5, Public Resources Code.

§ 15180. Redevelopment Projects.

(a) An EIR for a redevelopment plan may be a Master EIR, a program EIR, or a project EIR. An EIR for a redevelopment plan must specify whether it is a Master EIR, a program EIR, or a project EIR.
(b) If the EIR for a redevelopment plan is a project EIR, all public and private activities or undertakings pursuant to or in furtherance of the redevelopment plan shall constitute a single project, which shall be deemed approved at the time of adoption of the redevelopment plan by the legislative body. The EIR in connection with the redevelopment plan shall be submitted in accordance with Section 33352 of the Health and Safety Code.If a project EIR has been certified for the redevelopment plan, no subsequent EIRs are required for individual components of the redevelopment plan unless a subsequent EIR or a supplement to an EIR would be required by Section 15162 or 15163.
(c) If the EIR for a redevelopment plan is a Master EIR, subsequent projects which the lead agency determines as being within the scope of the Master EIR will be subject to the review required by Section 15177. If the EIR for a redevelopment plan is a program EIR, subsequent activities in the program will be subject to the review required by Section 15168.

Note: Authority cited: Section 21083, Public Resources Code. Reference: Sections 21090 and 21166, Public Resources Code.

Article 12. Special Situations

§ 15181. Housing and Neighborhood Commercial Facilities in Urbanized Areas.

Note: Authority cited: Sections 21083 and 21087, Public Resources Code. Reference: Section 21080.7, Public Resources Code.

§ 15182. Residential Projects Pursuant to a Specific Plan.

(a) Exemption. Where a public agency has prepared an EIR on a specific plan after January 1, 1980, no EIR or negative declaration need be prepared for a residential project undertaken pursuant to and in conformity to that specific plan if the project meets the requirements of this section.
(b) Scope. Residential projects covered by this section include but are not limited to land subdivisions, zoning changes, and residential planned unit developments.
(c) Limitation. This section is subject to the limitation that if after the adoption of the specific plan, an event described in Section 15162 should occur, this exemption shall not apply until the city or county which adopted the specific plan completes a subsequent EIR or a supplement to an EIR on the specific plan. The exemption provided by this section shall again be available to residential projects after the lead agency has filed a Notice of Determination on the specific plan as reconsidered by the subsequent EIR or supplement to the EIR.
(d) Fees. The lead agency has authority to charge fees to applicants for projects which benefit from this section. The fees shall be calculated in the aggregate to defray but not to exceed the cost of developing and adopting the specific plan including the cost of preparing the EIR.
(e) Statute of Limitations. A court action challenging the approval of a project under this section for failure to prepare a supplemental EIR shall be commenced within 30 days after the lead agency's decision to carry out or approve the project in accordance with the specific plan.

Note: Authority cited: Section 21083, Public Resources Code. Reference: Section 65453, Government Code.

§ 15183. Projects Consistent with a Community Plan, General Plan, or Zoning.

(a) CEQA mandates that projects which are consistent with the development density established by existing zoning, community plan, or general plan policies for which an EIR was certified shall not require additional environmental review, except as might be necessary to examine whether there are project-specific significant effects which are peculiar to the project or its site. This streamlines the review of such projects and reduces the need to prepare repetitive environmental studies.
(b) In approving a project meeting the requirements of this section, a public agency shall limit its examination of environmental effects to those which the agency determines, in an initial study or other analysis:
   (1) Are peculiar to the project or the parcel on which the project would be located,
   (2) Were not analyzed as significant effects in a prior EIR on the zoning action, general plan or community plan with which the project is consistent,
   (3) Are potentially significant off-site impacts and cumulative impacts which were not discussed in the prior EIR prepared for the general plan, community plan or zoning action, or
   (4) Are previously identified significant effects which, as a result of substantial new information which was not known at the time the EIR was certified, are determined to have a more severe adverse impact than discussed in the prior EIR.
(c) If an impact is not peculiar to the parcel or to the project, has been addressed as a significant effect in the prior EIR, or can be substantially mitigated by the imposition of uniformly applied development policies or standards, as contemplated by subdivision (e) below, then an additional EIR need not be prepared for the project solely on the basis of that impact.

(d) This section shall apply only to projects which meet the following conditions:
   (1) The project is consistent with:
      (A) A community plan adopted as part of a general plan,
      (B) A zoning action which zoned or designated the parcel on which the project would be located to accommodate a particular density of development, or
      (C) A general plan of a local agency, and
   (2) An EIR was certified by the lead agency for the zoning action, the community plan, or the general plan.
(e) This section shall limit the analysis of only those significant environmental effects for which:
   (1) Each public agency with authority to mitigate any of the significant effects on the environment identified in the EIR on the planning or zoning action undertakes or requires others to undertake mitigation measures specified in the EIR which the lead agency found to be feasible, and
   (2) The lead agency makes a finding at a public hearing as to whether the feasible mitigation measures will be undertaken.
(f) An effect of a project on the environment shall not be considered peculiar to the project or the parcel for the purposes of this section if uniformly applied development policies or standards have been previously adopted by the city or county with a finding that the development policies or standards will substantially mitigate that environmental effect when applied to future projects, unless substantial new information shows that the policies or standards will not substantially mitigate the environmental effect. The finding shall be based on substantial evidence which need not include an EIR. Such development policies or standards need not apply throughout the entire city or county, but can apply only within the zoning district in which the project is located, or within the area subject to the community plan on which the lead agency is relying. Moreover, such policies or standards need not be part of the general plan or any community plan, but can be found within another pertinent planning document such as a zoning ordinance. Where a city or county, in previously adopting uniformly applied development policies or standards for imposition on future projects, failed to make a finding as to whether such policies or standards would substantially mitigate the effects of future projects, the decisionmaking body of the city or county, prior to approving such a future project pursuant to this section, may hold a public hearing for the purpose of considering whether, as applied to the project, such standards or policies would substantially mitigate the effects of the project. Such a public hearing need only be held if the city or county decides to apply the standards or policies as permitted in this section.
(g) Examples of uniformly applied development policies or standards include, but are not limited to:
   (1) Parking ordinances,
   (2) Public access requirements,
   (3) Grading ordinances.
   (4) Hillside development ordinances.
   (5) Flood plain ordinances.
   (6) Habitat protection or conservation ordinances.
   (7) View protection ordinances.
   (8) Requirements for reducing greenhouse gas emissions, as set forth in adopted land use plans, policies, or regulations.
(h) An environmental effect shall not be considered peculiar to the project or parcel solely because no uniformly applied development policy or standard is applicable to it.
(i) Where the prior EIR relied upon by the lead agency was prepared for a general plan or community plan that meets the requirements of this section, any rezoning action consistent with the general plan or community plan shall be treated as a project subject to this section.
   (1) "Community plan" is defined as a part of the general plan of a city or county which applies to a defined geographic portion of the total area included in the general plan, includes or references each of the mandatory elements specified in Section 65302 of the Government Code, and contains specific development policies and implementation measures which will apply those policies to each involved parcel.
   (2) For purposes of this section, "consistent" means that the density of the proposed project is the same or less than the standard expressed for the involved parcel in the general plan, community plan or zoning action for which an EIR has been certified, and that the project complies with the density-related standards contained in that plan or zoning. Where the zoning ordinance refers to the general plan or community plan for its density standard, the project shall be consistent with the applicable plan.
(j) This section does not affect any requirement to analyze potentially significant offsite or cumulative impacts if those impacts were not adequately discussed in the prior EIR. If a significant offsite or cumulative impact was adequately discussed in the prior EIR, then this section may be used as a basis for excluding further analysis of that offsite or cumulative impact.

Note: Authority cited: Sections 21083 and 21083.05, Public Resources Code. Reference: Sections 21083.05 and 21083.3, Public Resources Code.

§ 15183.5. Tiering and Streamlining the Analysis of Greenhouse Gas Emissions.

(a) Lead agencies may analyze and mitigate the significant effects of greenhouse gas emissions at a programmatic level, such as in a general plan, a long range development plan, or a separate plan to reduce greenhouse gas emissions. Later project-specific environmental documents may tier from and/or incorporate by reference that existing programmatic review. Project-specific environmental documents may rely on an EIR containing a programmatic analysis of greenhouse gas emissions as provided in section 15152 (tiering), 15167 (staged EIRs) 15168 (program EIRs), 15175-15179.5 (Master EIRs), 15182 (EIRs Prepared for Specific Plans), and 15183 (EIRs Prepared for General Plans, Community Plans, or Zoning).
(b) Plans for the Reduction of Greenhouse Gas Emissions. Public agencies may choose to analyze and mitigate significant greenhouse gas emissions in a plan for the reduction of greenhouse gas emissions or similar document. A plan to reduce greenhouse gas emissions may be used in a cumulative impacts analysis as set forth below. Pursuant to sections 15064(h)(3) and 15130(d), a lead agency may determine that a project's incremental contribution to a cumulative effect is not cumulatively considerable if the project complies with the requirements in a previously adopted plan or mitigation program under specified circumstances.
   (1) Plan Elements. A plan for the reduction of greenhouse gas emissions should:
      (A) Quantify greenhouse gas emissions, both existing and projected over a specified time period, resulting from activities within a defined geographic area;
      (B) Establish a level, based on substantial evidence, below which the contribution to greenhouse gas emissions from activities covered by the plan would not be cumulatively considerable;
      (C) Identify and analyze the greenhouse gas emissions resulting from specific actions or categories of actions anticipated within the geographic area;
      D) Specify measures or a group of measures, including performance standards, that substantial evidence demonstrates, if implemented on a project-by-project basis, would collectively achieve the specified emissions level;
      (E) Establish a mechanism to monitor the plan's progress toward achieving the level and to require amendment if the plan is not achieving specified levels;
      (F) Be adopted in a public process following environmental review.
   (2) Use with Later Activities. A plan for the reduction of greenhouse gas emissions, once adopted following certification of an EIR or adoption of an environmental document, may be used in the cumulative impacts analysis of later projects. An environmental document that relies on a greenhouse gas reduction plan for a cumulative impacts analysis must identify those requirements specified in the plan that apply to the project, and, if those requirements are not otherwise binding and enforceable, incorporate those requirements as mitigation measures applicable to the project. If there is substantial evidence that the effects of a particular project may be cumulatively considerable notwithstanding the project's compliance with the specified requirements in the plan for the reduction of greenhouse gas emissions, an EIR must be prepared for the project.
(c) Special Situations. As provided in Public Resources Code sections 21155.2 and 21159.28, environmental documents for certain residential and mixed use projects, and transit priority projects, as defined in section 21155, that are consistent with the general use designation, density, building intensity, and applicable policies specified for the project area in an applicable sustainable communities strategy or alternative planning strategy need not analyze global warming impacts resulting from cars and light duty trucks. A lead agency should consider whether such projects may

result in greenhouse gas emissions resulting from other sources, however, consistent with these Guidelines.

Note: Authority cited: Sections 21083 and 21083.05, Public Resources Code. Reference: Section 65457, Government Code; Sections 21003, 21061, 21068.5, 21081(a)(2), 21081.6, 21083.05, 21083.3, 21093, 21094, 21100, 21151, 21155, 21155.2, 21156, 21157, 21157.1, 21157.5, 21157.6, 21158, 21158.5 and 21159.28, Public Resources Code; *California Native Plant Society v. County of El Dorado* (2009) 170 Cal. App. 4th 1026; and *Protect the Historic Amador Waterways v. Amador Water Agency* (2004) 116 Cal. App. 4th 1099.

§ 15184. State Mandated Local Projects.

Whenever a state agency issues an order which requires a local agency to carry out a project subject to CEQA, the following rules apply:

(a) If an EIR is prepared for the project, the local agency shall limit the EIR to considering those factors and alternatives which will not conflict with the order.

(b) If a local agency undertakes a project to implement a rule or regulation imposed by a certified state environmental regulatory program listed in Section 15251, the project shall be exempt from CEQA with regard to the significant effects analyzed in the document prepared by the state agency as a substitute for an EIR. The local agency shall comply with CEQA with regard to any site-specific effect of the project which was not analyzed by the certified state agency as a significant effect on the environment. The local agency need not re-examine the general environmental effects of the state rule or regulation.

Note: Authority cited: Section 21083, Public Resources Code. Reference: Sections 21080, 21080.5 and 21154, Public Resources Code.

§ 15185. Administrative Appeals.

(a) Where an agency allows administrative appeals upon the adequacy of an environmental document, an appeal shall be handled according to the procedures of that agency. Public notice shall be handled in accordance with individual agency requirements and Section 15202(e).

(b) The decisionmaking body to which an appeal has been made shall consider the environmental document and make findings under Sections 15091 and 15093 if appropriate.

Note: Authority cited: Section 21083, Public Resources Code. Reference: Sections 21082 and 21083, Public Resources Code.

§ 15186. School Facilities.

(a) CEQA establishes a special requirement for certain school projects, as well as certain projects near schools, to ensure that potential health impacts resulting from exposure to hazardous materials, wastes, and substances will be carefully examined and disclosed in a negative declaration or EIR, and that the lead agency will consult with other agencies in this regard.

(b) Before certifying an EIR or adopting a negative declaration for a project located within one-fourth mile of a school involves the construction or alteration of a facility that might reasonably be anticipated to emit hazardous air emissions, or that would handle an extremely hazardous substance or a mixture containing extremely hazardous substances in a quantity equal to or greater than the state threshold quantity specified in subdivision (j) of Section 25532 of the Health and Safety Code, that may impose a health or safety hazard to persons who would attend or would be employed at the school, the lead agency must do both of the following:

   (1) Consult with the affected school district or districts regarding the potential impact of the project on the school; and

   (2) Notify the affected school district or districts of the project, in writing, not less than 30 days prior to approval or certification of the negative declaration or EIR.

(c) When the project involves the purchase of a school site or the construction of a secondary or elementary school by a school district, the negative declaration or EIR prepared for the project shall not be adopted or certified unless:

   (1) The negative declaration, mitigated negative declaration, or EIR contains sufficient information to determine whether the property is:

      (A) The site of a current or former hazardous waste or solid waste disposal facility and, if so, whether wastes have been removed.

      (B) A hazardous substance release site identified by the Department of Toxic Substances Control in a current list adopted pursuant to Section 25356 of the Health and Safety Code for removal or remedial action pursuant to Chapter 6.8 (commencing with Section 25300) of Division 20 of the Health and Safety Code.

      (C) The site of one or more buried or above ground pipelines which carry hazardous substances, acutely hazardous materials, or hazardous wastes, as defined in Division 20 of the Health and Safety Code. This does not include a natural gas pipeline used only to supply the school or neighborhood.

      (D) Within 500 feet of the edge of the closest traffic lane of a freeway or other busy traffic corridor.

   (2) The lead agency has notified in writing and consulted with the county or city administering agency (as designated pursuant to Section 25502 of the Health and Safety Code) and with any air pollution control district or air quality management district having jurisdiction, to identify facilities within one-fourth mile of the proposed school site which might reasonably be anticipated to emit hazardous emissions or handle hazardous or acutely hazardous material, substances, or waste. The notice shall include a list of the school sites for which information is sought. Each agency or district receiving notice shall provide the requested information and provide a written response to the lead agency within 30 days of receiving the notification. If any such agency or district fails to respond within that time, the negative declaration or EIR shall be conclusively presumed to comply with this section as to the area of responsibility of that agency.

   (3) The school district makes, on the basis of substantial evidence, one of the following written findings:

      (A) Consultation identified none of the facilities specified in paragraph (2).

      (B) The facilities specified in paragraph (2) exist, but one of the following conditions applies:

         1. The health risks from the facilities do not and will not constitute an actual or potential endangerment of public health to persons who would attend or be employed at the proposed school.

         2. Corrective measures required under an existing order by another agency having jurisdiction over the facilities will, before the school is occupied, mitigate all chronic or accidental hazardous air emissions to levels that do not constitute any actual or potential public health danger to persons who would attend or be employed at the proposed school. When the school district board makes such a finding, it shall also make a subsequent finding, prior to occupancy of the school, that the emissions have been so mitigated.

         3. For a school site with boundary that is within 500 feet of the edge of the closest traffic lane of a freeway or other busy traffic corridor, the school district determines, through a health risk assessment pursuant to subdivision (b)(2) of Section 44360 of the Health and Safety Code, based on appropriate air dispersion modeling, and after considering any potential mitigation measures, that the air quality at the proposed site is such that neither short-term nor long-term exposure poses significant health risks to pupils.

      (C) The facilities or other pollution sources specified in subsection (c)(2) exist, but conditions in subdivisions (c)(3)(B)(1), (2) or (3) cannot be met, and the school district is unable to locate an alternative site that is suitable due to a severe shortage of sites that meet the requirements in subdivision (a) of Section 17213 of the Education Code. If the school district makes this finding, the school board shall prepare an EIR and adopt a statement of overriding considerations.

      This finding shall be in addition to any findings which may be required pursuant to Sections 15074, 15091 or 15093.

(d) When the lead agency has carried out the consultation required by paragraph (2) of subdivision (b), the negative declaration or EIR shall be conclusively presumed to comply with this section, notwithstanding any failure of the consultation to identify an existing facility.

(e) The following definitions shall apply for the purposes of this section:

   (1) "Acutely hazardous material," is as defined in 22 C.C.R. §66260.10.

(2) "Administering agency," is as defined in Section 25501 of the Health and Safety Code.
(3) "Extremely hazardous substance," is as defined in subdivision (g)(2)(B) of Section 25532 of the Health and Safety Code and listed in Section 2770.5, Table 3, of Title 19 of the California Code of Regulations.
(4) "Facilities" means any source with a potential to use, generate, emit or discharge hazardous air pollutants, including, but not limited to, pollutants that meet the definition of a hazardous substance, and whose process or operation is identified as an emission source pursuant to the most recent list of source categories published by the California Air Resources Board.
(5) "Freeway or other busy traffic corridors" means those roadways that, on an average day, have traffic in excess of 50,000 vehicles in a rural area, as defined in Section 50101 of the Health and Safety Code, and 100,000 vehicles in an urban area, as defined in Section 50104.7 of the Health and Safety Code.
(6) "Handle" means to use, generate, process, produce, package, treat, store, emit, discharge, or dispose of a hazardous material in any fashion.
(7) "Hazardous air emissions," is as defined in subdivisions (a) to (f), inclusive, of Section 44321 of the Health and Safety Code.
(8) "Hazardous substance," is as defined in Section 25316 of the Health and Safety Code.
(9) "Hazardous waste," is as defined in Section 25117 of the Health and Safety Code.
(10) "Hazardous waste disposal site," is as defined in Section 25114 of the Health and Safety Code.

Note: Authority cited: Section 21083, Public Resources Code. References: Sections 21151.4 and 21151.8, Public Resources Code.

§ 15187. Environmental Review of New Rules and Regulations.

(a) At the time of the adoption of a rule or regulation requiring the installation of pollution control equipment, establishing a performance standard, or establishing a treatment requirement, the California Air Resources Board, Department of Toxic Substances Control, Integrated Waste Management Board, State Water Resources Control Board, all regional water quality control boards, and all air pollution control districts and air quality management districts, as defined in Section 39025 of the Health and Safety Code, must perform an environmental analysis of the reasonably foreseeable methods by which compliance with that rule or regulation will be achieved.
(b) If an EIR is prepared by the agency at the time of adoption of a rule or regulation, it satisfies the requirements of this section provided that the document contains the information specified in subdivision (c) below. Similarly, for those State agencies whose regulatory programs have been certified by the Resources Agency pursuant to Section 21080.5 of the Public Resources Code, an environmental document prepared pursuant to such programs satisfies the requirements of this section, provided that the document contains the information specified in subdivision (c) below.
(c) The environmental analysis shall include at least the following:
   (1) An analysis of reasonably foreseeable environmental impacts of the methods of compliance;
   (2) An analysis of reasonably foreseeable feasible mitigation measures relating to those impacts; and
   (3) An analysis of reasonably foreseeable alternative means of compliance with the rule or regulation, which would avoid or eliminate the identified impacts.
(d) The environmental analysis shall take into account a reasonable range of environmental, economic, and technical factors, population and geographic areas, and specific sites. The agency may utilize numerical ranges and averages where specific data is not available, but is not required to, nor should it, engage in speculation or conjecture.
(e) Nothing in this section shall require the agency to conduct a project level analysis.
(f) Nothing in this section is intended, or may be used, to delay the adoption of any rule or regulation for which this section requires an environmental analysis.

Note: Authority cited: Section 21083, Public Resources Code. Reference: Sections 21159 and 21159.4, Public Resources Code.

§ 15188. Focused EIR for Pollution Control Equipment.

This section applies to projects consisting solely of the installation of pollution control equipment and other components necessary to the installation of that equipment which are undertaken for the purpose of complying with a rule or regulation which was the subject of an environmental analysis as described in Section 15187.
(a) The lead agency for the compliance project may prepare a focused EIR to analyze the effects of that project when the following occur:
   (1) The agency which promulgated the rule or regulation certified an EIR on that rule or regulation, or reviewed it pursuant to an environmental analysis prepared under a certified regulatory program and, in either case, the review included an assessment of growth inducing impacts and cumulative impacts of, and alternatives to, the project;
   (2) the focused EIR for the compliance project is certified within five years of the certified EIR or environmental analysis required by subdivision (a)(1); and
   (3) the EIR prepared in connection with the adoption of the rule or regulation need not be updated through the preparation of a subsequent EIR or supplemental EIR pursuant to section 15162 or section 15163.
(b) The discussion of significant environmental effects in the focused EIR shall be limited to project-specific, potentially significant effects which were not discussed in the environmental analysis required under Section 15187. No discussion of growth-inducing or cumulative impacts is required. Discussion of alternatives shall be limited to alternative means of compliance, if any, with the rule or regulation.

Note: Authority cited: Section 21083, Public Resources Code. Reference: Section 21159.1, Public Resources Code.

§ 15189. Compliance with Performance Standard or Treatment Requirement Rule or Regulation.

This section applies to projects consisting solely of compliance with a performance standard or treatment requirement which was the subject of an environmental analysis as described in Section 15187.
(a) If preparing a negative declaration, mitigated negative declaration or EIR on the compliance project the lead agency for the compliance project shall, to the greatest extent feasible, use the environmental analysis prepared pursuant to Section 15187. The use of numerical averages or ranges in the environmental analysis prepared under Section 15187 does not relieve the lead agency on the compliance project from its obligation to identify and evaluate the environmental effects of the project.
(b) Where the lead agency determines that an EIR is required for the compliance project, the EIR need address only the project-specific issues or other issues that were not discussed in sufficient detail in the environmental analysis prepared under Section 15187. The mitigation measures imposed by the lead agency shall be limited to addressing the significant effects on the environment of the compliance project. The discussion of alternatives shall be limited to a discussion of alternative means of compliance, if any, with the rule or regulation.

Note: Authority cited: Section 21083, Public Resources Code. Reference: Section 21159.2, Public Resources Code.

§ 15190. Deadlines for Compliance with Sections 15188 and 15189.

(a) The lead agency for a compliance project under either Section 15188 or Section 15189 shall determine whether an EIR or negative declaration should be prepared within 30 days of its determination that the application for the project is complete.
(b) Where the EIR will be prepared under contract to the lead agency for the compliance project, the agency shall issue a request for proposal for preparation of the EIR not later than 30 days after the deadline for response to the notice of preparation has expired. The contract shall be awarded within 30 days of the response date on the request for proposals.

Note: Authority cited: Section 21083, Public Resources Code. Reference: Section 21159.3, Public Resources Code.

§ 15190.5. Department of Defense Notification Requirement.

(a) For purposes of this section, the following definitions are applicable.
   (1) "Low-level flight path" means any flight path for any aircraft owned, maintained, or that is under the jurisdiction of the United States Department of Defense that flies lower than 1,500 feet above ground level, as indicated in the United States Department of Defense Flight Information Publication, "Area Planning Military Training Routes: North and South America (AP/1B)" published by the United States National Imagery and Mapping Agency, or its successor, as of the date the

military service gives written notification to a lead agency pursuant to subdivision (b).

(2) "Military impact zone" means any area, including airspace, that meets both of the following criteria:
  (A) Is within two miles of a military installation, including, but not limited to, any base, military airport, camp, post, station, yard, center, homeport facility for a ship, or any other military activity center that is under the jurisdiction of the United States Department of Defense; and
  (B) Covers greater than 500 acres of unincorporated land, or greater than 100 acres of city incorporated land.

(3) "Military service" means the United States Department of Defense or any branch of the United States Armed Forces.

(4) "Special use airspace" means the land area underlying the airspace that is designated for training, research, development, or evaluation for a military service, as that land area is established by the United States Department of Defense Flight Information Publication, "Area Planning: Special Use Airspace: North and South America (AP/1A)" published by the United States National Imagery and Mapping Agency, or its successor, as of the date the military service gives written notification to a lead agency pursuant to subdivision (b).

(b) A military service may give written notification to a lead agency of the specific boundaries of a low-level flight path, military impact zone, or special use airspace, and provide the lead agency, in writing, the military contact office and address for the military service. If the notice references the specific boundaries of a low-level flight path, such notification must include a copy of the applicable United States Department of Defense Flight Information Publication, "Area Planning Military Training Routes: North and South America (AP/1B)." If the notice references the specific boundaries of a special use airspace, such notification must include a copy of the applicable United States Department of Defense Flight Information Publication, "Area Planning: Special Use Airspace: North and South America (AP/1A)."

(c) If a military service provides the written notification specified in subdivision (b) of this section, a lead agency must include the specified military contact office in the list of organizations and individuals receiving a notice of intent to adopt a negative declaration or a mitigated negative declaration pursuant to Section 15072, in the list of organizations and individuals receiving a notice of preparation of an EIR pursuant to Section 15082, and in the list of organizations and individuals receiving a notice of availability of a draft EIR pursuant to Section 15087 for any project that meets all of the criteria specified below:
  (1) The project to be carried out or approved by the lead agency is within the boundaries specified in subdivision (b).
  (2) The project is one of the following:
    (A) a project that includes a general plan amendment; or
    (B) a project that is of statewide, regional, or areawide significance; or
    (C) a project that relates to a public use airport and the area surrounding such airport which is required to be referred to the airport land use commission, or appropriately designated body, pursuant to Sections 21670-21679.5 of the Public Utilities Code.
  (3) The project is not one of the actions described below. A lead agency does not need to send to the specified military contact office a notice of intent to adopt a negative declaration or a mitigated negative declaration, a notice of preparation of an EIR, or a notice of availability of a draft EIR for such actions.
    (A) a response action taken pursuant to Chapter 6.8 (commencing with Section 25300) of Division 20 of the Health and Safety Code.
    (B) a response action taken pursuant to Chapter 6.85 (commencing with Section 25396) of Division 20 of the Health and Safety Code.
    (C) a project undertaken at a site in response to a corrective action order issued pursuant to Section 25187 of the Health and Safety Code.

    The lead agency shall send the specified military contact office a notice of intent or a notice of availability sufficiently prior to adoption or certification of the environmental documents by the lead agency to allow the military service the review period provided under Section 15105.

(d) The effect or potential effect that a project may have on military activities does not itself constitute an adverse effect on the environment for the purposes of CEQA.

Note: Authority cited: Section 21083, Public Resources Code. Reference: Section 21098, Public Resources Code.

Article 12.5. Exemptions for Agricultural Housing, Affordable Housing, and Residential Infill Projects

§ 15191. Definitions.

For purposes of this Article 12.5 only, the following words shall have the following meanings:

(a) "Agricultural employee" means a person engaged in agriculture, including: farming in all its branches, and, among other things, includes: (1) the cultivation and tillage of the soil, (2) dairying,(3) the production, cultivation, growing, and harvesting of any agricultural or horticultural commodities (including commodities defined as agricultural commodities in Section 1141j(g) of Title 12 of the United States Code), (4) the raising of livestock, bees, furbearing animals, or poultry, and (5) any practices (including any forestry or lumbering operations) performed by a farmer or on a farm as an incident to or in conjunction with such farming operations, including preparation for market and delivery to storage or to market or to carriers for transportation to market. This definition is subject to the following limitations:This definition shall not be construed to include any person other than those employees excluded from the coverage of the National Labor Relations Act, as amended, as agricultural employees, pursuant to Section 2(3) of the Labor Management Relations Act (Section 152(3), Title 29, United States Code), and Section 3(f) of the Fair Labor Standards Act (Section 203(f), Title 29, United States Code).This definition shall not apply, or be construed to apply, to any employee who performs work to be done at the site of the construction, alteration, painting, or repair of a building, structure, or other work (as these terms have been construed under Section 8(e) of the Labor Management Relations Act, 29 U.S.C. Sec. 158(e)) or logging or timber-clearing operations in initial preparation of land for farming, or who does land leveling or only land surveying for any of the above. As used in this definition, "land leveling" shall include only major land moving operations changing the contour of the land, but shall not include annual or seasonal tillage or preparation of land for cultivation.

(b) "Census-defined place" means a specific unincorporated land area within boundaries determined by the United States Census Bureau in the most recent decennial census.

(c) "Community-level environmental review" means either of the following:
  (1) An EIR certified on any of the following:
    (A) A general plan.
    (B) A revision or update to the general plan that includes at least the land use and circulation elements.
    (C) An applicable community plan.
    (D) An applicable specific plan.
    (E) A housing element of the general plan, if the environmental impact report analyzed the environmental effects of the density of the proposed project.
  (2) A negative declaration or mitigated negative declaration adopted as a subsequent environmental review document, following and based upon an EIR on a general plan, an applicable community plan, or an applicable specific plan, provided that the subsequent environmental review document is allowed by CEQA following a master EIR or a program EIR, or is required pursuant to Section 21166.

(d) "Developed open space" means land that meets all of the following criteria:
  (1) land that is publicly owned, or financed in whole or in part by public funds,
  (2) is generally open to, and available for use by, the public, and
  (3) is predominantly lacking in structural development other than structures associated with open spaces, including, but not limited to, playgrounds, swimming pools, ball fields, enclosed child play areas, and picnic facilities.

  Developed open space may include land that has been designated for acquisition by a public agency for developed open space but does not include lands acquired by public funds dedicated to the acquisition of land for housing purposes.

(e) "Infill site" means a site in an urbanized area that meets one of the following criteria:
  (1) The site has been previously developed for qualified urban uses; or

(2) The site has not been developed for qualified urban uses but all immediately adjacent parcels are developed with existing qualified urban uses; or
(3) The site has not been developed for qualified urban uses, no parcel within the site has been created within the past 10 years, and the site is situated so that:
(A) at least 75 percent of the perimeter of the site is adjacent to parcels that are developed with existing qualified urban uses at the time the lead agency receives an application for an approval; and
(B) the remaining 25 percent of the perimeter of the site adjoins parcels that had been previously developed for qualified urban uses.

(f) "Low- and moderate-income households" means "persons and families of low or moderate income" as defined in Section 50093 of the Health and Safety Code to mean persons and families whose income does not exceed 120 percent of area median income, adjusted for family size by the Department of Housing and Community Development, in accordance with adjustment factors adopted and amended from time to time by the United States Department of Housing and Urban Development pursuant to Section 8 of the United States Housing Act of 1937.

(g) "Low-income households" means households of persons and families of very low and low income, which are defined in Sections 50093 and 50105 of the Health and Safety Code as follows:
(1) "Persons and families of low income" or "persons of low income" is defined in Section 50093 of the Health & Safety Code to mean persons or families who are eligible for financial assistance specifically provided by a governmental agency for the benefit of occupants of housing financed pursuant to this division.
(2) "Very low income households" is defined in Section 50105 of the Health & Safety Code to mean persons and families whose incomes do not exceed the qualifying limits for very low income families as established and amended from time to time pursuant to Section 8 of the United States Housing Act of 1937. "Very low income households" includes extremely low income households, as defined in Section 50106 of the Health & Safety Code.

(h) "Lower income households" is defined in Section 50079.5 of the Health and Safety Code to mean any of the following:
(1) "Lower income households," which means persons and families whose income does not exceed the qualifying limits for lower income families as established and amended from time to time pursuant to Section 8 of the United States Housing Act of 1937.
(2) "Very low income households," which means persons and families whose incomes do not exceed the qualifying limits for very low income families as established and amended from time to time pursuant to Section 8 of the United States Housing Act of 1937.
(3) "Extremely low income households," which means persons and families whose incomes do not exceed the qualifying limits for extremely low income families as established and amended from time to time by the Secretary of Housing and Urban Development and defined in Section 5.603(b) of Title 24 of the Code of Federal Regulations.

(i) "Major transit stop" means a site containing an existing rail transit station, a ferry terminal served by either a bus or rail transit service, or the intersection of two or more major bus routes with a frequency of service interval of 15 minutes or less during the morning and afternoon peak commute periods.

(j) "Project-specific effect" means all the direct or indirect environmental effects of a project other than cumulative effects and growth-inducing effects.

(k) "Qualified urban use" means any residential, commercial, public institutional, transit or transportation passenger facility, or retail use, or any combination of those uses.

(l) "Residential" means a use consisting of either of the following:
(1) Residential units only.
(2) Residential units and primarily neighborhood-serving goods, services, or retail uses that do not exceed 15 percent of the total floor area of the project.

(m) "Urbanized area" means either of the following:
(1) An incorporated city that either by itself or in combination with two contiguous incorporated cities has a population of at least 100,000 persons; or
(2) An unincorporated area that meets the requirements set forth in subdivision (m)(2)(A) and subdivision (m)(2)(B) below.
(A) The unincorporated area must meet one of the following location or density requirements:
1. The unincorporated area must be: (i) completely surrounded by one or more incorporated cities, (ii) have a population of at least 100,000 persons either by itself or in combination with the surrounding incorporated city or cities, and (iii) have a population density that at least equals the population density of the surrounding city or cities; or
2. The unincorporated area must be located within an urban growth boundary and have an existing residential population of at least 5,000 persons per square mile. For purposes of this subparagraph, an "urban growth boundary" means a provision of a locally adopted general plan that allows urban uses on one side of the boundary and prohibits urban uses on the other side.
(B) The board of supervisors with jurisdiction over the unincorporated area must have taken the following steps:
1. The board has prepared a draft document by which the board would find that the general plan, zoning ordinance, and related policies and programs applicable to the unincorporated area are consistent with principles that: (i) encourage compact development in a manner that promotes efficient transportation systems, economic growth, affordable housing, energy efficiency, and an appropriate balance of jobs and housing, and (ii) protects the environment, open space, and agricultural areas.
2. The board has submitted the draft document to OPR and allowed OPR thirty days to submit comments on the draft findings to the board.
3. No earlier than thirty days after submitting the draft document to OPR, the board has adopted a final finding in substantial conformity with the draft finding described in the draft document referenced in subdivision (m)(2)(B)(1) above.

Note: Authority cited: Section 21083, Public Resources Code. Reference: Sections 21159.20, 21159.21, 21159.22, 21159.23 and 21159.24, Public Resources Code.

§ 15192. Threshold Requirements for Exemptions for Agricultural Housing, Affordable Housing, and Residential Infill Projects.

In order to qualify for an exemption set forth in sections 15193, 15194 or 15195, a housing project must meet all of the threshold criteria set forth below.

(a) The project must be consistent with:
(1) Any applicable general plan, specific plan, or local coastal program, including any mitigation measures required by such plan or program, as that plan or program existed on the date that the application for the project pursuant to Section 65943 of the Government Code was deemed complete; and
(2) Any applicable zoning ordinance, as that zoning ordinance existed on the date that the application for the project pursuant to Section 65943 of the Government Code was deemed complete, unless the zoning of project property is inconsistent with the general plan because the project property has not been rezoned to conform to the general plan.

(b) Community-level environmental review has been adopted or certified.

(c) The project and other projects approved prior to the approval of the project can be adequately served by existing utilities, and the project applicant has paid, or has committed to pay, all applicable in-lieu or development fees.

(d) The site of the project:
(1) Does not contain wetlands, as defined in Section 328.3 of Title 33 of the Code of Federal Regulations.
(2) Does not have any value as an ecological community upon which wild animals, birds, plants, fish, amphibians, and invertebrates depend for their conservation and protection.
(3) Does not harm any species protected by the federal Endangered Species Act of 1973 (16 U.S.C. Sec. 1531 et seq.) or by the Native Plant Protection Act (Chapter 10 (commencing with Section 1900) of Division 2 of the Fish and Game Code), the California Endangered

Species Act (Chapter 1.5 (commencing with Section 2050) of Division 3 of the Fish and Game Code.
  (4) Does not cause the destruction or removal of any species protected by a local ordinance in effect at the time the application for the project was deemed complete.
(e) The site of the project is not included on any list of facilities and sites compiled pursuant to Section 65962.5 of the Government Code.
(f) The site of the project is subject to a preliminary endangerment assessment prepared by a registered environmental assessor to determine the existence of any release of a hazardous substance on the site and to determine the potential for exposure of future occupants to significant health hazards from any nearby property or activity. In addition, the following steps have been taken in response to the results of this assessment:
  (1) If a release of a hazardous substance is found to exist on the site, the release shall be removed, or any significant effects of the release shall be mitigated to a level of insignificance in compliance with state and federal requirements.
  (2) If a potential for exposure to significant hazards from surrounding properties or activities is found to exist, the effects of the potential exposure shall be mitigated to a level of insignificance in compliance with state and federal requirements.
(g) The project does not have a significant effect on historical resources pursuant to Section 21084.1 of the Public Resources Code.
(h) The project site is not subject to wildland fire hazard, as determined by the Department of Forestry and Fire Protection, unless the applicable general plan or zoning ordinance contains provisions to mitigate the risk of a wildland fire hazard.
(i) The project site does not have an unusually high risk of fire or explosion from materials stored or used on nearby properties.
(j) The project site does not present a risk of a public health exposure at a level that would exceed the standards established by any state or federal agency.
(k) Either the project site is not within a delineated earthquake fault zone or a seismic hazard zone, as determined pursuant to Section 2622 and 2696 of the Public Resources Code respectively, or the applicable general plan or zoning ordinance contains provisions to mitigate the risk of an earthquake or seismic hazard.
(l) Either the project site does not present a landslide hazard, flood plain, flood way, or restriction zone, or the applicable general plan or zoning ordinance contains provisions to mitigate the risk of a landslide or flood.
(m) The project site is not located on developed open space.
(n) The project site is not located within the boundaries of a state conservancy.
(o) The project has not been divided into smaller projects to qualify for one or more of the exemptions set forth in sections 15193 to 15195.

Note: Authority cited: Section 21083, Public Resources Code. Reference: Sections 21159.21 and 21159.27, Public Resources Code.

§ 15193. Agricultural Housing Exemption.

CEQA does not apply to any development project that meets the following criteria.

(a) The project meets the threshold criteria set forth in section 15192.
(b) The project site meets the following size criteria:
  (1) The project site is located in an area with a population density of at least 1,000 persons per square mile and is two acres or less in area; or
  (2) The project site is located in an area with a population density of less than 1,000 persons per square mile and is five acres or less in area.
(c) The project meets the following requirements regarding location and number of units.
  (1) If the proposed development project is located on a project site within city limits or in a census-defined place, it must meet the following requirements:
    (A) The proposed project location must be within one of the following:
      1. Incorporated city limits; or
      2. A census defined place with a minimum population density of at least 5,000 persons per square mile; or
      3. A census-defined place with a minimum population density of at least 1,000 persons per square mile, unless a public agency that is carrying out or approving the project determines that there is a reasonable possibility that the project, if completed, would have a significant effect on the environment due to unusual circumstances or that the cumulative impacts of successive projects of the same type in the same area, over time, would be significant.
    (B) The proposed development project must be located on a project site that is adjacent, on at least two sides, to land that has been developed.
    (C) The proposed development project must meet either of the following requirements:
      1. Consist of not more than 45 units, or
      2. Consist of housing for a total of 45 or fewer agricultural employees if the housing consists of dormitories, barracks, or other group living facilities.
  (2) If the proposed development project is located on a project site zoned for general agricultural use, it must meet either of the following requirements:
    (A) Consist of not more than 20 units, or
    (B) Consist of housing for a total of 20 or fewer agricultural employees if the housing consists of dormitories, barracks, or other group living facilities.
(d) The project meets the following requirements regarding provision of housing for agricultural employees:
  (1) The project must consist of the construction, conversion, or use of residential housing for agricultural employees.
  (2) If the project lacks public financial assistance, then:
    (A) The project must be affordable to lower income households; and
    (B) The developer of the development project must provide sufficient legal commitments to the appropriate local agency to ensure the continued availability and use of the housing units for lower income households for a period of at least 15 years.
  (3) If public financial assistance exists for the project, then:
    (A) The project must be housing for very low, low-, or moderate-income households; and
    (B) The developer of the development project must provide sufficient legal commitments to the appropriate local agency to ensure the continued availability and use of the housing units for low- and moderate-income households for a period of at least 15 years.

Note: Authority cited: Section 21083, Public Resources Code. Reference: Section 21159.22, Public Resources Code.

§ 15194. Affordable Housing Exemption.

CEQA does not apply to any development project that meets the following criteria:

(a) The project meets the threshold criteria set forth in section 15192.
(b) The project meets the following size criteria: the project site is not more than five acres in area.
(c) The project meets both of the following requirements regarding location:
  (1) The project meets one of the following location requirements relating to population density:
    (A) The project site is located within an urbanized area or within a census-defined place with a population density of at least 5,000 persons per square mile.
    (B) If the project consists of 50 or fewer units, the project site is located within an incorporated city with a population density of at least 2,500 persons per square mile and a total population of at least 25,000 persons.
    (C) The project is located within either an incorporated city or a census defined place with a population density of at least 1,000 persons per square mile and there is no reasonable possibility that the project would have a significant effect on the environment or the residents of the project due to unusual circumstances or due to the related or cumulative impacts of reasonably foreseeable projects in the vicinity of the project.
  (2) The project meets one of the following site-specific location requirements:
    (A) The project site has been previously developed for qualified urban uses; or
    (B) The parcels immediately adjacent to the project site are developed with qualified urban uses.
    (C) The project site has not been developed for urban uses and all of the following conditions are met:
      1. No parcel within the site has been created within 10 years prior to the proposed development of the site.
      2. At least 75 percent of the perimeter of the site adjoins parcels that are developed with qualified urban uses.
      3. The existing remaining 25 percent of the perimeter of the site adjoins parcels

that have previously been developed for qualified urban uses.

(d) The project meets both of the following requirements regarding provision of affordable housing.

(1) The project consists of the construction, conversion, or use of residential housing consisting of 100 or fewer units that are affordable to low-income households.

(2) The developer of the project provides sufficient legal commitments to the appropriate local agency to ensure the continued availability and use of the housing units for lower income households for a period of at least 30 years, at monthly housing costs deemed to be "affordable rent" for lower income, very low income, and extremely low income households, as determined pursuant to Section 50053 of the Health and Safety Code.

Note: Authority cited: Section 21083, Public Resources Code. Reference: Section 21159.23, Public Resources Code.

§ 15195. Residential Infill Exemption.

(a) Except as set forth in subdivision (b), CEQA does not apply to any development project that meets the following criteria:

(1) The project meets the threshold criteria set forth in section 15192; provided that with respect to the requirement in section 15192(b) regarding community-level environmental review, such review must be certified or adopted within five years of the date that the lead agency deems the application for the project to be complete pursuant to Section 65943 of the Government Code.

(2) The project meets both of the following size criteria:

(A) The site of the project is not more than four acres in total area.

(B) The project does not include any single level building that exceeds 100,000 square feet.

(3) The project meets both of the following requirements regarding location:

(A) The project is a residential project on an infill site.

(B) The project is within one-half mile of a major transit stop.

(4) The project meets both of the following requirements regarding number of units:

(A) The project does not contain more than 100 residential units.

(B) The project promotes higher density infill housing. The lead agency may establish its own criteria for determining whether the project promotes higher density infill housing except in either of the following two circumstances:

1. A project with a density of at least 20 units per acre is conclusively presumed to promote higher density infill housing.

2. A project with a density of at least 10 units per acre and a density greater than the average density of the residential properties within 1,500 feet shall be presumed to promote higher density infill housing unless the preponderance of the evidence demonstrates otherwise.

(5) The project meets the following requirements regarding availability of affordable housing: The project would result in housing units being made available to moderate, low or very low income families as set forth in either A or B below:

(A) The project meets one of the following criteria, and the project developer provides sufficient legal commitments to the appropriate local agency to ensure the continued availability and use of the housing units as set forth below at monthly housing costs determined pursuant to paragraph (3) of subdivision (h) of Section 65589.5 of the Government Code.

1. At least 10 percent of the housing is sold to families of moderate income, or

2. Not less than 10 percent of the housing is rented to families of low income, or

3. Not less than 5 percent of the housing is rented to families of very low income.

(B) If the project does not result in housing units being available as set forth in subdivision (A) above, then the project developer has paid or will pay in-lieu fees pursuant to a local ordinance in an amount sufficient to result in the development of an equivalent number of units that would otherwise be required pursuant to subparagraph (A).

(b) A project that otherwise meets the criteria set forth in subdivision (a) is not exempt from CEQA if any of the following occur:

(1) There is a reasonable possibility that the project will have a project-specific, significant effect on the environment due to unusual circumstances.

(2) Substantial changes with respect to the circumstances under which the project is being undertaken that are related to the project have occurred since community-level environmental review was certified or adopted.

(3) New information becomes available regarding the circumstances under which the project is being undertaken and that is related to the project that was not known, and could not have been known at the time that community-level environmental review was certified or adopted.

If a project is not exempt from CEQA due to subdivision (b), the analysis of the environmental effects of the project covered in the EIR or the negative declaration shall be limited to an analysis of the project-specific effect of the projects and any effects identified pursuant to subdivisions (b)(2) and (3).

Note: Authority cited: Section 21083, Public Resources Code. Reference: Section 21159.24, Public Resources Code. Resources Code.

§ 15196. Notice of Exemption for Agricultural Housing, Affordable Housing, and Residential Infill Projects.

(a) When a local agency determines that a project is not subject to CEQA under Section 15193, 15194, or 15195, and it approves or determines to carry out that project, the local agency or person seeking project approval shall file the notice required by Section 21152.1 of the Public Resources Code, pursuant to Section 15062.(b) Failure to file the notice required by this section does not affect the validity of a project.(c) Nothing in this section affects the time limitations contained in Section 21167.

Note: Authority cited: Section 21083, Public Resources Code. Reference: 21152.1, Public Resources Code.

Article 13. Review and Evaluation of EIRs and Negative Declarations

§ 15200. Purposes of Review.

The purposes of review of EIRs and negative declarations include:

(a) Sharing expertise,

(b) Disclosing agency analyses,

(c) Checking for accuracy,

(d) Detecting omissions,

(e) Discovering public concerns, and

(f) Soliciting counter proposals.

Note: Authority cited: Section 21083, Public Resources Code. Reference: Section 21000, 21108 and 21152, Public Resources Code; *Environmental Defense Fund v. Coastside County Water District* (1972) 27 Cal. App. 3d 695; *County of Inyo v. City of Los Angeles* (1977) 71 Cal. App. 3d 185.

§ 15201. Public Participation.

Public participation is an essential part of the CEQA process. Each public agency should include provisions in its CEQA procedures for wide public involvement, formal and informal, consistent with its existing activities and procedures, in order to receive and evaluate public reactions to environmental issues related to the agency's activities. Such procedures should include, whenever possible, making environmental information available in electronic format on the Internet, on a web site maintained or utilized by the public agency.

Note: Authority cited: Section 21083, Public Resources Code. Reference: Sections 21000, 21082, 21108 and 21152, Public Resources Code; *Environmental Defense Fund v. Coastside County Water District* (1972) 27 Cal. App. 3d 695; *People v. County of Kern* (1974) 39 Cal. App. 3d 830; *County of Inyo v. City of Los Angeles* (1977) 71 Cal. App. 3d 185.

§ 15202. Public Hearings.

(a) CEQA does not require formal hearings at any stage of the environmental review process. Public comments may be restricted to written communications.

(b) If an agency provides a public hearing on its decision to carry out or approve a project, the agency should include environmental review as one of the subjects for the hearing.

(c) A public hearing on the environmental impact of a project should usually be held when the lead agency determines it would facilitate the purposes and goals of CEQA to do so. The hearing may be held in conjunction with and as a part of normal planning activities.

(d) A draft EIR or negative declaration should be used as a basis for discussion at a public hearing. The hearing may be held at a place where public hearings are regularly conducted by the lead agency or at another location expected to be convenient to the public.

(e) Notice of all public hearings shall be given in a timely manner. This notice may be given in the same form and time as notice for other regularly conducted public hearings of the public agency. To the extent that the public agency maintains an Internet web site, notice of all public hearings should be made available in electronic format on that site.

(f) A public agency may include, in its implementing procedures, procedures for the conducting of public hearings pursuant to this section. The procedures may adopt existing notice and hearing requirements of the public agency for regularly conducted legislative, planning, and other activities.

(g) There is no requirement for a public agency to conduct a public hearing in connection with its review of an EIR prepared by another public agency.

Note: Authority cited: Section 21083, Public Resources Code. Reference: Sections 21000, 21082, 21108 and 21152, Public Resources Code; *Concerned Citizens of Palm Desert, Inc. v. Board of Supervisors* (1974) 38 Cal. App. 3d 272.

§ 15203. Adequate Time for Review and Comment.
The lead agency shall provide adequate time for other public agencies and members of the public to review and comment on a draft EIR or negative declaration that it has prepared.

(a) Public agencies may establish time periods for review in their implementing procedures and shall notify the public and reviewing agencies of the time for receipt of comments on EIRs. These time periods shall be consistent with applicable statutes, the State CEQA Guidelines, and applicable clearinghouse review periods.

(b) A review period for an EIR does not require a halt in other planning or evaluation activities related to a project. Planning should continue in conjunction with environmental evaluation.

Note: Authority cited: Section 21083, Public Resources Code. Reference: Sections 21082, 21108 and 21152, Public Resources Code. Formerly Sections 15160(a) and (e).

§ 15204. Focus of Review.

(a) In reviewing draft EIRs, persons and public agencies should focus on the sufficiency of the document in identifying and analyzing the possible impacts on the environment and ways in which the significant effects of the project might be avoided or mitigated. Comments are most helpful when they suggest additional specific alternatives or mitigation measures that would provide better ways to avoid or mitigate the significant environmental effects. At the same time, reviewers should be aware that the adequacy of an EIR is determined in terms of what is reasonably feasible, in light of factors such as the magnitude of the project at issue, the severity of its likely environmental impacts, and the geographic scope of the project. CEQA does not require a lead agency to conduct every test or perform all research, study, and experimentation recommended or demanded by commentors. When responding to comments, lead agencies need only respond to significant environmental issues and do not need to provide all information requested by reviewers, as long as a good faith effort at full disclosure is made in the EIR.

(b) In reviewing negative declarations, persons and public agencies should focus on the proposed finding that the project will not have a significant effect on the environment. If persons and public agencies believe that the project may have a significant effect, they should:
   (1) Identify the specfic effect,
   (2) Explain why they believe the effect would occur, and
   (3) Explain why they believe the effect would be significant.

(c) Reviewers should explain the basis for their comments, and should submit data or references offering facts, reasonable assumptions based on facts, or expert opinion supported by facts in support of the comments. Pursuant to Section 15064, an effect shall not be considered significant in the absence of substantial evidence.

(d) Reviewing agencies or organizations should include with their comments the name of a contact person who would be available for later consultation if necessary. Each responsible agency and trustee agency shall focus its comments on environmental information germane to that agency's statutory responsibility.

(e) This section shall not be used to restrict the ability of reviewers to comment on the general adequacy of a document or of the lead agency to reject comments not focused as recommended by this section.

(f) Prior to the close of the public review period for an EIR or mitigated negative declaration, a responsible or trustee agency which has identified significant effects on the environment may submit to the lead agency proposed mitigation measures which would address those significant effects. Any such measures shall be limited to impacts affecting those resources which are subject to the statutory authority of that agency. If mitigation measures are submitted, the responsible or trustee agency shall either submit to the lead agency complete and detailed performance objectives for the mitigation measures, or shall refer the lead agency to appropriate, readily available guidelines or reference documents which meet the same purpose.

Note: Authority cited: Section 21083, Public Resources Code. Reference: Sections 21080, 21081.6, 21080.4, 21104 and 21153, Public Resources Code, Formerly Section 15161; *San Joaquin Raptor/Wildlife Rescue Center v. County of Stanislaus* (1996) 42 Cal. App. 4th 608; and *Leonoff v. Monterey County Board of Supervisors* (1990) 222 Cal. App. 3d 1337.

§ 15205. Review by State Agencies.

(a) Draft EIRs and negative declarations to be reviewed by state agencies shall be submitted to the State Clearinghouse, 1400 Tenth Street, Sacramento, California 95814. For U.S. Mail, submit to P.O. Box 3044, Sacramento, California 95812-3044. When submitting such documents to the State Clearinghouse, the public agency shall include, in addition to the printed copy, a copy of the document in electronic form on a diskette or by electronic mail transmission, if available.

(b) The following environmental documents shall be submitted to the State Clearinghouse for review by state agencies:
   (1) Draft EIRs and negative declarations prepared by a state agency where such agency is a lead agency.
   (2) Draft EIRs and negative declarations prepared by a public agency where a state agency is a responsible agency, trustee agency, or otherwise has jurisdiction by law with respect to the project.
   (3) Draft EIRs and negative declarations on projects identified in Section 15206 as being of statewide, regional, or areawide significance.
   (4) Draft EIRs, environmental assessments, and findings of no significant impact prepared pursuant to NEPA, the Federal Guidelines (Title 40 CFR, Part 1500, commencing with Section 1500.1).

(c) Public agencies may send environmental documents to the State Clearinghouse for review where a state agency has special expertise with regard to the environmental impacts involved. The areas of statutory authorities of state agencies are identified in Appendix B. Any such environmental documents submitted to the State Clearinghouse shall include, in addition to the printed copy, a copy of the document in electronic format, on a diskette or by electronic mail transmission, if available.

(d) When an EIR or negative declaration is submitted to the State Clearinghouse for review, the review period set by the lead agency shall be at least as long as the period provided in the state review system operated by the State Clearinghouse. In the state review system, the normal review period is 45 days for EIRs and 30 days for negative declarations. In exceptional circumstances, the State Clearinghouse may set shorter review periods when requested by the lead agency.

(e) A sufficient number of copies of an EIR, negative declaration, or mitigated negative declaration, shall be submitted to the State Clearinghouse for review and comment by state agencies. The notice of completion form required by the State Clearinghouse must be submitted together with the copies of the EIR and may be submitted together with the copies of the negative declaration or mitigated negative declaration. The notice of completion form required by the State Clearinghouse is included in Appendix C. If the lead agency uses the on-line process for submittal of the notice of completion form to the State Clearinghouse, the form generated from the Internet shall satisfy this requirement (refer to www.ceqanet.ca.gov).

(f) While the lead agency is encouraged to contact the regional and district offices of state responsible agencies, the lead agency must, in all cases, submit documents to the State Clearinghouse for distribution in order to comply with the review requirements of this section.

Note: Authority cited: Section 21083, Public Resources Code. Reference: Sections 21083, 21091, 21104 and 21153, Public Resources Code.

§ 15206. Projects of Statewide, Regional, or Areawide Significance.

(a) Projects meeting the criteria in this section shall be deemed to be of statewide, regional, or areawide significance.
   (1) A draft EIR or negative declaration prepared by any public agency on a project described in this section shall be submitted to the State Clearinghouse and should be submitted also to the appropriate metropolitan area council of governments for review and comment. The notice of completion form required by the State Clearinghouse must be submitted together with the copies of the EIR and may be submitted together with the copies of the negative declaration. The notice of completion form required by the State Clearinghouse is included in Appendix C. If the lead agency uses the on-line process for submittal of the notice of completion form to the State Clearinghouse, the form generated from the Internet shall satisfy this requirement (refer to www.ceqanet.ca.gov).
   (2) When such documents are submitted to the State Clearinghouse, the public agency shall include, in addition to the printed copy, a copy of the document in electronic format on a diskette or by electronic mail transmission, if available.

(b) The lead agency shall determine that a proposed project is of statewide, regional, or areawide significance if the project meets any of the following criteria:
   (1) A proposed local general plan, element, or amendment thereof for which an EIR was prepared. If a negative declaration was prepared for the plan, element, or amendment, the document need not be submitted for review.
   (2) A project has the potential for causing significant effects on the environment extending beyond the city or county in which the project would be located. Examples of the effects include generating significant amounts of traffic or interfering with the attainment or maintenance of state or national air quality standards. Projects subject to this subdivision include:
      (A) A proposed residential development of more than 500 dwelling units.
      (B) A proposed shopping center or business establishment employing more than 1,000 persons or encompassing more than 500,000 square feet of floor space.
      (C) A proposed commercial office building employing more than 1,000 persons or encompassing more than 250,000 square feet of floor space.
      (D) A proposed hotel/motel development of more than 500 rooms.
      (E) A proposed industrial, manufacturing, or processing plant, or industrial park planned to house more than 1,000 persons, occupying more than 40 acres of land, or encompassing more than 650,000 square feet of floor area.
   (3) A project which would result in the cancellation of an open space contract made pursuant to the California Land Conservation Act of 1965 (Williamson Act) for any parcel of 100 or more acres.
   (4) A project for which an EIR and not a negative declaration was prepared which would be located in and would substantially impact the following areas of critical environmental sensitivity:
      (A) The Lake Tahoe Basin.
      (B) The Santa Monica Mountains Zone as defined by Section 33105 of the Public Resources Code.
      (C) The California Coastal Zone as defined in, and mapped pursuant to, Section 30103 of the Public Resources Code.
      (D) An area within 1/4 mile of a wild and scenic river as defined by Section 5093.5 of the Public Resources Code.
      (E) The Sacramento-San Joaquin Delta, as defined in Water Code Section 12220.
      (F) The Suisun Marsh as defined in Public Resources Code Section 29101.
      (G) The jurisdiction of the San Francisco Bay Conservation and Development Commission as defined in Government Code Section 66610.
   (5) A project which would substantially affect sensitive wildlife habitats including but not limited to riparian lands, wetlands, bays, estuaries, marshes, and habitats for endangered, rare and threatened species as defined by Section 15380 of this Chapter.
   (6) A project which would interfere with attainment of regional water quality standards as stated in the approved areawide waste treatment management plan.
   (7) A project which would provide housing, jobs, or occupancy for 500 or more people within 10 miles of a nuclear power plant.

Note: Authority cited: Section 21083, Public Resources Code. Reference. Section 21083, Public Resources Code.

§ 15207. Failure to Comment.

If any public agency or person who is consulted with regard to an EIR or negative declaration fails to comment within a reasonable time as specified by the lead agency, it shall be assumed, absent a request for a specific extension of time, that such agency or person has no comment to make. Although the lead agency need not respond to late comments, the lead agency may choose to respond to them.

Note: Authority cited: Section 21083, Public Resources Code. Reference: Sections 21104 and 21153, Public Resources Code; *Cleary v. County of Stanislaus* (1981) 118 Cal. App. 3d 348. Formerly Section 15162.

§ 15208. Retention and Availability of Comments.

Comments received through the consultation process shall be retained for a reasonable period and available for public inspection at an address given in the final EIR. Comments which may be received on a draft EIR or negative declaration under preparation shall also be considered and kept on file.

Note: Authority cited: Section 21083, Public Resources Code. Reference: Sections 21104, 21082.1 and 21153, Public Resources Code; Section 4, Chapter 480, Statutes of 1981; *People v. County of Kern* (1974) 39 Cal. App. 3d 830.

§ 15209. Comments on Initiative of Public Agencies.

Every public agency may comment on environmental documents dealing with projects which affect resources with which the agency has special expertise regardless of whether its comments were solicited or whether the effects fall within the legal jurisdiction of the agency.

Note: Authority cited: Section 21083, Public Resources Code. Reference: Sections 21002, 21104 and 21153, Public Resources Code.

Article 14. Projects Also Subject to the National Environmental Policy Act (Nepa)

§ 15220. General.

This article applies to projects that are subject to both CEQA and NEPA. NEPA applies to projects which are carried out, financed, or approved in whole or in part by federal agencies. Accordingly, this article applies to projects which involve one or more state or local agencies and one or more federal agencies.

Note: Authority cited: Section 21083, Public Resources Code. Reference: Sections 21083.5, 21083.6 and 21083.7, Public Resources Code; National Environmental Policy Act of 1969, Public Law 91-190 as amended, 42 U.S.C.A. 4321-4347; NEPA Regulations, 40 Code of Federal Regulations (C.F.R.) Parts 1500-1508.

§ 15221. NEPA Document Ready Before CEQA Document.

(a) When a project will require compliance with both CEQA and NEPA, state or local agencies should use the EIS or finding of no significant impact rather than preparing an EIR or negative declaration if the following two conditions occur:
   (1) An EIS or finding of no significant impact will be prepared before an EIR or negative declaration would otherwise be completed for the project; and
   (2) The EIS or finding of no significant impact complies with the provisions of these guidelines.

(b) Because NEPA does not require separate discussion of mitigation measures or growth inducing impacts, these points of analysis will need to be added, supplemented, or identified before the EIS can be used as an EIR.

Note: Authority cited: Section 21083, Public Resources Code. Reference: Sections 21083.5 and 21083.7, Public Resources Code; Section 102(2)(C) of NEPA, 43 U.S.C.A. 4322(2)(C).

§ 15222. Preparation of Joint Documents.

If a lead agency finds that an EIS or finding of no significant impact for a project would not be prepared by the federal agency by the time when the lead agency will need to consider an EIR or negative declaration, the lead agency should try to prepare a combined EIR-EIS or negative declaration-finding of no significant impact. To avoid the need for the federal agency to prepare a separate document for the same project, the lead agency must involve the federal agency in the preparation of the joint document. This involvement is necessary because federal law generally prohibits a federal agency from using an EIR prepared by a state agency unless the federal agency was involved in the preparation of the document.

Note: Authority cited: Section 21083, Public Resources Code. Reference: Sections 21083.5 and 21083.7, Public Resources Code; Section 102(2)(D) of NEPA, 43 U.S.C.A. 4322 (2)(D); 40 C.F.R. Part 1506.2.

§ 15223. Consultation with Federal Agencies.
When it plans to use an EIS or finding of no significant impact or to prepare such a document jointly with a federal agency, the lead agency shall consult as soon as possible with the federal agency.

Note: Authority cited: Section 21083, Public Resources Code. Reference: Sections 21083.5 and 21083.7, Public Resources Code.

§ 15224. Time Limits.
Where a project will be subject to both CEQA and the National Environmental Policy Act, the one year time limit and the 105 day time limit may be waived pursuant to Section 15110.

Note: Authority cited: Section 21083, Public Resources Code. Reference: Section 21083.6, Public Resources Code.

§ 15225. Circulation of Documents.

(a) Where the federal agency circulated the EIS or finding of no significant impact for public review as broadly as state or local law may require and gave notice meeting the standards in Section 15072(a) or 15087(a), the lead agency under CEQA may use the federal document in the place of an EIR or negative declaration without recirculating the federal document for public review. One review and comment period is enough. Prior to using the federal document in this situation, the lead agency shall give notice that it will use the federal document in the place of an EIR or negative declaration and that it believes that the federal document meets the requirements of CEQA. The notice shall be given in the same manner as a notice of the public availability of a draft EIR under Section 15087.

(b) If an EIS has been prepared and filed pursuant to NEPA on the closure and reuse of a military base and the Lead Agency decides that the EIS does not fully meet the requirements of CEQA or has not been circulated for public review as state and local law may require, the Lead Agency responsible for preparation of an EIR for a reuse plan for the same base may proceed in the following manner:

   (1) Prepare and circulate a notice of preparation pursuant to Section 15082. The notice shall include a description of the reuse plan, a copy of the EIS, an address to which to send comments, and the deadline for submitting comments. The notice shall state that the lead agency intends to utilize the EIS as a draft EIR and requests comments on whether the EIS provides adequate information to serve as a draft EIR and what specific additional information, if any, is necessary.

   (2) Upon the close of the comment period, the lead agency may proceed with preparation and circulation for comment of the draft EIR for the reuse plan. To the greatest extent feasible, the lead agency shall avoid duplication and utilize the EIS or information in the EIS as all or part of the draft EIR. The EIR shall be completed in compliance with the provisions of CEQA.

Note: Authority cited: Section 21083, Public Resources Code. Reference: Sections 21083.5 and 21092, Public Resources Code.

§ 15226. Joint Activities.
State and local agencies should cooperate with federal agencies to the fullest extent possible to reduce duplication between the California Environmental Quality Act and the National Environmental Policy Act. Such cooperation should, to the fullest extent possible, include:

(a) Joint planning processes,
(b) Joint environmental research and studies,
(c) Joint public hearings,
(d) Joint environmental documents.

Note: Authority cited: Section 21083, Public Resources Code. Reference: Sections 21083.5 and 21083.7, Public Resources Code; 40 C.F.R. Part 1506.2.

§ 15227. State Comments on a Federal Project.
When a state agency officially comments on a proposed federal project which may have a significant effect on the environment, the comments shall include or reference a discussion of the material specified in Section 15126. An EIS on the federal project may be referenced to meet the requirements of this section.

Note: Authority cited: Section 21083, Public Resources Code. Reference: Section 21101, Public Resources Code.

§ 15228. Where Federal Agency Will Not Cooperate.
Where a federal agency will not cooperate in the preparation of joint document and will require separate NEPA compliance for the project at a later time, the state or local agency should persist in efforts to cooperate with the federal agency. Because NEPA expressly allows federal agencies to use environmental documents prepared by an agency of statewide jurisdiction, a local agency should try to involve a state agency in helping prepare an EIR or negative declaration for the project. In this way there will be a greater chance that the federal agency may later use the CEQA document and not require the applicant to pay for preparation of a second document to meet NEPA requirements at a later time.

Note: Authority cited: Section 21083, Public Resources Code. Reference: Section 21083.5, Public Resources Code; Section 102(2)(D) of NEPA, 42 U.S.C.A. 4322(2)(D).

§ 15229. Baseline Analysis for Military Base Reuse Plan EIRs.
When preparing and certifying an EIR for a plan for the reuse of a military base, including when utilizing an Environmental Impact Statement pursuant to Section 21083.5 of the Public Resources Code, the determination of whether the reuse plan may have a significant effect on the environment may, at the discretion of the lead agency, be based upon the physical conditions which were present at the time that the federal decision for the closure or realignment of the base or reservation became final. These conditions shall be referred to as the "baseline physical conditions." Impacts which do not exceed the baseline physical conditions shall not be considered significant.

(a) Prior to circulating a draft EIR pursuant to the provisions of this Section, the lead agency shall do all of the following, in order:

   (1) Prepare proposed baseline physical conditions, identify pertinent responsible and trustee agencies and consult with those agencies prior to the public hearing required by subdivision (a)(2) as to the application of their regulatory authority and permitting standards to the proposed baseline physical conditions, the proposed reuse plan, and specific, planned future nonmilitary land uses of the base or reservation. The affected agencies shall have not less than 30 days prior to the public hearing to review the proposed baseline physical conditions and the proposed reuse plan and to submit their comments to the lead agency.

   (2) Hold a public hearing at which is discussed the federal EIS prepared for, or being prepared for, the closure or realignment of the military base or reservation. The discussion shall include the significant effects on the environment, if any, examined in the EIS, potential methods of mitigating those effects, including feasible alternatives, and the mitigative effects of federal, state, and local laws applicable to future nonmilitary activities. Prior to the close of the hearing, the lead agency shall specify whether it will adopt any of the baseline physical conditions for the reuse plan EIR and identify those conditions. The lead agency shall specify particular baseline physical conditions, if any, which it will examine in greater detail than they were examined in the EIS. Notice of the hearing shall be given pursuant to Section 15087. The hearing may be continued from time to time.

   (3) Prior to the close of the hearing, the lead agency shall do all of the following:

      (A) Specify the baseline physical conditions which it intends to adopt for the reuse plan EIR, and specify particular physical conditions, if any, which it will examine in greater detail than were examined in the EIS.

      (B) State specifically how it intends to integrate its discussion of the baseline physical conditions in the EIR with the reuse planning process, taking into account the adopted environmental standards of the community, including but not limited to, the adopted general plan, specific plan or redevelopment plan, and including other applicable provisions of adopted congestion management plans, habitat conservation or natural communities conservation plans, air quality management plans, integrated waste management plans, and county hazardous waste management plans.

      (C) State the specific economic or social reasons, including but not limited to, new job creation, opportunities for employment of skilled workers, availability of low and moderate-income housing, and economic continuity which support selection of the baseline physical conditions.

(b) An EIR prepared under this section should identify any adopted baseline physical conditions in the environmental setting section. The baseline physical conditions should be cited in discussions of effects. The no-project alternative analyzed in an EIR prepared under this section shall discuss the conditions on the base as they exist at the time of preparation, as well as what could be reasonably expected to occur in the foreseeable future if the reuse plan were not approved, based on current plans and consistent with available infrastructure and services.

(c) All public and private activities taken pursuant to or in furtherance of a reuse plan for which an EIR was prepared and certified pursuant to this section shall be deemed to be a single project. A subsequent or supplemental EIR shall be required only if the lead agency determines that any of the circumstances described in Section 15162 or 15163 exist.

(d) Limitations:

 (1) Nothing in this section shall in any way limit the scope of review or determination of significance of the presence of hazardous or toxic wastes, substances, and materials, including but not limited to, contaminated soils and groundwater. The regulation of hazardous or toxic wastes, substances, and materials shall not be constrained by this section.

 (2) This section does not apply to hazardous waste regulation and remediation projects undertaken pursuant to Chapter 6.5 (commencing with Section 25100) or Chapter 6.8 (commencing with Section 25300) of Division 20 of the Health and Safety Code or pursuant to the Porter-Cologne Water Quality Control Act (Water Code Section 13000, et seq.)

 (3) All subsequent development at the military base or reservation shall be subject to all applicable federal, state, or local laws, including but not limited to, those relating to air quality, water quality, traffic, threatened and endangered species, noise, and hazardous or toxic wastes, substances, or materials.

(e) "Reuse plan" means the initial plan for the reuse of military base adopted by a local government, including a redevelopment agency or joint powers authority, in the form of a general plan, general plan amendment, specific plan, redevelopment plan, or other planning document. For purposes of this section, a reuse plan also shall include a statement of development policies, a diagram or diagrams illustrating its provisions, including a designation of the proposed general distribution, location, and development intensity for housing, business, industry, open space, recreation, natural resources, public buildings and grounds, roads, and other transportation facilities, infrastructure, and other categories of proposed uses, whether public or private.

(f) This section may be applied to any reuse plan EIR for which a notice of preparation is issued within one year from the date that the federal record of decision was rendered for the military base or reservation closure or realignment and reuse, or prior to January 1, 1997, whichever is later, but only if the EIR is completed and certified within five years from the date that the federal record of decision was rendered.

Note: Authority cited: Section 21083, Public Resources Code. Reference: Section 21083.8.1, Public Resources Code.

Article 15. Litigation

§ 15230. Time Limits and Criteria.

Litigation under CEQA must be handled under the time limits and criteria described in Sections 21167 et seq. of the Public Resources Code and Section 15112 of these guidelines in addition to provisions in this article.

Note: Authority cited: Section 21083, Public Resources Code. Reference: Sections 21167 et seq., Public Resources Code.

§ 15231. Adequacy of EIR or Negative Declaration for Use by Lead and Responsible Agencies.

A final EIR prepared by a lead agency or a negative declaration adopted by a lead agency shall be conclusively presumed to comply with CEQA for purposes of use by responsible agencies which were consulted pursuant to Sections 15072 or 15082 unless one of the following conditions occurs:

(a) The EIR or negative declaration is finally adjudged in a legal proceeding not to comply with the requirements of CEQA, or

(b) A subsequent EIR is made necessary by Section 15162 of these guidelines.

Note: Authority cited: Section 21083, Public Resources Code. Reference: Sections 21080.1, 21166, 21167.2 and 21167.3, Public Resources Code.

§ 15232. Request for Hearing.

In a writ of mandate proceeding challenging approval of a project under CEQA, the petitioner shall, within 90 days of filing the petition, request a hearing or otherwise be subject to dismissal on the court's own motion or on the motion of any party to the suit.

Note: Authority cited: Section 21083, Public Resources Code. Reference: Section 21167.4, Public Resources Code.

§ 15233. Conditional Permits.

If a lawsuit is filed challenging an EIR or negative declaration for noncompliance with CEQA, responsible agencies shall act as if the EIR or negative declaration complies with CEQA and continue to process the application for the project according to the time limits for responsible agency action contained in Government Code Section 65952.

(a) If an injunction or a stay has been granted in the lawsuit prohibiting the project from being carried out, the responsible agency shall have authority only to disapprove the project or to grant a conditional approval of the project. A conditional approval shall constitute permission to proceed with a project only when the court action results in a final determination that the EIR or negative declaration does comply with the provisions of CEQA (Public Resources Code Section 21167.3a).(b) If no injunction or stay is granted in the lawsuit, the responsible agency shall assume that the EIR or negative declaration fully meets the requirements of CEQA. The responsible agency shall approve or disapprove the project within the time limits described in Article 8, commencing with Section 15100, of these guidelines and described in Government Code Section 65952. An approval granted by a responsible agency in this situation provides only permission to proceed with the project at the applicant's risk prior to a final decision in the lawsuit (Public Resources Code Section 21167.3b).

Note: Authority cited: Section 21083, Public Resources Code. Reference: Section 21167.3, Public Resources Code; *Kriebel v. City Council* (1980) 112 Cal. App. 3d 693.

Article 16. EIR Monitor

§ 15240. EIR Monitor.

The Secretary for Resources may provide for publication of a bulletin entitled "California EIR Monitor" on a subscription basis to provide public notice of amendments to the guidelines, the completion of draft EIRs, and other matters as deemed appropriate. Inquiries and subscription requests should be sent to the following address:Secretary for Resources Attention: California EIR Monitor 1416 Ninth Street, Room 1311 Sacramento, California 95814

Note: Authority cited: Section 21083, Public Resources Code. Reference: Section 21088, Public Resources Code.

Article 17. Exemption for Certified State Regulatory Programs

§ 15250. General.

Section 21080.5 of the Public Resources Code provides that a regulatory program of a state agency shall be certified by the Secretary for Resources as being exempt from the requirements for preparing EIRs, negative declarations, and initial studies if the Secretary finds that the program meets the criteria contained in that code section. A certified program remains subject to other provisions in CEQA such as the policy of avoiding significant adverse effects on the environment where feasible. This article provides information concerning certified programs.

Note: Authority cited: Section 21083, Public Resources Code. Reference: Section 21080.5, Public Resources Code.

§ 15251. List of Certified Programs.

The following programs of state regulatory agencies have been certified by the Secretary for Resources as meeting the requirements of Section 21080.5:

(a) The regulation of timber harvesting operations by the California Department of Forestry and the State Board of Forestry pursuant to Chapter 8, commencing with Section 4511 of Part 2 of Division 4 of the Public Resources Code.

(b) The regulatory program of the Fish and Game Commission pursuant to the Fish and Game Code.
(c) The regulatory program of the California Coastal Commission and the regional coastal commissions dealing with the consideration and granting of coastal development permits under the California Coastal Act of 1976, Division 20 (commencing with Section 30000) of the Public Resources Code.
(d) That portion of the regulatory program of the Air Resources Board which involves the adoption, approval, amendment, or repeal of standards, rules, regulations, or plans to be used in the regulatory program for the protection and enhancement of ambient air quality in California.
(e) The regulatory program of the State Board of Forestry in adopting, amending, or repealing standards, rules, regulations, or plans under the Z'berg-Nejedly Forest Practice Act, Chapter 8 (commencing with Section 4511) of Part 2 of Division 4 of the Public Resources Code.
(f) The program of the California Coastal Commission involving the preparation, approval, and certification of local coastal programs as provided in Sections 30500 through 30522 of the Public Resources Code.
(g) The Water Quality Control (Basin)/208 Planning Program of the State Water Resources Control Board and the Regional Water Quality Control Boards.
(h) The permit and planning programs of the San Francisco Bay Conservation and Development Commission under the McAteer-Petris Act, Title 7.2 (commencing with Section 66600) of the Government Code; and the planning program of the San Francisco Bay Conservation and Development Commission under the Suisun Marsh Preservation Act, Division 19 (commencing with Section 29000) of the Public Resources Code.
(i) The pesticide regulatory program administered by the Department of Pesticide Regulation and the county agricultural commissioners insofar as the program consists of:
   (1) The registration, evaluation, and classification of pesticides.
   (2) The adoption, amendment, or repeal of regulations and standards for the licensing and regulation of pesticide dealers and pest control operators and advisors.
   (3) The adoption, amendment, or repeal of regulations for standards dealing with the monitoring of pesticides and of the human health and environmental effects of pesticides.
   (4) The regulation of the use of pesticides in agricultural and urban areas of the state through the permit system administered by the county agricultural commissioners.
(j) The power plant site certification program of the State Energy Resources Conservation and Development Commission under Chapter 6 of the Warren-Alquist Act, commencing with Public Resources Code Section 25500.
(k) The regulatory program of the State Water Resources Control Board to establish instream beneficial use protection programs.
(l) That portion of the regulatory program of the South Coast Air Quality Management District which involves the adoption, amendment, and repeal of regulations pursuant to the provisions of the Health and Safety Code.
(m) The program of the Delta Protection Commission involving the preparation and adoption of a Resource Management Plan for the Sacramento-San Joaquin Delta (Pub. Resources Code § 29760 ff.), and the Commission's review and action on general plan amendments proposed by local governments to make their plans consistent with the provisions of the Commission's Resource Management Plan (Pub. Resources Code § 29763.5).
(n) The program of the Department of Fish and Game for the adoption of regulations under the Fish and Game Code.
(o) The program of the Department of Fish and Game implementing the incidental take permit application process under the California Endangered Species Act ("CESA"), Fish and Game Code sections 2080 and 2081, and specifically the regulation governing the Department of Fish and Game's role as a "lead agency" when issuing incidental take permits, found at California Code of Regulations, Title 14, section 783.5(d).
(p) The regulatory program of the Department of Fish and Game for review and approval of voluntary local programs for routine and ongoing agricultural activities, as authorized by the California Endangered Species Act, Fish and Game Code section 2086.

Note: Authority cited: Sections 21083 and 21080.5, Public Resources Code. Reference: Section 21080.5, Public Resources Code.

§ 15252. Substitute Document.

(a) The document used as a substitute for an EIR or negative declaration in a certified program shall include at least the following items:
   (1) A description of the proposed activity, and
   (2) Either:
      (A) Alternatives to the activity and mitigation measures to avoid or reduce any significant or potentially significant effects that the project might have on the environment, or
      (B) A statement that the agency's review of the project showed that the project would not have any significant or potentially significant effects on the environment and therefore no alternatives or mitigation measures are proposed to avoid or reduce any significant effects on the environment. This statement shall be supported by a checklist or other documentation to show the possible effects that the agency examined in reaching this conclusion.
(b) The notice of the decision on the proposed activity shall be filed with the Secretary for Resources.

Note: Authority cited: Section 21083, Public Resources Code. Reference: Section 21080.5, Public Resources Code.

§ 15253. Use of an EIR Substitute by a Responsible Agency.

(a) An environmental analysis document prepared for a project under a certified program listed in Section 15251 shall be used by another agency granting an approval for the same project where the conditions in subdivision (b) have been met. In this situation, the certified agency shall act as lead agency, and the other permitting agencies shall act as responsible agencies using the certified agency's document.
(b) The conditions under which a public agency shall act as a responsible agency when approving a project using an environmental analysis document prepared under a certified program in the place of an EIR or negative declaration are as follows:
   (1) The certified agency is the first agency to grant a discretionary approval for the project.
   (2) The certified agency consults with the responsible agencies, but the consultation need not include the exchange of written notices.
   (3) The environmental analysis document identifies:
      (A) The significant environmental effects within the jurisdiction or special expertise of the responsible agency.
      (B) Alternatives or mitigation measures that could avoid or reduce the severity of the significant environmental effects.
   (4) Where written notices were not exchanged in the consultation process, the responsible agency was afforded the opportunity to participate in the review of the property by the certified agency in a regular manner designed to inform the certified agency of the concerns of the responsible agency before release of the EIR substitute for public review.
   (5) The certified agency established a consultation period between the certified agency and the responsible agency that was at least as long as the period allowed for public review of the EIR substitute document.
   (6) The certified agency exercised the powers of a lead agency by considering all the significant environmental effects of the project and making a finding under Section 15091 for each significant effect.
(c) Certified agencies are not required to adjust their activities to meet the criteria in subdivision (b). Where a certified agency does not meet the criteria in subdivision (b):
   (1) The substitute document prepared by the agency shall not be used by other permitting agencies in the place of an EIR or negative declaration, and
   (2) Any other agencies granting approvals for the project shall comply with CEQA in the normal manner. A permitting agency shall act as a lead agency and prepare an EIR or a negative declaration. Other permitting agencies, if any, shall act as responsible agencies and use the EIR or negative declaration prepared by the lead agency.

Note: Authority cited: Section 21083, Public Resources Code. Reference: Sections 21002.1(d), 21080.5 and 21165, Public Resources Code.

Article 18. Statutory Exemptions.

§ 15260. General.

This article describes the exemptions from CEQA granted by the Legislature. The exemptions take several forms. Some exemptions are complete exemptions from CEQA. Other exemptions apply to only part of the requirements of CEQA, and still other exemptions apply only to the timing of CEQA compliance.

Note: Authority cited: Section 21083, Public Resources Code. Reference: Section 21080(b), Public Resources Code.

§ 15261. Ongoing Project.

(a) If a project being carried out by a public agency was approved prior to November 23, 1970, the project shall be exempt from CEQA unless either of the following conditions exists:

  (1) A substantial portion of public funds allocated for the project have not been spent, and it is still feasible to modify the project to mitigate potentially adverse environmental effects, or to choose feasible alternatives to the project, including the alternative of "no project" or halting the project; provided that a project subject to the National Environmental Policy Act (NEPA) shall be exempt from CEQA as an on-going project if, under regulations promulgated under NEPA, the project would be too far advanced as of January 1, 1970, to require preparation of an EIS.

  (2) A public agency proposes to modify the project in such a way that the project might have a new significant effect on the environment.

(b) A private project shall be exempt from CEQA if the project received approval of a lease, license, certificate, permit, or other entitlement for use from a public agency prior to April 5, 1973, subject to the following provisions:

  (1) CEQA does not prohibit a public agency from considering environmental factors in connection with the approval or disapproval of a project, or from imposing reasonable fees on the appropriate private person or entity for preparing an environmental report under authority other than CEQA. Local agencies may require environmental reports for projects covered by this paragraph pursuant to local ordinances during this interim period.

  (2) Where a project was approved prior to December 5, 1972, and prior to that date the project was legally challenged for noncompliance with CEQA, the project shall be bound by special rules set forth in Section 21170 of CEQA.

  (3) Where a private project has been granted a discretionary governmental approval for part of the project before April 5, 1973, and another or additional discretionary governmental approvals after April 5, 1973, the project shall be subject to CEQA only if the approval or approvals after April 5, 1973, involve a greater degree of responsibility or control over the project as a whole than did the approval or approvals prior to that date.

Note: Authority cited: Section 21083, Public Resources Code. Reference: Sections 21169, 21170 and 21171, Public Resources Code; *County of Inyo v. Yorty*, 32 Cal. App. 3d 795.

§ 15262. Feasibility and Planning Studies.

A project involving only feasibility or planning studies for possible future actions which the agency, board, or commission has not approved, adopted, or funded does not require the preparation of an EIR or negative declaration but does require consideration of environmental factors. This section does not apply to the adoption of a plan that will have a legally binding effect on later activities.

Note: Authority cited: Section 21083, Public Resources Code. Reference: Sections 21102 and 21150, Public Resources Code.

§ 15263. Discharge Requirements.

The State Water Resources Control Board and the regional boards are exempt from the requirement to prepare an EIR or a negative declaration prior to the adoption of waste discharge requirements, except requirements for new sources as defined in the Federal Water Pollution Control Act or in other acts which amend or supplement the Federal Water Pollution Control Act. The term "waste discharge requirements" as used in this section is the equivalent of the term "permits" as used in the Federal Water Pollution Control Act.

Note: Authority cited: Section 21083, Public Resources Code. Reference: Section 13389, Water Code.

§ 15264. Timberland Preserves.

Local agencies are exempt from the requirement to prepare an EIR or negative declaration on the adoption of timberland preserve zones under Government Code Sections 51100 et seq. (Gov. Code, Sec. 51119).

Note: Authority cited: Section 21083, Public Resources Code. Reference: Section 51119, Government Code.

§ 15265. Adoption of Coastal Plans and Programs.

(a) CEQA does not apply to activities and approvals pursuant to the California Coastal Act (commencing with Section 30000 of the Public Resources Code) by:

  (1) Any local government, as defined in Section 30109 of the Public Resources Code, necessary for the preparation and adoption of a local coastal program, or

  (2) Any state university or college, as defined in Section 30119, as necessary for the preparation and adoption of a long-range land use development plan.

(b) CEQA shall apply to the certification of a local coastal program or long-range land use development plan by the California Coastal Commission.(c) This section shifts the burden of CEQA compliance from the local agency or the state university or college to the California Coastal Commission. The Coastal Commission's program of certifying local coastal programs and long-range land use development plans has been certified under Section 21080.5, Public Resources Code. See Section 15192.

Note: Authority cited: Section 21083, Public Resources Code. Reference: Section 21080.9, Public Resources Code.

§ 15266. General Plan Time Extension.

CEQA shall not apply to the granting of an extension of time by the Office of Planning and Research to a city or county for the preparation and adoption of one or more elements of a city or county general plan.

Note: Authority cited: Section 21083, Public Resources Code. Reference: Section 21080.10(a), Public Resources Code.

§ 15267. Financial Assistance to Low or Moderate Income Housing.

CEQA does not apply to actions taken by the Department of Housing and Community Development to provide financial assistance for the development and construction of residential housing for persons and families of low or moderate income, as defined in Section 50093 of the Health and Safety Code. The residential project which is the subject of the application for financial assistance will be subject to CEQA when approvals are granted by another agency.

Note: Authority cited: Section 21083, Public Resources Code. Reference: Section 21080.10(b), Public Resources Code.

§ 15268. Ministerial Projects.

(a) Ministerial projects are exempt from the requirements of CEQA. The determination of what is "ministerial" can most appropriately be made by the particular public agency involved based upon its analysis of its own laws, and each public agency should make such determination either as a part of its implementing regulations or on a case-by-case basis.

(b) In the absence of any discretionary provision contained in the local ordinance or other law establishing the requirements for the permit, license, or other entitlement for use, the following actions shall be presumed to be ministerial:

  (1) Issuance of building permits.

  (2) Issuance of business licenses.

  (3) Approval of final subdivision maps.

  (4) Approval of individual utility service connections and disconnections.

(c) Each public agency should, in its implementing regulations or ordinances, provide an identification or itemization of its projects and actions which are deemed ministerial under the applicable laws and ordinances.

(d) Where a project involves an approval that contains elements of both a ministerial action and a discretionary action, the project will be deemed to be discretionary and will be subject to the requirements of CEQA.

Note: Authority cited: Section 21083, Public Resources Code. Reference: Section 21080(b)(1), Public Resources Code; *Day v. City of Glendale*, 51 Cal. App. 3d 817.

§ 15269. Emergency Projects.

The following emergency projects are exempt from the requirements of CEQA.

(a) Projects to maintain, repair, restore, demolish, or replace property or facilities damaged or destroyed as a result of a disaster in a disaster stricken area in which a state of emergency has been proclaimed by the Governor pursuant to the California Emergency Services Act, commencing with Section 8550 of the Government Code. This includes projects that will remove, destroy, or significantly alter an historical resource when that resource represents an imminent threat to the public of bodily harm or of damage to adjacent property or when the project has received a determination by the State Office of Historic

Preservation pursuant to Section 5028(b) of Public Resources Code.

(b) Emergency repairs to publicly or privately owned service facilities necessary to maintain service essential to the public health, safety or welfare.

(c) Specific actions necessary to prevent or mitigate an emergency. This does not include long-term projects undertaken for the purpose of preventing or mitigating a situation that has a low probability of occurrence in the short-term.

(d) Projects undertaken, carried out, or approved by a public agency to maintain, repair, or restore an existing highway damaged by fire, flood, storm, earthquake, land subsidence, gradual earth movement, or landslide, provided that the project is within the existing right of way of that highway and is initiated within one year of the damage occurring. This exemption does not apply to highways designated as official state scenic highways, nor any project undertaken, carried out, or approved by a public agency to expand or widen a highway damaged by fire, flood, storm, earthquake, land subsidence, gradual earth movement, or landslide.

(e) Seismic work on highways and bridges pursuant to Section180.2 of the Streets and Highways Code, Section 180 et seq.

Note: Authority cited: Section 21083, Public Resources Code. Reference: Sections 21080(b)(2), (3), and (4), 21080.33 and 21172, Public Resources Code; *Castaic Lake Water Agency v. City of Santa Clarita* (1995) 41 Cal. App. 4th 1257; and *Western Municipal Water District of Riverside County v. Superior Court of San Bernardino County* (1987) 187 Cal. App. 3d 1104.

§ 15270. Projects Which Are Disapproved.

(a) CEQA does not apply to projects which a public agency rejects or disapproves.

(b) This section is intended to allow an initial screening of projects on the merits for quick disapprovals prior to the initiation f the CEQA process where the agency can determine that the project cannot be approved.

(c) This section shall not relieve an applicant from paying the costs for an EIR or negative declaration prepared for his project prior to the lead agency's disapproval of the project after normal evaluation and processing.

Note: Authority cited: Section 21083, Public Resources Code. Reference: Section 21080(b)(5), Public Resources Code.

§ 15271. Early Activities Related to Thermal Power Plants.

(a) CEQA does not apply to actions undertaken by a public agency relating to any thermal power plant site or facility, including the expenditure, obligation, or encumbrance of funds by a public agency for planning, engineering, or design purposes, or for the conditional sale or purchase of equipment, fuel, water (except groundwater), steam, or power for such a thermal power plant, if the thermal power plant site and related facility will be the subject of an EIR or negative declaration or other document or documents prepared pursuant to a regulatory program certified pursuant to Public Resources Code Section 21080.5, which will be prepared by:
   (1) The State Energy Resources Conservation and Development Commission,
   (2) The Public Utilities Commission, or
   (3) The city or county in which the power plant and related facility would be located.

(b) The EIR, negative declaration, or other document prepared for the thermal power plant site or facility, shall include the environmental impact, if any, of the early activities described in this section.

(c) This section acts to delay the timing of CEQA compliance from the early activities of a utility to the time when a regulatory agency is requested to approve the thermal power plant and shifts the responsibility for preparing the document to the regulatory agency.

Note: Authority cited: Section 21083, Public Resources Code. Reference: Section 15080(b)(6), Public Resources Code.

§ 15272. Olympic Games.

CEQA does not apply to activities or approvals necessary to the bidding for, hosting or staging of, and funding or carrying out of, Olympic Games under the authority of the International Olympic Committee, except for the construction of facilities necessary for such Olympic Games. If the facilities are required by the International Olympic Committee as a condition of being awarded the Olympic Games, the lead agency need not discuss the "no project" alternative in an EIR with respect to those facilities.

Note: Authority cited: Section 21083, Public Resources Code. Reference: Section 21080(b)(7), Public Resources Code.

§ 15273. Rates, Tolls, Fares, and Charges.

(a) CEQA does not apply to the establishment, modification, structuring, restructuring, or approval of rates, tolls, fares, and other charges by public agencies which the public agency finds are for the purpose of:
   (1) Meeting operating expenses, including employee wage rates and fringe benefits,
   (2) Purchasing or leasing supplies, equipment, or materials,
   (3) Meeting financial reserve needs and requirements,
   (4) Obtaining funds for capital projects, necessary to maintain service within existing service areas, or
   (5) Obtaining funds necessary to maintain such intra-city transfers as are authorized by city charter.

(b) Rate increases to fund capital projects for the expansion of a system remain subject to CEQA. The agency granting the rate increase shall act either as the lead agency if no other agency has prepared environmental documents for the capital project or as a responsible agency if another agency has already complied with CEQA as the lead agency.

(c) The public agency shall incorporate written findings in the record of any proceeding in which an exemption under this section is claimed setting forth with specificity the basis for the claim of exemption.

Note: Authority cited: Section 21083, Public Resources Code. Reference: Section 21080(b)(8), Public Resources Code.

§ 15274. Family Day Care Homes.

(a) CEQA does not apply to establishment or operation of a large family day care home, which provides in-home care for up to fourteen children, as defined in Section 1596.78 of the Health and Safety Code.

(b) Under the Health and Safety Code, local agencies cannot require use permits for the establishment or operation of a small family day care home, which provides in-home care for up to eight children, and the establishment or operation of a small family day care home is a ministerial action which is not subject to CEQA.

Note: Authority cited: Section 21083, Public Resources Code. Reference: Section 21083, Public Resources Code.

§ 15275. Specified Mass Transit Projects.

CEQA does not apply to the following mass transit projects:

(a) The institution or increase of passenger or commuter service on rail lines or high-occupancy vehicle lanes already in use, including the modernization of existing stations and parking facilities;

(b) Facility extensions not to exceed four miles in length which are required for transfer of passengers from or to exclusive public mass transit guideway or busway public transit services.

Note: Authority cited: Section 21083, Public Resources Code. Reference: Section 21080(b)(11), (12), and (13), Public Resources Code.

§ 15276. Transportation Improvement and Congestion Management Programs.

(a) CEQA does not apply to the development or adoption of a regional transportation improvement program or the state transportation improvement program. Individual projects developed pursuant to these programs shall remain subject to CEQA.

(b) CEQA does not apply to preparation and adoption of a congestion management program by a county congestion management agency pursuant to Government Code Section 65089, et seq.

Note: Authority cited: Section 21083, Public Resources Code. Reference: Section 21080(b)(13), Public Resources Code.

§ 15277. Projects Located Outside California.

CEQA does not apply to any project or portion thereof located outside of California which will be subject to environmental impact review pursuant to the National Environmental Policy Act of 1969 or pursuant to a law of that state requiring preparation of a document containing essentially the same points of analysis as in an environmental impact statement prepared under the National Environmental Policy Act of 1969. Any emissions or discharges that would have a significant effect on the environment in the State of California are subject to CEQA where a California public agency has authority over the emissions or discharges.

Note: Authority cited: Section 21083, Public Resources Code. Reference: Section 21080(b)(15), Public Resources Code; 58 Opinions of the California Attorney General 614 (S.O. 75/50).

§ 15278. Application of Coatings.

(a) CEQA does not apply to a discretionary decision by an air quality management district for a project consisting of the application of coatings within an existing facility at an automotive manufacturing plant if the district finds all of the following:
  (1) The project will not cause a net increase in any emissions of any pollutant for which a national or state ambient air quality standard has been established after the internal emission accounting for previous emission reductions achieved at the facility and recognized by the district.
  (2) The project will not cause a net increase in adverse impacts of toxic air contaminants as determined by a health risk assessment. The term "net increase in adverse impacts of toxic air contaminants as determined by a health risk assessment" shall be determined in accordance with the rules and regulations of the district.
  (3) The project will not cause any other adverse effect on the environment.

(b) The district shall provide a 10-day notice, at the time of the issuance of the permit, of any such exemption. Notice shall be published in two newspapers of general circulation in the area of the project and shall be mailed to any person who makes a written request for such a notice. The notice shall state that the complete file on the project and the basis for the district's findings of exemption are available for inspection and copying at the office of the district.

(c) Any person may appeal the issuance of a permit based on an exemption under subdivision (a) to the hearing board as provided in Section 42302.1 of the Health and Safety Code. The permit shall be revoked by the hearing board if there is substantial evidence in light of the whole record before the board that the project may not satisfy one or more of the criteria established pursuant to subdivision (a). If there is no such substantial evidence, the exemption shall be upheld. Any appeal under this subdivision shall be scheduled for hearing on the calendar of the hearing board within 10 working days of the appeal being filed. The hearing board shall give the appeal priority on its calendar and shall render a decision on the appeal within 21 working days of the appeal being filed. The hearing board may delegate the authority to hear and decide such an appeal to a subcommittee of its body.

Note: Authority cited: Section 21083, Public Resources Code. Reference: Chapter 1131, Statutes of 1993, Section 1.

§ 15279. Housing for Agricultural Employees.

Note: Authority cited: Sections 21083 and 21087, Public Resources Code. Reference: Section 21080.10, Public Resources Code.

§ 15280. Lower-Income Housing Projects.

Note: Authority cited: Sections 21083 and 21087, Public Resources Code. Reference: Section 21080.14, Public Resources Code.

§ 15281. Air Quality Permits.

CEQA does not apply to the issuance, modification, amendment, or renewal of any permit by an air pollution control district or air quality management district pursuant to Title V, as defined in Section 39053.3 of the Health and Safety Code, or pursuant to an air district Title V program established under Sections 42301.10, 42301.11, and 42301.12 of the Health and Safety Code, unless the issuance, modification, amendment, or renewal authorizes a physical or operational change to a source or facility.

Note: Authority cited: Section 21083, Public Resources Code. Reference: Section 21080.24, Public Resources Code.

§ 15282. Other Statutory Exemptions.

The following is a list of existing statutory exemptions. Each subdivision summarizes statutory exemptions found in the California Code. Lead agencies are not to rely on the language contained in the summaries below but must rely on the actual statutory language that creates the exemption. This list is intended to assist lead agencies in finding them, but not as a substitute for them. This section is merely a reference tool.

(a) The notification of discovery of Native American burial sites as set forth in Section 5097.98(c) of the Public Resources Code.
(b) Specified prison facilities as set forth in Sections 21080.01, 21080.02, 21080.03 and 21080.07 of the Public Resources Code.
(c) The lease or purchase of the rail right-of-way used for the San Francisco Peninsula commute service between San Francisco and San Jose as set forth in Section 21080.05 of the Public Resources Code.
(d) Any activity or approval necessary for or incidental to project funding or authorization for the expenditure of funds for the project, by the Rural Economic Development Infrastructure Panel as set forth in Section 21080.08 of the Public Resources Code.
(e) The conversion of an existing rental mobilehome park to a resident initiated subdivision, cooperative, or condominium for mobilehomes as set forth in Section 21080.8 of the Public Resources Code.
(f) Settlements of title and boundary problems by the State Lands Commission and to exchanges or leases in connection with those settlements as set forth in Section 21080.11 of the Public Resources Code.
(g) Any railroad grade separation project which eliminates an existing grade crossing or which reconstructs an existing grade separation as set forth in Section 21080.13 of the Public Resources Code.
(h) The adoption of an ordinance regarding second units in a single-family or multifamily residential zone by a city or county to implement the provisions of Sections 65852.1 and 65852.2 of the Government Code as set forth in Section 21080.17 of the Public Resources Code.
(i) The closing of any public school or the transfer of students from that public school to another school in which kindergarten or any grades 1 through 12 is maintained as set forth in 21080.18 of the Public Resources Code.
(j) A project for restriping streets or highways to relieve traffic congestion as set forth in Section 21080.19 of the Public Resources Code.
(k) The installation of new pipeline or maintenance, repair, restoration, removal, or demolition of an existing pipeline as set forth in Section 21080.21 of the Public Resources Code, as long as the project does not exceed one mile in length.
(l) The activities and approvals by a local government necessary for the preparation of general plan amendments pursuant to Public Resources Code § 29763 as set forth in Section 21080.22 of the Public Resources Code. Section 29763 of the Public Resources Code refers to local government amendments made for consistency with the Delta Protection Commission's regional plan.
(m) Minor alterations to utilities made for the purposes of complying with Sections 116410 and 116415 of the Health and Safety Code as set forth in Section 21080.26 of the Public Resources Code.
(n) The adoption of an ordinance exempting a city or county from the provisions of the Solar Shade Control Act as set forth in Section 25985 of the Public Resources Code.
(o) The acquisition of land by the Department of Transportation if received or acquired within a statewide or regional priority corridor designated pursuant to Section 65081.3 of the Government Code as set forth in Section 33911 of the Public Resources Code.
(p) The adoption or amendment of a nondisposal facility element as set forth in Section 41735 of the Public Resources Code.
(q) Cooperative agreements for the development of Solid Waste Management Facilities on Indian country as set forth in Section 44203(g) of the Public Resources Code.
(r) Determinations made regarding a city or county's regional housing needs as set forth in Section 65584 of the Government Code.
(s) Any action necessary to bring a general plan or relevant mandatory element of the general plan into compliance pursuant to a court order as set forth in Section 65759 of the Government Code.
(t) Industrial Development Authority activities as set forth in Section 91543 of the Government Code.
(u) Temporary changes in the point of diversion, place of use, of purpose of use due to a transfer or exchange of water or water rights as set forth in Section 1729 of the Water Code.
(v) The preparation and adoption of Urban Water Management Plans pursuant to the provisions of Section 10652 of the Water Code.

Note: Authority cited: Section 21083, Public Resources Code. Reference: Sections 5097.98(c), 21080.01, 21080.02, 21080.03, 21080.05, 21080.07, 21080.08, 21080.8, 21080.11, 21080.13, 21080.17, 21080.18, 21080.19, 21080.21, 21080.22, 21080.26, 25985, 33911, 41735 and 44203(g), Public Resources Code.

§ 15283. Housing Needs Allocation.

CEQA does not apply to regional housing needs determinations made by the Department of Housing and

Community Development, a council of governments, or a city or county pursuant to Section 65584 of the Government Code.

Note: Authority cited: Section 21083, Public Resources Code. Reference: Section 65584, Government Code.

§ 15284. Pipelines.

(a) CEQA does not apply to any project consisting of the inspection, maintenance, repair, restoration, reconditioning, relocation, replacement, or removal of an existing hazardous or volatile liquid pipeline or any valve, flange, meter, or other piece of equipment that is directly attached to the pipeline.

(b) To qualify for this exemption, the diameter of the affected pipeline must not be increased and the project must be located outside the boundaries of an oil refinery. The project must also meet all of the following criteria:

(1) The affected section of pipeline is less than eight miles in length and actual construction and excavation activities are not undertaken over a length of more than one-half mile at a time.

(2) The affected section of pipeline is not less than eight miles distance from any section of pipeline that had been subject to this exemption in the previous 12 months.

(3) The project is not solely for the purpose of excavating soil that is contaminated by hazardous materials.

(4) To the extent not otherwise required by law, the person undertaking the project has, in advance of undertaking the project, prepared a plan that will result in notification of the appropriate agencies so that they may take action, if necessary, to provide for the emergency evacuation of members of the public who may be located in close proximity to the project, and those agencies, including but not limited to the local fire department, police, sheriff, and California Highway Patrol as appropriate, have reviewed and agreed to that plan.

(5) Project activities take place within an existing right-of-way and that right-of-way will be restored to its pre-project condition upon completion of the project.

(6) The project applicant will comply with all conditions otherwise authorized by law, imposed by the city or county as part of any local agency permit process, and to comply with the Keene-Nejedly California Wetlands Preservation Act (Public Resources Code Section 5810, et seq.), the California Endangered Species Act (Fish and Game Code Section 2050, et seq.), other applicable state laws, and all applicable federal laws.

(c) When the lead agency determines that a project meets all of the criteria of subdivisions (a) and (b), the party undertaking the project shall do all of the following:

(1) Notify in writing all responsible and trustee agencies, as well as any public agency with environmental, public health protection, or emergency response authority, of the lead agency's invocation of this exemption.

(2) Mail notice of the project to the last known name and address of all organizations and individuals who have previously requested such notice and notify the public in the affected area by at least one of the following procedures:

(A) Publication at least one time in a newspaper of general circulation in the area affected by the proposed project. If more than one area is affected, the notice shall be published in the newspaper of largest circulation from among the newspapers of general circulation in those areas.

(B) Posting of notice on and off site in the area where the project is to be located.

(C) Direct mailing to the owners and occupants of contiguous property shown on the latest equalized assessment roll.

The notice shall include a brief description of the proposed project and its location, and the date, time, and place of any public meetings or hearings on the proposed project. This notice may be combined with the public notice required under other law, as applicable, but shall meet the preceding minimum requirements.

(3) In the case of private rights-of-way over private property, receive from the underlying property owner permission for access to the property.

(4) Immediately inform the lead agency if any soil contaminated with hazardous materials is discovered.

(5) Comply with all conditions otherwise authorized by law, imposed by the city or county as part of any local agency permit process, and to comply with the Keene-Nejedly California Wetlands Preservation Act (Public Resources Code Section 5810, et seq.), the California Endangered Species Act (Fish and Game Code Section 2050, et seq.), other applicable state laws, and all applicable federal laws.

(d) For purposes of this section, "pipeline" is used as defined in subdivision (a) of Government Code Section 51010.5. This definition includes every intrastate pipeline used for the transportation of hazardous liquid substances or highly volatile liquid substances, including a common carrier pipeline, and all piping containing those substances located within a refined products bulk loading facility which is owned by a common carrier and is served by a pipeline of that common carrier, and the common carrier owns and serves by pipeline at least five such facilities in California.

Note: Authority cited: Section 21083, Public Resources Code. Reference: Section 21080.23, Public Resources Code.

§ 15285. Transit Agency Responses to Revenue Shortfalls.

(a) CEQA does not apply to actions taken on or after July 1,1995 to implement budget reductions made by a publicly owned transit agency as a result of a fiscal emergency caused by the failure of agency revenues to adequately fund agency programs and facilities. Actions shall be limited to those directly undertaken by or financially supported in whole or in part by the transit agency pursuant to Section 15378(a)(1) or (2), including actions which reduce or eliminate the availability of an existing publicly owned transit service, facility, program, or activity.

(b) When invoking this exemption, the transit agency shall make a specific finding that there is a fiscal emergency. Before taking its proposed budgetary actions and making the finding of fiscal emergency, the transit agency shall hold a public hearing. After this public hearing, the transit agency shall respond within 30 days at a regular public meeting to suggestions made by the public at that initial hearing. The transit agency may make the finding of fiscal emergency only after it has responded to public suggestions.

(c) For purposes of this subdivision, "fiscal emergency" means that the transit agency is projected to have negative working capital within one year from the date that the agency finds that a fiscal emergency exists. "Working capital" is defined as the sum of all unrestricted cash, unrestricted short-term investments, and unrestricted short-term accounts receivable, minus unrestricted accounts payable. Employee retirements funds, including deferred compensation plans and Section 401(k) plans, health insurance reserves, bond payment reserves, worker's compensation reserves, and insurance reserves shall not be included as working capital.

(d) This exemption does not apply to the action of any publicly owned transit agency to reduce or eliminate a transit service, facility, program, or activity that was approved or adopted as a mitigation measure in any environmental document certified or adopted by any public agency under either CEQA or NEPA. Further, it does not apply to actions of the Los Angeles County Metropolitan Transportation Authority.

Note: Authority cited: Section 21083, Public Resources Code. Reference: Sections 21080 and 21080.32, Public Resources Code.

Article 19. Categorical Exemptions

§ 15300. Categorical Exemptions.

Section 21084 of the Public Resources Code requires these guidelines to include a list of classes of projects which have been determined not to have a significant effect on the environment and which shall, therefore, be exempt from the provisions of CEQA.In response to that mandate, the Secretary for Resources has found that the following classes of projects listed in this article do not have a significant effect on the environment, and they are declared to be categorically exempt from the requirement for the preparation of environmental documents.

Note: Authority cited: Section 21083, Public Resources Code. Reference: Section 21084, Public Resources Code.

§ 15300.1. Relation to Ministerial Projects.

Section 21080 of the Public Resources Code exempts from the application of CEQA those projects over which public agencies exercise only ministerial authority. Since ministerial projects are already exempt, Categorical Exemptions should be applied only where a project is not ministerial under a public agency's statutes and ordinances. The inclusion of activities which may be ministerial within the classes and examples contained in this article shall not be construed as a finding by the Secretary for resources that such an activity is discretionary.

Note: Authority cited: Section 21083, Public Resources Code. Reference: Section 21084, Public Resources Code.

§ 15300.2. Exceptions.

(a) Location. Classes 3, 4, 5, 6, and 11 are qualified by consideration of where the project is to be located - a project that is ordinarily insignificant in its impact on the environment may in a particularly sensitive environment be significant. Therefore, these classes are considered to apply in all instances, except where the project may impact on an environmental resource of hazardous or critical concern where designated, precisely mapped, and officially adopted pursuant to law by federal, state, or local agencies.

(b) Cumulative Impact. All exemptions for these classes are inapplicable when the cumulative impact of successive projects of the same type in the same place, over time is significant.

(c) Significant Effect. A categorical exemption shall not be used for an activity where there is a reasonable possibility that the activity will have a significant effect on the environment due to unusual circumstances.

(d) Scenic Highways. A categorical exemption shall not be used for a project which may result in damage to scenic resources, including but not limited to, trees, historic buildings, rock outcroppings, or similar resources, within a highway officially designated as a state scenic highway. This does not apply to improvements which are required as mitigation by an adopted negative declaration or certified EIR.

(e) Hazardous Waste Sites. A categorical exemption shall not be used for a project located on a site which is included on any list compiled pursuant to Section 65962.5 of the Government Code.

(f) Historical Resources. A categorical exemption shall not be used for a project which may cause a substantial adverse change in the significance of a historical resource.

Note: Authority cited: Section 21083, Public Resources Code. Reference: Sections 21084 and 21084.1, Public Resources Code; Wildlife Alive v. Chickering (1977) 18 Cal.3d190; *League for Protection of Oakland's Architectural and Historic Resources v. City of Oakland* (1997) 52 Cal .App. 4th 896; *Citizens for Responsible Development in West Hollywood v. City of West Hollywood* (1995) 39 Cal. App. 4th 925; *City of Pasadena v. State of California* (1993) 14 Cal. App. 4th 810; *Association for the Protection etc. Values v. City of Ukiah* (1991) 2 Cal. App. 4th 720; and *Baird v. County of Contra Costa* (1995) 32 Cal. App. 4th 1464.

§ 15300.3. Revisions to List of Categorical Exemptions.

Any public agency may, at any time, request that a new class of Categorical Exemptions be added, or an existing one amended or deleted. This request must be made in writing to the Office of Planning and Research and shall contain detailed information to support the request. The granting of such request shall be by amendment to these guidelines.

Note: Authority cited: Section 21083, Public Resources Code. Reference: Section 21084, Public Resources Code.

§ 15300.4. Application by Public Agencies.

Each public agency shall, in the course of establishing its own procedures, list those specific activities which fall within each of the exempt classes, subject to the qualification that these lists must be consistent with both the letter and the intent expressed in the classes. Public agencies may omit from their implementing procedures classes and examples that do not apply to their activities, but they may not require EIRs for projects described in the classes and examples in this article except under the provisions of Section 15300.2.

Note: Authority cited: Section 21083, Public Resources Code. Reference: Section 21084, Public Resources Code.

§ 15301. Existing Facilities.

Class 1 consists of the operation, repair, maintenance, permitting, leasing, licensing, or minor alteration of existing public or private structures, facilities, mechanical equipment, or topographical features, involving negligible or no expansion of use beyond that existing at the time of the lead agency's determination. The types of "existing facilities" itemized below are not intended to be all-inclusive of the types of projects which might fall within Class 1. The key consideration is whether the project involves negligible or no expansion of an existing use.Examples include but are not limited to:

(a) Interior or exterior alterations involving such things as interior partitions, plumbing, and electrical conveyances;

(b) Existing facilities of both investor and publicly-owned utilities used to provide electric power, natural gas, sewerage, or other public utility services;

(c) Existing highways and streets, sidewalks, gutters, bicycle and pedestrian trails, and similar facilities (this includes road grading for the purpose of public safety).

(d) Restoration or rehabilitation of deteriorated or damaged structures, facilities, or mechanical equipment to meet current standards of public health and safety, unless it is determined that the damage was substantial and resulted from an environmental hazard such as earthquake, landslide, or flood;

(e) Additions to existing structures provided that the addition will not result in an increase of more than:
  (1) 50 percent of the floor area of the structures before the addition, or 2,500 square feet, whichever is less; or
  (2) 10,000 square feet if:
    (A) The project is in an area where all public services and facilities are available to allow for maximum development permissible in the General Plan and
    (B) The area in which the project is located is not environmentally sensitive.

(f) Addition of safety or health protection devices for use during construction of or in conjunction with existing structures, facilities, or mechanical equipment, or topographical features including navigational devices;

(g) New copy on existing on and off-premise signs;

(h) Maintenance of existing landscaping, native growth, and water supply reservoirs (excluding the use of pesticides, as defined in Section 12753, Division 7, Chapter 2, Food and Agricultural Code);

(i) Maintenance of fish screens, fish ladders, wildlife habitat areas, artificial wildlife waterway devices, stream flows, springs and waterholes, and stream channels (clearing of debris) to protect fish and wildlife resources;

(j) Fish stocking by the California Department of Fish and Game;

(k) Division of existing multiple family or single-family residences into common-interest ownership and subdivision of existing commercial or industrial buildings, where no physical changes occur which are not otherwise exempt;

(l) Demolition and removal of individual small structures listed in this subdivision;
  (1) A duplex or similar multifamily residential structure. In urbanized areas, this exemption applies to duplexes and similar structures where not more than six dwelling units will be demolished.
  (2) A store, motel, office, restaurant, and similar small commercial structure if designed for an occupant load of 30 persons or less. In urbanized areas, the exemption also applies to the demolition of up to three such commercial buildings on sites zoned for such use.
  (3) Accessory (appurtenant) structures including garages, carports, patios, swimming pools, and fences.

(m) Minor repairs and alterations to existing dams and appurtenant structures under the supervision of the Department of Water Resources.

(n) Conversion of a single family residence to office use.

(o) Installation, in an existing facility occupied by a medical waste generator, of a steam sterilization unit for the treatment of medical waste generated by that facility provided that the unit is installed and operated in accordance with the Medical Waste Management Act (Section 117600, et seq., of the Health and Safety Code) and accepts no offsite waste.

(p) Use of a single-family residence as a small family day care home, as defined in Section 1596.78 of the Health and Safety Code.

Note: Authority cited: Section 21083, Public Resources Code. Reference: Section 21084, Public Resources Code; Bloom v. McGurk (1994) 26 Cal.App.4th 1307.

§ 15302. Replacement or Reconstruction.

Class 2 consists of replacement or reconstruction of existing structures and facilities where the new structure will be located on the same site as the structure replaced and will have substantially the same purpose and capacity as the structure replaced, including but not limited to:

(a) Replacement or reconstruction of existing schools and hospitals to provide earthquake resistant structures which do not increase capacity more than 50 percent;

(b) Replacement of a commercial structure with a new structure of substantially the same size, purpose, and capacity.

(c) Replacement or reconstruction of existing utility systems and/or facilities involving negligible or no expansion of capacity.

(d) Conversion of overhead electric utility distribution system facilities to underground including connection to existing overhead electric utility distribution lines where the surface is restored to the condition existing prior to the undergrounding.

Note: Authority cited: Section 21083, Public Resources Code. Reference: Section 21084, Public Resources Code.

§ 15303. New Construction or Conversion of Small Structures.

Class 3 consists of construction and location of limited numbers of new, small facilities or structures; installation of small new equipment and facilities in small structures; and the conversion of existing small structures from one use to another where only minor modifications are made in the exterior of the structure. The numbers of structures described in this section are the maximum allowable on any legal parcel. Examples of this exemption include but are not limited to:

(a) One single-family residence, or a second dwelling unit in a residential zone. In urbanized areas, up to three single-family residences may be constructed or converted under this exemption.
(b) A duplex or similar multi-family residential structure totaling no more than four dwelling units. In urbanized areas, this exemption applies to apartments, duplexes, and similar structures designed for not more than six dwelling units.
(c) A store, motel, office, restaurant or similar structure not involving the use of significant amounts of hazardous substances, and not exceeding 2500 square feet in floor area. In urbanized areas, the exemption also applies to up to four such commercial buildings not exceeding 10,000 square feet in floor area on sites zoned for such use if not involving the use of significant amounts of hazardous substances where all necessary public services and facilities are available and the surrounding area is not environmentally sensitive.
(d) Water main, sewage, electrical, gas, and other utility extensions, including street improvements, of reasonable length to serve such construction.
(e) Accessory (appurtenant) structures including garages, carports, patios, swimming pools, and fences.
(f) An accessory steam sterilization unit for the treatment of medical waste at a facility occupied by a medical waste generator, provided that the unit is installed and operated in accordance with the Medical Waste Management Act (Section 117600, et seq., of the Health and Safety Code) and accepts no offsite waste.

Note: Authority cited: Section 21083, Public Resources Code. Reference: Section 21084, Public Resources Code.

§ 15304. Minor Alterations to Land.

Class 4 consists of minor public or private alterations in the condition of land, water, and/or vegetation which do not involve removal of healthy, mature, scenic trees except for forestry and agricultural purposes. Examples include but are not limited to:

(a) Grading on land with a slope of less than 10 percent, except that grading shall not be exempt in a waterway, in any wetland, in an officially designated (by federal, state, or local government action) scenic area, or in officially mapped areas of severe geologic hazard such as an Alquist-Priolo Earthquake Fault Zone or within an official Seismic Hazard Zone, as delineated by the State Geologist.
(b) New gardening or landscaping, including the replacement of existing conventional landscaping with water efficient or fire resistant landscaping.
(c) Filling of earth into previously excavated land with material compatible with the natural features of the site.
(d) Minor alterations in land, water, and vegetation on existing officially designated wildlife management areas or fish production facilities which result in improvement of habitat for fish and wildlife resources or greater fish production.
(e) Minor temporary use of land having negligible or no permanent effects on the environment, including carnivals, sales of Christmas trees, etc.
(f) Minor trenching and backfilling where the surface is restored.
(g) Maintenance dredging where the spoil is deposited in a spoil area authorized by all applicable state and federal regulatory agencies.
(h) The creation of bicycle lanes on existing rights-of-way.
(i) Fuel management activities within 30 feet of structures to reduce the volume of flammable vegetation, provided that the activities will not result in the taking of endangered, rare, or threatened plant or animal species or significant erosion and sedimentation of surface waters.This exemption shall apply to fuel management activities within 100 feet of a structure if the public agency having fire protection responsibility for the area has determined that 100 feet of fuel clearance is required due to extra hazardous fire conditions.

Note: Authority cited: Section 21083, Public Resources Code. Reference: Section 21084, Public Resources Code.

§ 15305. Minor Alterations in Land Use Limitations.

Class 5 consists of minor alterations in land use limitations in areas with an average slope of less than 20%, which do not result in any changes in land use or density, including but not limited to:

(a) Minor lot line adjustments, side yard, and set back variances not resulting in the creation of any new parcel;
(b) Issuance of minor encroachment permits;
(c) Reversion to acreage in accordance with the Subdivision Map Act.

Note: Authority cited: Section 21083, Public Resources Code. Reference: Section 21084, Public Resources Code.

§ 15306. Information Collection.

Class 6 consists of basic data collection, research, experimental management, and resource evaluation activities which do not result in a serious or major disturbance to an environmental resource. These may be strictly for information gathering purposes, or as part of a study leading to an action which a public agency has not yet approved, adopted, or funded.

Note: Authority cited: Section 21083, Public Resources Code. Reference: Section 21084, Public Resources Code.

§ 15307. Actions by Regulatory Agencies for Protection of Natural Resources.

Class 7 consists of actions taken by regulatory agencies as authorized by state law or local ordinance to assure the maintenance, restoration, or enhancement of a natural resource where the regulatory process involves procedures for protection of the environment. Examples include but are not limited to wildlife preservation activities of the State Department of Fish and Game. Construction activities are not included in this exemption.

Note: Authority cited: Section 21083, Public Resources Code. Reference: Section 21084, Public Resources Code.

§ 15308. Actions by Regulatory Agencies for Protection of the Environment.

Class 8 consists of actions taken by regulatory agencies, as authorized by state or local ordinance, to assure the maintenance, restoration, enhancement, or protection of the environment where the regulatory process involves procedures for protection of the environment. Construction activities and relaxation of standards allowing environmental degradation are not included in this exemption.

Note: Authority cited: Section 21083, Public Resources Code. Reference: Section 21084, Public Resources Code; *International Longshoremen's and Warehousemen's Union v. Board of Supervisors* (1981) 116 Cal. App. 3d 265.

§ 15309. Inspections.

Class 9 consists of activities limited entirely to inspections, to check for performance of an operation, or quality, health, or safety of a project, including related activities such as inspection for possible mislabeling, misrepresentation, or adulteration of products.

Note: Authority cited: Section 21083, Public Resources Code. Reference: Section 21084, Public Resources Code.

§ 15310. Loans.

Class 10 consists of loans made by the Department of Veterans Affairs under the Veterans Farm and Home Purchase Act of 1943, mortgages for the purchase of existing structures where the loan will not be used for new construction and the purchase of such mortgages by financial institutions. Class 10 includes but is not limited to the following examples:

(a) Loans made by the Department of Veterans Affairs under the Veterans Farm and Home Purchase Act of 1943.
(b) Purchases of mortgages from banks and mortgage companies by the Public Employees Retirement System and by the State Teachers Retirement System.

Note: Authority cited: Section 21083, Public Resources Code. Reference: Section 21084, Public Resources Code.

§ 15311. Accessory Structures.

Class 11 consists of construction, or placement of minor structures accessory to (appurtenant to) existing commercial, industrial, or institutional facilities, including but not limited to:

(a) On-premise signs;
(b) Small parking lots;
(c) Placement of seasonal or temporary use items such as lifeguard towers, mobile food units, portable restrooms, or similar items in generally the same locations from time to time in publicly owned parks, stadiums, or other facilities designed for public use.

Note: Authority cited: Section 21083, Public Resources Code. Reference: Section 21084, Public Resources Code.

§ 15312. Surplus Government Property Sales.
Class 12 consists of sales of surplus government property except for parcels of land located in an area of statewide, regional, or areawide concern identified in Section 15206(b)(4). However, even if the surplus property to be sold is located in any of those areas, its sale is exempt if:

(a) The property does not have significant values for wildlife habitat or other environmental purposes, and
(b) Any of the following conditions exist:
    (1) The property is of such size, shape, or inaccessibility that it is incapable of independent development or use; or
    (2) The property to be sold would qualify for an exemption under any other class of categorical exemption in these guidelines; or
    (3) The use of the property and adjacent property has not changed since the time of purchase by the public agency.

Note: Authority cited: Section 21083, Public Resources Code. Reference: Section 21084, Public Resources Code.

§ 15313. Acquisition of Lands for Wildlife Conservation Purposes.
Class 13 consists of the acquisition of lands for fish and wildlife conservation purposes including

(a) preservation of fish and wildlife habitat,
(b) establishing ecological reserves under Fish and Game Code Section 1580, and
(c) preserving access to public lands and waters where the purpose of the acquisition is to preserve the land in its natural condition.

Note: Authority cited: Section 21083, Public Resources Code. Reference: Section 21084, Public Resources Code.

§ 15314. Minor Additions to Schools.
Class 14 consists of minor additions to existing schools within existing school grounds where the addition does not increase original student capacity by more than 25% or ten classrooms, whichever is less. The addition of portable classrooms is included in this exemption.

Note: Authority cited: Section 21083, Public Resources Code. Reference: Section 21084, Public Resources Code.

§ 15315. Minor Land Divisions.
Class 15 consists of the division of property in urbanized areas zoned for residential, commercial, or industrial use into four or fewer parcels when the division is in conformance with the General Plan and zoning, no variances or exceptions are required, all services and access to the proposed parcels to local standards are available, the parcel was not involved in a division of a larger parcel within the previous 2 years, and the parcel does not have an average slope greater than 20 percent.

Note: Authority cited: Section 21083, Public Resources Code. Reference: Section 21084, Public Resources Code.

§ 15316. Transfer of Ownership of Land in Order to Create Parks.
Class 16 consists of the acquisition, sale, or other transfer of land in order to establish a park where the land is in a natural condition or contains historical or archaeological resources and either:

(a) The management plan for the park has not been prepared, or
(b) The management plan proposes to keep the area in a natural condition or preserve the historic or archaeological resources. CEQA will apply when a management plan is proposed that will change the area from its natural condition or cause substantial adverse change in the significance of the historic or archaeological resource.

Note: Authority cited: Section 21083, Public Resources Code. Reference: Sections 21084, 21083.2, and 21084.1, Public Resources Code.

§ 15317. Open Space Contracts or Easements.
Class 17 consists of the establishment of agricultural preserves, the making and renewing of open space contracts under the Williamson Act, or the acceptance of easements or fee interests in order to maintain the open space character of the area. The cancellation of such preserves, contracts, interests, or easements is not included and will normally be an action subject to the CEQA process.

Note: Authority cited: Section 21083, Public Resources Code. Reference: Section 21084, Public Resources Code.

§ 15318. Designation of Wilderness Areas.
Class 18 consists of the designation wilderness areas under the California Wilderness System.

Note: Authority cited: Section 21083, Public Resources Code. Reference: Section 21084, Public Resources Code.

§ 15319. Annexations of Existing Facilities and Lots for Exempt Facilities.
Class 19 consists of only the following annexations:

(a) Annexations to a city or special district of areas containing existing public or private structures developed to the density allowed by the current zoning or pre-zoning of either the gaining or losing governmental agency whichever is more restrictive, provided, however, that the extension of utility services to the existing facilities would have a capacity to serve only the existing facilities.
(b) Annexations of individual small parcels of the minimum size for facilities exempted by Section 15303, New Construction or Conversion of Small Structures.

Note: Authority cited: Section 21083, Public Resources Code. Reference: Section 21084, Public Resources Code.

§ 15320. Changes in Organization of Local Agencies.
Class 20 consists of changes in the organization or reorganization of local governmental agencies where the changes do not change the geographical area in which previously existing powers are exercised. Examples include but are not limited to:

(a) Establishment of a subsidiary district.
(b) Consolidation of two or more districts having identical powers.
(c) Merger with a city of a district lying entirely within the boundaries of the city.

Note: Authority cited: Section 21083, Public Resources Code. Reference: Section 21084, Public Resources Code.

§ 15321. Enforcement Actions by Regulatory Agencies.
Class 21 consists of:

(a) Actions by regulatory agencies to enforce or revoke a lease, permit, license, certificate, or other entitlement for use issued, adopted, or prescribed by the regulatory agency or enforcement of a law, general rule, standard, or objective, administered or adopted by the regulatory agency. Such actions include, but are not limited to, the following:
    (1) The direct referral of a violation of lease, permit, license, certificate, or entitlement for use or of a general rule, standard, or objective to the Attorney General, District Attorney, or City Attorney as appropriate, for judicial enforcement.
    (2) The adoption of an administrative decision or order enforcing or revoking the lease, permit, license, certificate, or entitlement for use or enforcing the general rule, standard, or objective.
(b) Law enforcement activities by peace officers acting under any law that provides a criminal sanction.
(c) Construction activities undertaken by the public agency taking the enforcement or revocation action are not included in this exemption.

Note: Authority cited: Section 21083, Public Resources Code. Reference: Section 21084, Public Resources Code.

§ 15322. Educational or Training Programs Involving No Physical Changes.
Class 22 consists of the adoption, alteration, or termination of educational or training programs which involve no physical alteration in the area affected or which involve physical changes only in the interior of existing school or training structures. Examples include but are not limited to:

(a) Development of or changes in curriculum or training methods.
(b) Changes in the grade structure in a school which do not result in changes in student transportation.

Note: Authority cited: Section 21083, Public Resources Code. Reference: Section 21084, Public Resources Code.

§ 15323. Normal Operations of Facilities for Public Gatherings.

Class 23 consists of the normal operations of existing facilities for public gatherings for which the facilities were designed, where there is a past history of the facility being used for the same or similar kind of purpose. For the purposes of this section, "past history" shall mean that the same or similar kind of activity has been occurring for at least three years and that there is a reasonable expectation that the future occurrence of the activity would not represent a change in the operation of the facility. Facilities included within this exemption include, but are not limited to, racetracks, stadiums, convention centers, auditoriums, amphitheaters, planetariums, swimming pools, and amusement parks.

Note: Authority cited: Section 21083, Public Resources Code. Reference: Section 21084, Public Resources Code.

§ 15324. Regulations of Working Conditions.

Class 24 consists of actions taken by regulatory agencies, including the Industrial Welfare Commission as authorized by statute, to regulate any of the following:

(a) Employee wages,
(b) Hours of work, or
(c) Working conditions where there will be no demonstrable physical changes outside the place of work.

Note: Authority cited: Section 21083, Public Resources Code. Reference: Section 21084, Public Resources Code.

§ 15325. Transfers of Ownership in Land to Preserve Existing Natural Conditions and Historical Resources.

Class 25 consists of the transfers of ownership of interests in land in order to preserve open space, habitat, or historical resources. Examples include but are not limited to:

(a) Acquisition, sale, or other transfer of areas to preserve the existing natural conditions, including plant or animal habitats.
(b) Acquisition, sale, or other transfer of areas to allow continued agricultural use of the areas.
(c) Acquisition, sale, or other transfer to allow restoration of natural conditions, including plant or animal habitats.
(d) Acquisition, sale, or other transfer to prevent encroachment of development into flood plains.
(e) Acquisition, sale, or other transfer to preserve historical resources.
(f) Acquisition, sale, or other transfer to preserve open space or lands for park purposes.

Note: Authority cited: Section 21083, Public Resources Code. Reference: Section 21084, Public Resources Code.

§ 15326. Acquisition of Housing for Housing Assistance Programs.

Class 26 consists of actions by a redevelopment agency, housing authority, or other public agency to implement an adopted Housing Assistance Plan by acquiring an interest in housing units. The housing units may be either in existence or possessing all required permits for construction when the agency makes its final decision to acquire the units.

Note: Authority cited: Section 21083, Public Resources Code. Reference: Section 21084, Public Resources Code.

§ 15327. Leasing New Facilities.

(a) Class 27 consists of the leasing of a newly constructed or previously unoccupied privately owned facility by a local or state agency where the local governing authority determined that the building was exempt from CEQA. To be exempt under this section, the proposed use of the facility:
   (1) Shall be in conformance with existing state plans and policies and with general, community, and specific plans for which an EIR or negative declaration has been prepared,
   (2) Shall be substantially the same as that originally proposed at the time the building permit was issued,
   (3) Shall not result in a traffic increase of greater than 10% of front access road capacity, and
   (4) Shall include the provision of adequate employee and visitor parking facilities.
(b) Examples of Class 27 include, but are not limited to:
   (1) Leasing of administrative offices in newly constructed office space.
   (2) Leasing of client service offices in newly constructed retail space.
   (3) Leasing of administrative and/or client service offices in newly constructed industrial parks.

Note: Authority cited: Section 21083, Public Resources Code. Reference: Section 21084, Public Resources Code.

§ 15328. Small Hydroelectric Projects at Existing Facilities.

Class 28 consists of the installation of hydroelectric generating facilities in connection with existing dams, canals, and pipelines where:

(a) The capacity of the generating facilities is 5 megawatts or less,
(b) Operation of the generating facilities will not change the flow regime in the affected stream, canal, or pipeline including but not limited to:
   (1) Rate and volume of flow,
   (2) Temperature,
   (3) Amounts of dissolved oxygen to a degree that could adversely affect aquatic life, and
   (4) Timing of release.
(c) New power lines to connect the generating facilities to existing power lines will not exceed one mile in length if located on a new right of way and will not be located adjacent to a wild or scenic river.
(d) Repair or reconstruction of the diversion structure will not raise the normal maximum surface elevation of the impoundment.
(e) There will be no significant upstream or downstream passage of fish affected by the project.
(f) The discharge from the power house will not be located more than 300 feet from the toe of the diversion structure.
(g) The project will not cause violations of applicable state or federal water quality standards.
(h) The project will not entail any construction on or alteration of a site included in or eligible for inclusion in the National Register of Historic Places, and
(i) Construction will not occur in the vicinity of any endangered, rare, or threatened species.

Note: Authority cited: Section 21083, Public Resources Code. Reference: Section 21084, Public Resources Code.

§ 15329. Cogeneration Projects at Existing Facilities.

Class 29 consists of the installation of cogeneration equipment with a capacity of 50 megawatts or less at existing facilities meeting the conditions described in this section.

(a) At existing industrial facilities, the installation of cogeneration facilities will be exempt where it will:
   (1) Result in no net increases in air emissions from the industrial facility, or will produce emissions lower than the amount that would require review under the new source review rules applicable in the county, and
   (2) Comply with all applicable state, federal, and local air quality laws.
(b) At commercial and industrial facilities, the installation of cogeneration facilities will be exempt if the installation will:
   (1) Meet all the criteria described in subdivision (a),
   (2) Result in no noticeable increase in noise to nearby residential structures,
   (3) Be contiguous to other commercial or institutional structures.

Note: Authority cited: Section 21083, Public Resources Code. Reference: Section 21084, Public Resources Code.

§ 15330. Minor Actions to Prevent, Minimize, Stabilize, Mitigate or Eliminate the Release or Threat of Release of Hazardous Waste or Hazardous Substances.

Class 30 consists of any minor cleanup actions taken to prevent, minimize, stabilize, mitigate, or eliminate the release or threat of release of a hazardous waste or substance which are small or medium removal actions costing $1 million or less.

(a) No cleanup action shall be subject to this Class 30 exemption if the action requires the onsite use of a hazardous waste incinerator or thermal treatment unit or the relocation of residences or businesses,or the action involves the potential release into the air of volatile organic compounds as defined in Health and Safety Code Section 25123.6, except for small scale in situ soil vapor extraction and treatment systems which have been permitted by the local Air Pollution Control District or Air Quality Management District. All actions must be consistent with applicable state and local environmental permitting requirements including, but not limited to, off-site disposal, air quality rules such as those governing volatile organic compounds and water quality standards, and approved by the regulatory body with jurisdiction over the site.
(b) Examples of such minor cleanup actions include but are not limited to:
   (1) Removal of sealed, non-leaking drums or barrels of hazardous waste or substances that have

been stabilized, containerized and are designated for a lawfully permitted destination;
(2) Maintenance or stabilization of berms, dikes, or surface impoundments;
(3) Construction or maintenance of interim or temporary surface caps;
(4) Onsite treatment of contaminated soils or sludges provided treatment system meets Title 22 requirements and local air district requirements;
(5) Excavation and/or offsite disposal of contaminated soils or sludges in regulated units;
(6) Application of dust suppressants or dust binders to surface soils;
(7) Controls for surface water run-on and run-off that meets seismic safety standards;
(8) Pumping of leaking ponds into an enclosed container;
(9) Construction of interim or emergency ground water treatment systems;
(10) Posting of warning signs and fencing for a hazardous waste or substance site that meets legal requirements for protection of wildlife.

Note: Authority cited: Section 21083, Public Resources Code. Reference: Section 21084, Public Resources Code.

§ 15331. Historical Resource Restoration/Rehabilitation.
Class 31 consists of projects limited to maintenance, repair, stabilization, rehabilitation, restoration, preservation, conservation or reconstruction of historical resources in a manner consistent with the Secretary of the Interior's Standards for the Treatment of Historic Properties with Guidelines for Preserving, Rehabilitating, Restoring, and Reconstructing Historic Buildings (1995), Weeks and Grimmer.

Note: Authority cited: Section 21083, Public Resources Code. Reference: Section 21084, Public Resources Code.

§ 15332. In-Fill Development Projects.
Class 32 consists of projects characterized as in-fill development meeting the conditions described in this section.
(a) The project is consistent with the applicable general plan designation and all applicable general plan policies as well as with applicable zoning designation and regulations.
(b) The proposed development occurs within city limits on a project site of no more than five acres substantially surrounded by urban uses.
(c) The project site has no value, as habitat for endangered, rare or threatened species.
(d) Approval of the project would not result in any significant effects relating to traffic, noise, air quality, or water quality.
(e) The site can be adequately served by all required utilities and public services.

Note: Authority cited: Section 21083, Public Resources Code. Reference: Section 21084, Public Resources Code.

§ 15333. Small Habitat Restoration Projects.
Class 33 consists of projects not to exceed five acres in size to assure the maintenance, restoration, enhancement, or protection of habitat for fish, plants, or wildlife provided that:
(a) There would be no significant adverse impact on endangered, rare or threatened species or their habitat pursuant to section 15065,
(b) There are no hazardous materials at or around the project site that may be disturbed or removed, and
(c) The project will not result in impacts that are significant when viewed in connection with the effects of past projects, the effects of other current projects, and the effects of probable future projects.(d) Examples of small restoration projects may include, but are not limited to:
(1) revegetation of disturbed areas with native plant species;
(2) wetland restoration, the primary purpose of which is to improve conditions for waterfowl or other species that rely on wetland habitat;
(3) stream or river bank revegetation, the primary purpose of which is to improve habitat for amphibians or native fish;
(4) projects to restore or enhance habitat that are carried out principally with hand labor and not mechanized equipment.
(5) stream or river bank stabilization with native vegetation or other bioengineering techniques, the primary purpose of which is to reduce or eliminate erosion and sedimentation; and
(6) culvert replacement conducted in accordance with published guidelines of the Department of Fish and Game or NOAA Fisheries, the primary purpose of which is to improve habitat or reduce sedimentation.

Note: Authority cited: Section 21083, Public Resources Code. Reference: Section 21084, Public Resources Code.

Article 20. Definitions

§ 15350. General.
The definitions contained in this article apply to terms used throughout the guidelines unless a term is otherwise defined in a particular section.

Note: Authority cited: Section 21083, Public Resources Code. Reference: Section 21083, Public Resources Code.

§ 15351. Applicant.
"Applicant" means a person who proposes to carry out a project which needs a lease, permit, license, certificate, or other entitlement for use or financial assistance from one or more public agencies when that person applies for the governmental approval or assistance.

Note: Authority cited: Section 21083, Public Resources Code. Reference: Section 21065, Public Resources Code.

§ 15352. Approval.
(a) "Approval" means the decision by a public agency which commits the agency to a definite course of action in regard to a project intended to be carried out by any person. The exact date of approval of any project is a matter determined by each public agency according to its rules, regulations, and ordinances. Legislative action in regard to a project often constitutes approval.
(b) With private projects, approval occurs upon the earliest commitment to issue or the issuance by the public agency of a discretionary contract, grant, subsidy, loan, or other form of financial assistance, lease, permit, license, certificate, or other entitlement for use of the project.

Note: Authority cited: Section 21083, Public Resources Code. Reference: Sections 21061 and 21065, Public Resources Code.

§ 15353. CEQA.
"CEQA" means the California Environmental Quality Act, California Public Resources Code Sections 21000 et seq.

Note: Authority cited: Section 21083, Public Resources Code. Reference: Section 21050, Public Resources Code.

§ 15354. Categorical Exemption.
"Categorical exemption" means an exemption from CEQA for a class of projects based on a finding by the Secretary for Resources that the class of projects does not have a significant effect on the environment.

Note: Authority cited: Section 21083, Public Resources Code. Reference: Sections 21080(b)(10) and 21084, Public Resources Code.

§ 15355. Cumulative Impacts.
"Cumulative impacts" refer to two or more individual effects which, when considered together, are considerable or which compound or increase other environmental impacts.
(a) The individual effects may be changes resulting from a single project or a number of separate projects.
(b) The cumulative impact from several projects is the change in the environment which results from the incremental impact of the project when added to other closely related past, present, and reasonably foreseeable probable future projects. Cumulative impacts can result from individually minor but collectively significant projects taking place over a period of time.

Note: Authority cited: Section 21083, Public Resources Code. Reference: Section 21083(b), Public Resources Code; *Whitman v. Board of Supervisors*, 88 Cal. App. 3d 397.

§ 15356. Decision-Making Body.
"Decision-making body" means any person or group of people within a public agency permitted by law to approve or disapprove the project at issue.

Note: Authority cited: Section 21083, Public Resources Code. Reference: Section 21003(b), Public Resources Code; *Kleist v. City of Glendale* (1976) 56 Cal. App. 3d 770.

§ 15357. Discretionary Project.
"Discretionary project" means a project which requires the exercise of judgment or deliberation when the public

agency or body decides to approve or disapprove a particular activity, as distinguished from situations where the public agency or body merely has to determine whether there has been conformity with applicable statutes, ordinances, or regulations. A timber harvesting plan submitted to the State Forester for approval under the requirements of the Z'berg-Nejedly Forest Practice Act of 1973 (Pub. Res. Code Sections 4511 et seq.) constitutes a discretionary project within the meaning of the California Environmental Quality Act. Section 21065(c).

Note: Authority cited: Section 21083, Public Resources Code. Reference: Section 21080(a), Public Resources Code; *Johnson v. State of California* (1968) 69 Cal. 2d 782; *People v. Department of Housing and Community Development* (1975) 45 Cal. App. 3d 185; *Day v. City of Glendale* (1975) 51 Cal. App. 3d 817; *N.R.D.C. v. Arcata National Corp.* (1976) 59 Cal. App. 3d 959.

§ 15358. Effects.

"Effects" and "impacts" as used in these guidelines are synonymous.

(a) Effects include:
  (1) Direct or primary effects which are caused by the project and occur at the same time and place.
  (2) Indirect or secondary effects which are caused by the project and are later in time or farther removed in distance, but are still reasonably foreseeable. Indirect or secondary effects may include growth-inducing effects and other effects related to induced changes in the pattern of land use, population density, or growth rate, and related effects on air and water and other natural systems, including ecosystems.

(b) Effects analyzed under CEQA must be related to a physical change.

Note: Authority cited: Section 21083, Public Resources Code. Reference: Sections 21068 and 21100, Public Resources Code.

§ 15359. Emergency.

"Emergency" means a sudden, unexpected occurrence, involving a clear and imminent danger, demanding immediate action to prevent or mitigate loss of, or damage to life, health, property, or essential public services. Emergency includes such occurrences as fire, flood, earthquake, or other soil or geologic movements, as well as such occurrences as riot, accident, or sabotage.

Note: Authority cited: Section 21083, Public Resources Code. Reference: Section 21080(b)(2), (3) and (4), Public Resources Code.

§ 15360. Environment.

"Environment" means the physical conditions which exist within the area which will be affected by a proposed project including land, air, water, minerals, flora, fauna, ambient noise, and objects of historic or aesthetic significance. The area involved shall be the area in which significant effects would occur either directly or indirectly as a result of the project. The "environment" includes both natural and man-made conditions.

Note: Authority cited: Section 21083, Public Resources Code. Reference: Section 21060.5, Public Resources Code.

§ 15361. Environmental Documents.

"Environmental documents" means initial studies, negative declarations, draft and final EIRs, documents prepared as substitutes for EIRs and negative declarations under a program certified pursuant to Public Resources Code Section 21080.5, and documents prepared under NEPA and used by a state or local agency in the place of an initial study, negative declaration, or an EIR.

Note: Authority cited: Section 21083, Public Resources Code. Reference: Sections 21061, 21080(b), 21080.5, 21108 and 21152, Public Resources Code.

§ 15362. EIR - Environmental Impact Report.

"EIR" or "environmental impact report" means a detailed statement prepared under CEQA describing and analyzing the significant environmental effects of a project and discussing ways to mitigate or avoid the effects. The contents of an EIR are discussed in Article 9, commencing with Section 15120 of these guidelines. The term "EIR" may mean either a draft or a final EIR depending on the context.

(a) Draft EIR means an EIR containing the information specified in Sections 15122 through 15131.

(b) Final EIR means an EIR containing the information contained in the draft EIR, comments either verbatim or in summary received in the review process, a list of persons commenting, and the response of the lead agency to the comments received. The final EIR is discussed in detail in Section 15132.

Note: Authority cited: Section 21083, Public Resources Code. Reference: Sections 21061, 21100 and 21151, Public Resources Code.

§ 15363. EIS - Environmental Impact Statement.

"EIS" or "Environmental Impact Statement" means an environmental impact document prepared pursuant to the National Environmental Policy Act (NEPA). NEPA uses the term EIS in the place of the term EIR which is used in CEQA.

Note: Authority cited: Section 21083, Public Resources Code. Reference: Sections 21083.5, 21083.6 and 21083.7, Public Resources Code; 43 U.S.C.A. 4322(2)(c).

§ 15364. Feasible.

"Feasible" means capable of being accomplished in a successful manner within a reasonable period of time, taking into account economic, environmental, legal, social, and technological factors.

Note: Authority cited: Section 21083, Public Resources Code. Reference: Sections 21002, 21002.1, 21004, 21061.1, 21080.5 and 21081, Public Resources Code; Section 4, Chapter 1438 of the Statutes of 1982.

§ 15364.5. Greenhouse Gas.

"Greenhouse gas" or "greenhouse gases" includes but is not limited to: carbon dioxide, methane, nitrous oxide, hydrofluorocarbons, perfluorocarbons and sulfur hexafluoride.

Note: Authority cited: Sections 21083 and 21083.05, Public Resources Code. Reference: Section 38505(g), Health and Safety Code; and Section 21083.05, Public Resources Code.

§ 15365. Initial Study.

"Initial study" means a preliminary analysis prepared by the lead agency to determine whether an EIR or a negative declaration must be prepared or to identify the significant environmental effects to be analyzed in an EIR. Use of the initial study is discussed in Article 5, commencing with Section 15060.

Note: Authority cited: Section 21083, Public Resources Code. Reference: Sections 21080.1, 21080.2, 21080.3 and 21100, Public Resources Code.

§ 15366. Jurisdiction by Law.

(a) "Jurisdiction by law" means the authority of any public agency:
  (1) To grant a permit or other entitlement for use,
  (2) To provide funding for the project in question, or
  (3) To exercise authority over resources which may be affected by the project.

(b) A city or county will have jurisdiction by law with respect to a project when the city or county having primary jurisdiction over the area involved is:
  (1) The site of the project;
  (2) The area in which the major environmental effects will occur; and/or
  (3) The area in which reside those citizens most directly concerned by any such environmental effects.

(c) Where an agency having jurisdiction by law must exercise discretionary authority over a project in order for the project to proceed, it is also a responsible agency, see Section 15381, or the lead agency, see Section 15367.

Note: Authority cited: Section 21083, Public Resources Code. Reference: Sections 21080.3, 21080.4, 21104 and 21153, Public Resources Code.

§ 15367. Lead Agency.

"Lead agency" means the public agency which has the principal responsibility for carrying out or approving a project. The lead agency will decide whether an EIR or negative declaration will be required for the project and will cause the document to be prepared. Criteria for determining which agency will be the lead agency for a project are contained in Section 15051.

Note: Authority cited: Section 21083, Public Resources Code. Reference: Section 21165, Public Resources Code.

§ 15368. Local Agency.

"Local agency" means any public agency other than a state agency, board, or commission. Local agency includes but is not limited to cities, counties, charter cities and counties, districts, school districts, special districts, redevelopment agencies, local agency formation commissions, and any board, commission, or organizational subdivision of a local agency when so designated by order or resolution of the governing legislative body of the local agency.

Note: Authority cited: Section 21083, Public Resources Code. Reference: Sections 21062 and 21151, Public Resources Code.

§ 15369. Ministerial.

"Ministerial" describes a governmental decision involving little or no personal judgment by the public official as to the wisdom or manner of carrying out the project. The public official merely applies the law to the facts as presented but uses no special discretion or judgment in reaching a decision. A ministerial decision involves only the use of fixed standards or objective measurements, and the public official cannot use personal, subjective judgment in deciding whether or how the project should be carried out. Common examples of ministerial permits include automobile registrations, dog licenses, and marriage licenses. A building permit is ministerial if the ordinance requiring the permit limits the public official to determining whether the zoning allows the structure to be built in the requested location, the structure would meet the strength requirements in the Uniform Building Code, and the applicant has paid his fee.

Note: Authority cited: Section 21083, Public Resources Code. Reference: Section 21080(b)(1), Public Resources Code; *Johnson v. State of California*, 69 Cal. 2d 782; *Day v. City of Glendale*, 51 Cal. App. 3d 817.

§ 15369.5. Mitigated Negative Declaration.

"Mitigated negative declaration" means a negative declaration prepared for a project when the initial study has identified potentially significant effects on the environment, but (1) revisions in the project plans or proposals made by, or agreed to by, the applicant before the proposed negative declaration and initial study are released for public review would avoid the effects or mitigate the effects to a point where clearly no significant effect on the environment would occur, and (2) there is no substantial evidence in light of the whole record before the public agency that the project, as revised, may have a significant effect on the environment.

Note: Authority cited: Section 21083, Public Resources Code. Reference: Section 21064.5, Public Resources Code.

§ 15370. Mitigation.

"Mitigation" includes:

(a) Avoiding the impact altogether by not taking a certain action or parts of an action.
(b) Minimizing impacts by limiting the degree or magnitude of the action and its implementation.
(c) Rectifying the impact by repairing, rehabilitating, or restoring the impacted environment.
(d) Reducing or eliminating the impact over time by preservation and maintenance operations during the life of the action.
(e) Compensating for the impact by replacing or providing substitute resources or environments.

Note: Authority cited: Section 21083, Public Resources Code. Reference: Sections 21002, 21002.1, 21081 and 21100(c), Public Resources Code.

§ 15371. Negative Declaration.

"Negative declaration" means a written statement by the lead agency briefly describing the reasons that a proposed project, not exempt from CEQA, will not have a significant effect on the environment and therefore does not require the preparation of an EIR. The contents of a negative declaration are described in Section 15071.

Note: Authority cited: Section 21083, Public Resources Code. Reference: Section 21080(c), Public Resources Code.

§ 15372. Notice of Completion.

"Notice of completion" means a brief notice filed with the Office of Planning and Research by a lead agency as soon as it has completed a draft EIR and is prepared to send out copies for review. The contents of this notice are explained in Section 15085.

Note: Authority cited: Section 21083, Public Resources Code. Reference: Section 21161, Public Resources Code.

§ 15373. Notice of Determination.

"Notice of determination" means a brief notice to be filed by a public agency after it approves or determines to carry out a project which is subject to the requirements of CEQA. The contents of this notice are explained in Sections 15075 and 15094.

Note: Authority cited: Section 21083, Public Resources Code. Reference: Sections 21108(a) and 21152, Public Resources Code.

§ 15374. Notice of Exemption.

"Notice of exemption" means a brief notice which may be filed by a public agency after it has decided to carry out or approve a project and has determined that the project is exempt from CEQA as being ministerial, categorically exempt, an emergency, or subject to another exemption from CEQA. Such a notice may also be filed by an applicant where such a determination has been made by a public agency which must approve the project. The contents of this notice are explained in Section 15062.

Note: Authority cited: Section 21083, Public Resources Code. Reference: Sections 21108(b) and 21152(b), Public Resources Code.

§ 15375. Notice of Preparation.

"Notice of preparation" means a brief notice sent by a lead agency to notify the responsible agencies, trustee agencies, the Office of Planning and Research, and involved federal agencies that the lead agency plans to prepare an EIR for the project. The purpose of the notice is to solicit guidance from those agencies as to the scope and content of the environmental information to be included in the EIR. Public agencies are free to develop their own formats for this notice. The contents of this notice are described in Section 15082.

Note: Authority cited: Section 21083, Public Resources Code. Reference: Section 21080.4, Public Resources Code.

§ 15376. Person.

"Person" includes any person, firm, association, organization, partnership, business, trust, corporation, limited liability company, company, district, city, county, city and county, town, the state, and any of the agencies and political subdivisions of such entities, and, to the extent permitted by federal law, the United States, or any of its agencies or political subdivisions.

Note: Authority cited: Section 21083, Public Resources Code. Reference: Section 21066, Public Resources Code.

§ 15377. Private Project.

A "private project" means a project which will be carried out by a person other than a governmental agency, but the project will need a discretionary approval from one or more governmental agencies for:

(a) A contract or financial assistance, or
(b) A lease, permit, license, certificate, or other entitlement for use.

Note: Authority cited: Section 21083, Public Resources Code. Reference: Section 21065, Public Resources Code.

§ 15378. Project.

(a) "Project" means the whole of an action, which has a potential for resulting in either a direct physical change in the environment, or a reasonably foreseeable indirect physical change in the environment, and that is any of the following:
   (1) An activity directly undertaken by any public agency including but not limited to public works construction and related activities clearing or grading of land, improvements to existing public structures, enactment and amendment of zoning ordinances, and the adoption and amendment of local General Plans or elements thereof pursuant to Government Code Sections 65100-65700.
   (2) An activity undertaken by a person which is supported in whole or in part through public agency contracts, grants, subsidies, loans, or other forms of assistance from one or more public agencies.
   (3) An activity involving the issuance to a person of a lease, permit, license, certificate, or other entitlement for use by one or more public agencies.
(b) Project does not include:
   (1) Proposals for legislation to be enacted by the State Legislature;
   (2) Continuing administrative or maintenance activities, such as purchases for supplies, personnel-related actions, general policy and procedure making (except as they are applied to specific instances covered above);
   (3) The submittal of proposals to a vote of the people of the state or of a particular community that does not involve a public agency sponsored initiative. (*Stein v.City of Santa Monica*, (1980) 110 Cal. App. 3d 458; *Friends of Sierra Madre v. City of Sierra Madre* (2001) 25 Cal. 4th 165);
   (4) The creation of government funding mechanisms or other government fiscal activities, which do not involve any commitment to any specific project which may result in a potentially significant physical impact on the environment.
   (5) Organizational or administrative activities of governments that will not result in direct or indirect physical changes in the environment.
(c) The term "project" refers to the activity which is being approved and which may be subject to several discretionary approvals by governmental agencies. The

term "project" does not mean each separate governmental approval.

(d) Where the lead agency could describe the project as either the adoption of a particular regulation under subdivision (a)(1) or as a development proposal which will be subject to several governmental approvals under subdivisions (a)(2) or (a)(3), the lead agency shall describe the project as the development proposal for the purpose of environmental analysis. This approach will implement the lead agency principle as described in Article 4.

Note: Authority cited: Section 21083, Public Resources Code. Reference: Section 21065, Public Resources Code; *Kaufman and Broad-South Bay, Inc. v. Morgan Hill Unified School District* (1992) 9 Cal. App. 4th 464; and *Fullerton Joint Union High School District v. State Board of Education* (1982) 32 Cal. 3d 779; *Simi Valley Recreation and Park District v. Local Agency Formation Commission of Ventura County* (1975) 51 Cal. App. 3d 648; and *Communities for a Better Environment v. California Resources Agency* (2002) 103 Cal. App. 4th 98.

§ 15379. Public Agency.

"Public agency" includes any state agency, board, or commission and any local or regional agency, as defined in these guidelines. It does not include the courts of the state. This term does not include agencies of the federal government.

Note: Authority cited: Section 21083, Public Resources Code. Reference: Section 21063, Public Resources Code.

§ 15380. Endangered, Rare or Threatened Species.

(a) "Species" as used in this section means a species or subspecies of animal or plant or a variety of plant.

(b) A species of animal or plant is:

  (1) "Endangered" when its survival and reproduction in the wild are in immediate jeopardy from one or more causes, including loss of habitat, change in habitat, overexploitation, predation, competition, disease, or other factors; or

  (2) "Rare" when either:

    (A) Although not presently threatened with extinction, the species is existing in such small numbers throughout all or a significant portion of its range that it may become endangered if its environment worsens; or

    (B) The species is likely to become endangered within the foreseeable future throughout all or a significant portion of its range and may be considered "threatened" as that term is used in the Federal Endangered Species Act.

(c) A species of animal or plant shall be presumed to be endangered, rare or threatened, as it is listed in:

  (1) Sections 670.2 or 670.5, Title 14, California Code of Regulations; or

  (2) Title 50, Code of Federal Regulations Sections 17.11 or 17.12 pursuant to the Federal Endangered Species Act as rare, threatened, or endangered.

(d) A species not included in any listing identified in subdivision (c) shall nevertheless be considered to be endangered, rare or threatened, if the species can be shown to meet the criteria in subdivision (b).

(e) This definition shall not include any species of the Class Insecta which is a pest whose protection under the provisions of CEQA would present an overwhelming and overriding risk to man as determined by:

  (1) The Director of Food and Agriculture with regard to economic pests; or

  (2) The Director of Health Services with regard to health risks.

Note: Authority cited: Section 21083, Public Resources Code. Reference: Section 21001(c), Public Resources Code.

§ 15381. Responsible Agency.

"Responsible agency" means a public agency which proposes to carry out or approve a project, for which a lead agency is preparing or has prepared an EIR or negative declaration. For the purposes of CEQA, the term "responsible agency" includes all public agencies other than the lead agency which have discretionary approval power over the project.

Note: Authority cited: Section 21083, Public Resources Code. Reference: Sections 21002.1, 21069, 21080.1, 21080.3, 21080.4, 21167.2 and 21167.3, Public Resources Code.

§ 15382. Significant Effect on the Environment.

"Significant effect on the environment" means a substantial, or potentially substantial, adverse change in any of the physical conditions within the area affected by the project including land, air, water, minerals, flora, fauna, ambient noise, and objects of historic or aesthetic significance. An economic or social change by itself shall not be considered a significant effect on the environment. A social or economic change related to a physical change may be considered in determining whether the physical change is significant.

Note: Authority cited: Section 21083, Public Resources Code. Reference: Sections 21068, 21083, 21100 and 21151, Public Resources Code; Hecton v. People of the State of California, 58 Cal. App. 3d 653.

§ 15383. State Agency.

"State agency" means a governmental agency in the executive branch of the State Government or an entity which operates under the direction and control of an agency in the executive branch of State Government and is funded primarily by the State Treasury.

Note: Authority cited: Section 21083, Public Resources Code. Reference: Section 21100, Public Resources Code.

§ 15384. Substantial Evidence.

(a) "Substantial evidence" as used in these guidelines means enough relevant information and reasonable inferences from this information that a fair argument can be made to support a conclusion, even though other conclusions might also be reached. Whether a fair argument can be made that the project may have a significant effect on the environment is to be determined by examining the whole record before the lead agency. Argument, speculation, unsubstantiated opinion or narrative, evidence which is clearly erroneous or inaccurate, or evidence of social or economic impacts which do not contribute to or are not caused by physical impacts on the environment does not constitute substantial evidence.

(b) Substantial evidence shall include facts, reasonable assumptions predicated upon facts, and expert opinion supported by facts.

Note: Authority cited: Section 21083, Public Resources Code. Reference: Sections 21080, 21082.2, 21168 and 21168.5, Public Resources Code; *No Oil, Inc. v. City of Los Angeles* (1974) 13 Cal. 3d 68; *Running Fence Corp. v. Superior Court* (1975) 51 Cal. App. 3d 400; *Friends of B Street v. City of Hayward* (1980) 106 Cal. App. 3d 988.

§ 15385. Tiering.

"Tiering" refers to the coverage of general matters in broader EIRs (such as on general plans or policy statements) with subsequent narrower EIRs or ultimately site-specific EIRs incorporating by reference the general discussions and concentrating solely on the issues specific to the EIR subsequently prepared. Tiering is appropriate when the sequence of EIRs is:

(a) From a general plan, policy, or program EIR to a program, plan, or policy EIR of lesser scope or to a site-specific EIR.

(b) From an EIR on a specific action at an early stage to a subsequent EIR or a supplement to an EIR at a later stage. Tiering in such cases is appropriate when it helps the lead agency to focus on the issues which are ripe for decision and exclude from consideration issues already decided or not yet ripe.

Note: Authority cited: Section 21083, Public Resources Code. Reference: Sections 21003, 21061 and 21100, Public Resources Code.

§ 15386. Trustee Agency.

"Trustee agency" means a state agency having jurisdiction by law over natural resources affected by a project which are held in trust for the people of the State of California. Trustee agencies include:

(a) The California Department of Fish and Game with regard to the fish and wildlife of the state, to designated rare or endangered native plants, and to game refuges, ecological reserves, and other areas administered by the department.

(b) The State Lands Commission with regard to state owned "sovereign" lands such as the beds of navigable waters and state school lands.

(c) The State Department of Parks and Recreation with regard to units of the State Park System.

(d) The University of California with regard to sites within the Natural Land and Water Reserves System.

Note: Authority cited: Section 21083, Public Resources Code. Reference: Sections 21080.3 and 21080.4, Public Resources Code.

§ 15387. Urbanized Area.

"Urbanized area" means a central city or a group of contiguous cities with a population of 50,000 or more, together with adjacent densely populated areas having a population density of at least 1,000 persons per square mile. A lead agency shall determine whether a particular area meets the criteria in this section either by examining the area or by referring to a map prepared by the U.S. Bureau of the Census which designates the area as urbanized. Maps of the designated urbanized areas can be found in the California EIR Monitor of February 7, 1979. The maps are also for sale by the Superintendent of Documents, U.S. Government Printing Office, Washington, D.C. 20402. The maps are sold in sets only as Stock Number 0301-3466. Use of the term "urbanized area" in Section 15182 is limited to areas mapped and designated as urbanized by the U.S. Bureau of the Census.

Note: Authority cited: Sections 21083 and 21087, Public Resources Code. Reference: Sections 21080.7, 21083 and 21084, Public Resources Code.

Appendix A

Appendix B
Appendix C
Appendix D Notice of Determination

Appendix E

Appendix F
Appendix G
Appendix H
Appendix I Notice of Preparation
Appendix J Examples of Tiering EIR's
Appendix K
Appendix L Notice of Completion of Draft EIR

Appendix A
CEQA Process Flow Chart

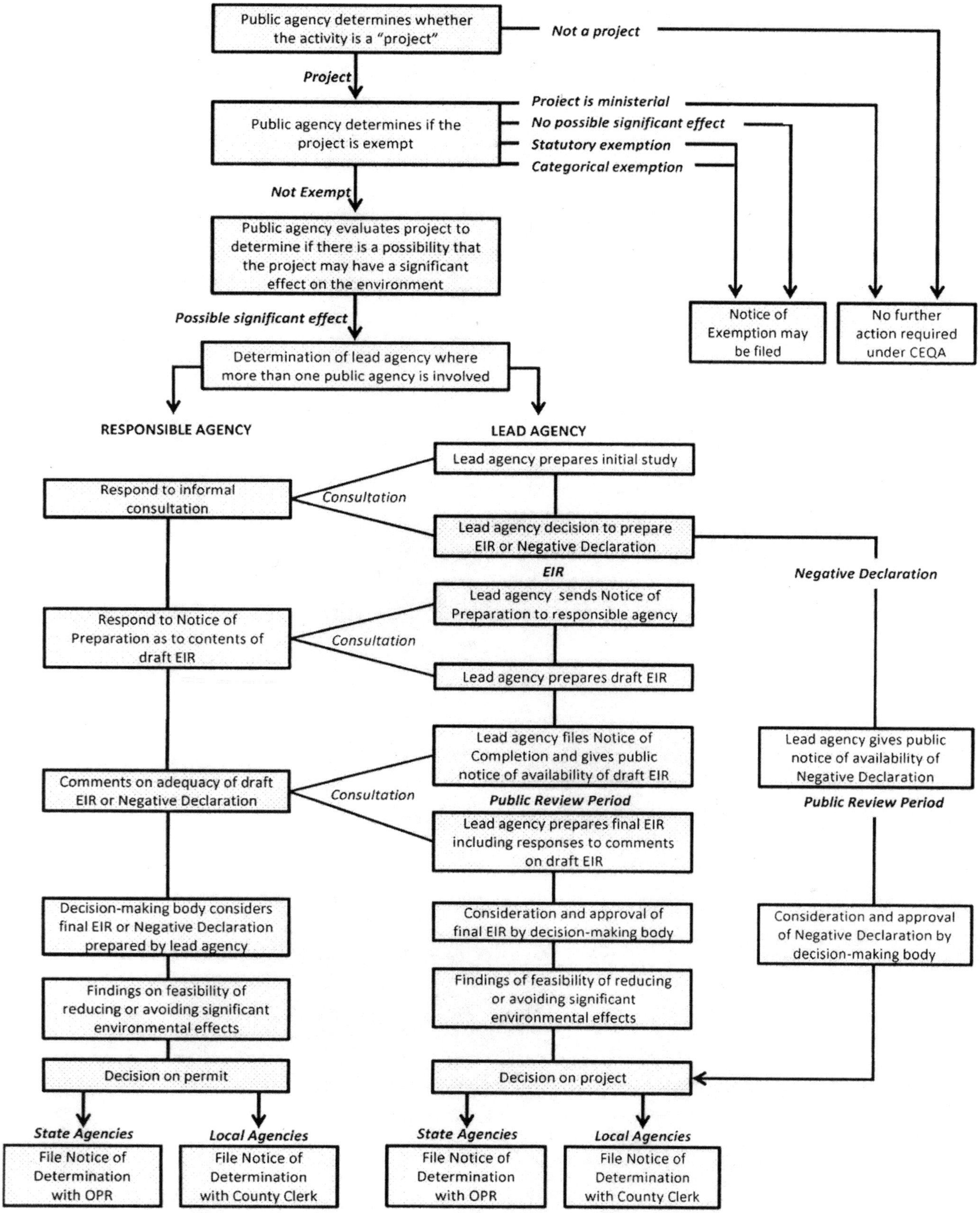

CEQA Appendix B:
Statutory Authority of State Departments

STATUTORY AUTHORITY OF STATE DEPARTMENTS

	Bay Conservation and Development Commission	Air Resources Board	Resources Agency	Health Services	Savings and Loan	Real Estate	Caltrans	Dept of Housing and Community Development	Dept of Motor Vehicles	Corporations	California Highway Patrol	Aeronautics	Food and Agriculture
1. Air quality and air pollution control		X		X					X		16	X	1
2. Chemical contamination and food products				X									X
3. Coastal areas, wetlands, estuaries, waterfowl refuges, and beaches	26			7									
4. Congestion in urban areas, housing, and building displacement		24		8		X		X					
5. Disease control				X									X
6. Electric energy generation and supply		X		X									
7. Environmental effects with special impact in low-income neighborhoods				9		X	X	X					
8. Flood plains and watersheds						X							X
9. Food additives and food sanitation				X									X
10. Herbicides			X	X									X
11. Historic and archaeological sites							X						
12. Human ecology		X		X									2
13. Microbiological contamination				X									X
14. Mineral land reclamation													
15. Natural gas energy development generation and supply													
16. Navigable airways		16		10								X	
17. Navigable waterways	25												
18. Noise control and abatement				X							X	X	
19. Parks, forests, trees and outdoor recreation areas	25												X
20. Pesticides			X	X									X
21. Radiation and radiological health			X	X									
22. Regional comprehensive planning		24		11	X	X	X	X				X	
23. Rodent control				X									X
24. Sanitation and waste systems				X									3
25. Shellfish sanitation				X									
26. Soil and plant life, sedimentation, erosion, and hydrologic conditions													X
27. Toxic Materials				X									X
28. Transportation and handling of hazardous materials				X					X		X		4
29. Water quality and water pollution control				X									X
30. Fish and wildlife				12									5
31. Activities with special impact on regional jurisdictions	25			13									
32. Water project formulation		24											
33. Geothermal energy		24											
34. Oil and petroleum development, generation and supply													
35. Statewide land use patterns													
36. Open space policy		24											
37. Statewide overview — cumulative impact of separate projects							X						
38. Seismic hazards								X					

Office of Planning & Research	Native American Heritage Commission	Water Resources	State Water Resources Control Board	State Reclamation Board	State Lands Commission	Solid Waste Mgmt Board	Parks and Recreation	Forestry	Fish and Game	Energy Commission	Conservation	Colorado River Board	CTRPA	Coastal Commission	Boating and Waterways	
			X								X		27			1. Air quality and air pollution control
			X						X							2. Chemical contamination and food products
		X	X		X		X		X		X	14	27	26	X	3. Coastal areas, wetlands, estuaries, waterfowl refuges, and beaches
			21										27	26		4. Congestion in urban areas, housing, and building displacement
			X					22	X			14				5. Disease control
		X					X	23	X	X		14		26	X	6. Electric energy generation and supply
							19									7. Environmental effects with special impact in low-income neighborhoods
		X		20	X		X		X		X	14	27	26		8. Flood plains and watersheds
																9. Food additives and food sanitation
			X				X	22	X			14				10. Herbicides
	X				X		X						27	26		11. Historic and archaeological sites
X							X		X				27	26		12. Human ecology
			X						X			14				13. Microbiological contamination
					X		X		X		X		27	26		14. Mineral land reclamation
					X				15	X	X			26		15. Natural gas energy development generation and supply
									16							16. Navigable airways
				20	X				X			14	27	26	X	17. Navigable waterways
									17							18. Noise control and abatement
	X				X		X		X		X	14	27	26	X	19. Parks, forests, trees and outdoor recreation areas
		X	X				X	22	X							20. Pesticides
									X	X		14				21. Radiation and radiological health
X		X	X		X		X		X	X	X	14	27	26	X	22. Regional comprehensive planning
							X	22	X							23. Rodent control
		X	X			X			18		X	14		26		24. Sanitation and waste systems
			X						X							25. Shellfish sanitation
		X	X		X		X		X		X	14	27	26		26. Soil and plant life, sedimentation, erosion, and hydrologic conditions
			X			X	X		X			14				27. Toxic Materials
			X							X	X					28. Transportation and handling of hazardous materials
		X	X						X		X	14	27	26	X	29. Water quality and water pollution control
			21				X		X			14	27	26		30. Fish and wildlife
		X		20			X					14	27	26		31. Activities with special impact on regional jurisdictions
		X	X	20			X	23	X			14			X	32. Water project formulation
		X	21		X				X	X	X	14				33. Geothermal energy
			21		X				X	X	X			26		34. Oil and petroleum development, generation and supply
X					X				X	X	X		27	26		35. Statewide land use patterns
X	X				X				X		X		27	26		36. Open space policy
X										X						37. Statewide overview — cumulative impact of separate projects
		X								X	X		27	26		38. Seismic hazards

Appendix B Footnotes

1. **Food and Agriculture**—Effects on plants and animals.
2. **Food and Agriculture**—Protection of food and fiber.
3. **Food and Agriculture**—Agricultural, dairy and feed ot systems.
4. **Food and Agriculture**—As pertains to transportation, handling, storage, and decontamination of pesticides.
5. **Food and Agriculture**—Pesticide effects, predatory animal control, bird control.
6. **California Highway Patrol**—Enforcement of motor vehicle regulations.
7. **Health Services**—Beach sanitation, water pollution, solid waste and mosquito contol.
8. **Health Services**—Pertains to health component.
9. **Health Services**—Most if these are strongly related to health.
10. **Health Services**—Pertains to noise.
11. **Health Services**—Pertains to personal and environmental health components.
12. **Health Services**—As it may pertain to human health hazards.
13. **Health Services**—Pertains to comprehensive health planning.
14. **Colorado River Board**—As pertains to the Colorado, New and Alamo rivers.
15. **Fish and Game**—As field development and distribution systems may affect fish and wildlife.
16. **Fish and Game**—As may affect migrating and resident wildlife.
17. **Fish and Game**—As excessive noise may affect wildlife.
18. **Fish and Game**—As water quality may affect fish and wildlife.
19. **Parks and Recreation**—In impacted areas only.
20. **Reclamation Board**—In areas of Board's jurisdiction only—the Sacramento-San Juaquin Valley.
21. **State Water Resources Control Board**—As may pertain to water quality.
22. **Forestry**—With respect to forest land.
23. **Forestry**—(6) and (32)—As related to fire protection of state (fire protection) responsibility land.
24. **Air Resources Board**—(4), (22), (32), (33), and (36)—As may pertain to residential, commercial, industrial or tranportation growth.
25. **San Francisco Bay Conservation and Development Commission**—(3), (17), (19), and (30)—With respect to San Francisco Bay, Suisun Bay, and adjacent shore areas.
26. **California Coastal Commission**—(3), (4), (6), (8), (11), (12), (14), (15), (17), (19), (22), (23), (26), (29), (30), (31), (34), (35), and (36)—With respect to effects within the California Coastal Zone.
27. **California Tahoe Regional Planning Agency**—With respect to effects in the Tahoe Basin.
28. **Native American Heritage Commission**—With respect to places of special religious or social significance to Native Americans including archaeological sites, cemeteries, and places of worship.

Note: Authority cited: Section 21083, Publc Resources Code; Reference: Sections 21080.3, 21080.4, 21104, and 21153, Public Resources Code.

CEQA Appendix C:
Notice of Completion & Environmental Document Transmittal

Mail to: State Clearinghouse, P.O. Box 3044, Sacramento, CA 95812-3044 (916) 445-0613
For Hand Delivery/Street Address: 1400 Tenth Street, Sacramento, CA 95814

SCH #

Project Title: ____________________

Lead Agency: ____________________ Contact Person: ____________________

Mailing Address: ____________________ Phone: ____________________

City: ____________________ Zip: __________ County: ____________________

Project Location: County: ____________________ City/Nearest Community: ____________________

Cross Streets: ____________________ Zip Code: __________

Longitude/Latitude (degrees, minutes and seconds): _____° _____′ _____″ N / _____° _____′ _____″ W Total Acres: __________

Assessor's Parcel No.: ____________________ Section: ________ Twp.: ________ Range: ________ Base: ________

Within 2 Miles: State Hwy #: ____________________ Waterways: ____________________

Airports: ____________________ Railways: ____________________ Schools: ____________________

Document Type:

CEQA: ☐ NOP ☐ Early Cons ☐ Neg Dec ☐ Mit Neg Dec ☐ Draft EIR ☐ Supplement/Subsequent EIR (Prior SCH No.) __________ Other: __________

NEPA: ☐ NOI ☐ EA ☐ Draft EIS ☐ FONSI

Other: ☐ Joint Document ☐ Final Document ☐ Other: __________

Local Action Type:

☐ General Plan Update
☐ General Plan Amendment
☐ General Plan Element
☐ Community Plan
☐ Specific Plan
☐ Master Plan
☐ Planned Unit Development
☐ Site Plan
☐ Rezone
☐ Prezone
☐ Use Permit
☐ Land Division (Subdivision, etc.)
☐ Annexation
☐ Redevelopment
☐ Coastal Permit
☐ Other: __________

Development Type:

☐ Residential: Units ______ Acres ______
☐ Office: Sq.ft. ______ Acres ______ Employees ______
☐ Commercial: Sq.ft. ______ Acres ______ Employees ______
☐ Industrial: Sq.ft. ______ Acres ______ Employees ______
☐ Educational: __________
☐ Recreational: __________
☐ Water Facilities: Type __________ MGD ______
☐ Transportation: Type __________
☐ Mining: Mineral __________
☐ Power: Type __________ MW ______
☐ Waste Treatment: Type __________ MGD ______
☐ Hazardous Waste: Type __________
☐ Other: __________

Project Issues Discussed in Document:

☐ Aesthetic/Visual
☐ Agricultural Land
☐ Air Quality
☐ Archeological/Historical
☐ Biological Resources
☐ Coastal Zone
☐ Drainage/Absorption
☐ Economic/Jobs
☐ Fiscal
☐ Flood Plain/Flooding
☐ Forest Land/Fire Hazard
☐ Geologic/Seismic
☐ Minerals
☐ Noise
☐ Population/Housing Balance
☐ Public Services/Facilities
☐ Recreation/Parks
☐ Schools/Universities
☐ Septic Systems
☐ Sewer Capacity
☐ Soil Erosion/Compaction/Grading
☐ Solid Waste
☐ Toxic/Hazardous
☐ Traffic/Circulation
☐ Vegetation
☐ Water Quality
☐ Water Supply/Groundwater
☐ Wetland/Riparian
☐ Growth Inducement
☐ Land Use
☐ Cumulative Effects
☐ Other: __________

Present Land Use/Zoning/General Plan Designation:

Project Description: *(please use a separate page if necessary)*

Reviewing Agencies Checklist

Lead Agencies may recommend State Clearinghouse distribution by marking agencies below with and "**X**".
If you have already sent your document to the agency please denote that with an "**S**".

- _____ Air Resources Board
- _____ Boating & Waterways, Department of
- _____ California Highway Patrol
- _____ Caltrans District # _____
- _____ Caltrans Division of Aeronautics
- _____ Caltrans Planning
- _____ Central Valley Flood Protection Board
- _____ Coachella Valley Mtns. Conservancy
- _____ Coastal Commission
- _____ Colorado River Board
- _____ Conservation, Department of
- _____ Corrections, Department of
- _____ Delta Protection Commission
- _____ Education, Department of
- _____ Energy Commission
- _____ Fish & Game Region # _____
- _____ Food & Agriculture, Department of
- _____ Forestry and Fire Protection, Department of
- _____ General Services, Department of
- _____ Health Services, Department of
- _____ Housing & Community Development
- _____ Integrated Waste Management Board
- _____ Native American Heritage Commission
- _____ Office of Emergency Services
- _____ Office of Historic Preservation
- _____ Office of Public School Construction
- _____ Parks & Recreation, Department of
- _____ Pesticide Regulation, Department of
- _____ Public Utilities Commission
- _____ Regional WQCB # _____
- _____ Resources Agency
- _____ S.F. Bay Conservation & Development Comm.
- _____ San Gabriel & Lower L.A. Rivers & Mtns. Conservancy
- _____ San Joaquin River Conservancy
- _____ Santa Monica Mtns. Conservancy
- _____ State Lands Commission
- _____ SWRCB: Clean Water Grants
- _____ SWRCB: Water Quality
- _____ SWRCB: Water Rights
- _____ Tahoe Regional Planning Agency
- _____ Toxic Substances Control, Department of
- _____ Water Resources, Department of

- _____ Other: ____________________
- _____ Other: ____________________

Local Public Review Period (to be filled in by lead agency)

Starting Date ____________________ Ending Date ____________________

Lead Agency (Complete if applicable):

Consulting Firm: ____________________
Address: ____________________
City/State/Zip: ____________________
Contact: ____________________
Phone: ____________________

Applicant: ____________________
Address: ____________________
City/State/Zip: ____________________
Phone: ____________________

Signature of Lead Agency Representative: ____________________ **Date:** __________

Authority cited: Section 21083, Public Resources Code. Reference: Section 21161, Public Resources Code.

CEQA Appendix D:
Notice of Determination

To:

☐ Office of Planning and Research

For U.S. Mail:	*Street Address:*
P.O. Box 3044	1400 Tenth St.
Sacramento, CA	Sacramento, CA
95812-3044	95814

☐ County Clerk
County of: ______________________
Address: ______________________
____

From:

Public Agency: ______________________
Address: ______________________
____
Contact: ______________________
Phone: ______________________

Lead Agency (if different from above):
____
Address: ______________________
____
Contact: ______________________
Phone: ______________________

SUBJECT: Filing of Notice of Determination in compliance with Section 21108 or 21152 of the Public Resources Code.

State Clearinghouse Number (if submitted to State Clearinghouse): ______________________

Project Title: ______________________
Project Location (include county): ______________________
Project Description:

This is to advise that the ______________________ has approved the above described project on
☐ Lead Agency or ☐ Responsible Agency
______________________ and has made the following determinations regarding the above described project:
(Date)

1. The project [☐ will ☐ will not] have a significant effect on the environment.
2. ☐ An Environmental Impact Report was prepared for this project pursuant to the provisions of CEQA.
   ☐ A Negative Declaration was prepared for this project pursuant to the provisions of CEQA.
3. Mitigation measures [☐ were ☐ were not] made a condition of the approval of the project.
4. A mitigation reporting or monitoring plan [☐ was ☐ was not] adopted for this project.
5. A statement of Overriding Consideration [☐ was ☐ was not] adopted for this project.
6. Findings [☐ were ☐ were not] made pursuant to the provisions of CEQA.

This is to certify that the final EIR with comments and responses and record of project approval, or the Negative Declaration, is available to the General Public at:

Signature (Public Agency) ______________________ Title ______________________
Date ______________________ Date Received for filing at OPR ______________________

Authority cited: Sections 21083, Public Resources Code.
References Section 21000-21174, Public Resources Code.

Revised 2005

CEQA Appendix E: Notice of Exemption

To: Office of Planning and Research
P.O. Box 3044, Room 212
Sacramento, CA 95812-3044

County Clerk
County of ______________________
____
____

From: Public Agency: ______________________
____
____
____

Project Title: ______________________
Project Location—Specific:

Project Location—City: ______________________ Project Location—County: ______________________
Description of Nature, Purpose, and Beneficiaries of Project:

Name of Public Agency Approving Project: ______________________

Name of Person or Agency Carrying Out Project: ______________________

Exempt Status: (check one)

- ☐ Ministerial (Sec. 21080(b)(1); 15268);
- ☐ Declared Emergency (Sec. 21080(b)(3); 15269(a));
- ☐ Emergency Project (Sec. 21080(b)(4); 15269(b)(c));
- ☐ Categorical Exemption. State type and section number: ______________________
- ☐ Statutory Exemptions. State code number: ______________________

Reasons why project is exempt:

Lead Agency
Contact Person ______________________ Area Code/Telephone/Extension: ______________________

If filed by applicant:

1. Attach certified document of exemption finding.
2. Has a Notice of Exemption been filed by the public agency approving the project? ☐ Yes ☐ No

Signature: ______________________ Date: ______________ Title: ______________

☐ Signed by Lead Agency
☐ Signed by Applicant

Date received for filing at OPR: ______________

revised 2005

CEQA Appendix F: Energy Conservation

I. Introduction

The goal of conserving energy implies the wise and efficient use of energy. The means of achieving this goal include:

(1) decreasing overall per capita energy consumption,

(2) decreasing reliance on fossil fuels such as coal, natural gas and oil, and

(3) increasing reliance on renewable energy sources.

In order to assure that energy implications are considered in project decisions, the California Environmental Quality Act requires that EIRs include a discussion of the potential energy impacts of proposed projects, with particular emphasis on avoiding or reducing inefficient, wasteful and unnecessary consumption of energy (see Public Resources Code section 21100(b)(3)). Energy conservation implies that a project's cost effectiveness be reviewed not only in dollars, but also in terms of energy requirements. For many projects, cost effectiveness may be determined more by energy efficiency than by initial dollar costs. A lead agency may consider the extent to which an energy source serving the project has already undergone environmental review that adequately analyzed and mitigated the effects of energy production.

II. EIR Contents

Potentially significant energy implications of a project shall be considered in an EIR to the extent relevant and applicable to the project. The following list of energy impact possibilities and potential conservation measures is designed to assist in the preparation of an EIR. In many instances specific items may not apply or additional items may be needed. Where items listed below are applicable or relevant to the project, they should be considered in the EIR.

A. Project Description may include the following items:
   1. Energy consuming equipment and processes which will be used during construction, operation and/or removal of the project. If appropriate, this discussion should consider the energy intensiveness of materials and equipment required for the project.
   2. Total energy requirements of the project by fuel type and end use.
   3. Energy conservation equipment and design features.
   4. Identification of energy supplies that would serve the project.
   5. Total estimated daily vehicle trips to be generated by the project and the additional energy consumed per trip by mode.

B. Environmental Setting may include existing energy supplies and energy use patterns in the region and locality.

C. Environmental Impacts may include:
   1. The project's energy requirements and its energy use efficiencies by amount and fuel type for each stage of the project including construction, operation, maintenance and/or removal. If appropriate, the energy intensiveness of materials maybe discussed.
   2. The effects of the project on local and regional energy supplies and on requirements for additional capacity.
   3. The effects of the project on peak and base period demands for electricity and other forms of energy.
   4. The degree to which the project complies with existing energy standards.
   5. The effects of the project on energy resources.
   6.
   7. The project's projected transportation energy use requirements and its overall use of efficient transportation alternatives.

D. Mitigation Measures may include:
   1. Potential measures to reduce wasteful, inefficient and unnecessary consumption of energy during construction, operation, maintenance and/or removal. The discussion should explain why certain measures were incorporated in the project and why other measures were dismissed.
   2. The potential of siting, orientation, and design to minimize energy consumption, including transportation energy, increase water conservation and reduce solid waste.
   3. The potential for reducing peak energy demand.
   4. Alternate fuels (particularly renewable ones) or energy systems.
   5. Energy conservation which could result from recycling efforts.

E. Alternatives should be compared in terms of overall energy consumption and in terms of reducing wasteful, inefficient and unnecessary consumption of energy.

F. Unavoidable Adverse Effects may include wasteful, inefficient and unnecessary consumption of energy during the project construction, operation, maintenance and/or removal that cannot be feasibly mitigated.

G. Irreversible Commitment of Resources may include a discussion of how the project preempts future energy development or future energy conservation.

H. Short-Term Gains versus Long-Term Impacts can be compared by calculating the project's energy costs over the project's lifetime.

I. Growth Inducing Effects may include the estimated energy consumption of growth induced by the project.

Note: Authority cited: Sections 21083 and 21087, Public Resources Code. Reference: Sections 21000-21176. Public Resources Code.

Revised 2009

CEQA Appendix G: Environmental Checklist Form

NOTE: The following is a sample form and may be tailored to satisfy individual agencies' needs and project circumstances. It may be used to meet the requirements for an initial study when the criteria set forth in CEQA Guidelines have been met. Substantial evidence of potential impacts that are not listed on this form must also be considered. The sample questions in this form are intended to encourage thoughtful assessment of impacts, and do not necessarily represent thresholds of significance.

1. Project title: ____________________

2. Lead agency name and address:

____

____

3. Contact person and phone number: ____________________

4. Project location: ____________________

5. Project sponsor's name and address:

____

____

6. General plan designation: ____________________ 7. Zoning: ____________________

8. Description of project: (Describe the whole action involved, including but not limited to later phases of the project, and any secondary, support, or off-site features necessary for its implementation. Attach additional sheets if necessary.)

____

____

____

____

9. Surrounding land uses and setting: Briefly describe the project's surroundings:

____

____

____

____

10. Other public agencies whose approval is required (e.g., permits, financing approval, or participation agreement.)

____

____

____

____

ENVIRONMENTAL FACTORS POTENTIALLY AFFECTED:

The environmental factors checked below would be potentially affected by this project, involving at least one impact that is a "Potentially Significant Impact" as indicated by the checklist below.

☐ Aesthetics	☐ Agriculture and Forestry Resources	☐ Air Quality
☐ Biological Resources	☐ Cultural Resources	☐ Geology /Soils
☐ Greenhouse Gas Emissions	☐ Hazards & Hazardous Materials	☐ Hydrology / Water Quality
☐ Land Use / Planning	☐ Mineral Resources	☐ Noise
☐ Population / Housing	☐ Public Services	☐ Recreation
☐ Transportation/Traffic	☐ Utilities / Service Systems	☐ Mandatory Findings of Significance

DETERMINATION: (To be completed by the Lead Agency)
On the basis of this initial evaluation:

☐ I find that the proposed project COULD NOT have a significant effect on the environment, and a NEGATIVE DECLARATION will be prepared.

☐ I find that although the proposed project could have a significant effect on the environment, there will not be a significant effect in this case because revisions in the project have been made by or agreed to by the project proponent. A MITIGATED NEGATIVE DECLARATION will be prepared.

☐ I find that the proposed project MAY have a significant effect on the environment, and an ENVIRONMENTAL IMPACT REPORT is required.

☐ I find that the proposed project MAY have a "potentially significant impact" or "potentially significant unless mitigated" impact on the environment, but at least one effect 1) has been adequately analyzed in an earlier document pursuant to applicable legal standards, and 2) has been addressed by mitigation measures based on the earlier analysis as described on attached sheets. An ENVIRONMENTAL IMPACT REPORT is required, but it must analyze only the effects that remain to be addressed.

☐ I find that although the proposed project could have a significant effect on the environment, because all potentially significant effects (a) have been analyzed adequately in an earlier EIR or NEGATIVE DECLARATION pursuant to applicable standards, and (b) have been avoided or mitigated pursuant to that earlier EIR or NEGATIVE DECLARATION, including revisions or mitigation measures that are imposed upon the proposed project, nothing further is required.

____________________________ ____________________________

Signature Date

____________________________ ____________________________

Signature Date

EVALUATION OF ENVIRONMENTAL IMPACTS:

1) A brief explanation is required for all answers except "No Impact" answers that are adequately supported by the information sources a lead agency cites in the parentheses following each question. A "No Impact" answer is adequately supported if the referenced information sources show that the impact simply does not apply to projects like the one involved (e.g., the project falls outside a fault rupture zone). A "No Impact" answer should be explained where it is based on project-specific factors as well as general standards (e.g., the project will not expose sensitive receptors to pollutants, based on a project-specific screening analysis).
2) All answers must take account of the whole action involved, including off-site as well as on-site, cumulative as well as project-level, indirect as well as direct, and construction as well as operational impacts.
3) Once the lead agency has determined that a particular physical impact may occur, then the checklist answers must indicate whether the impact is potentially significant, less than significant with mitigation, or less than significant. "Potentially Significant Impact" is appropriate if there is substantial evidence that an effect may be significant. If there are one or more "Potentially Significant Impact" entries when the determination is made, an EIR is required.
4) "Negative Declaration: Less Than Significant With Mitigation Incorporated" applies where the incorporation of mitigation measures has reduced an effect from "Potentially Significant Impact" to a "Less Than Significant Impact." The lead agency must describe the mitigation measures, and briefly explain how they reduce the effect to a less than significant level (mitigation measures from "Earlier Analyses," as described in (5) below, may be cross-referenced).
5) Earlier analyses may be used where, pursuant to the tiering, program EIR, or other CEQA process, an effect has been adequately analyzed in an earlier EIR or negative declaration. Section 15063(c)(3)(D). In this case, a brief discussion should identify the following:
   a) Earlier Analysis Used. Identify and state where they are available for review.
   b) Impacts Adequately Addressed. Identify which effects from the above checklist were within the scope of and adequately analyzed in an earlier document pursuant to applicable legal standards, and state whether such effects were addressed by mitigation measures based on the earlier analysis.
   c) Mitigation Measures. For effects that are "Less than Significant with Mitigation Measures Incorporated," describe the mitigation measures which were incorporated or refined from the earlier document and the extent to which they address site-specific conditions for the project.
6) Lead agencies are encouraged to incorporate into the checklist references to information sources for potential impacts (e.g., general plans, zoning ordinances). Reference to a previously prepared or outside document should, where appropriate, include a reference to the page or pages where the statement is substantiated.
7) Supporting Information Sources: A source list should be attached, and other sources used or individuals contacted should be cited in the discussion.
8) This is only a suggested form, and lead agencies are free to use different formats; however, lead agencies should normally address the questions from this checklist that are relevant to a project's environmental effects in whatever format is selected.
9) The explanation of each issue should identify:
   a) the significance criteria or threshold, if any, used to evaluate each question; and
   b) the mitigation measure identified, if any, to reduce the impact to less than significance

SAMPLE QUESTION

Issues:

	Potential Significant Impact	Less Than Significant with Mitigation Incorporated	Less Than Significant Impact	No Impact
I. AESTHETICS. Would the project:				
a) Have a substantial adverse effect on a scenic vista?	☐	☐	☐	☐
b) Substantially damage scenic resources, including, but not limited to, trees, rock outcroppings, and historic buildings within a state scenic highway?	☐	☐	☐	☐
c) Substantially degrade the existing visual character or quality of the site and its surroundings?	☐	☐	☐	☐
d) Create a new source of substantial light or glare which would adversely affect day or nighttime views in the area?	☐	☐	☐	☐
II. AGRICULTURE AND FORESTRY RESOURCES. In determining whether impacts to agricultural resources are significant environmental effects, lead agencies may refer to the California Agricultural Land Evaluation and Site Assessment Model (1997) prepared by the California Dept. of Conservation as an optional model to use in assessing impacts on agriculture and farmland. In determining whether impacts to forest resources, including timberland, are significant environmental effects, lead agencies may refer to information compiled by the California Department of Forestry and Fire Protection regarding the state's inventory of forest land, including the Forest and Range Assessment Project and the Forest Legacy Assessment project; and forest carbon measurement methodology provided in Forest Protocols adopted by the California Air Resources Board. Would the project:				
a) Convert Prime Farmland, Unique Farmland, or Farmland of Statewide Importance (Farmland), as shown on the maps prepared pursuant to the Farmland Mapping and Monitoring Program of the California Resources Agency, to non-agricultural use?	☐	☐	☐	☐
b) Conflict with existing zoning for agricultural use, or a Williamson Act contract?	☐	☐	☐	☐
c) Conflict with existing zoning for, or cause rezoning of, forest land (as defined in Public Resources Code section 12220(g)), timberland (as defined by Public Resources Code section 4526), or timberland zoned Timberland Production (as defined by Government Code section 51104(g))?	☐	☐	☐	☐
d) Result in the loss of forest land or conversion of forest land to non-forest use?	☐	☐	☐	☐
e) Involve other changes in the existing environment which, due to their location or nature, could result in conversion of Farmland, to non-agricultural use or conversion of forest land to non-forest use?	☐	☐	☐	☐

	Potential Significant Impact	Less Than Significant with Mitigation Incorporated	Less Than Significant Impact	No Impact
III. AIR QUALITY. Where available, the significance criteria established by the applicable air quality management or air pollution control district may be relied upon to make the following determinations. Would the project:				
a) Conflict with or obstruct implementation of the applicable air quality plan?	☐	☐	☐	☐
b) Violate any air quality standard or contribute substantially to an existing or projected air quality violation?	☐	☐	☐	☐
c) Result in a cumulatively considerable net increase of any criteria pollutant for which the project region is non-attainment under an applicable federal or state ambient air quality standard (including releasing emissions which exceed quantitative thresholds for ozone precursors)?	☐	☐	☐	☐
d) Expose sensitive receptors to substantial pollutant concentrations?	☐	☐	☐	☐
e) Create objectionable odors affecting a substantial number of people?	☐	☐	☐	☐
IV. BIOLOGICAL RESOURCES: Would the project:				
a) Have a substantial adverse effect, either directly or through habitat modifications, on any species identified as a candidate, sensitive, or special status species in local or regional plans, policies, or regulations, or by the California Department of Fish and Game or U.S. Fish and Wildlife Service?	☐	☐	☐	☐
b) Have a substantial adverse effect on any riparian habitat or other sensitive natural community identified in local or regional plans, policies, regulations or by the California Department of Fish and Game or US Fish and Wildlife Service?	☐	☐	☐	☐
c) Have a substantial adverse effect on federally protected wetlands as defined by Section 404 of the Clean Water Act (including, but not limited to, marsh, vernal pool, coastal, etc.) through direct removal, filling, hydrological interruption, or other means?	☐	☐	☐	☐
d) Interfere substantially with the movement of any native resident or migratory fish or wildlife species or with established native resident or migratory wildlife corridors, or impede the use of native wildlife nursery sites?	☐	☐	☐	☐
e) Conflict with any local policies or ordinances protecting biological resources, such as a tree preservation policy or ordinance?	☐	☐	☐	☐

	Potential Significant Impact	Less Than Significant with Mitigation Incorporated	Less Than Significant Impact	No Impact
f) Conflict with the provisions of an adopted Habitat Conservation Plan, Natural Community Conservation Plan, or other approved local, regional, or state habitat conservation plan?	☐	☐	☐	☐
V. CULTURAL RESOURCES. Would the project:				
a) Cause a substantial adverse change in the significance of a historical resource as defined in § 15064.5?	☐	☐	☐	☐
b) Cause a substantial adverse change in the significance of an archaeological resource pursuant to § 15064.5?	☐	☐	☐	☐
c) Directly or indirectly destroy a unique paleontological resource or site or unique geologic feature?	☐	☐	☐	☐
d) Disturb any human remains, including those interred outside of formal cemeteries?	☐	☐	☐	☐
VI. GEOLOGY AND SOILS. Would the project:				
a) Expose people or structures to potential substantial adverse effects, including the risk of loss, injury, or death involving:	☐	☐	☐	☐
i) Rupture of a known earthquake fault, as delineated on the most recent Alquist-Priolo Earthquake Fault Zoning Map issued by the State Geologist for the area or based on other substantial evidence of a known fault? Refer to Division of Mines and Geology Special Publication 42.	☐	☐	☐	☐
ii) Strong seismic ground shaking?	☐	☐	☐	☐
iii) Seismic-related ground failure, including liquefaction?	☐	☐	☐	☐
iv) Landslides?	☐	☐	☐	☐
b) Result in substantial soil erosion or the loss of topsoil?	☐	☐	☐	☐
c) Be located on a geologic unit or soil that is unstable, or that would become unstable as a result of the project, and potentially result in on- or off-site landslide, lateral spreading, subsidence, liquefaction or collapse?	☐	☐	☐	☐
d) Be located on expansive soil, as defined in Table 18-1-B of the Uniform Building Code (1994), creating substantial risks to life or property?	☐	☐	☐	☐
e) Have soils incapable of adequately supporting the use of septic tanks or alternative waste water disposal systems where sewers are not available for the disposal of waste water?	☐	☐	☐	☐

	Potential Significant Impact	Less Than Significant with Mitigation Incorporated	Less Than Significant Impact	No Impact
VII. GREENHOUSE GAS EMISSIONS. Would the project:				
a) Generate greenhouse gas emissions, either directly or indirectly, that may have a significant impact on the environment?	☐	☐	☐	☐
b) Conflict with an applicable plan, policy or regulation adopted for the purpose of reducing the emissions of greenhouse gases?	☐	☐	☐	☐
VIII. HAZARDS AND HAZARDOUS MATERIALS. Would the project:	☐	☐	☐	☐
a) Create a significant hazard to the public or the environment through the routine transport, use, or disposal of hazardous materials?	☐	☐	☐	☐
b) Create a significant hazard to the public or the environment through reasonably foreseeable upset and accident conditions involving the release of hazardous materials into the environment?	☐	☐	☐	☐
c) Emit hazardous emissions or handle hazardous or acutely hazardous materials, substances, or waste within one-quarter mile of an existing or proposed school?	☐	☐	☐	☐
d) Be located on a site which is included on a list of hazardous materials sites compiled pursuant to Government Code Section 65962.5 and, as a result, would it create a significant hazard to the public or the environment?	☐	☐	☐	☐
e) For a project located within an airport land use plan or, where such a plan has not been adopted, within two miles of a public airport or public use airport, would the project result in a safety hazard for people residing or working in the project area?	☐	☐	☐	☐
f) For a project within the vicinity of a private airstrip, would the project result in a safety hazard for people residing or working in the project area?	☐	☐	☐	☐
g) Impair implementation of or physically interfere with an adopted emergency response plan or emergency evacuation plan?	☐	☐	☐	☐
h) Expose people or structures to a significant risk of loss, injury or death involving wildland fires, including where wildlands are adjacent to urbanized areas or where residences are intermixed with wildlands?	☐	☐	☐	☐
IX. HYDROLOGY AND WATER QUALITY. Would the project:				
a) Violate any water quality standards or waste discharge requirements?	☐	☐	☐	☐

	Potential Significant Impact	Less Than Significant with Mitigation Incorporated	Less Than Significant Impact	No Impact
b) Substantially deplete groundwater supplies or interfere substantially with groundwater recharge such that there would be a net deficit in aquifer volume or a lowering of the local groundwater table level (e.g., the production rate of pre-existing nearby wells would drop to a level which would not support existing land uses or planned uses for which permits have been granted)?	☐	☐	☐	☐
c) Substantially alter the existing drainage pattern of the site or area, including through the alteration of the course of a stream or river, in a manner which would result in substantial erosion or siltation on- or off-site?	☐	☐	☐	☐
d) Substantially alter the existing drainage pattern of the site or area, including through the alteration of the course of a stream or river, or substantially increase the rate or amount of surface runoff in a manner which would result in flooding on- or off-site?	☐	☐	☐	☐
e) Create or contribute runoff water which would exceed the capacity of existing or planned stormwater drainage systems or provide substantial additional sources of polluted runoff?	☐	☐	☐	☐
f) Otherwise substantially degrade water quality?	☐	☐	☐	☐
g) Place housing within a 100-year flood hazard area as mapped on a federal Flood Hazard Boundary or Flood Insurance Rate Map or other flood hazard delineation map?	☐	☐	☐	☐
h) Place within a 100-year flood hazard area structures which would impede or redirect flood flows?	☐	☐	☐	☐
i) Expose people or structures to a significant risk of loss, injury or death involving flooding, including flooding as a result of the failure of a levee or dam?	☐	☐	☐	☐
j) Inundation by seiche, tsunami, or mudflow?	☐	☐	☐	☐
X. LAND USE AND PLANNING. Would the project:				
a) Physically divide an established community?	☐	☐	☐	☐
b) Conflict with any applicable land use plan, policy, or regulation of an agency with jurisdiction over the project (including, but not limited to the general plan, specific plan, local coastal program, or zoning ordinance) adopted for the purpose of avoiding or mitigating an environmental effect?	☐	☐	☐	☐
c) Conflict with any applicable habitat conservation plan or natural community conservation plan?	☐	☐	☐	☐

	Potential Significant Impact	Less Than Significant with Mitigation Incorporated	Less Than Significant Impact	No Impact
XI. MINERAL RESOURCES. Would the project:				
a) Result in the loss of availability of a known mineral resource that would be of value to the region and the residents of the state?	☐	☐	☐	☐
b) Result in the loss of availability of a locally-important mineral resource recovery site delineated on a local general plan, specific plan or other land use plan?	☐	☐	☐	☐
XII. NOISE. Would the project result in:				
a) Exposure of persons to or generation of noise levels in excess of standards established in the local general plan or noise ordinance, or applicable standards of other agencies?	☐	☐	☐	☐
b) Exposure of persons to or generation of excessive groundborne vibration or groundborne noise levels?	☐	☐	☐	☐
c) A substantial permanent increase in ambient noise levels in the project vicinity above levels existing without the project?				
d) A substantial temporary or periodic increase in ambient noise levels in the project vicinity above levels existing without the project?	☐	☐	☐	☐
e) For a project located within an airport land use plan or, where such a plan has not been adopted, within two miles of a public airport or public use airport, would the project expose people residing or working in the project area to excessive noise levels?				
f) For a project within the vicinity of a private airstrip, would the project expose people residing or working in the project area to excessive noise levels?	☐	☐	☐	☐
XIII. POPULATION AND HOUSING. Would the project:				
a) Induce substantial population growth in an area, either directly (for example, by proposing new homes and businesses) or indirectly (for example, through extension of roads or other infrastructure)?	☐	☐	☐	☐
b) Displace substantial numbers of existing housing, necessitating the construction of replacement housing elsewhere?	☐	☐	☐	☐
c) Displace substantial numbers of people, necessitating the construction of replacement housing elsewhere?	☐	☐	☐	☐
XIV. PUBLIC SERVICES.				
a) Would the project result in substantial adverse physical impacts associated with the provision of new or physically altered governmental facilities, need for new or physically altered governmental facilities, the construction of which could cause significant environmental impacts, in order to maintain acceptable service ratios, response times or other performance objectives for any of the public services:	☐	☐	☐	☐

	Potential Significant Impact	Less Than Significant with Mitigation Incorporated	Less Than Significant Impact	No Impact
Fire protection?	☐	☐	☐	☐
Police protection?	☐	☐	☐	☐
Schools?	☐	☐	☐	☐
Parks?	☐	☐	☐	☐
Other public facilities?	☐	☐	☐	☐
XV. RECREATION.				
a) Would the project increase the use of existing neighborhood and regional parks or other recreational facilities such that substantial physical deterioration of the facility would occur or be accelerated?	☐	☐	☐	☐
b) Does the project include recreational facilities or require the construction or expansion of recreational facilities which might have an adverse physical effect on the environment?	☐	☐	☐	☐
XVI. TRANSPORTATION/TRAFFIC. Would the project:				
a) Conflict with an applicable plan, ordinance or policy establishing measures of effectiveness for the performance of the circulation system, taking into account all modes of transportation including mass transit and non-motorized travel and relevant components of the circulation system, including but not limited to intersections, streets, highways and freeways, pedestrian and bicycle paths, and mass transit?	☐	☐	☐	☐
b) Conflict with an applicable congestion management program, including, but not limited to level of service standards and travel demand measures, or other standards established by the county congestion management agency for designated roads or highways?	☐	☐	☐	☐
c) Result in a change in air traffic patterns, including either an increase in traffic levels or a change in location that results in substantial safety risks?	☐	☐	☐	☐
d) Substantially increase hazards due to a design feature (e.g., sharp curves or dangerous intersections) or incompatible uses (e.g., farm equipment)?	☐	☐	☐	☐
e) Result in inadequate emergency access?	☐	☐	☐	☐
f) Conflict with adopted policies, plans, or programs regarding public transit, bicycle, or pedestrian facilities, or otherwise decrease the performance or safety of such facilities?	☐	☐	☐	☐

	Potential Significant Impact	Less Than Significant with Mitigation Incorporated	Less Than Significant Impact	No Impact
XVII. UTILITIES AND SERVICE SYSTEMS. Would the project:				
a) Exceed wastewater treatment requirements of the applicable Regional Water Quality Control Board?	☐	☐	☐	☐
b) Require or result in the construction of new water or wastewater treatment facilities or expansion of existing facilities, the construction of which could cause significant environmental effects?	☐	☐	☐	☐
c) Require or result in the construction of new storm water drainage facilities or expansion of existing facilities, the construction of which could cause significant environmental effects?	☐	☐	☐	☐
d) Have sufficient water supplies available to serve the project from existing entitlements and resources, or are new or expanded entitlements needed?	☐	☐	☐	☐
e) Result in a determination by the wastewater treatment provider which serves or may serve the project that it has adequate capacity to serve the project's projected demand in addition to the provider's existing commitments?	☐	☐	☐	☐
f) Be served by a landfill with sufficient permitted capacity to accommodate the project's solid waste disposal needs?	☐	☐	☐	☐
g) Comply with federal, state, and local statutes and regulations related to solid waste?	☐	☐	☐	☐
XVIII. MANDATORY FINDINGS OF SIGNIFICANCE.				
a) Does the project have the potential to degrade the quality of the environment, substantially reduce the habitat of a fish or wildlife species, cause a fish or wildlife population to drop below self-sustaining levels, threaten to eliminate a plant or animal community, reduce the number or restrict the range of a rare or endangered plant or animal or eliminate important examples of the major periods of California history or prehistory?	☐	☐	☐	☐
b) Does the project have impacts that are individually limited, but cumulatively considerable? ("Cumulatively considerable" means that the incremental effects of a project are considerable when viewed in connection with the effects of past projects, the effects of other current projects, and the effects of probable future projects)?	☐	☐	☐	☐
c) Does the project have environmental effects which will cause substantial adverse effects on human beings, either directly or indirectly?	☐	☐	☐	☐

Note: Authority cited: Sections 21083 and 21083.05, Public Resources Code. Reference: Section 65088.4, Gov. Code; Sections 21080(c), 21080.1, 21080.3, 21083, 21083.05, 21083.3, 21093, 21094, 21095, and 21151, Public Resources Code; *Sundstrom v. County of Mendocino*,(1988) 202 Cal.App.3d 296; *Leonoff v. Monterey Board of Supervisors*, (1990) 222 Cal.App.3d 1337; *Eureka Citizens for Responsible Govt. v. City of Eureka* (2007) 147 Cal.App.4th 357; *Protect the Historic Amador Waterways v. Amador Water Agency* (2004) 116 Cal.App.4th at 1109; *San Franciscans Upholding the Downtown Plan v. City and County of San Francisco* (2002) 102 Cal.App.4th 656.

Revised 2009

CEQA Appendix H: Environmental Information Form

Date Filed ______________________

General Information

1. Name and address of developer or project sponsor: ______________________________
2. Address of project: ______________________________
3. Name, address, and telephone number of person to be contacted concerning this project:

   ____

   ____
4. Indicate number of the permit application for the project to which this form pertains: ____________________
5. List and describe any other related permits and other public approvals required for this project, including those required by city, regional, state and federal agencies:

   ____
6. Existing zoning districts: ______________________________
7. Proposed use of site (Project for which this form is filed): ______________________________

   ____

Project Description

8. Site size.
9. Square footage.
10. Number of floors of construction.
11. Amount of off-street parking provided.
12. Attach plans.
13. Proposed scheduling.
14. Associated projects.
15. Anticipated incremental development.
16. If residential, include the number of units, schedule of unit sizes, range of sale prices or rents, and type of household size expected.
17. If commercial, include the number of units, whether neighborhood, city or regionally oriented, square footage of sales area, and loading facilities.
18. If industrial, indicate type, estimated employment per shift, and loading facilities.
19. If institutional, indicate the major function, estimated employment per shift, estimated occupancy, loading facilities, and community benefits to be derived from the project.
20. If the project involves a variance, conditional use or rezoning application, state this and indicate clearly why the application is required.

Are the following items applicable to the project or its effects? Discuss below all items checked yes (attach additional sheets as necessary).

	Yes	No
21. Change in existing features of any bays, tidelands, beaches, or hills, or substantial alteration of ground contours.	☐	☐
22. Change in scenic views or vistas from existing residential areas or public lands or roads.	☐	☐
23. Change in pattern, scale, or character of general area of project.	☐	☐
24. Significant amounts of solid waste or litter.	☐	☐
25. Change in dust, ash, smoke, fumes, or odors in vicinity.	☐	☐
26. Change in ocean, bay, lake, stream or ground water quality or quantity, or alteration of existing drainage patterns.	☐	☐
27. Substantial change in existing noise or vibration levels in the vicinity.	☐	☐
28. Site on filled land or on slope of ten percent or more.	☐	☐
29. Use of disposal of potentially hazardous materials, such as toxic substances, flammables or explosives.	☐	☐
30. Substantial change in demand for municipal services (police, fire, water, sewage, etc.).	☐	☐
31. Substantial increase in fossil fuel consumption (electricity, oil, natural gas, etc.).	☐	☐
32. Relationship to a larger project or series of projects.	☐	☐

Environmental Setting

33. Describe the project site as it exists before the project, including information on topography, soil, stability, plants and animals, and any cultural, historical or scenic aspects. Describe any existing structures on the site, and the use of the structures. Attach photographs of the site. Snapshots or polaroids photos will be accepted.

34. Describe the surrounding properties, including information on plant and animal and any cultural, historical or scenic aspects. Indicate the type of land use (residential, commercial, etc.), intensity of land use (one-family, apartment houses, shops, department stores, etc.), and scale of development (height, frontage, set-back, rear yard, etc.). Attach photographs of the vicinity. Snapshots or polaroid photos will be accepted.

Certification

I hereby certify that the statements furnished above and in the attached exhibits present the date and information required for this initial evaluation to the best of my ability, and that the facts, statements, and in formation presented are true and correct to the best of my knowledge and belief.

Date______________________________ Signature ______________________________

For ______________________________

CEQA Appendix I: Notice of Preparation

To: ______________________________

____
(Address)
____

From: ______________________________

____
(Address)
____

Subject: **Notice of Preparation of a Draft Environmental Impact Report**

______________________ will be the Lead Agency and will prepare an environmental impact report for the project identified below. We need to know the views of your agency as to the scope and content of the proposed project. Your agency will need to use the EIR prepared by our agency when considering your permit or other approval for the project.

The project description, location, and the potential environmental effects are contained in the attached materials. A copy of the Initial Study (☐ is ☐ is not) attached.

Due to the time limits mandated by state law, your response must be sent at the earliest possible date but not later than thirty (30) days after receipt of this notice.

Please send your response to ______________________________ at the address shown above. We will need the name for a contact person in your agency.

Project Title: ______________________________

Project Applicant, if any: ______________________________

Date ______________________

Signature ______________________

Title ______________________

Telephone ______________________

Reference: California Code of Regulations, Title 14 (CEQA Guidelines), Sections 15082(a), 15103, 15375.

CEQA Appendix J: Examples of Tiering EIRs

FIRST TIER EIR (15152)

- project encompasses separate but related projects such as general plan, zoning, development
- later tiers move from general to specific analysis of projects

Later Project EIR

- later project is consistent with general plan or zoning
- initial study must examine significant effects not covered in prior EIR
- later EIR must state lead agency is using tiering concept and must comply with section 15152

STAGED EIR (15167)

- one large project will require a number of discretionary approvals from govt. agencies and one of those approvals will occur more than two years before construction commences

Supplement to the Staged EIR

- supplements to the staged EIR are prepared for later government agency approvals on the same overall project if information available at the time of that later approval would permit consideration of additional environmental impacts, mitigation measures or reasonable alternatives

---

PROGRAM EIR (15168)

- series of actions or activities that can be characterized as one large project and are related either:
- geographically
- as logical parts of a chain of activities
- in connection with rules, regulations, plans or other general criteria governing a continuing program
- as individual activities carried out under common authority (statutory or regulatory) and having similar environmental effects which can be mitigated in similar ways

Subsequent Project EIR	• only if subsequent activity has effects not examined in the previously certified program EIR will additional environmental documentation be required (if subsequent activity has no new effects, that activity is covered by the program EIR)
MASTER EIR (15175)	• alternative to project, staged, or program EIR • can be used for: - general plan (or gen. plan element, amendment, or update) - redevelopment plan projects (public or private) - project consisting of phases of smaller individual projects - other activities described in 15175 • after five years from initial certification, adopting authority must review the Master EIR and prepare subsequent or supplemental EIR if substantial changes have occurred with respect to circumstances under which the original Master EIR was adopted • no new EIR is required for subsequent projects within the scope of the Master EIR which cause no additional significant effect
Focused EIR (15177)	• a subsequent, Focused EIR is required only where: - substantial new/additional information shows adverse environmental effects not examined in Master EIR or more significant than described in EIR, or - substantial new/additional information shows mitigation measures previously determined to be infeasible are now feasible and will avoid/reduce the significant effects to a level of insignificance

---

SPECIAL SITUATIONS / EIRs

Multiple-family residential development / residential and commercial or retail mixed-use development (PRC 21158.5 and Guideline §15179.5)

- project is multiple-family residential development up to 100 units or is a residential and commercial or retail mixed-use development of not more than 100,000 square feet
- if project complies with procedures in section 21158.5, only a focused EIR need be prepared, notwithstanding the fact that the project wasn't identified in the Master EIR

Redevelopment Project (15180)

- all public and private activities or undertakings in furtherance of a redevelopment plan (public or private) constitute a single project
- the redevelopment plan EIR is treated as a program EIR

- no subsequent EIR is required for individual components of the redevelopment plan unless substantial changes or substantial new information triggers a subsequent EIR or supplement to an EIR pursuant to (sections 15162 or 15163)

Housing/neighborhood commercial facilities (15181)
- a project involving construction of housing or neighborhood commercial facilities in an urbanized area
- a prior EIR for a specific plan, local coastal program, or port master plan may be used as the EIR for such a project (no new EIR need be prepared) provided section 15181 procedures are complied with

Projects Consistent with Community Plan, General Plan, or Zoning (15183)
- a project which is consistent with a community plan adopted as part of a general plan or zoning ordinance or a general plan of a local agency <u>and</u> where there was an EIR certified for the zoning action or master plan
- the EIR for the residential project need only examine certain significant environmental effects, as outlined in section 15183

Regulations on Pollution Control Equipment (PRC section 21159)
- section 21159 requires environmental analysis of reasonably foreseeable methods of compliance at the time of adoption of rule or regulation requiring the installation of pollution control equipment
- an EIR prepared at the time of adoption of the rule or regulation is deemed to satisfy the requirement of section 21159

Installation of Pollution Control Equipment (PRC section 21159.1)
- a focused EIR is permitted where project 1) consists solely of installation of pollution control equipment; 2) is required by rule or regulation adopted by the State Air Resources Board, an air pollution control district or air quality management district, the State Water Resources Control Board, a California regional water quality control board, the Dept. of Toxic Substances Control, or the California Integrated Waste Management Board; and 3) meets the procedural requirements outlined in section 21159.1

CEQA Appendix K:
Criteria for Shortened Clearinghouse Review

Under exceptional circumstances, and when requested in writing by the lead agency, the State Clearinghouse in the Office of Planning and Research (OPR) may shorten the usual review periods for proposed negative declarations, mitigated negative declarations and draft EIRs submitted to the Clearinghouse. A request must be made by the decision-making body of the lead agency, or by a properly authorized representative of the decision-making body.

A shortened review period may be granted when any of the following circumstances exist:

(1) The lead agency is operating under an extension of the one-year period for completion of an EIR and would not otherwise be able to complete the EIR within the extended period.

(2) The public project applicant is under severe time constraints with regard to obtaining financing or exercising options which cannot be met without shortening the review period.

(3) The document is a supplement to a draft EIR or proposed negative declaration or mitigated negative declaration previously submitted to the State Clearinghouse.

(4) The health and safety of the community would be at risk unless the project is approved expeditiously.

(5) The document is a revised draft EIR, or proposed negative declaration or mitigated negative declaration, where changes in the document are primarily the result of comments from agencies and the public.

Shortened review cannot be provided to a draft EIR or proposed negative declaration or mitigated negative declaration which has already begun the usual review process. Prior to requesting shortened review, the lead agency should have already issued a notice of preparation and received comments from applicable State agencies, in the case of an EIR, or consulted with applicable State agencies, in the case of a proposed negative declaration or mitigated negative declaration.

No shortened review period shall be granted unless the lead agency has contacted and obtained prior approval for a shortened review from the applicable state responsible and trustee agencies. No shortened review shall be granted for any project which is of statewide, regional, or areawide significance, as defined in Section 15206 of the guidelines.

CEQA Appendix L:
Notice of Completion of Draft EIR

Project Title: ______________________________

____
Project Location—Specific

____
Project Location—City Project
Location—County

Description of Nature, Purpose, and Beneficiaries of Project:

____

____

____

____

____

____
Lead Agency Division

____
Address Where Copy of EIR Is Available

____

____
Review Period

____
Contact Person Area Code Phone Extension

Glossary

Categorical Exemption
An exemption from CEQA for certain projects that the Secretary for Resources has determined generally do not have a significant effect on the environment.

Cumulative Impacts
Two or more environmental effects that, when considered together, are considerable or which compound or increase other environmental impacts.

Direct Impacts
Primary environmental effects that are caused by a project and occur at the same time and place.

Environment
The physical conditions that exist within an area that will be affected by a proposed project. The conditions include land, air, water, minerals, flora, fauna, noise, and objects of historical or aesthetic significance.

Environmental Impact Report
A detailed statement describing and analyzing the significant environmental effects and alternative identified in an EIR.

Findings
Written legal conclusions prepared by a public agency that explain the disposition of each significant environmental effect and alternative identified in an EIR.

Indirect Impacts
Also referred to as secondary effects, inirect impacts are caused by a project and occur later in time or at some distance from the project; however, they are still reasonably foreseeable.

Initial Study
A preliminary analysis prepared by a Lead Agency determining whether an EIR or Negative Declaration must be prepared, and identifying the significant environmental effects to be analyzed in and EIR.

Lead Agency
The public agency that has the principal responsibility for carrying out or approving a project.

Mitigation Measure
A change in a project designed to avoid, minimize, rectify, reduce or compensate for a significant environmental impact.

National Environmental Policy Act
The federal law that provided the model for CEQA and requires federal agencies to prepare Environmental Impact Statements (EIS) for federal actions significiantly affecting the human environment.

Negative Declaration
A written statement prepared by a Lead Agency that briefly describes the reasons why a proposed project will not have a significant effect on the environment and, therefore, does not require an EIR.

Notice of Completion
A brief notice filed withthe Office of Planning and Research by the Lead Agency, as soon as it has completed a draft EIR.

Notice of Determination
A brief notice filed by a public agency after it approves or determines to carry out a project.

Notice of Exemption
A brief notice that may be filed by a public agency after it has decided to carry out or approve a project for which an exemption to CEQA applies.

Notice of Preparation
A brief notice sent by a Lead Agency notifying Responsible, Trustee and involved federal agencies that it plans to prepare an EIR for a project.

Project
The entirety of an action that has a potential for resulting in a physical chance in the environment.

Responsible Agency
A public agency that proposes to carry out or approve a project for which a Lead Agency is preparing or has prepared an EIR.

Significant Effect
A substantial, or potentially substantial, adverse change in any of the physical conditions within the area affected by a project.

Statement of Overriding Consideration
A written explanation prepared by a public agency that explains why it approved a project, despite the presence of significant, unavoidable environmental impacts.

Tiering
Refers to the concept of a "multi-tiered" approach to preparing EIRs. The first-tier EIR covers general issues in a broader program-oriented analysis. Subsequent tiers incorporate by reference the general discussions from the broader EIR, while primarily concentrating on the issues specific to the action being evaluated.

Acromyms

ABAG
Association of Bay Area Governments

AEP
Association of Environmenta Professionals

APA
American Planning Association

BCDC
San Francisco Bay Conservation and Development Commission

CAL EPA
California Environmental Protection Acenty

Caltrans
California Department of Transportation

CEQA
California Environmental Quality Act

CFR
Code of Federal Regulations

DFG
Department of Five and Game

DHS
Department of Health Services

EIA
Environmental Impact Assessment

EIR
Environmental Impact Report

EIS
Environmental Impact Statement

FONSI
Finding of No Significant Effect

Gov. Code
California Government Code

Guidelines
State CEQA Guidelines

LAFCO
Local Agency Formation Commission

LESA
Land Evaluation and Site Assessment

MEA
Master Environmental Assessment

MOU
Memo of Understanding

NEPA
National Environmental Policy Act

NOP
Notice of Determination

NOP
Notice of Preparation

OPR
Office of Planning and Research

PSA
Permit Streamlining Act

Pub. Res. Code
Californina Public Resources Code

SCH
State Clearinghouse

SMUD
Sacramento Municipal Utility District

Index

Figures are indicated by italicized f following page numbers.

F

J

K

L

M

N